P9-EEU-742

WRITING

ABOUT THE WORLD

Susan McLeod

Washington State University

with the assistance of

Stacia Bates
Alan Hunt
John Jarvis
Shelley Spear

HBJ

Harcourt Brace Jovanovich, Publishers

San Diego • New York • Chicago • Austin • Washington, D.C.
London • Sydney • Tokyo • Toronto

To the Instructor

*W*riting about the World began as part of an initiative to revise the general education program and internationalize the curriculum at Washington State University. One goal of this curriculum revision was to include the study of women as well as men, and people of color as well as Western European figures in university courses. Thus, as we revised the English Composition curriculum, we set out to find readings that fit our introductory writing course (the main objective of which is to help students learn academic reading and writing strategies), but that also raised issues of cultural diversity and of gender. Our work is, therefore, in line with the resolution passed at the 1989 Conference on College Composition and Communication: "Resolved, that CCCC adopt a curriculum policy that represents the inclusion of women and people of color in the curriculum on all levels." We are pleased to help implement that curriculum policy through this book of readings.

Each reading in this book begins with a headnote that presents information on the author or information related to an understanding of the text. Each reading is followed by a list of questions for reading and classroom discussion. Where relevant, readings are cross-referenced for purposes of comparison. In addition to the general Table of Contents, two additional reference guides are offered in the appendices for those who might wish to organize courses thematically or by modes. One is a Thematic Table of Contents, and the other is a Rhetorical Table of Contents based on James Kinneavy's Modes and Aims.

Those who would like more detailed suggestions on how to teach a writing course using these readings should consult the *Instructor's Manual*. That manual is divided into four sections. Section 1, "Teaching Notes on Individual Readings," offers additional information on each selection, teaching strategies, and suggestions for further reading. Section 2, "In-Class Essay Writing Guide and Sample Writing Assignments," provides tips for effective in-class essay writing as well as a series of sample writing assignments based on the readings. Sample writing assignments include, among others, the following: the summary essay, the library research paper, the essay exam, the science and ethics essay, the analysis essay, the biographical profile, the creative response essay, the argument paper, and the evaluative paper. These assignments have been formatted so that they can be photocopied for classroom use. Section 3, "Preparing a Syllabus for the Course," offers tips on writing the syllabus as well as a sample syllabus. Section 4, "From Teacher to Teacher: Teaching Tips for Implementing a Multicultural Approach to College Composition," offers suggestions from teachers who have been using these readings since 1987, when we first began this project.

ACKNOWLEDGMENTS

Many people have helped us develop this project. In particular, we should like to thank Richard Law, Associate Dean of the College of Sciences and Arts, who, with Thomas Kennedy, wrote the National Endowment for the Humanities grant proposal for a core course in World Civilizations; with support from this project, this textbook was born. Professor Law's encouragement and support have been invaluable. We also value the help of the faculty involved in this World Civilizations project; in particular, we would like to thank Fritz Blackwell for his help with South Asian texts and Bonnie Frederick for her help with texts from South American and with translations of Spanish. We are also grateful to Richard Haswell for his expert advice and for his help with the pilot program in which we introduced the reader. Librarian Alice Spitzer worked tirelessly to help us find particular readings and was a valued collaborator in developing research assignments based on our readings.

For their helpful suggestions and guidance in revising the manuscript, we would like to thank the following reviewers: Chris M. Anson, University of Minnesota; Richard L. Larson, C.U.N.Y.-Herbert Lehman College; and Harry M. Solomon, Auburn University.

The professionals at Harcourt Brace Jovanovich were enormously helpful to us. For their guidance, patience, and good humor, we would like to thank Karen Allanson and Marlane Miriello, acquisitions editors; Eleanor Garner, permissions editor; Zanae Rodrigo, manuscript editior; Michael Ferreira, production editor; Cheryl Solheid and Diana Parks, designers; Elizabeth Banks, art editor; and Lynne Bush, production manager.

Finally, we would like to thank the Department of English at Washington State University, our students, and all of the instructors who advised us about the readings. Their help and suggestions have informed all parts of our work.

Susan McLeod
Stacia Bates
Alan Hunt
John Jarvis
Shelley Spear

To the Student

This book of readings for a writing class is based on several premises:

1. That reading and writing are interrelated; that you learn to write by *both* reading and writing.
2. That one of the purposes of a college writing class is to help you develop the critical reading, writing, and thinking strategies you need for other classes in the college curriculum.
3. That the best way to learn these strategies is to work with readings similar to the books you will encounter in other classes.
4. That writing is a mode of learning, a tool you can use to help you learn, as well as a method of testing that learning.

The readings included in this textbook are intended to help you think and write about important ideas associated with world cultures. The readings are not necessarily models for you to follow (although some are in fact excellent models); they are intended to provide you with a kind of minilibrary of books from which to write papers. Some are primary sources (for example, the selections from the Bible), and some are secondary (for example, the selection by Stephen Harris on understanding the Bible). Many are challenging, but no more so than readings in other courses in the university. We have chosen to focus on world cultures because we feel that this focus is important, given Americans' lack of knowledge about the rest of the world in a time of increasing global interdependence. It is our hope that the readings will help you not only with your writing, but also with your understanding of the complexity and richness of other cultures.

The readings are organized according to some of the ways cultures organize themselves. There are four major parts: Science and Technology, Government and Politics, Art and Literature, and Religion and Philosophy. Since many college-level writing tasks begin with defining terms carefully, each section contains readings having to do with definitions. We then move on to explore cultural diversity in each section, with readings from or about various world cultures. Finally, we have chosen particular issues (for example, science and ethics) to explore in depth. In this exploration, we have chosen readings that illustrate the complexity of the issues. The issue of gender is important enough to have been included in each section.

The multicultural focus for the readings should not obscure the fact that this is primarily a writing textbook. The writing assignments we suggest to go with this book are reading based. The most important of these is the reading journal, an assignment that is aimed at helping you develop your reading, writing, and thinking skills, while helping you see how the readings relate to you and your own culture. Suggestions for keeping this journal appear below. We also suggest some creative assignments, some assignments aimed at teaching certain forms of discourse needed for writing across the disciplines (definition, summary, argument), and some assignments that are like those you will encounter in other classes (the essay examination, the critique, the paper based on library research).

It is our hope that the readings in this book and the writing assignments we suggest to go with those readings will serve you in your other college classes and beyond the classroom, as an informed citizen of an interconnected world.

SUGGESTIONS FOR KEEPING A READING JOURNAL[1]

To help you develop your reading, writing, and thinking skills, the following suggestions are offered.

1. Summarize the main ideas of the selection you are reading. This need not be a long summary, but it should be as complete as possible. A good way to do a summary is to look at the first paragraph of a piece, to look at the last paragraph, and then to ask yourself questions about how the author got from beginning to end—what came between? Then skim the entire piece, underlining in your book the ideas that seem important. Finally, go back and read carefully and note the main ideas as you write.
2. Argue with the material. What do you disagree with? Why? Imagine that the writer is there to listen to you argue, and write down your points of disagreement. What do you agree with? Why? Where do you and the author have a meeting of the minds? For ease of writing, imagine that you are able to converse with the writer.
3. Ask yourself questions about the material. Why does the author structure his or her argument in a particular way? What perplexes you about the material? Try beginning your questions with such phrases as, "I don't understand why . . ." or "I was surprised when. . . ."
4. Make connections to your own experience. What does this reading make you think of? How does it connect with other readings in this class, or in your other classes? Are there other issues that are related to the issues raised in this reading that are important to you?
5. Write about the author and the author's point of view. For what audience is the author writing? What seems to be his or her attitude toward the subject matter and the audience? How can you tell?

Susan McLeod
Stacia Bates
Alan Hunt
John Jarvis
Shelley Spear

[1] Adapted from Sharon Flitterman-King, "The Role of the Response Journal in Active Reading," *The Quarterly* 10 (July, 1988): 4–11.

Contents

1
Science and Technology

EDWARD T. HALL
The Anthropology of Manners / 3

JULIUS ROBERT OPPENHEIMER
The Scientist in Society / 10

SHIGERU NAKAYAMA
Two Styles of Learning / 15

ANNE WALTON
Women Scientists: Are They Really Different? / 25

RAYMOND DAWSON
Science and China's Influence on the World / 39

JOHN B. CHRISTOPHER
Science / 41

FRITJOF CAPRA
The Tao of Physics / 49

CARL G. JUNG
Sigmund Freud / 52

CHIEF SEATTLE
Environmental Statement / 58

RACHEL CARSON
The Obligation to Endure / 60

MAC MARGOLIS
Amazon Ablaze / 65

JOHN W. MELLOR
The Intertwining of Environmental Problems and
Poverty / 75

CARL SAGAN
The Dragons of Eden: Speculations on the Evolution of
Human Intelligence / 83

ALBERT EINSTEIN
Religion and Science / 86

BERTRAND RUSSELL
Religion and Science / 90

CHARLES DARWIN
The Action of Natural Selection / 94

GEORGE E. SIMPSON
Early Social Darwinism / 97

CYNTHIA EAGLE RUSSETT
Darwin in America: The Intellectual Response,
1865–1912 / 100

MARGARET MEAD
Warfare: An Invention—Not a Biological
Necessity / 104

JOHN CONNOR
The U.S. Was Right / 109

GAR ALPEROVITZ
The U.S. Was Wrong / 111

SIDNEY SHALETT
First Atomic Bomb Dropped on Japan / 113

MASUJI IBUSE
Black Rain / 117

SUZANNE H. SANKOWSKY
Mainstreams of World History / 127

ANN SNITOW
The Paradox of Birth Technology / 128

S. OGBUAGU
Depo Provera—A Choice or an Imposition on the African
Woman? / 135

JO McGOWAN
In India, They Abort Females / 147

JEFFREY Z. RUBIN, FRANK J. PROVENZANO, and ZELLA LURIA
The Eye of the Beholder: Parents' View on Sex of
Newborns / 149

2
Government and Politics

KENNETH MINOGUE, ALFRED G. MEYER, PAUL HIRST, and ROGER WILLIAMS
Definitions of Democracy, Communism, Socialism, Nationalism, and Technocracy / 162

KAUTILYA
The Arthashastra / 173

NICCOLO MACHIAVELLI
The Prince / 180

PATRICIA J. SETHI
Pinochet: Destiny Gave Me the Job / 188

AMNESTY INTERNATIONAL
Chile / 190

PLATO
The Republic / 193

CONFUCIUS
The Sacred Books of Confucius / 195

JULIUS K. NYERERE
Ujamaa—The Basis of African Socialism / 200
The Arusha Declaration / 207

THOMAS JEFFERSON
The Declaration of Independence / 210

UNITED NATIONS
Universal Declaration of Human Rights / 215

RODERICK OGLEY
Extracts from the Declaration of the Belgrade Conference of Heads of State and Governments of Nonaligned Countries / 222

ALEXIS DE TOCQUEVILLE
Democracy in America / 226

KARL MARX and FRIEDRICH ENGELS
Bourgeois and Proletarians / 232

SIMONE DE BEAUVOIR
Women as Other / 242

AMAURY DE RIENCOURT
Women in Athens / 247

NANCY BARRETT
Women and the Economy / 251

ALBERT MEMMI
Racism and Oppression / 253

GEORGE ORWELL
Shooting an Elephant / 261

MOHANDAS K. GANDHI
Satyagraha / 266

MARTIN LUTHER KING, JR.
Letter from Birmingham Jail / 272

NELSON MANDELA
I Am Prepared to Die / 286

3

Art and Literature

ROYAL BANK OF CANADA NEWSLETTER
What Use Is Art? / 308

SUSANNE K. LANGER
The Cultural Importance of the Arts / 310

GLORIA ANZALDÚA
Tlilli, Tlapalli: The Path of the Red and Black Ink / 316

E. H. GOMBRICH
Art for Eternity: Egypt, Mesopotamia, and Crete / 325

ANANDA K. COOMARASWAMY
Understanding Indian Art / 333

HERMANN LIST
Chinese Painting / 337

J. P. HODIN
The Soviet Attitude to Art / 338

SYLVIA HOCHFIELD
Soviet Art: New Freedom, New Directions / 340

ROY SIEBER
Traditional Arts of Black Africa / 344

PHILIP RAWSON
Islamic Art: Calligraphy / 348

JON STALLWORTHY
Letter to a Friend / 351

ARCHIBALD MacLEISH
Ars Poetica / 352

JAVIER HERAUD
Ars Poetica / 354

MARIANNE MOORE
Poetry / 355

ALICE WALKER
In Search of Our Mothers' Gardens / 356

WOLE SOYINKA
Chimes of Silence / 364

PABLO NERUDA
The United Fruit Co. / 366

PAUL LAURENCE DUNBAR
We Wear the Mask / 369

EZEKIEL MPHAHLELE
The Master of Doornvlei / 370

ELLEN WRIGHT PRENDERGAST
Famous Are the Flowers (Patriot's Song) / 377

ANTHONY HECHT
More Light! More Light! / 378

MURIEL RUKEYSER
Letter to the Front / 380

WILLIAM BUTLER YEATS
Easter 1916 / 381

W. H. AUDEN
The Unknown Citizen / 384

CARL SANDBURG
The People, Yes *and* Men of Science Say Their Say / 386

MORRIS BISHOP
$E = mc^2$ / 390

JUNE JORDAN
A Poem About Intelligence for My Brothers and Sisters / 391

BARRY LOPEZ
Buffalo / 393

MARZIEH AHMADI OSKOOII
I'm a Woman / 397

YÜ HSÜAN-CHI
On a Visit to Ch'ung Chen Taoist Temple I See in the
South Hall the List of Successful Candidates in the Imperial
Examinations / 399

SOR JUANA INÉS DE LA CRUZ
She Proves the Inconsistency of the Desires and Criticism
of Men Who Accuse Women of What They Themselves
Cause / 400

MAXINE HONG KINGSTON
No Name Woman / 403

SAPPHO
Invocation to Aphrodite / 412

MURASAKI SHIKIBU
Lavender / 413

RABINDRANATH TAGORE
False Religion *and* The Evermoving / 435

HERMANN HESSE
The Brahmin's Son / 438

4

Religion and Philosophy

What the World Believes / 449

ÉMILE DURKHEIM
The Elementary Forms of the Religious Life / 449

WILL DURANT
The Story of Philosophy / 452

WINSTON L. KING
Religion and Nothingness / 455

JOHN JARVIS
Introduction to Buddhism / 458

NINIAN SMART and RICHARD D. HECHT
The Enlightenment of the Buddha: Buddhacarita / 461

DIANA L. ECK
Darśan: Seeing the Divine Image in India / 464
Muṇḍaka Upanishad / 473

BENJAMIN HOFF
The Tao of Pooh: The How of Pooh? *and* Nowhere and
Nothing / 481

LAO TZU
The Sayings of Lao Tzu / 488

STEPHEN L. HARRIS
Understanding the Bible: A Reader's Introduction / 491
Two Concepts of Deity: Exodus 32 *and* St. John 8 / 496

BENGT SUNDKLER
A Black Messiah: Acts of the Nazarites / 499

JOHN B. CHRISTOPHER
The Prophet / 501
The Teachings of Islam / 504
The Quran / 511

WILLIAM H. McNEILL and JEAN W. SEDLAR
Introduction to Confucius / 514
From the Analects of Confucius (Lun Yü) / 517

PLATO
The Allegory of the Cave / 519

CHARLES I. GLICKSBERG
The Literature of Nihilism / 528

GWENDOLYN BROOKS
the preacher: ruminates behind the sermon *and*
We Real Cool / 536

JEAN PAUL SARTRE
Existentialism / 537
Three Concepts of Creation: Genesis, Nu Kwa *and* Shakti / 542

NINIAN SMART and RICHARD D. HECHT
Women and the Order / 549

RIANE EISLER
Our Lost Heritage: New Facts on How God Became a
Man / 550

MARY DALY
After the Death of God the Father / 556

PHYLLIS SCHLAFLY
The Power of the Positive Woman / 560

HARVEY COX
Understanding Islam: No More Holy Wars / 566

MURTUZA MUTAHERY
The Martyr / 572

JOSEPH SMITH
The First Vision / 577

VOLTAIRE
Of Universal Tolerance / 581

BERTRAND RUSSELL
Why I Am Not a Christian / 584

C. S. LEWIS
What Christians Believe / 590

ELIE WIESEL
Night / 599

APPENDIX A
Thematic Table of Contents / 602

APPENDIX B
Rhetorical Table of Contents Based on Kinneavy's Modes
and Aims / 608

AUTHOR-TITLE INDEX / 615

WRITING
ABOUT THE WORLD

PART 1

Science and Technology

At nearly every institution of higher learning a distinction is made between the "arts" and the "sciences." Scholars from both fields claim to be attempting to find productive methods for examining the universe, and both are searching for knowledge; the clearest distinction between the two involves the method by which each approaches the subject matter. Scholars in the humanities spend time in libraries and use inductive and deductive reasoning and textual analysis as primary methods of study, while scientists use the scientific method of observing elements of the natural world, spending time in laboratories, forming hypotheses, testing hypotheses by experiments, and formulating theories based on the results of experiments.

According to J. Robert Oppenheimer, in *The Open Mind*, "We live today in a world in which poets and historians and men of affairs are proud that they wouldn't even begin to consider thinking about learning anything of science, regarding it as the far end of a tunnel too long for any wise man to put his head into."[1] An attitude of mutual distrust between scholars in the humanities and sciences has become widespread, but such an attitude ignores the recent blurring between methods of study in the humanities and the sciences; scholars in the humanities have come to view knowledge as "tentative" in the same way that many scientists have done for centuries, and many scientists, influenced by contemporary philosophy, have begun to question the effect of preconceived ideas on the scientific process.

The selections included in Part 1 explore the wide variety of fields of study within the realm of science, as well as the place of the scientist in society, the role of science in the future of the world, and the ways in which the sciences of different nations and cultures have developed and continue to develop. A mixture of primary and secondary selections has been included so that students can examine writing *by* important figures in science from around the world, as well as writing *about* the scientific developments of various nations. Part 1 can be conceptualized in three sections with the following labels: definitions, diversity, and issues in science.

The definitions section includes three essays which set the tone for the rest of Part 1. Edward Hall's "The Anthropology of Manners" introduces students to the variety of cultural norms by illustrating how manners and customs are different from one culture to the next. The essay argues that an awareness of cultural diversity is desirable and necessary for citizens of an interdependent world. The second article, J. Robert Oppenheimer's "The Scientist in Society," discusses the need for all people to be aware of scientific developments around the globe so that they can make informed, responsible decisions about the place of science in society. The third essay, "Two Styles of Learning" by Shigeru Nakayama, compares and contrasts the definitions and methods of science in the East and West.

The next section, which concerns diversity, continues the theme of the importance of understanding cultural similarities and differences presented in the

[1]J. Robert Oppenheimer, *The Open Mind* (New York: Simon and Schuster, 1975), 2.

2

introductory essays. Such articles as Raymond Dawson's "Science and China's Influence on the World" and John Christopher's "Science" illustrate both the differences in the sciences of various cultures as well as the sharing between cultures of scientific discoveries and developments. "Women Scientists: Are They Really Different?" by Anne Walton introduces the issue of gender into the area of diversity by exploring the ways in which women scientists have been considered outsiders in the scientific community. Other articles, like Fritjof Capra's excerpt from *The Tao of Physics* and Chief Seattle's "Environmental Statement," discuss the ways in which certain cultural approaches to the natural world seem alien to other cultures, while at the same time explaining the benefits of understanding the differences.

The final section, issues in science, centers on a second theme presented in the introductory essays: the responsibility of the individual to be aware of how values affect scientific and technological developments and to monitor the "advances" of science. These selections also pose the question of whether technological developments always lead to social progress. Two essays by Bertrand Russell and Albert Einstein discuss the conflicts between religion and science. Russell discusses the historical conflicts between various religious beliefs and scientific "truths," while Einstein's text focuses on the similarities between religious spiritual fervor and the devotion exhibited by humanitarian scientists. A group of essays on the issue of "social Darwinism" explores the question of what constitutes human nature, in an attempt to apply natural science to human history and behavior. Several articles involving the dropping of the atomic bomb on Japan at the end of World War II have been included to illustrate the interdependency of all nations in a nuclear age. Similarly, texts dealing with ecology and the impact of human activity on the environment explore the contemporary global concern for maintaining the "health" of the planet. Finally, the issue of science and gender is explored in regard to reproductive technology and individual responsibility; the science of psychology is applied to the issue of gender, as well, in an article titled "The Eye of the Beholder: Parents' View on Sex of Newborns," which provides an example of the type of text typical of scientific journals.

EDWARD T. HALL
The Anthropology of Manners

"The Anthropology of Manners," by Edward T. Hall (1914–   ), was written in 1955 for the journal, Scientific American. As an anthropologist, Hall is interested in the nature of human communication and other aspects of human behavior. In this essay, Hall, who served as director of a government program for training international diplomats, discusses the importance of manners in successful intercultural communication. He provides several examples of different standards of etiquette across cultures and discusses the problems that these differences can cause. Hall

demonstrates that an awareness of cultural diversity will provide substantial benefits in communication between the various peoples of the world.

The Goops they lick their fingers
  and the Goops they lick their knives;
They spill their broth on the table cloth—
  Oh, they lead disgusting lives.
The Goops they talk while eating,
  and loud and fast they chew;
And that is why I'm glad that I
  am not a Goop—are you?

In Gelett Burgess'[1] classic on the Goops we have an example of what anthropologists call "an enculturating device"—a means of conditioning the young to life in our society. Having been taught the lesson of the goops from childhood (with or without the aid of Mr. Burgess) Americans are shocked when they go abroad and discover whole groups of people behaving like goops—eating with their fingers, making noises and talking while eating. When this happens, we may (1) remark on the barbarousness or quaintness of the "natives" (a term cordially disliked all over the world) or (2) try to discover the nature and meaning of the differences in behavior. One rather quickly discovers that what is good manners in one context may be bad in the next. It is to this point that I would like to address myself.

The subject of manners is complex; if it were not, there would not be so many injured feelings and so much misunderstanding in international circles everywhere. In any society the code of manners tends to sum up the culture—to be a frame of reference for all behavior. Emily Post[2] goes so far as to say: "There is not a single thing that we do, or say, or choose, or use, or even think, that does not follow or break one of the exactions of taste, or tact, or ethics of good manners, or etiquette— call it what you will." Unfortunately many of the most important standards of acceptable behavior in different cultures are elusive: they are intangible, undefined and unwritten.

An Arab diplomat who recently arrived in the U. S. from the Middle East attended a banquet which lasted several hours. When it was over, he met a fellow countryman outside and suggested they go get something to eat, as he was starving. His friend, who had been in this country for some time, laughed and said: "But, Habib, didn't you know that if you say, 'No, thank you,' they think you really don't want any?" In an Arab country etiquette dictates that the person being served must refuse the proffered dish several times, while his host urges him repeatedly to partake. The other side of the coin is that Americans in the Middle East, until they learn better, stagger away from banquets having eaten more than they want or is good for them.

When a public-health movie of a baby being bathed in a bathinette was shown in India recently, the Indian women who saw it were visibly offended. They won-

[1] **Gelett Burgess (1866–1947)** American writer; the above stanza is taken from *Goops and How to Be Them* (1900). [Ed. note.]
[2] **Emily Post (1873–1900)** American expert on manners. [Ed. note.]

dered how people could be so inhuman as to bathe a child in stagnant (not running) water. Americans in Iran soon learn not to indulge themselves in their penchant for chucking infants under the chin and remarking on the color of their eyes, for the mother has to pay to have the "evil eye" removed. We also learn that in the Middle East you don't hand people things with your left hand, because it is unclean. In India we learn not to touch another person, and in Southeast Asia we learn that the head is sacred.

In the interest of intercultural understanding various U. S. Government agencies have hired anthropologists from time to time as technical experts. The State Department especially has pioneered in the attempt to bring science to bear on this difficult and complex problem. It began by offering at the Foreign Service Institute an intensive four-week course for Point 4 technicians. Later these facilities were expanded to include other foreign service personnel.

The anthropologist's job here is not merely to call attention to obvious taboos or to coach people about types of thoughtless behavior that have very little to do with culture. One should not need an anthropologist to point out, for instance, that it is insulting to ask a foreigner: "How much is this in real money?" Where technical advice is most needed is in the interpretation of the unconscious aspects of a culture—the things people do automatically without being aware of the full implications of what they have done. For example, an ambassador who has been kept waiting for more than half an hour by a foreign visitor needs to understand that if his visitor "just mutters an apology" this is not necessarily an insult. The time system in the foreign country may be composed of different basic units, so that the visitor is not as late as he may appear to us. You must know the time system of the country to know at what point apologies are really due.

Twenty years of experience in working with Americans in foreign lands convinces me that the real problem in preparing them to work overseas is not with taboos, which they catch on to rather quickly, but rather with whole congeries of habits and attitudes which anthropologists have only recently begun to describe systematically.

Can you remember tying your shoes this morning? Could you give the rules for when it is proper to call another person by his first name? Could you describe the gestures you make in conversation? These examples illustrate how much of our behavior is "out of awareness," and how easy it is to get into trouble in another culture.

Nobody is continually aware of the quality of his own voice, the subtleties of stress and intonation that color the meaning of his words or the posture and distance he assumes in talking to another person. Yet all these are taken as cues to the real nature of an utterance, regardless of what the words say. A simple illustration is the meaning in the tone of voice. In the U. S. we raise our voices not only when we are angry but also when we want to emphasize a point, when we are more than a certain distance from another person, when we are concluding a meeting and so on. But to the Chinese, for instance, overloudness of the voice is most characteristically associated with anger and loss of self-control. Whenever we become really interested in something, they are apt to have the feeling we are angry, in spite of many years' experience with us. Very likely most of their interviews with us, however cordial, seem to end on a sour note when we exclaim heartily: "WELL, I'M CER-TAINLY GLAD YOU DROPPED IN, MR. WONG."

The Latin Americans, who as a rule take business seriously, do not understand our mixing business with informality and recreation. We like to put our feet up on the desk. If a stranger enters the office, we take our feet down. If it turns out that the stranger and we have a lot in common, up go the feet again—a cue to the other fellow that we feel at ease. If the office boy enters, the feet stay up; if the boss enters and our relationship with him is a little strained at the moment, they go down. To a Latin American this whole behavior is shocking. All he sees in it is insult or just plain rudeness.

Differences in attitudes toward space—what would be territoriality in lower forms of life—raise a number of other interesting points. U. S. women who go to live in Latin America all complain about the "waste" of space in the houses. On the other hand, U. S. visitors to the Middle East complain about crowding, in the houses and on the streetcars and buses. Everywhere we go space seems to be distorted. When we see a gardener in the mountains of Italy planting a single row on each of six separate terraces, we wonder why he spreads out his crop so that he has to spend half his time climbing up and down. We overlook the complex chain of communication that would be broken if he didn't cultivate alongside his brothers and his cousin and if he didn't pass his neighbors and talk to them as he moves from one terrace to the next.

A colleague of mine was caught in a snowstorm while traveling with companions in the mountains of Lebanon. They stopped at the next house and asked to be put up for the night. The house had only one room. Instead of distributing the guests around the room, their host placed them next to the pallet where he slept with his wife—so close that they almost touched the couple. To have done otherwise in that country would have been unnatural and unfriendly. In the U. S. we distribute ourselves more evenly than many other people. We have strong feelings about touching and being crowded; in a streetcar, bus or elevator we draw ourselves in. Toward a person who relaxes and lets himself come into full contact with others in a crowded place we usually feel reactions that could not be printed on this page. It takes years for us to train our children not to crowd and lean on us. We tell them to stand up, that it is rude to slouch, not to sit so close or not to "breathe down our necks." After a while they get the point. By the time we Americans are in our teens we can tell what relationship exists between a man and woman by how they walk or sit together.

In Latin America, where touching is more common and the basic units of space seem to be smaller, the wide automobiles made in the U. S. pose problems. People don't know where to sit. North Americans are disturbed by how close the Latin Americans stand when they converse. "Why do they have to get so close when they talk to you?" "They're so pushy." "I don't know what it is, but it's something in the way they stand next to you." And so on. The Latin Americans, for their part, complain that people in the U. S. are distant and cold—*retraídos* (withdrawing and uncommunicative).

An analysis of the handling of space during conversations shows the following: A U. S. male brought up in the Northeast stands 18 to 20 inches away when talking face to face to a man he does not know very well; talking to a woman under similar circumstances, he increases the distance about four inches. A distance of only eight to 13 inches between males is considered either very aggressive or indicative of a closeness of a type we do not ordinarily want to think about. Yet in many parts of Latin America and the Middle East distances which are almost sexual in connotation are the only ones at which people can talk comfortably. In Cuba, for instance, there is nothing suggestive in a man's talking to an educated woman at a distance of 13 inches. If you are a Latin American, talking to a North American at the distance he insists on maintaining is like trying to talk across a room.

To get a more vivid idea of this problem of the comfortable distance, try starting a conversation with a person eight or 10 feet away or one separated from you by a wide obstruction in a store or other public place. Any normally enculturated person can't help trying to close up the space, even to the extent of climbing over benches or walking around tables to arrive within comfortable distance. U. S. businessmen working in Latin America try to prevent people from getting uncomfortably close by barricading themselves behind desks, typewriters or the like, but their Latin American office visitors will often climb up on desks or over chairs and put up with loss of dignity in order to establish a spatial context in which interaction can take place for them.

The interesting thing is that neither party is specifically aware of what is wrong when the distance is not right. They merely have vague feelings of discomfort or anxiety. As the Latin American approaches and the North American backs away, both parties take offense without knowing why. When a North American, having had the problem pointed out to him, permits the Latin American to get close enough, he will immediately notice that the latter seems much more at ease.

My own studies of space and time have engendered considerable cooperation and interest on the part of friends and colleagues. One case recently reported to me had to do with a group of seven-year-olds in a crowded Sunday school classroom. The children kept fighting. Without knowing quite what was involved, the teacher had them moved to a larger room. The fighting stopped. It is interesting to speculate as to what would have happened had the children been moved to a smaller room.

The embarrassment about intimacy in space applies also to the matter of addressing people by name. Finding the proper distance in the use of names is even more difficult than in space, because the rules for first-naming are unbelievably complex. As a rule we tend to stay on the "mister" level too long with Latins and some others, but very often we swing into first naming too quickly, which amounts to talking down to them. Whereas in the U. S. we use Mr. with the surname, in Latin America the first and last names are used together and señor (Sr.) is a title. Thus when one says, "My name is Sr. So-and-So," it is interpreted to mean, "I am the Honorable, his Excellency So-and-So." It is no wonder that when we stand away, barricade ourselves behind our desks (usually a reflection of status) and call ourselves mister, our friends to the south wonder about our so-called "good-neighbor" policy and think of us as either high-hat or unbelievably rude. Fortunately most North Americans learn some of these things after living in Latin America for a while, but the aversion to being touched and to touching sometimes persists after 15 or more years of residence and even under such conditions as intermarriage.

The difference in sense of time is another thing of which we are not aware. An Iranian, for instance, is not taught that it is rude to be late in the same way that we in the U. S. are. In a general way we are conscious of this, but we fail to realize that their time system is structured differently from ours. The different cultures simply place different values on the time units.

Thus let us take as a typical case of the North European time system (which has regional variations) the situation in the urban eastern U. S. A middle-class business man meeting another of equivalent rank will ordinarily be aware of being two minutes early or late. If he is three minutes late, it will be noted as significant but usually neither will say anything. If four minutes late, he will mutter something by way of apology; at five minutes he will utter a full sentence of apology. In other words, the major unit is a five-minute block. Fifteen minutes is the smallest significant period for all sorts of arrangements and it is used very commonly. A half hour of course is very significant, and if you spend three quarters of an hour or an hour, either the business you transact or the relationship must be important. Normally it is an insult to keep a public figure or a person of significantly higher status than yourself waiting even two or three minutes, though the person of higher position can keep you waiting or even break an appointment.

Now among urban Arabs in the Eastern Mediterranean, to take an illustrative case of another time system, the unit that corresponds to our five-minute period is 15 minutes. Thus when an Arab arrives nearly 30 minutes after the set time, by his reckoning he isn't even "10 minutes" late yet (in our time units). Stated differently, the Arab's tardiness will not amount to one significant period (15 minutes in our system). An American normally will wait no longer than 30 minutes (two significant periods) for another person to turn up in the middle of the day. Thereby he often unwittingly insults people in the Middle East who want to be his friends.

How long is one expected to stay when making a duty call at a friend's house in the U. S.? While there are regional variations, I have observed that the minimum is very close to 45 minutes, even in the face of pressing commitments elsewhere, such as a roast in the oven. We may think we can get away in 30 minutes by saying something about only stopping for "a minute," but usually we discover that we don't feel comfortable about leaving until 45 minutes have elapsed. I am referring to afternoon social calls; evening calls last much longer and operate according to a different system. In Arab countries an American paying a duty call at the house of a desert sheik causes consternation if he gets up to leave after half a day. There a duty call lasts three days—the first day to prepare the feast, the second for the feast itself and the third to taper off and say farewell. In the first half day the sheik has barely had time to slaughter the sheep for the feast. The guest's departure would leave the host frustrated.

There is a well-known story of a tribesman who came to Kabul, the capital of Afghanistan, to meet his brother. Failing to find him, he asked the merchants in the market place to tell his brother where he could be found if the brother showed up. A year later the tribesman returned and looked again. It developed that he and his brother had agreed to meet in Kabul but had failed to specify what year! If the Afghan time system were structured similarly to our own, which it apparently is not, the brother would not offer a full sentence of apology until he was five years late.

Informal units of time such as "just a minute," "a while," "later," "a long time," "a spell," "a long, long time," "years" and so on provide us with the culturological equivalent of Evil-Eye Fleegle's "double-whammy" (in *Li'l Abner*). Yet these expressions are not as imprecise as they seem. Any American who has worked in an office with someone else for six months can usually tell within five minutes when that person will be back if he says, "I'll be gone for a while." It is simply a matter of learning from experience the individual's system of time indicators. A reader who is interested in communications theory can fruitfully speculate for a while on the very wonderful way in which culture provides the means whereby the receiver puts back all the redundant material that was stripped from such a message. Spelled out, the message might go somewhat as follows: "I am going downtown to see So-and-So about the Such-and-Such contract, but I don't know what the traffic conditions will be like or how long it will take me to get a place to park nor do I know what shape So-and-So will be in today, but taking all this into account I think I will be out of the office about an hour but don't like to commit myself, so if anyone calls you can say I'm not sure how long I will be; in any event I expect to be back before 4 o'clock."

Few of us realize how much we rely on built-in patterns to interpret messages of this sort. An Iranian friend of mine who came to live in the U. S. was hurt and puzzled for the first few years. The new friends he met and liked would say on parting: "Well, I'll see you later." He mournfully complained: "I kept expecting to see them, but the 'later' never came." Strangely enough we ourselves are exasperated when a Mexican can't tell us precisely what he means when he uses the expression *mañana*.[3]

The role of the anthropologist in preparing people for service overseas is to open their eyes and sensitize them to the subtle qualities of behavior—tone of voice, gestures, space and time relationships—that so often build up feelings of frustration and hostility in other people with a different culture. Whether we are going to live in a particular foreign country or travel in many, we need a frame of reference that will enable us to observe and learn the significance of differences in manners. Progress is being made in this anthropological study, but it is also showing us how little is known about human behavior.

QUESTIONS FOR DISCUSSION

1. For what audience is Hall writing this piece? What is the purpose of the essay?
2. List synonyms for the word "Goop." What is the difference between a klutz and a Goop?
3. Pick out a sentence in the first paragraph that you would consider to encompass the main idea. How are manners related to context?
4. What is a cultural anthropologist? Why would such a person be an asset to a government's state department?
5. Discuss or freewrite about any encounters with people from other cultures that you have had. Have you had any experiences similar to the ones described in this article?
6. What is ethnocentrism? What causes an attitude of ethnocentrism to develop?

[3]*mañana* Spanish for "tomorrow."

JULIUS ROBERT OPPENHEIMER
The Scientist in Society

Julius Robert Oppenheimer (1904–1967) presented the following speech, titled "The Scientist in Society," to alumni of Princeton University in 1953. Oppenheimer, a physicist, is most famous for his work contributing to the development of the atomic bomb. Oppenheimer describes scientists, not as disinterested manipulators of the physical environment, but as individuals who must take personal responsibility for their experiments and discoveries in the laboratory. Scientists, he asserts, must evaluate the social consequences of their work as a part of the scientific process. Oppenheimer also notes the modern tendency of nonscientists to ignore scientific and technological advances. Questioning the notion that all scientific discovery is progressive, Oppenheimer urges people to recognize the importance of understanding and evaluating issues in science, which have global repercussions.

There is something inherently comforting about a panel of experts. One knows that the partial and inadequate and slanted and personal views that he expresses will be corrected by the less partial, less personal views of everyone else on the panel; it is not unlike the experience of the professor who always is glad that he has to meet his class again because he can correct the mistakes that he made the last time. It is with such tentativeness that I am going to talk to you.

This is a vast terrain—one full of strange precipices, chasms and terrors. What I thought I would do first is to run over in a quite synoptic way a few general opinions, almost words only, which seem to me involved in the relations between science and man's life. It is my hope that I will do this with enough baldness so that you will pick up some of these words and deal with them more fully and more wisely than in this summary. I will then devote a little time to one problem which seems to me singularly fit in this hall and in this company, which worries me a great deal, and as to a resolution for which I have only the most rudimentary notions.

For one thing, we have changed the face of the earth; we have changed the way men live. We may not change the condition of man's life, but we have changed all modes in which that condition occurs. I do not by this mean to say that from the existence of science, from the discovery, knowledge, technique and power of science the particularities of the present time follow. But we all know that if life today is very different from what it was two hundred years ago, if we meet our human and political problems in a quite new form, that has much to do with the fact that we know how to do a great many things, and that there are people who are eager to do them, not typically scientists, but people who are glad to use the knowledge and with it the control which science has made available.

I need not belittle two points. One is that the effect of science on the condition of man's life is also in part a cultural and intellectual one. I shall return to that because it is my persuasion that this is largely a happy symbiosis of the past; today we have very little of it. The ideas which have changed the thinking caps of men and which derived from experience in science are really not contemporary ideas but go back a century or two centuries or more.

The second, of course, is not to try to give to scientific life an autonomy of society. It is possible, manifestly, for society so to arrange things that there is no science. The Nazis made a good start in that direction; maybe the Communists will achieve it; and there is not one of us free of the worry that this flourishing tree may someday not be alive any more.

But nonetheless we *have* changed the face of the earth; any beginning of a talk about science and society must take that as a fact.

There is another theme. This is a time that tends to believe in progress. Our ways of thought, our ways of arranging our personal lives, our political forms, point to the future, point not merely to change, to decay, to alteration, but point with a hopeful note of improvement that our progress is inevitable. In the acquisition of knowledge, in the very notion of a cumulative discipline, tomorrow in a certain sense comprises today and yesterday. How much this built-in sense of progress in man's life—which is, I think, not a religious notion, not a Christian notion—how much this derives from the effects of science on philosophical and political thought I would leave to historians of ideas. It is probably not wholly trivial.

A third theme is that science in a certain sense is universal. It is not universal in the sense that all men participate in it. It is universal in the sense that all men can participate in it. It is nonnational, nonlocal and, although one would not say noncultural, singularly independent of the form of government, the immediate tradition, or the affective life of a people. It has to do with *humanitas*. This universality is not a trivial thing at a time when forms of unity, large forms of unity in the world, appear to be for other reasons rather necessary. This has been very much in all our minds in the years since the last war. I remember that on one occasion when I was in this hall, at the Bicentennial of the University, we were talking about the universality of science; and at that very moment the Soviet delegate to the United Nations Atomic Energy Commission was imploring his government for permission to accept the scientific and technical report of the subcommittee of this commission. This, I think, is the last time—the last time I remember—that the Soviet government has said *yes* to anything, has said *yes* to an agreement of fact. I know how bitterly disappointing the experiences of these years have been as to universality of science, but we all know that this is bad politics but not bad science. We all know that there is no such thing as German physics or Soviet genetics or American astronomy. These fields can open themselves to all reasonable men willing to take the trouble to inquire.

There is also what may first seem like the opposite of universality; I hope you will bear that in mind when I talk of science as a great and beautiful word. There *is* a unity to it; but there is also an even more striking and immense diversity. Both of your speakers this morning are physicists, and I think we are very different from our brothers the chemists and our brothers the mathematicians. In our values, in our style, we are different. Physics is perhaps the branch of science which has been most concerned to keep itself one. The Physical Society splits off divisions from time to time but is reluctant to do so; and the divisions largely have to do with semiapplied science. Physics has a history of close association with mathematics, with astronomy, with epistemology and cosmology too. And yet we do not know very much about the rest of the scientists. I know that it is a very happy occasion at the Institute when some piece of work turns up which is of interest to both the mathematicians and the physicists. It is a very rare occasion and we tend to ring bells when a small bit of cement can be found between their interests. I would stress especially that there is no systematic unity of techniques, of appreciation, of values, of style between the many things that we call science. There is a lot of difference between the nuclear physicist and the agricultural scientist exploring the possibility of improving crops in some poor island in the Caribbean. They are scientists, and they understand each other, and we hope love each other. But they are not very much alike.

There are perhaps two or three other general things. One I believe may be of more importance to some of the other panels than to this. This is one of the by-products of the great flowering of science that dates back to the time when science did have an effect on culture and on ideas. We have been impressed, and I must say I never stop being impressed, by the great sweep of general order in which particulars are recognized as united. You know the examples: electricity and light, the quantum theory and the theory of valence, places where things that appeared to be separate, and each having its own order, appear as illustrations of a more general order. And one may say, I suppose, that science is a search for regularity and order in those domains of experience which have proven accessible to it.

I am not sure that the effect of the impressive victory of man's mind in this enterprise has not been to make us a little obtuse to the role of the contingent and the particular in life. It is true that many particulars can be understood and subsumed by a general order. But it is probably no less a great truth that elements of abstractly irreconcilable general orders can be subsumed by a particular. And this notion might be more useful to our friends who study man and his life than an insistence on following the lines which in natural science have been so overwhelmingly successful.

There is another great complex of questions. These I feel reassured to mention hardly at all because my friend and successor Dr. Waterman has thought so deeply about them; he is perhaps as well informed as any man in the world. This has to do with the great variety of means whereby society patronizes science, whereby it is possible for the scientist to operate and live and eat and do his work, get in some sense a bit of encouragement and in some sense a bit of nourishment. The problem of patronage is a complex one; it is changing; it has changed enormously in the last decade in this country. I leave it with a good conscience to Alan Waterman that he may deal with it wisely.

What is it, then, that bothers me especially, that I want not merely to mention but to worry about here? I think that in this matter perhaps this panel is not so different than the panel on the role of the artist, or the panel on the role of the philosopher. To put it with great brutality, the point is that the scientist is not in society today, any more than is the artist or the philosopher.

Of course, he does get paid, he does get patronized and even, for odd reasons that he sometimes does not understand, respected. But he is not in society, in the sense that the ideas he has, the work he is doing, stop really rather short with the limits of his profession. They are not part of the intellectual and cultural life of the times. I am over and over again appalled by how ignorant, how incredibly ignorant of the most rudimentary things about my subject are my fellows the historians, my acquaintances the statesmen, my friends the men of affairs. They have no notion of what cooks in physics; I think that they have very little notion of what cooks in any other science. And I know that only by good luck and some hard work do I have even a rudimentary notion of what cooks in other parts of the house called science than the one that I live in. I read the *Physical Review* and work very hard to catch up with it every two weeks; and I think maybe I have some notion of what is going on in some parts of physics; but by and large we know little about one another, and the world outside knows nothing about us. I think this may vary a little from place to place. Perhaps it is tradition in Britain, where there is a sort of delicate tendency, a national tendency, to refuse to let things become obscure and recondite, that there is a little more effort to see that civilized men have a notion of what the mathematicians and astronomers and physicists are doing—not merely to know the by-products of their works, the practical products, but what they are thinking.

This is in very sharp contrast, this startling general ignorance of scientific ideas and discoveries at the edge of the technical disciplines, in very sharp contrast to the state of affairs two or three centuries ago; and some of the reasons for this are manifest. But I believe that the science of today is subtler, richer, more relevant to man's life and more useful to man's dignity than the science which had such a great effect on the age of the enlightenment, had such a great effect, among other things, on the forms and patterns, traditions and hopes—reflected in our Constitution—of human society. Science is not retrograde; and there is no doubt that the quantum mechanics represents a more interesting, more instructive, richer analogy of human life than Newtonian mechanics could conceivably be. There is no doubt that even the theory of relativity, which has been so much vulgarized and so little understood, that even the theory of relativity is a matter which would be of real interest to people at large. There is no doubt that the findings of biology and astronomy and chemistry are discoveries that would enrich our whole culture if they were understood. And what is perhaps more troublesome, there is a gulf between the life of the scientist and the life of a man who isn't actively a scientist, dangerously deep. The experience of science—to stub your toe hard and then notice that it was really a rock on which you stubbed it—this experience is something that is hard to communicate by popularization, by education, or by talk. It is almost as hard to tell a man what it is like to find out something new about the world as it is to describe a mystical experience to a chap who has never had any hint of such an experience.

The enlightenment was a peculiar time; it was hopeful, and superficial, and humane; and how much of the ideas of the enlightenment derived from an appreciation of science, it is perhaps not right for anyone but a careful historian to say. But we know that the same men who wrote about politics and philosophy—not very good philosophy, and not too good politics—also wrote about natural science, about physics, and astronomy, and mathematics. We know that on two very different planes Franklin and Jefferson managed to span the whole way from a living, and in some cases even practicing, interest in science to the world of affairs. And we know how full their writings are of the illumination which one sheds on the other.

Science in those days was connected with the practical arts; it was very close to common sense. Yet always there is in science little more than the infinitely diligent and patient and unremitting application of the practical arts and common sense. By now it has come to be a long chain. The mere process of carrying a boy through the elementary steps of this chain consumes so much of his life and is such an exhausting operation, to the teacher and student alike, that the simple means of communication and understanding, which sufficed in the seventeenth and eighteenth centuries, are clearly not good enough.

This is a problem that has had the thought of many wise people; I do not pretend to be talking of anything new or strange. I suppose the notion of having laboratory courses was an attempt to bring the young man and woman into this experience of really discovering something; yet my fear is that by the time it gets into the laboratory and the professor knows the answer, the whole operation is different; it is an imitation and not the real thing. I suppose all of you have read the eloquent pleas which a number of scientists, of whom perhaps President Conant is the best known, have made for attempting to communicate some understanding of science by what is essentially the historical method. These do, I think, establish the fact that science as a human activity is treatable by the historical method. They do not, I think, establish that a scientific method, or a scientific discovery, is communicable by these means. I have a great anxiety that our educational directions, far from making us a part of the world we live in, in this very special sense that we share ideas and some bit of experience with our fellow men, may even be moving rather in the opposite direction.

This is odd: we live in the world very much affected by science, and even our thinking caps, and our ideas and the terms in which we tend to talk about things, the notion of progress, the notion of a fraternity of scholars and scientists which is so familiar to a Christian life and which has a new twist because of the spread of science—all of these we can see originally at a time when science was understood by men of affairs, by artists, by poets. We live today in a world in which poets and historians and men of affairs are proud that they wouldn't even begin to consider thinking about learning anything of science, regarding it as the far end of a tunnel too long for any wise man to put his head into. We therefore have, in so far as we have at all, a philosophy that is quite anachronistic and, I am convinced, quite inadequate to our times. I think that whatever may have been thought of Cartesian[1] and Newtonian[2] reforms in the intellectual life of Europe, the time when these were what the doctor ordered—all that the doctor ordered—is long past. Far more subtle recognition of the nature of man's knowledge and of his relations to the universe is certainly long overdue, if we are to do justice to the wisdom which our tradition has in it and to the brilliant and ever-changing flower of discovery which is modern science.

Research is action; and the question I want to leave in a very raw and uncomfortable form with you is how to communicate this sense of action to our fellow men who are not destined to devote their lives to the professional pursuit of new knowledge.

[1]**Cartesian** Pertaining to the science and philosophy of Rene Descartes (1596–1650), a religious skeptic, author of the famous kernel, "I think; therefore I am." [Ed. note.]
[2]**Newtonian** Relating to Sir Isaac Newton (1642–1727), whose work included the theories of gravitation and differential calculus. [Ed. note.]

QUESTIONS FOR DISCUSSION

1. Look at the introduction to the article. Who is the audience that Oppenheimer is addressing? What might be some unique characteristics of such an audience? Try to discover three or four ways in which this article is addressed specifically to the stated audience.
2. What are the implications of the tentative nature of science?
3. What is Oppenheimer's concern about the relationship between the general population and the scientific community? Considering this concern, what might be the purpose of the article?
4. What does Oppenheimer mean by describing science as "cumulative" (par. 7)?
5. Why should/shouldn't science be universal, nonnational, and nonlocal?
6. Examine the final statement: "Research is action." What might this mean?
7. Look at the use of pronouns in this article. Does the use of the generic "he" imply a kind of gender bias? Does Oppenheimer's use of pronouns support Anne Walton's argument in "Women Scientists: Are They Really Different" (p. 25)?

SHIGERU NAKAYAMA
Two Styles of Learning

In "Two Styles of Learning" Shigeru Nakayama discusses the contrasting methods of scholarship which dominate in the East and the West. The "documentary" scholarship of the East develops out of a tradition involving the "objective" recording of fact in an attempt to discover empirical laws. The "rhetorical" scholarship of the West involves a tradition, characteristic of ancient Greece, of debating the "truths" of the universe. The two styles have at least one aspect of the scientific method in common: both depend on careful observation of the natural world.

One cannot examine the academic traditions of East and West in the earliest stages of their development without being struck by the remarkable parallels between them. Though this awareness has received a variety of expressions, writings on the subject can be roughly divided into two types: those that seek to compare Babylonia and archaic China and those that would compare and contrast classical Greece with the China of the Warring States period. Behind this duality of focus it is possible to see the presence, in both traditions, of two distinct styles of scholarly activity, styles ultimately grounded in the two general mediums by which human knowledge is communicated. The first, which I shall call the documentary, is centered around the keeping and ordering of written records. The other is characteristically cultivated and transmitted orally in and through polemical discourse and may be conveniently termed the rhetorical.

DOCUMENTARY SCHOLARSHIP

The notion that there was cultural contact between the civilizations of Babylonia and ancient China (chiefly in the form of the spread of Babylonian civilization toward China) has been the subject of a long-standing and as yet unsettled debate among Orientalists.[1] But whether or not there was contact, that there are many points of apparent similarity cannot be denied. Foremost among them are records of extraordinary occurrences in the heavens. Abundant both in ancient Chinese documents and on the cuneiform tablets of approximately the 7th century B.C. from the archives of King Ashurbanipal, these records evince an amazing likeness of purpose, method, and function in the activity that gave rise to them. In Babylonia as well as in China, people recorded changes in the heavens in order to ascertain their influence on earthly events. They were engaged, that is, in varieties of astrology.

The implicit suggestion that a discussion of documentary learning might properly begin with an account of ancient astrology may well meet with resistance. . . . But the issue is not the interpretation of events, but, rather, the records kept for this purpose. Moreover, in ancient times there was virtually no distinction between the historian and the astrologer. This is particularly evident in China where the term *shih* (史) comprehended both pursuits. Ssu-ma Ch'ien, the most famous of the Chinese astrologer-historians, is best known as an official historian charged with the compliation of court documents, but in his post as Grand Recorder (*t'ai shih ling*) he was also responsible for maintaining astrological records. In other words, "astrology" was originally regarded as historical, documentary science. If one thinks of learning as beginning with the oral traditions of the storyteller, traditions later written down, then these early records of strange and dramatic phenomena in the heavens may simply document what were perhaps the most impressive events recounted by the bard.

Information can be conveyed through written records only if readers are able to apprehend it more or less as the chronicler intended. In this imperative, one can recognize the first beginnings of a conscious orientation toward "objectivity." In recording ordinary historical events there is, of course, ample room for subjective interpretations. But the self-evident character of most events typically documented for astrological purposes (solar eclipses, for example) makes such records resistant to the biases of the transmitter-recorder. It is because they constitute an example of intended "pure objectivity" that I have chosen to look at astrological records as exemplary of scholarly activity in the documentary style.

But can one find in ancient astrology the search for lawful regularities that moderns have come to see as the goal of scientific activity? Both Babylonian and Chinese astrology begin with a recording of the appearance of extraordinary celestial phenomena—solar eclipses, comets, meteors, and the like. Should the outbreak

---

[1]In prewar Japan this question was the source of a celebrated controversy between Shinjō Shinzō, who claimed that Chinese astronomy represented an original development, and Iijima Tadao, who argued that it had Babylonian roots. See Shinjō Shinzō (1928).

of an earthly calamity such as war or famine coincide with one of these phenomena, then the two are seen as related in some way. For example, let us assume that on several occasions when the sun is in a certain position, a flood occurs in a particular region. The next time a solar eclipse occurs with the sun in the same position, it is taken as an omen of another flood in that region. Forecasts of the coming disaster are made and precautions taken. To those engaged in this activity, the mechanism that linked heavenly phenomena and earthly events remained unknown. But the whole enterprise rested on the conviction that there was a relationship between the two. It was in order to find out all they could about this relationship that people sought to assemble as much data as possible concerning extraordinary heavenly phenomena and natural disasters and to hypothesize about their relations.

Although speculative dogmas (such as the theory of Yin-yang and the Five Elements) were used in forging the interpretive link between occurrences in the heavens and events on earth, the records themselves have outlived the half-baked theories. Just as administrators and members of the legal profession tend to endow precedent with intrinsic significance, so the ancient astrologer regarded past records as an independent and virtually absolute source of authority. Every effort was made to resolve the discrepancy between the records and the new phenomenon within the established system of explanations, usually by an expanded interpretation of new and old data that made it possible to deal with both under the same classificatory rubric. Only unprecedented anomalies generated enough tension to require new interpretation. As a result, revolutionary theories were almost unheard of as the records continued to increase year after year.

Contemporary readers will not find this surprising. Believing with modern science that links between extraordinary celestial occurrences and terrestrial disasters are either nonexistent or irrelevant, they do not share the ancients' hope that the faithful accumulation of such data will eventually make possible the extrapolation of "empirical laws" governing this relationship. They are much more likely to be amazed that the ancients continued to pore through stack upon stack of old documents without becoming fed up with it all. Yet the discipline of the documentary style is readily recognizable. Although it does not necessarily call for a creative mind, it demands the same painstaking care, the same devotion to clerical routine, as bookkeeping.

The clerical collection and classification of documents also requires a pool of industrious, full-time workers, a condition that can be met only by a highly developed bureaucracy. In this sense, this style of scholarship seems particularly well suited to Chinese political culture. Its emergence under the "Oriental despotisms" of Babylonia and China is also suggestive. For unlike the horoscope astrology of today, the astrology of extraordinary occurrences in the heavens was not concerned with the fate of individuals as such, but with the divining of answers to questions of concern to the monarch as absolute ruler of the state (Nakayama, 1964). From the dawn of recorded history down to modern times, the major task of the Chinese observatory was to make and interpret the types of astrological observations that were deemed relevant to this task. This is the "astronomy" (t'ien-wen) so evident in the official dynastic histories of Imperial China.

RHETORICAL LEARNING

The ancient world also witnessed the emergence of another style of scholarly activity, one that stands in sharp contrast to that carried on in the routine of official business. Born from the heat of disputation, this "rhetorical scholarship" was largely the creation of the Greek natural philosophers and Sophists and the pre-Ch'in (3rd century B.C.) philosophers of China.

People often speak of the "miracle of Greece." They marvel that Thales (624–546 B.C.) and the other pre-Socratic natural philosophers should have approached nature with a sensibility so radically different from that of the astrologers and court historians who dominated cultural life before them. It is less often observed that the sequence of their discussions about a primary "stuff" that underlies and produces all things is finally intelligible only as the product of controversy, only as the issue of impassioned debate. The abstract logic of the Eleatics and the atomic theory of Democritus (460–370 B.C.) had their inception neither in official documents nor in the incantations of diviners, but in the midst of disputation and in the course of relentless pursuit of the issues. It was in this context that recognizable differences emerged and individual thinkers came to be identified with particular theories.

There is a conventional view of the scientist as one who does his thinking alone in the quiet of his room, eschewing the polemics of the political arena. In ancient Greece, the nature of the cosmos was discussed with the same combative spirit as were political matters. Forged and honed in the direct democracy of the Greek city-state where citizens hammered out public policy through discussion and debate, this was a spirit that regarded words as sovereign and saw in persuasive techniques a means to personal advancement.

The natural philosophers themselves seem to have been essentially publicists, itinerant moralists who had been attracted to Athens from the many outlying Greek colonies by the city's wealth. In fact, there is some indication that it was only after their political ambitions were thwarted and as they faced persecution and banishment that they escaped to mathematics or disguised themselves as students of nature (Africa, 1968). In the eyes of the upstanding citizens of Athens, the natural philosophers remained outsiders who lived off the city.

Yet it is the Sophists who were regarded as social parasites by later generations. When Nishi Amane first translated "Sophist" into Japanese in the latter half of the 19th century, his study of the history of Western thought led him to choose the term *nise-gakusha* (偽学者) or "purveyors of false learning."[2] Today, however, a century of scholarship has done much to redeem the Sophists' reputation, and scholars are more willing to view them as serious—if condescending—educators (Hunt, 1961). When they are taken seriously and seen in the context of what is apt to be a conservative profession, their manner and methods appear quite striking, even revolutionary.

---

[2]Nishi Amane, *Hyakugaku Renkan*. Although this work was not published until much later, Nishi wrote the manuscript in 1870 and used it as the basis for lectures at his private school.

The stage and setting for the men who have been called history's first professional teachers was the Greek *polis* of the 5th century B.C.[3] Greek society was then at the height of its prosperity, and Athenian forms of democracy were spreading throughout the region, but public educational institutions were as yet unknown, and learning remained something that each individual had to arrange for himself. Drawn to Athens by its wealth, like the natural philosophers, the Sophists were to find their opportunity here. Not being citizens, they sought private patrons, advertising their knowledge in the marketplace and going from street to street in search of an audience and students. To these efforts the mild Athenian climate lent a helping hand, drawing people out of doors and fostering a fondness for conversation and discussion. Moreover, under a democratic regime, people with political ambitions were glad to pay the Sophists for their expertise in rhetoric. For their part, the Sophists delighted the crowds with their unusual doctrines and shrewdly cultivated their public image. Protagoras (5th century B.C.) is perhaps the best case in point, for he is said to have amassed a considerable fortune from the teaching fees he collected. Increased competition after his time led to a decline in the going rate for instruction and "initial" fees, and later generations did not prosper to the same degree. Nevertheless, Plato, Aristotle, Isocrates, and other "teachers of mankind" supported themselves by giving oral instruction and operating private academies. The education in which the Sophists were engaged was thus an individualistic activity in which teachers peddled their skill and would-be students paid for it. This was the atmosphere in which Greek learning was born. As a result, polemical techniques and the dialectical style came to be closely associated with Greek philosophy, science, and culture.

The persuasive and oratorical arts the Sophists left behind are of more interest than what they had to say. What matter a few errors, so long as they were able to get the better of their rivals! In the *Gorgias*, Plato's Socrates forces the orator to acknowledge that his rhetoric is not an art which teaches knowledge of right and wrong but merely a means of persuasion that engenders belief without knowledge. An art designed solely to convince, he argues, is a "spurious counterfeit." Rhetoric is not bad in itself, but it must serve the search for truth. These views of Plato sound quite similar to our own. But what surprises us as we read the *Gorgias* today is how absolutely indispensable oratory appears to have been to scholarship of the time. Socrates himself emerges as an exceptionally capable rhetorician. Moreover, rhetoric is regarded, at least implicitly, as a method of discovery. Polemical discourse stimulates the mind, activating and nurturing creative thought. The locus of true education is dialogue, for it is here that new ideas and patterns of thought emerge. At least this is what Socrates and Plato believed. Hence they preferred to entrust their thought to the living minds of men rather than to the skins of dead sheep.

The breakdown of the Greek *polis* and the establishment of the Macedonian Empire resulted in the geographical diffusion of what had been a regional Athenian

---

[3]In discussing the Sophists, I have generally adopted the view of the outstanding French historian H. I. Marrou. His views are available in English in *A History of Education in Antiquity*, trans. George Lamb (London, 1956).

culture. This posed a new challenge for Greek learning. Persuading people with different languages, customs, and manners required more than clever plays on words and the skillful use of oratorical techniques. Attention to grammar became necessary, and logic replaced rhetoric as the primary tool of persuasion. Substance also received increasing attention, for stripped of the power of rhetoric, vacuous remarks were more readily exposed as such. In Isocrates (436–338 B.C.) one already sees a man more interested in substantive matters than the rhetorical forms of the Sophists, and in Plato (427–347) and Aristotle (348–322) there is a definite shift of emphasis from mere rhetoric to logic.

The expanded context in which Athenian culture now sought to make its way also served to accentuate another element of the Greek argumentative style. If one is to be successful as roving orator, one's remarks must have sufficient generality or universality about them that they can be readily understood by anyone. Within the narrow confines of a sect, knowledge to be transmitted may be treated as authoritative in itself or as the "divine wisdom" of the founder. But the relationship between a teacher and an audience of strangers is more like that between a salesman and a group of skeptical customers. Neither sweeping claims to authority nor smug complacency are effective in such a situation—nor in any context involving diverse assemblies of people. Knowledge and ways of thinking that are developed in and shaped by discussions among diverse participants tend inevitably to be refined in the direction of the general and the universal.

Disputation begins as ordinary human conversation, with talk of things that can be seen with the eye and touched with the hand—with concrete things. As the discussion proceeds, however, it departs from concrete objects and events. Thoughts coalesce, convictions become clarified, points of agreement and conflict are articulated and urged, and the conversation grows more and more abstract. Thus abstraction is born of persuasive discourse. The fact that the ancient atomic theorists seem to have approximated the atomic theory of modern science without the aid of experimentation or experimental facts, even though they approached the problem with a different set of concerns, is an example of the results obtainable on occasion through the vigorous pursuit of abstraction in a polemical context.

Ever since the emergence of Hellenist civilization, there have been two streams of thought in the Western academic tradition: the philosophical school that began with Plato, and the rhetorical tradition founded by Isocrates as he drew upon and absorbed the work of the Sophists.[4] The latter stream has seldom received the attention accorded the former. Presumably less readily committed to writing, rhetoric suffered historically from the fact that it was not in keeping with the cultural tastes of early modern Europe. Long subjected to the ruthless attacks of the Platonists, the Sophists in particular emerged as the enemy of the "philosophers," retaining a place in the history of philosophy only as "bad guys." Yet the fact that they were better remunerated than either the Platonic geometers or the teachers of the "three R's"

---

[4]We are accustomed to thinking of philosophers and rhetoricians as distinct groups, but in terms of their scholarly fields, no clear distinction can be made between the two. Mutual name-calling makes the distinction even more problematic. For instance, according to the "sophist" Isocrates, the Platonists were "sophists," while he and his followers were "philosophers." Thus one comes closer to the mark by referring to each of these scholarly groups by the name of the individual whose work was central to its tradition.

attests to the esteem they commanded in their society (Kōno, 1958). Nor can their lasting contributions be easily dismissed. They were the precursors of grammar and linguistics (Forbes, 1933), and the forensic techniques that they left behind played a significant role in the formation of the Roman legal tradition (Periphanakis, 1953).[5]

During the same 5th century in which the Sophists prospered in Greece, the so-called "hundred philosophers" were actively propagating their views among the "Warring States" of China. The decline of the Chou Dynasty had given rise to a plethora of small, independent, contending kingdoms, and, in the midst of a political crisis not unlike that which occurred in ancient Greece, similar intellectual conditions also emerged. A lower ruling stratum known as *shih* (土) began to come into its own as the lords and nobles of these principalities sought to enhance their power and prestige by attracting the most able and accomplished men to their kingdoms. In response to this demand, powerful *shih* became lecturers to kings or high officials, and groups of lesser *shih* began to form around them. The *shih* were wandering scholars who sought to change the world with their words—and win appointment to office by selling rulers on the value of what they had to offer.

The amount of information these scholars could bring with them on their travels was perforce minimal. Astrologer-officials might preserve huge stacks of records, classified and indexed for ready accessibility, but the wandering scholar was limited to what he could carry in a straw basket strapped to his back. Before the invention of paper, the Chinese kept their records on foot-long strips of bamboo or wood. For all practical purposes this meant that the only records available to the wandering scholar were those he kept in his head.

Clearly the knowledge the wandering *shih* had for sale was not bound in quantities of documents. They were purveyors of ideas, not encyclopedia salesmen. If a prospective buyer happened to be intelligent, the encounter could also be intellectually stimulating. But the *shih*'s wares were not limited to ideas. Merchandising methods—rhetoric and logic—were marketed as well, as Legalists, Confucianists, and Mohists vied with one another to make their product as attractive as possible. . . .

A more careful look at the Chinese rhetorical tradition, however, discloses a preference for arguing in terms of precedent and previous example that contrasts with the Greek style of logical persuasion. This tendency was reinforced in the Han period by Emperor Han Wu Ti's exclusive preference for Confucian teachings. Under his regime, the teachings of all other schools were suppressed. Even Mohism, which once had divided the intellectual world with the followers of Confucius, all but died out, not to be revived until the early 20th century when intellectuals under the influence of modern Western science welcomed its radical critique of Confucianism.[6]

PROPENSITIES AND FUNCTIONS

The distinctive character of the two scholarly styles should now be clear. The documentation of extraordinary occurrences in the heavens is cast in a settled, agri-

[5]This was first demonstrated by the famous 19th-century legal scholar F. K. Savigny.
[6]The best known work of the Mohist revival is by Hu Shih (1928).

cultural mode. The work is steady and the yield is stable, but the product is plain, restricted in scope, and conservatively inclined. The rhetorical style of the Sophists and pre-Ch'in debating scholars, on the other hand, is of the mobile, commercial type. It is pursued with a broader vision and tends to be progressive, but it cannot exist without an adversary and leads to the accumulation of substantive knowledge only in exceptional cases. New theories appear one after another, but rise and fall in such a manner that accumulation can be little more than another name for confusion.

Scholarship in the documentary style lacks the capacity to generate new problems. And when new problems are not forthcoming, the enthusiasm of scholars declines and their work goes flat. Rhetorical scholarship, on the other hand, is concerned with nothing if not the creation of problems. Posing and counterposing questions is its major function. But disputation seldom leads to firm conclusions. The adversaries advance their own doctrines and strive to persuade opponents of their own veracity. Such encounters provide opportunities for participants to refine their opinions, but the attainment of a "truth beyond" that transcends the particular views of the participants involved is not its object. Thus, whatever may eventually emerge from such discourse, it does not become generally accepted "truth." Indeed, the outcome is normally inconclusive. When interest wanes and the participants leave the scene, the controversy vanishes into thin air without becoming an academic tradition.

Documentary scholarship has as its proper object certain objective phenomena it is obliged to record, but scholarship in the rhetorical style is not likewise bound, though the polemicist may be constrained by his opponent. Thus its discussions occasionally digress from the subject at hand and end up as abstract debates over empty theories. Those who prefer proof to precept will always find such discussions unsatisfactory. And yet abstraction has always been a proper function of argumentative discourse.

During the early period with which I have been concerned, these two styles of scholarship were pursued largely without reference to each other. Disputation did not necessarily proceed on the basis of previously recorded data, as Plato's famous distinction between knowledge and opinion reminds us. Recent scholarship has increasingly embraced the view that the "miracle of Greece" was really no miracle at all, that Greek natural science was in fact largely built upon data accumulated by, and borrowed from, the empirical science of Babylon (Neugebauer, 1969). Yet it was a phenomenon of the late classical and early Hellenist period. The rhetorical scholarship of the Greek natural philosophers and Sophists neither required nor presupposed the Babylonian records of extraordinary occurrences in the heavens, and Greek influence on these records is inconceivable.

A mass of detailed, particular facts may supply the polemicist with data for argument, but one may point out many instances in the history of science and learning in which the weight of accumulated documents had become so great as to inhibit the emergence of a theory able to control all available data. An abstract notion such as the idea that all things come of water cannot be formulated while the mind is wholly absorbed in the details of things and events. Conversely, Chinese government records are said to have been rife with the controversies of the hundred philosophers before being edited as official histories.

Which of these two styles of scholarship should be called learning? Which deserves the name science? Although I have thus far seemed to view the rhetorical style slightly more sympathetically, this question cannot be answered unequivocally. It is, of course, easy enough to say that learning encompasses both functions and that healthy growth occurs when each type functions fully and a balance is maintained between them. But how is this balance to be maintained? And what is healthy growth? From the lofty heights of modern science, a kind of "victor's logic" readily leads us to assume that the course of Western science precisely reflects this balanced and healthy development. Yet such a view has no sanction. Moreover, insofar as our task is not to celebrate modern science but to understand from a comparative perspective the dynamic historical changes that have made the world of learning what it is today, such preconceptions can only impede. It will be more fruitful to ask not which scholarly style is better but rather how each has functioned in the history of science and learning wherever we find it.

Documentary scholarship finds little meaning in repeated recording of the same phenomenon; it is variety that is welcomed. Extraordinary phenomena are particularly worth documenting. It is such phenomena rather than the discovery of laws that constitute the chief concern of the astrologer and the historian. The ancients regarded both lunar and solar eclipses as extraordinary occurrences and recorded them. Since the prediction of lunar eclipses turned out to be comparatively simple, their nomological character was soon discovered. Once this occurred, astrologers lost interest and ceased to record them with any regularity. Solar eclipses, however, proved more difficult to forecast, and they continued to attract the attention of observers.

Even among the rhetorical traditions one can recognize degrees in the relative importance attached to documentation and demonstration. The contrast between the dialectic of the Greek philosophers and the tendency of the ancient Chinese philosophical schools to employ historical example as a persuasive device has already been noted (Graham, 1973). But differences obviously existed among the Greeks as well. Though extant records might well suggest otherwise, the first to advocate the preservation of knowledge in books was not Plato, whose quest for universal truth was accompanied by a distaste for writing, but the Sophists, with their interest in particular phenomena and their love of rhetoric.

As they became embroiled in actual controversies, the Sophists and the followers of Isocrates did of course strive to cast their remarks in general, universal terms. Yet they were clearly less thorough than the Platonists in this respect. Here one can already see two distinctive intellectual temperaments at work. The Sophists held that the world is in a state of constant change and flux. As relativists, they were interested in change, in variety, and in the particular. Avoiding the strict adherence to things eternal that dulls sensitivity to the actual, they cultivated a direct, empirical, pragmatic, and opportunistic attitude toward the changing world they saw around them. And compared to those who sought coherence, universality, and eternity, to those whose quest for law and order was liable to make them conservative, the Sophists were progressive, even radical.

The quarrel between sophist rhetoricians and philosophical polemicists has appeared in many guises throughout the course of history (Streuver, 1970), and still continues today. Historians, publicists, and journalists tend to be arrayed on the change-oriented side. This type does not seek eternal, unchanging laws, for it knows them to describe only the prosaic, the commonplace, the recurring. It responds enthusiastically only to the exceptional or extraordinary. Those who pursue unchanging regularities, on the other hand, are driven by a theorizing, systematizing impulse. They would reduce the actual diversity of the world to a series of generalizations, stop the flow of history at a given point in time, and force the world into a mold of their own making. As disturbed by the exceptional as the change-oriented are delighted, they are as a type inevitably oriented toward order.

Bibliography

Africa, Thomas W. *Science and the State in Greece and Rome*. New York: Wiley, 1968.

Forbes, P. B. R. "Greek Pioneers in Philology and Grammar," *Classical Review*, 47, 1933, p. 105ff.

Graham, A. C. "China, Europe and the Origins of Modern Science," in Nakayama, S. and Sivin, N. (eds.) *Chinese Science*. Cambridge, Mass.: Harvard University Press, 1973, p. 61.

Hu Shih. *The Development of the Logical Method in Ancient China*. Cambridge, Mass.: Harvard University Press, 1928.

Hunt, Everett Lee. "Plato and Aristotle on Rhetoric and Rhetoricians," in Howes, Raymond (ed.). *Historical Studies of Rhetoric and Rhetoricians*. Ithaca, N. Y.: Cornell University Press, 1961.

Kōno Yoichi. *Gakumon no Magarikado* [Learning at the Crossroads]. Tokyo: Iwanami Shoten, 1958.

Nakayama Shigeru. *Senseijutsu* [Astrology]. Tokyo: Kinokuniya Shoten, 1964.

Neugebauer, Otto. *The Exact Sciences in Antiquity*, 2nd ed. New York: Dover, 1969.

Periphanakis, Constantin. *Le Sophistes et le Droit*. Athens, 1953.

Shinjō Shinzō. *Tōyō Temmongakushi Kenkyū* [Studies in the History of East Asian Astronomy]. Kyoto: Kōbundō, 1928.

Struever, Nancy S. *The Language of History in the Renaissance*. Princeton, NJ: Princeton University Press, 1970.

QUESTIONS FOR DISCUSSION

1. According to Nakayama there are two types of scholarly activity—documentary and rhetorical. Briefly define each type. Discuss the source of each type.
2. Both styles of learning use observation as a source of gathering data. How do the methods employed by each differ?
3. The author remarks that in ancient China there was no distinction between the astrologer and the historian. Explain how this was true. The author also states that there was not a distinction between the astrologer and the astronomer. What is the difference between these two fields in the contemporary world?
4. Define the term "rhetoric" (par. 14). In what way is a writing course a course in rhetoric? What is a dialectic?
5. This article is set up as a comparison and contrast. Briefly outline the essay to show how the author uses comparison and contrast.

ANNE WALTON
Women Scientists:
Are They Really Different?

The following essay, "Women Scientists: Are They Really Different?" by Anne Walton, discusses the question of whether women are by nature unsuited to scientific study. Walton traces the prejudice against women scientists through the centuries and focuses on the barriers keeping women out of the sciences in the contemporary world. The article, which includes a number of interesting quotations from prominent scientists of the past and present, attempts to persuade the reader that the misogynistic attitudes toward women in science have no basis in empirical data.

INTRODUCTION

For most of my working life I have been a practising scientist. I have worked in industrial and academic laboratories—as a laboratory assistant—and as a consultant. I have also taught chemistry from 'O' level to the supervision of PhD students. But it is only in recent years that I have begun to look seriously beyond my own personal experience—to the role of women in science in a wider context.

To my dismay, it seemed that there had been little improvement since I had embarked on my own career. The dice are *still* so heavily loaded against girls and women choosing a scientific career that I was astonished that so *many* had succeeded, against all the odds, rather than that there were so few.

Many factors deter girls from choosing a scientific career and one of these is undoubtedly the attitudes adopted by parents, teachers, friends and society in general. It was this area which I decided to investigate and my studies so far have indicated that negative attitudes towards women scientists have always existed and still prevail. These attitudes need to be demonstrated and combated because they adversely affect women's careers, role models for girls and boys' expectations of women.

Science is dominated by men, most of its practitioners are men and it is said to have a masculine image. Society does not expect women to become scientists so those that do, know that they are 'stepping out of line'. This, in itself, makes them 'special' in some way because the men, in a male-dominated profession are not, in any sense, rebels. In an attempt to discover whether women scientists have any other characteristics in common, I have been gathering information about their lives, the way they work, the nature of that work and what they say about themselves.

If one includes both past and present women scientists one finds, superficially at least, a great diversity, particularly in their backgrounds, which range from poor, working-class to rich aristocracy. Some are married, with children, while some are unmarried and childless. However, it is evident that most of them developed habits of independent thought at an early age. Often these seem to have been fostered by parents who, in some cases, were subsequently dismayed when their daughters insisted on following their own inclinations and rejected traditional roles. Perhaps the parents *inadvertently* sowed the seeds of rebellion. Not all of the women scientists had to struggle against adversity as we normally think of it. The privileged ones who could have led idle, comfortable lives, chose not to, but all were quietly confident that what they were doing was *right for them*.

On the whole, I have limited my investigations so far mainly to women working in the physical and applied sciences because they represent a much smaller minority than women in the biological sciences. A consideration of the type of work which these women do may be significant. Interestingly, while most of them began by studying *pure* science and mathematics, as their careers developed, many of them seem to have been drawn to research areas with applications in everyday life, particularly in medicine. Their chosen fields of research, as intellectually tough as any in science, yet had strong humanitarian connotations.

This suggested to me that possibly science as constructed by males might prove to be a 'bad fit' for females. Certainly many girls seem to be ill at ease when confronted by science. Perhaps those women who had forged a career for themselves on the 'inside' of the scientific edifice were, consciously or unconsciously, adjusting and adapting their own function within that framework so as to derive more satisfaction from their work by relating it to a social context.

ATTITUDES TO WOMEN IN SCIENCE

It seemed to me that the fairest way to discuss attitudes would be to illustrate them using direct quotations by the women's contemporaries wherever possible. These fall into a number of categories each of which exemplifies a particular group of attitudes, although there is considerable overlap.

The idea that there might be innate differences between the intellectual powers of men and women has been bandied about for hundreds, if not thousands, of years. Indeed, a great deal of effort has been put into the search for differences, so far with limited success. At one time, brain size was thought to be an indicator of mental capacity. After the death of the eminent mathematician, Sonya (or Sofia) Kovalevskaia in 1891, her brain, which had been preserved in alcohol, was weighed and the weight compared with that of the brain of the scientist Herman van Helmholtz (Osen, 1974). Given the difference in body weight, her brain was proportionately larger. This practice was dropped when the brains of some idiots turned out to be heavier than those of the brilliant! More recently, there has been an interest in the functions of the left and right hemispheres of the brain and attempts have been made to relate these to gender stereotypes. In a book published in 1982 by Richter the question is asked 'Are there then some types of scientific work that women on the whole can do better than men?'. And later 'It may be concluded that women are not lacking in the abilities required for scientific research'. Then in the same paragraph 'The different fields of science offer a wide range of opportunities for people with many different kinds of abilities and so long as they do not expect too much, they offer a life that many find rewarding and enjoyable'. This is hardly encouraging to the budding female scientist.

Some further examples of these attitudes are shown in box 1.

Box 1—Inherent Differences

The female . . . seldom reach any farther than to a sleight superficial smattering in any deep science. (*The Compleat Midwifes Practice Enlarged*, 1659)

Women have no share in sciences and employments, because that they are not capable thereof. (Poulain de la Barre, 1673 (English translation, 1677))

Women are cast in too soft a mould, are made of too fine, too delicate a composure to endure the severity of study, the drudgery of contemplation, the fatigue of profound speculation. (*The British Apollo*, 1708)

The principal feature which appears to me to characterize the caucasian race . . . is the power that many of its *male* members have of advancing the horizon of science. (Bennett, 1870)

There can be no real question that the female mind stands considerably below the male . . . the ready firmness of decision which belongs by nature to the truly masculine mind is very rarely to be met with in the feminine. (Romanes, 1887)

When we come to science we find women are simply nowhere. The feminine mind is quite unscientific . . . (Swinburne, 1902)

We must put a stop to this, or we shall have Mary [Somerville] in a straight-jacket one of these days. (Mary Somerville's father about 1800 (Osen, 1974))

The reporter suggested to Irène (Joliot-Curie) that perhaps the career she had chosen would be too punishing for a woman. (Reid, 1978)

Nature herself prescribed to the woman her function as mother and housewife and that laws of nature cannot be ignored . . . without grave damage, which . . . would especially manifest itself in the following generation. (Max Planck, about 1897 (Krafft, 1978))

The notion that intense intellectual activity was damaging to women and particularly to their reproductive function and possible offspring, flourished towards the end of the nineteenth century. Rosenberg's *Beyond Separate Spheres* (Rosenberg, 1982) includes an interesting discussion on this issue and its significance for women then entering higher education in the United States.

It follows from the arguments outlined above that if women *do* become scientists they are only fit for work at the lower levels or under the direction of a man, or both. I recently talked to a woman chemist who was employed in industry in the 1920s and 1930s, she said 'I was expected to do all the boring jobs that came into the laboratory, while anything interesting was handed out to one of the men'. Later she said 'I was second in command in my own, now large department, and, as the head enjoyed rather poor health, I often had to run things for weeks or months on end'. When she left in 1935, she says 'they had difficulty in finding my successor, finally paying me the supreme compliment of replacing me by a young man to whom they paid a salary £100 greater than the figure I was receiving after ten years'.

Information on the type of work available to women scientists in America up to 1940 may be found in Rossiter's (1982) *Women Scientists in America* where she points out that promotion to senior positions was virtually confined to the women's colleges unless women were willing to move out of 'mainstream' science into such areas as home economics or nutrition which attracted relatively few men.

Some further examples are given in box 2. There are many more.

Box 2—What Women Can Do

[Women] make excellent assistants, and they could probably do the work of the assay, or city analyst's office, or of an observatory, better than most men. Ladies' names often appear as authors of papers, generally in organic chemistry, or in subjects involving tedious but accurate readings of instruments—. (Swinburne, 1902)

[Caroline Herschel] took care of all the laborious numerical calculations and reductions, all the record keeping, and the other tedious minutiae that required a trained mind but would have consumed too much of Sir William's time. (Osen, 1974)

All [woman's] perceptions of minute details, all her delicate observation of color, of form, of shape, of change, and her capability of patient routine, would be of immense value in the collection of scientific facts. (Professor Maria Mitchell, Vassar, 1876 (*Science*, 1979))

Even Professor A. accords me his sanction when I sew his papers or tie up a sore finger or dust the table etc . . . they can't say study spoils me for anything else . . . Professor Ordway trusts me to do his work for him . . . I am only too happy to do anything for him. (Ellen Swallow (became a founder of the American Home Economics Association) 1870–1873 at MIT (Bernard, 1964))

In the case of Pierre and Marie Curie, Pierre Curie was the creator, who with his genius established new laws of physics. Marie was outstanding for other qualities such as character, exceptional tenacity, precision and patience. (Leprince-Ringuet (Richter, 1982))

Some teachers encouraged me by saying that [anthropology] would be nice for a woman because there are . . . domestic aspects such as cooking and clothing. I did not like such remarks. (Chie Nakane, Tokyo—contemporary (Richter, 1982))

If a woman does manage to succeed in science, against all the odds, the commonest allegation made is that it is because she is collaborating with a man. Because most scientists are men and because in the experimental sciences most people work in a team, the chance of a woman collaborating with a man is very high. Certainly the support of a powerful male sponsor (Rossiter, 1982) can sometimes ensure that a woman is not overlooked, but receives the promotion she deserves. There is no doubt that women scientists have been helped in this way. Mary Fieser, for example, would not have been allowed to practise chemistry at Harvard (Pramer, 1985) had she not been married to Louis Fieser. She became his graduate student and continued as a research associate while other women were not taken on because the professors would not have women in their research teams. Agnes Pockels' work would probably never have been published unless she had received the support of Lord

Rayleigh (Giles and Forrester, 1971) who submitted her work for publication. It seems to me that there is nothing unfair or unreasonable in young persons of either sex being helped and encouraged by those who have already achieved success.

Another misleading allegation frequently levelled at successful women scientists is that they are 'exceptional' and therefore that there is no need to bother about any women who are less than outstanding. In a sense, men scientists are 'let off the hook' if they can point to a few women Nobel prize winners and say 'Ah, but *they* are exceptional'. True, but the majority of men practising science are doing no more than useful, competent jobs and why should women be excluded from making similar contributions?

Some quotations related to these themes are given in box 3.

Box 3—Helped by a Man or 'Exceptional'

Such work is either done in conjunction with men, or is obviously under their guidance and supervision, and much is made about it out of gallantry. (Swinburne, 1902)

There existed a vocal group very ready to revive the view that Marie Curie had ridden to success on her husband's coat-tails. (Reid, 1978)

Errors are notoriously hard to kill, but an error that ascribes to a man what was actually the work of a woman, has more lives than a cat. (Hertha Ayrton, of Marie Curie, approx. 1909 (Reid, 1978))

All the eminent women scientists have achieved their best work when collaborating with a male colleague. Sir William Ramsay, approx. 1910. (*ibid*)

There he [her husband] stood waiting while the President conferred the PhD degree . . . yet I could not help feeling that he was suggesting something: he was there when it all happened, a woman could never do it alone. W. Muta Maathai, Nairobi, Kenya—contemporary (Richter, 1982)

If a woman has a special gift—which does not happen often—I do not think it right to refuse her the chance and means of studying . . . [but] such a case must always be regarded just as an exception. (Max Planck, approx. 1897 (Krafft, 1978))

But when a person of the sex which . . . must encounter infinitely more difficulties than men . . . succeeds nevertheless . . . then without doubt she must have the noblest courage, quite extraordinary talents and a superior genius. (Gauss to Sophie Germain, 1807 (Ernest, 1976))

Because of the way that society is organized, I believe that it is still true to say that most women have greater social and domestic responsibilities than men. Experimental scientists cannot work at, or from, home for a lot of the time because they have to be in the laboratory. A family crisis often involves time off from work for the woman of the family rather than the man. It is still assumed that child-rearing and care for the sick and elderly is primarily a woman's job, and many a promising career has been damaged or even abandoned as a result.

Some quotations to illustrate these points are given in box 4. All except the first two are by contemporary women.

Box 4—Social and Domestic Responsibilities

A man can always command his time under the plea of business; a woman is not allowed any such excuse. At Chelsea I was always supposed to be at home when friends and acquaintances came out to see me. (Mary Somerville, 1780–1872 (Osen, 1974))

I wonder you let Mary waste her time in reading; she never sews more than if she were a man. [She hoped she] would give up her foolish manner of life and make a respectable and useful wife. (Mary Somerville's family (Osen, 1974))

I cannot emphasize too much the importance of his [her husband's] emotional support as well as his actual help with the tasks often considered to be 'women's work'. (Marian W. Kies, Bethesda, USA (Richter, 1982))

It was not very easy for me to take care of my child, his father and the house, together with my scientific work. (Liana Bolis, Messina, Sicily (*ibid*))

My parents became seriously ill when I was about to leave [for college]. I had to stay home and care for them. (R. Rajalakshmi, Baroda, India, (*ibid*))

But nobody knows the sense of guilt in having to leave the children to be looked after by somebody else for long periods. (Liana Bolis, Messina, Sicily (*ibid*))

I have never neglected any essential aspects of their upbringing, but I do not feel that I have done them any harm by delegating the washing of nappies and their supervision in playgrounds to others. (Tahereh M.Z. Rahmani, Tehran, Iran (*ibid*))

Many married women scientists are strongly supported in their career aspirations by their husbands. Nevertheless, if a conflict of interests arises between husband's and wife's career, it is nearly always the husband's career that wins. Examples abound but the two long quotations in box 5 (below) give a clear picture of a common situation. This was reinforced for me recently on hearing from an ex-student of mine—a woman chemist—who writes 'When my husband was moved to a new job, it was the economically most sensible thing for me to move too—and of course, while he got more money for moving, I would have to make do with anything I could get, so the salary differential just widened at each move'.

If it is difficult to get a job when you move to further your husband's career, it is often even worse if you stop work altogether to raise children and then try to re-enter your profession. The problems are exemplified in the last quotation in box 5.

Box 5—Marriage and Husband's Career

A married woman in science must therefore be very strongly motivated to enable her to overcome all kinds of difficulties. (Inga Fischer-Hjalmars, Stockholm, Sweden—contemporary (Richter, 1982))

I was under-ranked and under-paid, but 'they' told me I should not be ambitious for myself—only for my husband. I justified my career and my ambitions by being the 'best wife' I could. I did all the household chores and errands and all the entertaining. It seemed right and natural for us to organize our lives around his

career . . . it did not occur to either of us to make choices based on the opportunities for *both* of us. Twice we chose the best opportunity for him and each time I
changed direction, adapted and took a professional step backwards. We left Penn
in August because my husband was lured back to Columbia University . . . But
what of the wife who had relocated again? (Anne Briscoe, 1981—contemporary
American)

I protected my husband against all the daily annoyances of running a home and
rearing four children. During the years when he left us promptly after dinner to
return to the laboratory . . . or down to his study to work at home, I again took
over all the family problems. In this way he was free to devote himself to his work
and he was extremely successful, . . . when our last child was finally away at
school . . . I returned to my husband's university. I was given a section of the
introductory course to teach and a lab section. After a while I was being shunted
in whatever direction current registration or absent personnel indicated need.
(Anon—contemporary American (Bernard, 1964))

Many women scientists have had to endure some form of unpleasant sexual innu-
endo at some time in their lives. Anne Briscoe, an American biochemist, wrote in
1981 'I ignored my stepmother who said if I got a PhD, I would never get a rich
husband'. Later in the same article 'At times it was difficult not to feel the stigma of
the spinster status. After I married, it seemed as if my male colleagues had more
respect for me'. One infers from this that a clever girl is unattractive and an unmarried one is a failure or a freak. Other examples, some of which are given in box 6
(below) bear out these ideas. The woman scientist, because of her choice of a male-
dominated profession is at best 'unfeminine' and at worst, 'masculine'. This attitude,
however, does not prevent her from being appraised as a sex object in spite of the
fact that such a practice is totally inappropriate in the context of her work. When
objections were made to the appointment of the distinguished mathematician,
Emmy Noether, on the grounds of her sex, one of her supporters, David Hilbert,
retorted 'the Senate is not a bathhouse'.

Box 6—Masculine, Feminine or Neuter?

Such affectation never was part of her character, which was masculine and just.
(Voltaire of Emilie de Breteuil, Marquise du Châtelet (Osen, 1974))

What will our soldiers think when they return to the University and find that they
are expected to learn at the feet of a woman? (Faculty of the University of Göttingen, of Emmy Noether (Osen, 1974))

She was heavy of build and loud of voice . . . no one could contend that the graces
had stood by her cradle, but if we in Göttingen often chaffingly referred to her as
'Der Noether', it was also done with a respectful recognition of her power as a
creative thinker who seemed to have broken through the barrier of sex. (Hermann Weyl, 1935 (Ernest, 1976))

By choice she did not emphasize her feminine qualities, though her features were
strong, she was not unattractive and might have been quite stunning had she
taken even a mild interest in clothes. This she did not. There was never lipstick to

contrast with her straight black hair, while at the age of thirty-one her dresses showed all the imagination of English blue-stocking adolescents. (Watson (1978), of Rosalind Franklin)

If such a girl studies science and becomes successful, she will find it difficult to act as shy, inferior and apologetic. If she does not do so however, she may be accused of behaving 'like a man'. (W. Muta Maathai, Nairobi—contemporary (Richter, 1982))

Many people on hearing the words 'female mathematician' conjure up an image of a six-foot, grey-haired, tweed suited Oxford clad woman . . . this image, of course, doesn't attract the young woman who is continually being bombarded with messages . . . to be beautiful, 'feminine', and to catch a man. (Professor Martha Smith—contemporary American (Ernest, 1976))

I wondered how she would look if she took off her glasses and did something novel with her hair. (Watson (1968), of Rosalind Franklin)

Sonja Kovalevskaia was supposed to be pleased when a man said she was 'the first handsome mathematical lady I have ever seen' and Strindberg called her a 'monstrosity' (Koblitz, 1984). One of her recent biographers referred to her 'masculine energy' (Kennedy, 1983). In a discussion on the technology of thin films, a pioneer in this field, Katharine Blodgett, is described, as 'small, unassuming, bright-eyed and very sharp' (Tucker, 1982). A physics student, talking about her schooldays said, only last year 'All the girls thought I wasn't really a girl. The boys told me I was mad. 'You'll fail your exams' they scoffed. 'Physics is a boy's subject'.' (Couper, 1984).

It has been shown that women frequently over-qualify themselves in order to compensate for the prejudice against their sex. This so-called 'Madame Curie Effect' (Rossiter, 1982) may account for what seems to be fear of competition on the part of male colleagues. Various strategies have been used by men to prevent women becoming dominant and some examples are given in box 7. Presumably it is this fear which accounts for the apparently irrational prejudice which is not uncommon. The second quotation and the three quotations from Richter in box 7 are all by contemporary scientists so the problem has not disappeared.

Other examples exist showing the reluctance of some professors to let women work in the same laboratory as men. Mary Fieser (Pramer, 1985) was made to work 'in the deserted basement of an adjoining building where he [the professor] had no intention of supervising activity'. Otto Hahn says of Lise Meitner (Hahn, 1966) 'with the condition that she was not to enter the laboratories where male students were working, she was permitted to work with me in the wood shop'.

The fact that most European and American universities were closed to women for so long and that Cambridge University did not award degrees to women until 1948 cannot be justified on rational grounds. Neither can a company justify the statement 'We do not employ women chemists' nor another paying a woman 80 per cent of the man's rate of pay and also having a scale for women which rose much more slowly than that for men. In 1960 the same company offered me a job doing fundamental long-term research on the grounds that there was no chance of me moving into sales or management and so I would remain 'at the bench'. I suppose one could regard this as an example of 'positive discrimination'!

Box 7—Male Prejudice

Clearly Rosy had to go or be put in her place. The former was obviously preferable because . . . it would be very difficult for Maurice to maintain a dominant position. (Watson (1968), of Rosalind Franklin)

My record was good but they did not want to hire a woman. One of them was a third-rate biochemist from a tenth rate medical school. It did not matter that I had a first-rate record from a top drawer university, they preferred men of their own calibre. (Anne Briscoe (1981))

I was mostly left to myself because my colleagues were not accustomed to working with women. [However] when the post of director fell vacant, a man with inferior qualifications to mine was appointed. (Kamala Sohonie, Bombay (Richter, 1982))

Attacks on women colleagues come always from men who are lacking in self-confidence and distinguished achievement. Strong support for women comes from elderly men of distinction. (Chie Nakane, Tokyo (*ibid*))

Mistakes made by women are still *women's* mistakes, while much more serious mistakes made by a man are always the mistakes of a concrete Ivan or Piotr. (Natalie P. Bechtereva, Leningrad (*ibid*))

Women cannot be part of the Institute of France. (M. Amagat, quoted by Eve Curie (Curie, 1939))

Emil Fischer cherished a strong aversion to women in the laboratories . . . this dislike stemmed from his constant worry with a Russian student lest her rather exotic hairstyle result in its catching fire on the bunsen burner. (Krafft (1978))

If I were to pick out one theme which has constantly recurred during my studies on women scientists it would be that of 'invisibility'. By that I mean that their work has been discounted, under-rated, unacknowledged and ignored and they themselves have been belittled. Inevitably this theme has been implicit in much of what has been said already. There is a mass of evidence and, thanks particularly to some recent work, many sources of information are now available. Reference has already been made to *Women Scientists in America* (Rossiter, 1982). Cole's careful analysis (1979) in *Fair Science: Women in the Scientific Community* includes an important chapter on the marginality of women scientists and in *Machina ex Dea* (Rothschild, 1983) the contributors show that women's achievements in technology have been far greater than has generally been supposed. (The book also examines many of the issues surrounding the relationship between women and technology). These works go a long way to redress the balance.

Turning now to some specific examples, Agnes Pockels invented the slide trough for the investigation of surface films on water in 1882. Fortunately, she sent an account of her work to Lord Rayleigh who arranged for it to be published in *Nature* in 1891. An improved version of the Pockels trough became known as the Langmuir trough and is described in Langmuir's paper of 1917. All this is well-documented and accessible (Giles and Forrester, 1971; Derrick, 1982) but I doubt whether one could claim that Pockels was a household word in most surface science circles.

Interestingly, another woman made a major contribution in surface science. She was Katharine Blodgett, born in 1898. After receiving her master's degree in 1918 she went to work at the General Electric Laboratory with Langmuir on the transfer of thin films from water to a solid surface. In his paper of 1919, Langmuir acknowledged Blodgett's contribution saying that she had carried out 'most of the experimental work'. Langmuir-Blodgett films, or LB films as they are now called, have many applications such as the manufacture of anti-glare glass, in integrated optics and lasers and in creating new types of semiconductor (Tucker, 1982; Davis, 1984). But again, Blodgett's name is not a familiar one.

A number of women have made important contributions to the earth sciences but it has been pointed out (Arnold, 1975) that these are ignored in earth science curriculum materials for American schools. The case of Florence Bascom is cited. She was the first woman to be awarded a PhD by Johns Hopkins and this was the first geology doctorate in the United States (in 1893). She was the first woman Fellow of the Geological Society of America and became a Vice-President in 1930.

Among biologists, two outstanding examples of women whose work has been unappreciated for too long or under-estimated are Barbara McClintock who discovered genetic transposition (Keller, 1983) and Nettie Stevens who played a major rôle in the discovery of chromosomal sex determination (Brush, 1978).

Some quotations illustrating the 'belittlement' theme particularly, are given in box 8.

Box 8—The Invisible Woman

You must have been amused at all the furor created by the visit of Madame Curie to this country . . . I was quite pleasantly surprised to find that she was quite keen about scientific matters and in an unusually amiable mood . . . I felt sorry for the old girl, she was a distinctly pathetic figure. (Boltwood, on Marie Curie's visit to the USA in 1921 (Reid, 1978))

Perhaps you have seen that Monsieur Ramsay has published some work on the atomic weight of radium. He arrives at exactly the same result as I did and his measurements are less consistent than mine. In spite of that he concludes that his work is the first good work on this subject. (Marie Curie in a letter to Rutherford (*ibid*))

My husband suggested to Hahn . . . that he should at least make some reference, in his lectures and publications, to my criticism of Fermi's experiments. Hahn answered that he did not wish to make me look ridiculous as my assumption . . . was really absurd. (Ida Noddack, 1935 (Jungk, 1960))

When the assistants of the Chemical Institute met her [Lise Meitner] and Hahn they somewhat obviously greeted them with 'Guten Tag, Herr Hahn'. (Krafft, (1978))

All a male competitor has to say of a female scientist is that her work is not very original. When such a remark is made to a grants review panel immeasurable harm is done. (Marian W. Kies, USA—contemporary (Richter, 1982))

When the question is asked 'Who are the top ten in your field?' the woman is not likely to be among those named. (Bernard, (1964))

> My former students often write to me appreciatively of my work but they do not
> find it necessary to cite it in their own. (Anon,—contemporary quoted in Bernard
> (1964))

The allegation of non-citation is quite common. It is very discouraging and depressing to *know* that you have made a significant contribution in a particular field and then to find that no-one acknowledges it.

A woman chemist wrote to me of her experiences in World War II. 'Although it was so often publicly stated that industry was short of scientists, the Appointments Board were not able to tell me of a single opening for which a woman would be considered. Well-qualified women were not wanted, only quite inexperienced women as handmaidens.' And 'I was set to serve a former wages clerk . . . He was good enough to show me how to work percentages.'

Another of my correspondents has, I think, managed to identify one aspect of the problem. She says 'There is a real, and usually unspoken, set of attitudes . . . unfortunately not uncommon . . . which come into play when a woman's work, or personality, is at issue. I see it as a *fundamental lack of seriousness*, as if these matters can be dealt with negligently because they are *never of real consequence*' (my emphasis).

I know I used to wonder how old I had to be before I would be taken seriously as a scientist. I hoped it would be 30, but this was not the case, and it seemed to me that I was well past 40 before I felt that I had been accepted as a member of the scientific community.

In an article in the *New Scientist* last year Koblitz comments 'It is sobering to think that the achievements of nineteenth century women scientists had so little impact on the attitude of scientists, educationalists and women themselves that now a century later, we still need special initiatives such as WISE (Women into Science and Engineering) to increase the numbers of women practising science' (Koblitz, 1984).

The variety of attitudes which women scientists have expressed about themselves, their work and their colleagues has already been demonstrated to some extent and some others are shown in box 9.

Box 9—Women Scientists' Own Attitudes

> I objected to myself that it was not the profession of a lady to teach, that she should remain silent, listen and learn, without displaying her own knowledge. That it is above her station to offer a work to the public and that a reputation gained thereby is not ordinarily to her advantage since men always scorn and blame the products of a woman's wit. (Marie Meurdrac, 1666 (Bishop and Deloach, 1970))

> In writing these pages, the author was more than once checked in her progress by the apprehension that such an attempt might be considered by some, either as unsuited to the ordinary pursuits of her sex, or ill-justified by her own imperfect knowledge of the subject. (Jane Marcet, *Conversations on Chemistry*, 10th ed. 1825 (Marcet, 1825))

> I believe that men and women's scientific aptitudes are exactly the same—a woman of science should renounce worldly obligations. I consider science to be the primordial interest of my life. (Irene Joliot-Curie (Reid, 1978))

> I do not like being made conscious of being a woman, and particularly I don't like having to take account of sex in matters concerned with research. (Chie Nakane, Tokyo—contemporary (Richter, 1982))

> Two X chromosomes have . . . spelled the destiny for endless generations of individuals, irrespective of their natural talents and inclinations. (Rita Levi, Montalcini, Rome—contemporary (*ibid*))

Some women even give men credit for their own ideas. According to Kitteringham (1982), 'Margaret Bryan writing on natural philosophy in 1806, offered herself "merely as a reflector of the intrinsic light of superior genius and erudition . . . "'.

Elizabeth Fulhame, however, in her *Essay on Combustion*, published in 1794, went in appropriately, with all guns blazing:

> But censure is perhaps inevitable, for some are so ignorant, that they grow sullen and silent, and are chilled with horror at the sight of anything that bears the resemblance of learning, in whatever shape it may appear; and should the spectre appear in the shape of a woman, the pangs which they suffer are truly dismal. (Rayner-Canham, 1983)

MEN OF GOODWILL

Those of us who did manage to become women scientists owe a great debt to those men who were willing to teach, train and encourage us. Negative attitudes abound, as we have seen, but it is important to acknowledge the existence also of positive ones. Naming names can be invidious but mention must be made in this context of the Braggs and Bernal who encouraged women crystallographers and of the biochemist Gowland Hopkins who took on women research students. Katharine Blodgett worked with Rutherford at the Cavendish Laboratory and was the first woman to be awarded a PhD in Physics from Cambridge (Tucker, 1982). Agnes Pockels' work would have been unknown without Rayleigh's help (Giles and Forrester, 1971) and Weierstrass gave private tuition to Sonja Kovalevskaia (Koblitz, 1983). Gauss was very encouraging to Sophie Germain and he wrote an appreciative letter of thanks to Caroline Herschel on receipt of her edited and up-dated version of Flamsteed's catalogue (Osen, 1974). Evelyn Wilson said of Louis Fieser that 'he was one of the few professors who treated female students as seriously as male students' (Pramer, 1985). Perhaps I should end this necessarily selective section by paying tribute to Professor William Klyne, the first head of the chemistry department at Westfield College, University of London, who declared 'other things being equal' he wanted women on his staff and, as a result, appointed me and one other woman among the founder members of the department in 1961.

CONCLUDING REMARKS

There are obvious practical reasons why it is important that the prejudices outlined in this paper should be exposed and combated. More scientists and technologists are needed; industry is increasingly based on these disciplines. Girls and women need jobs and can fulfil these requirements if they are appropriately trained.

There has been much discussion of late about whether there is such a thing as feminist science. I believe that women do have a different perspective to offer which would enrich science and that they could contribute to the process of change which seems to me to be necessary.

I would like to close with a quotation on the subject of change from the eminent astronomer, Cecilia Payne-Gaposchkin written in 1979, the year of her death, at the age of 79.

> For we spend our lives in trying to overthrow obsolete ideas and to replace them with something that represents Nature better. There is no joy more intense than that of coming upon a fact that cannot be understood in terms of currently accepted ideas . . . Only those who have shared this activity can understand the joy of it. Science is a living thing, not a dead dogma. (Haramundanis, 1984)

APPENDIX

Some women scientists and mathematicians of the past, mentioned in this chapter.

Name	Dates	Discipline(s)
Emile de Breteuil	1706–1749	Mathematics/theoretical physics
Marie Curie	1867–1934	Chemistry/physics
Rosalind Franklin	1920–1958	Chemistry/crystallography
Sophie Germain	1776–1831	Mathematics/physics
Caroline Herschel	1750–1848	Mathematics/astronomy
Irene Jolit-Curie	1897–1956	Physics
Sonja Kovalevskaia	1850–1891	Mathematics
Jane Marcet	1769–1858	Chemistry
Lise Meitner	1878–1968	Physics
Ida Noddack	1896–1979	Chemistry
Emmy Noether	1882–1935	Mathematics
Mary Somerville	1780–1872	Mathematics/astronomy

REFERENCES

Arnold, L. (1975) *Journal of Geological Education*, 23, 110.
Bennett, J. H. (1870) *The Lancet*, 2, 887 (see Easlea, p. 139).
Bernard, J. (1964) *Academic Women*, New York, Meridian.
Bishop, L. O. and De Loach, W. S. (1970) *Journal of Chemical Education*, 47, 448.
Briscoe, A. (1981) *International Journal of Women's Studies*, 4, 420.
British Apollo, The, (1708) (see Easlea, p. 69).
Brush, S. G. (1978) *Isis*, 69, 163.
Cole, J. R. (1979) *Fair Science: Women in the Scientific Community*, New York and London, Macmillan.
Compleat Midwifes Practice Enlarged, The, (1659) (see Easlea, p. 69).
Couper, H. (1984) *SHE*, March, 78.
Curie, E. (1939) *Madame Curie*, London, Readers Union/Heinemann.
Davis, K. A. (1984) *Journal of Chemical Education*, 61, 437.
Derrick, M. E. (1982) *Journal of Chemical Education*, 59, 1030.

Easlea, B. (1981) *Science and Sexual Oppression*, London, Weidenfeld and Nicolson.

Ernest, J. (1976) *American Mathematics Monthly*, 83, 595.

Giles, C. H. and Forrester, S. D. (1971) *Chemistry and Industry*, 9 January.

Hahn, O. (1966) *Otto Hahn: A Scientific Autobiography*, New York, Charles Scribner & Sons.

Haramundanis, K. (Ed.), (1984) *Cecilia Payne-Gaposchkin*, Cambridge, Cambridge University Press.

Jungk, R. (1960) *Brighter than a Thousand Suns*, Harmondsworth, Penguin.

Keller, E. F. (1983) *A Feeling for the Organism: The Life and Work of Barbara McClintock*, New York, W. E. Freeman.

Kennedy, D. H. (1983) *Little Sparrow: A Portrait of Sophia Kovalevsky*, Athens, O.H. Ohio University Press.

Kitteringham, G. (1982) in *Times Higher Educational Supplement*, 21 May.

Koblitz, A. H. (1983) *A Convergence of Lives, Sofia Kovalevskaia: Scientist, Writer and Revolutionary*, Boston, MA, Birkhäuser.

Koblitz, A. H. (1984) *Sofia Kovalevskaia: 'Muse of the Heavens', New Scientist*, 16 February.

Krafft, F. (1978) *Agnew. Chem. Int. Engl. Ed.*, 17, 826.

Langmuir, I. (1917) *Journal of the American Chemical Society*, 39, 1848.

Marcet, J. (1825) *Conversations on Chemistry . . .*, 10th ed., London, Longman, Hurst, Rees and Orme.

Osen, L. M. (1974) *Women in Mathematics*, Cambridge, MA, and London, MIT Press.

Poulain de la Barre (1673) English translation, (1677) (see Easlea, p. 71).

Pramer, S. (1985) *Journal of Chemical Education*, 62, 186.

Rayner-Canham, G. W. (1983) *Education in Chemistry*, 20, 140.

Reid, R. (1978) *Marie Curie*, St. Albans, Paladin.

Richter, D. (1982) *Women Scientists: The Road to Liberation*, London and Basingstoke, Macmillan.

Romanes, G. J. (1887) *The Nineteenth Century*, 21, 189, (see Easlea, p. 146).

Rosenberg, R. (1982) *Beyond Separate Spheres: Intellectual Roots of Modern Feminism*, New Haven, C.T., and London, Yale University Press.

Rossiter, M. W. (1982) *Women Scientists in America: Struggles and Strategies to 1940*, Baltimore, Johns Hopkins University Press.

Rothschild, J. (Ed.), (1983) *Machina ex Dea*, New York and Oxford, Pergamon Press. *Science*, (1979) 203, 150.

Swinburne, J. (1902) *Westminster Review*, 158, 189.

Tucker, A. (1982) in *The Guardian*, 8 March.

Watson, J. D. (1968) *The Double Helix*, London, Weidenfeld and Nicolson.

QUESTIONS FOR DISCUSSION

1. Why do you think Walton has written this article? For whom is the article intended?
2. Walton begins the essay with a brief description of her experience as a woman scientist. Why does she begin in this way?
3. What cultural factors contribute to the low percentage of women in the scientific professions? Discuss your own experience with these aspects of your culture.
4. Are there any physical differences between men and women which explain the paucity of women scientists? Explain.
5. Discuss the organization of the essay. How does the organization contribute to the method of argument? How does the information in the boxes contribute to Walton's argument? Why do you think the quotes are presented in lists?

6. What can women do to help remove the prejudices against women in science? What can men do? Why would she separate these two in the essay?
7. Summarize the main idea in Walton's conclusion. How is the conclusion persuasive to persons of either gender?
8. Examine the use of pronouns in the articles by Hall, Oppenheimer, and Nakayama. Is a gender bias apparent? How does the use of pronouns illustrate Walton's point?

RAYMOND DAWSON
Science and China's Influence on the World

In The Legacy of China *(1964) Raymond Dawson describes Chinese science in its historical context. "Science and China's Influence on the World" discusses the prominence of Chinese scientific achievements before and after the European Renaissance. Pointing out that Chinese scientists were responsible for such world-shattering developments as the production of gunpowder and the making of clocks, Dawson emphasizes the international connections between scientific inventions and discoveries and subsequent technological development. Read in conjunction with the text on Islamic science and the excerpt from Fritjof Capra's* Tao of Physics *(p. 49), this text provides insight into the weblike interrelationship that has developed in the area of science between the many cultures of the world.*

In technological influences before and during the Renaissance China occupies a quite dominating position. In the body of this contribution we shall mention among other things the efficient equine harness, the technology of iron and steel, the inventions of gunpowder and paper, the mechanical clock, and basic engineering devices such as the driving-belt, the chain-drive, and the standard method of converting rotary to rectilinear motion, together with segmental arch bridges and nautical techniques such as the stern-post rudder. The world owes far more to the relatively silent craftsmen of ancient and medieval China than to the Alexandrian mechanics, articulate theoreticians though they were.

We have next to think of those achievements of Asian and Chinese science which, though not genetically connected with the first rise of modern science, yet deserve close attention. They may or may not be directly related genetically to their corresponding developments in post-Renaissance modern science. Perhaps the most outstanding Chinese discovery which was so related, even though it influenced the West relatively late (the end of the eighteenth and the beginning of the nineteenth centuries), was that of the first successful immunization technique. Variolation, the forerunner of Jennerian vaccination, had been in use in China certainly since the beginning of the sixteenth century, and if tradition is right since the eleventh; it consisted in the inoculation of a minute amount of the contents of the smallpox pustule itself into the nostril of the patient to be immunized, and Chinese physicians had gradually worked out methods of attenuating the virus so as to give greater safety. The origins of the whole science of immunology lie in a practice based on medieval Chinese medical thought. A case of direct theoretical influence which springs to mind concerns cosmology—the old Chinese doctrine of infinite empty space as opposed to the solid crystalline celestial spheres of medieval Europe, but again it did not exert its full effect towards their dissolution until after Galileo's time. Examples of later incorporation would be the development of undulatory theory in eighteenth-century physics, which immensely elaborated characteristically Chinese ideas without knowing anything of them; or the use of ancient and medieval Chinese records of novae and supernovae by modern radio-astronomers. A good case of the probable absence of any stimulus would be the seismograph as used in China from the second to the seventh centuries A.D.; though an outstanding achievement and a permanent legacy to the history of geology, it was almost certainly unknown to any of the scientific men who developed seismographs again in post-Renaissance Europe. Chinese biological and pathological classification systems occupy the same position; they were clearly unknown to Linnaeus and Sydenham, but none the less worthy of study, for only by drawing up the balance-sheet in full shall we ever ascertain what each civilization has contributed to human advancement. Similarly, it is now becoming clear that medieval Chinese anatomy was far more advanced than has generally been thought, for judgments have been based by Western anatomists only on the few remaining block-print illustrations, since they were unable to read the texts themselves and to pursue the complex and elaborate nomenclature. But it exerted no influence on the revival and development of anatomy in Renaissance Europe. Nor did the outstandingly good iconographic tradition of the pharmaceutical compendia of the *Pen-ts'ao* genre, centuries ahead of the West in accurate botanical illustration, which has gained appreciation only in our own time.

Lastly we have to think of technical inventions which only became incorporated, whether or not by re-invention, into the corpus of modern technology after the Renaissance period. A case in point might be the paddle-wheel boat, but it is uncertain, for we do not know whether the first European successes were based on a Byzantine idea never executed, or on a vast fund of practical Chinese achievement during the preceding millennium, or on neither. A clearer example is the iron-chain suspension bridge, for while the first European description came towards the end of the sixteenth century, the first realization occurred only in the eighteenth, and in knowledge of the Chinese antecedents, going back, as we now know, for more than a thousand years previously. Independent invention occurred, no doubt, with the differential gear, for though this was present in the south-pointing carriages of ancient China, their construction has been revealed only by modern historical research and could hardly have inspired the later mechanics of the West who fitted up again this important form of enmeshing wheel-work. So also the Chinese methods of steel-making by the co-fusion process and by the direct oxygenation of cast iron, though of great seniority to the siderurgy of Europe, were not able to exert any influence upon it, if indeed they did, which is still uncertain, until long after the Renaissance. At the same time one must always refrain from being too positive about the absence of influence. In human intercourse there have been innumerable capillary channels which we cannot see, and especially for earlier times we should never be tempted to dogmatism in the denial of transmissions. Sometimes one wonders whether humanity ever forgets anything. The sailing-carriage of early seventeenth-century Europe was consciously modelled on supposed Chinese prototypes which had in fact been rather different, but it is possible that they in their turn derived from the model boats with sails outspread which, supported upon low wooden wagons, conveyed the coffins of ancient Egyptian gods or kings across the deserts to their tombs. Broadly speaking, experience shows that the further one goes back in history the more unlikely independent invention was; we cannot infer it from the conditions of modern science today, where it frequently occurs.

QUESTIONS FOR DISCUSSION

1. What does the phrase "attenuating a virus" (par. 2) mean? Why was the invention of immunization so important at this point in time?
2. Explain Dawson's contention that "independent invention" is "unlikely" (par. 3). What does this imply about the tendency of our society to point to inventors as absolute creators?
3. List the scientific achievements of China during the Renaissance. Which items surprise you? Which did you know about? How does the rest of the world continue to develop some of these discoveries—gunpowder? Clocks? Others?
4. Discuss the common point of Dawson and Oppenheimer—that science is/should be universal (nonnational).
5. Analyze the organization of this excerpt. Why might the points be ordered in this way?

JOHN B. CHRISTOPHER
Science

John B. Christopher, in The Islamic Tradition *(1972), discusses the science of the Islamic empire of the Middle Ages. Not only Muslim scientists, but Christians and Jews living in the geographical area dominated by Islam made substantial contributions to some of the major fields of scientific inquiry, including medicine, mathematics, and the physical sciences. Physicians such as Avicenna received acclaim and respect for their work, while mathematicians developed the Arabic numeral system, a far more practically useful tool than the system of Roman numerals. Mathematical developments contributed to the rise of the physical sciences, particularly astronomy. The syncretism (cross-cultural borrowing) which characterized medieval Islamic science reflects that described by Raymond Dawson in "Science and China's Influence on the World" (p. 39).*

Several of the great names in Islamic philosophy—ar-Razi, al-Farabi, Avicenna— also figure prominently in the history of Islamic science. Scientists, too, built on the work of older civilizations, Greek, Persian, Hindu, and even Chinese (it is possible that the Arabic word *alchemy* is derived from the Chinese for *gold-extracting juice*). In science as in philosophy, many of the men responsible for transmitting older traditions were non-Muslims; Christians translated Greek works, and in Baghdad certain Christian and Jewish families, generation after generation, supplied the physicians and pharmacists who served the upper classes.

The extremely important contributions made by non-Muslims to Islamic culture suggest that in this context the term *Islamic* has such broad and syncretistic implications that, unlike *Muslim*, it does not necessarily refer to participation in a particular religious faith. Some historians refer to the Abbasid caliphate as the *Islamic empire* to point up the contrast between its cosmopolitanism and the more primitive, more soldierly, and predominantly Muslim qualities of the Umayyads' *Arab kingdom*. Medieval Spain furnished striking examples of a kind of cultural free trade between Muslims and non-Muslims. The Jew Maimonides (1134–1204) is a significant personage in the Islamic tradition because he was physician to Saladin, wrote in Arabic not Hebrew, and carried forward the philosophical inquiries of his master, Averroes. Jews and Christians participated significantly in the intellectual and scientific life of Toledo, which continued almost without interruption after the city passed permanently from Muslim to Christian control in 1085. In the twelfth and thirteenth centuries the archbishops of Toledo, the ranking prelates of Spain, made the city far and away the most important center for translating works by Muslim intellectuals into Latin.

The linguistic preeminence of Arabic and the relative ease of travel across the length and breadth of the medieval Islamic world permitted the development of important scientific centers all the way from Spain and Morocco to Samarkand in Central Asia, capital of the conqueror Tamerlane, who established a great school there at the close of the Middle Ages. In the first two Muslim centuries the major scientific center was the city of Jundishapur in south-western Persia, founded by the Sasanid emperor Shapur, who defeated the legions of Rome in the third century A.D. Renowned for its hospital and its medical and scientific academics, Jundishapur attracted many Nestorian refugees from Byzantine persecution. Under the early Abbasid caliphs leadership passed to Baghdad, where the caliphs' House of Wisdom established a vigorous intellectual tradition continued by the city's schools and hospitals. In the tenth and eleventh centuries the energy of the Ismaili movement and the patronage of the Fatimid caliphs, particularly in establishing a great library, brought Cairo to the first rank. It remained there during many later political vicissitudes thanks to the continuity provided by institutions such as its famous hospitals and the university of al-Azhar.

MEDICINE

In the medieval Islamic world the medical profession was established and recognized to a degree unknown in Catholic Europe. Reputable physicians were on the whole highly esteemed and well paid; an outstanding doctor such as Avicenna served Persian princes not only as a physician but also as a political counsellor. The starting point of Islamic medicine was the legacy of Hindu and Persian medical lore preserved at Jundishapur, supplemented by the Arabic translation of the Greek physician Galen, who had summarized the medical legacy of the ancient Mediterranean world in the second century A.D.

Past authorities did not necessarily command uncritical deference from Muslim physicians. For example, ar-Razi, who flourished about A.D. 900, cited Greek, Syriac, Persian, and Hindu opinions on a given question and then presented his own views. This independent attitude enabled ar-Razi to make some important discoveries, above all to distinguish for the first time the differences between smallpox and measles. Here is an excerpt from his monograph on these two diseases:

> The outbreak of small-pox is preceded by continuous fever, aching in the back, itching in the nose and shivering during sleep. The main symptoms of its presence are: back-ache with fever, stinging pain in the whole body, congestion of the face, sometimes shrinkage, violent redness of the cheeks and eyes, a sense of pressure in the body, creeping of the flesh, pain in the throat and breast accompanied by difficulty of respiration and coughing, dryness of the mouth, thick salivation, hoarseness of the voice, headache and pressure in the head, excitement, anxiety, nausea and unrest. Excitement, nausea and unrest are more pronounced in measles than in small-pox, whilst the aching in the back is more severe in small-pox than in measles.[1]

Through careful detailed observation, ar-Razi added much to the store of clinical data about infectious diseases that had been accumulating since the pioneering work of Hippocrates 1300 years earlier.

Ar-Razi's contribution to Islamic medicine was the more remarkable because he only began his studies in middle age, when he already had many other intellectual irons in the fire. He directed a hospital in his native Rayy, then another at Baghdad, and wrote more than fifty clinical studies in addition to more ambitious general works. The latter included the *Comprehensive Book*, the longest medical work in the Arabic language (over eighteen volumes in an incomplete modern edition), which Renaissance Europeans much respected in its Latin translation. In the present century ar-Razi has attracted attention because of his *Spiritual Physick* (see pp. 109–110) and other original works on the psychological and sociological aspects of medicine. A few pertinent titles are: *On the Fact That Even Skillful Physicians Cannot Heal All Diseases; Why Frightened Patients Easily Forsake Even the Skilled Physician; Why People Prefer Quacks and Charlatans*.

A hundred years later, Avicenna also placed considerable stress on psychosomatic medicine and reportedly was able to cure a prince suffering from a severe depression. The patient imagined himself to be a cow, made lowing noises, and demanded to be butchered and converted into stew beef; Avicenna, posing as a cheerful butcher, refused to oblige, claiming that the intended victim was too scrawny and needed to be fattened up; whereupon the patient began eating heartily and eventually recovered his health. Avicenna compiled an encyclopedia, *The Canon of Medicine*, which was more systematic than Razi's *Comprehensive Book* and was widely consulted in the Arab world down to the last century and in Western Europe until the 1600s. Avicenna appears to have been the first doctor to describe and identify meningitis and the first to recommend alcohol as a disinfectant.

---

[1] Quoted by Max Meyerhof, "Science and Medicine," in T. Arnold and A. Guillaume, eds., *The Legacy of Islam* (London: Oxford University Press, 1931), pp. 323–324.

The more scholars examine the sources, the more "firsts" can be claimed for Islamic medicine. The work of Avicenna and others on eye diseases, very prevalent in the Middle East, and on the nature of vision helped to found the study of optics. These studies also made possible rather complicated operations on the eye. Muslim surgeons used opium for anesthesia and attempted experimental operations, including the extraction of teeth and their replacement by ones made from animal bones, the removal of kidney stones lodged in the bladder, and possibly even colostomy (opening of an artificial anus after removal of cancerous tissue).

However, it is important to keep a proper perspective on Islamic medical achievements and not to magnify them unduly. Mortality among surgical patients appears to have been very high, because doctors knew little about either antiseptic measures or the details of anatomy. Muslim tradition forbade dissecting corpses, though a little clandestine dissection may have occurred, mainly in Spain. Some scholars, therefore, discount reports that a thirteenth-century Egyptian physician discovered the existence of the pulmonary circulation, which accounts for the passage of the blood from one chamber of the heart to another via the lungs. He may have advanced this theory three centuries before it was confirmed by European scientists; but it was a purely speculative hypothesis, untested clinically or experimentally.

MATHEMATICS AND THE PHYSICAL SCIENCES

To describe certain procedures mathematicians borrowed from the vocabulary of surgery the term *al-jabr*, meaning restoration or reestablishment of something broken (Spaniards still call a bone-setter an *algebrista*). Islamic algebra was built on Greek and Hindu foundations and closely linked to geometry; its principal architects were the ninth-century Zoroastrian, al-Khuwarizmi, and the twelfth-century Persian, Omar Khayyam. Al-Khuwarizmi, who worked at the House of Wisdom in Baghdad, wrote a very influential book on algebra and also contributed to the development of trigonometry. He described an angle by an Arabic word meaning *pocket* or *pouch*, which was translated into the Latin *sinus*—whence our *sine*. Omar Khayyam, who was also a poet and a Sufi as well as an astronomer, is an excellent instance of the Muslim who sought both the rationalist and the gnostic paths to truth. Indeed, many Islamic mathematicians, like the Pythagoreans of ancient Greece, believed that through numbers men could ascend beyond the world of bewildering phenomena into a higher realm of abstractions and eternal verities. Because the science of numbers was regarded as "the tongue which speaks of unity and transcendence," it was appropriate to use as charms magic squares based on the numerical value of some of the ninety-nine names of God.

To the average Westerner, Arabic numbers have the merit of great simplicity, in contrast to the cumbersome Roman system based on letters. The simplicity of the Arabic system, however, is somewhat deceptive. The numerals used in the West, except for 1 and 9, do not look much like those used today by Arabs and Persians: their numerals are derived from those used in medieval Iraq, whereas ours come through medieval Spain. All of them, except for zero, almost certainly go back ultimately to the Hindus. The most revolutionary innovation of Arabic numbers was not their greater convenience, valuable and time-saving though this was; it lay in the

Arabs' use of a dot to indicate an empty column, ten, for example, being 1·, one hundred one 1·1, and one million and one 1 · · · · · 1. The dot was called *sifr* ("empty"), whence our *cipher* and, through an Italian translation, our *zero*. This system made possible a whole new world of arithmetical operations.

Islamic mathematicians opened new worlds to science, or at least freshened understanding of older worlds. Increased knowledge of geometry and algebra aided the development of optics. The tables compiled by observers systematically recording their findings were utilized by later astronomers both in the Islamic world and in Europe. Islamic advances in trigonometry allowed computations that refined the picture of the earth-centered universe drawn by Ptolemy, the Greco-Egyptian astronomer of the second century A.D. One such refinement disclosed the eccentric behavior of Venus, which would have been easier to explain if the planet had been viewed as orbiting around the sun rather than around the earth. But, as in the medieval West, acceptance of the Ptolemaic system was too ingrained to countenance such a radical innovation as the heliocentric universe.

In certain instances theoretical science was turned to practical account. Astronomical tables enabled the faithful to determine the direction of Mecca and to schedule the five daily prayers and fix the annual festivals and holy days of the lunar calendar. Astronomy and geography facilitated navigation of the monsoon-swept Indian ocean, and mathematics and physics encouraged improvement of water clocks and of water wheels and other irrigation apparatus. Mechanical devices were sometimes remarkably ingenious, as in this thirteenth-century clock consisting of an elephant and a fantastic contrivance mounted on its back:

> Every half-hour the bird on top of the cupola whistles and turns while the mahout hits the elephant with his pick-axe and sounds a tattoo with his drumstick. In addition, the little man who seems to be looking out of a window . . . moves his arms and legs to induce the falcon below to release a pellet. This moving downward, makes the dragon turn until it is finally ejected into the little vase on the elephant's back. From there it drops into the animal, hits a gong, and finally comes to rest in a little bowl where the observer can establish the half-hours passed by counting the number of little balls collected there.[2]

ASTROLOGY AND ALCHEMY

Modern Westerners, who are amused by the talent expended on such fanciful gadgets, are uneasy when they learn that many Islamic astronomers were also astrologers and that a pioneer psychologist and physician such as ar-Razi could also be an alchemist. Astrology is based on the belief that the universe is, as the name suggests, a totality in which the stars do determine and indeed predestine activities on earth. Alchemy is based on the theory that there is a hierarchy of metals, from the base to the pure; if man can find the magical philosopher's stone or elixir, he will be able to change one to the other, iron to gold, or lead to silver, and perhaps also to make glass or quartz into emeralds or some other precious stone.

[2]Richard Ettinghausen, *Arab Painting* (World, 1962), p. 95.

To us today all this seems an unfortunate confusion between true science and occult or pseudo science; our medieval forebears accepted the occult as a matter of course. Ancient traditions, together with the gnostic elements present in both Christianity and Islam, nourished the widely held conviction that there were other pathways to truth beside the one that we call rationalist or scientific. The more radical Shiites, especially the Ismailis with their concern for discovering the hidden message of the Koran, endeavored to unlock the secrets of nature by esoteric means as well as by scientific ones. The Sufis strove to release themselves from the physical restraints of body and mind to enable the soul to penetrate the veils concealing God.

A modern Persian scholar, familiar both with the history of science and with the Shii and Sufi traditions, advances this explanation for the popularity of alchemy:

> We must remember that ancient and medieval man did not separate the material order from the psychological and spiritual in the categorical manner that has become customary today. There was a "naiveness" in the mentality of premodern man which made it possible for him . . . to see a deeper significance in physical phenomena than just plain facts. . . . The basic symbols and principles of alchemy stem from the earliest periods of history and convey through their very concreteness the primordial character of this point of view. Ancient man, during the millennia before recorded history, considered metals to be a special class of beings, which did not belong to the natural environment of the "Adamic race." The earliest iron probably came from meteorites which, in falling from the heavens, gave that metal special virtues and powers.[3]

Although this hypothesis is controversial, there seems little doubt that alchemy was regarded as a quasi-religious pursuit. It has been argued that, just as the alchemist sought to transmute baser metals into gold, so he also sought a kind of transmutation of the soul, which would release it from the sin imposed by the fall of Adam from Eden and allow it to reach a nobler state. The alchemist has likewise been compared to a Sufi sheik, guiding his disciples on their way to God, and to the Christian priest, celebrating the miracle of the mass, which transforms the bread and wine into the body and blood of Christ.

Astrology and alchemy were, in effect, the face and obverse of the same coin, the one turned toward the heavens and the other toward the earth. The seven metals of the alchemist were the earthly symbols of the astrologer's seven planets—gold symbolized the sun, silver the moon, quicksilver Mercury, copper Venus, iron Mars, tin Jupiter, and lead Saturn. From the ancient Greeks Islamic alchemists borrowed the concept of four fundamental elements—fire, air, earth, and water. Each of these, they argued, combined two of the four fundamental characteristics or qualities of nature, heat, cold, dryness, and wetness: fire was hot and dry, air hot and wet, earth cold and dry, and water cold and wet.

Islamic physicians, also borrowing from the Greeks, put the four humors of the human body into this pattern, noting that each produced a characteristic temperament. Yellow bile, which was hot and dry, made a man fiery or choleric; blood, which was hot and wet, made him sanguine or cheerful; black bile, which was cold

---

[3]Seyyed Hossein Nasr, *Science and Civilization in Islam* (Harvard University Press, 1968), p. 243.

and dry, made him melancholy; and phlegm, cold and wet, made him phlegmatic. When the humors were reasonably balanced, the individual was in good health. In illness, the balance was destroyed; and treatment consisted in prescribing for the patient drugs and a diet that would supply the humors in which he was deficient until his normal balance was restored.

The doctrines of astrology and alchemy did not win universal approval in the medieval Islamic world. The ulema[4] proclaimed them contrary to the faith, and several distinguished philosophers rejected them as contrary to reason. Ibn-Khaldun concluded:

> The worthlessness of astrology from the point of view of the religious law, as well as the weakness of its achievements from the rational point of view, are evident. In addition, astrology does harm to human civilization. It hurts the faith of the common people when an astrological judgment occasionally happens to come true. . . . Ignorant people are taken in by that and suppose that all the other astrological judgments must be true.[5]

And Avicenna flatly denied the possibility of physical transmutation:

> As to the claims of the alchemists, it must be clearly understood that it is not in their power to bring about any true change of species. They can, however, produce excellent imitations, dyeing the red metal white so that it resembles silver, or dyeing it yellow so that it closely resembles gold. They can, too, dye the white metal with any colour they desire, until it bears a close resemblance to gold or copper; and they can free the leads from most of their defects and impurities. Yet in these dyed metals the essential nature remains unchanged.[6]

This last passage nevertheless suggests how the Arabic *al-kimiya* was to furnish modern chemistry both with its name and with some of its techniques and apparatus. In addition to being expert dyers, the alchemists developed methods of refining metals and of applying varnish to protect iron or waterproof cloth. They employed such chemical processes as distillation, evaporation, sublimation, crystallization, and filtration. Ar-Razi, in his writings on alchemy, describes vials, beakers, mortars and pestles, flasks, smelters, and other items of equipment. A modern scholar has compared the power attributed to the elusive philosopher's stone with that actually present in a chemical catalyst.[7]

MUSIC

At first glance it seems strange that the quantitative sciences of the medieval Islamic curriculum should have included arithmetic, geometry, astronomy, optics—and music, a discipline that we tend to bracket with the arts and humanities. Yet the

---

[4]**ulema** Doctors of Muslim religion and law; learned men. [Ed. note.]
[5]Ibn-Khaldun, *The Muqaddimah*, abridged (Princeton University Press, 1969), p. 408.
[6]Quoted in A. C. Crombie, "Avicenna's Influence on the Medieval Scientific Tradition," in G. M. Wickens, ed., *Avicenna: Scientist and Philosopher* (Luzac, 1952), p. 96.
[7]A. Mieli, *La Science Arabe et Son Rôle dans l'Evolution Scientifique Mondiale* (Brill, 1938), pp. 131–132.

same list of subjects, except for optics, formed the quadrivium (fourfold way to knowledge) in the schools of the medieval West. Many of the leading Islamic scientists wrote on music—ar-Razi, who was a talented lute-player; Avicenna, who was an expert in rhythm; and, above all, al-Farabi, who compiled the *Grand Book of Music*, considered the most important work on musical theory written in the Middle Ages.

In theory Islamic musicians relied heavily on Pythagoras and other ancient Greeks and also on Byzantine and Persian precedents and on rhythmical early Arab poetry. Their greatest innovation was technical, indeed quantitative: it was a system of measures that assigned each sound a time value, in contrast to the unmeasured plain song of the early medieval West. Measures endowed music with greater structure, encouraged new concepts of rhythm, and ultimately led to the full, half, quarter, and other notes we use today. Islamic musicians applied mathematics to stringed instruments by the device of frets, which allowed the player to tune a string to a desired note. These musicians provided the West with the lute (in Arabic, *al-oud*), with the rebec, a pioneering two-stringed instrument played with a bow rather than plucked, and possibly with the guitar (*qitara* in Arabic), though the instrument, like its name, *kithara*, may have been of Greek origin. The tambourine ("little drum") is of Islamic origin, as is *fanfare*, a word derived from the Arabic for *trumpets* and reflecting Muslim enthusiasm for martial music.

Music had no recognized formal role in Islamic life. The chanting of Koranic passages and the intonation of prayers were not regarded as musical activities, and fundamentalists opposed free indulgence in music as conducive to debauchery and paganism. Al-Ghazali once recommended that the best way to disarm the temptations of secular music was to break the instruments used and rout the singers. Yet the same al-Ghazali wrote *Music and Ecstasy*, praising the contribution of music to the Sufi dhikr; and visitors to Konya may still hear the strains of flute, rebec, and drum to which the Mevlevi dervishes danced their way to a mystical trance.

In practice, then, music played an important informal role in Islamic life. It accompanied the recital of poetry, and it was recommended to relieve the distress of the ill or the depressed (musical therapy is not a twentieth-century invention). Music was a central ingredient in military and palace ceremonies; and it underscored the capers of jesters, which inspired those morris dances that sound so very English but were actually Moorish and performed by dancers with faces blackened to resemble Moors. Music illustrates once again the complexity of the Islamic tradition, the coexistence of the sacred and the profane, the gnostic and the scientific.

QUESTIONS FOR DISCUSSION

1. Describe the kinds of sharing between cultures that contributed to the science of Islam.
2. What does the writer's purpose seem to be in this article? Who is the audience?
3. What does "linguistic preeminence" (par. 3) mean? Give an example of linguistic pre-eminence in another context.
4. List the developments in medicine mentioned by Christopher. Evaluate their significance.

5. Why was the invention of Arabic numerals such a great contribution to the field of mathematics?
6. How have the inventions and developments mentioned in this article been developed by or influenced by other cultures?

FRITJOF CAPRA
The Tao of Physics

Fritjof Capra, in his book titled The Tao of Physics *(1975), discusses the connections between modern physics and concepts in the Eastern philosophy of mysticism. Capra asserts that the revolutionary ideas uncovered in the study of atomic and subatomic physics have their roots in the ancient philosophy of the Far East. Capra's thesis reinforces that of Raymond Dawson in "Science and China's Influence on the World" (p. 39): scientific learning involves a complex web of influence and interrelationships between cultures.*

EPILOGUE

The Eastern religious philosophies are concerned with timeless mystical knowledge which lies beyond reasoning and cannot be adequately expressed in words. The relation of this knowledge to modern physics is but one of its many aspects and, like all the others, it cannot be demonstrated conclusively but has to be experienced in a direct intuitive way. What I hope to have achieved, to some extent, therefore, is not a rigorous demonstration, but rather to have given the reader an opportunity to relive, every now and then, an experience which has become for me a source of continuing joy and inspiration; that the principal theories and models of modern physics lead to a view of the world which is internally consistent and in perfect harmony with the views of Eastern mysticism.

For those who have experienced this harmony, the significance of the parallels between the world views of physicists and mystics is beyond any doubt. The interesting question, then, is not *whether* these parallels exist, but *why*; and, furthermore, what their existence implies.

In trying to understand the mystery of Life, man has followed many different approaches. Among them, there are the ways of the scientist and mystic, but there are many more; the ways of poets, children, clowns, shamans, to name but a few. These ways have resulted in different descriptions of the world, both verbal and non-verbal, which emphasize different aspects. All are valid and useful in the context in which they arose. All of them, however, are only descriptions, or representations, of reality and are therefore limited. None can give a complete picture of the world.

The mechanistic world view of classical physics is useful for the description of the kind of physical phenomena we encounter in our everyday life and thus appropriate for dealing with our daily environment, and it has also proved extremely successful as a basis for technology. It is inadequate, however, for the description of physical phenomena in the submicroscopic realm. Opposed to the mechanistic conception of the world is the view of the mystics which may be epitomized by the word 'organic', as it regards all phenomena in the universe as integral parts of an inseparable harmonious whole. This world view emerges in the mystical traditions from meditative states of consciousness. In their description of the world, the mystics use concepts which are derived from these non-ordinary experiences and are, in general, inappropriate for a scientific description of macroscopic phenomena. The organic world view is not advantageous for constructing machines, nor for coping with the technical problems in an overpopulated world.

In everyday life, then, both the mechanistic and the organic views of the universe are valid and useful; the one for science and technology, the other for a balanced and fulfilled spiritual life. Beyond the dimensions of our everyday environment, however, the mechanistic concepts lose their validity and have to be replaced by organic concepts which are very similar to those used by the mystics. This is the essential experience of modern physics which has been the subject of our discussion. Physics in the twentieth century has shown that the concepts of the organic world view, although of little value for science and technology on the human scale, become extremely useful at the atomic and subatomic level. The organic view, therefore, seems to be more fundamental than the mechanistic. Classical physics, which is based on the latter, can be derived from quantum theory, which implies the former, whereas the reverse is not possible. This seems to give a first indication why we might expect the world views of modern physics and Eastern mysticism to be similar. Both emerge when man enquires into the essential nature of things—into the deeper realms of matter in physics; into the deeper realms of consciousness in mysticism—when he discovers a different reality behind the superficial mechanistic appearance of everyday life.

The parallels between the views of physicists and mystics become even more plausible when we recall the other similarities which exist in spite of their different approaches. To begin with, their method is thoroughly empirical. Physicists derive their knowledge from experiments; mystics from meditative insights. Both are observations, and in both fields these observations are acknowledged as the only source of knowledge. The object of observation is of course very different in the two cases. The mystic looks within and explores his or her consciousness at its various levels, which include the body as the physical manifestation of the mind. The experience of one's body is, in fact, emphasized in many Eastern traditions and is often seen as the key to the mystical experience of the world. When we are healthy, we do not feel any separate parts in our body but are aware of it as an integrated whole, and this awareness generates a feeling of well-being and happiness. In a similar way, the mystic is aware of the wholeness of the entire cosmos which is experienced as an extension of the body. In the words of Lama Govinda,

> To the enlightened man . . . whose consciousness embraces the universe, to him the universe becomes his 'body', while his physical body becomes a manifestation of the Universal Mind, his inner vision an expression of the highest reality, and his speech an expression of eternal truth and mantric power.[1]

[1] Lama Anagarika Govinda, *Fountains of Tibetan Mysticism*. New York: Samuel Weiser (1974), p. 225.

In contrast to the mystic, the physicist begins his enquiry into the essential nature of things by studying the material world. Penetrating into ever deeper realms of matter, he has become aware of the essential unity of all things and events. More than that, he has also learnt that he himself and his consciousness are an integral part of this unity. Thus the mystic and the physicist arrive at the same conclusion; one starting from the inner realm, the other from the outer world. The harmony between their views confirms the ancient Indian wisdom that *Brahman*, the ultimate reality without, is identical to *Atman*, the reality within.

A further similarity between the ways of the physicist and mystic is the fact that their observations take place in realms which are inaccessible to the ordinary senses. In modern physics, these are the realms of the atomic and subatomic world; in mysticism they are non-ordinary states of consciousness in which the sense world is transcended. Mystics often talk about experiencing higher dimensions in which impressions of different centres of consciousness are integrated into a harmonious whole. A similar situation exists in modern physics where a four-dimensional 'space-time' formalism has been developed which unifies concepts and observations belonging to different categories in the ordinary three-dimensional world. In both fields, the multi-dimensional experiences transcend the sensory world and are therefore almost impossible to express in ordinary language.

We see that the ways of the modern physicist and the Eastern mystic, which seem at first totally unrelated, have, in fact, much in common. It should not be too surprising, therefore, that there are striking parallels in their descriptions of the world. Once these parallels between Western science and Eastern mysticism are accepted, a number of questions will arise concerning their implications. Is modern science, with all its sophisticated machinery, merely rediscovering ancient wisdom, known to the Eastern sages for thousands of years? Should physicists, therefore, abandon the scientific method and begin to meditate? Or can there be a mutual influence between science and mysticism; perhaps even a synthesis?

I think all these questions have to be answered in the negative. I see science and mysticism as two complementary manifestations of the human mind; of its rational and intuitive faculties. The modern physicist experiences the world through an extreme specialization of the rational mind; the mystic through an extreme spe-cialization of the intuitive mind. The two approaches are entirely different and in-volve far more than a certain view of the physical world. However, they are comple-mentary, as we have learned to say in physics. Neither is comprehended in the other, nor can either of them be reduced to the other, but both of them are necessary, supplementing one another for a fuller understanding of the world. To paraphrase an old Chinese saying, mystics understand the roots of the *Tao* but not its branches; scientists understand its branches but not its roots. Science does not need mysticism and mysticism does not need science; but man needs both. Mystical experience is necessary to understand the deepest nature of things, and science is essential for modern life. What we need, therefore, is not a synthesis but a dynamic interplay between mystical intuition and scientific analysis.

So far, this has not been achieved in our society. At present, our attitude is too *yang*—to use again Chinese phraseology—too rational, male and aggressive. Scien-tists themselves are a typical example. Although their theories are leading to a world view which is similar to that of the mystics, it is striking how little this has affected the attitudes of most scientists. In mysticism, knowledge cannot be separated from a certain way of life which becomes its living manifestation. To acquire mystical knowledge means to undergo a transformation; one could even say that the knowledge *is* the transformation. Scientific knowledge, on the other hand, can often stay abstract and theoretical. Thus most of today's physicists do not seem to realize the philosophical, cultural and spiritual implications of their theories. Many of them actively support a society which is still based on the mechanistic, fragmented world view, without seeing that science points beyond such a view, towards a oneness of the universe which includes not only our natural environment but also our fellow human beings. I believe that the world view implied by modern physics is inconsistent with our present society, which does not reflect the harmonious interrelatedness we observe in nature. To achieve such a state of dynamic balance, a radically different social and economic structure will be needed: a cultural revolution in the true sense of the word. The survival of our whole civilization may depend on whether we can bring about such a change. It will depend, ultimately, on our ability to adopt some of the *yin* attitudes of Eastern mysticism; to experience the wholeness of nature and the art of living with it in harmony.

QUESTIONS FOR DISCUSSION

1. Define the term "tao." Why is this word used in the title?
2. Discuss the related concepts of yin and yang. How might such separations be universal?
3. Discuss the limitations of the Western world view, as Capra presents them. How is the Eastern world view different from the Western?
4. What is meant by the words "mystic" (par. 2) and "mysticism" (par. 5)? What is mysticism presented in opposition to? Discuss the cultural advantages and limitations of focusing exclusively on either one or the other.
5. How are the concepts of tao interconnected with concepts of Western science?

CARL G. JUNG
Sigmund Freud[1]

An early supporter of the theories and practices of Sigmund Freud, Carl G. Jung (1875–1961) revealed, in his autobiography Memories, Dreams, Reflections *(1963), several reasons for the subsequent break with his mentor. Those reasons are explained in the following text, "Sigmund Freud." Sigmund Freud (1856–1939) lived in Vienna, Austria, until he was forced to leave during*

---

[1]This chapter should be regarded as a supplement to Jung's numerous writings on Freud. The most important of these are contained in *Freud and Psychoanalysis* (CW 4). Cf. also "Sigmund Freud in His Historical Setting" (1934) and "In Memory of Sigmund Freud" (1939), in *The Spirit in Man, Art, and Literature* (CW 15). (CW refers to Jung's *Collected Works*; the initials *A. J.* are those of his editor, Aniela Jaffe. Ed. note.)

the Nazi invasion of 1938. Freud, a medical doctor, was led by his interest in the field of mental illness to devise radically innovative psychological theories, based largely on issues of gender and sexuality. Freud invented the technique of psychoanalysis to treat various psychological "disorders." Like Einstein, also a European Jewish scientist, Freud revolutionized his field of study. Freud's theories, however, have been the subject of much controversy in recent years.

Jung, like Freud, was one of the premier influences on contemporary psychology. His writings deal with such concepts as the archetype, the collective unconscious, introversion and extroversion, and the interpretation of dreams.

I embarked on the adventure of my intellectual development by becoming a psychiatrist. In all innocence I began observing mental patients, clinically, from the outside, and thereby came upon psychic processes of a striking nature. I noted and classified these things without the slightest understanding of their contents, which were considered to be adequately evaluated when they were dismissed as "pathological." In the course of time my interest focused more and more upon cases in which I experienced something understandable—that is, cases of paranoia, manic-depressive insanity, and psychogenic disturbances. From the start of my psychiatric career the studies of Breuer and Freud, along with the work of Pierre Janet, provided me with a wealth of suggestions and stimuli. Above all, I found that Freud's technique of dream analysis and dream interpretation cast a valuable light upon schizophrenic forms of expression. As early as 1900 I had read Freud's *The Interpretation of Dreams.*[2] I had laid the book aside, at the time, because I did not yet grasp it. At the age of twenty-five I lacked the experience to appreciate Freud's theories. Such experience did not come until later. In 1903 I once more took up *The Interpretation of Dreams* and discovered how it all linked up with my own ideas. What chiefly interested me was the application to dreams of the concept of the repression mechanism, which was derived from the psychology of the neuroses. This was important to me because I had frequently encountered repressions in my experiments with word association; in response to certain stimulus words the patient either had no associative answer or was unduly slow in his reaction time. As was later discovered, such a disturbance occurred each time the stimulus word had touched upon a psychic lesion or conflict. In most cases the patient was unconscious of this. When questioned about the cause of the disturbance, he would often answer in a peculiarly artificial manner. My reading of Freud's *The Interpretation of Dreams* showed me that the repression mechanism was at work here, and that the facts I had observed were consonant with his theory. Thus I was able to corroborate Freud's line of argument.

The situation was different when it came to the content of the repression. Here I could not agree with Freud. He considered the cause of the repression to be a sexual trauma. From my practice, however, I was familiar with numerous cases of neurosis in which the question of sexuality played a subordinate part, other factors standing in the foreground—for example, the problem of social adaptation, of oppression by tragic circumstances of life, prestige considerations, and so on. Later I

[2]In his obituary on Freud (1939), Jung calls this work "epoch-making" and "probably the boldest attempt that has ever been made to master the riddles of the unconscious psyche upon the apparently firm ground of empiricism. For us, then young psychiatrists, it was . . . a source of illumination, while for our older colleagues it was an object of mockery." —A. J.

presented such cases to Freud; but he would not grant that factors other than sexuality could be the cause. That was highly unsatisfactory to me.

At the beginning it was not easy for me to assign Freud the proper place in my life, or to take the right attitude toward him. When I became acquainted with his work I was planning an academic career, and was about to complete a paper that was intended to advance me at the university. But Freud was definitely *persona non grata* in the academic world at the time, and any connection with him would have been damaging in scientific circles. "Important people" at most mentioned him surreptitiously, and at congresses he was discussed only in the corridors, never on the floor. Therefore the discovery that my association experiments were in agreement with Freud's theories was far from pleasant to me.

Once, while I was in my laboratory and reflecting again upon these questions, the devil whispered to me that I would be justified in publishing the results of my experiments and my conclusions without mentioning Freud. After all, I had worked out my experiments long before I understood his work. But then I heard the voice of my second personality: "If you do a thing like that, as if you had no knowledge of Freud, it would be a piece of trickery. You cannot build your life upon a lie." With that, the question was settled. From then on I became an open partisan of Freud's and fought for him.

I first took up the cudgels for Freud at a congress in Munich where a lecturer discussed obsessional neuroses but studiously forbore to mention the name of Freud. In 1906, in connection with this incident, I wrote a paper[3] for the *Münchner Medizinische Wochenschrift* on Freud's theory of the neuroses, which had contributed a great deal to the understanding of obsessional neuroses. In response to this article, two German professors wrote to me, warning that if I remained on Freud's side and continued to defend him, I would be endangering my academic career. I replied: "If what Freud says is the truth, I am with him. I don't give a damn for a career if it has to be based on the premise of restricting research and concealing the truth." And I went on defending Freud and his ideas. But on the basis of my own findings I was still unable to feel that all neuroses were caused by sexual repression or sexual traumata. In certain cases that was so, but not in others. Nevertheless, Freud had opened up a new path of investigation, and the shocked outcries against him at the time seemed to me absurd.[4]

I had not met with much sympathy for the ideas expressed in "The Psychology of Dementia Praecox." In fact, my colleagues laughed at me. But through this book I came to know Freud. He invited me to visit him, and our first meeting took place in Vienna in March 1907. We met at one o'clock in the afternoon and talked virtually

---

[3]"Die Hysterielehre Freuds: Eine Erwiderung auf die Aschaffenburgsche Kritik," *Münchener medizinische Wochenschrift*, LIII (November, 1906), 47; English trans.: "Freud's Theory of Hysteria: A Reply to Aschaffenburg," in *Freud and Psychoanalysis* (CW 4).

[4]In 1906, after Jung sent Freud *Diagnostische Assoziationsstudien* (1906; English trans. of Jung's contributions in *Experimental Researches*, CW 2), the correspondence between the two men began, and went on until 1913. In 1907 Jung sent Freud his book *Über die Psychologie der Dementia Praecox* (English trans.: "The Psychology of Dementia Praecox," in *The Psychogenesis of Mental Disease*, CW 3). —A. J.

without a pause for thirteen hours. Freud was the first man of real importance I had encountered; in my experience up to that time, no one else could compare with him. There was nothing the least trivial in his attitude. I found him extremely intelligent, shrewd, and altogether remarkable. And yet my first impressions of him remained somewhat tangled; I could not make him out.

What he said about his sexual theory impressed me. Nevertheless, his words could not remove my hesitations and doubts. I tried to advance these reservations of mine on several occasions, but each time he would attribute them to my lack of experience. Freud was right; in those days I had not enough experience to support my objections. I could see that his sexual theory was enormously important to him, both personally and philosophically. This impressed me, but I could not decide to what extent this strong emphasis upon sexuality was connected with subjective prejudices of his, and to what extent it rested upon verifiable experiences.

Above all, Freud's attitude toward the spirit seemed to me highly questionable. Wherever, in a person or in a work of art, an expression of spirituality (in the intellectual, not the supernatural sense) came to light, he suspected it, and insinuated that it was repressed sexuality. Anything that could not be directly interpreted as sexuality he referred to as "psychosexuality." I protested that this hypothesis, carried to its logical conclusion, would lead to an annihilating judgment upon culture. Culture would then appear as a mere farce, the morbid consequence of repressed sexuality. "Yes," he assented, "so it is, and that is just a curse of fate against which we are powerless to contend." I was by no means disposed to agree, or to let it go at that, but still I did not feel competent to argue it out with him.

There was something else that seemed to me significant at that first meeting. It had to do with things which I was able to think out and understand only after our friendship was over. There was no mistaking the fact that Freud was emotionally involved in his sexual theory to an extraordinary degree. When he spoke of it, his tone became urgent, almost anxious, and all signs of his normally critical and skeptical manner vanished. A strange, deeply moved expression came over his face, the cause of which I was at a loss to understand. I had a strong intuition that for him sexuality was a sort of *numinosum*. This was confirmed by a conversation which took place some three years later (in 1910), again in Vienna.

I can still recall vividly how Freud said to me, "My dear Jung, promise me never to abandon the sexual theory. That is the most essential thing of all. You see, we must make a dogma of it, an unshakable bulwark." He said that to me with great emotion, in the tone of a father saying, "And promise me this one thing, my dear son: that you will go to church every Sunday." In some astonishment I asked him, "A bulwark—against what?" To which he replied, "Against the black tide of mud"—and here he hesitated for a moment, then added—"of occultism." First of all, it was the words "bulwark" and "dogma" that alarmed me; for a dogma, that is to say, an undisputable confession of faith, is set up only when the aim is to suppress doubts once and for all. But that no longer has anything to do with scientific judgment; only with a personal power drive.

This was the thing that struck at the heart of our friendship. I knew that I would never be able to accept such an attitude. What Freud seemed to mean by "occultism" was virtually everything that philosophy and religion, including the rising contemporary science of parapsychology, had learned about the psyche. To me the sexual theory was just as occult, that is to say, just as unproven an hypothesis, as many other speculative views. As I saw it, a scientific truth was a hypothesis which might be adequate for the moment but was not to be preserved as an article of faith for all time.

Although I did not properly understand it then, I had observed in Freud the eruption of unconscious religious factors. Evidently he wanted my aid in erecting a barrier against these threatening unconscious contents.

The impression this conversation made upon me added to my confusion; until then I had not considered sexuality as a precious and imperiled concept to which one must remain faithful. Sexuality evidently meant more to Freud than to other people. For him it was something to be religiously observed. In the face of such deep convictions one generally becomes shy and reticent. After a few stammering attempts on my part, the conversation soon came to an end.

I was bewildered and embarrassed. I had the feeling that I had caught a glimpse of a new, unknown country from which swarms of new ideas flew to meet me. One thing was clear: Freud, who had always made much of his irreligiosity, had now constructed a dogma; or rather, in the place of a jealous God whom he had lost, he had substituted another compelling image, that of sexuality. It was no less insistent, exacting, domineering, threatening, and morally ambivalent than the original one. Just as the psychically stronger agency is given "divine" or "daemonic" attributes, so the "sexual libido" took over the role of a *deus absconditus*, a hidden or concealed god. The advantage of this transformation for Freud was, apparently, that he was able to regard the new numinous principle as scientifically irreproachable and free from all religious taint. At bottom, however, the numinosity, that is, the psychological qualities of the two rationally incommensurable opposites—Yahweh and sexuality—remained the same. The name alone had changed, and with it, of course, the point of view: the lost god had now to be sought below, not above. But what difference does it make, ultimately, to the stronger agency if it is called now by one name and now by another? If psychology did not exist, but only concrete objects, the one would actually have been destroyed and replaced by the other. But in reality, that is to say, in psychological experience, there is not one whit the less of urgency, anxiety, compulsiveness, etc. The problem still remains: how to overcome or escape our anxiety, bad conscience, guilt, compulsion, unconsciousness, and instinctuality. If we cannot do this from the bright, idealistic side, then perhaps we shall have better luck by approaching the problem from the dark, biological side.

Like flames suddenly flaring up, these thoughts darted through my mind. Much later, when I reflected upon Freud's character, they revealed their significance. There was one characteristic of his that preoccupied me above all: his bitterness. It had struck me at our first encounter, but it remained inexplicable to me until I was able to see it in connection with his attitude toward sexuality. Although, for Freud, sexuality was undoubtedly a *numinosum*, his terminology and theory seemed to define it exclusively as a biological function. It was only the emotionality with which he spoke of it that revealed the deeper elements reverberating within him. Basically, he wanted to teach—or so at least it seemed to me—that, regarded from within, sexuality included spirituality and had an intrinsic meaning. But his concretistic terminology was too narrow to express this idea. He gave me the impression that at bottom he was working against his own goal and against himself; and there is, after all, no harsher bitterness than that of a person who is his own worst enemy. In his own words, he felt himself menaced by a "black tide of mud"—he who more than anyone else had tried to let down his buckets into those black depths.

Freud never asked himself why he was compelled to talk continually of sex, why this idea had taken such possession of him. He remained unaware that his "monotony of interpretation" expressed a flight from himself, or from that other side of him which might perhaps be called mystical. So long as he refused to acknowledge that side, he could never be reconciled with himself. He was blind toward the paradox and ambiguity of the contents of the unconscious, and did not know that everything which arises out of the unconscious has a top and a bottom, an inside and an outside. When we speak of the outside—and that is what Freud did—we are considering only half of the whole, with the result that a countereffect arises out of the unconscious.

There was nothing to be done about this one-sidedness of Freud's. Perhaps some inner experience of his own might have opened his eyes; but then his intellect would have reduced any such experience to "mere sexuality" or "psychosexuality." He remained the victim of the one aspect he could recognize, and for that reason I see him as a tragic figure; for he was a great man, and what is more, a man in the grip of his daimon.

QUESTIONS FOR DISCUSSION

1. This text is an excerpt from Jung's autobiography. How does an awareness of the context of the writing contribute to your ability to understand it? Who might the audience be?
2. What is the purpose of an autobiography? What is the particular purpose of this section of Jung's autobiography? In what sense can it be said that all autobiography is "fiction"? How is autobiographical writing different from biography?
3. What aspects of Freud's psychological theories does Jung support? What aspects of Freud's theories does Jung criticize?
4. What kind of a person does Jung portray Freud to be? Freewrite for about a half a page (in your reading journal) describing his portrait of Freud.
5. As a result of reading this article, what kind of a person do you imagine Jung to be? Write a brief description of some of the characteristics you see in the author.
6. Analyze the conflicts between Jung and Freud that caused the two to end their friendship. How might Freud have explained the conflict? (Apply what you know about Oedipal theory.)

CHIEF SEATTLE
Environmental Statement

Chief Seattle (1788–1866) reputedly delivered the speech presented here as an "Environmental Statement" in which he responded to a treaty proposed by the United States government to buy two million acres of land occupied by his people for $150,000. Seattle was an environmentalist who, late in life, also became known as an antiwar activist. In this essay Seattle questions the notion that people can own land, that the Earth is a material commodity. Presenting the lifestyle of his people, the Duwamish tribe of the Puget Sound region, as communal, Seattle argues in favor of a responsible, forward-looking perspective on land use. Seattle's concerns prefigure the ethical questions raised by contemporary ecologists like Rachel Carson and Carl Sagan.

How can you buy or sell the sky, the warmth of the land? The idea is strange to us.

If we do not own the freshness of the air and the sparkle of the water, how can you buy them?

Every part of this earth is sacred to my people. Every shining pine needle, every sandy shore, every mist in the dark woods, every clearing and humming insect is holy in the memory and experience of my people. The sap which courses through the trees carries the memories of the red man.

The white man's dead forget the country of their birth when they go to walk among the stars. Our dead never forget this beautiful earth, for it is the mother of the red man. We are part of the earth and it is part of us. The perfumed flowers are our sisters; the deer, the horse, the great eagle, these are our brothers. The rocky crests, the juices in the meadows, the body heat of the pony, and man—all belong to the same family.

So, when the Great Chief in Washington sends word that he wishes to buy our land, he asks much of us. The Great Chief sends word he will reserve us a place so that we can live comfortably to ourselves. He will be our father and we will be his children.

So we will consider your offer to buy our land. But it will not be easy. For this land is sacred to us. This shining water that moves in the streams and rivers is not just water but the blood of our ancestors. If we sell you land, you must remember that it is sacred, and you must teach your children that it is sacred and that each ghostly reflection in the clear water of the lakes tells of events and memories in the life of my people. The water's murmur is the voice of my father's father.

The rivers are our brothers, they quench our thirst. The rivers carry our canoes, and feed our children. If we sell you our land, you must remember, and teach your children, that the rivers are our brothers and yours, and you must henceforth give the rivers the kindness you would give any brother.

We know that the white man does not understand our ways. One portion of land is the same to him as the next, for he is a stranger who comes in the night and takes from the land whatever he needs. The earth is not his brother, but his enemy, and when he has conquered it, he moves on. He leaves his father's grave behind, and he does not care. He kidnaps the earth from his children, and he does not care. His father's grave, and his children's birthright are forgotten. He treats his mother, the earth, and his brother, the sky, as things to be bought, plundered, sold like sheep or bright beads. His appetite will devour the earth and leave behind only a desert.

I do not know. Our ways are different from your ways. The sight of your cities pains the eyes of the red man. There is no quiet place in the white man's cities. No place to hear the unfurling of leaves in spring or the rustle of the insect's wings. The clatter only seems to insult the ears. And what is there to life if a man cannot hear the lonely cry of the whippoorwill or the arguments of the frogs around the pond at night? I am a red man and do not understand. The Indian prefers the soft sound of the wind darting over the face of a pond and the smell of the wind itself, cleansed by a midday rain, or scented with piñon pine.

The air is precious to the red man for all things share the same breath, the beast, the tree, the man, they all share the same breath. The white man does not seem to notice the air he breathes. Like a man dying for many days he is numb to the stench. But if we sell you our land, you must remember that the air is precious to us, that the air shares its spirit with all the life it supports.

The wind that gave our grandfather his first breath also receives his last sigh. And if we sell you our land, you must keep it apart and sacred as a place where even the white man can go to taste the wind that is sweetened by the meadow's flowers.

You must teach your children that the ground beneath their feet is the ashes of our grandfathers. So that they will respect the land, tell your children that the earth is rich with the lives of our kin. Teach your children that we have taught our children that the earth is our mother. Whatever befalls the earth befalls the sons of the earth. If men spit upon the ground, they spit upon themselves.

This we know: the earth does not belong to man; man belongs to the earth. All things are connected. We may be brothers after all. We shall see. One thing we know which the white man may one day discover: our God is the same God.

You may think now that you own Him as you wish to own our land; but you cannot. He is the God of man, and His compassion is equal for the red man and the white. This earth is precious to Him, and to harm the earth is to heap contempt on its creator. The whites too shall pass; perhaps sooner than all other tribes. Contaminate your bed and you will one night suffocate in your own waste.

But in your perishing you will shine brightly fired by the strength of the God who brought you to this land and for some special purpose gave you dominion over this land and over the red man.

That destiny is a mystery to us, for we do not understand when the buffalo are all slaughtered, the wild horses are tame, the secret corners of the forest heavy with scent of many men and the view of the ripe hills blotted by talking wires.

Where is the thicket? Gone. Where is the eagle? Gone.

The end of living and the beginning of survival.

QUESTIONS FOR DISCUSSION

1. To whom is Seattle's statement addressed? Why did he give the speech?
2. Why is the idea of ownership of land alien to Seattle and his people? Why is it "natural" to the white settlers?

3. The belief that the land is sacred imposes certain responsibilities on those who use the land. What are those responsibilities? Why is it important to Seattle that the white people recognize those obligations?
4. How does Seattle's use of the analogy of the family help support his main idea?
5. In what ways do Chief Seattle's concerns look forward to the problems that contemporary ecologists point out?
6. Compare and contrast the concerns of Seattle with those of Rachel Carson in her essay "The Obligation to Endure," which follows.

RACHEL CARSON
The Obligation to Endure

Rachel Carson (1907–1964) was an American biologist and writer known for her books about the sea and her writings concerning the use of pesticides. Beginning in 1947, she worked as editor in chief of the U.S. Fish and Wildlife Service. In her essay titled "The Obligation to Endure," from Silent Spring *(1961), Carson describes the ways in which humankind, in its relatively short time on Earth, has drastically altered the natural world. An ardent and eloquent environmentalist, Carson questions the value of the gains achieved by the sacrifice of natural resources. Most specifically, Carson indicts chemical insecticides as an instrument which may well work the destruction of much plant and animal life. Like several of the other scientists represented here, Carson warns that "the obligation to endure" endows each person with a responsibility to be aware of scientific activities and to make sound decisions based on that awareness.*

The history of life on earth has been a history of interaction between living things and their surroundings. To a large extent, the physical form and the habits of the earth's vegetation and its animal life have been molded by the environment. Considering the whole span of earthly time, the opposite effect, in which life actually modifies its surroundings, has been relatively slight. Only within the moment of time represented by the present century has one species—man—acquired significant power to alter the nature of his world.

During the past quarter century this power has not only increased to one of disturbing magnitude but it has changed in character. The most alarming of all man's assaults upon the environment is the contamination of air, earth, rivers, and sea with dangerous and even lethal materials. This pollution is for the most part irrecoverable; the chain of evil it initiates not only in the world that must support life but in living tissues is for the most part irreversible. In this now universal contamination of the environment, chemicals are the sinister and little-recognized partners of radiation in changing the very nature of the world—the very nature of its life. Strontium 90, released through nuclear explosions into the air, comes to earth in rain or drifts down as fallout, lodges in soil, enters into the grass or corn or wheat grown there, and in time takes up its abode in the bones of a human being, there to remain until his death. Similarly, chemicals sprayed on croplands or forests or gardens lie long in soil, entering into living organisms, passing from one to another in a chain of poisoning and death. Or they pass mysteriously by underground streams until they emerge and, through the alchemy of air and sunlight, combine into new forms that kill vegetation, sicken cattle, and work unknown harm on those who drink from once pure wells. As Albert Schweitzer[1] has said, "Man can hardly even recognize the devils of his own creation."

It took hundreds of millions of years to produce the life that now inhabits the earth—eons of time in which that developing and evolving and diversifying life reached a state of adjustment and balance with its surroundings. The environment, rigorously shaping and directing the life it supported, contained elements that were hostile as well as supporting. Certain rocks gave out dangerous radiation; even within the light of the sun, from which all life draws its energy, there were short-wave radiations with power to injure. Given time—time not in years but in millennia—life adjusts, and a balance has been reached. For time is the essential ingredient; but in the modern world there is no time.

The rapidity of change and the speed with which new situations are created follow the impetuous and heedless pace of man rather than the deliberate pace of nature. Radiation is no longer merely the background radiation of rocks, the bombardment of cosmic rays, the ultraviolet of the sun that have existed before there was any life on earth; radiation is now the unnatural creation of man's tampering with the atom. The chemicals to which life is asked to make its adjustment are no longer merely the calcium and silica and copper and all the rest of the minerals washed out of the rocks and carried in rivers to the sea; they are the synthetic creations of man's inventive mind, brewed in his laboratories, and having no counterparts in nature.

To adjust to these chemicals would require time on the scale that is nature's; it would require not merely the years of a man's life but the life of generations. And even this, were it by some miracle possible, would be futile, for the new chemicals come from our laboratories in an endless stream; almost five hundred annually find their way into actual use in the United States alone. The figure is staggering and its implications are not easily grasped—500 new chemicals to which the bodies of men and animals are required somehow to adapt each year, chemicals totally outside the limits of biologic experience.

Among them are many that are used in man's war against nature. Since the mid-1940's over 200 basic chemicals have been created for use in killing insects, weeds, rodents, and other organisms described in the modern vernacular as "pests"; and they are sold under several thousand different brand names.

These sprays, dusts, and aerosols are now applied almost universally to farms, gardens, forests, and homes—nonselective chemicals that have the power to kill every insect, the "good" and the "bad," to still the song of birds and the leaping of fish in the streams, to coat the leaves with a deadly film, and to linger on in soil—all this though the intended target may be only a few weeds or insects. Can anyone believe it is possible to lay down such a barrage of poisons on the surface of the earth without making it unfit for all life? They should not be called "insecticides," but "biocides."

---

[1] **Albert Schweitzer (1875–1965)** Alsatian theologian, musician, and medical missionary. [Ed. note.]

The whole process of spraying seems caught up in an endless spiral. Since DDT was released for civilian use, a process of escalation has been going on in which ever more toxic materials must be found. This has happened because insects, in a triumphant vindication of Darwin's principle of the survival of the fittest, have evolved super races immune to the particular insecticide used, hence a deadlier one has always to be developed—and then a deadlier one than that. It has happened also because, for reasons to be described later, destructive insects often undergo a "flareback," or resurgence, after spraying, in numbers greater than before. Thus the chemical war is never won, and all life is caught in its violent crossfire.

Along with the possibility of the extinction of mankind by nuclear war, the central problem of our age has therefore become the contamination of man's total environment with such substances of incredible potential for harm—substances that accumulate in the tissues of plants and animals and even penetrate the germ cells to shatter or alter the very material of heredity upon which the shape of the future depends.

Some would-be architects of our future look toward a time when it will be possible to alter the human germ plasm by design. But we may easily be doing so now by inadvertence, for many chemicals, like radiation, bring about gene mutations. It is ironic to think that man might determine his own future by something so seemingly trivial as the choice of an insect spray.

All this has been risked—for what? Future historians may well be amazed by our distorted sense of proportion. How could intelligent beings seek to control a few unwanted species by a method that contaminated the entire environment and brought the threat of disease and death even to their own kind? Yet this is precisely what we have done. We have done it, moreover, for reasons that collapse the moment we examine them. We are told that the enormous and expanding use of pesticides is necessary to maintain farm production. Yet is our real problem not one of *overproduction?* Our farms, despite measures to remove acreages from production and to pay farmers *not* to produce, have yielded such a staggering excess of crops that the American taxpayer in 1962 is paying out more than one billion dollars a year as the total carrying cost of the surplus-food storage program. And is the situation helped when one branch of the Agriculture Department tries to reduce production while another states, as it did in 1958, "It is believed generally that reduction of crop acreages under provisions of the Soil Bank will stimulate interest in use of chemicals to obtain maximum production on the land retained in crops."

All this is not to say there is no insect problem and no need of control. I am saying, rather, that control must be geared to realities, not to mythical situations, and that the methods employed must be such that they do not destroy us along with the insects.

The problem whose attempted solution has brought such a train of disaster in its wake is an accompaniment of our modern way of life. Long before the age of man, insects inhabited the earth—a group of extraordinarily varied and adaptable beings. Over the course of time since man's advent, a small percentage of the more than half a million species of insects have come into conflict with human welfare in two principal ways: as competitors for the food supply and as carriers of human disease.

Disease-carrying insects become important where human beings are crowded together, especially under conditions where sanitation is poor, as in time of natural disaster or war or in situations of extreme poverty and deprivation. Then control of some sort becomes necessary. It is a sobering fact, however, as we shall presently see, that the method of massive chemical control has had only limited success, and also threatens to worsen the very conditions it is intended to curb.

Under primitive agricultural conditions the farmer had few insect problems. These arose with the intensification of agriculture—the devotion of immense acreages to a single crop. Such a system set the stage for explosive increases in specific insect populations. Single-crop farming does not take advantage of the principles by which nature works; it is agriculture as an engineer might conceive it to be. Nature has introduced great variety into the landscape, but man has displayed a passion for simplifying it. Thus he undoes the built-in checks and balances by which nature holds the species within bounds. One important natural check is a limit on the amount of suitable habitat for each species. Obviously then, an insect that lives on wheat can build up its population to much higher levels on a farm devoted to wheat than on one in which wheat is intermingled with other crops to which the insect is not adapted.

The same thing happens in other situations. A generation or more ago, the towns of large areas of the United States lined their streets with the noble elm tree. Now the beauty they hopefully created is threatened with complete destruction as disease sweeps through the elms, carried by a beetle that would have only limited chance to build up large populations and to spread from tree to tree if the elms were only occasional trees in a richly diversified planting.

Another factor in the modern insect problem is one that must be viewed against a background of geologic and human history: the spreading of thousands of different kinds of organisms from their native homes to invade new territories. This worldwide migration has been studied and graphically described by the British ecologist Charles Elton in his recent book *The Ecology of Invasions*. During the Cretaceous Period, some hundred million years ago, flooding seas cut many land bridges between continents and living things found themselves confined in what Elton calls "colossal separate nature reserves." There, isolated from others of their kind, they developed many new species. When some of the land masses were joined again, about 15 million years ago, these species began to move out into new territories—a movement that is not only still in progress but is now receiving considerable assistance from man.

The importation of plants is the primary agent in the modern spread of species, for animals have almost invariably gone along with the plants, quarantine being a comparatively recent and not completely effective innovation. The United States Office of Plant Introduction alone has introduced almost 200,000 species and varieties of plants from all over the world. Nearly half of the 180 or so major insect enemies of plants in the United States are accidental imports from abroad, and most of them have come as hitchhikers on plants.

In new territory, out of reach of the restraining hand of the natural enemies that kept down its numbers in its native land, an invading plant or animal is able to become enormously abundant. Thus it is no accident that our most troublesome insects are introduced species.

These invasions, both the naturally occurring and those dependent on human assistance, are likely to continue indefinitely. Quarantine and massive chemical campaigns are only extremely expensive ways of buying time. We are faced, according to Dr. Elton, "with a life-and-death need not just to find new technological means of suppressing this plant or that animal"; instead we need the basic knowledge of animal populations and their relations to their surroundings that will "promote an even balance and damp down the explosive power of outbreaks and new invasions."

Much of the necessary knowledge is now available but we do not use it. We train ecologists in our universities and even employ them in our governmental agencies but we seldom take their advice. We allow the chemical death rain to fall as though there were no alternative, whereas in fact there are many, and our ingenuity could soon discover many more if given opportunity.

Have we fallen into a mesmerized state that makes us accept as inevitable that which is inferior or detrimental, as though having lost the will or the vision to demand that which is good? Such thinking, in the words of the ecologist Paul Shepard, "idealizes life with only its head out of water, inches above the limits of toleration of the corruption of its own environment . . . Why should we tolerate a diet of weak poisons, a home in insipid surroundings, a circle of acquaintances who are not quite our enemies, the noise of motors with just enough relief to prevent insanity? Who would want to live in a world which is just not quite fatal?"

Yet such a world is pressed upon us. The crusade to create a chemically sterile, insect-free world seems to have engendered a fanatic zeal on the part of many specialists and most of the so-called control agencies. On every hand there is evidence that those engaged in spraying operations exercise a ruthless power. "The regulatory entomologists . . . function as prosecutor, judge and jury, tax assessor and collector and sheriff to enforce their own orders," said Connecticut entomologist Neely Turner. The most flagrant abuses go unchecked in both state and federal agencies.

It is not my contention that chemical insecticides must never be used. I do contend that we have put poisonous and biologically potent chemicals indiscriminately into the hands of persons largely or wholly ignorant of their potentials for harm. We have subjected enormous numbers of people to contact with these poisons, without their consent and often without their knowledge. If the Bill of Rights contains no guarantee that a citizen shall be secure against lethal poisons distributed either by private individuals or by public officials, it is surely only because our forefathers, despite their considerable wisdom and foresight, could conceive of no such problem.

I contend, furthermore, that we have allowed these chemicals to be used with little or no advance investigation of their effect on soil, water, wildlife, and man himself. Future generations are unlikely to condone our lack of prudent concern for the integrity of the natural world that supports all life.

There is still very limited awareness of the nature of the threat. This is an era of specialists, each of whom sees his own problem and is unaware of or intolerant of the larger frame into which it fits. It is also an era dominated by industry, in which the right to make a dollar at whatever cost is seldom challenged. When the public protests, confronted with some obvious evidence of damaging results of pesticide applications, it is fed little tranquilizing pills of half truth. We urgently need an end to these false assurances, to the sugar coating of unpalatable facts. It is the public that is being asked to assume the risks that the insect controllers calculate. The public must decide whether it wishes to continue on the present road, and it can do so only when in full possession of the facts. In the words of Jean Rostand, "The obligation to endure gives us the right to know."

QUESTIONS FOR DISCUSSION

1. Who might be the intended audience of this text? Is the vocabulary suited to a general audience? List words that might be too specialized for the lay reader.
2. What is Carson's purpose in writing this essay? Look for a statement of purpose in the text.
3. What is meant by the phrase "the obligation to endure"? Compare and contrast this obligation with the duties described by Chief Seattle in his "Environmental Statement" (p. 58).
4. Describe the ways in which the use of certain pesticides has endangered the environment.
5. What solution to the problem does Carson offer? Is it a viable one? Explain.
6. Is the conclusion persuasive? Analyze the language of the last paragraph to locate elements of persuasion.
7. Discuss other threats to the environment. Propose possible solutions to the problems.
8. Analyze Carson's practice of questioning the reader. In what ways is this an effective strategy for argument?

MAC MARGOLIS
Amazon Ablaze

In "Amazon Ablaze" Mac Margolis describes the decimation of the Brazilian rain forest. Battling the farmers who have been burning down the forest to clear land for agriculture, ecologists are concerned that the loss of the rain forests will devastate not only the local environment, but eventually, the global ecosystem. Margolis, a reporter for Newsweek *and* The Christian Science Monitor *who specializes in writing about Latin America, documents the history of the problem and proposes a complex but urgently needed solution.*

*"Here in Brazil the soil had been first violated, then destroyed. Agriculture had been a matter of looting for quick profits. Within a hundred years, in fact, the pioneers had worked their way like a slow fire across the state of São Paulo, eating into virgin territory on the one side, leaving nothing but exhausted fallow land on the other."—**Claude Levi-Strauss, "Tristes Tropiques."***

The air was getting thick inside José Pedro Gonçalves' office. "Burnings," he was saying, "are a part of our culture." Mr. Gonçalves, the chief of environmental protection for Mato Grosso, a state on Brazil's western frontier, was wearing a smallish smile and shook his head from time to time. "It's an age-old myth," he said, "that fire renews the soil and makes the next crop better." As he spoke, wisps of black ash floated down onto the coffee table between us. I could make out yellowish smoke seeping through the air conditioner, which seemed to groan in protest. My eyes began to tear and itch. "You don't have to go far to see the destruction."

Gonçalves got up and went to the window of his fifth-floor suite. He pointed to a brawny man clad only in tattered shorts and rubber sandals, poking a blackened stick at a brush fire that was burning away on an acre lot below. I had gone to the state of Mato Grosso last October to see up close once more Brazil's, and perhaps the planet's, most publicized ecological problem, the destruction of the Amazon rain forest. Suddenly, there it was, smoldering away in downtown Cuiabá, a bustling state capital of 700,000 inhabitants. There, shouting distance from the region's highest environmental authority, another small acre of Amazonia was going up in smoke.

Later, during that visit to the sprawling pioneer state, the problem became vivid. The twin-engine Fokker F-27 Friendship plane that took me to Alta Floresta, a boom town of loggers and gold prospectors in the north, droned endless circles in a sky opaque with smoke, soot, and ash. Hundreds of forest fires had turned the atmosphere into an acrid soup of carbon gases and particulate matter. After an hour of searching in vain for a glimpse of the landing strip, the pilots were forced to veer off to another city, where we put down and waited for "the dry clouds" to blow away.

At that time, a good deal of the Brazilian Amazon region was on fire, literally. September and October mark the end of the dry season in the north, a time Brazilians have come to designate as a season all its own: the *"Queimadas"* or "Burnings." This is the time just before the torrential winter rains when smallholders and ranchers prepare their crops and pastures for the coming wet season. Some homesteaders use machetes or handsaws. Land barons sling great link chains between two tractors to drag down the forest. But fire has become the preferred tool.

Amerindian tribes and New World pilgrim farmers used fire for centuries to clear small plots for subsistence agriculture. But, as Brazil's settler civilization has advanced relentlessly west, from São Paulo and Rio de Janeiro into the empty spaces of this country, the burnings have gotten out of hand. You can spot them from 10,000 feet in the air, from a plane window at night, and they look like giant undulating rings of primary red and orange, licking away at an inky emptiness. In Alta Floresta, the smoke hung low, a gray pall that mingled with billows of dust kicked up by vehicles pounding up and down the city's unpaved streets.

During the last burnings, weather satellites detected 80,000 square miles of forest fires, an area bigger than New England, New Jersey, and Delaware put together. Sixty percent of the fires were to reclaim overgrown pastures, but the rest destroyed virgin forest nearly three times the size of Belgium.

Fires of that size raise more than local concern. Much of the industrialized world has been ringing the alarm bell—aware of the effect of the carbon dioxide buildup and the smoke pall on global climate, of the threatened decimation of plant and animal species, and of other equally devastating ecological damage. But the only realistic fire brigade is the Brazilian government. Finally that government is responding to the alarm over the burning, logging, erosion, river poisoning, and other dangers.

After a spate of shrill headlines worldwide and protests at home, the government was forced to act. In October, on the eve of a trip to Europe, President José Sarney issued a decree meant to overhaul the country's entire Amazonian policy. The measures, dubbed "Our Nature," called for a 90-day moratorium on initiatives in the Amazon. Among other items, Sarney mandated a temporary halt to government subsidies for Amazon development projects and suspended exports of round logs from Amazonia, practices which have encouraged deforestation. Study groups were given until late January this year to deliver their plans, which will become the basis of a new Amazon policy.

"In a country with continental dimensions, ecology has to be given top priority," the President announced before a group of foreign journalists, summoned to the nation's capital, Brasília. "The times are over when we thought our natural resources were inexhaustible."

The burnings that first attracted world attention are only the most spectacular threat to the Amazon. Scientists suspect mercury, used by prospectors to amalgamate gold, has damaged the lungs of untold gold prospectors and has contaminated river fish—a staple in the diet of millions of Amazon dwellers. Pig-iron smelters erected at the giant Carajás mine demand tremendous amounts of timber, threatening dwindling forests. Settlers steered to Amazonia during land-reform campaigns have ignored preservation laws and wantonly sold away their stands of timber.

In recent months, such destruction has touched off further 12-alarm headlines in the Brazilian and the world press. It sent thousands of youths to the streets of Berlin, during the IMF-World Bank annual meeting last September, and mobilized ecology groups from Queensland to Washington. The burning Amazon has become not only the *casus belli* [opportunity for battle] between Brazil and environmentalists but also a diplomatic embarrassment and a financial threat. Doubled over by debt, Brazil has come to depend more and more on the largess of institutions like the World Bank and the Inter-American Development Bank to supply the badly needed sources of credit that dried up after the world debt crisis of 1982. In recent years, these lenders have held up, and sometimes outright canceled, loans for projects judged to be harmful to the environment. Last November, officials of the West German government informed Brazil that even private banks would veto loans if they were not linked to ecological safeguards.

Until very recently the overwhelming impression explorers and naturalists took away from the Amazon was one of the forest's absolute dominion. The woodland named for the New World's largest river system was immense and majestic, endowed by newcomers with primordial qualities. Euclides da Cunha, a celebrated turn-of-the-century journalist and explorer, was dazzled by Amazonia's lushness and bounty. The Amazon, this "excess of heavens above an excess of waters," he wrote in 1903, was "the last page of Genesis, that has yet to be written." In the iconography of Brazilian novelist Alberto Rangel, the forest was an indomitable "Green Hell."

"It's big," an expatriate English barman in the seaport city of Pará told a marvelling British journalist, H. M. Tomlinson in 1901. "It's a world with no light yet. You get lost in it . . . [It's] as if something dark was coming and you couldn't move.

There the forest is all around us. Nobody knows what's at the back of it. Men leave Pará, going up river. We have a drink here, and they go up river, and they don't go back."

This epic tone, of awe and majesty, runs throughout most Amazon narratives. Against this current runs another leitmotif, the obsession of glint-eyed explorers and frontiersmen to dominate the unruly region. Indeed, this lush, humid rain forest has been as fecund for fantasy as for its bountiful wildlife. A host of fortune seekers, Sir Walter Raleigh, and Spain's conquistadors plunged into the jungle in disastrous searches for Eldorado, the mythic Indian chief said to rule a city "where gold was more plentiful than cloth"—the kind of legendary land of wealth still known by the name of Eldorado. Much later, there were the visionary capitalists, Henry Ford[1] and Daniel Ludwig, who attempted, and failed, in megalomaniacal ventures to extract natural riches—rubber and wood pulp—from the niggardly forest. In the 1970s, the US-based Hudson Institute, a public policy think tank, even suggested damming the mighty river itself, to turn the region into a great lake, to facilitate transit across the border.

There was perhaps no more zealous an Amazon promoter than Theodore Roosevelt. In 1914, America's lyric advocate of the strenuous life teamed up with a Brazilian colonel, Candido Mariano Rondon, and trekked off to darkest Amazonia for yet another of his patented adventures in the outback. Rondon, a Brazilian explorer and Indianist, was on a strategic government mission to map uncharted territory. For Roosevelt it was another chance to shoot things and to wax imperial about the prosperous future of America's great southern neighbor.

"Here the soil was fertile; it will be a fine site for a coffee plantation when this region is open to settlement," he wrote in Scribner's Magazine in 1913. "Surely such a rich and fertile land cannot be permitted to remain idle, to lie as a tenantless wilderness, while there are such teeming swarms of human beings in the overcrowded, overpeopled countries of the Old World. The very rapids and waterfalls which now make the navigation of the river so difficult and dangerous would drive electric trolleys up and down its whole length and far out on either side, and run mills and factories, and lighten the labor on farms. A land like this is a hard land for the first explorers, and perhaps for their immediate followers, but not for the people who come after them."

But times have tempered such bully forecasts. The narrative has changed as well. It is no longer the forest that is mean and implacable, but rather man, the most reckless of the earth's fauna. The demonology has also been amended. Hell is no longer green and vine-entangled but two-legged and pale-faced. The seasonal Amazonian fires are his infernal tools, the once villainous forest less his adversary than his victim.

Today the wild territory Roosevelt and Rondon traveled—Mato Grosso and Rondônia—is traversed by a two-lane blacktop superhighway, overrun by settlers, studded with microwave telecommunications towers, and dotted with agribusiness. Settlers have streamed in from the farmed-out lands in the south, mentioned

---

[1]**Henry Ford (1863–1947)** American industrialist, famous automobile manufacturer. [Ed. note.]

by Claude Levi-Strauss,[2] and from the crowded coastal cities. They represent the most massive human migration since the wagons pushed west of the Mississippi. In their wake, they have indeed left some monuments of prosperity, but there is also crowding out, poverty, disease, land conflict, and devastation.

The critics, who are legion, have pointed an accusing finger at reckless developers, loggers, and landgrabbers on the one hand and ignorant peasants on the other as the chief agents of destruction. Each has its parcel of blame. But by far the worst culprit appears to have been a succession of Brazilian rulers.

Part of the problem is that authorities, from Emperor Pedro II to the generals and technocrats of the 1970s, have looked at the Amazon not as a complex biosystem, with particular characteristics and requirements, but as a natural treasure chest to pilfer at will, or else as a piece of national real estate to serve as a foundation for nation building.

To battalions of Brazilian military men and intellectuals, driven by the positivist teachings of Auguste Comte,[3] the taking of the Amazon was the fulfillment of national identity. More urgently, the forest was the "splendid stage where sooner or later the globe's civilization would concentrate," forecast Euclides da Cunha, one of the leading positivists. The task was to occupy the empty forest land before Brazil's neighbors in South America, or any other of the planet's covetous races, did. A heady elixir of manifest destiny and xenophobia propelled government missions headlong into Amazonia.

The official ideologies encouraged occupation and settlement of this forest region long before anyone understood it. The lessons have often been costly. During the two rubber booms of this century, governments dispatched "rubber-tapper armies" into the forest in search of latex—and nothing else. When world rubber prices collapsed, so did this sylvan Eldorado. The rubber soldiers began the region's new lumpen proletariat, and Amazonia returned to its timeless torpor as an economic and social backwater.

More recently, military leaders saw the Amazon as an instrument to solve two different and unrelated problems, national security and abject regional poverty. The empty forest would be, in the often quoted phrase of Gen. Emilio Garrastazu Médici, "a land without men for men without land." The enormous 3,000-mile trans-Amazon highway scattered homesteaders from the starving northeast in "agrovillas" all up and down its length. But though millions of dollars were poured into the project, technical help was scarce, markets for produce precarious, and the settlers from the arid northeast confounded by the alien tropical climate. After eight years, according to a World Bank study, the government had managed to settle only 3,000 northeasterners, a fraction of the target.

Despite the disappointments, official designs for the Amazon have grown only more ambitious. In 1960, there were only 3,726 miles of roads into the Amazon, and only 186 miles of blacktop. A quarter century later, there are 31,050 miles of improved roads and two interstate superhighways, the Belém-Brasília, which connects

---

[2]**Claude Levi-Strauss (b. 1908)** French anthropologist, founder of structural anthropology. [Ed. note.]
[3]**Auguste Comte (1798–1857)** French philosopher, founder of philosophy known as "Positivism," in which knowledge is based only on observable, scientific data. [Ed. note.]

a seaport city to Brazil's capital, in the central Amazon, and BR-364 in the northwest. Roads have become to this forest land what railways were to the Russian steppe and the American West.

Now, more than 160,000 pilgrims come flooding every year into Rondônia, the state named for the intrepid explorer who strung a 900-mile telegraph line there at the turn of the century. The population of Mato Grosso, the immense state directly to the south, increases by 12% a year, four times the national average. Boom towns, schools, bus depots, and banks have followed, just as Roosevelt predicted. But destruction has not lagged far behind. In Pará, the settler assault laid waste to 9% of the state forest in 1987.

Much of this rush to the frontier has been spontaneous, propelled by rumors of opportunity that fly along the new Amazon frontier highways. However, a number of government policies have encouraged the waste. In the 1960s and 1970s, Brasília created a number of generous tax credits and subsidies for settlers, especially cattle ranchers, in the Amazon. In the last 20 years, according to a recent World Bank document, the government spent $700 million on subsidies to 950 Amazon settlement projects, 631 of them for livestock. But the returns have been dismal—only 16% of original productivity targets, according to the Brazilian Planning Ministry.

Though some ranchers have succeeded by experimenting with different grasses and fertilizers, generally the pastures carved out of forest turned out to be poor grazing lands. According to the World Bank, ranches that supported one cow per hectare (2.5 acres) in the first year could maintain only one cow for every four hectares five years later. "Cattle ranching under conditions commonly prevailing in Amazonia is intrinsically uneconomic," the World Bank paper flatly concluded.

The wave of *colonos*, or smallholders, has also been a major menace. Rondônia, where 18% of the forest has been destroyed in a decade, has been the site of a settler deluge. Again, government policies have worked at cross purposes. The federal settlement agency that handed out lots to newcomers also conditioned continued land tenure on the improvements shown on a settler's plot. "Improvements" has generally meant cutting down the forest. Also, although the forestry agency mandated half of each property be preserved, lax inspection procedures coupled with the widespread activities of unscrupulous loggers made short work of the reserves. "Some settlers . . . have already cleared as much as 90% of their lots," according to the World Bank, which lent Brazil half a billion dollars for the Rondônia highway and settlement project.

Although much of Rondônia is endowed with good "terra roxa," or rich red volcanic soil, many other Amazon soils are nutrient-poor and highly acid. Yearly crops, such as corn and beans—precisely those crops planners envisioned for smallholders—have proven to be too hard on the weaker soils. Today, perennial or tree crops, such as coffee, cocoa, and citrus fruits have proven far more viable, but only after painful experimentation and a number of failed farms.

As a result, many of these frontier settlements are still threatened by inappropriate cultivation, lack of seeds and credit, and, especially in Rondônia, epidemic malaria and other diseases. Land turnover is common, and many bankrupt smallholders have wound up squatting on some unoccupied corner of a vast estate, opening the way for land conflicts.

The other Amazonian tenants, the scattered Indian tribes, have fared even worse. Surly resisters to white incursion during the Roosevelt-Rondon expedition, they are every day losing ground to the forests' new icons of prosperity—hydro-electric dams that flood their villages, gold miners who invade their reservations, and colonial settlements which encroach on protected areas. At the turn of the century there were almost a million Indians inhabiting the forests, plus a few scattered white people. Today there are 220,000 Indians in all of Brazil and a settler stampede.

Of course, many Indians married into the local peasant population, becoming *caboclos*, the squat, nimble, dark-skinned people of the north whose features mingle those of blacks, Portuguese, and Indians. And some tribes, such as the Tucuna on the upper Río Negro, have been able to organize and meet white society on its own terms. They are seeking formal education, language training, and mining skills, and are going to Brasília to lobby for their rights.

The situation is most critical for Brazil's 9,000 Yanomami, one of the world's few remaining tribes of forest Indians, whose lands have been inundated by some 15,000 *garimpeiros*, or gold prospectors. The government has finally demarcated their lands, but critics say the reservation is a fraction of the traditional Yanomamo reserve. Worse, it has been fractured into 19 islands, or "homelands," according to the Roman Catholic church.

There is no easy solution on the horizon. Both the gold miners, who are producing more than 964.50 oz. of gold a day (which would be worth about $415,000 if in the form of refined gold bars instead of raw gold), and the Indians' defenders, who want the miners expelled, say they are equally determined. "I've seen governments rise and fall because of gold finds, but I've never seen a government close down a gold mine," says José Altino Machado, influential leader of a federation of *garimpeiros* unions, representing some 600,000 Amazonian prospectors. "Acculturation is one thing, but this is one culture crushing another," answers Walter Ivan de Azevedo, bishop of São Gabriel de Cachoeira. We're not here to give final unction to a dying race."

In this land of seemingly endless frontiers and boundless riches, environmental consciousness has evolved only slowly. Even today, the vastness of Amazonia, which comprises fully 30% of the world's tropical woodlands, seems to defy description and mocks the cataclysmic pronouncements of world ecologists. One may fly for hours over the ocean of mottled green treetops and see not a trace of humankind except perhaps a glimpse of a road, a tiny brown seam in the spreading forest canopy, or the mobile black speck of the airplane's shadow.

But the rest of the world has not been so complacent. A highly organized and militant ecology lobby has arisen in Europe and the US. Some, like Greenpeace,[4] engage in civil disobedience, disabling loggers' bulldozers or hammering spikes into tree trunks to make it dangerous to use a chain saw for lumbering. But most have turned to a more sophisticated form of political activism, using computers, scientific laboratories, and mass-mailing lists. They know, with the best of lobbyists, their

[4]**Greenpeace** A twentieth-century ecological movement devoted to the preservation of the natural environment. [Ed. note.]

way around the halls of Congress, Parliament, and the Bundestag.[5] They have been effective in creating an environmental agenda among institutions from the World Bank to the International Tropical Timber Organization, a 42-nation group monitoring trade in tropical woods. They have mobilized public opinion and even shamed policymakers into action.

This sprawling South American nation, which is trying to tread the long way from the third world to the first, has suddenly come face to face with this new, daunting challenge: the jungle of environmental politics, larger and in some ways more intractable than the Amazon itself.

The message of alarm and criticism from much of the rest of the world was echoed by the Brazilian news media and environmentalists. That led to President Sarney's 90-day moratorium on government support for Amazon projects and on the export of logs.

Sarney's measures were hailed as a welcome, if tardy, effort at damage control. But all those forces that expressed concern are now watching to see what the Sarney-designated study groups propose—and how the proposals are honored. These environmental forces have become more militant.

A respected head of the federal Environmental Protection Agency, SEMA, had quit in disgust the month before Sarney's moratorium announcement, complaining that his agency was underfunded and his advice routinely ignored. What's more, researchers at the prestigious National Space Institute released a report revealing exhaustive hard data on the extent of the seasonal burnings, documented by satellite and aerial photos compiled in cooperation with the US National Space Agency, NASA. What's more, officials at the Brazilian Forestry Institute, an embattled agency which has often been accused of furthering destruction of woodland, were riven by dissent.

"We are treated like a fifth-rate agency, and run by an archaic and neglectful structure. We are losing skilled personnel to the private sector," said an exasperated senior official at the Brazilian Institute of Forestry and Development, which has a shoestring budget and only 600 inspectors for all of Brazil's three million square miles of territory.

Though the doomsayers may speak loudest, the political fallout from the Amazon debate has, fortuitously, reenfranchised a fairly neglected class of laborers: experts.

Biologists, botanists, anthropologists, and even entomologists are studying the forest's mysteries in places like the National Institute for Amazon Research in Manaus and the Museu Goeldi in Belém. They are preparing "zoning" maps to classify the stubborn Amazonian soils. They are measuring the land's "carrying capacity" to understand when there is an overload of human settlement and livestock. Researchers at agricultural experimental stations are developing new seeds and determining the sort of agriculture possible on the region's fragile soils.

Geologists are emerging as key protagonists in Amazonia, and for good reason. In the forest's subsoil, ancient pre-Cambrian layers hold some of the most valu-

---

[5]**Bundestag** The lower house of the parliament in West Germany. [Ed. note.]

able minerals known to man. While the major gold reserves are stagnant or steadily dwindling in the major gold-producing nations (South Africa, Canada, and the Soviet Union) Brazil's production has leapt from next to nothing 20 years ago to 100 tons a year, worth about $1.2 billion. Geologists say Brazil's potential is double or triple that amount, which would make Brazil one of the most promising gold producers in the world.

The Amazon's treasures include not only gold but iron ore, manganese, and bauxite. The Carajás iron mine in Pará state sits on 18 million tons of high-grade ore, the world's largest known reserves. A former São Paulo-based construction company, Paranapanema, discovered cassiterite 10 years ago in the Amazon and has become the world's single largest producer of tin ore. Amazonia also harbors the largest known reserves of niobium, a mineral used for special steels and, more recently, as a superconductor.

"The future of Amazonia is mineral exploration," said João Orestes Santos, a geologist at the Company for Mineral Research and Resources in Manaus. "It's the best way to use and at the same time protect the Amazon's resources."

Increasingly, in fact, many argue that the key to preserving Amazonia is to make it economically viable. Until today, only four or five of the myriad species of Amazon timber have proved commercially viable. The forest's fabulous abundance has worked hand in hand with waste and destruction. The sparse stands of mahogany and *cerejeira* (cherry tree of Brazil)—"noble woods"—are plucked out of the forest while the rest are simply burned down or bulldozed. Almost nothing is replanted. But economy and ecology could become allies instead of enemies. "If the government promoted the lesser-known woods, we could triple the commercial output. We are wasting untold natural assets," said one government forestry agency official.

These researchers and scientists are Brazil's techno-pioneers who have replaced sporadic plunder with systematic schemes of development. They have begun to take on the jungle with science and determination, often at perilous costs.

All of them are probing a single question: how to harness the resources of this delicate ecosystem without destroying it. As Brazil completes its inexorable push toward the northern frontier, that question is no longer one of detached science, floated about in antiseptic laboratories by white-coated academics. Rather, it is becoming a matter of social and economic necessity—and, in a world of dwindling resources, perhaps a matter of survival.

QUESTIONS FOR DISCUSSION

1. Describe how the article begins. Is the beginning effective in catching the reader's attention? Explain why the author might have chosen to begin the article in such a way.
2. How has fire been used by farmers in the Amazon region? Why are such fires so dangerous, not only to local people but to people all over the planet?
3. What has the Brazilian government done to stop the destruction of the rain forest? Have these actions been effective? Explain.

4. Describe the history of the Amazon region over the last century. How has the rain forest changed?
5. The author of the article points out that certain attitudes toward the land have led to the problems we are experiencing today. Describe these attitudes. How do these attitudes differ from the approach to the land explained by Chief Seattle in his "Environmental Statement" (p. 58)?
6. What actions do you think it will be necessary to take to save the rain forests? Speculate about the future of the rain forests (and of the planet) if such actions are not taken.

JOHN W. MELLOR
The Intertwining of Environmental Problems and Poverty

John W. Mellor's "The Intertwining of Environmental Problems and Poverty" discusses the ways in which rural poverty contributes to environmental devastation and how environmental problems then cause even more hardship for the poor. Mellor, who is director of the International Food Policy Research Institute and an expert in the field of economics and agriculture, explains the interrelationships between population growth, mismanagement of natural resources, and the continuance of extreme poverty in many developing countries in Asia, Africa, and Latin America. Like Mac Margolis, in "Amazon Ablaze" (p. 65), Mellor presents problem-solving strategies that will require the assistance of wealthier countries, but solving the problems will benefit both the developing and the developed parts of the world.

In developing countries, environmental problems and poverty are inseparable. At least three-quarters of a billion people in these countries cannot afford sufficient food to maintain minimum activity levels for healthy, productive lives. Such extreme poverty is especially prevalent in rural areas; in Asia and Africa, 80 to 90 percent of the poor live outside cities. Even in Latin America, the countryside is home to 60 percent of the poor. Half of these rural poor live on resources with the potential to increase substantially production and income in environmentally sustainable ways. Increasingly, however, as development raises incomes in these countries' more productive regions, rural poverty concentrates in environmentally fragile areas.

The rural poor largely depend directly or indirectly on agriculture and therefore on the environment for their income. As a result, environmental problems are inextricably linked with the problems of growing populations. Increasing numbers of people survive by subsistence farming, growing just the crops they need to eat to survive. The growing population also forces land appropriate only to perennial crops, such as tree crops or grasses, to be farmed for annual crops, particularly food crops, which the soil cannot sustain indefinitely. Thus environmental preservation depends on a complex interaction of income and population pressures that contribute to both environmental and agricultural instability.

As leaders of developing countries work to preserve their environments and eliminate poverty, they face several difficult questions. First, they must determine what environmental damage is irreversible and how much damage they can afford to tolerate for their citizens' current well-being. They must also consider to what extent environmental destruction impedes their ability to ensure the well-being of future generations. In other words, people in developing countries are forced to decide how much of the future they can or must give up to ensure today's survival.

Meanwhile, the people of developed countries also must ask important questions: How does environmental damage in developing countries affect the quality of life? How much will it cost to contain the damage? What common threads connect concerns about poverty and the environment? Should concerns be focused locally, nationally, or internationally? Considering the unequal distribution of wealth around the globe, does not the universal concern for the environment require payment not only commensurate with the damage done, but also with the ability to pay? Should the richer nations provide financial assistance to the poorest people of the poorest countries to assist their progress toward sustainable, self-reliant growth to reduce environmental stress?

It is important to note that the environmental destruction in developed countries is immensely more threatening and costly than that in developing countries and has yet to be tackled adequately. Environmental destruction in developing countries mostly affects the people of those countries, whereas the destruction wrought by the rich countries—for example, destruction of the ozone layer and air pollution that causes the greenhouse effect—has major consequences for *all* the world. Nevertheless, developed countries must not forget about the environmental problems of developing countries.

Many less developed countries are falling into the extreme poverty associated with rapid population growth, poor nutrition and hygiene, and low levels of education. All these trends make population control and environmental programs less effective. As a result, environmental exploitation and abuse are increasing in ever more damaging ways. Developed nations have a responsibility to help them break this cycle and replace it with an agenda that ensures sustainable population patterns, improved education levels, and increased production and employment rates.[1]

POPULATION AND INCOME

The most pervasive manifestation of environmentally destructive poverty in developing countries is the dangerous exploitation of fragile resources by burgeoning populations. Deforestation and cultivation of easily eroded land and overgrazing of natural pastures are the most obvious examples. In South Asia and other developing regions, half of the poor occupy one-quarter of the land area that could most easily be developed with high-yield crop varieties. However, as the income of people raising high-yield crops on fertile land rise, rural poverty is progressively concentrated

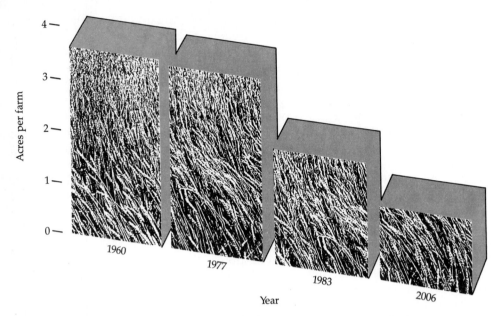

FIGURE 1.   Average Farm Size in Bangladesh in 1960, 1977, 1983 and Projected to 2006.
SOURCE: R. Ahmed, "A Structural Perspective of Farm and Non-Farm Households in Bangladesh," *Bangladesh Development Studies* 55 (June 1987):87–112.

in pockets of land less responsive to high-yield crops. . . . Within growing populations, farmers are rarely able to increase the sizes of their farms; even if they do, their
incomes do not necessarily rise proportionally with the extra land and effort involved. For instance, in Bangladesh the growing population has forced a decline in
farm sizes, shrinking opportunities to expand income (see Figure 1 . . .). As agricultural productivity declines, the land loses its ability to sustain a growing population, and pressures on the forests increase. With shorter crop rotations and subsequent soil erosion, incomes decrease and destabilize. In bad years, incomes in
Bangladesh fall to the lowest level of poverty, which forces people to destroy more of
the physical environment to provide short-term survival. This year, distant, upstream deforestation greatly increased the ferocity of floods inundating highly productive soils.

The forces of population and poverty can also be seen dramatically at work in
the hill regions of Nepal. With few advances in available agricultural technology for
the relatively favorable lowland soils, Nepalese farmers cannot maintain their incomes as the population rises and farms become smaller.[2] Farmers are forced to clear
and crop the hillsides. Cultivating this less productive land exacerbates soil erosion
problems on the hillsides and may flood and pollute the lowlands. In fact, between
the late 1960s and early 1980s, the forested area in Nepal's hills dropped from between 55 and 60 percent, depending on specific location, to 40 percent of total area.
The tree cover shrank even more substantially when the remaining forest was
thinned. In contrast, the area under agricultural production expanded from between 15 and 35 percent to far more than 40 percent during that same period.

Nepal's forests have been pushed so far back from rural populations that it takes, on average, 1.4 additional hours each day for women to collect firewood and fodder than it did just a decade ago. The extra hours are taken, in part, from women's work time in agricultural production, reducing total farm labor by as much as 24 percent per household and thus lowering household productivity. By lowering agricultural productivity, this deforestation has reduced food consumption on average more than 100 calories per capita per day. In addition, time for food preparation and child care have also been lost; this loss furthers the decline in nutrition, especially for children. Expanded planting on hillsides shifts cropping patterns away from rice and other high-quality calorie sources, reducing the nutritional content of the families' diets even more. The combined effect is a downward spiral of incomes and health, as malnourished individuals are less and less able to overcome the problems caused by deforestation.

To relieve population pressure on the environment in developing countries, population control must be combined with increased intensity of land use in high-potential agricultural areas. Therefore, a long-term strategy for poverty abatement must be planned and should include an adequate agricultural research and extension system that can develop new, high-yield crop varieties for developing countries' flat valleys. This new technology will allow farmers to increase their productivity by intensifying production so that they can feed more people on less land and earn higher incomes. Larger incomes will also help create the social environment within which other measures can effectively reduce population growth.

Intensified agriculture on good land will also relieve population pressures on more fragile lands. Increased farm incomes allow people to spend more on goods and services that are produced in labor-intensive ways in nonagricultural sectors and on labor-intensive agricultural commodities that are less harmful to the environment. As their incomes rise, farmers typically spend about 40 percent of their additional income on locally produced, labor-intensive, nonagricultural goods and services.[3] They spend another 20 percent on livestock and horticultural commodities. Therefore, in a country like Nepal, more land could be planted with perennial tree crops such as fruit orchards, which preserve the hillsides, and more land could be accorded to perennial grasses to feed more livestock. Thus, higher rural incomes are conducive to more environmentally sound land use.

Important environmental tradeoffs occur under the pressures of population growth and falling per capita incomes. For instance, to maintain their incomes, farmers must often clear more and more land. One way to overcome this kind of tradeoff is to increase fertilizer use on lowland areas, which boosts productivity and helps to prevent cultivation on hillsides. These efforts require cheap, reliable fertilizers and crop varieties that respond to increased fertilizer. Today, these fertilizers can be produced most cheaply from the vast quantities of gas that are going to waste in the Middle East and the Soviet Union. The question remains how those gas resources can best be mobilized to protect the even more easily exhaustible land resources.

The effects of poverty on the environment are endlessly complex. Thomas Reardon of the International Food Policy Research Institute points out that in the Sahel of Burkina Faso, with highly variable crop production, households have developed complex mechanisms to lessen extreme variations of income. For instance, in economically good times, livestock numbers rise well above the range carrying capacity of the Sahel. In these circumstances, foreign assistance increases income, livestock numbers, and therefore environmental degradation. Thus incomes rise but people's food security problems are not properly addressed. Providing food security requires greater integration with the outside world and effort by the international community. In contrast, on Burkina Faso's somewhat rainier Mossi plateau, poverty is more intense than in the Sahel, and higher incomes often lead to investment in bunds and other land-protecting devices. Even for such village-level cooperation, the investment structure needs to be reviewed and funds channeled effectively. Peter A. Oram in "Moving Toward Sustainability: Building the Agroecological Framework" treats the important issue of how to classify the agroecological conditions to facilitate those investment decisions. . . .

As the complex relationships between technology, input intensification, and environmental preservation are examined, the importance of commercialization and infrastructure to the environment becomes apparent. Land resources in developing countries are very diverse; optimal land use requires growing a wide variety of crops. However, marketing this variety of crops requires demand for those crops, which in turn requires higher incomes. To achieve higher incomes and the trade associated with diversity, low-cost transport is necessary. If people are to diversify their agricultural strategies enough to preserve the land, there must be broad demand for the products. Such demand cannot occur when incomes are at the minimal survival levels. For example, hill lands must generate income from perennial tree crops. The demand for these crops must come in part from local areas, but the income to buy the crops requires intensification of agriculture on other land. In part, the demand must also come from outside.

Increasing income and demand requires commercialization and development of the rural infrastructure. In Senegal, the introduction of cowpeas (legumes beneficial to the soil) to the rapidly degrading peanut basin is being delayed by lack of marketing infrastructure. Roads and communication systems also have a powerful impact on the environment. In Bangladesh, for example, in villages with good physical infrastructure (which generally means roads usable in all weather) only 12 percent of the population falls under the absolute poverty line, while 21 percent of the people are below the poverty line in villages without this infrastructure.[4] In villages with good infrastructure, employment per hectare of land is 4 percent higher; in nonagricultural sectors, employment is 30 percent higher; and wage rates are 12 percent higher than in villages without good infrastructure.[5] All those forces reduce the pressure to abuse the land for short-term survival.

A perennial problem for many developing countries is land tenure. The land often belongs to someone other than the people who are farming it. Since the farmers do not know how long they will be able to continue working on a parcel of land, they have little incentive to make long-term investments in it. In Africa, poorly defined land rights cause insecurity, and labor productivity is so low that farmers are preoccupied with wresting a minimum subsistence. Even with improved tenure conditions, only the research thrusts that E. T. York spells out in "Improving Sustainability with Agricultural Research" . . . can raise agricultural productivities.

POVERTY AND HEALTH

Much of the anxiety over environmental destruction in developed countries stems from health concerns. Pollution of cities, streams, and rivers cause serious illnesses. In developing countries, this concern is even greater because the state of health is so poor. For example, a lack of sanitation facilities creates serious health threats in densely populated rural areas—a problem that rarely exists in developed countries. Without adequate disposal facilities, not only the streams but the land around small towns in developing countries is heavily polluted.

Although rising incomes lead to improved food intake, they do not necessarily improve health. For example, a study of women and children at different economic levels in southwestern Kenya found no significant differences in total illness (see Table 1 . . .). However, a significant relationship exists between illness and the presence of general health and sanitation services in Kenya.[6] These problems are particularly severe in areas with dense rural populations and limited sanitation and health facilities. These areas also may have poorly drained alluvial soils, which add to the problems of population density and sanitation. In deforested regions, the quality of drinking water has dropped as water sources shift from fresh forest streams to increasingly contaminated rivers and ponds. Poor health cuts labor productivity and income in this "Catch 22" cycle.

Solving these problems requires tremendous investments of resources. However, solutions to environmental problems do not necessarily compete for resources with efforts to alleviate poverty and vice versa. However, many forms of investment benefit both endeavors. In Bangladesh, for example, the quality of the water supply and sanitary conditions are strongly influenced by improved rural infrastructure.[7] Also, health problems such as river blindness in Africa, tsetse fly infestation, and malaria all lend themselves to solution through modern biological research. Solving these problems would make it possible to populate more densely areas that are not environmentally fragile, thus relieving pressure on the fragile areas.

TABLE 1   Percentage of Time Preschoolers and Women in Southwestern Kenya are Sick with Any Illness and with Diarrhea, Measured by Per Capita Income Quartile, for 1984–1985.

Illness	Poorest Quartile	Poorer Than Average Quartile	Richer Than Average Quartile	Richest Quartile
Preschoolers				
All illness[a]	27.5%	26.0%	29.5%	26.5%
Diarrhea[a]	4.9	6.4	6.2	4.6
Women				
All illness[a]	30.2	26.8	29.8	26.6
Diarrhea[b]	1.2	1.4	2.2	3.7

Note: The quartiles are based on total household income per capita.
[a]There was no significant difference across income quartiles.
[b]Women in the poorest and poorer than average quartiles reported significantly shorter duration of diarrhea at the 0.05 level than women did in the richest quartile.
Source: Eileen Kennedy, International Food Policy Research Institute, "Survey 1984/85," South Nyanza, Kenya.

EDUCATION'S ROLE

Education affects the environment in three ways. First, some environmental destruction occurs simply because people do not understand the harm of what they are doing. Education can bring understanding of the environmental impacts of certain actions and lead to acceptance of complex technologies such as the biological control of insects and diseases. However, there is not much correlation between education and acceptance of a simple technology like high-yield wheat. Thus, educational levels in rural areas of developing countries must be raised to permit environmental improvements. This educational expansion must occur at all levels. At the secondary level, farmers must be taught to work with more complex technologies. At the college level, people need to be trained to teach this knowledge to farmers.

Second, education influences population growth. With all else equal, including income, rural people with more education tend to have somewhat smaller families. Perhaps with educated children who can get better jobs, parents need fewer children to support them in their old age.

Third, education increases income. In an increasingly complex world, education is necessary to understand the technological changes and the institutional interactions that can be used to raise farmers' incomes. So educational opportunities must grow to increase incomes.

AGRICULTURE AND STABILITY

Agriculture is innately and notoriously unstable, and the instability of production and prices is increasing. In bad times, instability drives poor people below the line of minimum subsistence. This drop cuts their ability to plan for the long term and leads them (and their animals) to assault the environment for short-run gains in ways they would never do if their incomes were stable above the subsistence level.

Areas with fragile environmental resources often have either low rainfall or rainfall that fluctuates around the critical level for arable agriculture. These areas in particular need to be returned to grassland or other perennial crops such as trees to counter the destruction that occurs, especially during periods of low rainfall. People must be provided with some means of support to carry them through these bad periods so they will not destroy the environment. Agricultural instability causes greater problems in areas of excessive poverty and environmental fragility, but the damage also carries into the middle classes.

Food scarcity wreaks devastating consequences on the poorest of a population rather than on the wealthiest. In India, a 10 percent reduction in food supplies reduces the consumption of the wealthiest 5 percent of the people by 8 percent, whereas the poorest 20 percent of the people are forced to reduce their consumption by 40 percent.[8]

Thus, ways must be found to stabilize the incomes of the very poor in the face of agricultural instability. Modern mechanisms do exist for just this purpose. Food aid can be useful. The International Monetary Fund,* through its cereal facility,

---

*International Monetary Fund A specialized agency of the United Nations, established in 1945 to discharge international indebtedness and stabilize exchange rates. [Ed. note.]

loans money to countries so that they can stabilize their food supply with imports during periods of extreme stress. Still, the recipient governments must have the facilities and institutions to utilize grain imports.

To reduce instability, unviable areas must, in the long run, lose population density through emigration to areas able to accept new technology and to realize rapid growth in nonagricultural employment. Those processes require infrastructure to facilitate specialization and trade.

A SHARED FUTURE

Unfortunately, income problems require solutions much more complex than just alleviating the grinding poverty of one-third to one-half of the population of the Third World. Quite simply, reversing the downward spiral of poverty and environmental destruction requires financial resources. Problems will be solved only through substantial expenditure on public goods, including investments in research, infrastructure, services, and education. But the tax base is thin and shallow in developing countries. The combination of high proportions of populations living at subsistence levels, little administrative capacity, and inadequate commercialization shrinks the proportion of the gross national product spent in the public sector (to levels one-half to three-quarters of that spent in the United States, for example). Developing countries are constrained from generating resources because high taxation on those who live above the subsistence level and on the commercial sector discourages work and enterprise. Thus, a vital link in the poverty-environment nexus is to obtain adequate public resources for the physical and institutional infrastructure needed to raise incomes, reduce population growth, improve health, and increase education, as well as to undertake direct public action to protect and rehabilitate rural areas.

Given that people in poor countries often must sacrifice long-term environmental stability for short-run survival, wealthy countries must put aside the common belief that the poor can solve these problems on their own without enhanced resources and face up to the reality that substantial financial assistance in the short run is crucial to saving the environment from irreversible damage. However, if that assistance concurrently enhances progress toward self-reliant growth, it will be necessary only for a short while and can be beneficial to the donors themselves.

Developed countries must recognize that environmental protection and the growth of incomes of very poor people in developing countries will demand scientific and financial assistance to develop improved agricultural technologies. Investments in infrastructure and food aid will also help to dissolve poverty.

The leaders of developed countries need to understand how trade relationships can accelerate processes, allowing developing countries to import some agricultural commodities that they would otherwise be forced to produce on very fragile land resources, and to export commodities that are more suitable to those resources. Perennial crops, for example, could help pay for the imported commodities. Developed countries need to work toward an ecologically optimal global allocation of production systems. Most important, the rich nations need to consider the environmental problems of developing countries in a positive way, looking for solutions rather than criticizing their attempts to struggle with such complex problems.

NOTES

1. See J. W. Mellor, *The New Economics of Growth* (Ithaca, N.Y.: Cornell University Press, 1976), for a description of the role of agriculture and employment growth in development.
2. S. K. Kumar and D. Hotchkiss, *Energy and Nutrition Links to Agriculture in a Hill Region of Nepal* (Washington, D.C.: International Food Policy Research Institute, 1988).
3. P. B. R. Hazell and A. Roell, *Rural Growth Linkages: Household Expenditure Patterns in Malaysia and Nigeria*, Research Report 41 (Washington, D.C.: International Food Policy Research Institute, 1983), 28.
4. S. K. Kumar, *Rural Infrastructure in Bangladesh: Effects on Food Consumption and Nutrition of the Population* (Washington, D.C.: International Food Policy Research Institute, 1988). Poverty is defined here as the inability to secure more than 80 percent of the minimum requirement of daily calories.
5. R. Ahmed and M. Hossain, *Infrastructure and Development of a Rural Economy* (Washington, D.C.: International Food Policy Research Institute, 1987).
6. E. T. Kennedy and B. Cogill, *Income and Nutritional Effects of the Commercialization of Agriculture in Southwestern Kenya*, Research Report 63 (Washington, D.C.: International Food Policy Research Institute, 1987), 42–49.
7. Kumar, note 4 above.
8. J. W. Mellor and S. Gavian, "Famine: Causes, Prevention, and Relief," *Science* 235 (1987):539–45.

QUESTIONS FOR DISCUSSION

1. Why is this author particularly qualified to write about the relationship between environmental problems and poverty? Why might he have written this article? For what audience is it intended?
2. What resources do the rural poor use to sustain life? Describe how the use of these resources contributes to environmental concerns.
3. What specific problems do developing countries most need to focus on? Consider the questions posed by Mellor in the third and fourth paragraphs.
4. Why should developed countries take an interest in the environmental concerns of developing countries?
5. Describe the problems of poverty and the environment in Bangladesh and Nepal. What factors contribute to the problems?
6. How is the issue of birth control related to environmental problems? How can the use of fertilizer help to alleviate these problems? What other technological assistance might be used?
7. What is meant by the phrase "rural infrastructure" (par. 15)? What contextual clues lead you to this meaning? What conclusions does the author make about the rural infrastructure?
8. How does environmental damage affect the health of the native population? What actions can be taken to reduce such health risks?
9. Discuss possible solutions to the problems described in the article. Explain why a combination of actions must be taken.

CARL SAGAN
The Dragons of Eden: Speculations on the Evolution of Human Intelligence

Carl Sagan's The Dragons of Eden: Speculations on the Evolution of Human Intelligence
*(1977) begins with an insightful discussion of the vastness of geologic time. Sagan compares the time
since the Big Bang to the span of a single day. The astonishing conclusions he reaches raise questions
about the relative significance of human beings in the universe. In his preface Sagan quotes Darwin:
"The main conclusion arrived at in this work* [On the Origin of the Species, 1859], *namely, that
man is descended from some lowly-organized form, will, I regret to think, be highly distasteful to
many persons." Sagan, rather than being disturbed, finds delight in the idea that humanity is closely
related to the other species which inhabit the planet.*

The world is very old, and human beings are very young. Significant events in our
personal lives are measured in years or less; our lifetimes in decades; our family
genealogies in centuries; and all of recorded history in millennia. But we have been
preceded by an awesome vista of time, extending for prodigious periods into the
past, about which we know little—both because there are no written records and
because we have real difficulty in grasping the immensity of the intervals involved.

Yet we are able to date events in the remote past. Geological stratification and
radioactive dating provide information on archaeological, paleontological and geological events; and astrophysical theory provides data on the ages of planetary surfaces, stars, and the Milky Way Galaxy, as well as an estimate of the time that has
elapsed since that extraordinary event called the Big Bang[1]—an explosion that involved all of the matter and energy in the present universe. The Big Bang may be the
beginning of the universe, or it may be a discontinuity in which information about
the earlier history of the universe was destroyed. But it is certainly the earliest event
about which we have any record.

The most instructive way I know to express this cosmic chronology is to imagine the fifteen-billion-year lifetime of the universe (or at least its present incarnation
since the Big Bang) compressed into the span of a single year. Then every billion
years of Earth history would correspond to about twenty-four days of our cosmic
year, and one second of that year to 475 real revolutions of the Earth about the sun.
[Following] I present the cosmic chronology in three forms: a list of some representative pre-December dates; a calendar for the month of December; and a closer look
at the late evening of New Year's Eve. On this scale, the events of our history
books—even books that make significant efforts to deprovincialize the present—are
so compressed that it is necessary to give a second-by-second recounting of the last
seconds of the cosmic year. Even then, we find events listed as contemporary that
we have been taught to consider as widely separated in time. In the history of life, an

---

[1] **the Big Bang** Theory of the origin of the known universe which speculates that at the beginning of time all the
matter in the universe was concentrated in a very small volume that exploded; the resulting expansion continues
today. [Ed. note.]

PRE-DECEMBER DATES

Big Bang	January 1
Origin of the Milky Way Galaxy	May 1
Origin of the solar system	September 9
Formation of the Earth	September 14
Origin of life on Earth	~September 25
Formation of the oldest rocks known on Earth	October 2
Date of oldest fossils (bacteria and blue-green algae)	October 9
Invention of sex (by microorganisms)	~November 1
Oldest fossil photosynthetic plants	November 12
Eukaryotes (first cells with nuclei) flourish	November 15

~ = approximately

COSMIC CALENDAR
DECEMBER

SUNDAY	MONDAY	TUESDAY	WEDNESDAY	THURSDAY	FRIDAY	SATURDAY
	1 Significant oxygen atmosphere begins to develop on Earth.	**2**	**3**	**4**	**5** Extensive vulcanism and channel formation on Mars.	**6**
7	**8**	**9**	**10**	**11**	**12**	**13**
14	**15**	**16** First worms.	**17** Precambrian ends. Paleozoic Era and Cambrian Period begin. Invertebrates flourish.	**18** First oceanic plankton. Trilobites flourish.	**19** Ordovician Period. First fish, first vertebrates.	**20** Silurian Period. First vascular plants. Plants begin colonization of land.
21 Devonian Period begins. First insects. Animals begin colonization of land.	**22** First amphibians. First winged insects.	**23** Carboniferous Period. First trees. First reptiles.	**24** Permian Period begins. First dinosaurs.	**25** Paleozoic Era ends. Mesozoic Era begins.	**26** Triassic Period. First mammals.	**27** Jurassic Period. First birds.
28 Cretaceous Period. First flowers. Dinosaurs become extinct.	**29** Mesozoic Era ends. Cenozoic Era and Tertiary Period begin. First cetaceans. First primates.	**30** Early evolution of frontal lobes in the brains of primates. First hominids. Giant mammals flourish.	**31** End of the Pliocene Period. Quatenary (Pleistocene and Holocene) Period. First humans.			

DECEMBER 31

Origin of *Proconsul* and *Ramapithecus*, probable ancestors of apes and men	~1:30 P.M.
First humans	~10:30 P.M.
Widespread use of stone tools	11:00 P.M.
Domestication of fire by Peking man	11:46 P.M.
Beginning of most recent glacial period	11:56 P.M.
Seafarers settle Australia	11:58 P.M.
Extensive cave painting in Europe	11:59 P.M.
Invention of agriculture	11:59:20 P.M.
Neolithic civilization; first cities	11:59:35 P.M.
First dynasties in Sumer, Ebla and Egypt; development of astronomy	11:59:50 P.M.
Invention of the alphabet; Akkadian Empire	11:59:51 P.M.
Hammurabic legal codes in Babylon; Middle Kingdom in Egypt	11:59:52 P.M.
Bronze metallurgy; Mycenaean culture; Trojan War; Olmec culture; invention of the compass	11:59:53 P.M.
Iron metallurgy; First Assyrian Empire; Kingdom of Israel; founding of Carthage by Phoenicia	11:59:54 P.M.
Asokan India; Ch'in Dynasty China; Periclean Athens; birth of Buddha	11:59:55 P.M.
Euclidean geometry; Archimedean physics; Ptolemaic astronomy; Roman Empire; birth of Christ	11:59:56 P.M.
Zero and decimals invented in Indian arithmetic; Rome falls; Moslem conquests	11:59:57 P.M.
Mayan civilization; Sung Dynasty China; Byzantine empire; Mongol invasion; Crusades	11:59:58 P.M.
Renaissance in Europe; voyages of discovery from Europe and from Ming Dynasty China; emergence of the experimental method in science	11:59:59 P.M.
Widespread development of science and technology; emergence of a global culture; acquisition of the means for self-destruction of the human species; first steps in spacecraft planetary exploration and the search for extraterrestrial intelligence	Now: The first second of New Year's Day

equally rich tapestry must have been woven in other periods—for example, between 10:02 and 10:03 on the morning of April 6th or September 16th. But we have detailed records only for the very end of the cosmic year.

The chronology corresponds to the best evidence now available. But some of it is rather shaky. No one would be astounded if, for example, it turns out that plants colonized the land in the Ordovician rather than the Silurian Period; or that segmented worms appeared earlier in the Precambrian Period than indicated. Also, in the chronology of the last ten seconds of the cosmic year, it was obviously impossible for me to include all significant events; I hope I may be excused for not having explicitly mentioned advances in art, music and literature or the historically significant American, French, Russian and Chinese revolutions.

The construction of such tables and calendars is inevitably humbling. It is disconcerting to find that in such a cosmic year the Earth does not condense out of interstellar matter until early September; dinosaurs emerge on Christmas Eve; flowers arise on December 28th; and men and women originate at 10:30 P.M. on New Year's Eve. All of recorded history occupies the last ten seconds of December 31; and the time from the waning of the Middle Ages to the present occupies little more than one second. But because I have arranged it that way, the first cosmic year has just ended. And despite the insignificance of the instant we have so far occupied in cosmic time, it is clear that what happens on and near Earth at the beginning of the second cosmic year will depend very much on the scientific wisdom and the distinctly human sensitivity of mankind.

QUESTIONS FOR DISCUSSION

1. The first sentence of this text summarizes the rest. How does Sagan develop the two related ideas in the first sentence?
2. Evaluate the use of analogy in this text. Is the analogy between the span of geologic time and the span of a single year effective in inspiring a certain awe in the reader? Explain.
3. Analyze the last paragraph. What does the paragraph lead you to believe is the purpose of the text?
4. Contrast Sagan's discussion of geologic evolution with Darwin's description of biological evolution.

ALBERT EINSTEIN
Religion and Science

Albert Einstein (1879–1955) was the most influential scientist of this century. His quantum theory and the famous theory of relativity (which includes the equation $E = mc^2$) revolutionized contemporary physics, making possible such inventions as the atomic bomb and the moon rocket. Einstein, a German Jew, was ousted from his native country during the Nazi regime; at that time, fearing that the Germans would develop the atomic bomb first, a group of American scientists asked Einstein to sign a letter to President Roosevelt, requesting that he expedite research in that area. Although he signed the letter, Einstein was deeply dismayed by the destruction caused by America's use of the bomb against Japan. (For a description of that destruction, see the excerpt from Ibuse's Black Rain, *which begins on p. 117.) In the essay here, "Religion and Science" (1934), Einstein poses philosophical questions in response to issues in science. Compare this essay with the text from Bertrand Russell (p. 90).*

Everything that the human race has done and thought is concerned with the satisfaction of deeply felt needs and the assuagement of pain. One has to keep this constantly in mind if one wishes to understand spiritual movements and their development. Feeling and desire are the motive force behind all human endeavour and human creation, in however exalted a guise the latter may present itself to us. Now what are the feelings and needs that have led men to religious thought and belief in the widest sense of the words? A little consideration will suffice to show us that the most varying emotions preside over the birth of religious thought and experience. With primitive man it is above all fear that evokes religious notions—fear of hunger, wild beasts, sickness, death. Since at this stage of existence understanding of causal connexions is usually poorly developed, the human mind creates for itself more or less analogous beings on whose wills and actions these fearful happenings depend. Thus one tries to secure the favour of these beings by carrying out actions and offering sacrifices which, according to the tradition handed down from generation to generation, propitiate them or make them well disposed towards a mortal. I am speaking now of the religion of fear. This, though not created, is in an important degree stabilised by the formation of a special priestly caste which sets itself up as a mediator between the people and the beings they fear, and erects a hegemony on this basis. In many cases a leader or ruler whose position depends on other factors, or a privileged class, combines priestly functions with its secular authority in order to make the latter more secure; or the political rulers and the priestly caste make common cause in their own interests.

The social impulses are another source of the crystallisation of religion. Fathers and mothers and the leaders of larger human communities are mortal and fallible. The desire for guidance, love and support prompts men to form the social or moral conception of God. This is the God of Providence, who protects, disposes, rewards and punishes; the God who, according to the width of the believer's outlook, loves and cherishes the life of the tribe or of the human race, or even life itself; the comforter in sorrow and unsatisfied longing; he who preserves the souls of the dead. This is the social or moral conception of God.

The Jewish scriptures admirably illustrate the development from the religion of fear to moral religion, a development continued in the New Testament. The religions of all civilised peoples, especially the peoples of the Orient, are primarily moral religions. The development from a religion of fear to moral religion is a great step in a nation's life. And yet, that primitive religions are based entirely on fear and the religions of civilised peoples purely on morality is a prejudice against which we must be on our guard. The truth is that all religions are a varying blend of both types, with this differentiation: that on the higher levels of social life the religion of morality predominates.

Common to all these types is the anthropomorphic character of their conception of God. Only individuals of exceptional endowments and exceptionally high-minded communities, as a general rule, get in any real sense beyond this level. But there is a third stage of religious experience which belongs to all of them, even though it is rarely found in a pure form, and which I will call cosmic religious feeling. It is very difficult to explain this feeling to any one who is entirely without it, especially as there is no anthropomorphic conception of God corresponding to it.

The individual feels the nothingness of human desires and aims and the sublimity and marvellous order which reveal themselves both in Nature and in the world of thought. He looks upon individual existence as a sort of prison and wants to experience the universe as a single significant whole. The beginnings of cosmic religious feeling already appear in earlier stages of development, e.g., in many of the Psalms of David and in some of the Prophets. Buddhism, as we have learnt from the wonderful writings of Schopenhauer[1] especially, contains a much stronger element of this.

The religious geniuses of all ages have been distinguished by this kind of religious feeling, which knows no dogma and no God conceived in man's image; so that there can be no church whose central teachings are based on it. Hence it is precisely among the heretics of every age that we find men who were filled with the highest kind of religious feeling and were in many cases regarded by their comtemporaries as atheists, sometimes also as saints. Looked at in this light, men like Democritus,[2] Francis of Assisi,[3] and Spinoza[4] are closely akin to one another.

How can cosmic religious feeling be communicated from one person to another, if it can give rise to no definite notion of a God and no theology? In my view, it is the most important function of art and science to awaken this feeling and keep it alive in those who are capable of it.

We thus arrive at a conception of the relation of science to religion very different from the usual one. When one views the matter historically one is inclined to look upon science and religion as irreconcilable antagonists, and for a very obvious reason. The man who is thoroughly convinced of the universal operation of the law of causation cannot for a moment entertain the idea of a being who interferes in the course of events—provided, of course, that he takes the hypothesis of causality really seriously. He has no use for the religion of fear and equally little for social or moral religion. A God who rewards and punishes is inconceivable to him for the simple reason that a man's actions are determined by necessity, external and internal, so that in God's eyes he cannot be responsible, any more than an inanimate object is responsible for the motions it undergoes. Hence science has been charged with undermining morality, but the charge is unjust. A man's ethical behaviour should be based effectually on sympathy, education, and social ties; no religious basis is necessary. Man would indeed be in a poor way if he had to be restrained by fear and punishment and hope of reward after death.

It is therefore easy to see why the churches have always fought science and persecuted its devotees. On the other hand I maintain that the cosmic religious feeling is the strongest and noblest incitement to scientific research. Only those who realise the immense efforts and, above all, the devotion which pioneer work in theoretical science demands can grasp the strength of the emotion out of which alone such work, remote as it is from the immediate realities of life, can issue. What a deep conviction of the rationality of the universe and what a yearning to understand, were it but a feeble reflection of the mind revealed in this world, Kepler and Newton must have had to enable them to spend years of solitary labour in disentangling the principles of the celestial sphere! Those whose acquaintance with scientific research is derived chiefly from its practical results easily develop a completely false notion of

[1] **Arthur Schopenhauer (1788–1860)** Author of *The World as Will and Representation* (1819), a philosophical treatise in which God, freewill, and immortality are seen as illusions. [Ed. note.]
[2] **Democritus (b. 460 B.C.E.)** Greek philosopher who wrote on the natural sciences, mathematics, morals, and music, and who advanced a theory that the world was formed by the interaction of atoms. [Ed. note.]
[3] **Saint Francis of Assisi (1181?–1226)** Founded the Franciscan order based on joyousness and love of nature, devoted to relief of those in need. [Ed. note.]
[4] **Benedict de Spinoza (1632–1677)** Philosopher who viewed God as immanent, that is, existing within all the elements of nature; Spinoza denied personal immortality and believed in determinism. [Ed. note.]

the mentality of the men who, surrounded by a sceptical world, have shown the way to those fellow spirits scattered wide through the world and the centuries. Only one who has devoted his life to similar ends can have a vivid realisation of what has inspired these men and given them the strength to remain true to their purpose in spite of countless failures. It is cosmic religious feeling that gives a man strength of this sort. A contemporary has said, not unjustly, that in this materialistic age of ours the serious scientific workers are the only profoundly religious people.

THE RELIGIOUSNESS OF SCIENCE

You will hardly find one among the profounder sort of scientific minds without a peculiar religious feeling of his own. But it is different from the religion of the naive man. For the latter, God is a being from whose care one hopes to benefit and whose punishment one fears; a sublimation of a feeling similar to that of a child for its father, a being to whom one stands to some extent in a personal relation, however deeply it may be tinged with awe.

But the scientist is possessed by the sense of universal causation. The future, to him, is every whit as necessary and determined as the past. There is nothing divine about morality; it is a purely human affair. His religious feeling takes the form of a rapturous amazement at the harmony of natural law, which reveals an intelligence of such superiority that, compared with it, all the systematic thinking and acting of human beings is an utterly insignificant reflection. This feeling is the guiding principle of his life and work, insofar as he succeeds in keeping himself from the shackles of selfish desire. It is beyond question closely akin to that which has possessed the religious geniuses of all ages.

QUESTIONS FOR DISCUSSION

1. Outline the organizational pattern of this essay. How does Einstein build his argument?
2. Define the words "religion" and "science" in your own words. How does Einstein define religion and science? How are these definitions different from your own?
3. What are the two motivating factors, according to Einstein, of all human behavior? What other factors might he have left out?
4. Einstein remarks, "With primitive man it is above all fear that evokes religious notions" (par.1). Explain this statement. What does he mean by "primitive"? Examine the possible cultural bias in this remark. Is modern religious belief in developed countries ever motivated by fear? Explain.
5. According to Einstein, the "most important function of art and science" is to awaken a "cosmic religious feeling" (par. 4). What does this statement mean? How is the statement related to the author's purpose in writing the article? Who is the intended audience?
6. For what reason has science "been charged with undermining morality" (par. 8)? Why does Einstein say the charge is "unjust"? Do you agree with his argument? Why or why not?
7. Explain what you think "the religiousness of science" might entail.

BERTRAND RUSSELL
Religion and Science

Bertrand Russell (1872–1970) was a mathematician and philosopher. An English lord and a Nobel laureate, Russell applied mathematical thinking processes to questions of ethics, religion, and politics. In Religion and Science *(1960), Russell explores the controversies that have arisen between the two fields over the centuries. Russell claims that religion has waged a war "against scientific discovery" which has been generally unsuccessful until recent times. His introductory chapter, reproduced here, explains the "grounds and history" of that war. Interesting similarities can be seen between Russell's essay and the essay of the same title by Albert Einstein (p. 86). (For additional information, see the note on Russell on p. 584.)*

Religion and Science are two aspects of social life, of which the former has been important as far back as we know anything of man's mental history, while the latter, after a fitful flickering existence among the Greeks and Arabs, suddenly sprang into importance in the sixteenth century, and has ever since increasingly moulded both the ideas and the institutions among which we live. Between religion and science there has been a profound conflict, in which, until the last few years, science has invariably proved victorious. But the rise of new religions in Russia and Germany, equipped with new means of missionary activity provided by science, has again put the issue in doubt, as it was at the beginning of the scientific epoch, and has made it again important to examine the grounds and the history of the warfare waged by traditional religion against scientific knowledge.

Science is the attempt to discover, by means of observation, and reasoning based upon it, first, particular facts about the world, and then laws connecting facts with one another and (in fortunate cases) making it possible to predict future occurrences. Connected with this theoretical aspect of science there is scientific technique, which utilizes scientific knowledge to produce comforts and luxuries that were impossible, or at least much more expensive, in a pre-scientific era. It is this latter aspect that gives such great importance to science even for those who are not scientists.

Religion, considered socially, is a more complex phenomenon than science. Each of the great historical religions has three aspects: (1) a Church, (2) a creed, and (3) a code of personal morals. The relative importance of these three elements has varied greatly in different times and places. The ancient religions of Greece and Rome, until they were made ethical by the Stoics,[1] had not very much to say about personal morals; in Islam the Church has been unimportant in comparison with the temporal monarch; in modern Protestantism there is a tendency to relax the rigors of the creed. Nevertheless, all three elements, though in varying proportions, are essential to religion as a social phenomenon, which is what is chiefly concerned in the conflict with science. A purely personal religion, so long as it is content to avoid assertions which science can disprove, may survive undisturbed in the most scientific age.

---

[1] **Stoics** A group of Greek philosophers founded by Zeno of Citium about 310 B.C.E.; Stoics held that happiness is achieved through freeing oneself from the passions and appetites, and that virtue is the highest good while suffering is a necessary part of experience. [Ed. note.]

Creeds are the intellectual source of the conflict between religion and science, but the bitterness of the opposition has been due to the connection of creeds with Churches and with moral codes. Those who questioned creeds weakened the authority, and might diminish the incomes, of Churchmen; moreover, they were thought to be undermining morality, since moral duties were deduced by Churchmen from creeds. Secular rulers, therefore, as well as Churchmen, felt that they had good reason to fear the revolutionary teaching of the men of science.

In what follows, we shall not be concerned with science in general, nor yet with religion in general, but with those points where they have come into conflict in the past, or still do so at the present time. So far as Christendom is concerned, these conflicts have been of two kinds. Sometimes there happens to be a text in the Bible making some assertion as to a matter of fact, for example, that the hare chews the cud. Such assertions, when they are refuted by scientific observation, cause difficulties for those who believe, as most Christians did until science forced them to think otherwise, that every word of the Bible is divinely inspired. But when the Biblical assertions concerned have no inherent religious importance, it is not difficult to explain them away, or to avoid controversy by deciding that the Bible is only authoritative on matters of religion and morals. There is, however, a deeper conflict when science controverts some important Christian dogma, or some philosophical doctrine which theologians believe essential to orthodoxy. Broadly speaking, the disagreements between religion and science were, at first, of the former sort, but have gradually become more and more concerned with matters which are, or were, considered a vital part of Christian teaching.

Religious men and women, in the present day, have come to feel that most of the creed of Christendom, as it existed in the Middle Ages, is unnecessary, and indeed a mere hindrance to the religious life. But if we are to understand the opposition which science encountered, we must enter imaginatively into the system of ideas which made such opposition seem reasonable. Suppose a man were to ask a priest why he should not commit murder. The answer "because you would be hanged" was felt to be inadequate, both because the hanging would need justification, and because police methods were so uncertain that a large proportion of murderers escaped. There was, however, an answer which, before the rise of science, appeared satisfactory to almost everyone, namely, that murder is forbidden by the Ten Commandments, which were revealed by God to Moses on Mount Sinai. The criminal who eluded earthly justice could not escape from the Divine wrath, which had decreed for impenitent murderers a punishment infinitely more terrible than hanging. This argument, however, rests upon the authority of the Bible, which can only be maintained intact if the Bible is accepted as a whole. When the Bible seems to say that the earth does not move, we must adhere to this statement in spite of the arguments of Galileo,[2] since otherwise we shall be giving encouragement to murderers and all other kinds of malefactors. Although few would now accept this argument, it cannot be regarded as absurd, nor should those who acted upon it be viewed with moral reprobation.

---

[2] **Galileo Galilei (1564–1642)** Italian astronomer and physicist who observed laws of gravity; Galileo was forced to repudiate the Copernican view of the universe by the Inquisition (1633). [Ed. note.]

The mediaeval outlook of educated men had a logical unity which has now been lost. We may take Thomas Aquinas[3] as the authoritative exponent of the creed which science was compelled to attack. He maintained—and his view is still that of the Roman Catholic Church—that some of the fundamental truths of the Christian religion could be proved by the unaided reason, without the help of revelation. Among these was the existence of an omnipotent and benevolent Creator. From His omnipotence and benevolence it followed that He would not leave His creatures without knowledge of His decrees, to the extent that might be necessary for obeying His will. There must therefore be a Divine revelation, which, obviously, is contained in the Bible and the decisions of the Church. This point being established, the rest of what we need to know can be inferred from the Scriptures and the pronouncements of œcumenical Councils. The whole argument proceeds deductively from premises formerly accepted by almost the whole population of Christian countries, and if the argument is, to the modern reader, at times faulty, its fallacies were not apparent to the majority of learned contemporaries.

Now logical unity is at once a strength and a weakness. It is a strength because it insures that whoever accepts one stage of the argument must accept all later stages; it is a weakness because whoever rejects any of the later stages must also reject some, at least, of the earlier stages. The Church, in its conflict with science, exhibited both the strength and the weakness resulting from the logical coherence of its dogmas.

The way in which science arrives at its beliefs is quite different from that of mediaeval theology. Experience has shown that it is dangerous to start from general principles and proceed deductively, both because the principles may be untrue and because the reasoning based upon them may be fallacious. Science starts, not from large assumptions, but from particular facts discovered by observation or experiment. From a number of such facts a general rule is arrived at, of which, if it is true, the facts in question are instances. This rule is not positively asserted, but is accepted, to begin with, as a working hypothesis. If it is correct, certain hitherto unobserved phenomena will take place in certain circumstances. If it is found that they do take place, that so far confirms the hypothesis; if they do not, the hypothesis must be discarded and a new one must be invented. However many facts are found to fit the hypothesis, that does not make it certain, although in the end it may come to be thought in a high degree probable; in that case, it is called a theory rather than a hypothesis. A number of different theories, each built directly upon facts, may become the basis for a new and more general hypothesis from which, if true, they all follow; and to this process of generalization no limit can be set. But whereas, in mediaeval thinking, the most general principles were the starting point, in science they are the final conclusion—final, that is to say, at a given moment, though liable to become instances of some still wider law at a later stage.

A religious creed differs from a scientific theory in claiming to embody eternal and absolutely certain truth, whereas science is always tentative, expecting that modifications in its present theories will sooner or later be found necessary, and aware that its method is one which is logically incapable of arriving at a complete

---

[3]**Saint Thomas Aquinas (1225–1274)** Italian philosopher and theologian whose Christian philosophy is based on Aristotle. [Ed. note.]

and final demonstration. But in an advanced science the changes needed are generally only such as serve to give slightly greater accuracy; the old theories remain serviceable where only rough approximations are concerned, but are found to fail when some new minuteness of observation becomes possible. Moreover, the technical inventions suggested by the old theories remain as evidence that they had a kind of practical truth up to a point. Science thus encourages abandonment of the search for absolute truth, and the substitution of what may be called "technical" truth, which belongs to any theory that can be successfully employed in inventions or in predicting the future. "Technical" truth is a matter of degree: a theory from which more successful inventions and predictions spring is truer than one which gives rise to fewer. "Knowledge" ceases to be a mental mirror of the universe, and becomes merely a practical tool in the manipulation of matter. But these implications of scientific method were not visible to the pioneers of science, who, though they practised a new method of pursuing truth, still conceived truth itself as absolutely as did their theological opponents.

An important difference between the mediaeval outlook and that of modern science is in regard to authority. To the schoolmen, the Bible, the dogmas of the Catholic faith, and (almost equally) the teachings of Aristotle,[4] were above question; original thought and even investigation of facts, must not overstep the limits set by these immutable boundaries of speculative daring. Whether there are people at the antipodes, whether Jupiter has satellites, and whether bodies fall at a rate proportional to their mass were questions to be decided, not by observation, but by deduction from Aristotle or the Scriptures. The conflict between theology and science was quite as much a conflict between authority and observation. The men of science did not ask that propositions should be believed because some important authority had said they were true; on the contrary, they appealed to the evidence of the senses, and maintained only such doctrines as they believed to be based upon facts which were patent to all who chose to make the necessary observations. The new method achieved such immense successes, both theoretical and practical, that theology was gradually forced to accommodate itself to science. Inconvenient Bible texts were interpreted allegorically or figuratively; Protestants transferred the seat of authority in religion, first from the Church and the Bible to the Bible alone, and then to the individual soul. It came gradually to be recognized that the religious life does not depend upon pronouncements as to matters of fact, for instance, the historical existence of Adam and Eve. Thus religion, by surrendering the outworks, has sought to preserve the citadel intact—whether successfully or not remains to be seen.

There is, however, one aspect of the religious life, and that perhaps the most desirable, which is independent of the discoveries of science, and may survive whatever we may come to believe as to the nature of the universe. Religion has been associated, not only with creeds and churches, but with the personal life of those who felt its importance. In the best of the saints and mystics, there existed in combination the belief in certain dogmas and a certain way of feeling about the purposes of human life. The man who feels deeply the problems of human destiny, the desire

---

[4]**Aristotle (384–322 B.C.E.)** Greek philosopher who studied under Plato; Aristotle's works cover logic, moral philosophy, metaphysics, poetry, physics, zoology, politics, and rhetoric; he created "logic," the science of reasoning. [Ed. note.]

to diminish the sufferings of mankind, and the hope that the future will realize the best possibilities of our species, is nowadays often said to have a religious outlook, however little he may accept of traditional Christianity. In so far as religion consists in a way of feeling, rather than in a set of beliefs, science cannot touch it. Perhaps the decay of dogma may, psychologically, make such a way of feeling temporarily more difficult, because it has been so intimately associated with theological belief. But this difficulty need not endure for ever; in fact, many freethinkers have shown in their lives that this way of feeling has no essential connection with a creed. No real excellence can be inextricably bound up with unfounded beliefs; and if theological beliefs are unfounded, they cannot be necessary for the preservation of what is good in the religious outlook. To think otherwise is to be filled with fears as to what we may discover, which will interfere with our attempts to understand the world; but it is only in the measure in which we achieve such understanding that true wisdom becomes possible.

QUESTIONS FOR DISCUSSION

1. What is the purpose of the article? Who might the intended audience be?
2. How does Russell define science? Religion? Compare and contrast Russell's definitions with those of Einstein (p. 86). Then compare and contrast them with your own.
3. What is a "purely personal religion" (par. 3)? Give an example from your own experience.
4. What are creeds and how are they "the source of the conflict between religion and science" (par. 4)?
5. Describe the conflict between scientific inquiry and religious assertions as to matters of "fact." How has religion solved the conflict?
6. Analyze the method for ascertaining truths in science, and contrast that method with the practices of religion in proving its beliefs.
7. Discuss the difference between the "tentative" nature of scientific hypotheses (review Oppenheimer's explanation, par. 10) and the "absolute" nature of religious truth.
8. Outline the essay's pattern of organization. How does Russell build his argument? Compare and contrast the structure with that of Einstein's essay.

CHARLES DARWIN
The Action of Natural Selection

Charles Darwin (1809–1882) was a British geologist and biologist. He developed the theory that animals evolve by a natural process of selection. In the following essay from Darwin's On the Origin of the Species *(1859), the process of natural selection is described. Although several European scientists were formulating similar theories at the same time, Darwin became known as the founder of the Theory of Evolution because his writings on the subject were the most widely read.*

In order to make it clear how, as I believe, natural selection acts, I must beg permission to give one or two imaginary illustrations. Let us take the case of a wolf, which preys on various animals, securing some by craft, some by strength, and some by fleetness; and let us suppose that the fleetest prey, a deer for instance, had from any change in the country increased in numbers, or that other prey had decreased in numbers, during that season of the year when the wolf is hardest pressed for food. I can under such circumstances see no reason to doubt that the swiftest and slimmest wolves would have the best chance for surviving, and so be preserved or selected,— provided always that they retained strength to master their prey at this or at some other period of the year, when they might be compelled to prey on other animals. I can see no more reason to doubt this, than that man can improve the fleetness of his grayhounds by careful and methodical selection, or by that unconscious selection which results from each man trying to keep the best dogs without any thought of modifying the breed.

Even without any change in the proportional numbers of the animals on which our wolf preyed, a cub might be born with an innate tendency to pursue certain kinds of prey. Nor can this be thought very improbable; for we often observe great differences in the natural tendencies of our domestic animals; one cat, for instance, taking to catch rats, another mice; one cat, according to Mr. St. John, bringing home winged game, another hares or rabbits, and another hunting on marshy ground and almost nightly catching woodcocks or snipes. The tendency to catch rats rather than mice is known to be inherited. Now, if any slight innate change of habit or of structure benefited an individual wolf, it would have the best chance of surviving and of leaving offspring. Some of its young would probably inherit the same habits or structure, and by the repetition of this process, a new variety might be formed which would either supplant or coexist with the parent-form of wolf. Or, again, the wolves inhabiting a mountainous district, and those frequenting the lowlands, would naturally be forced to hunt different prey; and from the continued preservation of the individuals best fitted for the two sites, two varieties might slowly be formed. These varieties would cross and blend where they met; but to this subject of intercrossing we shall soon have to return. I may add, that, according to Mr. Pierce, there are two varieties of the wolf inhabiting the Catskill Mountains in the United States, one with a light greyhound-like form, which pursues deer, and the other more bulky, with shorter legs, which more frequently attacks the shepherd's flocks.

Let us now take a more complex case. Certain plants excrete a sweet juice, apparently for the sake of eliminating something injurious from their sap: this is effected by glands at the base of the stipules in some Leguminosae, and at the back of the leaf of the common laurel. This juice, though small in quantity, is greedily sought by insects. Let us now suppose a little sweet juice or nectar to be excreted by the inner bases of the petals of a flower. In this case insects in seeking the nectar would get dusted with pollen, and would certainly often transport the pollen from one flower to the stigma of another flower. The flowers of two distinct individuals of the same species would thus get crossed; and the act of crossing, we have good reason to believe (as will hereafter be more fully alluded to), would produce very vigorous seedlings, which consequently would have the best chance of flourishing and surviving. Some of these seedlings would probably inherit the nectar-excreting power. Those individual flowers which had the largest glands or nectaries, and which excreted most nectar, would be oftenest visited by insects, and would be oftenest crossed; and so in the long-run would gain the upper hand. Those flowers, also, which had their stamens and pistils placed, in relation to the size and habits of the particular insects which visited them, so as to favor in any degree the transportal of their pollen from flower to flower, would likewise be favored or selected. We might have taken the case of insects visiting flowers for the sake of collecting pollen instead of nectar; and as pollen is formed for the sole object of fertilization, its destruction appears a simple loss to the plant; yet if a little pollen were carried, at first occasionally and then habitually, by the pollen-devouring insects from flower to flower, and a cross thus effected, although nine-tenths of the pollen were destroyed, it might still be a great gain to the plant; and those individuals which by us, might profit a bee or other insect, so that an individual so characterized would be able to obtain its food more quickly, and so have a better chance of living and leaving descendants. Its descendants would probably inherit a tendency to a similar slight deviation of structure. The tubes of the corollas of the common red and incarnate clovers (Trifolium pratense and incarnatum) do not on a hasty glance appear to differ in length; yet the hive-bee can easily suck the nectar out of the incarnate clover, but not out of the common red clover, which is visited by humble-bees alone; so that whole fields of the red clover offer in vain an abundant supply of precious nectar to the hive-bee. Thus it might be a great advantage to the hive-bee to have a slightly longer or differently constructed proboscis. On the other hand, I have found by experiment that the fertility of clover greatly depends on bees visiting and moving parts of the corolla, so as to push the pollen on to the stigmatic surface. Hence, again, if humble-bees were to become rare in any country, it might be a great advantage to the red clover to have a shorter or more deeply divided tube to its corolla, so that the hive-bee could visit its flowers. Thus I can understand how a flower and a bee might slowly become, either simultaneously or one after the other, modified and adapted in the most perfect manner to each other, by the continued preservation of individuals presenting mutual and slightly favorable deviations of structure.

I am well aware that this doctrine of natural selection, exemplified in the above imaginary instances, is open to the same objections which were at first urged against Sir Charles Lyell's[1] noble views on "the modern changes of the earth, as illustrative of geology;" but we now very seldom hear the action, for instance, of the coast-waves, called a trifling and insignificant cause, when applied to the excavation of gigantic valleys or to the formation of the longest lines of inland cliffs. Natural selection can act only by the preservation and accumulation of infinitesimally small inherited modifications, each profitable to the preserved being; and as modern geology has almost banished such views as the excavation of a great valley by a single diluvial wave, so will natural selection, if it be a true principle, banish the belief of the continued creation of new organic beings, or of any great and sudden modification in their structure.

---

[1]**Sir Charles Lyell (1797–1875)** English geologist who completely revolutionized the prevailing ideas about the age of the earth. [Ed. note.]

QUESTIONS FOR DISCUSSION

1. What might be Darwin's purpose in writing this text? Who is his intended audience?
2. Outline the structure of the article. How does the organization of the article help to persuade the reader of the validity of Darwin's theory regarding natural selection?
3. What is "natural selection" (par. 1)? How do the examples of the wolf and deer help to explain this concept? What other examples does Darwin use? How do those illustrations add to your understanding of the concept?
4. Explain the point Darwin is making in the last paragraph. How is this point supported by Carl Sagan in the excerpt from *The Dragons of Eden* (p. 83)?

GEORGE E. SIMPSON
Early Social Darwinism

In "Early Social Darwinism" (1959) George Simpson discusses the application of Darwin's theories to human culture. The idea of the "survival of the fittest" is applied to society to explain why some people attain power and wealth while others are the victims of poverty and hunger. The Social Darwinists use this application of Darwin's theories to argue in favor of unrestricted economic competition and imperialism. The view of human nature explained here by George Simpson is similar to that described by Cynthia Eagle Russett in Darwin in America: The Intellectual Response, 1865–1912 *(p. 100). Margaret Mead, however, takes an opposing view in "Warfare: An Invention— Not a Biological Necessity" (p. 104).*

The application of Darwin's principle of natural selection to human society, with special emphasis on competition and struggle, became known as "Social Darwinism." This doctrine, congenial to the intellectual climate of the end of the nineteenth century, was endorsed by the advocates of unrestricted competition in private enterprise, the colonial expansionists, and the opponents of voluntary social change. Among others, Ernest Haeckel[1] provided scientific sanction for this point of view:

> The theory of selection teaches that in human life, as in animal and plant life, everywhere and at all times, only a small and chosen minority can exist and flourish, while the enormous majority starve and perish miserably and more or less prematurely. . . . The cruel and merciless struggle for existence which rages through living nature, and in the course of nature must rage, this unceasing and inexorable competition of all living creatures is an incontestable fact; only the picked minority of the qualified fittest is in a position to resist it successfully,

[1] **Ernest Haeckel (1834–1919)** German biologist and natural philosopher. [Ed. note.]

while the great majority of the competitors must necessarily perish miserably. We may profoundly lament this tragical state of things, but we can neither controvert nor alter it. "Many are called, but few are chosen." This principle of selection is as far as possible from democratic, on the contrary it is aristocratic in the strictest sense of the word.

Herbert Spencer and William Graham Sumner were prominent in advancing the doctrine of the social Darwinists. Despite differences in their philosophies, both saw the poor as the "unfit." Because they are the result of the operations of the laws of evolution, they cannot be assisted and efforts to help them through legislation, public charity, and social reconstruction are evil. According to Spencer, "The whole effort of nature is to get rid of them, and make room for better . . . If they are sufficiently complete to live, they do live, and it is well they should live. If they are not sufficiently complete to live, they die, and it is best they should die."

Although Darwin pointed out that militarism and war occasion reverse selection by exposing the biologically soundest young men to early death or preventing them from marrying during the prime of life and, at the same time, by providing those with poorer constitutions with greater opportunity to marry and propagate their kind, many of the social Darwinists praised war as a means of furthering social progress. An English scientist, Karl Pearson, wrote: "History shows me one way and one way only, in which a high state of civilization has been produced, namely the struggle of race with race, and the survival of the physically and mentally fitter race. If men want to know whether the lower races of man can evolve a higher type, I fear the only course is to leave them to fight it out among themselves."

Nineteenth century imperialists, calling upon Darwinism in defense of the subjugation of "backward" races, could point to *The Origin of Species* which had referred in its sub-title to *The Preservation of Favored Races in the Struggle for Life*. Darwin had been talking about pigeons but they saw no reason why his theories should not apply to men, and the whole spirit of the naturalistic world view seemed to call for a vigorous and unrelenting thoroughness in the application of biological concepts. Darwinian theory was utilized to justify the conflicts of rival empires, the ententes and the alliances of the "balance of power." Bismarck in Germany, Chamberlain in England, and Theodore Roosevelt in the United States found in social Darwinism a sanction for their theories of force and expansion.

Another aspect of social Darwinism at the turn of the century was the eugenics movement. Like other early social Darwinists, the eugenicists equated the "fit" with the upper classes and the "unfit" with the poor. Believing that disease, poverty, and crime are due largely to heredity, they warned against the high reproductive rates of the lower classes.

SOCIAL DARWINISM IN RECENT YEARS

Adolf Hitler's racism and Nazism have been called perversions of Darwinism. Hitler's virulent doctrines were the culmination of a half-century of social Darwinistic thinking in Germany. One of his most influential immediate predecessors was

General Freidrich von Bernhardi, who said of the Germans that "no nation on the face of the globe is so able to grasp and appropriate all the elements of culture, to add to them from the stores of its own spiritual endowment, and to give back to mankind richer gifts than it received." Bernhardi glorified war as a biological necessity, as the greatest factor in the furtherance of culture and power, and claimed that the Germans could fulfill their great and urgent duty toward civilization only by the sword.

Hitler's doctrines are so well-known that extended reference to them here is unnecessary. According to *Mein Kampf*, the "Aryan" alone "furnishes the great building-stones and plans for all human progress." The Aryan had subjugated "lower races" and made them do his will, the Jew's "intellect is never constructive," "the mingling of blood . . . is the sole reason for the dying-out of old cultures," and hyperindividualism had cheated Germany of world domination and a peace "founded on the victorious sword of a lordly people. . . ." Hitlerism represents the most extreme variety of social Darwinism and the one which has had the most powerful effects on the destinies of modern peoples.

CONCLUSION

One hundred years after the publication of *The Origin of Species*, and eighty-eight years after the appearance of *The Descent of Man*, natural selection remains an important concept in biology, anthropology, sociology, even in international relations. Modern man is subject to selection, natural and artificial. If this were not so, all human genotypes would produce surviving children in the same ratio as the occurrence of these genotypes in existing populations. Today the adaptive value of cooperation is more widely acknowledged and the role of ruthless aggression as a factor in the evolution of man, society, and culture is given smaller significance. Social Darwinistic thinking has not disappeared, but increasingly the "nature, red in tooth and claw" version of natural selection is regarded as an outdated brand of Darwinism.

QUESTIONS FOR DISCUSSION

1. Who is the audience of this text? What is its purpose?
2. Outline the pattern of organization. How does the organization of the article reflect its purpose?
3. What is Social Darwinism? Who were its early proponents? Discuss their theories about human nature.
4. According to the Social Darwinist, why do humans compete with one another?
5. Do you agree with the Social Darwinists' view that human beings are naturally warlike? Defend your answer.

CYNTHIA EAGLE RUSSETT
Darwin in America:
The Intellectual Response, 1865–1912

Cynthia Eagle Russett explains the emergence of Social Darwinism in the following excerpt from her book Darwin in America: The Intellectual Response, 1865–1912. *Extrapolated from the Theory of Evolution presented by Charles Darwin in the mid-nineteenth century, Social Darwinism applies the principles of natural selection to the lives of individual human beings and to society as a whole. Russett discusses the use of Social Darwinist theory to explain the "necessity" of war and human suffering, and to justify such social evils as racism and the oppression of the working class.*

SOCIAL DARWINISM: WEEDING OUT THE WEAK

[S]ome hardier souls were quite prepared to accept Darwin's account of nature at face value and apply it to human affairs. These hardy ones, the Social Darwinists, drew on Darwin and even more on Spencer[1] to adapt the struggle for existence and survival of the fittest into a paradigm for the behavior of men and nations. In certain moods Darwin could himself give voice to some characteristic Social Darwinian anxieties. "We civilized men," he noted, "do our utmost to check the process of elimination; we build asylums for the imbecile, the maimed, and the sick; we institute poor-laws. . . . Thus the weak members of civilized society propagate their kind. No one who has attended to the breeding of domestic animals will doubt that this must be highly injurious to the race of man." But Darwin did not therefore give eugenic human breeding first place in his catalogue of values as some of his contemporaries did. He was too tenderhearted for that.[2]

Less tenderhearted was Herbert Spencer, who sternly adjudged that "fostering the good-for-nothing at the expense of the good, is an extreme cruelty," a "storing-up of miseries for future generations." Spencer was convinced that there was no surer path to ultimate woe than cosseting the unfortunate: "To aid the bad in multiplying, is, in effect, the same as maliciously providing for our descendants a multitude of enemies." Doubtless, individual altruism was all very well, but organized charity was intolerable: " . . . An unquestionable injury is done by agencies which undertake in a wholesale way to foster good-for-nothings; putting a stop to that natural process of elimination by which society continually purifies itself." Nor need one feel excessive pity for these underprivileged ones, the idlers, the imbeciles, the incompetent of every strain; for the most part, they brought their troubles on themselves.[3] The same robust outlook on the international level produced a school of theorists who justified war as the purifying agent among nations, a beneficial if rigorous tonic against the softening effects of effete civilization.

---

[1] **Herbert Spencer (1820–1903)** Founder of evolutionary philosophy in which all phenomena in the universe are subject to the process of evolution; often referred to as the originator of the theory of Social Darwinism. [Ed. note.]
[2] Charmian London, *The Book of Jack London* (2 vols., London, 1921), 2:69.
[3] Jack London, *A Daughter of the Snows* (Philadelphia: J. B. Lippincott, 1902), p. 76.

Social Darwinism spoke to the needs of several different groups in American society. Still, it may not have been quite so important an influence on the ethics of the Gilded Age as some historians have supposed. There can be no doubt, for example, that Social Darwinism in Europe often took the form of nationalism and militarism, but American society was only rarely congenial to its fiercer variants. Few, indeed, were the number of those in America willing to join the European voices raised in tribute to war, "not merely a necessary element in the life of nations but an indispensable factor of culture, in which a truly civilized nation finds the highest expression of strength and vitality."[4] Even among the few genuine militarists Darwinism tended not so much to initiate theory as to confirm ideas already established. In the words of Richard Hofstadter,[5] "Neither the philosophy of force nor doctrines of *Machtpolitik* had to wait upon Darwin to make their appearance."[6]

Captain Alfred Thayer Mahan wrote his enormously influential *Influence of Sea Power Upon History* without benefit of Darwin. Mahan's arguments on behalf of a strong navy and a vigorous policy of expansion, cordially received by Theodore Roosevelt among others, rested on a close study of contemporary international relations and intimate familiarity with the great European military and naval theorists of the previous century. Reflection upon the lessons of history had led Mahan to a frank avowal of the supremacy of force in world affairs: "Force, the organized force of the community as the means of assuring its will, is and must remain the basis of social order so long as evil exists to be repressed." The use of force might at times appear coercive, Mahan conceded, but it was both natural and irresistible, and worked, in the main, for righteousness. "To such a view aggression, in its primary sense of onward movement, is inevitable. Those who will not move must be swept aside. They may be drawn into the movement by moral forces, as Japan has been; but if not, they must be brought despite themselves into external conditions favorable to their welfare and the general good, as has been done in India, in Egypt, and in the Philippines."[7] This virile imperialism, so apparently Darwinian in tone and temper, in reality owed nothing at all to the *Origin*.

So also with racism and the cult of the Anglo-Saxon that blossomed around the turn of the century. Darwinian concepts were brandished in support of ideas that had circulated long before 1859. In the United States popular racism dated back to the founding of the colonies and the introduction of black slaves. During the nineteenth century theories of racial determinism and white supremacy were given scientific foundation, so it was believed, by physiological studies differentiating the human species into groups on the basis of color, physique, or head shape. To this dubious anthropology Darwinism gave some support, emphasizing as it did the preservation of some species at the expense of others in the great struggle for life. It seemed plausible to view the Anglo-Saxon race as one of Darwin's fittest species, preeminently suited not only to survive but to furnish the main impetus to the progress of civilization.

---

[4]London, *The Sea Wolf* (New York: The Macmillan Co., 1904), p. 75.
[5]**Richard Hofstadter (1916–1970)** American social and political historian. [Ed. note.]
[6]London, *A Daughter of the Snows*, p. 135.
[7]Letter of Dec. 12, 1899, in *Letters from Jack London* (New York: Odyssey Press, 1965), p. 74.

At the same time Darwinism provided only ambiguous support for racist doctrine. For one thing, it discredited the notion of the separate and distinct origin of races, in favor of the evolution of races from a single source. This was discomfiting to racists, for, as Asa Gray[8] noted, "the very first step backward [on the evolutionary scale] makes the Negro and the Hottentot[9] our blood-relations."[10] For another thing, Darwinism did not answer the question of how traits were inherited (though Darwin did speculate, wrongly, as it turned out, about the mechanism of inheritance), and so could not establish the preponderance of heredity over environment, belief in which was crucial to racist ideology.[11] Indeed, many Darwinians, including Herbert Spencer, were also convinced Lamarckians, committed to the view that parents could transmit to their offspring traits acquired in their own lifetime. Such a view would be difficult to reconcile with the racist ideology of fixed and unchanging racial characteristics. Until Lamarckianism was scientifically disproven and an alternative theory of genetics supplied—developments which occurred well after 1900—Darwinism could only provide a set of rather vague though undeniably suggestive phrases and ideas to strengthen the ideology of race.[12]

BUSINESS DARWINISM

The impact of Darwinism is often presumed to have been greatest on the business world. Richard Hofstadter's *Social Darwinism* disclosed to view the Darwinian social ethics of the Rockefellers, Hills, Carnegies, Vanderbilts, and Goulds, known collectively to history as the "robber barons." Along with the wit to capitalize on the unparalleled business opportunities of the Gilded Age, these men combined, so Hofstadter alleged, the ethics of the jungle. Of postbellum America Hofstadter wrote: "Its rapid expansion, its exploitative methods, its desperate competition, and its peremptory rejection of failure" made it "a vast human caricature of the Darwinian struggle for existence and survival of the fittest."[13]

There is some truth to this view, insofar as competition was intense, economic activity perilous, and the harshness of the industrial system unmitigated by any remedial public policy. But much the same thing could be said of early-industrial England in the first half of the nineteenth century. Some observers, indeed, have turned the tables on the chronology which gives Darwinism a causal role in the development of a predatory industrial ethic by speculating that the genesis of the *Origin* might be traced to Darwin's own knowledge of the rigors of British industrialism. Oswald Spengler, who described the *Origin* as "the application of economics to biology," remarked that it reeked of the atmosphere of the English factory. So also Nietzsche observed with distaste: "Over the whole of English Darwinism there hovers something of the suffocating air of over-crowded England, something of the odour of humble people in need and in straits."[14] These comments, though extreme,

---

[8]**Asa Gray (1810–1888)** American botanist. [Ed. note.]
[9]**Hottentot** A person from Southern Africa, related to the Bantu and Bushmen. [Ed. note.]
[10]London, *A Daughter of the Snows*, p. 83.
[11]Letter of Jan. 6, 1902, in *Letters from Jack London*, p. 128.
[12]London, *A Daughter of the Snows*, p. 184.
[13]*Letters from Jack London*, p. 128.
[14]Jack London, *The Call of the Wild* (New York: The Macmillan Co., 1903), pp. 59–60.

gain a certain plausibility when it is recalled that Darwin found the clue to the operation of natural selection in Malthus's essay on population. If it is true that Darwin generalized the insights of Malthus to include animals as well as human beings, then descriptions of the business world as a caricature of the Darwinian universe obviously invert the chronological sequence, even as the evils of unregulated industrialism predate the *Origin*.

Subsequent scholarship has cast doubt, in any case, on the picture of American businessmen as Social Darwinists who seized on the theories of Darwin and Spencer to cloak their rapacity. Evidence for that conclusion turns out to be remarkably scanty. There were, to be sure, a few businessmen who referred to their work in Darwinian terms, or who were familiar with Spencer's evolutionary philosophy, men like the publisher Richard R. Bowker, the textile manufacturer Daniel A. Tompkins, the sugar magnate Henry O. Havemeyer. The outstanding example is Andrew Carnegie, the steelmaster, a devoted disciple of Spencer. "Man was not created with an instinct for his own degradation," Carnegie learned from Darwin and Spencer. "From the lower he has risen to the higher forms, and there is no conceivable end to his march to perfection. His face is turned to the light; he stands in the sun and looks upward."[15]

But such men were few in number. A good bit of the material adduced as evidence for the Social Darwinian cast of American businessmen was in fact produced by intellectuals, social theorists, or publicists rather than by businessmen themselves. Such is the case with the well-known work of James H. Bridge, literary assistant successively to Herbert Spencer and Andrew Carnegie, who preached the benevolence of trusts as the industrial stage in which cooperation replaced competition. Bridge looked forward to a "rational industrialism," prefigured by the trusts, in which "we are to pass from the cruel egoism of old systems to the kindly altruism of the new."[16]

A careful search by Irvin G. Wyllie some years ago turned up remarkably little evidence of Social Darwinism among American entrepreneurs. It is hard to see how the case could be otherwise. A consciously Darwinian social philosophy would have required the kind of education few businessmen received in the late nineteenth century. . . .

QUESTIONS FOR DISCUSSION

1. Who might be the audience for the book from which this excerpt is taken? What aspects of the text lead you to make these inferences about the audience?
2. How would you define Social Darwinism? Discuss the passages in the text that helped you to form your definition.
3. What aspects of human life seem to be the best "proof" of the theory of Social Darwinism?

---

[15] Alfred Kazin, "Theodore Dreiser: His Education and Ours," in Alfred Kazin, ed., *The Stature of Theodore Dreiser* (Bloomington, Ind.: Indiana University Press, 1955), p. 158.
[16] Frank Norris, *Vandover and the Brute* (Garden City, N.Y.: Doubleday, Page & Co., 1914).

4. How might the theory of Social Darwinism be used to discriminate against certain groups of people? Describe examples of such discrimination from your own experience and from your study of history.
5. What is "Business Darwinism"? What individuals or groups of people would probably benefit most by supporting this application of Darwin's theory? Give examples of business practices that illustrate the concepts of Business Darwinism.

MARGARET MEAD
Warfare: An Invention— Not a Biological Necessity

Dr. Margaret Mead (1901–1979) was a cultural anthropologist and a popularizer of cultural anthropology. She did much of her fieldwork in the South Pacific; her dissertation, Coming of Age in Samoa *(1928), in which she demonstrated that adolescence is not a time of strife and difficulties in all cultures, made her famous. Mead's "Warfare: An Invention—Not a Biological Necessity" (1940) was intended to educate the English-speaking world about nonaggressive cultures, questioning the assumption that war is an inevitable part of human experience.*

Is war a biological necessity, a sociological inevitability or just a bad invention? Those who argue for the first view endow man with such pugnacious instincts that some outlet in aggressive behavior is necessary if man is to reach full human stature. It was this point of view which lay back of William James's[1] famous essay, "The Moral Equivalent of War," in which he tried to retain the warlike virtues and channel them in new directions. A similar point of view has lain back of the Soviet Union's attempt to make competition between groups rather than between individuals. A basic, competitive, aggressive, warring human nature is assumed, and those who wish to outlaw war or outlaw competitiveness merely try to find new and less socially destructive ways in which these biologically given aspects of man's nature can find expression. Then there are those who take the second view: warfare is the inevitable concomitant of the development of the state, the struggle for land and natural resources of class societies springing, not from the nature of man, but from the nature of history. War is nevertheless inevitable unless we change our social system and outlaw classes, the struggle for power, and possessions; and in the event of our success warfare would disappear, as a symptom vanishes when the disease is cured.

One may hold a compromise position between these two extremes; one may claim that all aggression springs from the frustration of man's biologically determined drives and that, since all forms of culture are frustrating, it is certain each new generation will be aggressive and the aggression will find its natural and inevitable expression in race war, class war, nationalistic war, and so on.

---

[1]**William James (1842–1910)** American philosopher and psychologist. [Ed. note.]

All three positions are very popular today among those who think seriously about the problems of war and its possible prevention, but I wish to urge another point of view, less defeatist perhaps than the first and third, and more accurate than the second: that is, that warfare, by which I mean organized conflict between two groups as *groups*, in which each group puts an army (even if the army is only fifteen Pygmies) into the field to fight and kill, if possible, some of the members of the army of the other group—that warfare of this sort is an invention like any other of the inventions in terms of which we order our lives, such as writing, marriage, cooking our food instead of eating it raw, trial by jury, or burial of the dead, and so on. Some of this list any one will grant are inventions: trial by jury is confined to very limited portions of the globe; we know that there are tribes that do not bury their dead but instead expose or cremate them; and we know that only part of the human race has had a knowledge of writing as its cultural inheritance. But, whenever a way of doing things is found universally, such as the use of fire or the practice of some form of marriage, we tend to think at once that it is not an invention at all but an attribute of humanity itself. And yet even such universals as marriage and the use of fire are inventions like the rest, very basic ones, inventions which were perhaps necessary if human history was to take the turn it has taken, but nevertheless inventions. At some point in his social development man was undoubtedly without the institution of marriage or the knowledge of the use of fire.

The case for warfare is much clearer because there are peoples even today who have no warfare. Of these the Eskimo are perhaps the most conspicuous example, but the Lepchas of Sikkim are an equally good one.[2] Neither of these peoples understands war, not even defensive warfare. The idea of warfare is lacking, and this idea is as essential to carrying on war as an alphabet or a syllabary is to writing. But whereas the Lepchas are a gentle, unquarrelsome people, and the advocates of other points of view might argue that they are not full human beings or that they had never been frustrated and so had no aggression to expend in warfare, the Eskimo case gives no such possibility of interpretation. The Eskimo are not a mild and meek people; many of them are turbulent and troublesome. Fights, theft of wives, murder, cannibalism occur among them—all outbursts of passionate men goaded by desire or intolerable circumstance. Here are men faced with hunger, men faced with loss of their wives, men faced with the threat of extermination by other men, and here are orphan children, growing up miserably with no one to care for them, mocked and neglected by those about them. The personality necessary for war, the circumstances necessary to goad men to desperation are present, but there is no war. When a traveling Eskimo entered a settlement he might have to fight the strongest man in the settlement to establish his position among them, but this was a test of strength and bravery, not war. The idea of warfare, of one *group* organizing against another *group* to maim and wound and kill them was absent. And without that idea passions might rage but there was no war.

But, it may be argued, isn't this because the Eskimo have such a low and undeveloped form of social organization? They own no land, they move from place to place, camping, it is true, season after season on the same site, but this is not something to fight for as the modern nations of the world fight for land and raw materials.

[2]**Sikkim** A small kingdom between India and Tibet that became an Indian state in 1975. [Ed. note.]

They have no permanent possessions that can be looted, no towns that can be burned. They have no social classes to produce stress and strains within the society which might force it to go to war outside. Doesn't the absence of war among the Eskimo, while disproving the biological necessity of war, just go to confirm the point that it is the state of development of the society which accounts for war, and nothing else?

We find the answer among the Pygmy peoples of the Andaman Islands in the Bay of Bengal. The Andamans also represent an exceedingly low level of society; they are a hunting and food-gathering people; they live in tiny hordes without any class stratification; their houses are simpler than the snow houses of the Eskimo. But they knew about warfare. The army might contain only fifteen determined pygmies marching in a straight line, but it was the real thing none the less. Tiny army met tiny army in open battle, blows were exchanged, casualties suffered, and the state of warfare could only be concluded by a peace-making ceremony.

Similarly, among the Australian aborigines, who built no permanent dwellings but wandered from water hole to water hole over their almost desert country, warfare—and rules of "international law"—were highly developed. The student of social evolution will seek in vain for his obvious causes of war, struggle for lands, struggle for power of one group over another, expansion of population, need to divert the minds of a populace restive under tyranny, or even the ambition of a successful leader to enhance his own prestige. All are absent, but warfare as a practice remained, and men engaged in it and killed one another in the course of a war because killing is what is done in wars.

From instances like these it becomes apparent that an inquiry into the causes of war misses the fundamental point as completely as does an insistence upon the biological necessity of war. If a people have an idea of going to war and the idea that war is the way in which certain situations, defined within their society, are to be handled, they will sometimes go to war. If they are a mild and unaggressive people, like the Pueblo Indians, they may limit themselves to defensive warfare; but they will be forced to think in terms of war because there are peoples near them who have warfare as a pattern, and offensive, raiding, pillaging warfare at that. When the pattern of warfare is known, people like the Pueblo Indians will defend themselves, taking advantage of their natural defenses, the *mesa* village site, and people like the Lepchas, having no natural defenses and no idea of warfare, will merely submit to the invader. But the essential point remains the same. There is a way of behaving which is known to a given people and labeled as an appropriate form of behavior. A bold and warlike people like the Sioux or the Maori may label warfare as desirable as well as possible;[3] a mild people like the Pueblo Indians may label warfare as undesirable; but to the minds of both peoples the possibility of warfare is present. Their thoughts, their hopes, their plans are oriented about this idea, that warfare may be selected as the way to meet some situation.

So simple peoples and civilized peoples, mild peoples and violent, assertive peoples, will all go to war if they have the invention, just as those peoples who have the custom of dueling will have duels and peoples who have the pattern of vendetta

[3]**Maori** The aboriginal people of New Zealand. [Ed. note.]

will indulge in vendetta. And, conversely, peoples who do not know of dueling will not fight duels, even though their wives are seduced and their daughters ravished; they may on occasion commit murder but they will not fight duels. Cultures which lack the idea of the vendetta will not meet every quarrel in this way. A people can use only the forms it has. So the Balinese have their special way of dealing with a quarrel between two individuals:[4] if the two feel that the causes of quarrel are heavy they may go and register their quarrel in the temple before the gods, and, making offerings, they may swear never to have anything to do with each other again. Under the Dutch government they registered such mutual "not-speaking" with the Dutch government officials. But in other societies, although individuals might feel as full of animosity and as unwilling to have any further contact as do the Balinese, they cannot register their quarrel with the gods and go on quietly about their business because registering quarrels with the gods is not an invention of which they know.

Yet, if it be granted that warfare is after all an invention, it may nevertheless be an invention that lends itself to certain types of personality, to the exigent needs of autocrats, to the expansionist desires of crowded peoples, to the desire for plunder and rape and loot which is engendered by a dull and frustrating life. What, then, can we say of this congruence between warfare and its uses? If it is a form which fits so well, is not this congruence the essential point? But even here the primitive material causes us to wonder, because there are tribes who go to war merely for glory, having no quarrel with the enemy, suffering from no tyrant within their boundaries, anxious neither for land nor loot nor women, but merely anxious to win prestige which within that tribe has been declared obtainable only by war and without which no young man can hope to win his sweetheart's smile of approval. But if, as was the case with the Bush Negroes of Dutch Guiana,[5] it is artistic ability which is necessary to win a girl's approval, the same young man would have to be carving rather than going out on a war party.

In many parts of the world, war is a game in which the individual can win counters—counters which bring him prestige in the eyes of his own sex or of the opposite sex; he plays for these counters as he might, in our society, strive for a tennis championship. Warfare is a frame for such prestige-seeking merely because it calls for the display of certain skills and certain virtues; all of these skills—riding straight, shooting straight, dodging the missiles of the enemy and sending one's own straight to the mark—can be equally well exercised in some other framework and, equally, the virtues—endurance, bravery, loyalty, steadfastness—can be displayed in other contexts. The tie-up between proving oneself a man and proving this by a success in organized killing is due to a definition which many societies have made of manliness. And often, even in those societies which counted success in warfare a proof of human worth, strange turns were given to the idea, as when the Plains Indians gave their highest awards to the man who touched a live enemy rather than to the man who brought in a scalp—from a dead enemy—because killing a man was less risky. Warfare is just an invention known to the majority of

---

[4]**Balinese** The people of Bali, a province of Indonesia. [Ed. note.]
[5]**Dutch Guiana** Formerly Surinam in northern South America. [Ed. note.]

human societies by which they permit their young men either to accumulate prestige or avenge their honor or acquire loot or wives or slaves or sago lands or cattle or appease the blood lust of their gods or the restless souls of the recently dead. It is just an invention, older and more widespread than the jury system, but none the less an invention.

But, once we have said this, have we said anything at all? Despite a few instances, dear to the hearts of controversialists, of the loss of the useful arts, once an invention is made which proves congruent with human needs or social forms, it tends to persist. Grant that war is an invention, that it is not a biological necessity nor the outcome of certain special types of social forms, still, once the invention is made, what are we to do about it? The Indian who had been subsisting on the buffalo for generations because with his primitive weapons he could slaughter only a limited number of buffalo did not return to his primitive weapons when he saw that the white man's more efficient weapons were exterminating the buffalo. A desire for the white man's cloth may mortgage the South Sea Islander to the white man's plantation, but he does not return to making bark cloth, which would have left him free. Once an invention is known and accepted, men do not easily relinquish it. The skilled workers may smash the first steam looms which they feel are to be their undoing, but they accept them in the end, and no movement which has insisted upon the mere abandonment of usable inventions has ever had much success. Warfare is here, as part of our thought; the deeds of warriors are immortalized in the words of our poets; the toys of our children are modeled upon the weapons of the soldier; the frame of reference within which our statesmen and our diplomats work always contains war. If we know that it is not inevitable, that it is due to historical accident that warfare is one of the ways in which we think of behaving, are we given any hope by that? What hope is there of persuading nations to abandon war, nations so thoroughly imbued with the idea that resort to war is, if not actually desirable and noble, at least inevitable whenever certain defined circumstances arise?

In answer to this question I think we might turn to the history of other social inventions, inventions which must once have seemed as firmly entrenched as warfare. Take the methods of trial which preceded the jury system: ordeal and trial by combat. Unfair, capricious, alien as they are to our feeling today, they were once the only methods open to individuals accused of some offense. The invention of trial by jury gradually replaced these methods until only witches, and finally not even witches, had to resort to the ordeal. And for a long time the jury system seemed the one best and finest method of settling legal disputes, but today new inventions, trial before judges only or before commissions, are replacing the jury system. In each case the old method was replaced by a new social invention; the ordeal did not go out because people thought it unjust or wrong, it went out because a method more congruent with the institutions and feelings of the period was invented. And, if we despair over the way in which war seems such an ingrained habit of most of the human race, we can take comfort from the fact that a poor invention will usually give place to a better invention.

For this, two conditions at least are necessary. The people must recognize the defects of the old invention, and some one must make a new one. Propaganda against warfare, documentation of its terrible cost in human suffering and social waste, these prepare the ground by teaching people to feel that warfare is a defective social institution. There is further needed a belief that social invention is possible and the invention of new methods which will render warfare as out-of-date as the tractor is making the plow, or the motor car the horse and buggy. A form of behavior becomes out-of-date only when something else takes its place, and in order to invent forms of behavior which will make war obsolete, it is a first requirement to believe that an invention is possible.

QUESTIONS FOR DISCUSSION

1. Who is the audience for the essay? (Reread the headnote.) How might the author's awareness of her audience affect the content?
2. What do you consider to be the purpose of the essay? Outline the structure of the argument. Discuss how each point builds on the last.
3. The essay begins with a question. What is Mead's answer? How do you know?
4. What peoples have no warfare? Why is this important to Mead's thesis?
5. What points does Mead concede to her assumed opposition? Is her argument weakened by these concessions? Explain.
6. What other points does Mead present to prove that war is an invention?
7. If war is a bad invention, why does it persist? How does Mead suggest that the world get rid of war?
8. Do you think it is possible or even desirable to end war? Why or why not?
9. Contrast Mead's position with that of the Social Darwinists who favor war as a means for ensuring the survival of the fittest.

JOHN CONNOR
The U.S. Was Right

GAR ALPEROVITZ
The U.S. Was Wrong

The two short newspaper articles which follow, "The U.S. Was Right" by John Connor, and "The U.S. Was Wrong" by Gar Alperovitz, appeared in the New York Times *in August of 1985, forty years after the atomic bomb was dropped on Hiroshima, Japan. Connor, who supports the U.S. military action, worked out of General Douglas MacArthur's headquarters in Tokyo during the period just after World War II. Alperovitz, who criticizes the U.S. government action as unnecessary, is a historian, political economist, and author of* Atomic Diplomacy: Hiroshima and Potsdam. *The arguments presented by each writer use different persuasive modes and are written in contrasting journalistic styles.*

JOHN CONNOR
The U.S. Was Right

Forty years ago this week in Hiroshima: the dreadful flash, the wrist watches fused forever at 8:16 A.M. The question still persists: Should we have dropped the atomic bomb?

History seldom gives decisive answers, but recently declassified documents point to a clear judgment: Yes, it was necessary to drop the bomb. It was needed to end the war. It saved countless American and Japanese lives.

In the early summer of 1945, Japan, under tight control of the militarists, was an implacable, relentless adversary. The Japanese defended territory with a philosophy we had seldom encountered: Soldiers were taught that surrender was worse than death. There was savage resistance to the end in battle after battle.

Of the 5,000-man Japanese force at Tarawa in November 1943, only 17 remained alive when the island was taken. When Kwajalein was invaded in February 1944, Japanese officers slashed at American tanks with samurai swords; their men held grenades against the sides of tanks in an effort to disable them.

On Saipan, less than 1,000 of the 32,000 defending Japanese troops survived. Casualties among the Japanese-ruled civilians on the island numbered 10,000. Parents bashed their babies' brains out on rocky cliff sides, then leaped to their deaths. Others cut each other's throats; children threw grenades at each other. America suffered 17,000 casualties.

Just 660 miles southeast of Tokyo, Iwo Jima's garrison was told to defend the island as if it were Tokyo itself. They did. In the first day of fighting, there were more American casualties then during "D-Day" in Normandy. At Okinawa—only 350 miles south of Kyushu—more than 110,000 Japanese soldiers and 100,000 civilians were killed. Kamikaze attacks cost the Navy alone some 10,000 casualties. The Army and Marines lost more than 50,000 men.

In the early summer of 1945, the invasion of Japan was imminent and everyone in the Pacific was apprehensive. The apprehension was justified, because our intelligence was good: With a system code named "Magic," it had penetrated Japanese codes even before Pearl Harbor. "Magic" would play a crucial role in the closing days of the war.

Many have maintained that the bomb was unnecessary because in the closing days of the war intercepted Japanese diplomatic messages disclosed a passionate desire for peace. While that is true, it is irrelevant. The Japanese Government remained in the hands of the militarists: *Their* messages indicated a willingness to fight to the death.

Japanese planes, gasoline and ammunition had been hoarded for the coming invasion. More than 5,000 aircraft had been hidden everywhere to be used as suicide weapons, with only enough gas in their tanks for a one-way trip to the invasion beaches. More than two million men were moving into positions to defend the home islands.

The object was to inflict such appalling losses that the Americans would agree to a treaty more favorable than unconditional surrender. The Army Chief of Staff, Gen. George C. Marshall, estimated potential American casualties as high as a million.

The willingness of the Japanese to die was more than empty bravado. Several of my colleagues at Kyushu University told me that as boys of 14 or 15, they were being trained to meet the Americans on the beaches with little more than sharpened bamboo spears. They had no illusions about their chances for survival.

The Potsdam declaration calling for unconditional surrender was beamed to Japan on July 27. On July 30, the Americans were informed that Japan would officially ignore the ultimatum. A week later, the bomb was dropped.

Could we not have warned the Japanese in advance, critics asked, and dropped a demonstration bomb? That alternative was vetoed on the grounds the bomb might not work, or that the plane carrying it might be shot down. Moreover, it is questionable how effective a demonstration bomb might have been. The militarists could have imposed a news blackout as complete as the one imposed after the disastrous battle of Midway and continued on their suicidal course. That is exactly what happened at Hiroshima. Within hours, the Japanese Government sent in a team of scientists to investigate the damage. Their report was immediately suppressed and was not made public until many years after the war.

After midnight on Aug. 10, a protracted debate took place in an air-raid shelter deep inside the Imperial Palace. The military insisted that Japan should hold out for terms far better than unconditional surrender. The peace faction favored accepting the Potsdam declaration, providing that the Emperor would be retained. The two factions remained at an impasse. At 2 A.M., Prime Minister Kantaro Suzuki asked the Emperor to decide. In a soft, deliberate voice, the Emperor expressed his great longing for peace. The war had ended.

It was impossible, in August 1945, to predict the awesome shadow the bomb would cast on humanity. The decision to drop it seemed both simple and obvious. Without it, the militarists might have prevailed, an invasion ordered. And the loss of both American and Japanese lives would have been awesome.

The atomic bomb accomplished what it had been designed to do. It ended the war.

GAR ALPEROVITZ
The U.S. Was Wrong

Though it has not yet received broad public attention, there exists overwhelming historical evidence that President Harry S Truman knew he could almost certainly end World War II without using the atomic bomb: The United States had cracked the Japanese code, and a stream of documents released over the last 40 years show that Mr. Truman had two other options.

The first option was to clarify America's surrender terms to assure the Japanese we would not remove their Emperor. The second was simply to await the expected Soviet declaration of war—which, United States intelligence advised, appeared likely to end the conflict on its own.

Instead, Hiroshima was bombed on Aug. 6, 1945, and Nagasaki on Aug. 9. The planned date for the Soviet Union's entry into the war against Japan was Aug. 8.

The big turning point was the Emperor's continuing June-July decision to open surrender negotiations through Moscow. Top American officials—and, most critically, the President—understood the move was extraordinary: Mr. Truman's secret diaries, lost until 1978, call the key intercepted message "the telegram from Jap Emperor asking for peace."

Other documents—among them newly discovered secret memorandums from William J. Donovan, director of the Office of Strategic Services—show that Mr. Truman was personally advised of Japanese peace initiatives through Swiss and Portuguese channels as early as three months before Hiroshima. Moreover, Mr. Truman told several officials he had no objection in principle to Japan's keeping the Emperor, which seemed the only sticking point.

American leaders were sure that if he so chose "the Mikado could stop the war with a royal word"—as one top Presidential aide put it. Having decided to use the bomb, however, Mr. Truman was urged by Secretary of State James F. Byrnes not to give assurances to the Emperor before the weapon had been demonstrated.

Additional official records, including minutes of top-level White House planning meetings, show the President was clearly advised of the importance of a Soviet declaration of war: It would pull the rug out from under Japanese military leaders who were desperately hoping the powerful Red Army would stay neutral.

Gen. George C. Marshall in mid-June told Mr. Truman that "the impact of Russian entry on the already hopeless Japanese may well be the decisive action levering them into capitulation at that time or shortly thereafter if we land."

A month later, the American-British Combined Intelligence Staffs advised their chiefs of the critical importance of a Red Army attack. As the top British general, Sir Hastings Ismay summarized the conclusions for Prime Minister Winston Churchill: "If and when Russia came into the war against Japan, the Japanese would probably wish to get out on almost any terms short of the dethronement of the Emperor."

Mr. Truman's private diaries also record his understanding of the significance of this option. On July 17, 1945, when Stalin confirmed that the Red Army would march, Mr. Truman privately noted: "Fini Japs when that comes about."

There was plenty of time: The American invasion of Japan was not scheduled until the spring of 1946. Even a preliminary landing on the island Kyushu was still three months in the future.

Gen. Dwight D. Eisenhower, appalled that the bomb would be used in these circumstances, urged Mr. Truman and Secretary of War Henry L. Stimson not to drop it. In his memoirs, he observed that weeks before Hiroshima, Japan had been seeking a way to surrender. "It wasn't necessary," he said in a later interview, "to hit them with that awful thing."

The one man who presided over the Joint Chiefs of Staff, Adm. William D. Leahy, was equally shocked: "The use of this barbarous weapon at Hiroshima and Nagasaki was of no material assistance in our war against Japan. The Japanese were already defeated and ready to surrender."

Why, then, was the bomb used?

American leaders rejected the most obvious option—simply waiting for the Red Army attack—out of political, not military, concerns.

As the diary of one official put it, they wanted to end the war before Moscow got "in so much on the kill." Secretary of the Navy James V. Forrestal's diaries record that Mr. Byrnes "was most anxious to get the Japanese affair over with before the Russians got in."

United States leaders had also begun to think of the atomic bomb as what Secretary Stimson termed the "master card" of diplomacy. President Truman postponed his Potsdam meeting with Stalin until July 17, 1945—one day after the first successful nuclear test—to be sure the atomic bomb would strengthen his hand before confronting the Soviet leader on the shape of a postwar settlement.

To this day, we do not know with absolute certainty Mr. Truman's personal attitudes on several key issues. Yet we do know that his most important adviser, Secretary of State Byrnes, was convinced that dropping the bomb would serve crucial long-range diplomatic purposes.

As one atomic scientist, Leo Szilard, observed: "Mr. Byrnes did not argue that it was necessary to use the bomb against the cities of Japan in order to win the war. Mr. Byrnes' . . . view [was] that our possessing and demonstrating the bomb would make Russia more manageable."

QUESTIONS FOR DISCUSSION

1. What is the purpose of each of the two articles? Who are the writers trying to persuade? (Reread the headnote.)
2. List the arguments made by Connor. Then list the arguments made by Alperovitz. Determine whether each argument is basically an appeal to reason or to emotion. Justify your categorization.
3. Which of the two articles do you find the more persuasive? Why?
4. What arguments might you add to Connor's essay? To Alperovitz's?

SIDNEY SHALETT
First Atomic Bomb Dropped on Japan

The following article by Sidney Shalett appeared in the New York Times *just after the first atomic bomb was dropped on Hiroshima, Japan, in August of 1945. Shalett's celebratory, patriotic tone sharply contrasts with that of Masuji Ibuse (p. 117) in his description of the event. The lack of details in Shalett's account results, at least in part, from U.S. government censorship of information regarding nuclear technology. Ibuse's description, translated into English by John Bester in 1979, is a much more graphic rendering of the devastation which occurred.*

The White House and War Department announced today that an atomic bomb, possessing more power than 20,000 tons of TNT, a destructive force equal to the load of 2,000 B-29s and more than 2,000 times the blast power of what previously was the world's most devastating bomb, had been dropped on Japan.

The announcement, first given to the world in utmost solemnity by President Truman, made it plain that one of the scientific landmarks of the century had been passed, and that the "age of atomic energy," which can be a tremendous force for the advancement of civilization as well as for destruction, was at hand.

At 10:45 o'clock this morning, a statement by the President was issued at the White House that sixteen hours earlier—about the time that citizens on the Eastern seaboard were sitting down to their Sunday suppers—an American plane had dropped the single atomic bomb on the Japanese city of Hiroshima, an important army center.

What happened at Hiroshima is not yet known. The War Department said it "as yet was unable to make an accurate report" because "an impenetrable cloud of dust and smoke" masked the target area from reconnaissance planes. The Secretary of War will release the story "as soon as accurate details of the results of the bombing become available."

But in a statement vividly describing the results of the first test of the atomic bomb in New Mexico, the War Department told how an immense steel tower had been "vaporized" by the tremendous explosion, how a 40,000-foot cloud rushed into the sky, and two observers were knocked down at a point 10,000 yards away. And President Truman solemnly warned:

It was to spare the Japanese people from utter destruction that the ultimatum of July 26 was issued at Potsdam. Their leaders promptly rejected that ultimatum. If they do not now accept our terms, they may expect a rain of ruin from the air the like of which has never been seen on this earth.

The President referred to the joint statement issued by the heads of the American, British and Chinese governments, in which terms of surrender were outlined to the Japanese and warning given that rejection would mean complete destruction of Japan's power to make war.

[The atomic bomb weighs about 400 pounds and is capable of utterly destroying a town, a representative of the British Ministry of Aircraft Production said in London, the United Press reported.]

What is this terrible new weapon, which the War Department also calls the "Cosmic Bomb"? It is the harnessing of the energy of the atom, which is the basic power of the universe. As President Truman said, "the force from which the sun draws its power has been loosed against those who brought war to the Far East."

The imagination-sweeping experiment in harnessing the power of the atom has been the most closely guarded secret of the war. America to date has spent nearly $2,000,000,000 in advancing its research. Since 1939, American, British and Canadian scientists have worked on it. The experiments have been conducted in the United States, both for reasons of achieving concentrated efficiency and for security; the consequences of having the material fall into the hands of the enemy, in case Great Britain should have been successfully invaded, were too awful for the Allies to risk.

All along, it has been a race with the enemy. Ironically enough, Germany started the experiments, but we finished them. Germany made the mistake of expelling, because she was a "non-Aryan," a woman scientist who held one of the keys to the mystery, and she made her knowledge available to those who brought it to the United States. Germany never quite mastered the riddle, and the United States, Secretary Stimson declared, is "convinced that Japan will not be in a position to use an atomic bomb in this war."

Not the slightest spirit of braggadocio is discernible either in the wording of the official announcements or in the mien of the officials who gave out the news. There was an element of elation in the realization that we had perfected this devastating weapon for employment against an enemy who started the war and has told us she would rather be destroyed than surrender, but it was grim elation. There was sobering awareness of the tremendous responsibility involved.

Secretary Stimson said that this new weapon "should prove a tremendous aid in the shortening of the war against Japan," and there were other responsible officials who privately thought that this was an extreme understatement and that Japan might find herself unable to stay in the war under the coming rain of atom bombs.

It was obvious that officials at the highest levels made the important decision to release news of the atomic bomb because of the psychological effect it may have in forcing Japan to surrender. However, there are some officials who feel privately it might have been well to keep this completely secret. Their opinion can be summed up in the comment by one spokesman: "Why bother with psychological warfare against an enemy that already is beaten and hasn't sense enough to quit and save herself from utter doom?"

No details were given on the plane that carried the bomb. Nor was it stated whether the bomb was large or small. The President, however, said the explosive charge was "exceedingly small." It is known that tremendous force is packed into tiny quantities of the element that constitutes these bombs. Scientists, looking to the peacetime uses of atomic power envisage submarines, ocean liners and planes traveling around the world on a few pounds of the element. Yet, for various reasons, the bomb used against Japan could have been extremely large.

Hiroshima, first city on earth to be the target of the "Cosmic Bomb," is a city of 318,000 which is—or was—a major quartermaster depot and port of embarkation for the Japanese. In addition to large military supply depots, it manufactured ordnance, mainly large guns and tanks, and machine tools and aircraft-ordnance parts.

President Truman grimly told the Japanese that "the end is not yet. In their present form these bombs are now in production," he said, "and even more powerful forms are in development."

He sketched the story of how the late President Roosevelt and Prime Minister Churchill agreed that it was wise to concentrate research in America, and how great secret cities sprang up in this country, where, at one time, 125,000 men and women labored to harness the atom. Even today more than 65,000 workers are employed.

"What has been done," he said, "is the greatest achievement of organized science in history. We are now prepared to obliterate more rapidly and completely every productive enterprise the Japanese have above ground in any city. We shall destroy their docks, their factories and their communications. Let there be no mistake; we shall completely destroy Japan's power to make war."

The President emphasized that the atomic discoveries were so important, both for the war and for the peace, that he would recommend to Congress that it consider promptly establishing "an appropriate commission to control the production and use of atomic power within the United States."

"I shall give further consideration and make further recommendations to the Congress as to how atomic power can become a powerful and forceful influence toward the maintenance of world peace," he said.

Secretary Stimson called the atomic bomb "the culmination of years of herculean effort on the part of science and industry, working in cooperation with the military authorities." He promised that "improvements will be forthcoming shortly which will increase by several fold the present effectiveness."

"But more important for the long-range implications of this new weapon," he said, "is the possibility that another scale of magnitude will be developed after considerable research and development." The scientists are confident that over a period of many years atomic bombs may well be developed which will be very much more powerful than the atomic bombs now at hand.

[The plants which manufactured the atom bombs] were amazing phenomena in themselves. They grew into large, self-sustaining cities, employing thousands upon thousands of workers. Yet, so close was the secrecy that not only were the citizens of the area kept in darkness about the nature of the project, but the workers themselves had only the sketchiest ideas—if any—as to what they were doing. This was accomplished, Mr. Stimson said, by "compartmentalizing" the work so "that no one had been given more information than was absolutely necessary to his particular job."

A special laboratory also has been set up near Santa Fe, N.M., under direction of Dr. J. Robert Oppenheimer of the University of California. Dr. Oppenheimer also supervised the first test of the atomic bomb on July 16, 1945. This took place in a remote section of the New Mexico desert lands, with a group of eminent scientists gathered, frankly fearful to witness the results of the invention which might turn out to be either the salvation or the Frankenstein's monster of the world.

"Atomic fission holds great promise for sweeping developments by which our civilization may be enriched when peace comes, but the overriding necessities of war have precluded the full exploration of peacetime applications of this new knowledge," Mr. Stimson said. "However, it appears inevitable that many useful contributions to the well-being of mankind will ultimately flow from these discoveries when the world situation makes it possible for science and industry to concentrate on these aspects."

Although warning that many economic factors will have to be considered "before we can say to what extent atomic energy will supplement coal, oil and water as fundamental sources of power," Mr. Stimson acknowledged that "we are at the threshold of a new industrial art which will take many years and much expenditure of money to develop."

The War Department gave this supplementary background on the development of the atomic bomb:

The series of discoveries which led to the development of the atomic bomb started at the turn of the century when radioactivity became known to science. Prior to 1939, the scientific work in this field was world-wide, but more particularly so in the United States, the United Kingdom, Germany, France, Italy, and Denmark. One of Denmark's great scientists, Dr. Neils Bohr, a Nobel prize winner, was whisked from the grasp of the Nazis in his occupied homeland and later assisted in developing the atomic bomb.

It is known that Germany worked desperately to solve the problem of controlling atomic energy.

QUESTIONS FOR DISCUSSION

1. Like the articles by Connor and Alperovitz (pp. 109–113), this article was written for a newspaper. Does the article answer the five Ws (who, what, when, where, and why) of journalistic writing? Describe those answers.
2. How might an article for a newspaper be organized differently from a magazine article? How do you account for the difference?
3. How does the solemnity of Truman's announcement contrast with the tone of the rest of the article?
4. Was the ultimatum for the benefit of sparing the Japanese? What other motives might be involved?
5. No other nation besides the United States has ever used a nuclear weapon against another nation. How might this fact affect the attitudes of citizens of other nations toward the U.S.?
6. The author seems aware of the risk of a nuclear arms race and the possible annihilation of human life ("Frankenstein's monster"). So does Truman in setting up a commission. Are the benefits of nuclear technology worth the risks?
7. Discuss the anticipated positive outcomes of nuclear technology mentioned in the article. Remember that this article was written the day after the bomb was dropped.
8. What justifications do the President and the military officials offer for dropping the bomb?
9. Why isn't human destruction described? Consider Shalett's audience and purpose.

MASUJI IBUSE
Black Rain

Masuji Ibuse's Black Rain *(1969) describes the experiences of a Japanese family in Hiroshima before, during, and after the dropping of the atomic bomb in 1945. This fictional account is based on Ibuse's research of the stories of actual victims of the bombing. In the segment reprinted here, a couple— Shigematsu (husband) and Shigeko (wife)—and their niece Yasuko are traveling through the atomic rubble in an absurd quest for normalcy. While Shigematsu and Shigeko have escaped extreme exposure to radiation, Yasuko, playing in the schoolyard during the bombing, was drenched by the "black rain" which fell on some areas of the city. Although some American officials of the time claimed that the black rain was harmless, Yasuko later in the novel becomes critically ill. This selection presents several contrasts with the account of the bombing presented by Shalett (p. 113), and with the American high school textbook representation of the event (p. 127).*

Still Shigematsu continued the transcription of his "Journal of the Bombing." This month, he reflected, was a succession of festivals. The Mass for Dead Insects had gone by already; the Rice-Planting Festival came on the eleventh, and the Iris Festival, by the old lunar calendar, on the fourteenth. On the fifteenth there was the River Imp Festival, and on the twentieth the Bamboo-Cutting Festival. In all these countless little festivals he seemed to sense the affection that the peasants of the past, poor though they were, had lavished on each detail of their daily lives. And as he wrote on, and the horrors of that day came back to him ever more vividly, it seemed to him that in their very insignificance these farmers' festivals were something to be loved and cherished. . . .

We reached the streetcar stop at Kamiya-chō. The streetcar tracks crossed each other here, and broken overhead wires and cables hung down in tangled profusion over the road. I had a terrifying feeling that one or the other of them must be live, since these were the same wires that one usually saw emitting fierce, bluish-white sparks. The occasional refugees who passed to and fro had the sense to crouch down as they passed beneath them.

I wanted to take the left-hand edge of the road across Aioi Bridge to Sakan-chō, but the heat from the still-smoldering fires seemed likely to bar the way. I tried turning to the right, but a blast of hot air swept over me with an authority that would have made the bravest man waver, so I turned back again. Even so, as I approached a Western-style brick building, a great lump of glowing charcoal came hurtling down from what had been the window frames.

The only alternative was to go along the middle of the road. Since the overhead wires were cut at various points, there was no likelihood of their being live, but the very fact that they were crossing and touching each other made one fear some display of the mysterious properties of electricity. Beneath one of the dangling wires lay the blackened bodies of a man and two women. We, too, numbered two women and one man.

"Come on, under the wires after me!" I called. "Whatever you do, don't touch the wires. I'll hold them out of the way. If I get a shock don't touch anything except my clothes. Do you understand?—you get hold of the end of my trouser leg and drag me away." I followed the example of the other refugees, and pushed the wires away to either side with a piece of stick, crawling on all fours when necessary, crouching down when necessary.

"Look," I yelled back again. "Wrap a towel round your left elbow like those people have done. Your left elbow goes on the ground."

Time and again it was necessary to crouch down beneath the wires, but at last we were safely past. We stopped and took stock of each other. Shigeko was completely unscathed, but Yasuko, who had wound the towel round her arm in the wrong way, had a painful-looking graze on her elbow.

Shigeko sat down beside her on a stone by the roadside and attended to her elbow with mentholatum and a triangular bandage. Suddenly, it occurred to me that we were directly in front of an entrance that I knew.

"Just a moment—" I said, "Surely that stone's one from Mr. Ōmuro's garden?"

The Ōmuros in question were an old family, said to date back to the Edo period, and the present head was engaged in chemical research on spinning thread. He was a man of property, owning mills in three different places, as well as dabbling in calligraphy, painting, and art-collecting. I had visited the house myself several times during the past year for the benefit of his advice on matters concerning textile products. It had been an imposing mansion, with a splendid old-style garden. Now, however, it was completely razed to the ground. Where the main building and clay-walled storehouse had once stood was an arid waste scattered with broken tiles. The stone on which Shigeko and Yasuko were sitting was almost certainly a rock from the garden inside the grounds. Rock though it was, a thin layer had been burned away all over it.

"That rock's granite, you know," I said. "I expect it was covered with moss only this morning."

"Do you think the whole household was wiped out, then?" said Shigeko.

I did not reply. It was a scene of cruel desolation. Where the ornamental pond had been was an uneven stretch of blackish mud, and at the foot of a rounded hillock of earth lay the blackened skeletons of three large pine trees. Beside the trunk of the thickest of the three stood a narrow, square pillar of stone. Why it alone should have remained standing was a mystery. Mr. Ōmuro had once told me that an ancestor of his, several generations back, had had it erected there. It was somewhat over ten feet tall, and instead of the usual long inscription it had the single character "Dream" carved on it, about two and a half feet from the top. Some high-ranking priest was said to have written the original, and the effect was doubtless considered stylish and rather sophisticated in its day, but at present, style and sophistication alike failed utterly.

Both Shigeko and Yasuko were deathly pale. My throat was so dry it felt as though it might close up entirely, and a slight tic affected my eye as I walked.

We reached the entrance to the West Parade Ground. The grass on the west side of the embankment had been burned away, leaving the earth smooth and bare. The trees seemed to have been carbonized where they stood, and retained their branches, but not a single leaf. The divisional commander's residence, the temporary army hospital, the Gokoku Shrine and, of course, the keep of Hiroshima Castle, were all gone.

My eyes began to hurt, so I massaged them as I walked by rubbing the eyelids with my fingers. They smarted, and at the same time felt as though there was grit in them. Shigeko and Yasuko had cheered up a little, and were talking about the now vanished mushroom cloud—its size, its shape, its color, the shape of its stalk, and the way it had moved. Concluding that my eyes hurt because I had too much blood in the head, I had Yasuko give me the treatment they used to give children who had nosebleed. It consisted of no more than pulling out three hairs from the back of the head, but it helped the pain a little.

The West Parade Ground was an unbroken expanse of sand. It reminded me of a vast desert I had seen in a movie called "Morocco." Even in the film, the desert had seemed to exhale a smell of sand, and it had been quite empty, with not a single footprint visible. The sandy waste of the parade ground, however, was rather different: the hot breath it gave off stank of smoke, and there were a number of human trails leading away in the direction of the hills. It must have been raining. The sand was fine enough for holes the size of broad beans to be visible all over its surface, and the newspapers scattered here and there were covered with countless bean-sized black spots. The black rain had evidently fallen here. I had realized that the stalk of the mushroom cloud was a shower, but I had not imagined that the drops were as big as this.

At the western edge of the ground, we found a number of what looked like round black balls lying in the sand. At first I could not identify them, but as I got closer I realized they were lumps of what had been tin sheeting. They must have been torn away by the blast and have risen up into the sky, where they had been softened by the intense heat, then kneaded into balls by the wind before falling. To have gone quite round, like dumplings, they must have been sucked up into the great whirlwind of flame and have spun round and round furiously before finally descending to earth.

I glanced back across the sandy waste. A solitary figure—a boy wearing his underpants and an undershirt that flapped in the breeze at the front, exposing his naked belly—was walking rapidly in the direction of the hills. "Hi!" he called, turning in our direction and waving his hand at us. It seemed a peculiarly pointless gesture.

We walked on northwards. By the bank skirting the Gokoku Shrine a sentry stood with his rifle at order. Closer to, we found he was dead at his post, his back propped against the embankment, his eyes wide and staring. The badge on his collar showed him to be a private first-class in the army. He was about thirty-seven or eight, and old for a ranker, yet his features had an indefinable air of breeding.

"Why—just like the soldier with his bugle," said Shigeko.

"Come woman, mind your tongue," I said sternly, though if the truth be told I, too, had been reminded of the same story—of the bugler found dead at his post during the Sino-Japanese War, with his bugle still held to his lips.

The area was near the point where the bomb had been dropped. We saw another of them at the west corner of the grounds of Hiroshima Castle: a young man, still on his bicycle and carrying a wooden box as though on his way to deliver an order from a restaurant, propped dead against the stone ramparts. This one was a mere youth, and as skinny as a grasshopper.

We had often been taught during air raid drill that one must always breathe out steadily while a bomb was falling. Perhaps the sentry and the delivery boy had been breathing in at the moment the bomb burst? I did not understand the physiology of it, but it occurred to me that a blast just as one had filled one's lungs to capacity might well press on them and cause instant death.

We were taking a rest just this side of the embankment when we were hailed by an acquaintance, Police Sergeant Susumu Satō.

"Hello—I'm glad to see you safe," I said.

"Why, your face has caught it, hasn't it?" he said.

I spoke to him for a while before joining the others, and he told me that Superintendent-General Ōtsuka of the Chūgoku District Commissary had been trapped under his home and burned to death.

I had not known that Satō had been transferred from the police station to the Chūgoku District Commissary. I had not even known, in fact, that there existed a government office of that name. It was most remiss of me. I learned for the first time from Satō that the enemy's attacks had grown so fierce recently that it had been decided that Japan must prepare to do battle on home territory. Local governing agencies known as "district commissaries" had been set up, so that the struggle could be continued in each region independently should the country be split up by enemy forces. With the same objective, war materials had been stored at factories and primary schools throughout the area in which Hiroshima stood.

"So that's what it meant—" I said, "the slogan about the war only just beginning."

"Yes," said Satō, "the idea is to go ahead with the grand policy of a wealthy and militarily powerful nation launched over half a century ago. It's not for you or me to assume that this is a kind of tragic finale. *This* is precisely what we've been brought up for. It's fate."

The Chūgoku Commissary, located in the Hiroshima University of Liberal Arts and Science, had had responsibility for the five prefectures of the Chūgoku district. The Superintendent-General himself—Isei Ōtsuka, a man with the bearing of an old-time samurai—had been in the Superintendent-General's official residence at Kami-Nagaregawa-machi when the bomb fell, and had been caught beneath the house. His wife had managed with great difficulty to crawl out of the wreckage, but the Superintendent-General had been hopelessly trapped. The good lady had been beside herself, but the Superintendent-General had insisted on her leaving him. "I'm ready for whatever comes," he had said. "Get yourself away, woman, as fast as you can." The flames were already close at hand, so she had had no choice but to flee.

"The Superintendent-General was cremated where he lay. A ghastly business," Satō said. "I myself didn't know which way to run from the flames." His eyes filled with tears. Normally, his manner of speech was cheerful and his face gave an immediate impression of openness and sunniness, but today his eyes were bloodshot and his face grim.

Arriving on the embankment, we found the middle section of Misasa Bridge missing. Changing my plan, I set off along the embankment downstream with the idea of crossing Aioi Bridge. Countless dead bodies were lying in the undergrowth at the foot of the embankment on our right. Other bodies came floating in steady succession along the river. Every so often, one of them would catch on the roots of a riverside willow, swing round with the current, and suddenly rear its face out of the water. Or one would come along rocking in the water, so that first its upper half then its lower half bobbed to the surface. Or another would swing round beneath a willow tree and raise its arms as though to grasp at a branch, so that it almost seemed, for a moment, to be alive.

We had sighted from some way off the body of a woman who lay stretched out dead across the path on top of the embankment. Suddenly Yasuko, who was walking ahead of us, came running back with a cry of "Uncle! Uncle!" and burst into tears. As I drew closer, I saw a baby girl of about three who had opened the corpse's dress at the top and was playing with the breasts. When we came up to her, she clutched tight at both breasts and gazed up at us with apprehensive eyes.

What could we possibly do for her? To ask ourselves this was our only recourse. I stepped gently over the corpse's legs so as not to frighten the little girl, and walked briskly on another ten yards or so downstream. Here I spotted another group of four or five women dead together in the undergrowth, and a boy of five or six crouched on the ground as though caught between the bodies.

"Come along," I called waving with both arms to the others, who were still hesitating. "Just step over it as quietly as possible and come on." Shigeko and Yasuko stepped over the body and joined me.

At the end of Aioi Bridge we found a carter and the ox harnessed to his cart both seated, dead, on the electric car tracks. The ropes around the load had come undone, and the goods had been rifled.

Here, too, the corpses came floating one after the other down the river, and it was a sickening sight to see them butt their heads against the piers of the bridge and swivel round in the water. Near its center, the bridge reared in a hump about a yard high, and on what one might have called the crest of the wave a young foreigner with fair hair lay dead with his arms clasped about his head. The surface of the bridge was distorted and undulating.

Around Sakan-chō and Sorazaya-chō, it was clear that the flames had swept evenly across the whole area. The corpses lay scattered in every conceivable condition—one with only the upper half of the body burned to the bone, one completely skeletonized save for one arm and one leg, another lying face down, consumed from the knees down, yet another with the two legs alone cremated—and an unspeakable stench hanging over all. Nauseating though the odor was, there was no way to escape it.

In Tera-machi, the "temple quarter," not a single temple was standing. All that remained was clay walls crumbled and collapsed till they were barely recognizable, and venerable trees with their limbs torn open to expose the naked wood within. Even the branch of the Honganji temple, famed as the greatest temple building in the whole quarter, had vanished without trace. The smoke still rising from the embers drifted menacingly over the crumbling walls, then crept low over the surface of the river till it vanished at the other bank.

On the other side of Yokogawa Bridge the flames were still rising. Fanned by the wind, fires were swirling white-hot up to the skies from the whole area on the opposite bank. To approach was out of the question.

We found the road ahead completely blocked on this side of the bridge. The iron girders forming the bow-shaped framework of the bridge were discolored up to a height of some twelve to fifteen feet, and close to one of the piers of the bridge that rested on a stretch of grass stood a horse badly burned on its back and the back of its head. It was trembling violently and looked as though it might collapse at any moment. Close by its side a corpse, the upper half burned away, lay face downwards. The lower half, which was untouched, wore army breeches and boots with spurs. The spurs actually gleamed gold. If the owner had been an army man, then he had been an officer, for only an officer could wear boots with gold spurs like that. I pictured the scene to myself: the officer running to the stables, mounting his horse barebacked, rushing outside. . . . The horse must have been a favorite of the soldier's. Though it was on the verge of collapse, it still seemed—or was it my imagination?—to be yearning for some sign from the man in the spurred boots. How immeasurable the pain it must have felt, with the west-dipping sun beating down unmercifully on its burned flesh; how immeasurable its love for the man in the boots! But pity eluded me: I felt only a shudder of horror.

Our only choice was to walk on through the river. Close to the bank there were grassy shoals, but in places they were too far apart for us to tread dry ground all the time. We stepped into the flowing water and set off walking upstream. Even at its deepest, the water only came up to our knees. The district we were passing through would have been Hirose Kitamachi or thereabouts. On the sandy parts, where the river had dried up, our shoes spouted water with a squelching sound. No sooner did the water empty out of them a little, and walking become a little pleasanter, than the sand would start getting in our shoes and almost lame us with the pain.

We decided it was actually better to walk in the water, and splashed on regardless. On a pebbly shoal a man lay with both hands thrust in the water, drinking. We approached, thinking to join him, and found he was not drinking water but dead, with his face thrust down into the water.

"I wonder if the water in this river is poisonous, then?" said Yasuko, voicing my own unspoken question.

"There's no telling," I replied, setting off through the water again. "But perhaps we'd better not drink it."

The smoke blowing across from the town gradually diminished, and paddy fields appeared on our right, so we clambered up a crumbling stone wall and onto the bank.

We reached the rice fields. Walking along the raised paths between them in the direction of the electric car tracks, we came across a number of schoolgirls and schoolboys lying here and there in the fields, dead. They must have fled in disorder from the factory where they had been doing war work. There were adults lying about too. One of them, an elderly man, had fallen across the path, and the front of his jacket was soaked with water. He had evidently drunk to bursting point from the paddy field water, then—either unable to care any more or in a fit of vertigo—subsided onto the ground and expired where he lay.

We stepped over the body and wound our way, first left then right, along the paths between the fields, till finally they led us into a bamboo grove. The grove must have been kept for the purpose of gathering bamboo shoots, for the undergrowth was well cut back. Finding ourselves in cool, leafy shade at last, we sank to the ground without exchanging a word.

I unfastened my first-aid kit, took off my air raid hood and my shoes, and sprawled out on my back. At once my body seemed to be dissolving into thin air, and before I knew it I had slipped into a deep slumber.

I awoke, I knew not how long after, to a raging thirst and a pain in my throat. My wife and Yasuko were both lying with their heads pillowed on their arms. I rolled onto my belly, and, filching the quart bottle of water out of my wife's rucksack, drank. It was a heaven-sent nectar. I had had no idea that water was so good. The ecstasy was touched, almost, with a kind of pride. I must have drunk all of a third of a pint.

My wife and Yasuko awoke too. By now, the sun was sinking toward the west. Without a word Shigeko took the bottle I handed her and, lifting it with both hands, drank greedily. She probably drank another third of a pint. Then she passed the bottle to Yasuko, also without a word. Yasuko in her turn raised it with both hands. She paused between each mouthful, but every time she upended the bottle a stream of bubbles ran up through it and the remaining water decreased visibly. I was almost despairing of her leaving any at all, when she finally put the bottle down with about one-third of a pint still in it.

From her rucksack, my wife took out the cucumbers she had brought for want of anything better, and opened a packet of salt. The cucumbers were blackened and discolored on one side. "Where did you buy these?" I asked. "Mrs. Murakami from Midori-chō brought them for us this morning," she said.

Early that morning, apparently, Mrs. Murakami had brought us three cucumbers and a dozen or so tiny dried fish, of the kind used in flavoring soup, in return for a share of some tomatoes that Shigeko's people in the country had sent us. Shigeko had left the cucumbers in a bucket of water by the pool in the garden, and the flash from the bomb had discolored them.

"It's funny," I said. "When I went back to the house from the university sports ground, the basket worms were eating the leaves of the azalea. The cucumber was burned, but the insects were still alive."

I dipped the cucumber in the salt and turned the question over in my mind as I ate. Some physical reaction had obviously taken place on the surface of the water in the bucket. Could it be that reflection inside the bucket had stepped up the amount of heat and light? Glancing at the pond as I went to sink the mosquito net in the water, I had noticed basket worms on the azalea that grew out over the water, busily eating the new summer buds. I shook the branch, and they drew back into their baskets, but when I got back from collecting pieces of brick to sink the net with, they were busily eating once more. The buds themselves were not discolored, nor were the worms' baskets burned, which suggested that light and heat had caused some chemical change when it came up against metal. Or had the basket worms and azalea been sheltered by the house, or by some other obstacle, when the bomb had burst? The rice plants in the open paddy fields seemed to have been affected by the flash. It seemed likely that they, too, would have turned black by the following morning.

I washed my small towel in a ditch at the edge of the bamboo grove, wiped my right cheek and the sinews of my neck, then rinsed the towel time and time again. I wrung it out and rinsed it, wrung it out and rinsed it, repeating the same seemingly pointless procedure over and over again. To wring out my towel was the one thing, it seemed to me, that I was free to do as I pleased at that moment. My left cheek smarted painfully. A shoal of minnows was swimming in the ditch, and in a patch of still water the flags were growing in profusion. Here is shadow, they seemed to say, here is safety. . . .

Smoke came drifting from deep within the bamboo grove. Going to investigate, I peered through the bamboos and saw a group of refugees who had built a shelter of green bamboo and branches and were preparing a meal. They seemed to have been burned out of their homes and to be making ready to spend the night out.

I strained my ears to catch their conversation. It seemed from what they said that the houses along the main highway had all closed their shutters in order to keep out refugees. At one sundry goods store this side of Mitaki Station on the Kabe line, they had found a woman who had got in unnoticed and died in one of their closets. When the owner of the store dragged the body out, he found that the garment it was wearing was his own daughter's best summer kimono. Scandalized, he had torn the best kimono off the body, only to find that it had no underwear on underneath. She must have been burned out of her home and fled all the way there naked, yet still— being a young woman—sought something to hide her nakedness even before she sought water or food. The refugees were wondering whether bombs like today's would be dropped on other cities besides Hiroshima. What were Japan's battleships and land forces up to, they were asking each other. It would be a wonder if there weren't a civil war. . . .

I made my way back quietly through the bamboo, and with a "Come on" to the others started to get ready. I had a stabbing pain in my toes. "Come on," I urged them again, but neither Shigeko nor Yasuko made any reply. They seemed utterly exhausted. "Well, then, I'm off!" I said sharply, and this time they reluctantly got to their feet and started to get ready.

Walking made my toes hurt so that I nearly danced with the pain. The others were complaining of the pain too. I myself must have walked some ten or eleven miles already. My wife had walked five or six, and Yasuko about five. We ate parched rice as we walked. We would thrust a hand into the cloth bag my wife was carrying, take out a handful and, putting it in our mouths, chew on it as we walked. It gradually turned to sugar, and tasted sweet in the mouth; it was better than either the water or the cucumber. The most effective way seemed to be to chew as one walked, and I could understand why travelers in olden times took parched rice with them as rations for the journey. Finally, one gulped it down, then took another handful out of the cloth bag and put it in one's mouth. Parched rice may be very unappetizing-looking, but I gave thanks in my heart to my wife's folk for sending it.

The main highway was dotted with refugees. Just as I had overheard the people in the bamboo grove saying, the houses by the roadside all had their doors and shutters fastened. Where there was a roofed gateway, its doors were shut fast. Outside one of the gates with shut doors lay a bundle of straw scorched by fire. I wondered if passing refugees had set fire to it.

However far we went, still the houses along the road had their doors shut. Here the breeze was cool, unlike the hot breath of the town, and ripples were running over the rice plants in the paddy fields. The fathers from the Catholic church on the north side of Yamamoto Station went running past us at top speed, carrying a stretcher. With them was one father, a man past middle age, whom I had often seen on the Kabe-bound train on my way to work. He came panting along far behind the others carrying the stretcher, and as he passed me he glanced into my face and nodded briefly in recognition. "Good luck to you," I called after him.

At last, we reached Yamamoto Station. From here on, the trains were running. A train was standing in the station, every coach full, but we managed to squeeze our way into the vestibule of one of them. Wedged tight, I tried to make more room by nudging at a bundle directly in front of me. Wrapped in a cloth, it rested on the shoulders of a woman of about thirty. Somehow, it felt different from a bundle of belongings, so I tried touching it furtively with my hand. I contacted what felt like a human ear: a child seemed to be in the bundle. To carry a child in such a fashion was outrageous. It was almost certain to suffocate in such a crush.

"Excuse me Ma'am," I said softly. "Is it your child in here?"

"Yes," she said in a scarcely audible voice. "He's dead."

"I'm sorry," I said, taken aback. "I didn't know. . . . I really must apologize, to be pushing and. . . ."

"Not at all," she said gently. "None of us can help it in such a crowd." She hitched the bundle up, bent her head, and was seized with a fit of weeping.

"It was when the bomb burst," she said through her sobs. "The sling of his hammock broke, and he was dashed against the wall and killed. Then the house started to burn, so I wrapped him in a quilt cover and brought him away on my back. I'm taking him to my old home in Iimori, so I can bury him in the cemetery there."

She stopped weeping, and ceased talking at the same time. I could not bring myself to address her any further.

A kite was wheeling in the air above the wires. The cicadas were chirping, and a dabchick was bustling about the pond with waterlilies by the side of the highway. A perfectly commonplace scene that somehow seemed quite extraordinary. . . .

The conductor announced the train's imminent departure, and a fiercer clamor arose from those who had not succeeded in getting on. The train lurched forward and stopped, lurched and stopped again.

"What the hell're you up to? Are you starting or aren't you?" bellowed a voice, to be followed by another voice that launched into a speech somewhere inside the coach: "Ladies and gentlemen, you can see for yourselves how sadly decadent the National Railways have become. Concerned only with carrying black market goods, they have nothing but contempt for the ordinary passenger. . . ." But this time the train glided smoothly into motion, and the rest of the speech was lost forever in the clatter of its wheels.

QUESTIONS FOR DISCUSSION

1. This text is a fictional account of the bombing based on the diaries of survivors. Contrast the impact of this style of writing with the journalistic style of Shalett (p. 113). Discuss the effectiveness of such fictional techniques as dialogue, characterization, and irony.
2. How might the festivals mentioned in the first paragraph have been affected by the bombing?

3. What is the narrator of the story describing? What are the characters looking for? Their search for normalcy is clearly absurd: why do they continue?
4. What are some of the horrors the three encounter as they return through the wreckage to their home?
5. What surprises you about the way the victims react to the bombing?
6. Some scientists asserted that the "black rain" that fell after the bomb was dropped was completely harmless. What effects do you think the black rain will have on the niece?
7. How could the information presented in this fictionalized account of the bombing be synthesized into a historical account? How would the impact of the information be affected?

SUZANNE H. SANKOWSKY
Mainstreams of World History

The following excerpt from the high school textbook Mainstreams of World History *describes the use of the atomic bomb by America on the Japanese cities of Hiroshima and Nagasaki. The bombing is placed in the context of the American war effort. Contrast this text with the account of the bombing presented by Ibuse (p. 117).*

The Japanese are defeated. Even while the main military effort was being directed against Germany, the Allied offensive in the Pacific was making progress. But after Germany's defeat the Americans and the British greatly intensified their struggle against Japan. This was a war in which naval vessels, especially aircraft carriers, and planes played major roles. In the fall of 1944, U.S. forces retook the Philippines and Guam from Japan, while the British drove the enemy out of Burma. In the following months, the British pushed toward Malaya, while American forces continued the "island hopping" drive toward the main islands of Japan. The fighting was especially severe on the islands of Saipan, Iwo Jima, and Okinawa. Thousands of American lives were lost before these places were taken.

In July, 1945, Japan received an official ultimatum from the United Nations leaders: surrender unconditionally or be completely destroyed. The military rulers of Japan ignored the ultimatum, and the country paid a most terrible penalty. On August 6 and 9 two atomic bombs were dropped, the first one on Hiroshima and the second on Nagasaki, destroying most of each city and killing or injuring vast numbers of the inhabitants. Only then did the Japanese leaders surrender and ask for peace.

The whole world was shocked and startled at the announcement of the atomic bombs, which had been developed in utmost secrecy. (This spectacular accomplishment was made possible by the contributions of scientists of several countries who had been working on nuclear fission—the splitting of the atom.) Never before had such a destructive force been known, and people were therefore greatly alarmed at the new possibilities of warfare.

On the day before the second atom bombing, Soviet Russia had declared war against Japan and had sent troops into Manchuria and Korea. On August 14, Japan surrendered. But formal surrender took place on the U.S.S. *Missouri* September 2. General Douglas MacArthur was put in command of the occupation of the defeated country. The war was now over and the United Nations celebrated V-J (Victory in Japan) Day.

QUESTIONS FOR DISCUSSION

1. Who is this book written for? In what ways do you think the information presented here is modified for its audience? What is the purpose of the account? How might the content have been modified to accord with that purpose?
2. What information is given? What is left out? Why might this information have been omitted?
3. How might a Japanese textbook be different from this American one?
4. What information about the use of the atomic bomb do you think should be included in American high school textbooks? Justify your changes.
5. Analyze Sankowsky's diction. (Why does she describe the bombing as a "spectacular accomplishment," [par. 3] for example?) Compare and contrast Sankowsky's diction with that of Shalett (p. 113) and Ibuse (p. 117).

ANN SNITOW
The Paradox of Birth Technology

A teacher of literature in New York City at Eugene Lang College of the New School for Social Research, Ann Snitow wrote "The Paradox of Birth Technology" (1986) for a symposium titled "The Politics of the New Reproductive Technologies," sponsored by New York University. Snitow presents a case in favor of legal abortion; she also discusses prenatal genetic testing, test tube fertilization, and fetal therapy as areas of potential controversy equal to that surrounding the issue of abortion.
Arguing that scientific intervention in the birth process could take choices out of the hands of women and place them within the realm of medical responsibility, Snitow, like Margaret Mead and Rachel Carson, warns that all people must understand and carefully evaluate the advantages and disadvantages of such technology.

Activists used to call reproduction "gut level" material. To have dignity and self-determination, women need the right to safe, legal, affordable abortions, in other words, the power to intervene in the biological processes of our own bodies. As a feminist, I expected that—in this area at least—I would always be unambivalent, would always know my own best interests and true desires.

But no. Though I'm still as unambivalent as ever about abortion, abortion is now only one in a swiftly proliferating number of possible ways to intervene in reproduction. These developments, which have come to be called collectively "the new reproductive technologies," are of very different kinds, and pose a disturbing array of questions. The new technologies have the potential to take control and autonomy away from women in newfangled ways. But, at the same time, I'm attracted by the possibilities, which I see as part of a long line of social developments—like easily available contraception and assisted childbirth—that have changed women's lives fundamentally, and for the better. After all, why not start an embryo in a petri dish? Or take an egg from one woman and plant it in another's uterus? Isn't it an unlooked-for advance that doctors can now lift a fetus from the womb, operate on it for problems discovered by new methods, then return it again?

But the pace of these changes makes them particularly hard to assess as social events. People working in the field themselves say that 10 years ago they would not have guessed how fast developments would unfold in prenatal genetic testing, in vitro fertilization, and fetal therapy (and, one might add, how fast they would be capitalized, would turn into big business). The social fallout of the technologies is beginning to register on the highly gendered culture of reproduction. Lately, as each innovation has rushed by on the news, I have felt tried in my essential metal as a feminist. What are women's short- and long-term best interests in each case?

I want to suggest that women might have grounds for responding to the new possibilities with hope and excitement. But as soon as I say this my next impulse is to bury my enthusiasm under an avalanche of second thoughts and cautionary tales. Why trust the experts with their infernal, only half-tested machines? I am struggling to locate myself between my typically American faith in a fatherly doctor and his devices, and my equally deep impulse to spurn the sexist pig for the arrogant impostor I have so often found him. (To give technology its due: I would probably be dead now if we still had only 19th-century medicine.)

Trying for a dialectical position, I find instead I'm making loops. Here's one: I begin by thinking it is useful and promising that embryos can be started outside a woman's body (the so-called test-tube baby). The procedure gives the infertile another chance, a new choice. But then an internal voice whispers, Must we all have our own genetic offspring or none at all? Such an idea narrows rather than broadens choice. If many of us feel that only the blood ties are deep and real, then an oppressive desperation lies behind the mushrooming high-tech baby business. Which leads me to the nasty underside of any new choice in American society: the price. How much do test-tube babies cost? And the services of a woman who might be hired to do the risky work of carrying the fetus to term? Who will be buying these new consumer options, who selling them in the form of blood and sweat and nine months of hard work? (Men get paid for sperm donations at about $50 a shot; surrogate mothers get about $10,000 for a live birth—sometimes nothing for a miscarriage. Do the math if you want to get depressed about the current, relative value of women's work in America. And yes, yes, I know: comically and maddeningly, the "work" is different in kind.)

My only comfort on these circular mental journeys is that the big social institutions surrounding the new reproductive technologies (the medical profession, the state legislatures, the judiciary) are confused, too—which can translate: still fluid. For example, in a current New Jersey case, the court is pondering whether a surrogate mother who decided after the baby was born that she wanted to keep it as a renegade contract-breaker or a distraught parent with a strong custody claim. My first impulse is to insist that Mary Beth Whitehead, the woman who went through pregnancy, must be able to keep the baby she agreed to bear for an infertile couple, Elizabeth and William Stern. Mr. Stern gave his semen, but Ms. Whitehead gave not only an egg but also nine months. The body makes its great and proper claim. But how *far* do feminists want to take this claim, that pregnancy makes women more naturally the privileged parent in a custody suit? How would we feel if the court turned around and said that biology is destiny, that mothers and children are linked by umbilical cords, which can never be socially severed?

Many feminists decry what is happening under current laws, such as custody and no-fault divorce statutes that take no note of gender and operate as if women come to court with the same needs, interests, and resources as men. But women have much to lose, too, when we are defined as a special case. Such patronizing public gestures are often part of a larger movement to separate women from change, to ensure that we will continue to be—and see ourselves—first and foremost as the bearers of children and the nurturers of everyone.

In fact, the paradox of the new reproductive technologies is that once the imagery of the miraculous and exotic is stripped away, a woman who tries to use these services is likely to find herself a partner in long-established duets that are sadly traditional—between men and women, doctors and patients, husbands and wives. Maybe it should be no surprise, but it is downright impressive how fast antifeminist politics have moved in on the new ground, setting up the old totem poles: the mother, to blame for her baby's so-called defects (Did she drink while pregnant? Did she smoke?) and responsible for handling whatever fortune dishes out, and the father, guardian of his own sperm. Sometimes by default of the imagination, sometimes by design, the more unruly possibilities—the new wine of the new technologies—are often poured back into old bottles.

Look what happened to Mary K., a single woman who decided to have a baby and raise the child jointly with a close friend, Victoria T., who lived nearby. The two women sought a sperm donor, interviewed several, and chose one Jhordan C. They did not know that in the state of California the civil code requires that in artificial insemination the sperm donation be made to a licensed physician if the mother is to be protected from future paternity claims from the sperm donor. (Statutes in Connecticut, Georgia, Oklahoma, and Oregon make it *illegal* for a person other than a physician to perform artificial insemination.) The day after baby Devin's birth, Jhordan went to see him and began to make visits on a limited basis. Mary, willing to be friendly up to a point and even to allow Jhordan to set up a trust fund for the baby, must have gotten alarmed; she stopped the visits. Jhordan sued, demanding both legal recognition as Devin's natural father and visitation rights. By March, 1986, he had won in two courts. The trial judge said: " . . . you are going to have a hard time convincing this court to call him [Jhordan] anything but the father of that child because I will not do that to that boy. . . . He wants to be a normal kid like any other kid."

Mary K. meant Jhordan C. to be her sperm donor, not the father of her child, and certainly not a permanent family member. Jhordan, essentially a stranger, is now an ongoing part of Mary, Devin, and Victoria's life together. Mary K.'s lawyer,

Roberta Achtenberg, points out that if Mary K. had been a married woman, Jhordan would never have won his paternity suit, since statutory law, in a majority of states, says the husband of an inseminated woman is considered the baby's father. The judge saw nothing wrong in Mary's powerlessness to control the shape of her family, but was deeply upset at the idea of lost fathers and of sons who are not "normal," not fathered. In other words, only a doctor (one of American society's most patriarchal figures) or a husband can protect a woman from that other rival patriarch, her sperm donor. So ruled two judges in the state of California, Anno Domini 1986.

This case demonstrates the troubling depth of the questions feminists must now face. If the *biology* of parenthood can be shifted around (think of parenthood without intercourse or of two biological mothers: egg donor and egg bearer) and, in addition, the *social* parents can boundlessly increase (think of the new parents children acquire through separation and divorce and of the varied emotional stakes of sperm donors and surrogates), what will be the relationship among all these people? Feminist thought includes a range of trial answers from hopefulness that the more parents, the more opportunities for love, to the belief that whatever the weaknesses of the nuclear family, as long as such families are a social ideal, women must have an equal right to form them and keep them private, excluding whom they choose. The unsettling scenarios multiply: When there are potentially two fathers (a woman's partner and her sperm donor), should the official "husband" figure (including Victoria T.) *always* have the sole claim in spite of the biological contribution of the sperm donor? When one woman gives the egg and another gestates it, how can *both* be protected from old and new forms of exploitation?

And such questions about rights are only the beginning. What about feelings? In the Whitehead-Stern surrogacy case, no one ever mentions Mr. Stern's wife; a silence surrounds the infertile, adopting mother, whose legal claim to the contested baby she is now caring for comes last on every list. But what pressure there must be on her: she is caring for a baby she may well lose. The boundaries of relatedness may be changeable, but just how flexible can our emotions about relatedness be? And even assuming that we are very flexible indeed, as I believe we are, flexibility is but one value among many. The task of imagining actual forms for the enduring ties of love among the generations remains.

These new worries confirm what feminists have been saying all along: childbirth and child-rearing are socially produced, not timeless, unchanging activities. The new reproductive technologies are contributing to a larger social shift. It's getting harder and harder to call parenting simple, natural, or unquestionable anymore. But now we're up against it: if parenting is *this* malleable, women's struggle for reproductive autonomy is only just beginning.

Feminists have always had a forked reaction to this unnervingly broad range of possibilities. In 1970, radical feminist Shulamith Firestone called pregnancy "barbaric" and demanded that women be freed from the "tyranny of their reproductive biology." The female doctor was a great Zeitgeist[1] figure that year. (In Myrna Lamb's play *But What Have You Done for Me Lately?*, a woman researcher invented the advanced technology to make a man pregnant.) But at the same time, the women's health movement was beginning its radical critique of how doctors manipulate their

---

[1]**Zeitgeist** German for "the spirit of the age"; refers to the particular outlook of a generation or period. [Ed. note.]

female patients, often creating their illnesses. These feminists refused to see pregnancy as women's problem, and blamed medicine for treating it as an incapacity rather than a strength.

The present feminist reaction to the new reproductive technologies includes—as it must—elements of both these earlier (and perennial) responses. At a first look, the negative take is far more compelling. The new technical "choices" are often a mockery of that treasured word. Take prenatal genetic screening: Is it a choice to know your baby *might* be born with a certain health problem, and this problem *might* be either mild or serious, and you *might* abort this so-called questionable fetus even though by the time you've got these inconclusive test results you're already in your fifth month? Some prenatal conditions, such as Down's syndrome, can be tested for quite accurately, but as disability-rights activist Anne Finger has said, such tests rule out only a small percentage of the problems a baby can have, while fostering the social fantasy that perfect babies are easy to engineer; that disabilities are a thing of the past; that the disabled are a dwindling minority. In fact, many disabilities come during or after birth, and as biologist Ruth Hubbard has pointed out, poor health care and workplace hazards are the real mass threats to fertility and fetal health. And, of course, the technologies themselves carry their own multiple risks. For example, sonograms are now used routinely. No one knows if they will turn out to have long-term ill effects, so large numbers of pregnant women are really test animals for future generations whose health the medical profession may be carelessly compromising.

For low-income women, such irresponsible medical practices are ironically compounded. First, women without money are underserved by doctors in the more routine, preventive side of health care; then, this initial deprivation leads to complications in pregnancy, making poor women particularly likely to need the fancy reproductive technologies they are the least able to afford.

The capital-intensive new technologies are typical of American medicine, which reaches for the high-tech response to disease rather than for more systemic, social solutions. We should view with skepticism the very way the medical establishment has defined the problems that the new technologies are being invented to solve. For example, is difficulty with conception most clearly identified as "rising infertility"? Or should we look at where infertility comes from and name the problem "toxic work environments" or "overpriced, hence postponed medical treatment," or "deferred childbearing due to inadequate child-care programs"? These diagnostic names are not catchy, but they come closer to describing the full situation.

The nasty underbelly of American medical priorities shows up with particular clarity in the statistics. Black women, who are disproportionately poor, are about one and a half times as likely as white women to have infertility problems. A black baby has a 12.4 percent chance of having a clinically low birth weight compared to a 5.6 percent chance for a white baby. Low birth weight is a predictor of a whole range of health problems that are not on the high-tech agenda at all. It's not that women don't need the new technologies, but that the technologies are not enough. They only make sense as part of expanded opportunities for reproductive health in general.

Statistics like these put the new medicine in its place. Each therapy or test invented enters where gender, race, and class set the stage, determining its use and its users. None is neutral, none blandly safe, none dependably offered with either fairness or restraint. As health care activist Laurie Nsiah-Jefferson has wryly pointed out, public family-planning agencies are not in the business of helping black women have more babies—even though fertility problems are supposed to be as much their province as birth control. Though most women using the new technologies are currently guinea pigs, black and Third World women are particularly vulnerable to being the objects of studies—like those early tests of the Pill in Puerto Rico—that provide low-cost health care because they are experimental.

This is the status quo that makes Firestone's high hopes for technology seem dreamy or callow. Certainly, times are bad for revolutionary enthusiasms. But the shamelessness with which Firestone celebrated the idea of separating women from fetuses is a reminder of the kind of radical feminism that demands to have abortion without ambivalence, public child care without guilt, lesbianism without giving up the right to have children, heterosexuality without isolation in the family.

And, right now, under our noses, women like Mary K. are galloping away with the possibilities. They are accepting the *idea* of intervention in pregnancy and are going ahead without fancy (or risky) inventions. With increasing visibility, they are carrying on the feminist self-help tradition, rejecting medical authority, inseminating themselves with donor sperm, using homey implements like turkey basters. They are bringing the resulting children into situations quite different from those laid down by either genetics or conventional social expectations. Often set adrift by the general loosening of family continuities implied by high divorce and single-parent rates, they are sailing right into the challenging high wind of complex recombinations—some with regrets but many, also, with exuberance.

In these hard times, I rejoice in this exuberance, in the panache of single mothers and the courage and wit of all those raising children with grace under pressure. As writer and historian Barbara Omolade wrote recently in an article that explored the rich survival tactics of black single mothers, "In a society where men are taught to dominate and women to follow, we all have a lot to overcome in learning to build relationships, with each other and with our children, based on love and justice. For many black single mothers, this is what the struggle is about." Right-wing politicians lump these struggles, these lively inventions, together as "breakdowns"—of the family, of conventional morals. And they are. But for women, ambivalence and skepticism about what "breakdown" may mean are always in order. The new technologies offer an occasion to speculate, and to organize. Those who want to add flexibility to present gender arrangements have the tactical advantage just now of surprise—our own as well as other people's.

I don't want to overstate the liberating possibilities. Women have a long memory of changes—in work, divorce, child custody—that we fought for but couldn't control. Our success has been ragged and costly, and many of the big changes in women's working and family lives don't line up solidly in the victory-and-progress column. With the new reproductive technologies it's particularly easy to project ironic nightmares in which mechanical devices steal our experience of intact, bodily reproductive power away, without giving us one iota of real liberation. Only today a disturbingly jubilant press packet arrived from a private fertility clinic in New Orleans, complete with a blue bubble-gum cigar marked "It's a boy," announcing the world's first test-tube baby to have its gender preselected. (Price tag, about $4,200.)

It's too early to know yet what "choice" is going to look like in *this* context. Will people choose boys as firstborns, or prefer them as only children? Certainly the mostly Newspeak[2] press release from New Orleans hints at these darker themes when fatuous boosterism flags: the father of the first in vitro sex selection in the world was an only son; now, he has replicated himself.

What the new reproductive technologies could do in a world of women's choosing may seem largely beside the point when a woman is trudging off to her doctor or clinic, waiting for hours, receiving information it is impossible to assess, undergoing procedures that are new and strange and that no one knows nearly enough about. (If her presenting symptom is infertility, success rates are only 50 percent; though 40 percent of fertility problems turn out to be the man's, it is women who usually run the first test gauntlet.) As she pays a huge bill or tries to convince an insurer that genetic testing, pregnancy, and problems with fertility deserve to be included in the definition of necessary health care, neither feminist self-help nor social revolution is likely to be the image uppermost in her mind. In the context of the cheerful sales rap from the clinic in New Orleans, it is not appropriate to end on a rising note.

But the case of Mary, her friend and coparent, Victoria, and her sperm donor, Jhordan, has a more positive fascination. Oh, to be King Solomon, test Jhordan C. and Victoria T., and choose which one is Devin's true parent with the kingly finality now affected by the courts. But both are connected to Devin, and the meaning of these connections is being fought out now; we live on this battleground. For good reason, women are reluctant to cede any of the ground of motherhood while we are relatively powerless. Right now it's obviously necessary to protect Mary K.'s family plans from Jhordan C.'s intrusion. Right now Jhordan's precedent-setting lawsuit makes him an enemy of women's reproductive autonomy. When Mary excluded Jhordan, she didn't necessarily mean to exclude men in general; what she *did* unequivocally do, however, is reject the overvalued category "father," with all the symbolic and actual clout the word implies. Feminists feel enraged for Mary, who has not been allowed to shape her childbearing, who has been invaded by Jhordan and the judge.

In the longer term, though, some moments of loss, of scary free-fall will be inevitable if we really want shifts in the shape of "home," "family," child care, and work. Where is it written that women, the childbearers, must *always* be much more enmeshed in child-rearing than men? Certainly, the Jhordan C.'s of this world are going to have to come to grips with how they feel about childbearing and intimacy. It seems fair to guess that Jhordan didn't *know* he would care so much about Devin. More than anything, this kind of ignorance threatens women's chances of making real childbearing alliances with men.

I don't know these people; I'm only inventing emotions for them. But the quadrille of Mary and Victoria, Jhordan and Devin feels like a new dance to me, inviting these flights of anxious speculation. A feminist lost in the thicket of the new reproductive technologies, at least I know savage gender politics when it comes my

---

[2]**Newspeak** Coined by George Orwell in the novel *1984* (1948); refers to the language of a bureaucracy, which confuses listeners, paralyzes action, and covers up truth. [Ed. note.]

way: in California, Jhordan C. has been allowed to ignore his verbal understanding with Mary K. that she was looking for a sperm donor, not a father. In New Jersey, William Stern may well win his case by having *his* contractual understanding with Mary Beth Whitehead legally supported. If that happens, in each case the rule of the father will have prevailed—the deal upheld or abrogated depending on what each father wants.

It falls to women to assert a counterorder—without reestablishing the myth of the eternal mother with her unending maternal responsibility. The new reproductive technologies cause unease because they insert a scalpel between mother and father, parent and child, egg and sperm, X chromosome and Y. Whether we win or lose any particular fight for reproductive self-determination, in these struggles we are seeing the underlying laws of gender quiver and shake.

QUESTIONS FOR DISCUSSION

1. This essay was written for *Ms.* magazine. What characteristics might be attributed to this particular audience? How might the writer's awareness of her audience affect the content of the article and the tone in which it is written?
2. What opinion does the author express in the first paragraph? Who might oppose such a view? What arguments does the author present in the first few paragraphs to support her opinion? Why does she arrange her arguments as she does?
3. Besides abortion and birth control, what other controversial issues relating to reproductive technology are mentioned? Why are these issues controversial?
4. Discuss the advantages and disadvantages of the new reproductive technologies described by Snitow. What is Snitow's major concern?
5. Examine the last three or four paragraphs. What is Snitow's main concluding idea? Do you see scientific involvement in the birth process as a threat to a woman's autonomy? Why or why not?

S. OGBUAGU
Depo Provera—A Choice or an Imposition on the African Woman?

In certain parts of Africa millions of women are using depo provera, a long-acting injectable form of birth control. S. Ogbuagu describes a study of the use of this controversial contraceptive in her article, "Depo Provera—A Choice or an Imposition on the African Woman?" Although the use of this drug has been banned in the United States, a United States corporation is promoting its use in many developing countries. Ogbuagu questions whether the use of the drug is voluntary or whether the choice has gone out of the hands of the women involved and into the hands of corporations and governments. Ogbuagu's concern for a woman's right to choose reflects that of Ann Snitow in her essay on "The Paradox of Birth Technology" (p. 128), as well as that of Jo McGowan in her article "In India, They Abort Females" (p. 147).

While the controversy over the use of *Depo Provera* (a long-acting injectable contraceptive) goes on unabated, millions of women in Africa, and in Nigeria in particular, are being subjected to it. The perplexing question remains whether these women choose to have depo provera or whether it is imposed on them. A sequel to this question is whether the African woman user is in any position to be able to make a fully considered choice with regard to the family planning technique she adopts. How many of the numerous health hazards of the drugs are made known to her at the outset?

In the light of these concerns it is argued that, since women bear the brunt of childbearing and raising, it is their basic human right to be able to decide on the family planning methods they wish to adopt. Furthermore, that the introduction and the use of depo provera on African women is a violation of this right. Consequently, it can be posited that it is morally objectionable that a drug banned in its country of manufacture finds a ready, profitable and quite often unsuspecting market in Nigeria and the Third World in general. Can it be that the profit interest of multi-national corporations (in this case Upjohn) is placed high above the health considerations of Third World women?

The primary purpose of this study is to establish the extent of the use of depo provera in Maiduguri. A second aim is to draw the attention of policy makers, implementers and drug-procuring officers in Nigeria and elsewhere to the unresolved controversial status of depo provera.

THE DRUG AND ITS HISTORY

Depo provera (medroxyprogesterone acetate) is a synthetic steroid, used as a long-acting, injectable contraceptive. Minkin points out that "depending on the dose, each shot of the drug can cause sterility from three to six months".[1]

At its inception in 1960, depo provera was approved by the United States Food and Drug Administration (F.D.A.) as "safe for endometriosis".[2] This approval was withdrawn in 1962 when the "efficacy" had not been demonstrated as required by the 1962 Drug Amendment Act. In 1972, it again received F.D.A.'s approval for palliative treatment of certain kinds of inoperable cancer of the uterus. It had also been used for the treatment of breast cancer, threatened abortion, idiopathic precocious puberty, and psychiatric disorders.[3] In 1974, the F.D.A. delayed its final approval of the drug while waiting for further assessment of the findings about an association said to exist between depo provera and cervical cancer. In 1978, following continued reviews, the F.D.A. eventually refused the approval of the drug as an injectable contraceptive for use in the United States.

Scientific studies aimed at evaluating the health implications of depo provera usage started in 1963. According to Kennedy (1978), two of these studies dealt with beagle dogs and rhesus monkeys which were given various doses of depo provera.[4] In each case, there was evidence of the presence of cancer. Two of the beagle dogs developed malignant breast tumors while two of the rhesus monkeys are reported to have died of endometrial carcinoma or cancer of the uterine lining.[5]

Much of the controversy about depo provera is related to these findings. The opponents are asking for a delay in the use of the drug while further studies about its safety are carried out. The argument is that it will be a human tragedy to have another (thalidomide[6]) situation. It was also mostly because of this suspected drug-cancer linkage that the F.D.A. withheld its final approval of the drug while waiting for positive findings of its safety. That is why, the F.D.A. argued, that the "benefits of the drug have not been shown to outweigh the potential risks".[7] It further stated, among other things, that:

a. health risks had been indicated by studies of beagle dogs in the early 1970s;
b. the simultaneous use of estrogen with depo provera increased the health risks; and
c. there is the risk of congenital malformations of the fetus exposed to depo provera if failure occurred.

In addition, it expressed reservations about the post-marketing study for breast and cervical cancers proposed by Upjohn Company (the manufacturer of depo provera).[8]

Despite this disapproval, Upjohn and population control enthusiasts (such as the International Planned Parenthood Federation) continue to agitate for the drug's approval. They argue that the drug is safe, long-acting, almost 100 per cent effective, and therefore convenient, for use, especially by rural women. Usually, they cite the Potts-McDaniel study. This study, conducted in Thailand, was an investigation of[9] Thai women who had endometrial cancer. It was found that none of them had used depo provera. The study yielded very little information because it used a very small sample in areas (Chiang Mai and Lumpoon Provinces of Thailand) where over 80,000 women had used the drug. As Minkin rightly points out its methodology and procedures have also been seriously questioned.[10]

Claims by Upjohn and its supporters, notwithstanding, the drug has many distressful side effects. They include: long- and short-term infertility, possible sterility, severe menstrual disorders, menstrual chaos, hair loss, weight gain, depression, diabetic stress, etc.[11] In addition to this list, there is the fear of depo provera having a possible association with breast and cervical cancers.

Although there are these debilitating side effects, fear of the drug-cancer linkage, and the possible effects on the fetus should failure occur (none of which has successfully been laid to rest or dismissed), the International Planned Parenthood Federation (IPPF), the World Health Organization (WHO), and the United States Agency for International Development (USAID) endorse its continued use. The IPPF and other international agencies in collaboration with Upjohn Company distribute the drug to over sixty countries. Unfortunately, most of the countries are in the Third World and appear not to be fully aware of the concerns, controversy and uncertainties surrounding depo provera.

THE AFRICAN SCENE

Many countries in Africa use depo provera for contraceptive purposes. Prominent among these countries are Angola, Uganda, Zaire, Kenya, Zimbabwe,[12] Sierra Leone, Nigeria and South Africa to name only a few. In the African countries south of the Sahara, excluding South Africa, the demographic parameters indicate a need for family planning. The women experience high birth rates of over 46 per 100; their total fertility rate is about 6.5; while their life expectancy at birth is below 50 years. About 80 per cent are still engaged in agriculture and petty trading; less than 30 per cent are literate and about the same percentage live in the urban areas. In Nigeria the picture is even more depressing since the annual population growth rate is about 3 per cent. These socio-demographic variables point to the existence of a need for family planning. However, the question is what kind of family planning methods? Who decides on the technique to be used—the women, the international organizations, or the male administrators?

Family planning is aimed at helping interested couples, especially the women, to plan the number and spacing of their children. It is considered a basic human right. It should be given to any woman who needs it. Although two adults are involved in the reproductive process the woman bears the brunt. Her body, and quite often her life, is at risk in the process. It becomes extremely important, therefore, that the decision on what type of contraceptive to use should in the end be hers. The problem is how she can effectively make the decision.

Self-determination, according to the United Nations, is experienced when one has the will, the choice and the freedom to decide on a course that one considers best and when one has the resources to pursue that course. Factors that aid in self-determination include education, access to chosen jobs with appropriate income, social recognition and acceptance; and freedom to pursue one's life ambitions.[13] The African woman is very low on these self-determination variables. Placed in this situation, can the African woman successfully determine her fate in the area of family planning?

THE STUDY

Background of Study

Maiduguri is the capital city of Borna State in the North-eastern part of Nigeria. Its founding dates back to the 17th century; it has a population of about 0.7 million people and is still growing. Although it has a cosmopolitan composition, the major ethnic groups are the Kunuris, the Shuwa-Arabs, and the Kwayam. English is the official language for transacting business although Kanuri and Hausa are widely spoken.

The population is predominantly Moslem and Islamic culture predominates. Polygamy is quite common. Children are very highly valued; numbers of children being regarded as blessings from Allah. Women are respected but are traditionally restricted from open closeness to men. They are involved mainly in agriculture and petty trading. Their educational background (especially with regard to modern education) is very low, though improving.[14]

Generally in the country, there is a *laissez-faire* official attitude to family planning, possibly due to the different religions' opposition which could have political repercussions for the leaders. Instead, whatever support the government gives to family planning is through subventions to voluntary organisations operating in

Nigeria, such as the Planned Parenthood of Nigeria. This body has about eighteen clinics in the country but as yet has none in Borno State which includes Maiduguri. This notwithstanding, contraceptives are available in private and government pharmacies and hospitals. There is also a proliferation of "quacks" who carry and sell different family planning items. In effect people can buy most contraceptive items over the counter of numerous drug stores run by qualified and unqualified personnel. Among the items that can be easily acquired is the controversial depo provera.

With the above background, it is perhaps difficult to see what role the Maiduguri women play in the decision to include depo provera as part of the family planning package in the city. Equally puzzling is how they can possibly know the health hazards associated with the drug before they are advised to use it.

Method of Study

It is intended that the present paper will be part of longer research which will survey the overall usage of depo provera in the country. This paper focuses on the present status of the drug in Maiduguri. It explores the extent of use and the age, number, educational and rural/urban background of the users. It also examines what screening and follow-up procedures are adopted, who administers the drug, and how much information or literature the doctor-prescribers have on the drug.

Information about the use of depo provera in Maiduguri was gathered in the first instance from doctors employed in the Obstetrics and Gynecology departments of three hospitals. The three pharmacists in charge of the pharmacies in the hospitals were also interviewed since they procure the drug and quite often are aware of the regularity or otherwise of its usage. In the second stage of the work, the actual users will be interviewed. It must be emphasized at this point that the study is extremely exploratory, since demographic data in the town are very limited. This initial study is intended to provide data to sharpen the procedure to be adopted in the follow-up research.

Since this is a preliminary study, it was necessary to study the general institutions that handle most of the cases in the town. These are, moreover, institutions that are likely to have records of their activities. Those selected for study, therefore, were:

1. the Government General Hospital (which handles people from all walks of life but especially the poorer urban groups and villagers);
2. the Specialist Hospital which runs a women's clinic and advises on family planning and has a team of well-qualified doctors (it is supposed to serve everybody but it is selective towards the higher socio-economic class); and
3. the University of Maiduguri Clinic which deals with salaried University staff and their families.

Besides these three hospitals, there are other hospitals and clinics which are privately owned, expensive, and limited to those who can afford their services. There are also the patent medicine stores where people pick up items for family planning. It may be worthwhile including these in a later study to find out how much depo provera is prescribed in the private institutions.

The Interviews

The researcher did all the interviewing using an informal schedule of questions and since the number of respondents was small, comprising three pharmacists and five doctors, there was no need for any sample selection. A factor that facilitated the interviewing process was that the three hospitals are linked by the exchange of medical doctors. It happens that the only consultant gynecologist at the University Clinic is one of the five gynecologists at the Teaching Hospital. Similarly, the consultant gynecologist at the General Hospital is also the professor-in-charge of the Teaching Hospital Gynecology staff. With this arrangement it was possible to gather information about two institutions from one person.

Although the subject of family planning in Maiduguri remains a mooted issue rather than one openly discussed, co-operation was given by the respondents. The three pharmacists suggested that depo provera is procured from an agent of the Upjohn company in Nigeria. It is available and can always be purchased on demand from the government and private institutions as well as from roadside hawkers. At the University Clinic, although the doctor who prescribed depo provera had left the University, the pharmacist was able to give the information that two women had used the drug and discontinued it because of the harsh side effects—especially abnormal bleeding and weight gain.

Generally, the more experienced doctors (those who have had upwards of seven years experience in the field) were very much aware of the controversies surrounding depo provera and its non-approved status in the country of its origin—the United States. They, therefore, tended not to use it at all. Their main reason was that it creates more problems than it seems to solve. Again they stressed the difficulty in using it because "once it is given it is hard to retract", as it takes at least three months for its effects to wear off. Most of the patients (fifteen) reported in this work were patients of a young doctor who had read Upjohn's list of side effects but not much more.

In all, the doctors interviewed admitted prescribing depo provera for twenty women. This number may appear small. However, when it is considered that this is a Moslem town where family planning is seriously frowned upon and discouraged, the above number assumes some significance. Furthermore, if it is remembered that there are many roadside medicine peddlers and stores where people can pick up contraceptives, it is possible that many more women may be using the drug than the twenty recorded here. Also, doctors show that the rate of contraceptive acceptance in the clinics is below one per cent. Most of the acceptors use them for spacing their children rather than for limiting numbers. Moreover, the more experienced doctors prefer either the I.U.D. or the pill for their patients. According to them too, the women who have had some education tend to prefer the pill or the I.U.D. When all these facts are considered, the relevance of the twenty depo provera users becomes pronounced. They may be representing a much larger population of women users.

From the interviews, it was observed that the doctors were not sure of the relevant personal data of the patients. But it was gathered that most of the depo provera users were young, unmarried women aged 25 years and above, ten of them having no children. All were semi-illiterate and, although they lived within the limits of the city, most were from very poor socio-economic backgrounds.

Findings and Discussions

One of the first striking features of the family planning services in Maiduguri is that those who procure the drugs are all men—the pharmacists. What items are secured for use are, therefore, the choice of men. Another factor highlighted is that, with their generally poor socio-educational background, women tend to have, as Brown observed, "an unquestioning respect for medical authority, and thereby do put their trust in the medical staff".[15] In a discussion with one of the consultant gynecologists—a Pole—he disclosed that the women who come to his clinic in Maiduguri do not know much about family planning techniques. He advises them, or rather recommends a certain method for them. In this case he does not favor "the pill" and is averse to the use of depo provera. As an advocate of I.U.D. it follows, of course, that all his patients in this particular clinic receive the I.U.D. Thus, it seems clear that the medical or clinic personnel, rather than the women themselves, are deciding on the kind of contraceptive used.

A third observable factor, which is also of major concern to opponents of depo provera, is the fact that the medical and clinic personnel are inadequate to handle the proper screening and follow-up of users. For example, in the case of the doctors interviewed, the only screening procedures adopted were checking the patients' pulse, blood pressure and pelvis. In all the cases, the doctors neither supervised nor did the actual injection by themselves, that being the nurses' task.

In the few developed countries such as Belgium, Denmark, France, and West Germany, where depo provera is used, Silverman notes that it is normally used in conjunction with regular medical check-ups.[16] In Maiduguri such regular check-ups are rarely available. Firstly, the doctor/patient ratio is low. Secondly, because of the above, doctors and clinics are generally over-crowded and over-worked. Moreover, even when the doctor is able to set up appointments, the patients rarely show up. Some of the doctors interviewed explained that after prescribing the injections at the first instance they usually ask the patients to come for check-ups after two weeks, after two months, and again when their period resumes. However, their experience is that most of the women (90 per cent) do not report for the two-week check-up. Nonetheless, some of the women do come back (66 per cent) when the side effects (bleeding and disturbed menstrual periods) start. It can be seen from this that there are no proper follow-up procedures for checking on the effects of depo provera on users.

To support this assertion, one of the young doctors who has prescribed depo provera for fifteen women in the last two years argued that unless the women come back to the hospital to report on their conditions there is no way of knowing what their fate is. In his particular case, out of the fifteen to whom he gave depo provera, three have dropped out—one married and so stopped usage of the drug in the hope of becoming pregnant; the second, he suspects, must have moved out of town; and the third woman just did not show up again, so there is no means of checking on her.

From the more experienced and mature doctor colleagues of the young practitioner, I gathered that quite often the patients who have problems with depo provera refuse to go back to the prescribing doctors. Instead, they take their problems and complaints to other doctors hoping for a rectification of their circumstance. One consultant gynecologist, who has had practical experience for over twelve years, said he had to treat women who have received depo provera from other doctors. They often went to him to complain essentially of abnormal bleeding. Usually they would be reduced to tears in explaining what was happening to them and how little information the doctors had given them at the time of the injection. All the patients who went to him (three in number) refused to have anything to do with the drug ever again. They discontinued its use. In this situation it is not surprising that women users of depo provera in Maiduguri are often ignorant of what to expect from the injection.

Of the twenty patients doctors admitted prescribing the injection for, none has used it for more than twelve months. Two have used it for about nine to twelve months, ten for about six months, and eight stopped after the first injection. The usual complaints for those who stopped were bleeding, disturbed menstrual cycle and weight gain. These are known side effects, but the difficulty is that the patients are often ignorant of what to expect. When the problems arise, their reaction is to stop usage. It is unthinkable to sue the doctor who is held in high esteem. Rather, the women take their complaints to other doctors in the hope of finding some relief.

This highlights one of those problems facing women in underdeveloped countries. As citizens, women often do not know their rights within the legal system. Doctors, in situations as described above, go unchallenged and unquestioned. In Britain, for example, Miss Shirley Rayner is reported to have been paid an out-of-court settlement of $3,750 by a hospital, which she alleged prescribed the controversial contraceptive injection—depo provera—without warning her of the side effects.[17] In the United States there are also cases of women who have sued their doctors or hospital for inadequate information about the drug before it was given to them.[18] The great problem in Maiduguri remains the low level of education of the women and the implicit belief and confidence placed in the doctor and the medical personnel.

The following tables give the status of depo provera usage, the stoppage rate, and the congruence between doctors' and patients' preferences for certain contraceptive methods.

It is clear from Table 1 that depo provera usage in Maiduguri is relatively recent. This is hardly surprising considering the conservative nature of the society. It also indicates that the more harmful effects of depo provera may not have started to show up yet in Maiduguri. The time lapse is too short (6.8 months for current users). However, the fact that 40 per cent of the reported users stopped usage after the first injection supports the view that the side effects are disabling.[19] It is to be expected

TABLE 1   State of Depo Usage in the Three Public Hospitals in Maiduguri

| | Depo Provera Usage | | |
	Ever Used	Currently Using	Stopped Usage
Total Numbers	20	12	8
Percentage	100	60	40
Mean Length of Usage in Months	6.2	6.8	3

Source: Author's interviews at three public hospitals in Maiduguri.

TABLE 2   Reasons for Stopping Usage of Depo Provera

	Reasons				
	Excessive Bleeding & Weight Gain	*To Get Married*	*Move Out of Town*	*Unknown*	*Total*
Numbers	5	1	1	1	8
Percentage	12.5	12.5	12.5	62.5	100

Source: Author's interviews.

that with prolonged usage the rate of drop-out might increase as other anticipated or unanticipated side effects are experienced. The reasons for stoppage are given below, as remembered by the doctors. The patients themselves may have other reasons.

Thus, it is seen that the majority of those who stopped did so because of immediate side effects. It will be revealing to know whether the one who stopped to get married did become pregnant as infertility is one of the side effects of depo provera. Also the fate of the remaining two is unknown since they are no longer in contact with their doctor. In all, this 40 per cent stoppage rate among such short-time users indicates that the claims of Upjohn, the IPPF, and other population control groups about the convenience and safety of depo provera are not borne out in the experiences of the users.

On the question of decision-making, all the doctors admitted the patients do not know much about the contraceptives. They depend mostly on the doctors' recommendations. It is in this regard that doctors' preference for certain methods corresponds to their preferred use by the patients.

Table 2 has one message, which is that doctors most often make decisions for, or recommendations to, their patients which are rarely refused. The young doctor already mentioned indicated that some of his patients (five) had heard about the three-monthly injection but knew nothing more about it. The usual practice is that the doctor mentions the different methods. To the uninformed, the three-monthly injection sounds convenient and therefore seems to be acceptable.

TABLE 3   Doctors' Most Frequently Prescribed Contraceptives by Patients' Preferred Methods

Doctors'/Patients' Methods	*Pills*	*Diaphram/I.U.D.*	*Depo Provera*	*Percentage Totals*
First	80	20	0	100
Second	50	10	40	100
Third	10	90	0	100
Fourth	60	40	0	100
Fifth	70	30	0	100

Source: Author's interviews.

Most of the time the patient is unsuspecting about the side effects. According to two of the more experienced doctors, "If we explain the detailed side effects of the different methods, we may probably end up with no users. So we give them only what is necessary." Quite often, what is considered "necessary" is so inadequate that the woman is virtually ignorant.

CONCLUSION

From the foregoing discussions one thing is clear. Depo provera is used even in the furthest parts of Nigeria. Maiduguri is the last large town in the northeast of Nigeria and suffers from relative isolation from the rest of the country. That depo provera is used in this town, where there is no established family planning clinic and where the Moslem faith is very strong, suggests a much wider use in the rest of the country.

The discontinuation rate is also indicative of not only the dissatisfaction the patients have for it but also the lack of proper understanding of what to expect. Evidence from the study shows that the choice is usually more the doctors' than the patients.

Perhaps the most disconcerting issue is the fact that the follow-up or monitoring procedure is non-existent. In effect, patients or users are left to their fate. If a drug is well established as safe, it may be that follow-up is not so very necessary. However, when a drug is as severe in its side effects, and as controversial, as depo provera is then there is reason to be concerned that there is no proper way of monitoring its effects on the users. All the people involved in the approval for its purchase, its introduction in the health care system, and the doctors who actually prescribe it are responsible for whatever harm is caused to the users. The health of the women should be the concern of all involved. A drug produced in America but considered unsafe for American women should also be seen as unsafe for women everywhere in the world. To impose it on Maiduguri women is to jeopardize their health and that is morally objectionable.

Finally, it is recommended that depo provera be banned in Nigeria until its safety has been proved beyond any doubt.

NOTES

1. Minkin, S; 1981 "Nine Thai Women Had Cancer . . . Therefore Depo Provera Is Safe."
2. Kennedy, D; 1978 Statement Before the Select Committee on Population, House Representation (August) p 1 USA.
3. *ibid.*
4. Kennedy *op cit.*
5. Minkin, S; *op cit.* See also the feature article in *Thailand Update* January/February 1981 p 7.
6. **thalidomide** A sedative and hypnotic drug withdrawn from sale because of its association with fetal abnormalities. [Ed. note.]
7. *HEW News* 1978 U.S. Department of Health, Education and Welfare, October 25 pp 1–2.
8. International Planned Parenthood Federation 1978 "U.S. Decision on Depo Provera" *Mailing* 3.
9. Minkin, S; *op cit.* pp 38–39.

10. Cowan, B n.d. "Women's Health Group Establishes Registry for Birth Control Shot" *National Women's Network Inc.*
11. Population Reference Bureau 1981 *Data Sheet.*
12. Zimbabwe banned the use of depo provera in 1981 after its commissioner for Health became convinced of the health risks involved.
13. United Nations 1975 *Status of Women and Family Planning* (New York).
14. Taiwo, O. A; 1982 "Universal Primary Education Problems and Prospects in Maiduguri Metropolis" (B.A. Ed. Long Essay Faculty of Education University of Maiduguri).
15. Brown quoted in Corea G 1979 *The Depo Provera Weapon* Paper written for the Women's Wing of the American Friendship Society Committee.
16. Silverman, J; 1980 "U.S. Banned Drug Used by Refugees" *Oakland Tribune.*
17. Charlton, P; 1980 "Singer receives $3,750 Award for Contraceptive Injection: Hospital Settles Claim Over One Drug's Effects" *The Guardian* May 29.
18. *New Haven Register* 1978 "Woman Claims Her Cancer Caused by Contraceptive" October 26.
19. Minkin, S; 1980 *Depo Provera: A Critical Analysis* (Institute of Food and Development Policy San Francisco).

BIBLIOGRAPHY

American Friendship Society Committee n.d. "Depo Provera: Upjohn and Third World Health" *AFSC Women's Newsletter*, p. 11.
Beral, V; 1979 "Maternal Mortality is an Inadequate Indicator of Deaths Associated with Reproduction in a Community" *British Medical Journal*, Vol. 632–34.
Black, H. R; et al 1979 "The Effect of Medroxyprogesterone Acetate on Blood Pressure" *International Journal of Gynaecology and Obstetrics*, Vol. 17, pp. 83–7.
Cassidy, M. M; 1980 "Depo Provera and Sterilization: Abuse Overview" in Homes H. B, B Hoskins & M Gross (eds) *Birth Control and Controlling Birth: Women-Centered Perspectives* (HZUMAN Press: Clifton NJ).
Castle, W. M; et al 1973 "Efficacy and Acceptability of Injectable Medroxyprogesterone" *South African Medical Journal*, Vol. 53, pp. 842–5.
Chorlton, P; 1980 "Singer Receives $3,750 Award for Contraceptive Injection: Hospital Settles Claim Over Drug's Effects" *The Guardian* May 29.
Ciira, J; 1981 "The Depo Provera Issue: Mother's Health Ignored" *The Standard* (Kenya) August 31.
Corea, G; 1979 *The Depo Provera Weapon* (Paper written for the Women's Wing of the American Friendship Society Committee.)
    1979 Memo to Commissioner Kennedy on Depo Provera in *Women Wise* Spring/Summer.
    1980 "The Depo Provera Weapon" in Holmes et al *op cit.*
Higg, V; 1977 "La Leche Women Attack Drugs" *Midweek Magazine Auckland Star* October 26.
HEW News 1978 U.S. Department of Health, Education and Welfare "Release on Depo Provera" October 25.
International Planned Parenthood Federation 1978 "U.S. Decision on Depo Provera" *Mailing* 3.
1975 IPPF Central Medical Committee *Statement on Injectable Contraception.*
Kadhi, J; 1981 "Dr. Koinange Should be Told to Ban Depo Provera" *Sunday Nation* (Kenya) August.
Kasper, A; 1980 "New Law Would Release Potentially Lethal Drugs" *New Direction for Women* January/February.
Kennedy, D; 1978 Statement Before the Select Committee on Population (U.S. House of Representatives).

Minkin, S; 1981 "Nine Thai Women Had Cancer . . . Therefore Depo Provera is Safe" *Mother Jones* November, pp. 34–38.

1981 *Depo Provera: A Critical Analysis* (Institute for Food Development Policy San Francisco).

Multinational Monitor 1981 "Zimbabwe Bans Dangerous Contraceptive, Depo Provera: A Victory for Women's Groups" September 4.

Munyakho, D. K; 1981 "Depo: Birth Control Drug Only Suitable for Certain Women" *Sunday Nation* (Kenya) July 26.

Nash, H. A; 1975 "Depo Provera: A Review" *Contraception* 12377–393.

National Women's Health Network n.d. "Women's Health Group Establishes Registry for Birth Control Shot" (Press release from Washington).

New Haven Register 1978 "Woman Claims Her Cancer Caused by Contraceptive" October 26.

Nordland, R; 1980 "Birth Control: Injections of a Drug Banned in the U.S." *Philadelphia Inquirer*.

Rogow, D; 1980 "Disease Outcomes Associated with the Use of DepoMedroxy Progesterone Acetate Contraception: A Review of the Literature" (Course Paper School of Public Health Berkeley).

Silverman, J; 1980 "U.S. Banned Drug Used by Refugees" *Oakland Tribune* November 5.

Sapire, E; 1978 "An Injectable Contraceptive: A Decade of Experience" *British Journal of Family Planning* 4 pp. 49–57.

Saymour, R. J; & L. C. Powerl 1970 "Depo Medroxy Progesterone Acetate as Contraceptive" *Obstetrics and Gynaecology* 36 pp. 589–95.

Thailand Update 1981 "The Incredible Injectable Contraceptive, Depo Provera" January/February.

USAID 1980 Report to USAID of the Ad Hoc Consultative Panel on Depo Medroxyprogesterone Acetate.

Van der Tak 1979 "Family Planning Booms in Thailand and Bali" *Intercom* August/September.

Washington Post 1978 "The Depo Provera Question" January 7.

Wolfe, S. M; 1976 "Sex Hormones Used in Pregnancy and Birth Defects: Another Thalidomide" *Public Citizen* (Washington).

Wyrick, B; 1977 "Doctors Found Prescribing Questionable Birth Control Drug" *Washington Post* November.

QUESTIONS FOR DISCUSSION

1. What is the purpose of this article? (See especially the third paragraph.) Explain the ideas in the statement of purpose in your own words.
2. What is depo provera and how does it work as a form of birth control? What are the advantages of using depo provera? What are the disadvantages?
3. This article is organized in a fashion typical of scientific journal articles. Describe the organization. Discuss the functions of each section of the article.
4. Look at the tables toward the end of the article. Explain the results that the tables illustrate.
5. Summarize the conclusion of the article. Do you agree or disagree with the statements in the conclusion? Defend your answer.
6. What are some possible methodological problems with the study as described in this article? Explain.
7. What action do you think the author would like the reader to take? Whom does she blame for the problems involving the use of depo provera?

JO MCGOWAN
In India, They Abort Females

The following essay, "In India, They Abort Females," was written by Jo McGowan for the "My Turn" column which appears regularly in Newsweek *magazine. McGowan is a Roman Catholic who lives in India with her husband and children; her political position against abortion is consistent with the articulated views of the Catholic church. The point of view in this essay contrasts interestingly with that of Ann Snitow in "The Paradox of Birth Technology" (p. 128), although both articles attempt to persuade through logical argument and appeals to the reader's emotions.*

Beware what you set your heart upon, for it surely shall be yours. Pro-choice feminists would be wise to heed this old-fashioned warning. By insisting upon the right of every woman to have an abortion, they have opened a Pandora's box[1] of which they are only now realizing the depths.

I say this as an American resident of India where an updated version of female infanticide is being practiced. Amniocentesis, a medical procedure used to detect certain fetal abnormalities, almost always reveals the sex of the unborn child—a side benefit doctors in India now put to use in a culture that prizes sons. Or, as one doctor was quoted in the Indian Express last year: "Yes, I do sex-determination tests. It's better for an unwanted girl not to be born than to suffer later." The birth of a boy is cause for great rejoicing, but that of a daughter can lead some women to consider suicide.

In India, being female is an economic handicap. A girl means trouble. She must be married off at great expense (the custom of dowry was outlawed in 1961 but is still prevalent), only to be lost to her family. Anything she earns belongs to her in-laws. Her parents, who may incur a lifetime of debt to pay for her wedding, can expect to see her only once or twice a year and then in strained, formal visits. The more daughters they have, the worse off they become. It's no wonder then that the idea of sex determination, with abortion as an option if the sex turns out to be "wrong," is so popular here that sex-selection clinics have become a big business.

But as amniocentesis has become widely available in the subcontinent, it has also become more and more controversial. Pro-choice feminists decry its inherent sexism—their vigorous fight against its use for sex selection won them a victory recently when the western Indian state of Maharashtra (of which Bombay is the capital) outlawed the procedure for any but strictly defined medical reasons.

To undergo amniocentesis in Maharashtra now, a woman must be at least 35 years old or must have a medical history that suggests the possibility of a genetic disease. The new law, applauded by women's groups, is seen as a promise of things to come. In my opinion, however, the victory it represents will remain an isolated one simply because the feminist position on this issue is illogical and inconsistent.

What is the feminist position? Very simply put—it is wrong to abort babies just because they are girls. In making their arguments, women in India use highly

---

[1] **Pandora's box** Pandora was the first human woman, according to Greek mythology. She was given a box into which were put all the evils that have since afflicted the human race; Epimetheus, Pandora's husband, opened the box. [Ed. note.]

emotional terms like "feticide" and marshal grim statistics (out of 8,000 cases of abortion in Bombay, 7,999 involved a female fetus, according to one study) to support their case.

All very sad and very compelling but for one large fact: pro-choice feminists (in India and all over the world, for the feminist community is at one on this issue) are speaking out of both sides of their mouths. When the issue is sex determination and the "selective" abortion of girls, they call it female feticide. But when the issue is reproductive freedom and the abortion of male and female fetuses, they call it a "woman's right to choose." It won't work. They can't have it both ways. Either they accept abortion or they don't.

For years now, feminists have made the abortion issue a top priority and have worked tirelessly to create a climate in which the destruction of unborn children is acceptable. They have done their work well: millions of fetuses are aborted all over the world and very few people give it a second thought.

Special interest: The basic principle of the abortion-on-demand movement is that the decision to abort should rest entirely with the woman. No special-interest group or individual (be it the church, the state, her parents or her husband or lover) should have any say in the matter. Free choice means just that—the woman chooses.

Yet some mothers, indeed many mothers in India and other countries and cultures where males are highly prized, have very legitimate reasons in believing that giving birth to a girl is unacceptable. What gives anyone the right to tell them they are wrong? Certainly no traditional feminist should dare, any more than she would tell the mother of a hemophiliac that she should carry her pregnancy to term.

"Selective" is the term used to describe the specific targeting of girls for abortion, as if the word somehow proves the essential evil of the act. But which abortion is *not* selective? The handicapped fetus of the mother who only wants a perfect baby, the third child of a mother who only wants two, the unplanned baby of a mother who wants total control of her life—all of these can be "selectively" aborted. What changes in each case is only the mother's view of what is acceptable and what is not.

From where I sit, pro-choice feminists have no moral standing from which to speak out against the selective abortion of girls. In insisting that they do, they have become just another special-interest group, like the church or the state, trying to prevent women from exercising their right to choose. Once it is permitted to kill some fetuses for some reasons, I don't see why it isn't permitted to kill all for any reason.

As a feminist opposed to abortion, I would almost have welcomed this turn of events, were it not so tragic and wrong. But perhaps now the real nature of abortion will be revealed in all its horror. Perhaps from the undeniable truth that it is wrong to kill a baby simply because she is a girl will emerge the larger truth that it is wrong to kill a baby at all.

QUESTIONS FOR DISCUSSION

1. This essay was written for *Newsweek*'s "My Turn" column. What seems to be the purpose of this regular feature? What might be some common characteristics of essays which appear in the column? (Check other examples in *Newsweek*.)

2. Describe the conflict between the feminists' "pro-choice" position on abortion and the feminists' position on abortion of female fetuses.
3. Why do many Indian women choose to abort female fetuses? What cultural values might contribute to this choice?
4. What is McGowan's position on the issue? What arguments does she present to support her position? What cultural values might contribute to her political views? Can you detect any flaws in the logic of her argument?
5. Examine the conclusion of the article. Is it persuasive? Why or why not?

JEFFREY Z. RUBIN, FRANK J. PROVENZANO, AND ZELLA LURIA

The Eye of the Beholder: Parents' View on Sex of Newborns

The "battle of the sexes" is one type of cultural clash that seems to cut across differences in age, affluence, and even national and ethnic boundaries. Most people would agree that an individual's sex is a major influence upon that individual's behavior, their role in society, and even the opportunities for fulfillment that the person may enjoy. But how much of our so-called sex differences are the result of our "biological" gender? In the following article, "The Eye of the Beholder: Parents' View on Sex of Newborns," psychologists Jeffrey Rubin, Frank Provenzano, and Zella Luria illustrate that the cultural sex-role socialization defining much of what we mean by "masculine" and "feminine" begins almost at birth. This article, reprinted from the American Journal of Orthopsychiatry, *is written in a style typical of scientific journals which report the results of experiments. Notice the distinctive organization and style of the writing.*

ABSTRACT

Thirty pairs of primiparous parents, fifteen with sons and fifteen with daughters, were interviewed within the first 24 hours postpartum. Although male and female infants did not differ in birth length, weight, or Apgar scores, daughters were significantly more likely than sons to be described as little, beautiful, pretty, and cute, and as resembling their mothers. Fathers made more extreme and stereotyped rating judgments of their newborns than did mothers. Findings suggest that sex-typing and sex-role socialization have already begun at birth.

As Schaffer[10] has observed, the infant at birth is essentially an asocial, largely undifferentiated creature. It appears to be little more than a tiny ball of hair, fingers, toes, cries, gasps, and gurgles. However, while it may seem that "if you've seen one, you've seen them all," babies are *not* all alike—a fact that is of special importance to their parents, who want, and appear to need, to view their newborn child as a creature that is special. Hence, much of early parental interaction with the infant may be focused on a search for distinctive features. Once the fact that the baby is normal has been established, questions such as, "Who does the baby look like?" and "How much does it weigh?" are asked.

Of all the questions parents ask themselves and each other about their infant, one seems to have priority: "Is it a boy or a girl?" The reasons for and consequences of posing this simple question are by no means trivial. The answer, "boy" or "girl," may result in the parents' organizing their perception of the infant with respect to a wide variety of attributes—ranging from its size to its activity, attractiveness, even its future potential. It is the purpose of the present study to examine the kind of verbal picture parents form of the newborn infant, as a function both of their own and their infant's gender.

As Asch[2] observed years ago, in forming our impressions of others, we each tend to develop a *Gestalt*—a global picture of what others are like, which permits us to organize our perceptions of the often discrepant, contradictory aspects of their behavior and manner into a unified whole. The awareness of another's status,[13] the belief that he is "warm" or "cold,"[2,5] "extroverted" or "introverted,"[6] even the apparently trivial knowledge of another's name[4]—each of these cues predisposes us to develop a stereotypic view of that other, his underlying nature, and how he is likely to behave. How much more profound, then, may be the consequences of a cue as prominent in parents' minds as the gender of their own precious, newborn infant.

The study reported here is addressed to parental perceptions of their infants at the point when these infants first emerge into the world. If it can be demonstrated that parental sex-typing has already begun its course at this earliest of moments in the life of the child, it may be possible to understand better one of the important antecedents of the complex process by which the growing child comes to view itself as boy-ish or girl-ish.

Based on our review of the literature, two forms of parental sex-typing may be expected to occur at the time of the infant's birth. First, it appears likely that parents will view and label their newborn child differentially, as a simple function of the infant's gender. Aberle and Naegele[1] and Tasch,[12] using only fathers as subjects, found that they had different expectations for sons and daughters: sons were expected to be aggressive and athletic, daughters were expected to be pretty, sweet, fragile, and delicate. Rebelsky and Hanks[9] found that fathers spent more time talking to their daughters than their sons during the first three months of life. While the sample size was too small for the finding to be significant, they suggest that the role of father-of-daughter may be perceived as requiring greater nurturance. Similarly, Pedersen and Robson[8] reported that the fathers of infant daughters exhibited more behavior labeled (by the authors) as "apprehension over well being" than did the fathers of sons.

A comparable pattern emerges in research using mothers as subjects. Sears, Maccoby and Levin,[11] for example, found that the mothers of kindergartners reported tolerating more aggression from sons than daughters, when it was directed toward parents and peers. In addition, maternal nurturance was seen as more important for the daughter's than the son's development. Taken together, the findings in this body of research lead us to expect parents (regardless of their gender) to view their newborn infants differentially—labeling daughters as weaker, softer, and therefore in greater need of nurturance, than sons.

The second form of parental sex-typing we expect to occur at birth is a function both of the infant's gender *and* the parent's own gender. Goodenough[3] interviewed the parents of nursery school children, and found that mothers were less concerned with sex-typing their child's behavior than were fathers. More recently, Meyer and Sobieszek[7] presented adults with videotapes of two seventeen-month-old children (each of whom was sometimes described as a boy and sometimes as a girl), and asked their subjects to describe and interpret the children's behavior. They found that male subjects, as well as those having little contact with small children, were more likely (although not always significantly so) to rate the children in sex-stereo-typic fashion—attributing "male qualities" such as independence, aggressiveness, activity, and alertness to the child presented as a boy, and qualities such as cuddli-ness, passivity, and delicacy to the "girl." We expect, therefore, that sex of infant and sex of parent will interact, such that it is fathers, rather than mothers, who emerge as the greater sex-typers of their newborn.

In order to investigate parental sex-typing of their newborn infants, and in order, more specifically, to test the predictions that sex-typing is a function of the infant's gender, as well as the gender of both infant and parent, parents of newborn boys and girls were studied in the maternity ward of a hospital, within the first 24 hours postpartum, to uncover their perceptions of the characteristics of their new-born infants.

METHOD

Subjects

The subjects consisted of 30 pairs of primiparous [first-time] parents, fifteen of whom had sons, and fifteen of whom had daughters. The subjects were drawn from the available population of expecting parents at a suburban Boston hospital serving local, predominantly lower–middle-class families. Using a list of primiparous expectant mothers obtained from the hospital, the experimenter made contact with families by mail several months prior to delivery, and requested the subjects' assistance in "a study of social relations among parents and their first child." Approximately one week after the initial contact by mail, the experimenter telephoned each family, in order to answer any questions the prospective parents might have about the study, and to obtain their consent. Of the 43 families reached by phone, eleven refused to take part in the study. In addition, one consenting mother subsequently gave birth to a low birth weight infant (a 74-ounce girl), while another delivered an unusually large son (166 ounces). Because these two infants were at the two ends of the distri-bution of birth weights, and because they might have biased the data in support of our hypotheses, the responses of their parents were eliminated from the sample.

All subjects participated in the study within the first 24 hours postpartum—the fathers almost immediately after delivery, and the mothers (who were often under sedation at the time of delivery) up to but not later than 24 hours later. The mothers typically had spoken with their husbands at least once during this 24 hour period.

There were no reports of medical problems during any of the pregnancies or deliveries, and all infants in the sample were full-term at time of birth. Deliveries were made under general anesthesia, and the fathers were not allowed in the delivery room. The fathers were not permitted to handle their babies during the first 24 hours, but could view them through display windows in the hospital nursery. The mothers, on the other hand, were allowed to hold and feed their infants. The subjects participated individually in the study. The fathers were met in a small, quiet waiting room used exclusively by the maternity ward, while the mothers were met in their hospital rooms. Every precaution was taken not to upset the parents or interfere with hospital procedure.

Procedure

After introducing himself to the subjects, and after congratulatory amenities, the experimenter (FJP) asked the parents: "Describe your baby as you would to a close friend or relative." The responses were tape-recorded and subsequently coded.

The experimenter then asked the subjects to take a few minutes to complete a short questionnaire. The instructions for completion of the questionnaire were as follows:

> On the following page there are 18 pairs of opposite words. You are asked to rate your baby in relation to these words, placing an "x" or a checkmark in the space that best describes your baby. The more a word describes your baby, the closer your "x" should be to that word.
>
> Example: Imagine you were asked to rate Trees.
> Good   : ____ : ____ : ____ : ____ : ____ : ____ : ____ : ____ : ____ :   Bad
> Strong   : ____ : ____ : ____ : ____ : ____ : ____ : ____ : ____ : ____ :   Weak
>
> If you cannot decide or your feelings are mixed, place your "x" in the center space. Remember, the more you think a word is a good description of your baby, the closer you should place your "x" to that word. If there are no questions, please begin. Remember, you are rating your baby. Don't spend too much time thinking about your answers. First impressions are usually the best.

Having been presented with these instructions, the subjects then proceeded to rate their baby on each of the eighteen following, eleven-point, bipolar adjective scales: firm-soft; large featured-fine featured; big-little; relaxed-nervous; cuddly-not cuddly; easy going-fussy; cheerful-cranky; good eater-poor eater; excitable-calm; active-inactive; beautiful-plain; sociable-unsociable; well coordinated-awkward; noisy-quiet; alert-inattentive; strong-weak; friendly-unfriendly; hardy-delicate.

Upon completion of the questionnaire, the subjects were thanked individually, and when both parents of an infant had completed their participation, the underlying purposes of the study were fully explained.

Hospital Data

In order to acquire a more objective picture of the infants whose characteristics were being judged by the subjects, data were obtained from hospital records concerning each infant's birth weight, birth length, and Apgar scores. Apgar scores are typically assigned at five and ten minutes postpartum, and represent the physician's ratings of the infant's color, muscle tonicity, reflex irritability, and heart and respiratory rates. No significant differences between the male and female infants were found for birth weight, birth length, or Apgar scores at five and ten minutes postpartum.*

Results

In Table 1, the subjects' mean ratings of their infant, by condition, for each of the eighteen bipolar adjective scales, are presented. The right-extreme column of Table 1 shows means for each scale, which have been averaged across conditions. Infant stimuli, overall, were characterized closer to the scale anchors of soft, fine featured, little, relaxed, cuddly, easy going, cheerful, good eater, calm, active, beautiful, sociable, well coordinated, quiet, alert, strong, friendly, and hardy. Our parent-subjects, in other words, appear to have felt on Day 1 of their babies' lives that their newborn infants represented delightful, competent new additions to the world!

Analysis of variance of the subjects' questionnaire responses (1 and 56 degrees of freedom) yielded a number of interesting findings. There were *no* rating differences on the eighteen scales as a simple function of Sex of Parent: parents appear to agree with one another, on the average. As a function of Sex of Infant, however, several significant effects emerged: Daughters, in contrast to sons, were rated as significantly softer ($F = 10.67$, $p < .005$), finer featured ($F = 9.27$, $p < .005$), littler ($F = 28.83$, $p < .001$), and more inattentive ($F = 4.44$, $p < .05$). In addition, significant interaction effects emerged for seven of the eighteen scales: firm-soft ($F = 11.22$, $p < .005$), large featured-fine featured ($F = 6.78$, $p < .025$), cuddly-not cuddly ($F = 4.18$, $p < .05$), well coordinated-awkward ($F = 12.52$, $p < .001$), alert-inattentive ($F = 5.10$, $p < .05$), strong-weak ($F = 10.67$, $p < .005$), and hardy-delicate ($F = 5.32$, $p < .025$).

The meaning of these interactions becomes clear in Table 1, in which it can be seen that six of these significant interactions display a comparable pattern: fathers were more extreme in their ratings of *both* sons and daughters than were mothers. Thus, sons were rated as firmer, larger featured, better coordinated, more alert, stronger, and hardier—and daughters as softer, finer featured, more awkward, more inattentive, weaker, and more delicate—by their fathers than by their mothers. Finally, with respect to the other significant interaction effect (cuddly-not cuddly), a rather different pattern was found. In this case, mothers rated sons as cuddlier than daughters, while fathers rated daughters as cuddlier than sons—a finding we have dubbed the "oedipal" effect.

Responses to the interview question were coded in terms of adjectives used and references to resemblance. Given the open-ended nature of the question, many adjectives were used—healthy, for example, being a high frequency response cutting across sex of babies and parents. Parental responses were pooled, and recurrent adjectives were analyzed by X^2 analysis for sex of child. Sons were described as big

---

*Birth weight ($\overline{X}_{Sons} = 114.43$ ounces, $\overline{X}_{Daughters} = 110.00$, $t (28) = 1.04$); Birth length ($\overline{X}_{Sons} = 19.80$ inches, $\overline{X}_{Daughters} = 19.96$, $t (28) = 0.52$); 5 minute Apgar score ($\overline{X}_{Sons} = 9.07$, $\overline{X}_{Daughters} = 9.33$, $t (28) = 0.69$); and 10 minute Apgar score ($\overline{X}_{Sons} = 10.00$, $\overline{X}_{Daughters} = 10.00$).

TABLE 1 Mean Ratings on the 18 Adjective Scales, as a Function of Sex of Parent (Mother vs. Father) and Sex of Infant (Son vs. Daughter)[a]

Scale	Experimental Condition				
(I) — (II)	M–S	M–D	F–S	F–D	X̄
Firm–Soft	7.47	7.40	3.60	8.93	6.85
Large featured–Fine featured	7.20	7.53	4.93	9.20	7.22
Big–Little	4.73	8.40	4.13	8.53	6.45
Relaxed–Nervous	3.20	4.07	3.80	4.47	3.88
Cuddly–Not cuddly	1.40	2.20	2.20	1.47	1.82
Easy going–Fussy	3.20	4.13	3.73	4.60	3.92
Cheerful–Cranky	3.93	3.73	4.27	3.60	3.88
Good eater–Poor eater	3.73	3.80	4.60	4.53	4.16
Excitable–Calm	6.20	6.53	5.47	6.40	6.15
Active–Inactive	2.80	2.73	3.33	4.60	3.36
Beautiful–Plain	2.13	2.93	1.87	2.87	2.45
Sociable–Unsociable	4.80	3.80	3.73	4.07	4.10
Well coordinated–Awkward	3.27	2.27	2.07	4.27	2.97
Noisy–Quiet	6.87	7.00	5.67	7.73	6.82
Alert–Inattentive	2.47	2.40	1.47	3.40	2.44
Strong–Weak	3.13	2.20	1.73	4.20	2.82
Friendly–Unfriendly	3.33	3.40	3.67	3.73	3.53
Hardy–Delicate	5.20	4.67	3.27	6.93	5.02

[a]The larger the mean, the greater the rated presence of the attribute denoted by the second (right-hand) adjective in each pair.

more frequently than were daughters (X^2 (1) = 4.26, $p < .05$); daughters were called little more often than were sons (X^2 (1) = 4.28, $p < .05$). The "feminine" cluster—beautiful, pretty, and cute—was used significantly more often to describe daughters than sons (X^2 (1) = 5.40, $p < .05$). Finally, daughters were said to resemble mothers more frequently than were sons (X^2 (1) = 3.87, $p < .05$).

Discussion

The data indicate that parents—especially fathers—differentially label their infants, as a function of the infant's gender. These results are particularly striking in light of the fact that our sample of male and female infants did *not* differ in birth length, weight, or Apgar scores. Thus, the results appear to be a pure case of parental labeling—what a colleague has described as "nature's first projective test" (personal communication, Leon Eisenberg). Given the importance parents attach to the birth of their first child, it is not surprising that such ascriptions are made.

But why should posing the simple question, "Is it a boy or a girl?", be so salient in parents' minds, and have such important consequences? For one thing, an infant's gender represents a truly *distinctive* characteristic. The baby is either a boy or a girl—there are no ifs, ands, or buts about it. A baby may be active sometimes, and quiet at others, for example, but it can always be assigned to one of two distinct classes: boy or girl. Secondly, an infant's gender tends to assume the properties of a *definitive* characteristic. It permits parents to organize their questions and answers about the infant's appearance and behavior into an integrated *Gestalt*. Finally, an infant's gender is often a *normative* characteristic. It is a property that seems to be of special importance not only to the infant's parents, but to relatives, friends, neighbors, and even casual passersby in the street. For each of these reasons, an infant's gender is a property of considerable importance to its parents, and is therefore one that is likely to lead to labeling and the investment of surplus meaning.

The results of the present study are, of course, not unequivocal. Although it was found, as expected, that the sex-typing of infants varied as a function of the infant's gender, as well as the gender of both infant and parent, significant differences did not emerge for all eighteen of the adjective scales employed. Two explanations for this suggest themselves. First, it may simply be that we have overestimated the importance of sex-typing at birth. A second possibility, however, is that sex-typing is more likely to emerge with respect to certain classes of attributes—namely, those which denote physical or constitutional, rather than "internal," dispositional, factors. Of the eight different adjective pairs for which significant main or interaction effects emerged, six (75%) clearly refer to external attributes of the infant. Conversely, of the ten adjective pairs for which no significant differences were found, only three (30%) clearly denote external attributes. This suggests that it is physical and constitutional factors that specially lend themselves to sex-typing at birth, at least in our culture.

Another finding of interest is the lack of significant effects, as a simple function of sex of parent. Although we predicted no such effects, and were therefore not particularly surprised by the emergence of "non-findings," the implication of these results is by no means trivial. If we had omitted the sex of the infant as a factor in the present study, we might have been led to conclude (on the basis of simply varying the sex of the parent) that *no* differences exist in parental descriptions of newborn infants—a patently erroneous conclusion! It is only when the infant's and the parent's gender are considered together, in interaction, that the lack of differences between overall parental mean ratings can be seen to reflect the true differences between the parents. Mothers rate both sexes closer together on the adjective pairs than do fathers (who are the stronger sex-typers), but *both* parents agree on the direction of sex differences.

An issue of considerable concern, in interpreting the findings of the present study appropriately, stems from the fact that fathers were not permitted to handle their babies, while mothers were. The question then becomes: Is it possible that the greater sex-typing by fathers is simply attributable to their lesser exposure to their infants? This, indeed, may have been the case. However, it seems worthwhile to consider some of the alternative possibilities. Might not the lesser exposure of fathers to their infants have led not to greater sex-typing, but to a data "wash out"—with no differences emerging in paternal ratings? After all, given no opportunity to handle their babies, and therefore deprived of the opportunity to obtain certain first-hand information about them, the fathers might have been expected to make a series of neutral ratings—hovering around the middle of each adjective scale. The fact that they did not do this suggests that they brought with them a variety of sex stereotypes that they then imposed upon their infant. Moreover, the fact that

mothers, who were allowed to hold and feed their babies, made distinctions between males and females that were in keeping with cultural sex-stereotypes (see
Table 1), suggests that even if fathers had had the opportunity of holding their infants, similar results might have been obtained. We should also not lose sight of the
fact that father-mother differences in exposure to infants continue well into later
years. Finally, one must question the very importance of the subjects' differential
exposure on the grounds that none of the typical "exposure" effects reported in the
social psychological literature[14] were observed. In particular, one might have expected mothers to have come to rate their infants more favorably than fathers, simply as a result of greater exposure. Yet such was not the case.

The central implication of the study, then, is that sex-typing and sex-role socialization appear to have already begun their course at the time of the infant's birth,
when information about the infant is minimal. The *Gestalt* parents develop, and the
labels they ascribe to their newborn infant, may well affect subsequent expectations
about the manner in which their infant ought to behave, as well as parental behavior
itself. This parental behavior, moreover, when considered in conjunction with the
rapid unfolding of the infant's own behavioral repertoire, may well lead to a modification of the very labeling that affected parental behavior in the first place. What
began as a one-way street now bears traffic in two directions. In order to understand
the full importance and implications of our findings, therefore, research clearly
needs to be conducted in which delivery room stereotypes are traced in the family
during the first several months after birth, and their impact upon parental behavior
is considered. In addition, further research is clearly in order if we are to understand
fully the importance of early paternal sex-typing in the socialization of sex-roles.

REFERENCES

1. Aberle, D. and Naegele, K. 1952. Middleclass fathers' occupational role and attitudes
   toward children. Amer. J. Orthopsychiat. 22(2):366–378.
2. Asch, S. 1946. Forming impressions of personality. J. Abnorm. Soc. Psychol. 41:258–290.
3. Goodenough, E. 1957. Interest in persons as an aspect of sex differences in the early
   years. Genet. Psychol. Monogr. 55:287–323.
4. Harari, H. and McDavid, J. Name stereotypes and teachers' expectations. J. Educ. Psychol. (in press)
5. Kelley, H. 1950. The warm-cold variable in first impressions of persons. J. Pers. 18:
   431–439.
6. Luchins, A. 1957. Experimental attempts to minimize the impact of first impressions. *In*
   The Order of Presentation in Persuasion, C. Hovland, ed. Yale University Press, New
   Haven, Conn.
7. Meyer, J. and Sobieszek, B. 1972. Effect of a child's sex on adult interpretations of its
   behavior. Develpm. Psychol. 6:42–48.
8. Pedersen, F. and Robson, K. 1969. Father participation in infancy. Amer. J. Orthopsychiat. 39(3):466–472.
9. Rebelsky, F. and Hanks, C. 1971. Fathers' verbal interaction with infants in the first three
   months of life. Child Develpm. 42:63–68.
10. Schaffer, H. 1971. The Growth of Sociability. Penguin Books, Baltimore.
11. Sears, R., Maccoby, E. and Levin, H. 1957. Patterns of Child Rearing. Row, Peterson,
    Evanston, Ill.

12. Tasch, R. 1952. The role of the father in the family. J. Exper. Ed. 20:319–361.
13. Wilson, P. 1968. The perceptual distortion of height as a function of ascribed academic status. J. Soc. Psychol. 74:97–102.
14. Zajonc, R. 1968. Attitudinal effects of mere exposure. J. Pers. Soc. Psychol. Monogr. Supplement 9:1–27.

QUESTIONS FOR DISCUSSION

1. Who is the audience for this article? How does the language and structure reflect that audience?
2. Why do parents focus so intensely on the gender of their newborn babies?
3. What are the two kinds of parental behavior that illustrate gender discrimination regarding newborns?
4. Do the differences that parents discriminate actually exist, according to the authors? What might account for the perceptual problems?
5. This text is structured according to a pattern typical of articles in scientific journals. Analyze the organization of the essay. Why are the sections separated? What function does each section serve?

PART 2

Politics and Government

I n *The Lincoln Nobody Knows*, the historian Richard N. Current states that, "Among Americans the words *politics* and *politician* long have been terms of reproach. [To many Americans] politics generally means 'dirty' politics."[1] Recent political scandals like Watergate and the Iran-Contra affair may only confirm people's suspicions that many politicians manipulate language to deceive people. One response to political deception is to over-generalize that all politicians are corrupt and that political involvement is hopeless. But simply ignoring public officials and their decisions does not make public issues go away; it is more effective to identify deception and to develop educated opinions on public affairs by learning to ask questions and to think critically.

The link between politics and deception is not likely to disappear, even at the best of times; the use of deceptive means is not new to contemporary American culture or to any other world culture. More than 2,000 years ago an Indian advisor named Kautilya advocated the use of spies to control those who opposed the ruler. Likewise, the 15th century Italian Niccolo Machiavelli advised the ruler of Florence to lie when it would further the ruler's plans. The deceptive means advocated by these authors have raised ethical questions about a ruler's means and ends: Is it ever justifiable for public officials to use deceptive means to accomplish their ends? If so, in what situations? And, what are the consequences of such decisions?

While these questions are crucial to an understanding of the role of politics and governments around the world, the arena of politics and government also includes debates over the best way to organize a society. Thus, writers like Confucius, Plato, Karl Marx, Thomas Jefferson, Julius Nyerere, Simone de Beauvoir, and Nelson Mandela all have proposed ideas that they believe would create better societies. But once again, the thoughtful reader will pose further questions: What are the reader's and the writer's social, political, economic, and cultural assumptions? How do they shape our definitions of a better society? Are political ideas and governments like Soviet communism, Tanzania's socialism, or American constitutional democracy universal or are they relative, depending on the time, place, and culture? What could Americans learn from other governments, and vice versa?

This part can be divided into three sections, with readings having to do with definitions, with diversity, and with issues of race and gender. The definitions section presents a brief historical context for the ideas of democracy, communism, socialism, nationalism, and technocracy. Unlike simpler dictionary definitions, these selections suggest that political and economic ideas change with time. Because these terms have no simple, static definition, they may seem quite different from the stereotyped concepts featured in our early education, in the news media, and in traditional political rhetoric. These definitions can be used as a reference for such readings in this part as the interview with Augusto Pinochet,

---

[1]Richard N. Current. *The Lincoln Nobody Knows* (New York, 1958), p. 187.

Julius Nyerere's "African Socialism," Karl Marx's "Bourgeois and Proletarians," Thomas Jefferson's *The Declaration of Independence*, and Alexis de Tocqueville's *Democracy in America*.

The readings that illustrate diversity feature a collection of influential political ideas that form a number of dialogues in which the ideas explicitly and implicitly comment on each other. Serving as political advisors, Kautilya and Machiavelli focus on "practical" issues of political power. In the tradition of *realpolitik* (politics based on practical and material needs), Kautilya and Machiavelli are less concerned with questions of ethics, freedom, justice, or equality than with questions of how leaders can retain power, deceive the public, and control their opposition. These realpolitik approaches might then be applied to any of the readings in this part, but are most clearly featured in the *Newsweek* interview with the Chilean ruler Augusto Pinochet. The Amnesty International selection on "Chile" documents cases of torture, adding to the controversy over Pinochet's rule.

In contrast to realpolitik, the rest of the diversity readings present a variety of idealistic proposals for better governments. For Plato, the solution to poor government requires that philosophers become kings; for Confucius, it requires a virtuous ruler. In contrast to this emphasis on individual rulers, the selection from Karl Marx argues that an inevitable class struggle between the bourgeois (the middle class) and proletarians (working class) would lead to a workers' revolution that would end class oppression. Unlike Marx's European tradition of communism, Julius Nyerere's "African Socialism" and *The Arusha Declaration* draw upon the extended family as a model for a cooperative society that rejects class struggle and economic exploitation. Like Thomas Jefferson's *The Declaration of Independence*, *The Arusha Declaration* sets forth ideal principles for government. These declarations can be further compared to the "Declaration of the Belgrade Conference . . . of Nonaligned Countries" and to the United Nations' *Universal Declaration of Human Rights*. Finally, Alexis de Tocqueville's *Democracy in America* reflects de Tocqueville's concern that America's democratic principles are threatened by the tyranny of the majority.

The final set of readings focuses upon the issues of power and politics, specifically sexism, racism, and imperialism. Simone de Beauvoir discusses the concept of the woman as the "Other" to explain the psychology of sexism. The selections from Amaury de Riencourt on the roles of women in ancient Greece and Nancy Barrett on the economic status of women in contemporary America further illustrate the consequences of sexism. Like de Beauvoir's theoretical account of sexism, Albert Memmi's text delves into the psychology of racism. "Shooting an Elephant," George Orwell's classic essay, graphically illustrates the ambiguity of British imperialism in Burma. *Satyagraha* presents Gandhi's philosophy of nonviolent protest which he used against British Colonialism in India. Martin Luther King, Jr.'s "Letter from Birmingham Jail" calls for nonviolent protest as a way to challenge racism in America while Nelson Mandela's "I Am Prepared to Die" defends sabotage as a means of challenging South Africa's system of apartheid.

KENNETH MINOGUE, ALFRED G. MEYER, PAUL HIRST, AND ROGER WILLIAMS

Definitions of Democracy, Communism, Socialism, Nationalism, and Technocracy

Politicians often play on the fears and hopes of an audience when using such terms as "communism," "socialism," and "democracy." But, while many politicians only vaguely define such terms, critical thinkers carefully define key abstract terms for their readers. The definitions presented in this selection demonstrate a general principle of language—that language is historical and that meaning changes depending upon time, place, and context. Hence, the definition of communism has changed from that used to describe Plato's ideal society of philosopher kings and the actual society of the early Christians to the varied nineteenth and twentieth century versions of Marx and Engels, Lenin, Stalin, Trotsky, Mao, and Gorbachev. Other European, African, South American, and Asian groups have traditions which they may label communist, even though they differ greatly from one another. Likewise, the definition of democracy can refer to the ancient Athenian style of democracy which did not rely solely upon representatives and, hence, was direct, but which excluded women and slaves. In the eighteenth, nineteenth, and much of the twentieth century, democracy in England and America focused on political rights, such as universal suffrage for women and people of color. But, since the mid-twentieth century, when many countries in Africa and Asia gained their independence from European colonial powers, the meaning has shifted toward economic rights and the right to self-determination. In these newly independent countries and in less industrialized nations, the egalitarian principles of land reform and redistribution of wealth are often considered essential for creating more democratic societies.

"Nationalism" and "technocracy" also are essential terms when discussing modern political issues. Since World War II, American political leaders often have mislabeled nationalist movements (such as in Iran and Guatemala), that called for social reform, as "communist." In Vietnam, for example, American politicians thought mostly in anticommunist terms and ignored the broader nationalist sentiment that perceived the U.S. government as being another foreign invader. Like nationalism, technocracy has been and continues to be a great shaper of the modern world. As the technology of industrial nations grows increasingly complex, the roles of scientists and specialists have gained in importance, and have influenced the way industrial nations handle their own social, economic, and military problems, as well as the way experts in industrial nations approach the problems of the less-industrialized nations of this world.

DEMOCRACY

In the classical Greek *polis*, democracy was the name of a constitution in which the poorer people (*demos*) exercised power in their own interest as against the interest of the rich and aristocratic. Aristotle thought it a debased form of constitution, and it played relatively little part in subsequent political thought, largely because Polybius and other writers diffused the idea that only mixed and balanced constitutions (incorporating monarchic, aristocratic and democratic elements) could be stable. Democracies were commonly regarded as aggressive and unstable and likely to lead (as in Plato's *Republic*) to tyranny. Their propensity to oppress minorities (especially the propertied) was what Burke meant when he described a perfect democracy as the most shameless thing in the world.

Democracy as popular power in an approving sense may occasionally be found in early modern times (in the radical thinkers of the English Civil War, the constitution of Rhode Island of 1641, and in the deliberations of the framers of the American Constitution), but the real vogue for democracy dates from the French Revolution. The main reason is that 'democracy' came to be the new name for the long-entrenched tradition of classical republicanism which, transmitted through Machiavelli, had long constituted a criticism of the dominant monarchical institutions of Europe. This tradition had often emphasized the importance of aristocratic guidance in a republic, and many of its adherents throughout Europe considered that British constitutional monarchy with an elected parliament was the very model of a proper republic. This idea fused in the nineteenth century with demand to extend the franchise, and the resulting package came generally to be called 'democracy'.

It is important to emphasize that democracy *was* a package, because the name had always previously described a source of power rather than a manner of governing. By the nineteenth century, however, the idea of democracy included representative parliaments, the separation of powers, the rule of law, civil rights and other such liberal desirabilities. All of these conditions were taken to be the culmination of human moral evolution, and the politics of the period often revolved around extensions of the franchise, first to adult males, then to women, and subsequently to such classes as young people of 18 (rather than 21) and, recently in Great Britain, to voluntary patients in mental hospitals.

Democracy proved to be a fertile and effervescent principle of political perfection. Inevitably, each advance towards democracy disappointed many adherents, but the true ideal could always be relocated in new refinements of the idea. The basis of many such extensions had been laid by the fact that 'democracy' was a Greek term used, for accidental reasons, to describe a complicated set of institutions whose real roots were medieval. The most important was representation, supported by some American founding fathers precisely because it might moderate rather than reflect the passions of an untutored multitude. The Greekness of the name, however, continually suggests that the practice of representation is not intrinsic to modern democracy, but rather a contingent imperfection resulting from the sheer size of modern nations by comparison with ancient city states. In fact, modern constitutional government is quite unrelated to the democracy of the Greeks.

Although modern democracy is a complicated package, the logic of the expression suggests a single principle. The problem is: what precisely is the principle? And a further question arises: how far should it extend? So far as the first question is concerned, democracy might be identified with popular sovereignty, majority rule, protection of minorities, affability, constitutional liberties, participation in decisions at every level, egalitarianism,[1] and much else. Parties emphasize one or other of these principles according to current convenience, but most parties in the modern world (the fascist parties between 1918 and 1945 are the most important exception) have seldom failed to claim a democratic legitimacy. The principle of democracy was thus a suitably restless principle for a restless people ever searching for constitutional perfection.

---

[1] **egalitarianism** A belief in human equality that argues for reducing or eliminating social, political, and economic inequalities. [Ed. note.]

Democracy is irresistible as a slogan because it seems to promise a form of government in which rulers and ruled are in such harmony that little actual governing will be required. Democracy was thus equated with a dream of freedom. For this reason, the nationalist theories which helped destroy the great European empires were a department of the grand principle of democracy, since everybody assumed that the people would want to be ruled by politicians of their own kind. The demographic complexities of many areas, however, were such that many people would inevitably be ruled by foreigners; and such people often preferred to be ruled on an imperial principle—in which all subjects are, as it were, foreigners—rather than on a national principle, which constitutes some as the nation, and the rest as minorities. In claiming to be democratic, rulers might hope to persuade their subjects that they ruled in the popular interest.

Democracy is possible only when a population can recognize both sectional and public interests, and organize itself for political action. Hence no state is seriously democratic unless an opposition is permitted to criticize governments, organize support, and contest elections. But in many countries, such oppositions are likely to be based upon tribes, nations or regions, which do not recognize a common or universal good in the state. Where political parties are of this kind, democratic institutions generate quarrels rather than law and order. In these circumstances, democracy is impossible, and the outcome has been the emergence of some other unifying principle: sometimes an army claiming to stand above 'politics', and sometimes an ideological party in which a doctrine supplies a simulacrum of the missing universal element. One-party states often lay claim to some eccentric (and superior) kind of democracy—basic, popular, guided and so on. In fact, the very name 'party' requires pluralism. Hence, in one-party states, the party is a different kind of political entity altogether, and the claim to democracy is merely window-dressing. This does not necessarily mean, however, that such governments are entirely without virtue. It would be foolish to think that one manner of government suited all peoples.

Democracy as an ideal in the nineteenth century took for granted citizens who were rationally reflective about the voting choices open to them. Modern political scientists have concentrated their attention upon the actual irrationalities of the democratic process. Some have even argued that a high degree of political apathy is preferable to mass enthusiasm which endangers constitutional forms.

Kenneth Minogue

FURTHER READING

Macpherson, C. B. (1973), *Democratic Theory: Essays in Retrieval*, Oxford.
Plamenatz, J. (1973), *Democracy and Illusion*, London.
Sartori, G. (1962), *Democracy*, Detroit.
Schumpeter, J. (1943), *Capitalism, Socialism and Democracy*, London.

COMMUNISM

Communism connotes any societal arrangement based on communal ownership, production, consumption, self-government, perhaps even communal sexual mating. The term refers both to such societies and practices and to any theory advocating them. Examples of the former can be found in religious orders throughout history and in radical communities, from the sixteenth-century Anabaptists to the contemporary 'counterculture'; and the most famous example of advocacy of communism may well be the regime proposed for the guardian caste in Plato's *Republic*.

In the middle of the nineteenth century, the most radical schools of the growing socialist movement, including that of Marx and Engels, called themselves communists in order to dissociate themselves from other, allegedly less consistent, socialist groups. Hence when reference is made to that period, communism often is synonymous with the system of ideas developed by Engels and Marx, even though they often used the terms 'communism' and 'socialism' interchangeably. Communism in this sense connotes the sum-total of Marxist doctrines; hence it is the Marxist critique of capitalism and liberal theory and the project for the proletarian revolution, though at times it connotes specifically the ultimate goal of that revolution—the society visualized as emerging out of it, which is dimly foreseen as a society without property, without classes or a division of labour, without institutions of coercion and domination. The precise features of this society are not delineated in the writings of Marx and Engels, and among Marxists there are controversies about the degree of residual alienation and oppression (if any) that one ought to expect in the communist society of the future. Some of the hints Marx and Engels themselves gave come from their notion of a primitive communism allegedly prevailing among the savage early ancestors of the human race.

Among the earliest followers of Engels and Marx, the term fell into disuse; most Marxists around the turn of the century called themselves Social-Democrats. The term was revived after the Russian Revolution of 1917 by V. I. Lenin, who renamed his faction of the Russian Marxist movement the 'Communist Party' and compelled all those parties who wished to join the newly-created Third (or Communist) International to adopt the same designation, so as to dissociate themselves from the Social-Democratic parties. As a consequence, communism since then connotes that interpretation of Marxism which considers the ideas and actions of Lenin and his Bolshevik faction to be the only correct interpretation of Marxism, and the sum-total of parties that subscribe to this interpretation.

Leninism is characterized by the insistence that meaningful social change can come only through revolution, while reforms threaten to corrupt the oppressed. Further, it implies the application of Marxism to countries where capitalism is underdeveloped, hence the development of flexible political strategies, including the mobilization of peasants and ethnic minorities for revolution. Foremost, it insists on the need for a 'vanguard party' of revolutionaries-by-profession to whom correct knowledge of the laws of history and politics ('consciousness') is attributed. Within the party and its numerous auxiliary organizations designed to mobilize the working class and its presumed allies, the vanguard is expected to ensure the prevalence of enlightened 'consciousness' over blind passion by a combination of mass initiative and bureaucratic control that Lenin called 'democratic centralism'. Finally, Leninism implies the accumulated experience of the Russian Communist Party in governing their country. Communism thus connotes the theory and practice of rule by communist parties.

Although the leaders of ruling communist parties have generally refrained from claiming that the systems they were ruling were communist, it has become customary in the Western world to refer to them as communist systems. Communism thus refers to any society or group of societies governed by communist parties.

The mature form of communist rule was developed in the USSR under the rule of J. V. Stalin. Hence Communism since the 1930s has become synonymous with Stalinism or Neo-Stalinism. This is a system in which the communist party proclaims itself the enlightened leadership and claims authority to speak for the entire nation. It enforces this claim through control over all organizations and associations, all forms of communication, education, and entertainment, individual appointments and careers. The chief aim of these systems is rapid economic growth through crash programmes of industrialization, carried out through a centralized command economy. Communism in its Stalinist form thus is a species of entrepreneurship.

Contemporary communist societies thus bear no resemblance to the vision of communism sketched by Marx and Engels or even to that provided by Lenin in his unfinished work, *The State and Revolution*. Yet the memory of that vision lingers and has repeatedly led to attempts within communist parties to define alternatives to Leninist and Stalinist theories and practices. Contemporary communism therefore is not one single orthodoxy, but an ever growing cluster of orthodoxies and heresies, all of them backing up their arguments by reference to Engels and Marx, yet fiercely contending with each other.

Alfred G. Meyer

FURTHER READING

Claudin, F. (1975), *The Communist Movement: From Comintern to Cominform*, London.
Daniels, R. V. (ed.) (1965), *Marxism and Communism: Essential Readings*, New York.
Kolakowski, L. (1978), *Main Currents of Marxism*, 3 vols, Oxford.
Meyer, A. G. (1984), *Communism* (4th edn), New York.
Rosenberg, A. (1967), *A History of Bolshevism*, New York.

SOCIALISM

Socialism is the name for a varied group of political theories and movements. Socialist ideas and agitation began in the early nineteenth century in England and France. The period between the 1820s and the 1850s was marked by a plethora of diverse and distinguished theorists, among them, Saint-Simon, Fourier, Owen, Blanc and Proudhon, and also many lesser thinkers. It was also marked by the foundation of co-operative societies, model utopian communities and the advocacy—and in the case of Blanc's national workshops half-hearted adoption—of schemes to be put into action by governments.

Socialism was brought into existence by the rise of industrial production and the intensification of wage labour in handicraft enterprises alongside it. Prior to the large-scale existence of workshops, factories and machines, most radical conceptions of a reorganization of society were agrarian, as in Rousseau's constitution for an imaginary republic of Corsica. Socialist doctrines sought to 'organize' society in order to replace the anarchy of the market-place and large-scale poverty with an orderly system based on greater or lesser degrees of central control, co-operation and mutuality. Organization offered a rational solution to the 'social question'—the problems of mass poverty and poor urban living conditions. Most of the early social- ists were middle-class reformers, concerned philanthropists who sought to better the lot of the poor by changes in social organization rather than charitable works.

The radical and revolutionary movements in this period were nationalist in countries like Hungary or Poland or Italy under foreign domination, and popular- democratic in England and France. Such political movements were not dominated by socialist ideas. Between 1848 and 1871 the popular democratic and revolutionary traditions exhausted themselves in the European countries in a series of political defeats, at the barricades in countries like France, or through political containment in the case of the Chartists in England.

In the period between 1848 and 1871, Marx and Engels made radical attempts to recast socialist theory. They attacked the utopianism[2] of their predecessors, refusing to promulgate schemes of social reform. In essence they argued that:

1. the class struggle is the objective basis of socialist victory, socialism is identified with the proletariat and its struggle to eliminate exploitation and oppression;
2. the class struggle arises from the system of social production and that the development of the forces of production would secure the objective basis for a planned economy;
3. the overthrow of the exploiting class and its ruling machinery, the state, would usher in a new period of popular self-government in which the domination of man by man would be replaced by the administration of things.

Marx and Engels insisted on the necessity of revolution, and the seizure of power by the working class, but they did recognize that universal suffrage might facilitate the downfall of capitalism.

Actually, it did nothing of the sort. Between 1870 and 1914 the institutional foundations of modern socialism were developed in Britain and Germany. Universal suffrage created the modern political party—a permanent machine with paid offi- cials whose task is to mobilize the mass electorate. The SPD became the dominant force in German socialism, not because it came to treat Marx's ideas as party ortho- doxy, but because it started early and effectively to compete for votes in elections for the Reichstag. In Britain and Germany, large-scale industrialism was accompanied by the growth of trade unionism. The British Labour Party was created to facilitate the parliamentary representation of the trade unions, and the links between the SPD and the unions were similarly close.

As a mass electoral party and the political representative of unionized labour, any socialist movement in an advanced industrial country had to relegate to vir- tual impotence the popular insurrectionary politics of the old European 'left'. Even

[2]**utopianism** A belief in an ideal state. [Ed. note.]

Engels conceded as much, and Eduard Bernstein did no more than carry the conclusion to its logical extreme. Bernstein's *Evolutionary Socialism* (1899) represented the
first articulate advocacy of 'social democracy' as against socialism, and it displaced
the goal of 'revolution' for a never-ending struggle for attainable reforms. Others,
like Karl Kautsky, argued that by parliamentary and legal means the workers could
engineer a revolutionary change in the social system.

   To the mass party and the labour union must be added the rise of big government as a key institutional support of modern socialist movements. In the period
1870–1914 in Britain and Germany, central state and municipal authorities came to
provide, administer and organize an increasing range of activities, mass schooling,
social insurance, public health, sewerage and electric light, and so on. This administration of mass needs and utilities provided another base for socialist advocacy
and practice. Fabian socialism consciously sought to intervene in central and local
government's provision, to provide an organizing core of intellectuals equipped to
shape the extent and character of 'big government'. The success of the Fabian position stands in stark contrast to the failure of the anti-statist doctrines of Guild Socialists and others. For all the forceful advocacy by able thinkers like G. D. H. Cole
(1953–61), the Guild Socialist movement was dead by the early 1920s. Likewise,
British syndicalism perished in the same period, while institutional unionism survived and flourished.

   After 1914 the landscape of the socialist movement in Europe was changed by
World War I, the split in socialism and the rise of Communism. The Communist
parties for a considerable period in the 1920s and early 1930s emphasized revolutionary insurrectionary politics, going so far as to stigmatize the still existent European
socialist parties like the SPD as 'social fascist'. World War II, the consolidation of
Soviet rule in Eastern Europe and the stabilization of parliamentary democracy in
Western Europe led to a radical change in the Communist parties. Where legally
permitted or successful, they became mass electoral parties and developed links
with their own labour unions, as in France and Italy, for example, and sought to
participate in government. The split between Communism and socialism in Europe,
bitter into the 1950s, ceased to have much meaning with the rise of Eurocommunism.

   Since 1945 socialist and social democratic parties have participated in government to a hitherto unprecedented degree. The post-war boom was a period of intensification of 'big government' and welfarism. In Scandinavia, the UK and Germany,
socialist parties became accepted parties of government, and in the Swedish case
ruled uninterruptedly for over thirty years. In this period, traditional socialist ideas,
centering on publicly-owned planned production, suffered at the expense of social-
democratic views of redistribution and welfare in a state-managed, full-employment,
capitalist system. Anthony Crosland's *The Future of Socialism* (1964) advocated, like
Bernstein, a change in British Labour Party doctrine to match the Party's practice.

   Since the end of the post-war boom in 1973, social democratic ideas have had to
compete with a revitalized socialist fundamentalism in the UK. At the same time
throughout Europe many intellectuals have begun to rethink the goals of socialism.
Many are chastened by the experience of centrally-planned production and distribution in the USSR, but also by the consequences of the growth of statist welfarism in

Western Europe. Many favour the sort of anti-authoritarian, decentralizing and self-management views advocated by Cole and the Guild Socialists. The problem with much of this rethinking is the failure to provide a new political base comparable to that provided by the mass party, the union and big government. A good example of such views is André Gorz's *Farewell to the Working Class* (1982). Socialist doctrine has entered a period of diversity and productivity comparable to the 1820s–50s; its institutional supports, however, remain those developed in the period 1870–1914.

Socialism has been treated as an exclusively European phenomenon. Socialism in the United States, having grown spectacularly between the formation of the American Socialist Party in 1901 and 1912, thereafter underwent a process of decline such that in 1938 it had been reduced to a mere 7,000 members. This failure is attributable to many causes but most important is the character of American trade unionism which made it impossible to create the links between a united union movement and a socialist political party so important in Germany and England. Socialist doctrines in the Third World, where they are not modelled on those of Europe, have tried to offer a vision of social organization different from that based on large-scale industry, as in the case of 'African Socialism'. Julius Nyerere (1969) offers perhaps the most systematic version of this alternative to European ideas. Some commentators would contend that not only have such doctrines been a dismal failure in practice, but also that as a doctrine they are better conceived as a variant of agrarian populism. Socialism is an outgrowth of advanced industrialism but, as the United States shows, is by no means an inevitable one.

Paul Hirst

REFERENCES

Berstein, E. (1961 [1899]), *Evolutionary Socialism*, New York.
Cole, G. D. H. (1953–61), *A History of Socialist Thought*, Vols I–V, London.
Crosland, A. (1964), *The Future of Socialism*, London.
Gorz, A. (1982), *Farewell to the Working Class*, London.
Nyerere, J. K. (1969), *Freedom and Socialism*, Dar-es-Salaam.

FURTHER READING

Wright, A. W. (1979), *G. D. H. Cole and Socialist Democracy*, Oxford.

NATIONALISM

Nationalism is the belief that each nation has both the right and the duty to constitute itself as a state. There are many difficulties in specifying what a nation is—in Europe, for example, the candidates range from the Welsh and the Basques to Occitanians and Northumbrians—but some common culture is indispensable and a shared language highly desirable. The Swiss have so far got by without a common language, but its lack has sorely tried the rulers of Belgium. Nationalist theory usually attributes conflict to cross-national oppression, and thus offers a promise of world peace when self-determination has become a global reality.

Nationalism emerged in the hatred of cosmopolitanism which registered the resentment of Germans and other Europeans who were coming to feeling marginal in terms of the universalistic rationalism of the French Enlightenment. The romantic idea that true humanity must be mediated by a deep involvement in one's own unique culture led to an admiration for songs, poems, stories, plays and other creations understood as emanations of the national soul. The language of a people was accorded a unique value, no less as the medium of cultural self-expression than as a practical rule of thumb about how far the boundaries of a putative nation might stretch. The conquests of Napoleon turned these particularistic passions in a practical direction, and Fichte's *Addresses to the German Nation* delivered at Berlin in 1807–8 struck a responsive chord throughout Germany. Italy and Germany were both plausible candidates for state creation and both duly became states, though Italy remains imperfectly national to this day, while German unity owed more to Bismarck than to popular passion for nationhood.

The spread of nationalist ideas to Eastern Europe and beyond, where very different peoples were inextricably intertwined, was bound to create difficulties. Doctrinal diffusion was facilitated by the growth of industry, and of cities. Teachers, journalists, clergymen and other intellectuals found in nationalist ideas an identity for the present and a vision for the future. Some set to work writing down languages previously purely oral; others constructed a literature and elicited a suitable history. Opera and the novel were favourite vehicles of nationalist feeling. The politics of these endeavours triumphed with the Treaty of Versailles in 1918, which settled Europe in terms of the principle of national self-determination.

Throughout Africa and Asia, nationalist ideas fuelled the campaigns to replace the old European empires with home grown rulers, but since there were few plausible nations in this area, successor states which had been constructed on a variety of principles claimed freedom in order to *begin* the process of cultural homogenization which might lead to nationhood. Pakistan, based upon the religious identity of Islam, attempted to hold together two separated areas inherited from the British raj, and could not be sustained in that form; the eastern region broke off as Bangladesh in 1971. The artificial boundaries of imperial Africa have, however, been a surprisingly successful container of the often chaotic mixture of tribes they contained, though virtually all have had to compensate for lack of homogeneity by centralizing and frequently tyrannizing governments.

Political scientists often find in nationalism an attractive form of explanation because it promises to explain the hidden causes of conflict between different ethnic groups. In this usage, nationalism is not a belief, but rather a force supposed to move people to both action and belief. Such a concept provokes a search for the conditions under which the force is triggered. The promise of this research programme, like many another in political science, far exceeds the performance. Nationalism is better treated as a complex of ideas and sentiments which respond flexibly, decade by decade, to new situations, usually situations of grievance, in which peoples may find themselves.

Kenneth Minogue

FURTHER READING

Hertz, F. (1944), *Nationality in History and Politics*, London.
Kedourie, E. (1960), *Nationalism*, London.
Minogue, K. R. (1963), *Nationalism*, London.
Smith, A. D. (1971), *Theories of Nationalism*, London.

TECHNOCRACY

Rule or tendency to rule by technical experts. In *The Rise of the Technocrats* (1965), W. H. G. Armytage describes the St Simonians, followers of Count Henri de Saint-Simon (1760–1825), as 'the first technocrats: apostles of the religion of industry'. The term itself was coined by Californian engineer William H. Smyth in 1919 for an organization, Technocracy Inc. This arose from a group, the 'technical alliance', for whom Thorstein Veblen's book *The Engineers and the Price System* (1921) and especially its final chapter, 'A memorandum on a practical soviet of technicians', became a central text. In the early 1930s, thanks largely to Howard Scott, the concept achieved some popular resonance, only to be overtaken by the New Deal. Jean Meynaud in *Technocracy* (1968, p. 212) found the term 'common' in France but 'comparatively unknown' elsewhere in Europe. Several authors have coined similar neologisms. For example: President Eisenhower in his Farewell Address, 17 January 1961 warned that public policy could become the 'captive of a scientific-technological elite'; J. K. Galbraith defined the Technostructure as 'all who participate in group decision-making or the organisation which they form'; Nigel Calder (*Technopolis*, pp. 22–3) states that 'we inhabit Technopolis, a society not only shaped but continuously modified in drastic ways by scientific and technical novelty'; Zbigniew Brzezinski argues that 'the post-industrial society is becoming a technocratic society: a society shaped by the impact of technology and electronics'.

Economic planning, operations research, systems analysis and technology assessment, etc. are evidently all technocratic activities, and the technocratic tendency is seemingly inevitable in advanced industrial societies. However, political disagreements arise over ends as much as means and here technocrats have no special advantage. They can also disagree among themselves. Alvin M. Weinberg defines 'trans-scientific' questions as questions 'which can be asked by science and yet *which cannot be answered by science*'. It follows that although some societies (for example France under the Fourth Republic) and institutions (such as the Pentagon when Robert McNamara was Defence Secretary) seem to be more technocratic than most, true government by technocracy is an unrealized, and unlikely, extreme.

Roger Williams

FURTHER READING

Armytage, W. H. G.: *The Rise of the Technocrats*. London: Routledge & Kegan Paul, 1965.
Brzezinski, Z.: *Between Two Ages*. New York: Viking, 1970; London: Greenwood, 1982.
Calder, N.: *Technopolis*. London: MacGibbon & Kee, 1969.

Galbraith, J. K.: *The New Industrial State*, chs 2 and 6. New York and Harmondsworth: Pelican, 1967, 1969.
Meynaud, J.: *Technocracy*, trans. P. Barnes. New York: Free Press, 1968.
Public Papers of the Presidents: Dwight D. Eisenhower, pp. 1035–40. Washington, DC: US Government Printing Office, 1961.
Veblen, T.: *The Engineers and the Price System*. New York: Viking, 1921.
Weinberg, A. M.: Science and trans-science. *Minerva* 10.2 (1972) 204–22.

QUESTIONS FOR DISCUSSION

Before reading and discussing the preceding definitions, how would you have defined democracy, communism, socialism, nationalism, and technocracy?

Democracy

1. How has the definition of democracy changed over time? Compare the meaning of the term in ancient Greece (where citizens, excluding women and slaves, had a direct democracy) to the West's representative democracy in the 19th century. What problems might arise if we don't specify the time, place, and culture that uses the term "democracy"? Do you agree that a direct democracy is not practical in a modern nation as implied by the author? Explain.
2. The author describes democracy as a "complicated package." What do you think he means by this?
3. Why is democracy "irresistible as a slogan"?
4. According to the author, what is the one criterion necessary for all "seriously democratic" states? Do you agree that a one-party system cannot be democratic? Explain. If a one-party system is less democratic than a two-party system, is a two-party system less democratic than a multi-party system?

Communism and Socialism

1. What connotations do these terms often have in American culture? In what ways do politicians use them? How does the common usage of these terms differ from these definitions?
2. What is the basic definition of communism according to the reading?
3. Compare and contrast pre-Marxist communism with 19th century Marxist communism, Lenin's communism, Stalin's communism, and contemporary European versions. How has European communism changed over time?
4. What is the relationship between communism and socialism over time? How have social democrats in Europe gotten along with the communists in the 20th century?
5. Why might Marx and Engels use the terms "communism" and "socialism" interchangeably? Why might they want to "recast socialist theory"? How did they view Utopian socialism?
6. Some writers have claimed that independence movements often are motivated by nationalism rather than by theories of democracy, communism, and social-

ism. Did revolutionary movements in the 19th and 20th centuries necessarily have a communist or socialist ideology? What other factors might be of greater importance as the basis for revolution?

7. How do Germany's SPD, Britain's Labor Party, and modern European socialist movements differ from Marx and Engel's communism?

8. How might the recent changes in the Soviet Union and Eastern Europe change this definition of communism?

Nationalism

1. Why is self-determination necessary for world peace according to nationalist theory? Look up a definition of imperialism and discuss how nationalism might or might not lead to imperialism.

2. Why might cultural uniqueness be an important aspect for nationalism?

3. In your opinion, what might be the positive and negative aspects of nationalism?

Technocracy

1. President Eisenhower warned that America could be dominated by "a scientific-technological elite" and also warned that a "military-industrial complex" (an unrestrained partnership between the military and business) was a threat to democracy. Why might technocracy be a threat to democratic ideals? How might technocracy be necessary for a modern industrial society? Can the two be reconciled?

KAUTILYA
The Arthashastra

The Arthashastra, *which means "a treatise on wealth and power," is attributed to the Indian minister Kautilya, a man well-known for his cleverness. Helping to overthrow the Nanda dynasty, Kautilya became an advisor to the despotic king Chandragupta Maurya, who reigned from 322–298 B.C.E. As advisor to the king, Kautilya composed* The Arthashastra. *This manual, written to further promote the autocratic style of government, discusses everything from rearing princes and promoting trade to spying on opponents and suppressing rebellions. The ideal government, according to* The Arthashastra, *is a well-organized bureaucratic state that could control dissent, much like the state proposed by Machiavelli in* The Prince *(p. 180).*

CHAPTER 6: CONTROL OF SENSES

By conquering the six enemies of living (lust, anger, greed, vanity, haughtiness and exuberance) he (the ruler) shall acquire balanced wisdom. He shall keep company with the learned. He shall get information through his spies. By his actions, he shall set up safety and security. By enforcing his authority, he shall keep his subjects observing their duties and obligations. He shall exercise control over himself by learning sciences. He shall help his subjects to acquire wealth and do good to them.

In this manner, with control over his impulses, he shall abstain from hurting the women and the property of others. He shall avoid lust, falsehood, hauteur and evil inclinations. He shall keep away from wrong and wasteful transactions.

He shall enjoy his lawful desires in conformity with the right and the economic. He shall pursue the three merits of living: charity, wealth and desire.[1] Any one of these merits carried to excess not only hurts the other two, but itself.

Wealth is the foundation of the other two because charity and desire depend upon it for their fulfilment.

Teachers and ministers should keep the ruler away from dangers and warn him of time-schedules even in private.[2] Such teachers and ministers are always respected.

Authority is possible only with assistance. A single wheel cannot move by itself. The ruler, therefore, shall employ ministers and hear their advice.

CHAPTER 10: ON SPIES

Advised and assisted by a tried council of officers, the ruler should proceed to institute spies.

Spies are in the guise of pseudo-student, priest, householder, trader, saint practising renunciation, classmate or colleague, desperado, poisoner and woman mendicant.

An artful person, capable of reading human nature, is a pseudo-student. Such a person should be encouraged with presents and purse and be told by the officer: "Sworn to the ruler and myself you shall inform us what wickedness you find in others."

One initiated in scripture and of pure character is a priest-spy. This spy should carry on farming, cattle culture and commerce with resources given to him. Out of the produce and profit accrued, he should encourage other priests to live with him and send them on espionage work. The other priests also should send their followers on similar errands.

A householder-spy is a farmer fallen in his profession but pure in character. This spy should do as the priest.[3]

A trader-spy is a merchant in distress but generally trustworthy. This spy should carry on espionage, in addition to his profession.

A person with proper appearance and accomplishments as an ascetic is a saint-spy. He surrounds himself with followers and may settle down in the suburb of a big city and may pretend prayer and fasting in public. Trader-spies may associate with this class of spies. He may practise fortune-telling, palmistry, and pretend supernatural and magical powers by predictions. The followers will adduce proof for the

---

[1]I.e., *dharma, artha, kama*.
[2]This refers to a later chapter (18) which directs the ruler to set an example of energy and activity and assign his various functions to specific parts of the day. Here he is directed to maintain his schedule even when unobserved by others.
[3]I.e., carry on farming, as in the previous paragraph.

predictions of their saint. He may even foretell official rewards and official changes, which the officers concerned may substantiate by reciprocating.

Rewarded by the rulers with money and titles, these five institutions of espionage should maintain the integrity of the country's officers.

CHAPTER 12: HOME AND OPPOSITION PARTIES

Having instituted spies over his chief officers, the ruler should spread his intelligence network over the citizens and the country folk.

Social spies, forming into opposite camps, should carry propaganda into places of confluence of people, tourist centres, associations and general congregations. . . .

Spies should also know all news current in the state. Special spies should collect news of joy or distress among those who professionalise in grains, cattle and gold of the ruler, among those who supply them to the ruler (or administration); among those who harbour a relative or restrain a troubled area and those who check a wild tribe or an invading enemy. The greater the contentment of such groups of people, the greater the rewards given to them. Those who demur should be propitiated by presents or conciliation, or disputes may be created to break their alliance with each other, as from a neighbouring enemy, a wild tribe or a disputant to the ruler's position.

Failing this measure, they must be commissioned to collect unpopular fines and taxes. Those in severe opposition may be quelled by punishment in secret, or by exposing them to the wrath of the people of the land. Or having hostaged their families, they may be sent to the mines to break contact with the enemies [of the state].

The enemies [of the state] employ as instruments those who are incensed, those who are ambitious, as well as those who despise the ruler. Special spies, parading as fortune tellers, should be instituted to spy on such persons in their relation with each other and with foreigners.

Thus, in his own state, the ruler should preserve parties and factions among the people, friendly or opposed, powerful or puerile, against the intrigues and machinations of the foreigners.

CHAPTER 14: ADMINISTRATIVE COUNCILS

After consolidating the attitude of both internal and external parties, both within and abroad, the ruler should consider administrative affairs.

Deliberation in well-constituted councils precedes administrative measures. The proceedings of a council should be in camera and deliberations made top secret so that not even a bird can whisper. The ruler should be guarded against disclosure.

Whoever divulges secret deliberations should be destroyed. Such guilt can be detected by physical and attitudinal changes of ambassadors, ministers and heads.

Secrecy of proceedings in the council and guarding of officers participating in the council must be organised.

The causes of divulgence of counsels are recklessness, drink, talking in one's sleep and infatuation with women which assail councillors.

He of secretive nature or who is not regarded well will divulge council matters. Disclosure of council secrets is of advantage to persons other than the ruler and his high officers. Steps should be taken to safeguard deliberations. . . .

CHAPTER 16: PROTECTION OF PRINCES

. . . The prince should be protected from wicked influences. He should be taught properly, since he is at an age of trust. He should be told about right, but not of non-right; he should be told of wealth, but not of non-wealth. He should be scared of drink and women by a process of making him drunk and of confronting him with blackmailing women. If fond of gambling, he should be blackmailed by tricksters. If fond of hunting, by forest brigands. If he shows proclivities[4] for rebelling, he should be scared by narration of hardships and even ignominious death attending such ventures.

When a prince is of commendable disposition, he should be made commander-in-chief or nominated successor.

Princes are of three categories: those of dynamic intelligence; those of stagnant intelligence; and those who are mentally deficient.

He who carries out mandates of right and leading to wealth is of dynamic intelligence. He who never carries out good instructions is of stagnant intelligence. He who entangles himself in avoidable dangers leading to wickedness and poverty is mentally incompetent.

If a ruler has a deficient son, attempt should be made to beget a grandson by him. Or to get sons from his daughters.

If a ruler is too old or diseased to beget children, he may mandate a close relation or any neighbouring ruler of high qualities to beget a son for him through his queen.

Never should a mentally deficient son be made to sit on the seat of power.

Unless in times of grave danger, the eldest son should succeed the ruler. Sometimes sovereignty may reside in a corporation. Corporate sovereignty is the most invincible form of authority in the world.[5]

CHAPTER 20: PERSONAL SECURITY

. . . The ruler should employ as his security staff only such persons as have noble and proven ancestry and are closely related to him and are well trained and loyal. No foreigners, or anonymous persons, or persons with clouded antecedents are to be employed as security staff for the ruler.

In a securely guarded chamber, the chief should supervise the ruler's food arrangements.

Special precautions are to be taken against contaminated and poisoned food. The following reveal poison: rice sending out deep blue vapour; unnaturally col-

---

[4]**proclivities** Inclinations or predispositions toward something. [Ed. note.]
[5]Because each member acts as a check on the others.

oured and artificially dried-up and hard vegetables; unusually bright and dull vessels; foamy vessels; streaky soups, milk and liquor; white streaked honey; strange-tempered food; carpets and curtains stained with dark spots and threadbare; polishless and lustreless metallic vessels and gems.

The poisoner reveals himself by parched and dry mouth, hesitating talk, perspiration, tremour, yawning, evasive demeanour and nervous behaviour.

Experts in poison detection should be in attendance on the ruler. The physicians attending the ruler should satisfy themselves personally as to the purity of the drugs which they administer to the ruler. The same precaution is indicated for liquor and beverages which the ruler uses. Scrupulous cleanliness should be insisted on in persons in charge of the ruler's dress and toilet requisites. This should be ensured by seals. . . .

In any entertainment meant for the amusement of the ruler, the actors should not use weapons, fire and poison. Musical instruments and accoutrements for horses, elephants and vehicles should be secured in the palace.

The ruler should mount beasts and vehicles only after the traditional rider or driver has done so. If he has to travel in a boat, the pilot should be trustworthy and the boat itself secured to another boat. There should be a proper convoy on land or water guarding the ruler. He should swim only in rivers which are free of larger fishes and crocodiles and hunt in forests free from snakes, man-eaters and brigands.

He should give private audience only attended by his security guards. He should receive foreign ambassadors in his full ministerial council. While reviewing his militia, the ruler should also attend in full battle uniform and be on horseback or on the back of an elephant. When he enters or exits from the capital city, the path of the ruler should be guarded by staffed officers and cleared of armed men, mendicants and the suspicious. He should attend public performances, festivals, processions or religious gatherings accompanied by trained bodyguards. The ruler should guard his own person with the same care with which he secures the safety of those around him through espionage arrangements.

CHAPTER 41: DECAY, STABILISATION, AND PROGRESS OF STATES

Every state can be said to have a sixfold policy as against any other state.

Ancient thinkers hold that armistice, war, neutrality, invasion, alliance and peace are the six principal policy-relations. Sixfold policy can be reduced into peace, which means concord supported by pacts; war, implying armed aggression; neutrality involving nonchalance; armed invasion against another power; alliance involving appeal for assistance to another power; bilateral policy involving making war with one and suing for peace with another.

Any power inferior to another should sue for peace; any power superior in might to another should launch into war; any power which fears no external attack and which has no strength to wage war should remain neutral; any power with high war-potential should indulge in invasion; any debilitated power should seek new alliances; any power which tries to play for time in mounting an offensive should indulge in a bilateral policy of making war with one and suing for peace with another.

A state should always observe such a policy as will help it strengthen its defensive fortifications and life-lines of communications, build plantations, construct villages, and exploit the mineral and forest wealth of the country, while at the same time preventing fulfilment of similar programmes in the rival state.

Whoever estimates that the rate of growth of the state's potential is higher than that of the enemy can afford to ignore such an enemy.

Any two states hostile to each other, finding that neither has an advantage over the other in fulfilment of their respective programmes, should make peace with each other.

No state should pursue a policy which, while not enabling it to have means to fulfil its own programmes, does not impose a similar handicap on its neighbour: this is the path to reversion.

When any state evaluates that its loss over time would be much less than its acquisition as compared with its rivals, it can afford to ignore its present recession.

When any two states which are rivals expect to acquire equal possessions over the same span of time, they should keep peace with each other.

Stagnation occurs when there is neither progression nor regression. When a temporary stagnation is expected to lead to greater rate of growth than that of the rival, the stagnation can be ignored.

A state can augment its resources by observing peaceful pacts with an enemy in the following situations:

Where, maintaining peace, productive operations of strategic importance can be planned and executed, preventing the rival state at the same time from fulfilling similar programmes;

When under the terms of the peace pact, the state can enjoy the resources created by the productive projects of its enemy in addition to its own resources;

When the state can plan works of sabotage through espionage on the plans and projects of its enemy;

Where under powerful incentives of happy settlements, immigration concessions, tax exemptions, pleasant work-conditions, large profits and high wages, immigration can be induced of strategic workers from an enemy state;

Where because of a prior pact, the enemy can harass another state which is also hostile;

Where because of invasion of the enemy state by another power, the workers of the enemy state immigrate and settle down in the state;

Where because of damage to the productive sectors of the enemy, his potential for offensive is reduced;

Where the state can, by pacts with other states, increase its own resources;

Where a sphere of alliance is formed of which an enemy state is a member, the alliance can be broken by forming fresh alliances.

A state can increase its own resources by preserving hostility with another state in the following situations:

Where the state is composed of military races and war-like corporations;

Where the state has natural defensive fortifications like mountains, woods, rivers and forts and is capable of liquidating the enemy's offensive;

Where harassing operations can be launched on an attacking enemy from powerful fortifications in the states;

Where internal disorders sabotage the war potential of the enemy;

Where invasion of the enemy by another hostile power can be expected to create strategic immigration of skilled workers into the state.

A policy of neutrality can be sustained in the following situations:

Where the balance of power between states is even: as when neither state can immobilise the other;

Where, in the event of an attack, the state can intensify the tribulations of the enemy without loss of its own strategic power.

A state can indulge in armed invasion only:

Where, by invasion, it can reduce the power of an enemy without in any way reducing its own potential, by making suitable arrangements for protection of its own strategic works.

A state should form an alliance with a powerful power where its potential is strong neither to harass its enemy nor to withstand its offensive. It should also attempt reconstruction of its potential from the stage of regression to that of stabilisation and from that of stabilisation to that of progress.

A state can pursue a bilateral policy where it can benefit in resources by maintaining peace with one enemy, and waging war with another.

The central aim of inter-state sixfold policy is to enable a state to advance from a condition of regression to progress through the intermediary state of stabilisation or balance of the forces of advance.

CHAPTER 54: RESTORATION OF LOST BALANCE OF POWER

When an invader is assailed by an alliance of his enemies, he should try to purchase the leader of the alliance with offers of gold and his own alliance and by diplomatic camouflage of the threat of treachery from the alliance of powers. He should instigate the leader of the allied enemies to break up his alliance.

The invader should also attempt to break the allied enemies' formation by setting up the leader of the alliance against the weaker of his enemies, or attempt to forge a combination of the weaker allies against their leader. He may also form a pact with the leader through intrigue, or offer of resources. When the confederation is shattered, he may form alliances with any of his former enemies.

If the allied enemies have no leader, the invader can form a pact with the most influential member of the confederated allies. Or with a powerful member, or with a popular member or with a designing member or with a transient ally, bent on protecting and advancing his own self-interest.

If a state is weak in treasury or in striking power, attention should be directed to strengthen both through stabilisation of authority. Irrigational projects are a source of agricultural prosperity. Good highways should be constructed to facilitate movements of armed might and merchandise. Mines should be developed, as they supply ammunition. Forests should be conserved, as they supply material for defence, communication and vehicles. Pasture lands are the source of cattle wealth.

Thus, a state should build up its striking power through development of the exchequer, the army and wise counsel; and, till the proper time, should conduct itself as a weak power towards its neighbours, to evade conflict or envy from enemy or allied states. If the state is deficient in resources, it should acquire them from related or allied states. It should attract to itself capable men from corporations, from wild and ferocious tribes, and foreigners, and organise espionage that will damage hostile powers.

QUESTIONS FOR DISCUSSION

1. How does Kautilya define the wise ruler? What qualities should a ruler have? Why must *he* control *his* impulses? Why should the ruler not overindulge the merits of "charity, wealth, and desire"?
2. Do modern political candidates need to conquer the "six enemies"? Explain.
3. What roles do ministers and spies play according to Kautilya? How did spies disguise themselves? How might contemporary spies disguise themselves? Could there be a country that does not need spies? When, if ever, is it ethical or just to use spies? Explain, using your imagination or recent news stories.
4. Kautilya states that "those in severe opposition may be quelled by punishment in secret." What does this mean? Compare this to Amnesty International's reading on "Chile" (p. 190). What ethical principles, if any, can justify torture?
5. Discuss Kautilya's illustrations supporting his claim that "the prince [unlike Machiavelli's usage, this refers to a future ruler] should be protected from wicked influences." How effective do you think this education would be?

NICCOLO MACHIAVELLI
The Prince

Niccolo Machiavelli (1469–1527), a native Florentine, was a statesman and political theorist who lived in Florence during a period when Italy was divided into city-states. The year before Machiavelli wrote The Prince, *Giuliano de Medici began his short reign as the ruler of Florence (1512–1513) and imprisoned the republican Machiavelli, whom Giuliano had suspected of conspiring against him. Nevertheless, seeking to regain a position in the government, Machiavelli dedicated* The Prince *to the powerful Lorenzo Medici, father of Giuliano. He further hoped that* The Prince *would inspire the Medicis to defend Italy from France and Spain. The work is notorious for its pragmatic, amoral advice that a prince should use any means to maintain his power. The term "Machiavellian" was coined to describe deceptive and manipulative practices that became associated with* The Prince. *This treatise on power can be compared to* The Arthashastra *(p. 173), which preceded it by eighteen centuries.*

CHAPTER XV

Of the Things for Which Men, and Especially Princes, Are Praised or Blamed

It now remains to be seen what are the methods and rules for a prince as regards his subjects and friends. And as I know that many have written of this, I fear that my writing about it may be deemed presumptuous, differing as I do, especially in this matter, from the opinions of others. But my intention being to write something of use to those who understand, it appears to me more proper to go to the real truth of the matter than to its imagination; and many have imagined republics and principalities which have never been seen or known to exist in reality; for how we live is so far removed from how we ought to live, that he who abandons what is done for what ought to be done, will rather learn to bring about his own ruin than his preservation. A man who wishes to make a profession of goodness in everything must necessarily come to grief among so many who are not good. Therefore it is necessary for a prince, who wishes to maintain himself, to learn how not to be good, and to use this knowledge and not use it, according to the necessity of the case.

Leaving on one side, then, those things which concern only an imaginary prince, and speaking of those that are real, I state that all men, and especially princes, who are placed at a greater height, are reputed for certain qualities which bring them either praise or blame. Thus one is considered liberal, another *misero* or miserly (using a Tuscan term, seeing that *avaro* with us still means one who is rapaciously acquisitive and *misero* one who makes grudging use of his own); one a free giver, another rapacious; one cruel, another merciful; one a breaker of his word, another trustworthy; one effeminate and pusillanimous, another fierce and high-spirited; one humane, another haughty; one lascivious, another chaste; one frank, another astute; one hard, another easy; one serious, another frivolous; one religious, another an unbeliever, and so on. I know that every one will admit that it would be highly praiseworthy in a prince to possess all the above-named qualities that are reputed good, but as they cannot all be possessed or observed, human conditions not permitting of it, it is necessary that he should be prudent enough to avoid the scandal of those vices which would lose him the state, and guard himself if possible against those which will not lose it him, but if not able to, he can indulge them with less scruple. And yet he must not mind incurring the scandal of those vices, without which it would be difficult to save the state, for if one considers well, it will be found that some things which seem virtues would, if followed, lead to one's ruin, and some others which appear vices result in one's greater security and wellbeing.

CHAPTER XVI

Of Liberality and Niggardliness

Beginning now with the first qualities above named, I say that it would be well to be considered liberal; nevertheless liberality such as the world understands it will injure you, because if used virtuously and in the proper way, it will not be known, and you will incur the disgrace of the contrary vice. But one who wishes to obtain the reputation of liberality among men, must not omit every kind of sumptuous display, and to such an extent that a prince of this character will consume by such means all his resources, and will be at last compelled, if he wishes to maintain his name for liberality, to impose heavy taxes on his people, become extortionate, and do everything possible to obtain money. This will make his subjects begin to hate him, and he will be little esteemed being poor, so that having by this liberality injured many and benefited but few, he will feel the first little disturbance and be endangered by every peril. If he recognises this and wishes to change his system, he incurs at once the charge of niggardliness.

A prince, therefore, not being able to exercise this virtue of liberality without risk if it be known, must not, if he be prudent, object to be called miserly. In course of time he will be thought more liberal, when it is seen that by his parsimony his revenue is sufficient, that he can defend himself against those who make war on him, and undertake enterprises without burdening his people, so that he is really liberal to all those from whom he does not take, who are infinite in number, and niggardly to all to whom he does not give, who are few. In our times we have seen nothing great done except by those who have been esteemed niggardly; the others have all been ruined. Pope Julius II, although he had made use of a reputation for liberality in order to attain the papacy, did not seek to retain it afterwards, so that he might be able to wage war. The present King of France has carried on so many wars without imposing an extraordinary tax, because his extra expenses were covered by the parsimony he had so long practised. The present King of Spain, if he had been thought liberal, would not have engaged in and been successful in so many enterprises.

For these reasons a prince must care little for the reputation of being a miser, if he wishes to avoid robbing his subjects, if he wishes to be able to defend himself, to avoid becoming poor and contemptible, and not to be forced to become rapacious; this niggardliness is one of those vices which enable him to reign. If it is said that Cæsar attained the empire through liberality, and that many others have reached the highest positions through being liberal or being thought so, I would reply that you are either a prince already or else on the way to become one. In the first case, this liberality is harmful; in the second, it is certainly necessary to be considered liberal. Cæsar was one of those who wished to attain the mastery over Rome, but if after attaining it he had lived and had not moderated his expenses, he would have destroyed that empire. And should any one reply that there have been many princes, who have done great things with their armies, who have been thought extremely liberal, I would answer by saying that the prince may either spend his own wealth and that of his subjects or the wealth of others. In the first case he must be sparing, but for the rest he must not neglect to be very liberal. The liberality is very necessary to a prince who marches with his armies, and lives by plunder, sack and ransom, and is dealing with the wealth of others, for without it he would not be followed by his soldiers. And you may be very generous indeed with what is not the property of yourself or your subjects, as were Cyrus, Cæsar, and Alexander; for spending the wealth of others will not diminish your reputation, but increase it, only spending your own resources will injure you. There is nothing which destroys itself so much as liberality, for by using it you lose the power of using it, and become either poor and despicable, or, to escape poverty, rapacious and hated. And of all things that a prince must guard against, the most important are being despicable or hated, and liberality will lead you to one or other of these conditions. It is, therefore, wiser to have the name of a miser, which produces disgrace without hatred, than to incur of necessity the name of being rapacious, which produces both disgrace and hatred.

CHAPTER XVII

Of Cruelty and Clemency, and Whether It Is Better to Be Loved or Feared

Proceeding to the other qualities before named, I say that every prince must desire to be considered merciful and not cruel. He must, however, take care not to misuse this mercifulness. Cesare Borgia was considered cruel, but his cruelty had brought order to the Romagna, united it, and reduced it to peace and fealty. If this is considered well, it will be seen that he was really much more merciful than the Florentine people, who, to avoid the name of cruelty, allowed Pistoia to be destroyed. A prince, therefore, must not mind incurring the charge of cruelty for the purpose of keeping his subjects united and faithful; for, with a very few examples, he will be more merciful than those who, from excess of tenderness, allow disorders to arise, from whence spring bloodshed and rapine; for these as a rule injure the whole community, while the executions carried out by the prince injure only individuals. And of all princes, it is impossible for a new prince to escape the reputation of cruelty, new states being always full of dangers. Wherefore Virgil through the mouth of Dido says:

> Res dura, et regni novitas me talia cogunt
> Moliri, et late fines custode tueri.[1]

Nevertheless, he must be cautious in believing and acting, and must not be afraid of his own shadow, and must proceed in a temperate manner with prudence and humanity, so that too much confidence does not render him incautious, and too much diffidence does not render him intolerant.

From this arises the question whether it is better to be loved more than feared, or feared more than loved. The reply is, that one ought to be both feared and loved,

---

[1] Hard times, and the newness of my reign, have forced me to post guards far and wide along our borders for our own safety. [Ed. trans.]

but as it is difficult for the two to go together, it is much safer to be feared than loved, if one of the two has to be wanting. For it may be said of men in general that they are ungrateful, voluble, dissemblers, anxious to avoid danger, and covetous of gain; as long as you benefit them, they are entirely yours; they offer you their blood, their goods, their life, and their children, as I have before said, when the necessity is remote; but when it approaches, they revolt. And the prince who has relied solely on their words, without making other preparations, is ruined; for the friendship which is gained by purchase and not through grandeur and nobility of spirit is bought but not secured, and at a pinch is not to be expended in your service. And men have less scruple in offending one who makes himself loved than one who makes himself feared; for love is held by a chain of obligation which, men being selfish, is broken whenever it serves their purpose; but fear is maintained by a dread of punishment which never fails.

Still, a prince should make himself feared in such a way that if he does not gain love, he at any rate avoids hatred; for fear and the absence of hatred may well go together, and will be always attained by one who abstains from interfering with the property of his citizens and subjects or with their women. And when he is obliged to take the life of any one, let him do so when there is a proper justification and manifest reason for it; but above all he must abstain from taking the property of others, for men forget more easily the death of their father than the loss of their patrimony. Then also pretexts for seizing property are never wanting, and one who begins to live by rapine will always find some reason for taking the goods of others, whereas causes for taking life are rarer and more fleeting.

But when the prince is with his army and has a large number of soldiers under his control, then it is extremely necessary that he should not mind being thought cruel; for without this reputation he could not keep an army united or disposed to any duty. Among the noteworthy actions of Hannibal is numbered this, that although he had an enormous army, composed of men of all nations and fighting in foreign countries, there never arose any dissension either among them or against the prince, either in good fortune or in bad. This could not be due to anything but his inhuman cruelty, which together with his infinite other virtues, made him always venerated and terrible in the sight of his soldiers, and without it his other virtues would not have sufficed to produce that effect. Thoughtless writers admire on the one hand his actions, and on the other blame the principal cause of them.

And that it is true that his other virtues would not have sufficed may be seen from the case of Scipio (famous not only in regard to his own times, but all times of which memory remains), whose armies rebelled against him in Spain, which arose from nothing but his excessive kindness, which allowed more licence to the soldiers than was consonant with military discipline. He was reproached with this in the senate by Fabius Maximus, who called him a corrupter of the Roman militia. Locri having been destroyed by one of Scipio's officers was not revenged by him, nor was the insolence of that officer punished, simply by reason of his easy nature; so much so, that some one wishing to excuse him in the senate, said that there were many men who knew rather how not to err, than how to correct the errors of others. This disposition would in time have tarnished the fame and glory of Scipio had he persevered in it under the empire, but living under the rule of the senate this harmful quality was not only concealed but became a glory to him.

I conclude, therefore, with regard to being feared and loved, that men love at their own free will, but fear at the will of the prince, and that a wise prince must rely on what is in his power and not on what is in the power of others, and he must only contrive to avoid incurring hatred, as has been explained.

CHAPTER XVIII

In What Way Princes Must Keep Faith

How laudable it is for a prince to keep good faith and live with integrity, and not with astuteness, every one knows. Still the experience of our times shows those princes to have done great things who have had little regard for good faith, and have been able by astuteness to confuse men's brains, and who have ultimately overcome those who have made loyalty their foundation.

You must know, then, that there are two methods of fighting, the one by law, the other by force: the first method is that of men, the second of beasts; but as the first method is often insufficient, one must have recourse to the second. It is therefore necessary for a prince to know well how to use both the beast and the man. This was covertly taught to rulers by ancient writers, who relate how Achilles and many others of those ancient princes were given to Chiron the centaur to be brought up and educated under his discipline. The parable of this semi-animal, semi-human teacher is meant to indicate that a prince must know how to use both natures, and that the one without the other is not durable.

A prince being thus obliged to know well how to act as a beast must imitate the fox and the lion, for the lion cannot protect himself from traps, and the fox cannot defend himself from wolves. One must therefore be a fox to recognise traps, and a lion to frighten wolves. Those that wish to be only lions do not understand this. Therefore, a prudent ruler ought not to keep faith when by so doing it would be against his interest, and when the reasons which made him bind himself no longer exist. If men were all good, this precept would not be a good one; but as they are bad, and would not observe their faith with you, so you are not bound to keep faith with them. Nor have legitimate grounds ever failed a prince who wished to show colourable excuse for the non-fulfilment of his promise. Of this one could furnish an infinite number of modern examples, and show how many times peace has been broken, and how many promises rendered worthless, by the faithlessness of princes, and those that have been best able to imitate the fox have succeeded best. But it is necessary to be able to disguise this character well, and to be a great feigner and dissembler; and men are so simple and so ready to obey present necessities, that one who deceives will always find those who allow themselves to be deceived.

I will only mention one modern instance. Alexander VI did nothing else but deceive men, he thought of nothing else, and found the occasion for it; no man was ever more able to give assurances, or affirmed things with stronger oaths, and no man observed them less; however, he always succeeded in his deceptions, as he well knew this aspect of things.

It is not, therefore, necessary for a prince to have all the above-named qualities, but it is very necessary to seem to have them. I would even be bold to say that to possess them and always to observe them is dangerous, but to appear to possess them is useful. Thus it is well to seem merciful, faithful, humane, sincere, religious, and also to be so; but you must have the mind so disposed that when it is needful to be otherwise you may be able to change to the opposite qualities. And it must be understood that a prince, and especially a new prince, cannot observe all those things which are considered good in men, being often obliged, in order to maintain the state, to act against faith, against charity, against humanity, and against religion. And, therefore, he must have a mind disposed to adapt itself according to the wind, and as the variations of fortune dictate, and, as I said before, not deviate from what is good, if possible, but be able to do evil if constrained.

A prince must take great care that nothing goes out of his mouth which is not full of the above-named five qualities, and, to see and hear him, he should seem to be all mercy, faith, integrity, humanity, and religion. And nothing is more necessary than to seem to have this last quality, for men in general judge more by the eyes than by the hands, for every one can see, but very few have to feel. Everybody sees what you appear to be, few feel what you are, and those few will not dare to oppose themselves to the many, who have the majesty of the state to defend them; and in the actions of men, and especially of princes, from which there is no appeal, the end justifies the means. Let a prince therefore aim at conquering and maintaining the state, and the means will always be judged honourable and praised by every one, for the vulgar is always taken by appearances and the issue of the event; and the world consists only of the vulgar, and the few who are not vulgar are isolated when the many have a rallying point in the prince. A certain prince of the present time, whom it is well not to name, never does anything but preach peace and good faith, but he is really a great enemy to both, and either of them, had he observed them, would have lost him state or reputation on many occasions.

CHAPTER XXIII

How Flatterers Must Be Shunned

I must not omit an important subject, and mention of a mistake which princes can with difficulty avoid, if they are not very prudent, or if they do not make a good choice. And this is with regard to flatterers, of which courts are full, because men take such pleasure in their own things and deceive themselves about them that they can with difficulty guard against this plague; and by wishing to guard against it they run the risk of becoming contemptible. Because there is no other way of guarding one's self against flattery than by letting men understand that they will not offend you by speaking the truth; but when every one can tell you the truth, you lose their respect. A prudent prince must therefore take a third course, by choosing for his council wise men, and giving these alone full liberty to speak the truth to him, but only of those things that he asks and of nothing else; but he must ask them about everything and hear their opinion, and afterwards deliberate by himself in his own way, and in these councils and with each of these men comport himself so that every one may see that the more freely he speaks, the more he will be acceptable. Beyond these he should listen to no one, go about the matter deliberately, and be deter-mined in his decisions. Whoever acts otherwise either acts precipitately through flattery or else changes often through the variety of opinions, from which it follows that he will be little esteemed.

I will give a modern instance of this. Pre' Luca, a follower of Maximilian, the present emperor, speaking of his majesty said that he never took counsel with any-body, and yet that he never did anything as he wished; this arose from his following the contrary method to the aforesaid. As the emperor is a secret man he does not communicate his designs to any one or take any advice, but as on putting them into effect they begin to be known and discovered, they begin to be opposed by those he has about him, and he is easily diverted from his purpose. Hence it comes to pass that what he does one day he undoes the next, no one ever understands what he wishes or intends to do, and no reliance is to be placed on his deliberations.

A prince, therefore, ought always to take counsel, but only when he wishes, not when others wish; on the contrary he ought to discourage absolutely attempts to advise him unless he asks it, but he ought to be a great asker, and a patient hearer of the truth about those things of which he has inquired; indeed, if he finds that any one has scruples in telling him the truth he should be angry. And since some think that a prince who gains the reputation of being prudent is so considered, not by his nature but by the good counsellors he has about him, they are undoubtedly de-ceived. It is an infallible rule that a prince who is not wise himself cannot be well advised, unless by chance he leaves himself entirely in the hands of one man who rules him in everything, and happens to be a very prudent man. In this case he may doubtless be well governed, but it would not last long, for that governor would in a short time deprive him of the state; but by taking counsel with many, a prince who is not wise will never have united councils and will not be able to bring them to una-nimity for himself. The counsellors will all think of their own interests, and he will be unable either to correct or to understand them. And it cannot be otherwise, for men will always be false to you unless they are compelled by necessity to be true. Therefore it must be concluded that wise counsels, from whoever they come, must necessarily be due to the prudence of the prince, and not the prudence of the prince to the good counsels received.

QUESTIONS FOR DISCUSSION

1. Outline Machiavelli's argument in each chapter and note the rhetorical purpose of each paragraph in his argument. What assumptions does he make about power and human nature? Do you agree with these assumptions? Are they con-vincing? Which of Machiavelli's assumptions might you consider realistic? Cyni-cal? Cite specific passages.
2. Use a Machiavellian interpretation to analyze the behavior of a current political figure or of one of the political thinkers whom you have read. Do you agree or disagree with a Machiavellian view of this person's motives and program?
3. What is the rhetorical purpose of Machiavelli's opening line in Chapter XV?
4. Compare and contrast the means and ends of Kautilya's (p. 173) advice with Machiavelli's advice. What means are justified for what ends in both of these readings?

5. What ways can a ruler use to control the opposition? What is the value of appearing to have the "five good qualities" according to Machiavelli?
6. What does Machiavelli's analogy of the fox and the lion seek to prove? Explain.
7. Machiavelli states a prince must "learn how not to be good." Do you agree? Why or why not?
8. Discuss Machiavelli's opinion on advisors. In your own opinion, why might flattery be an effective means of persuasion? Illustrate, using your own examples.
9. Compare the attitude of Machiavelli and Kautilya on the issue of power and its proper use.

PATRICIA J. SETHI
Pinochet: Destiny Gave Me the Job

The socialist land reform programs during the mid-1960s spurred the Chilean lower classes to participate in politics, leading to the election of the socialist candidate Salvador Allende Gossens as the president of Chile in 1970. Interpreting Allende's policy of nationalization as a communist threat, it is alleged that President Nixon, the CIA, and International Telephone and Telegraph (IT&T) supported a military coup in which Allende was killed and out of which Augusto Pinochet became the military dictator of Chile. Afterwards, Pinochet repressed moderate and socialist opposition parties. In 1980, Pinochet helped to write a new constitution that allowed him to rule until 1990; after 1990, the constitution allows him to remain in control of the army and remain a senator for life. Because of an economic collapse in 1982–83 and the growing discontent of the left, moderates, and the Roman Catholic Church, Pinochet declared a "state of emergency," outlawed all opposition parties, and exiled many of Chile's leading activists. In 1987 moderate and right-wing parties were legalized while socialist and communist parties continue to be outlawed. In a 1989 special election, a majority of Chilean voters chose to have multi-party elections rather than to have Pinochet remain as ruler. Some opposition members believe that, even if free elections depose Pinochet, reform will be impossible if he remains the head of the army since Chile's 1980 constitution gives the military a veto over the executive and legislative branches of government. This interview can be read in conjunction with Pablo Neruda's "The United Fruit Co." (p. 366), which is a poetic response to the political tyranny of dictators in Chile prior to Pinochet's rise to power.

At 68, Chile's President Augusto Pinochet is a strongman with problems. For 10 years after the 1973 coup that ousted the Marxist government of Salvador Allende, Pinochet ran the country largely unchallenged. These days economic difficulties beset him, and demonstrators bang pots and pans to protest his autocratic rule. In a rare, 90-minute interview with Newsweek's United Nations Bureau Chief Patricia J. Sethi last week, Pinochet still said he was confident of the future. Excerpts:

SETHI: *After the strife in Chile last year, many predicted that you would be squeezed out. You survived. How?*

PINOCHET: The difficulties arising from the world recession created a restlessness here. The opposition used these difficulties politically, attributing them to the government. Their purpose, quite obviously, was to create a climate of agitation in order to destabilize the government. But they were mistaken. The majority of the Chilean people understood that demagogy, violence and political maneuvering were not the path to resolving the economic crisis. . . . As for the secret to my survival, it is not a secret. I am a man fighting for a just cause: the fight between Christianity and spiritualism on one hand, and Marxism and materialism on the other. I get my strength from God.

Q. *The opposition is planning a general strike and rallies for later this month.*

A. During the year, some sporadic agitation might occur in an attempt by the opposition to create a fictitious climate of instability. But they will be engineered by forces which are directly or indirectly at the service of Soviet imperialism. . . . I do not only operate through the military. The majority of the Chilean people are with me.

Q. *What about relations with the United States?*

A. Except for some misunderstandings about Chile in certain sectors of U.S. public opinion, relations are very good.

Q. *Washington sources say the administration has been "encouraging" Chile to liberalize faster. The U.S. ambassador to Chile, James Theberge, said only a few days ago that the political process appears to be stagnating.*

A. I don't like it when an ambassador gets involved in the internal affairs of a country—even if he comes from a country as powerful as the United States. We have always had problems with the United States—before, during and after independence. . . . We don't like anyone, even the powerful U.S., telling us how to run our lives. We will never accept it.

Q. *But you yourself talk about returning Chile to democracy.*

A. I am a better democrat than those who call themselves democrats, because the democracy I speak of is a protected democracy—not a license which will be used by totalitarian groups to destroy it.

Q. *Does this mean protected democracy will not permit any left-wing parties?*

A. All antidemocratic parties must be excluded from political life; they work against the institutional order of the republic. Our past experience will not be repeated. . . . Political parties do not exist legally today, but in a few months I might go to the people to ask them to decide on the fate of the parties. The government would then make laws relating to a national congress, political parties and an electoral system.

Q. *Amnesty International, the U.N., the U.S. State Department and the Chilean Roman Catholic Vicariate have all issued reports of human-rights abuses in Chile. Can all of them be fabrications?*

A. There is a well-mounted campaign against Chile and its government, organized and orchestrated by international Marxism, which projects Chile as a primary violator of human rights. . . . There is a double standard at the U.N., where, out of 158 countries, Chile, Guatemala and El Salvador alone are singled out for human-rights abuses. As for Amnesty International, they at least study abuse in the majority of countries in the world. But they have never recognized the circumstances under which this government came to power, nor do they recognize the improvement in the situation since then. With regard to the Vicariate of Solidarity in Chile, there is a Dr. Manuel Almeida who was primarily responsible for verification of tortures for the Vicariate. He is now in jail because he called for a Marxist revolution against my government. Can such a person's word be trusted?

Q. *Now that Chile's economy is suffering, do you envisage any changes in economic policy?*

A. Chile is currently suffering from the same negative effects of a world recession as is most of the developing world. . . . After the Marxist government of Allende, we were effecting an 8 percent growth rate, which means Chile is capable of repeating that performance if conditions are good. We plan to return to the same levels of growth without renouncing our accepted principles of an open market and a free-market economy. . . . We will pull through—and most important, we will repay our external debts.

Q. *Will you permit Walter Rauff, the notorious Nazi war criminal, to go to Germany to stand trial?*

A. The highest court in the land decided that Rauff could stay. I couldn't care less for Rauff as a person. I don't know him at all. I regret that he committed so many crimes as the Israelis and the Germans say. But that was a long time ago. I can't do anything about it once the courts have decided.

Q. *Have you ever considered retiring?*

A. I am here because my people ask me to stay. Go on, they say, please don't leave us. I wasn't looking for this job. Destiny gave it to me. I have to sacrifice myself for this privilege. I don't misuse power for my personal gain. I don't socialize, I don't go to parties, I am a teetotaler. I wake at 5 in the morning, I am at the office by 7 and I work till after 10 at night. I am a man of principle. All politicians want to be president. I never wanted to be president. But I am.

Q. *Will you run for re-election when your term expires in 1989?*

A. It will be the sovereign people of Chile who will have to decide. At this moment my position is strong. I have everything going for me. Five more years down the road, things could be different. So it is too soon to think about 1989.

AMNESTY INTERNATIONAL
Chile

Founded in 1961 in London, Amnesty International (AI) won the Nobel Peace Prize in 1977 for its extensive involvement in promoting fundamental human rights. AI is a worldwide organization that seeks the release of prisoners of conscience, those who have not used violence to promote their ideas. These prisoners are detained and often tortured because of their political, religious, or philosophical beliefs. Basing its principles on the United Nations' Universal Declaration of Human Rights, AI believes that such basic rights as fair and speedy trials, protection from torture or execution while in detention, and a right to life (AI is opposed to the death penalty) transcend the claims of other national or cultural beliefs. Thus AI's human rights campaign applies to all countries, regardless of their political ideologies or economic systems. Because of its careful documentation of human rights abuses (AI uses two independent sources to confirm cases of detention and torture), AI's investigations are often cited by the UN and by other human rights organizations. This reading can be compared to the poetic account of imprisonment and torture in Wole Soyinka's "Chimes of Silence" (p. 364) and Pablo Neruda's "The United Fruit Co." (p. 366).

Torture of political detainees by members of the security forces has been reported regularly since the present military government under General Augusto Pinochet Ugarte seized power in 1973 and has continued during the period under review. Although most of the information available to Amnesty International refers to cases of a political nature, allegations of torture and ill-treatment of detainees accused of ordinary crimes have also been widespread.

No political party has been allowed to function legally since 11 September 1973 and those who were detained and tortured on account of their alleged political activities came from a broad spectrum of sectors and professions of Chilean society— teachers, students, peasants, doctors, lawyers, trade unionists, workers, and shanty-town dwellers.

Although torture and ill-treatment (especially of detainees suspected of ordinary crimes) was reportedly used by both *Carabineros*, uniformed police, and *Investigaciones*, plain-clothes police, in police stations, it was the *Centrál Nacional de Informaciones* (CNI) which was by far the most frequently cited as responsible for torturing people suspected of political activity. The CNI was created in 1977, taking over the personnel and functions of the *Dirección de Inteligencia Nacional* (DINA). People detained by, or handed over to, the CNI for interrogation were usually taken to secret detention centres where they may be held in incommunicado detention for up to 20 days. It was during this period of incommunicado detention that torture was used, apparently to obtain information and self-incriminatory statements from political detainees, to intimidate them and, in some cases, to obtain their collaboration with the security forces.

According to Transitory Provision 24 of the 1981 constitution, the President may order the detention of political suspects for up to 20 days. Although the text of the law restricts the 20-day period to cases of people suspected of being involved in "terrorist activities with serious consequences," the executive and the courts have taken a very broad view of the scope of its application. In fact, most of those detained for up to 20 days have not been charged with any offence related to terrorism.

Amnesty International has gathered information on torture in Chile from a wide variety of sources: directly from victims, lawyers, victims' families, and human rights groups working in Chile.

The most common physical tortures described in testimonies available to Amnesty International (some collected by an Amnesty International mission to Chile in 1982) were: beating; administration of electric shocks and burns on the head and sensitive parts of the body; rape and other sexual abuse of women; non-therapeutic use of drugs; sleep deprivation; use of a form of torture known as *el teléfono*, the telephone, consisting of blows with the palms of the hands on both ears simultaneously; *la parrilla*, the metal grill, consisting of electric shocks on the most sensitive parts of the victim's body (usually the genitals, mouth, temples, toes, wrists) while he or she is tied to a metal bed frame; the *pau de arara*, parrot's perch, in which the victim is trussed into a crouching position, with the arms hugging the legs, a pole being then passed through the narrow gap between the bent knees and the elbows, the ends resting on two trestles or desks—with the victim in a position in which the head hangs downwards, electric current is then administered to sensitive parts of the body, and water squirted under high pressure into the mouth and nose until the victim is on the verge of suffocation; the *submarino* or *bañera*, in which the victim's head is held under water almost to the point of suffocation.

The Chilean courts have not taken effective action to prevent detainees from being tortured: they have usually failed to respond to *recursos de amparo*, similar to petitions for *habeas corpus*, within the 48-hour period stipulated by law. When detainees have filed complaints before the courts, and military personnel were suspected of being involved, they were normally dealt with by military tribunals which have consistently failed to charge or convict any member of the security forces for the torture or ill-treatment of detainees. This was true of the several hundreds of complaints filed with the courts since 1980.

Amnesty International has frequently issued appeals in cases since 1980 where the organization feared that detainees faced the possibility of torture after arrest. The organization has published numerous testimonies of torture victims and sent documentary evidence to the United Nations Commission on Human Rights and the Inter-American Commission on Human Rights.

In 1983 Amnesty International published its report *Chile: Evidence of Torture*, describing the use of torture in that country as systematic and widespread. This report was based on the findings of an Amnesty International delegation which visited the country in 1982 and included two doctors who carried out in-depth medical examinations of 19 people, 18 of whom alleged they had been tortured. They found that the results of the medical examinations were consistent with the allegations of torture. Documentary evidence collected by Amnesty International included formal complaints by the victims submitted to the courts, medical certificates both from independent doctors and from the official Institute of Forensic Medicine in Santiago, and reports from autopsies of people who died allegedly as a result of injuries sustained during torture. One of the more disturbing findings in the report was that medically trained personnel—probably doctors—had taken part in the torture of detainees.

The report concluded that, based on its information, the organization regards it as beyond reasonable doubt that the use of torture has been a constant feature of the security forces' practice over the past nine years. The report recommended, among other measures, that the Government of Chile institute promptly a public, open and independent inquiry into the allegations of torture filed before the courts—more than 200 were pending in the courts in mid-1982—the results of which should be made public and redress and compensation secured for the victims. No response was received from the government.

QUESTIONS FOR DISCUSSION

1. Who is the audience in the interview with Pinochet? How does this affect the interview?
2. How does he define Marxism? What purpose does his definition have? (Consider the audience.) How does he justify a "protected democracy"? How does this differ from the definition of democracy at the beginning of this chapter?
3. How does he respond to Amnesty International's and the Catholic Church's accusation of human rights abuses?
4. Evaluate Amnesty International's reporting and use of sources. Is their information specific and verifiable? Can we trust their information?
5. Compare and contrast the two readings. Consider the different audiences, purposes, and styles of argument in your response. Which do you find more persuasive? Why?
6. Evaluate Pinochet according to Machiavelli's advice for the ruler. Does Pinochet seem to apply Machiavellian principles in his interview? Cite specific examples from the interview for discussion.

PLATO
The Republic

Plato (428–348 B.C.E.) rejected politics in favor of philosophy after the Athenian democracy executed his mentor, Socrates. In The Republic, *he argues that to rule wisely, statesmen need to become philosophers. Because the goal of the "true" philosopher is to seek wisdom rather than distinction or self-gratification, an aristocracy of the most talented citizens should be the best form of government, according to Plato. (He envisioned women as well as men in this aristocracy of an ideal government; this fact might be compared to de Riencourt's depiction of women's roles in Athens during the time of Plato.) In this selection he justifies the need for "philosopher kings" as rulers; his ideas may be compared to de Tocqueville's criticisms of democracy (p. 226), Pinochet's notions of government (p. 188), Jefferson's and Nyerere's democratic theories (p. 210 and p. 207), Confucius's idea of the ethical ruler (p. 195), and Marx's utopian socialism (p. 232).*

Then when we were discussing the nature of absolute justice and injustice—as well as the perfectly just man (supposing that he exists) and the completely unjust man—we were looking for ideals and patterns of instruction. We wanted to bring them into focus as models so that we might judge our own happiness or unhappiness according to the standards they set and according to the degree we reflect them. It was not our purpose to demonstrate the possibility of fully realizing these ideals.

You are right.

Suppose an artist painted an ideally beautiful man, so that his portrait should lack nothing that could contribute to its perfection. Were he then unable to prove that any such man could exist, would that make him any less an artist?

No, by Zeus.

And have we not been trying to create a model of an ideal state in words?

We have.

Then do you think our words are any less compelling simply because we are unable to prove that it would be possible to govern a state in accord with what the words prescribe?

No.

Then we have spoken truly. However, if you wish it, I shall strive to show how a real city might most nearly approach the ideal. But you must reaffirm the concessions you made earlier.

What concessions?

Can deeds perfectly match words? Is it not true, whether some deny it or not, that action stands further from truth than speech? How do you stand on these questions?

I stand with you.

Then you won't insist that all the words we have been using so far must find their precise counterparts in practice. But if we can show how a city might be constituted most nearly approximating what we have previously described, then you must concede that we have demonstrated the possibility of its realization. I should be very content with that. Would that satisfy you, too?

It would.

Now we must try to find out what it is that causes our cities to be so badly governed and what prevents them from being governed well. What might be the least change that would transform bad government into good government? It would surely be preferable to manage this with a single change. If not one change then two; if not two, then the fewest and most moderate changes possible.

Proceed.

I think there is one change that could bring about the transformation we desire. It is no small change, nor would it be easy to implement. But it is possible.

What is it?

So. At last I come face to face with what I have called the greatest of the waves. But I will speak even if it break over my head and drown me in a flood of laughter and derision. Mark my words.

I am all attention.

Unless philosophers become kings in our cities, or unless those who now are kings and rulers become true philosophers, so that political power and philosophic intelligence converge, and unless those lesser natures who run after one without the other are excluded from governing, I believe there can be no end to troubles, my dear Glaucon, in our cities or for all mankind. Only then will our theory of the state spring to life and see the light of day, at least to the degree possible. Now you see why I held back so long from speaking out about so troublesome a proposition. For it points to a vexing lesson: whether in private or public life there is no other way to achieve happiness.

Socrates, after launching such an assault you must expect to be attacked by hordes of our leading men of learning. They will at once cast off their garments and strip for action—metaphorically speaking, of course. Snatching the first handy weapon, they will rush at you full tilt, fully prepared to do dreadful deeds. If you can't find arguments to fend them off and make your escape, you will learn what it means to be scorned and despised.

It was you who got me into this.

A good thing, too. But I won't desert you; I'll help defend you as best I can. My good will and encouragement may be of use, and perhaps I shall be able to offer more suitable answers than others. With such a helpmate at your side you should be able to be at your best in convincing the unbelievers that you are right.

Your invaluable offer of assistance obliges me to try. If we are going to find some way to elude our assailants, I think we must explain what we mean by our daring suggestion that philosophers ought to be rulers. First, we must make clear what it is to be a philosopher. Then, we should be able to vindicate ourselves by explaining that philosophy and political leadership are inherent qualities of the philosopher's nature, so that it behooves the others to let philosophy alone and to follow the leaders.

QUESTIONS FOR DISCUSSION

1. How does Plato view the notion of an ideal state? What is his version of it?
2. Compare Plato's ideas to the definition of democracy at the beginning of this part. Why might Plato be antagonistic to Athenian democracy?
3. Review the definition of technocracy at the beginning of this part and make a list of contemporary occupations that require expertise. How is Plato's notion of the philosopher king parallel to the roles of these experts and professionals in a modern industrial society? How might a faith in experts be in tension with the concept of democracy?
4. How might Plato defend his ideas against charges of elitism?

CONFUCIUS
The Sacred Books of Confucius

The Chinese philosopher, teacher, and political reformer, K'ung Fu-tzu ("Master K'ung," 551–479 B.C.E.) known in the West as Confucius, was a highly influential figure. He lived in a period of warring feudal states and sought to reform the government so as to alleviate the sufferings of the people who often starved or were victims of heavy taxation. Ethics and education are central to Confucius's notions of government. According to Confucius, education was a means to strengthen the ruler's character and personal conduct. The right to govern depended upon the ruler's virtue—his love for the people and his ability to understand the governed and to make them happy. Because of the emphasis on an ethical education, those who wanted to enter government service had to pass grueling civil service examinations. Women were excluded from these exams, as is pointed out in Yu Hsuan-chi's poem, "On a Visit to Ch'ung Chen Taoist Temple" (see p. 399).

CHAPTER VI. PATERNAL GOVERNMENT

Confucius, as a great humanist, looked at all political problems in terms of human relations. He based all his judgments on the moral codes, from which he evolved his ethical-political system of a paternal government. The good behavior of the ruler was a prerequisite for successful government. As taught by Confucius, a ruler had nine basic duties:

1. To cultivate his personal conduct
2. To honor men of worth
3. To cherish affection for his kinsmen
4. To show respect to great ministers
5. To have an interest in the welfare of all officials
6. To take paternal care of the common people
7. To promote all useful crafts
8. To be hospitable to strangers
9. To be friendly to the neighboring princes

It was especially important for a ruler to cultivate his own conduct, so that he could set a perfect moral example for his officials and for his people. The moral attributes of a ruler were the same as those of a *chün-tzu*. For a ruler, as well as for a *chün-tzu*, the cardinal virtues were *jen, li, yi*, and *hsin* [good faith], as illustrated in his teachings. . . .

244. The Master said: "To rule a state of a thousand chariots, there must be reverent attention to duties and sincerity, economy in expenditure and love for the people, working them only at the proper seasons." [I-5]

245. The Master said: "One who governs by virtue is comparable to the polar star, which remains in its place while all the stars turn towards it." [II-1]

246. The Master said: "Govern the people by laws and regulate them by penalties, and the people will try to do no wrong, but they will lose the sense of shame. Govern the people by virtue and restrain them by rules of propriety, and the people will have a sense of shame and be reformed of themselves." [II-3]

247. Duke Ai asked: "What should I do to secure the submission of the people?" "Promote the upright and banish the crooked," said the Master; "then the people will be submissive. Promote the crooked and banish the upright; then the people will not be submissive." [II-19]

248. Chi Kang Tzu asked: "What should be done to make the people respectful and be encouraged to cultivate virtues?" "Approach the people with dignity," said the Master, "and they will be respectful. Show filial piety and kindness, and they will be loyal. Promote those who are worthy, and train those who are incompetent; and they will be encouraged to cultivate virtues." [II-20]

249. Duke Ting asked how a prince should employ his ministers and how ministers should serve their prince. Master K'ung said: "A prince should employ his ministers with propriety; ministers should serve their prince with loyalty." [III-19]

250. The Master said: "If a prince governs his state with propriety and courtesy, what difficulty will he have? But if not, of what use are rituals?" [IV-13]

251. The Master said: "Yung would be a ruler." Then Chung Kung [Yung] asked about Tzu-sang Po-tzu. "He would be, too," said the Master, "but he is lax." "Such a man might be a ruler," said Chung Kung, "if he were scrupulous in his own conduct and lax only in his dealing with the people. But a man who was lax in his own conduct as well as in government would be too lax." The Master said: "What Yung says is true." [VI-1]

252. [Alluding to the States of Ch'i and Lu], the Master said: "Ch'i, by one change, might attain to the level of Lu; and Lu, by one change, might attain to the *Tao!*" [VI-22]

253. The Master said: "A cornered vessel that has no corners. What a cornered vessel! What a cornered vessel!" [VI-23]

254. The Master said: "The people may be made to follow but not to understand." [VIII-9]

255. Tzu Kung asked about government, and the Master said: "The essentials [of good government] are sufficient food, sufficient arms, and the confidence of the people." "But," asked Tzu Kung, "if you have to part with one of the three, which would you give up?" "Arms," said the Master. "But suppose," said Tzu Kung, "one of the remaining two has to be relinquished, which would it be?" "Food," said the Master. "From time immemorial, death has been the lot of all men, but a people without confidence is lost indeed." [XII-7]

256. Duke Ching asked Master K'ung about government, and Master K'ung said: "Let the ruler be ruler; the minister, minister; the father, father; and the son, son." "Good!" said the Duke. "For truly if the ruler be not ruler, the minister not minister; if the father be not father, and the son not son, then with all the grain in my possession, should I be able to relish it?" [XII-11]

257. The Master said: "In hearing lawsuits, I am no better than other men, but my aim is to bring about the end of lawsuits." [XII-13]

258. Tzu Chang asked about government, and the Master said: "Attend to its affairs untiringly, and carry it out loyally." [XII-14]

259. Chi Kang Tzu asked Master K'ung about government, and Master K'ung said: "To govern means to rectify. If you, Sir, lead the people in rectitude, who dares not to be rectified?" [XII-17]

260. Chi Kang Tzu, being troubled by burglars, asked Master K'ung what he should do, and Master K'ung said: "If only you, Sir, are free from desire [for wealth], they will not steal even though you pay them." [XII-18]

261. Chi Kang Tzu asked Master K'ung about government, saying: "Suppose I kill the *Tao*-less for the good of the *Tao*-abiding, what do you think of it?" "What need, Sir," said Master K'ung, "is there of killing in your administration? Let you desire good, and the people will be good. The virtue of the prince [*chün-tzu*] is the wind, and that of the common people [*hsiao-jen*] the grass. The grass bends in the direction of the wind." [XII-19]

262. Tzu Lu asked about government, and the Master said: "Go before the people and be diligent in their affairs." When asked for further instruction, the Master said: "Be not weary." [XIII-1]

263. Chung Kung, chief minister of the Chi family, asked about government, and the Master said: "Employ first the services of your men, overlook minor faults, and then promote men of worth and talents." "How do I know a man of worth and talents in order to promote him?" said Chung Kung. "Promote those whom you know," said the Master. "Those whom you do not know others will certainly not neglect." [XIII-2]

264. Tzu Lu said: "The prince of Wei is awaiting you, Sir, to join his government. What will you do first, Sir?"

The Master said: "The first thing needed is the rectification of names."

"So, indeed!" said Tzu Lu. "How pedantic it sounds! Why must there be such rectification?" "Yu! How rude you are!" said the Master. "*Chün-tzu* abstains from what he does not know. If names are not correct, then words are inappropriate; when the words are inappropriate, then things cannot be accomplished. Then rites and music will not flourish, punishments will not be properly administered, and the people have nowhere to put hand or foot. Therefore *chün-tzu* designates what can be properly stated, and only speaks of what can be properly carried into effect. *Chün-tzu*, in what he says, leaves nothing that is remiss." [XIII-3]

265. The Master said: "If a prince himself is upright, all will go well without orders. But if he himself is not upright, even though he gives orders, they will not be obeyed." [XIII-6]

266. The Master said: "In their governments, Lu and Wei are still brothers." [XIII-7]

267. When the Master went to Wei, Jan Yu acted as driver of his carriage. The Master said: "How thriving is the population here!" "Since it is so thriving," asked Jan Yu, "what more shall be done for the people?" "Enrich them!" was the Master's reply. "And when they are enriched, what more shall be done?" "Educate them!" said the Master. [XIII-9]

268. The Master said: "Were any prince to employ me, in a year something could be done; in three years, the work could be completed." [XIII-10]

269. The Master said: "'Only if good men were to govern a country for one hundred years, would it be really possible to transform the evil and do away with killings.' How true is the saying!" [XIII-11]

270. The Master said: "If a prince has rendered himself upright, he will have no difficulty in governing the people. But if he cannot rectify himself, how can he hope to rectify the people?" [XIII-13]

271. The Master said: "If a sage-king were to arise, *jen*[1] would prevail within one generation." [XIII-12] . . .

281. Yen Yuen asked how to rule a state, and the Master said: "Follow the calendar of Hsia; ride in the carriage of Yin; wear the cap of Chou. Adopt the music of *Shao* with its pantomime; banish the songs of *Cheng*; and keep away from glib talkers. For the song of *Cheng* is licentious and glib talkers are dangerous." [XV-10]

---

[1]*jen* Humanity or human heartedness. [Ed. note.]

282. The Master said: "Suppose a prince has sufficient wisdom to attain power, but he has no *jen* to secure it. Though he gets it, he will certainly lose it. Suppose his wisdom brings him to power, and he has *jen* to secure it; if there is no dignity in his rule, the people will not show respect. Suppose his wisdom has brought him into power; he has *jen* to secure it and rules with dignity. However, if he acts contrary to the code of rituals, he is still not a good ruler." [XV-32]

283. Master K'ung said: "When the *Tao*[2] prevails in the world, ceremonies, music, and punitive expeditions proceed from the Emperor. When the *Tao* fails in the world, ceremonies, music, and military expeditions proceed from the feudal princes. When they proceed from a feudal prince, his power can seldom survive for ten generations. When they proceed from a state minister, his power can seldom survive for five generations. When a subordinate officer holds power in the kingdom, his power can seldom survive for three generations. When there is *Tao* in the world, the power is not in the hands of ministers. And when there is *Tao* in the world, the people do not even discuss government affairs." [XVI-2]

284. Master K'ung said: "For five generations the revenue has departed from the Ducal House [of Lu], and for four generations the government has been in the hands of ministers. That is why the descendants of the three Huan [the three powerful families] are so losing their powers!" [XVI-3]

285. Tzu Chang asked Master K'ung: "What must a man do to qualify himself for government position?" "Let him honor the five merits and banish the four demerits," said the Master, "then may he serve in the government." "What are the five merits?" asked Tzu Chang. "A *chün-tzu* is bounteous without extravagance; he works the people without causing their resentment; he has desires, but he is not covetous; he is dignified but not arrogant; he is majestic but not ferocious." "What do you mean by 'being bounteous without extravagance'?" said Tzu Chang. "Let him spend on what the people find advantageous; is this not being bounteous without extravagance? Let him work the people during the proper seasons; who will resent? Let him long for *jen* and become *jen*-minded; how can he be covetous? Whether he deals with many people or few, with the small or with the great, he never presumes to be arrogant; is this not being dignified but not arrogant? When he is properly dressed, with dignified manners, he will inspire awe on the onlookers; is this not being majestic but not ferocious?" Then Tzu Chang asked again: "What are the four demerits?" "To put the people to death without giving instruction," said the Master; "this is cruelty. To require accomplishment without previous warning; this is tyranny. To delay orders and hasten its execution; this is oppression. And to make offers but grudge to carry them out; this is the way of the petty officials." [XX-2]

QUESTIONS FOR DISCUSSION

1. What does Confucius value in a ruler? What are his assumptions?
2. How does this compare with Kautilya's and Machiavelli's (p. 173 and p. 180) versions of the ideal ruler?

---

[2]**Tao** In Confucianism: "the right way of life; the path of virtuous conduct." [Ed. note.]

3. Compare this reading to Plato's dialogue (p. 193). How are they similar? How are they different?
4. Do you agree with Confucius's statements about the essentials of good government? Discuss.

JULIUS K. NYERERE
Ujamaa—The Basis of African Socialism

The orator and statesman Julius Nyerere (1922–   ) became president of the Tanganyikan African National Union (TANU) in the 1950s, when his country was still a British colony. TANU advocated replacing tribal and racial discrimination with the goals of a peaceful society that promoted greater social and economic equality and racial harmony. In 1961 Nyerere became the first prime minister of an independent Tanganyika. In 1964 Tanganyika was renamed Tanzania and between 1964 and 1985 the TANU party, the backbone of Tanzania's single-party democracy, reelected Nyerere to the presidency for four consecutive terms before he stepped down from the office. Nyerere's definition of African socialism—"Ujamaa" or "familyhood"—sets itself apart from the European definitions of socialism by claiming to be indigenous to Africa and by rejecting the notion of class struggle. In its opposition to class division, exploitation, and corruption, Ujamaa draws upon the cooperative work ethic and life of the traditional extended family in Tanzania. These ideals shaped the famous Arusha Declaration which the TANU party adopted in 1967.

Socialism—like democracy—is an attitude of mind. In a socialist society it is the socialist attitude of mind, and not the rigid adherence to a standard political pattern, which is needed to ensure that the people care for each other's welfare.

The purpose of this paper is to examine that attitude. It is not intended to define the institutions which may be required to embody it in a modern society.

In the individual, as in the society, it is an attitude of mind which distinguishes the socialist from the non-socialist. It has nothing to do with the possession or non-possession of wealth. Destitute people can be potential capitalists—exploiters of their fellow human beings. A millionaire can equally well be a socialist; he may value his wealth only because it can be used in the service of his fellow men. But the man who uses wealth for the purpose of dominating any of his fellows is a capitalist. So is the man who would if he could!

I have said that a millionaire can be a good socialist. But a socialist millionaire is a rare phenomenon. Indeed he is almost a contradiction in terms. The appearance of millionaires in any society is no proof of its affluence; they can be produced by very poor countries like Tanganyika just as well as by rich countries like the United States of America. For it is not efficiency of production, nor the amount of wealth in a country, which make millionaires; it is the uneven distribution of what is produced. The basic difference between a socialist society and a capitalist society does not lie in their methods of producing wealth, but in the way that wealth is distributed. While, therefore, a millionaire could be a good socialist, he could hardly be the product of a socialist society.

Since the appearance of millionaires in a society does not depend on its affluence, sociologists may find it interesting to try and find out why our societies in Africa did not, in fact, produce any millionaires—for we certainly had enough wealth to create a few. I think they would discover that it was because the organization of traditional African society—its distribution of the wealth it produced—was such that there was hardly any room for parasitism. They might also say, of course, that as a result of this Africa could not produce a leisured class of landowners, and therefore there was nobody to produce the works of art or science which capitalist societies can boast. But works of art and the achievements of science are products of the intellect—which, like land, is one of God's gifts to man. And I cannot believe that God is so careless as to have made the use of one of His gifts depend on the *misuse* of another!

Defenders of capitalism claim that the millionaire's wealth is the just reward for his ability or enterprise. But this claim is not borne out by the facts. The wealth of the millionaire depends as little on the enterprise or abilities of the millionaire himself as the power of a feudal monarch depended on his own efforts, enterprise or brain. Both are users, exploiters, of the abilities and enterprise of other people. Even when you have an exceptionally intelligent and hard-working millionaire, the difference between his intelligence, his enterprise, his hard work, and those of other members of society, cannot possibly be proportionate to the difference between their 'rewards'. There must be something wrong in a society where one man, however hard-working or clever he may be, can acquire as great a 'reward' as a thousand of his fellows can acquire between them.

Acquisitiveness for the purpose of gaining power and prestige is unsocialist. In an acquisitive society wealth tends to corrupt those who possess it. It tends to breed in them a desire to live more comfortably than their fellows, to dress better, and in every way to outdo them. They begin to feel they must climb as far above their neighbours as they can. The visible contrast between their own comfort and the comparative discomfort of the rest of society becomes almost essential to the enjoyment of their wealth, and this sets off the spiral of personal competition—which is then anti-social.

Apart from the anti-social effects of the accumulation of personal wealth, the very desire to accumulate it must be interpreted as a vote of 'no confidence' in the social system. For when a society is so organized that it cares about its individuals, then, provided he is willing to work, no individual within that society should worry about what will happen to him tomorrow if he does not hoard wealth today. Society itself should look after him, or his widow, or his orphans. This is exactly what traditional African society succeeded in doing. Both the 'rich' and the 'poor' individual were completely secure in African society. Natural catastrophe brought famine, but it brought famine to everybody—'poor' or 'rich'. Nobody starved, either of food or of human dignity, because he lacked personal wealth; he could depend on the wealth possessed by the community of which he was a member. That was socialism. That *is* socialism. There can be no such thing as acquisitive socialism, for that would be another contradiction in terms. Socialism is essentially distributive. Its concern is to see that those who sow reap a fair share of what they sow.

The production of wealth, whether by primitive or modern methods, requires three things. First, land. God has given us the land, and it is from the land that we get the raw materials which we reshape to meet our needs. Secondly, tools. We have found by simple experience that tools do help! So we make the hoe, the axe, or the modern factory or tractor, to help us to produce wealth—the goods we need. And, thirdly, human exertion—or labour. We don't need to read Karl Marx or Adam Smith to find out that neither the land nor the hoe actually produces wealth. And we don't need to take degrees in Economics to know that neither the worker nor the landlord produces land. Land is God's gift to man—it is always there. But we do know, still without degrees in Economics, that the axe and the plough were produced by the labourer. Some of our more sophisticated friends apparently have to undergo the most rigorous intellectual training simply in order to discover that stone axes were produced by that ancient gentleman 'Early Man' to make it easier for him to skin the impala he had just killed with a club, which he had also made for himself!

In traditional African society *everybody* was a worker. There was no other way of earning a living for the community. Even the Elder, who appeared to be enjoying himself without doing any work and for whom everybody else appeared to be working, had, in fact, worked hard all his younger days. The wealth he now appeared to possess was not *his*, personally; it was only 'his' as the Elder of the group which had produced it. He was its guardian. The wealth itself gave him neither power nor prestige. The respect paid to him by the young was his because he was older than they, and had served his community longer; and the 'poor' Elder enjoyed as much respect in our society as the 'rich' Elder.

When I say that in traditional African society everybody was a worker, I do not use the word 'worker' simply as opposed to 'employer' but also as opposed to 'loiterer' or 'idler'. One of the most socialistic achievements of our society was the sense of security it gave to its members, and the universal hospitality on which they could rely. But it is too often forgotten, nowadays, that the basis of this great socialistic achievement was this: that it was taken for granted that every member of society—barring only the children and the infirm—contributed his fair share of effort towards the production of its wealth. Not only was the capitalist, or the landed exploiter, unknown to traditional African society, but we did not have that other form of modern parasite—the loiterer, or idler, who accepts the hospitality of society as his 'right' but gives nothing in return! Capitalistic exploitation was impossible. Loitering was an unthinkable disgrace.

Those of us who talk about the African way of life and, quite rightly, take a pride in maintaining the tradition of hospitality which is so great a part of it, might do well to remember the Swahili saying: *'Mgeni siku mbili; siku ya tatu mpe jembe'*—or in English, 'Treat your guest as a guest for two days; on the third day give him a hoe!' In actual fact, the guest was likely to ask for the hoe even before his host had to give him one—for he knew what was expected of him, and would have been ashamed to remain idle any longer. Thus, working was part and parcel, was indeed the very basis and justification of this socialist achievement of which we are so justly proud.

There is no such thing as socialism without work. A society which fails to give its individuals the means to work, or, having given them the means to work, prevents them from getting a fair share of the products of their own sweat and toil, needs putting right. Similarly, an individual who can work—and is provided by society with the means to work—but does not do so, is equally wrong. He has no right to expect anything from society because he contributes nothing to society.

The other use of the word 'worker', in its specialized sense of 'employee' as opposed to 'employer', reflects a capitalist attitude of mind which was introduced into Africa with the coming of colonialism and is totally foreign to our own way of thinking. In the old days the African had never aspired to the possession of personal wealth for the purpose of dominating any of his fellows. He had never had labourers or 'factory hands' to do his work for him. But then came the foreign capitalists. They were wealthy. They were powerful. And the African naturally started wanting to be wealthy too. There is nothing wrong in our wanting to be wealthy; nor is it a bad thing for us to want to acquire the power which wealth brings with it. But it most certainly is wrong if we want the wealth and the power so that we can dominate somebody else. Unfortunately there are some of us who have already learnt to covet wealth for that purpose—and who would like to use the methods which the capitalist uses in acquiring it. That is to say, some of us would like to use, or exploit, our brothers for the purpose of building up our own personal power and prestige. This is completely foreign to us, and it is incompatible with the socialist society we want to build here.

Our first step, therefore, must be to re-educate ourselves; to regain our former attitude of mind. In our traditional African society we were individuals within a community. We took care of the community, and the community took care of us. We neither needed nor wished to exploit our fellow men.

And in rejecting the capitalist attitude of mind which colonialism brought into Africa, we must reject also the capitalist methods which go with it. One of these is the individual ownership of land. To us in Africa land was always recognized as belonging to the community. Each individual within our society had a right to the use of land, because otherwise he could not earn his living and one cannot have the right to life without also having the right to some means of maintaining life. But the African's right to land was simply the right to use it; he had no other right to it, nor did it occur to him to try and claim one.

The foreigner introduced a completely different concept—the concept of land as a marketable commodity. According to this system, a person could claim a piece of land as his own private property whether he intended to use it or not. I could take a few square miles of land, call them 'mine', and then go off to the moon. All I had to do to gain a living from 'my' land was to charge a rent to the people who wanted to use it. If this piece of land was in an urban area I had no need to develop it at all; I could leave it to the fools who were prepared to develop all the other pieces of land surrounding 'my' piece, and in doing so automatically to raise the market value of mine. Then I could come down from the moon and demand that these fools pay me through their noses for the high value of 'my' land—a value which they themselves had created for me while I was enjoying myself on the moon! Such a system is not only foreign to us, it is completely wrong. Landlords, in a society which recognizes individual ownership of land, can be, and usually are, in the same class as the loiterers I was talking about: the class of parasites.

We must not allow the growth of parasites here in Tanganyika. The TANU Government must go back to the traditional African custom of land-holding. That is to say a member of society will be entitled to a piece of land *on condition that he uses it*. Unconditional, or 'freehold', ownership of land (which leads to speculation and parasitism) must be abolished. We must, as I have said, regain our former attitude of mind—our traditional African socialism—and apply it to the new societies we are building today. TANU has pledged itself to make socialism the basis of its policy in every field. The people of Tanganyika have given us their mandate to carry out that policy, by electing a TANU Government to lead them. So the Government can be relied upon to introduce only legislation which is in harmony with socialist principles.

But, as I said at the beginning, true socialism is an attitude of mind. It is therefore up to the people of Tanganyika—the peasants, the wage-earners, the students, the leaders, all of us—to make sure that this socialist attitude of mind is not lost through the temptations to personal gain (or to the abuse of positions of authority) which may come our way as individuals, or through the temptation to look on the good of the whole community as of secondary importance to the interests of our own particular group.

Just as the Elder, in our former society, was respected for his age and his service to the community, so, in our modern society, this respect for age and service will be preserved. And in the same way as the 'rich' Elder's apparent wealth was really only held by him in trust for his people, so, today, the apparent extra wealth which certain positions of leadership may bring to the individuals who fill them, can be theirs only in so far as it is a necessary aid to the carrying out of their duties. It is a 'tool' entrusted to them for the benefit of the people they serve. It is not 'theirs' personally; and they may not use any part of it as a means of accumulating more for their own benefit, nor as an 'insurance' against the day when they no longer hold the same positions. That would be to betray the people who entrusted it to them. If they serve the community while they can, the community must look after them when they are no longer able to do so.

In tribal society, the individuals or the families within a tribe were 'rich' or 'poor' according to whether the whole tribe was rich or poor. If the tribe prospered all the members of the tribe shared in its prosperity. Tanganyika, today, is a poor country. The standard of living of the masses of our people is shamefully low. But if every man and woman in the country takes up the challenge and works to the limit of his or her ability for the good of the whole society, Tanganyika will prosper; and that prosperity will be shared by all her people.

But it must be shared. The true socialist may not exploit his fellows. So that if the members of any group within our society are going to argue that, because they happen to be contributing more to the national income than some other groups, they must therefore take for themselves a greater share of the profits of their own industry than they actually need; and if they insist on this in spite of the fact that it would mean reducing their group's contribution to the general income and thus slowing down the rate at which the whole community can benefit, then that group is exploiting (or trying to exploit) its fellow human beings. It is displaying a capitalist attitude of mind.

There are bound to be certain groups which, by virtue of the 'market value' of their particular industry's products, will contribute more to the nation's income than others. But the others may actually be producing goods or services which are of equal, or greater, intrinsic value although they do not happen to command such a high artificial value. For example, the food produced by the peasant farmer is of greater social value than the diamonds mined at Mwadui. But the mine-workers of Mwadui could claim, quite correctly, that their labour was yielding greater financial profits to the community than that of the farmers. If, however, they went on to demand that they should therefore be given most of that extra profit for themselves, and that no share of it should be spent on helping the farmers, they would be potential capitalists!

This is exactly where the attitude of mind comes in. It is one of the purposes of trade unions to ensure for the workers a fair share of the profits of their labour. But a 'fair' share must be fair in relation to the whole society. If it is greater than the country can afford without having to penalize some other section of society, then it is not a fair share. Trade union leaders and their followers, as long as they are true socialists, will not need to be coerced by the Government into keeping their demands within the limits imposed by the needs of society as a whole. Only if there are potential capitalists amongst them will the socialist government have to step in and prevent them from putting their capitalist ideas into practice!

As with groups, so with individuals. There are certain skills, certain qualifications, which, for good reasons, command a higher rate of salary for their possessors than others. But, here again, the true socialist will demand only that return for his skilled work which he knows to be a fair one in proportion to the wealth or poverty of the whole society to which he belongs. He will not, unless he is a would-be capitalist, attempt to blackmail the community by demanding a salary equal to that paid to his counterpart in some far wealthier society.

European socialism was born of the Agrarian Revolution and the Industrial Revolution which followed it. The former created the 'landed' and the 'landless' classes in society; the latter produced the modern capitalist and the industrial proletariat.

These two revolutions planted the seeds of conflict within society, and not only was European socialism born of that conflict, but its apostles sanctified the conflict itself into a philosophy. Civil war was no longer looked upon as something evil, or something unfortunate, but as something good and necessary. As prayer is to Christianity or to Islam, so civil war (which they call 'class war') is to the European version of socialism—a means inseparable from the end. Each becomes the basis of a whole way of life. The European socialist cannot think of his socialism without its father—capitalism!

Brought up in tribal socialism, I must say I find this contradiction quite intolerable. It gives capitalism a philosophical status which capitalism neither claims nor deserves. For it virtually says, 'Without capitalism, and the conflict which capitalism creates within society, there can be no socialism'! This glorification of capitalism by the doctrinaire European socialists, I repeat, I find intolerable.

African socialism, on the other hand, did not have the 'benefit' of the Agrarian Revolution or the Industrial Revolution. It did not start from the existence of conflicting 'classes' in society. Indeed I doubt if the equivalent for the word 'class' exists in any indigenous African language; for language describes the ideas of those who speak it, and the idea of 'class' or 'caste' was non-existent in African society.

The foundation, and the objective, of African socialism is the extended family. The true African socialist does not look on one class of men as his brethren and another as his natural enemies. He does not form an alliance with the 'brethren' for the extermination of the 'non-brethren'. He rather regards *all* men as his brethren—as members of his ever extending family. That is why the first article of TANU's Creed is: *'Binadamu wote ni ndugu zangu, na Afrika ni moja'*. If this had been originally put in English, it could have been: 'I believe in Human Brotherhood and the Unity of Africa'.

'Ujamaa', then, or 'Familyhood', describes our socialism. It is opposed to capitalism, which seeks to build a happy society on the basis of the exploitation of man by man; and it is equally opposed to doctrinaire socialism which seeks to build its happy society on a philosophy of inevitable conflict between man and man.

We, in Africa, have no more need of being 'converted' to socialism than we have of being 'taught' democracy. Both are rooted in our own past—in the traditional society which produced us. Modern African socialism can draw from its traditional heritage the recognition of 'society' as an extension of the basic family unit. But it can no longer confine the idea of the social family within the limits of the tribe, nor, indeed, of the nation. For no true African socialist can look at a line drawn on a map and say, 'The people on this side of that line are my brothers, but those who happen to live on the other side of it can have no claim on me'; every individual on this continent is his brother.

It was in the struggle to break the grip of colonialism that we learnt the need for unity. We came to recognize that the same socialist attitude of mind which, in the tribal days, gave to every individual the security that comes of belonging to a widely extended family, must be preserved within the still wider society of the nation. But we should not stop there. Our recognition of the family to which we all belong must be extended yet further—beyond the tribe, the community, the nation, or even the continent—to embrace the whole society of mankind. This is the only logical conclusion for true socialism.

QUESTIONS FOR DISCUSSION

1. How does Nyerere define Ujamaa?
2. Who does Nyerere's audience seem to be? What might be Nyerere's purposes in describing and arguing for Ujamaa?
3. List the characteristics of Ujamaa. How does Nyerere's socialism compare to Marx's communism? What African traditions does Nyerere appeal to?
4. How effective are Nyerere's arguments about the millionaire and the African worker? What analogies does he use? Are they clear? Are they convincing?

JULIUS NYERERE
The Arusha Declaration

Julius Nyerere wrote The Arusha Declaration *and made it public in the town of Arusha, Tanzania. This declaration embodies Nyerere's ideals of Ujamaa as expressed in "Ujamaa—The Basis of African Socialism." It was adopted by the Tanzanian African National Union (TANU), the one official party in Tanzania's single-party democracy. A primary goal of* The Arusha Declaration *was to set forth the principles that would establish a democratic socialist government in Tanzania. This declaration calls for self-reliance (as opposed to dependence on foreign aid), collective farms, and literacy programs. Following TANU's adoption of the declaration, the Tanzanian government nationalized banks, insurance companies, grain mills, and the assets of multinational corporations.*

The Arusha Declaration[1] and Tanu's Policy on Socialism and Self-Reliance
5 February 1967

PART ONE

The TANU Creed

The policy of TANU is to build a socialist state. The principles of socialism are laid down in the TANU Constitution and they are as follows:

WHEREAS TANU believes:

a. That all human beings are equal;
b. That every individual has a right to dignity and respect;
c. That every citizen is an integral part of the nation and has the right to take an equal part in Government at local, regional and national levels;
d. That every citizen has the right to freedom of expression, of movement, of religious belief and of association within the context of the law;
e. That every individual has the right to receive from society protection of his life and of property held according to law;
f. That every individual has the right to receive a just return for his labour;
g. That all citizens together possess all the natural resources of the country in trust for their descendants;
h. That in order to ensure economic justice the state must have effective control over the principal means of production; and
i. That it is the responsibility of the state to intervene actively in the economic life of the nation so as to ensure the well-being of all citizens, and so as to prevent

---

[1] The Declaration was discussed and then published in Swahili. This revised English translation clarifies ambiguities which existed in the translation originally issued.

the exploitation of one person by another or one group by another, and so as to prevent the accumulation of wealth to an extent which is inconsistent with the existence of a classless society.

NOW, THEREFORE, the principal aims and objects of TANU shall be as follows:

a. To consolidate and maintain the independence of this country and the freedom of its people;
b. To safeguard the inherent dignity of the individual in accordance with the Universal Declaration of Human Rights;
c. To ensure that this country shall be governed by a democratic socialist government of the people;
d. To co-operate with all political parties in Africa engaged in the liberation of all Africa;
e. To see that the Government mobilizes all the resources of this country towards the elimination of poverty, ignorance and disease;
f. To see that the Government actively assists in the formation and maintenance of co-operative organizations;
g. To see that wherever possible the Government itself directly participates in the economic development of this country;
h. To see that the Government gives equal opportunity to all men and women irrespective of race, religion or status;
i. To see that the Government eradicates all types of exploitation, intimidation, discrimination, bribery and corruption;
j. To see that the Government exercises effective control over the principal means of production and pursues policies which facilitate the way to collective ownership of the resources of this country;
k. To see that the Government co-operates with other states in Africa in bringing about African unity;
l. To see that Government works tirelessly towards world peace and security through the United Nations Organization.

PART TWO

The Policy of Socialism

Absence of Exploitation   A truly socialist state is one in which all people are workers and in which neither capitalism nor feudalism exists. It does not have two classes of people, a lower class composed of people who work for their living, and an upper class of people who live on the work of others. In a really socialist country no person exploits another; everyone who is physically able to work does so; every worker obtains a just return for the labour he performs; and the incomes derived from different types of work are not grossly divergent.

In a socialist country, the only people who live on the work of others, and who have the right to be dependent upon their fellows, are small children, people who are too old to support themselves, the crippled, and those whom the state at any one time cannot provide with an opportunity to work for their living.

Tanzania is a nation of peasants and workers, but it is not yet a socialist society. It still contains elements of feudalism and capitalism—with their temptations. These feudalistic and capitalistic features of our society could spread and entrench themselves.

The Major Means of Production and Exchange are under the Control of the Peasants and Workers   To build and maintain socialism it is essential that all the major means of production and exchange in the nation are controlled and owned by the peasants through the machinery of their Government and their co-operatives. Further, it is essential that the ruling Party should be a Party of peasants and workers.

The major means of production and exchange are such things as: land; forests; minerals; water; oil and electricity; news media; communications; banks, insurance, import and export trade, wholesale trade; iron and steel, machine-tool, arms, motor-car, cement, fertilizer, and textile industries; and any big factory on which a large section of the people depend for their living, or which provides essential components of other industries; large plantations, and especially those which provide raw materials essential to important industries.

Some of the instruments of production and exchange which have been listed here are already owned or controlled by the people's Government of Tanzania.

The Existence of Democracy   A state is not socialist simply because its means of production and exchange are controlled or owned by the government, either wholly or in large part. For a country to be socialist, it is essential that its government is chosen and led by the peasants and workers themselves. If the minority governments of Rhodesia or South Africa controlled or owned the entire economies of these respective countries, the result would be a strengthening of oppression, not the building of socialism. True socialism cannot exist without democracy also existing in the society.

Socialism is a Belief   Socialism is a way of life, and a socialist society cannot simply come into existence. A socialist society can only be built by those who believe in, and who themselves practise, the principles of socialism. A committed member of TANU will be a socialist, and his fellow socialists—that is, his fellow believers in this political and economic system—are all those in Africa or elsewhere in the world who fight for the rights of peasants and workers. The first duty of a TANU member, and especially of a TANU leader, is to accept these socialist principles, and to live his own life in accordance with them. In particular, a genuine TANU leader will not live off the sweat of another man, nor commit any feudalistic or capitalistic actions.

The successful implementation of socialist objectives depends very much upon the leaders, because socialism is a belief in a particular system of living, and it is difficult for leaders to promote its growth if they do not themselves accept it.

QUESTIONS FOR DISCUSSION

1. What is the purpose of this declaration and who might be the audience(s) for it?
2. Summarize the key ideas of this declaration. Discuss the relationship between the state and the people according to Nyerere.
3. Compare the idea of the peasants and workers owning the means of production to the idea of a manager or entrepreneur as the owner. In what ways would society be affected if the peasants and workers owned the means of production?
4. Discuss some key similarities and differences between *The Arusha Declaration* and one of the following: The United Nations *Universal Declaration of Human Rights* (p. 215), *The Declaration of Independence* (p. 210), or the "Extracts from the Belgrade Conference of . . . Nonaligned Countries" (p. 222). What are some of the factors that might account for the differences? (Consider the context of each piece.)

THOMAS JEFFERSON
The Declaration of Independence

Thomas Jefferson (1743–1826), political philosopher and third president of the U.S., wrote The Declaration of Independence *in June 1776 to persuade some of the more reluctant members of the Continental Congress to break away from Britain and its colonial rule. In addition,* The Declaration *was aimed at persuading France to supply arms and aid to the colonies. In writing* The Declaration, *Jefferson drew upon the political theories of John Locke, a social philosopher whose concept of social contract argued that those who govern had obligations to the governed. He completed* The Declaration *in a period of seventeen days, redrafting it two or three times after he submitted it to a committee which included himself, John Adams, and Benjamin Franklin, among others.*

A Declaration by the Representatives of the United States of America, in General Congress Assembled[1]
July 4, 1776

When, in the course of human events, it becomes necessary for one people to dissolve the political bands which have connected them with another, and to assume among the powers of the earth

---

[1]This was Jefferson's original title. Congress changed it, on July 19, 1776, to "The Unanimous Declaration of the thirteen united States of America."

Since this is Jefferson's most famous paper, the text is given here as he first wrote it and as it was finally corrected. The parts stricken out by Congress are shown in brackets and in italics, and insertions are given in the margin or in a parallel column.

the separate and equal station to which the laws of nature and of nature's God entitle them, a decent respect to the opinions of mankind requires that they should declare the causes which impel them to the separation.

certain   We hold these truths to be self-evident; that all men are created equal; that they are endowed by their creator with [*inherent and*] inalienable rights; that among these are life, liberty, and the pursuit of happiness; that to secure these rights, governments are instituted among men, deriving their just powers from the consent of the governed; that whenever any form of government becomes destructive of these ends, it is the right of the people to alter or to abolish it, and to institute new government, laying its foundation on such principles, and organizing its powers in such form, as to them shall seem most likely to effect their safety and happiness. Prudence, indeed, will dictate that governments long established should not be changed for light and transient causes; and accordingly all experience hath shown that mankind are more disposed to suffer while evils are sufferable, than to right themselves by abolishing the forms to which they are accustomed. But when a long train of abuses and usurpations [*begun at a distinguished period and*] pursuing invariably the same object, evinces a design to reduce them under absolute despotism, it is their right, it is their duty to throw off such government, and to provide new guards for their future security. Such has been the patient sufferance of these Colonies; and such is now the neces-

alter   sity which constrains them to [*expunge*] their former systems of government. The history of the present King of Great Britain is a

repeated   history of [*unremitting*] injuries and usurpations, [*among which ap-*

all having   *pears no solitary fact to contradict the uniform tenor of the rest, but all have*] in direct object the establishment of an absolute tyranny over these States. To prove this, let facts be submitted to a candid world [*for the truth of which we pledge a faith yet unsullied by falsehood*].

He has refused his assent to laws the most wholesome and necessary for the public good.

He has forbidden his governors to pass laws of immediate and pressing importance, unless suspended in their operation till his assent should be obtained; and, when so suspended, he has utterly neglected to attend to them.

He has refused to pass other laws for the accommodation of large districts of people, unless those people would relinquish the right of representation in the Legislature, a right inestimable to them, and formidable to tyrants only.

He has called together legislative bodies at places unusual, uncomfortable, and distant from the depository of their public records, for the sole purpose of fatiguing them into compliance with his measures.

He has dissolved representative houses repeatedly [*and continually*] for opposing with manly firmness his invasions on the rights of the people.

He has refused for a long time after such dissolutions to cause others to be elected, whereby the legislative powers, incapable of annihilation, have returned to the people at large for their exercise, the State remaining, in the meantime, exposed to all the dangers of invasion from without and convulsions within.

He has endeavored to prevent the population of these States; for that purpose obstructing the laws for naturalization of foreigners, refusing to pass others to encourage their migrations hither, and raising the conditions of new appropriations of lands.

obstructed   He has [*suffered*] the administration of justice [*totally to cease*
by   *in some of these States*] refusing his assent to laws for establishing judiciary powers.

He has made [*our*] judges dependent on his will alone for the tenure of their offices, and the amount and payment of their salaries.

He has erected a multitude of new offices, [*by a self-assumed power*] and sent hither swarms of new officers to harass our people and eat out their substance.

He has kept among us in times of peace standing armies [*and ships of war*] without the consent of our Legislatures.

He has affected to render the military independent of, and superior to, the civil power.

He has combined with others to subject us to a jurisdiction foreign to our constitutions and unacknowledged by our laws, giving his assent to their acts of pretended legislation for quartering large bodies of armed troops among us; for protecting them by a mock trial from punishment for any murders which they should commit on the inhabitants of these States; for cutting off our trade with all parts of the world; for imposing taxes on us
in many cases   without our consent; for depriving us [   ] of the benefits of trial by jury; for transporting us beyond seas to be tried for pretended offences; for abolishing the free system of English laws in a neighboring province, establishing therein an arbitrary government, and enlarging its boundaries, so as to render it at once an example and fit instrument for introducing the same absolute
Colonies   rule into these [*States*]; for taking away our charters, abolishing our most valuable laws, and altering fundamentally the forms of our governments; for suspending our own Legislatures, and declaring themselves invested with power to legislate for us in all cases whatsoever.

by declaring us out of his protection, and waging war against us.

He has abdicated government here [*withdrawing his governors, and declaring us out of his allegiance and protection*].

He has plundered our seas, ravaged our coasts, burnt our towns, and destroyed the lives of our people.

He is at this time transporting large armies of foreign mercenaries to complete the works of death, desolation, and tyranny already begun with circumstances of cruelty and perfidy [   ] unworthy the head of a civilized nation.

scarcely paralleled in the most barbarous ages, and totally

He has constrained our fellow-citizens taken captive on the high seas to bear arms against their country, to become the executioners of their friends and brethren, or to fall themselves by their hands.

excited domestic insurrection among us, and has

He has [   ] endeavored to bring on the inhabitants of our frontiers the merciless Indian savages, whose known rule of warfare is an undistinguished destruction of all ages, sexes, and conditions [*of existence*].

[*He has incited treasonable insurrections of our fellow-citizens, with the allurements of forfeiture and confiscation of our property.*

He has waged cruel war against human nature itself, violating its most sacred rights of life and liberty in the persons of a distant people who never offended him, captivating and carrying them into slavery in another hemisphere, or to incur miserable death in their transportation thither. This piratical warfare, the opprobrium[1] *of* INFIDEL *powers, is the warfare of the* CHRISTIAN *King of Great Britain. Determined to keep open a market where* MEN *should be bought and sold, he has prostituted his negative for suppressing every legislative attempt to prohibit or to restrain this execrable commerce. And that this assemblage of horrors might want no fact of distinguished die, he is now exciting those very people to rise in arms among us, and to purchase that liberty of which he has deprived them, by murdering the people on whom he also obtruded them: thus paying off former crimes committed against the* LIBERTIES *of one people with crimes which he urges them to commit against the* LIVES *of another.*]

In every stage of these oppressions we have petitioned for redress in the most humble terms: our repeated petitions have been answered only by repeated injuries.

free

A Prince whose character is thus marked by every act which may define a tyrant is unfit to be the ruler of a [   ] people [*who mean to be free. Further ages will scarcely believe that the hardiness of one man adventured, within the short compass of twelve years only, to lay a foundation so broad and so undisguised for tyranny over a people fostered and fixed in principles of freedom.*]

Nor have we been wanting in attentions to our British brethren. We have warned them from time to time of attempts by

---

[1] **opprobrium** An action or behavior considered to be disgraceful. [Ed. note.]

an unwarrantable

us

their legislature to extend [*a*] jurisdiction over [*these our States*]. We have reminded them of the circumstances of our emigration and settlement here, [*no one of which could warrant so strange a pretension: that these were effected at the expense of our own blood and treasure, unassisted by the wealth or the strength of Great Britain: that in constituting indeed our several forms of government, we had adopted one common king, thereby laying a foundation for perpetual league and amity with them: but that submission to their parliament was no part of our Constitution, nor ever in idea, if history may be credited: and,*] we

have

and we have

conjured them by

would inevitably

[ ] appealed to their native justice and magnanimity[2] [*as well as to*] the ties of our common kindred to disavow these usurpations which [*were likely to*] interrupt our connection and correspondence. They too have been deaf to the voice of justice and of consanguinity,[3] [*and when occasions have been given them, by the regular course of their laws, of removing from their councils the disturbers of our harmony, they have, by their free election, reestablished them in power. At this very time too, they are permitting their chief magistrate to send over not only soldiers of our common blood, but Scotch and foreign mercenaries to invade and destroy us. These facts have given the last stab to agonizing affection, and manly spirit bids us to renounce forever these unfeeling brethren. We must endeavor to forget our former love for them, and hold them as we hold the rest of mankind, enemies in war, in peace friends. We might have been a free and a great people together; but a communication of grandeur and of freedom, it seems, is below their dignity. Be it so, since they will have it. The road to happiness and to glory is*]

We must therefore

and hold them as

we hold the rest of

mankind, enemies

in war, in peace

friends.

[*open to us too. We will tread it apart from them, and*] acquiesce in the necessity which denounces our [*eternal*] separation [ ]!

We therefore the representatives of the United States of America in General Congress assembled, appealing to the supreme judge of the world for the rectitude of our intentions, do in the name, and by the authority of the good people of these Colonies, solemnly publish and declare, that these united Colonies are, and of right ought to be, free and independent States; that they are absolved from all allegiance to the British crown, and that all political connection between them and the state of Great Britain is, and ought to be, totally dissolved; and that as free and independent States, they have full power to levy war, conclude peace, contract alliances, establish commerce, and to do all other acts and things which independent States may of right do.

And for the support of this declaration, with a firm reliance on the protection of divine providence, we mutually pledge to each other our lives, our fortunes, and our sacred honor.

---

[2]**magnanimity** A generosity that suggests a noble action. [Ed. note.]
[3]**consanguinity** The state of being related by blood. [Ed. note.]

We therefore the representatives of the United States of America in General Congress assembled, do in the name, and by the authority of the good people of these [*States reject and renounce all allegiance and subjection to the kings of Great Britain and all others who may hereafter claim by, through, or under them; we utterly dissolve all political connection which may heretofore have subsisted between us and the people or parliament of Great Britain: and finally we do assert and declare these Colonies to be free and independent States,*] and that as free and independent States, they have full power to levy war, conclude peace, contract alliances, establish commerce, and to do all other acts and things which independent States may of right do.

And for the support of this declaration, we mutually pledge to each other our lives, our fortunes, and our sacred honor.

QUESTIONS FOR DISCUSSION

1. What are the various purposes and audiences for *The Declaration of Independence?* How might the second to last paragraph be an appeal to aid?
2. Why might the long passage on slavery have been taken out?
3. Read selected portions of this aloud and notice Jefferson's word choices. If you were a loyalist, an American supporter of the King, how might you react to the declaration?
4. What is the tone (the apparent attitude) of this declaration? How is this effective for the purposes suggested in the introduction?
5. Compare *The Declaration of Independence* to *The Arusha Declaration* (p. 207). How are their purposes similar? How are they different?
6. Choose one of the revisions made in *The Declaration of Independence* and speculate why the change might have been made.

UNITED NATIONS
Universal Declaration of Human Rights

Eleanor Roosevelt served as the first chairperson of the United Nations Human Rights Commission (1946–1951) and played a major role in drafting the Universal Declaration of Human Rights, *which was adopted by the UN General Assembly in 1948. Although defining human rights in a way that is agreed upon by all nations is an ongoing process, the* Universal Declaration of Human Rights *serves as an international standard to judge the actions of governments. It has created a moral and political authority for ending such human rights abuses as torture and detaining people without charge. It is often cited by human rights organizations like Amnesty International when reporting on human rights violations. In addition to influencing international law, emerging nations after World War II have borrowed from it for their national constitutions.*

Adopted and Proclaimed by General Assembly Resolution 217 A (III) of 10 December 1948

PREAMBLE

Whereas recognition of the inherent dignity and of the equal and inalienable rights of all members of the human family is the foundation of freedom, justice and peace in the world.

Whereas disregard and contempt for human rights have resulted in barbarous acts which have outraged the conscience of mankind, and the advent of a world in which human beings shall enjoy freedom of speech and belief and freedom from fear and want has been proclaimed as the highest aspiration of the common people,

Whereas it is essential, if man is not to be compelled to have recourse, as a last resort, to rebellion against tyranny and oppression, that human rights should be protected by the rule of law,

Whereas it is essential to promote the development of friendly relations between nations,

Whereas the peoples of the United Nations have in the Charter reaffirmed their faith in fundamental human rights, in the dignity and worth of the human person and in the equal rights of men and women and have determined to promote social progress and better standards of life in larger freedom,

Whereas Member States have pledged themselves to achieve, in cooperation with the United Nations, the promotion of universal respect for and observance of human rights and fundamental freedoms,

Whereas a common understanding of these rights and freedoms is of the greatest importance for the full realization of this pledge,

Now, Therefore,

The General Assembly

Proclaims this Universal Declaration of Human Rights as a common standard of achievement for all peoples and all nations, to the end that every individual and every organ of society, keeping this Declaration constantly in mind, shall strive by teaching and education to promote respect for these rights and freedoms and by progressive measures, national and international to secure their universal and effective recognition and observance, both among the peoples of Member States themselves and among the peoples of territories under their jurisdiction.

ARTICLE 1

All human beings are born free and equal in dignity and rights. They are endowed with reason and conscience and should act towards one another in a spirit of brotherhood.

ARTICLE 2

Everyone is entitled to all the rights and freedoms set forth in this Declaration, without distinction of any kind, such as race, colour, sex, language, religion, political or other opinion, national or social origin, property, birth or other status.

Furthermore, no distinction shall be made on the basis of the political, jurisdictional or international status of the country or territory to which a person belongs, whether it be independent, trust, non-self-governing or under any other limitation of sovereignty.

ARTICLE 3

Everyone has the right to life, liberty and the security of person.

ARTICLE 4

No one shall be held in slavery or servitude; slavery and the slave trade shall be prohibited in all their forms.

ARTICLE 5

No one shall be subjected to torture or to cruel, inhuman or degrading treatment or punishment.

ARTICLE 6

Everyone has the right to recognition everywhere as a person before the law.

ARTICLE 7

All are equal before the law and are entitled without any discrimination to equal protection of the law. All are entitled to equal protection against any discrimination in violation of this Declaration and against any incitement to such discrimination.

ARTICLE 8

Everyone has the right to an effective remedy by the competent national tribunals for acts violating the fundamental rights granted him by the constitution or by law.

ARTICLE 9

No one shall be subjected to arbitrary arrest, detention or exile.

ARTICLE 10

Everyone is entitled in full equality to a fair and public hearing by an independent and impartial tribunal, in the determination of his rights and obligations and of any criminal charge against him.

ARTICLE 11

1. Everyone charged with a penal offence has the right to be presumed innocent until proved guilty according to law in a public trial at which he has had all the guarantees necessary for his defence.
2. No one shall be held guilty of any penal offence on account of any act or omission which did not constitute a penal offence, under national or international law, at the time when it was committed. Nor shall a heavier penalty be imposed than the one that was applicable at the time the penal offence was committed.

ARTICLE 12

No one shall be subjected to arbitrary interference with his privacy, family, home or correspondence, nor to attacks upon his honour and reputation. Everyone has the right to the protection of the law against such interference or attacks.

ARTICLE 13

1. Everyone has the right to freedom of movement and residence within the borders of each State.
2. Everyone has the right to leave any country, including his own, and to return to his country.

ARTICLE 14

1. Everyone has the right to seek and to enjoy in other countries asylum from persecution.
2. This right may not be invoked in the case of prosecutions genuinely arising from non-political crimes or from acts contrary to the purposes and principles of the United Nations.

ARTICLE 15

1. Everyone has the right to a nationality.
2. No one shall be arbitrarily deprived of his nationality nor denied the right to change his nationality.

ARTICLE 16

1. Men and women of full age, without any limitation due to race, nationality or religion, have the right to marry and to found a family. They are entitled to equal rights as to marriage, during marriage and at its dissolution.
2. Marriage shall be entered into only with the free and full consent of the intending spouses.
3. The family is the natural and fundamental group unit of society and is entitled to protection by society and the State.

ARTICLE 17

1. Everyone has the right to own property alone as well as in association with others.
2. No one shall be arbitrarily deprived of his property.

ARTICLE 18

Everyone has the right to freedom of thought, conscience and religion; this right includes freedom to change his religion or belief, and freedom, either alone or in community with others and in public or private, to manifest his religion or belief in teaching, practice, worship and observance.

ARTICLE 19

Everyone has the right to freedom of opinion and expression; this right includes freedom to hold opinions without interference and to seek, receive and impart information and ideas through any media and regardless of frontiers.

ARTICLE 20

1. Everyone has the right to freedom of peaceful assembly and association.
2. No one may be compelled to belong to an association.

ARTICLE 21

1. Everyone has the right to take part in the government of his country, directly or through freely chosen representatives.
2. Everyone has the right of equal access to public service in his country.
3. The will of the people shall be the basis of the authority of government; this will shall be expressed in periodic and genuine elections which shall be by universal and equal suffrage and shall be held by secret vote or by equivalent free voting procedures.

ARTICLE 22

Everyone, as a member of society, has the right to social security and is entitled to realization, through national effort and international co-operation and in accordance with the organization and resources of each State, of the economic, social and cultural rights indispensable for his dignity and the free development of his personality.

ARTICLE 23

1. Everyone has the right to work, to free choice of employment, to just and favourable conditions of work and to protection against unemployment.
2. Everyone, without any discrimination, has the right to equal pay for equal work.
3. Everyone who works has the right to just and favourable remuneration ensuring for himself and his family an existence worthy of human dignity, and supplemented, if necessary, by other means of social protection.
4. Everyone has the right to form and to join trade unions for the protection of his interests.

ARTICLE 24

Everyone has the right to rest and leisure, including reasonable limitation of working hours and periodic holidays with pay.

ARTICLE 25

1. Everyone has the right to a standard of living adequate for the health and well-being of himself and of his family, including food, clothing, housing and medical care and necessary social services, and the right to security in the event of unemployment, sickness, disability, widowhood, old age or other lack of livelihood in circumstances beyond his control.
2. Motherhood and childhood are entitled to special care and assistance. All children, whether born in or out of wedlock, shall enjoy the same social protection.

ARTICLE 26

1. Everyone has the right to education. Education shall be free, at least in the elementary and fundamental stages. Elementary education shall be compulsory. Technical and professional education shall be made generally available and higher education shall be equally accessible to all on the basis of merit.
2. Education shall be directed to the full development of the human personality and to the strengthening of respect for human rights and fundamental

freedoms. It shall promote understanding, tolerance and friendship among all nations, racial or religious groups, and shall further the activities of the United Nations for the maintenance of peace.

3. Parents have a prior right to choose the kind of education that shall be given to their children.

ARTICLE 27

1. Everyone has the right freely to participate in the cultural life of the community, to enjoy the arts and to share in scientific advancement and its benefits.
2. Everyone has the right to the protection of the moral and material interests resulting from any scientific, literary or artistic production of which he is the author.

ARTICLE 28

Everyone is entitled to a social and international order in which the rights and freedoms set forth in this Declaration can be fully realized.

ARTICLE 29

1. Everyone has duties to the community in which alone the free and full development of his personality is possible.
2. In the exercise of his rights and freedoms, everyone shall be subject only to such limitations as are determined by law solely for the purpose of securing due recognition and respect for the rights and freedoms of others and of meeting the just requirements of morality, public order and the general welfare in a democratic society.
3. These rights and freedoms may in no case be exercised contrary to the purposes and principles of the United Nations.

ARTICLE 30

Nothing in this Declaration may be interpreted as implying for any State, group or person any right to engage in any activity or to perform any act aimed at the destruction of any of the rights and freedoms set forth herein.

QUESTIONS FOR DISCUSSION

1. What is the purpose of this declaration and who is the audience?
2. What is the rhetorical effect of dividing the essay into a preamble followed by the articles? What is the effect of repeating certain phrases?
3. This declaration has been criticized for its emphasis on legal and civil rights while neglecting economic rights (poverty, starvation, and distribution of land and

wealth). Classify the thirty articles under the two categories of either legal/civil rights or economic rights. Then compare this declaration to *The Arusha Declaration* (p. 207). Discuss why the two documents might be different in their emphases.
4. What are the political implications of some of the articles? What might they imply about the political climate at the time this was written?

RODERICK OGLEY
Extracts from the Declaration of the Belgrade Conference of Heads of State and Government of Nonaligned Countries

After World War II, many countries in Asia and Africa gained their independence from colonial powers and many of these chose neutralism as a means to express their independence. Unlike the word neutrality, *which refers to the refusal to form alliances during wartime,* neutralism *means that these nations, during peacetime, preferred to follow their own national interests rather than side with the economic, political, or ideological systems of the United States or the Soviet Union. In 1961, many nonaligned nations gathered for the first nonaligned conference in Belgrade, which produced this declaration. Not surprisingly, this declaration takes a decisive stand on the issue of colonialism, which was an important issue in the post-World War II era when many nations successfully achieved their independence.*

Document 30. Extracts from the Declaration of the Belgrade Conference of Heads of State and Government of Nonaligned Countries, 1–6 September 1961.

The Conference of Heads of State or Government of the following non-aligned countries:

1. Afghanistan
2. Algeria
3. Burma
4. Cambodia
5. Ceylon
6. Congo
7. Cuba
8. Cyprus
9. Ethiopia
10. Ghana
11. Guinea
12. India
13. Indonesia
14. Iraq
15. Lebanon
16. Mali
17. Morocco
18. Nepal
19. Saudi Arabia
20. Somalia
21. Sudan
22. Tunisia
23. United Arab Republic
24. Yemen
25. Yugoslavia

and of the following countries represented by observers:

1. Bolivia   3. Ecuador
2. Brazil

was held in Belgrade from September 1 to 6, 1961, for the purpose of exchanging views on international problems with a view to contributing more effectively to world peace and security and peaceful co-operation among peoples.

The Heads of State or Government of the aforementioned countries have met at a moment when international events have taken a turn for the worst and when world peace is seriously threatened. Deeply concerned for the future of peace, voicing the aspirations of the vast majority of people of the world, aware that, in our time, no people and no government can or should abandon its responsibilities in regard to the safeguarding of world peace, the participating countries—having examined in detail, in an atmosphere of equality, sincerity and mutual confidence, the current state of international relations and trends prevailing in the present-day world—make the following declaration: . . .

I

War has never threatened mankind with graver consequences than today. On the other hand, never before has mankind had at its disposal stronger forces for eliminating war as an instrument of policy in international relations.

Imperialism is weakening. Colonial empires and other forms of foreign oppression of peoples in Asia, Africa and Latin America are gradually disappearing from the stage of history. Great successes have been achieved in the struggle of many peoples for national independence and equality. . . .

Prompted by such developments in the world, the vast majority of people are becoming increasingly conscious of the fact that war between peoples constitutes not only an anachronism but also a crime against humanity. This awareness of peoples is becoming a great moral force, capable of exercising a vital influence on the development of international relations.

Relying on this and on the will of their peoples, the Governments of countries participating in the Conference resolutely reject the view that war, including the cold war, is inevitable, as this view reflects a sense both of helplessness and hopelessness and is contrary to the progress of the world. They affirm their unwavering faith that the international community is able to organize its life without resorting to means which actually belong to a past epoch of human history.

However, the existing military blocs, which are growing into more and more powerful military, economic and political groupings, which, by the logic and nature of their mutual relations, necessarily provoke periodical aggravations of international relations the cold war and the constant and acute danger of its being transformed into actual war have become a part of the situation prevailing in international relations. . . .

II

The present-day world is characterized by the existence of different social systems. The participating countries do not consider that these differences constitute an insurmountable obstacle for the stabilization of peace, provided attempts at domination and interference in the internal development of other peoples and nations are ruled out. . . .

Furthermore, any attempt at imposing upon peoples one social or political system or another by force and from outside is a direct threat to world peace.

The participating countries consider that under such conditions the principles of peaceful co-existence are the only alternative to the cold war and to a possible general nuclear catastrophe. Therefore, by these principles which include the right of peoples to self-determination, to independence and to the free determination of the forms and methods of economic, social and cultural development—must be the only basis of all international relations. . . .

III

The non-aligned countries represented at this Conference do not wish to form a new bloc and cannot be a bloc. They sincerely desire to co-operate with any Government which seeks to contribute to the strengthening of confidence and peace in the world. . . .

The participants in the Conference consider that, under present conditions, the existence and the activities of non-aligned countries in the interests of peace are one of the more important factors for safeguarding world peace.

The participants in the Conference consider it essential that the non-aligned countries should participate in solving outstanding international issues concerning peace and security in the world as none of them can remain unaffected by or indifferent to these issues.

They consider that the further extensions of the non-committed area of the world constitutes the only possible and indispensable alternative to the policy of total division of the world into blocs, and intensification of cold war policies. The non-aligned countries provide encouragement and support to all peoples fighting for their independence and equality.

The participants in the Conference are convinced that the emergence of newly-liberated countries will further assist in narrowing of the area of bloc antagonisms and thus encourage all tendencies aimed at strengthening peace and promoting peaceful co-operation among independent and equal nations.

1. The participants in the Conference solemnly reaffirm their support to the "Declaration on the Granting of Independence to Colonial Countries and Peoples", adopted at the 15th Session of the General Assembly of the United Nations and recommend the immediate unconditional, total and final abolition of colonialism and resolved to make a concerted effort to put an end to all types of new colonialism and imperialist domination in all its forms and manifestations. . . .

3. The participating countries consider the struggle of the people of Algeria for freedom, self-determination and independence, and for the integrity of its national territory including the Sahara, to be just and necessary and are, therefore, determined to extend to the people of Algeria all the possible support and aid. The Heads of State or Government are particularly gratified that Algeria is represented at this Conference by its rightful representative, the Prime Minister of the Provisional Government of Algeria.

4. The participating countries draw attention with great concern to the developments in Angola and to the intolerable measures of repression taken by the Portuguese colonial authorities against the people of Angola and demand that an immediate end should be put to any further shedding of blood of the Angolan people, and the people of Angola should be assisted by all peace-loving countries, particularly member states of the United Nations, to establish their free and independent state without delay. . . .

6. The participating countries demand the immediate evacuation of French armed forces from the whole of the Tunisian territory in accordance with the legitimate right of Tunisia to the exercise of its full national sovereignty. . . .

8. The participants in the Conference resolutely condemn the policy of apartheid practised by the Union of South Africa and demand the immediate abandonment of this policy. They further state that the policy of racial discrimination anywhere in the world constitutes a grave violation of the Charter of the United Nations and the Universal Declaration of Human Rights. . . .

10. The participants in the Conference condemn the imperialist policies pursued in the Middle East, and declare their support for the full restoration of all the rights of the Arab people of Palestine in conformity with the Charter and resolutions of the United Nations.

11. The participating countries consider the establishment and maintenance of foreign military bases in the territories of other countries, particularly against their express will, a gross violation of the sovereignty of such States. They declare their full support to countries who are endeavouring to secure the vacation of these bases. They call upon those countries maintaining foreign bases to consider seriously their abolition as a contribution to world peace.

12. They also acknowledge that the North American military base at Guantanamo, Cuba, to the permanence of which the Government and people of Cuba have expressed their opposition, affects the sovereignty and territorial integrity of that country. . . .

18. The participants in the Conference urge the Great Powers to sign without further delay a treaty for general and complete disarmament in order to save mankind from the scourge of war and to release energy and resources now being spent on armaments to be used for the peaceful economic and social development of all mankind. The participating countries also consider that:
   a. The non-aligned Nations should be represented at all further world conferences on disarmament;
   b. All discussions on disarmament should be held under the auspices of the United Nations;

   c. General and complete disarmament should be guaranteed by an effective
      system of inspection and control, the teams of which should include
      members of non-aligned Nations.
19. The participants in the Conference consider it essential that an agreement on
    the prohibition of all nuclear and thermonuclear tests should be urgently
    concluded. With this aim in view, it is necessary that negotiations be
    immediately resumed, separately or as part of negotiations on general
    disarmament. Meanwhile, the moratorium on the testing of all nuclear
    weapons should be resumed and observed by all countries. . . .
26. Those of the countries participating in the Conference who recognize the
    Government of the People's Republic of China recommend that the General
    Assembly in its forthcoming Session should accept the representatives of the
    Government of the People's Republic of China as the only legitimate
    representatives of that country in the United Nations.

QUESTIONS FOR DISCUSSION

1. What is the purpose of this declaration and who is the audience?
2. This declaration was written during the Cold War between the United States and
   the Soviet Union and at a time when peoples in Asia and Africa were gaining
   independence from European domination. How is this historical context reflected in the stance of this document?
3. Summarize this declaration and compare it to one other declaration (see *The Arusha Declaration* [p. 207], *The Declaration of Independence* [p. 210], and the *Universal
   Declaration of Human Rights* [p. 215]). How are the two similar? How are they
   different? What might account for the differences?

ALEXIS DE TOCQUEVILLE
Democracy in America

*A French aristocrat, political theorist, historian, and politician, Alexis de Tocqueville (1805–1859)
traveled throughout the United States in 1831 and 1832 and observed American democracy and
society in action. After returning to France, he began writing* Democracy in America.
*De Tocqueville was impressed by the local self-government, the relative equality of political and social
conditions, and the talent he found among the citizens. But the lack of talented leaders and the
conformist pressure that restricted independent thinking could, he believed, easily lead to a "tyranny
of the majority." De Tocqueville feared that "individualism" led to conformity because it perpetuated
a self-centered concern for the acquisition of wealth at the expense of participation in public issues.
An apathy toward public duty would in turn allow the government to become centralized and would
reduce the number of checks against state power. Furthermore, the assumption that authority should
be placed in the hands of the majority would cause individuals to feel powerless and would cause them
to internalize the idea that dissent was somehow wrong because it opposed the majority.*

POWER EXERCISED BY THE MAJORITY IN AMERICA UPON OPINION

In America, when the Majority has once irrevocably decided a Question, all Discussion ceases.—Reason of this.—Moral Power exercised by the Majority upon Opinion.—Democratic Republics have applied Despotism to the Minds of Men.

It is in the examination of the exercise of thought in the United States, that we clearly perceive how far the power of the majority surpasses all the powers with which we are acquainted in Europe. Thought is an invisible and subtle power, that mocks all the efforts of tyranny. At the present time, the most absolute monarchs in Europe cannot prevent certain opinions hostile to their authority from circulating in secret through their dominions, and even in their courts. It is not so in America; as long as the majority is still undecided, discussion is carried on; but as soon as its decision is irrevocably pronounced, every one is silent, and the friends as well as the opponents of the measure unite in assenting to its propriety. The reason of this is perfectly clear: no monarch is so absolute as to combine all the powers of society in his own hands, and to conquer all opposition, as a majority is able to do, which has the right both of making and of executing the laws.

The authority of a king is physical, and controls the actions of men without subduing their will. But the majority possesses a power which is physical and moral at the same time, which acts upon the will as much as upon the actions, and represses not only all contest, but all controversy.

I know of no country in which there is so little independence of mind and real freedom of discussion as in America. In any constitutional state in Europe, every sort of religious and political theory may be freely preached and disseminated; for there is no country in Europe so subdued by any single authority, as not to protect the man who raises his voice in the cause of truth from the consequences of his hardihood. If he is unfortunate enough to live under an absolute government, the people are often upon his side; if he inhabits a free country, he can, if necessary, find a shelter behind the throne. The aristocratic part of society supports him in some countries, and the democracy in others. But in a nation where democratic institutions exist, organized like those of the United States, there is but one authority, one element of strength and success, with nothing beyond it.

In America, the majority raises formidable barriers around the liberty of opinion: within these barriers, an author may write what he pleases; but woe to him if he goes beyond them. Not that he is in danger of an *auto-da-fé*,[1] but he is exposed to continued obloquy and persecution. His political career is closed forever, since he has offended the only authority which is able to open it. Every sort of compensation, even that of celebrity, is refused to him. Before publishing his opinions, he imagined that he held them in common with others; but no sooner has he declared them, than he is loudly censured by his opponents, whilst those who think like him, without

---

[1] **auto-da-fé** Literally, "act of faith" in Portuguese. During the Inquisition it referred to the act of burning heretics. [Ed. note.]

having the courage to speak out, abandon him in silence. He yields at length, overcome by the daily effort which he has to make, and subsides into silence, as if he felt remorse for having spoken the truth.

Fetters and headsmen were the coarse instruments which tyranny formerly employed; but the civilization of our age has perfected despotism itself, though it seemed to have nothing to learn. Monarchs had, so to speak, materialized oppression: the democratic republics of the present day have rendered it as entirely an affair of the mind, as the will which it is intended to coerce. Under the absolute sway of one man, the body was attacked in order to subdue the soul; but the soul escaped the blows which were directed against it, and rose proudly superior. Such is not the course adopted by tyranny in democratic republics; there the body is left free, and the soul is enslaved. The master no longer says, "You shall think as I do, or you shall die"; but he says, "You are free to think differently from me, and to retain your life, your property, and all that you possess; but you are henceforth a stranger among your people. You may retain your civil rights, but they will be useless to you, for you will never be chosen by your fellow-citizens, if you solicit their votes; and they will affect to scorn you, if you ask for their esteem. You will remain among men, but you will be deprived of the rights of mankind. Your fellow-creatures will shun you like an impure being; and even those who believe in your innocence will abandon you, lest they should be shunned in their turn. Go in peace! I have given you your life, but it is an existence worse than death."

Absolute monarchies had dishonored despotism; let us beware lest democratic republics should reinstate it, and render it less odious and degrading in the eyes of the many, by making it still more onerous to the few.

Works have been published in the proudest nations of the Old World, expressly intended to censure the vices and the follies of the times: Labruyère inhabited the palace of Louis XIV when he composed his chapter upon the Great, and Molière criticised the courtiers in the pieces which were acted before the court. But the ruling power in the United States is not to be made game of. The smallest reproach irritates its sensibility, and the slightest joke which has any foundation in truth renders it indignant; from the forms of its language up to the solid virtues of its character, everything must be made the subject of encomium. No writer, whatever be his eminence, can escape paying this tribute of adulation to his fellow-citizens. The majority lives in the perpetual utterance of self-applause; and there are certain truths which the Americans can only learn from strangers or from experience.

If America has not as yet had any great writers, the reason is given in these facts; there can be no literary genius without freedom of opinion, and freedom of opinion does not exist in America. The Inquisition has never been able to prevent a vast number of anti-religious books from circulating in Spain. The empire of the majority succeeds much better in the United States, since it actually removes any wish to publish them. Unbelievers are to be met with in America, but there is no public organ of infidelity. Attempts have been made by some governments to protect morality by prohibiting licentious books. In the United States, no one is punished for this sort of books, but no one is induced to write them; not because all the citizens are immaculate in conduct, but because the majority of the community is decent and orderly.

In this case the use of the power is unquestionably good; and I am discussing the nature of the power itself. This irresistible authority is a constant fact, and its judicious exercise is only an accident.[2]

EFFECTS OF THE TYRANNY OF THE MAJORITY UPON THE NATIONAL CHARACTER OF THE AMERICANS—THE COURTIER-SPIRIT IN THE UNITED STATES

Effects of the Tyranny of the Majority more sensibly felt hitherto on the Manners than on the Conduct of Society.—They check the Development of great Characters.—Democratic Republics, organized like the United States, infuse the Courtier-spirit into the Mass of the People.—Proofs of this Spirit in the United States,—Why there is more Patriotism in the People than in those who govern in their Name.

The tendencies which I have just mentioned are as yet but slightly perceptible in political society; but they already exercise an unfavourable influence upon the national character of the Americans. I attribute the small number of distinguished men in political life to the ever-increasing despotism of the majority in the United States.

When the American Revolution broke out, they arose in great numbers; for public opinion then served, not to tyrannize over, but to direct the exertions of individuals. Those celebrated men, sharing the agitation of mind common at that period, had a grandeur peculiar to themselves, which was reflected back upon the nation, but was by no means borrowed from it.

In absolute governments, the great nobles who are nearest to the throne flatter the passions of the sovereign, and voluntarily truckle[3] to his caprices. But the mass of the nation does not degrade itself by servitude; it often submits from weakness, from habit, or from ignorance, and sometimes from loyalty. Some nations have been known to sacrifice their own desires to those of the sovereign with pleasure and pride, thus exhibiting a sort of independence of mind in the very act of submission. These nations are miserable, but they are not degraded. There is a great difference between doing what one does not approve, and feigning to approve what one does; the one is the weakness of a feeble person, the other befits the temper of a lackey.

In free countries, where every one is more or less called upon to give his opinion on affairs of state,—in democratic republics, where public life is incessantly mingled with domestic affairs, where the sovereign authority is accessible on every side, and where its attention can always be attracted by vociferation,[4]—more persons are to be met with who speculate upon its weaknesses, and live upon minister-

---

[2]De Tocqueville's remarks on this subject are rhetorical, and altogether too highly colored. It is notorious, that, in politics, morality, and religion, the most offensive opinions are preached and printed every week here in America, apparently for no other purpose than that of shocking the sentiments of the great bulk of the community. Instead of complaining of the bondage of thought, the judicious observer will rather grieve at the extreme licentiousness of the rostrum and the press. [Ed. note.]
[3]**truckle** Submit. [Ed. note.]
[4]**vociferation** Shouting. [Ed. note.]

ing to its passions, than in absolute monarchies. Not because men are naturally worse in these states than elsewhere, but the temptation is stronger and of easier access at the same time. The result is a more extensive debasement of character.

Democratic republics extend the practice of currying favor with the many, and introduce it into all classes at once: this is the most serious reproach that can be addressed to them. This is especially true in democratic states organized like the American republics, where the power of the majority is so absolute and irresistible that one must give up his rights as a citizen, and almost abjure[5] his qualities as a man, if he intends to stray from the track which it prescribes.

In that immense crowd which throngs the avenues to power in the United States, I found very few men who displayed that manly candor and masculine independence of opinion which frequently distinguished the Americans in former times, and which constitutes the leading feature in distinguished characters wheresoever they may be found. It seems, at first sight, as if all the minds of the Americans were formed upon one model, so accurately do they follow the same route. A stranger does, indeed, sometimes meet with Americans who dissent from the rigor of these formularies,—with men who deplore the defects of the laws, the mutability and the ignorance of democracy,—who even go so far as to observe the evil tendencies which impair the national character, and to point out such remedies as it might be possible to apply; but no one is there to hear them except yourself, and you, to whom these secret reflections are confided, are a stranger and a bird of passage. They are very ready to communicate truths which are useless to you, but they hold a different language in public.

If ever these lines are read in America, I am well assured of two things;—in the first place, that all who peruse them will raise their voices to condemn me; and, in the second place, that many of them will acquit me at the bottom of their conscience.

I have heard of patriotism in the United States, and I have found true patriotism among the people, but never among the leaders of the people. This may be explained by analogy: despotism debases the oppressed much more than the oppressor: in absolute monarchies, the king often has great virtues, but the courtiers are invariably servile. It is true that American courtiers do not say "Sire," or "Your Majesty,"—a distinction without a difference. They are forever talking of the natural intelligence of the people whom they serve: they do not debate the question which of the virtues of their master is pre-eminently worthy of admiration, for they assure him that he possesses all the virtues without having acquired them, or without caring to acquire them; they do not give him their daughters and their wives to be raised at his pleasure to the rank of his concubines; but, by sacrificing their opinions, they prostitute themselves. Moralists and philosophers in America are not obliged to conceal their opinions under the veil of allegory; but before they venture upon a harsh truth, they say, "We are aware that the people whom we are addressing are too superior to the weaknesses of human nature to lose the command of their temper for an instant. We should not hold this language if we were not speaking to men whom their virtues and their intelligence render more worthy of freedom than all the rest of the world." The sycophants of Louis XIV could not flatter more dexterously.

---

[5]**abjure** Reject. [Ed. note.]

For my part, I am persuaded that, in all governments, whatever their nature may be, servility will cower to force, and adulation[6] will follow power. The only means of preventing men from degrading themselves is to invest no one with that unlimited authority which is the sure method of debasing them.

THE GREATEST DANGERS OF THE AMERICAN REPUBLICS PROCEED FROM THE OMNIPOTENCE OF THE MAJORITY

Democratic Republics liable to perish from a Misuse of their Power, and not from Impotence.—The Governments of the American Republics are more Centralized and more Energetic than those of the Monarchies of Europe.—Dangers resulting from this.—Opinions of Madison and Jefferson upon this Point.

Governments usually perish from impotence or from tyranny. In the former case, their power escapes from them; it is wrested from their grasp in the latter. Many observers who have witnessed the anarchy of democratic states, have imagined that the government of those states was naturally weak and impotent. The truth is, that, when war is once begun between parties, the government loses its control over society. But I do not think that a democratic power is naturally without force or resources; say, rather, that it is almost always by the abuse of its force, and the misemployment of its resources, that it becomes a failure. Anarchy is almost always produced by its tyranny or its mistakes, but not by its want of strength.

It is important not to confound stability with force, or the greatness of a thing with its duration. In democratic republics, the power which directs[7] society is not stable; for it often changes hands, and assumes a new direction. But, whichever way it turns, its force is almost irresistible. The governments of the American republics appear to me to be as much centralized as those of the absolute monarchies of Europe, and more energetic than they are. I do not, therefore, imagine that they will perish from weakness.[8]

If ever the free institutions of America are destroyed, that event may be attributed to the omnipotence of the majority, which may at some future time urge the minorities to desperation, and oblige them to have recourse to physical force. Anarchy will then be the result, but it will have been brought about by despotism.

Mr. Madison expresses the same opinion in the Federalist, No. 51. "It is of great importance in a republic, not only to guard the society against the oppression of its rulers, but to guard one part of the society against the injustice of the other part. Justice is the end of government. It is the end of civil society. It ever has been, and ever will be, pursued until it be obtained, or until liberty be lost in the pursuit. In a society, under the forms of which the stronger faction can readily unite and oppress the weaker, anarchy may as truly be said to reign as in a state of nature, where

---

[6]**adulation** Excessive praise. [Ed. note.]

[7]This power may be centralized in an assembly, in which case it will be strong without being stable; or it may be centralized in an individual, in which case it will be less strong, but more stable.

[8]I presume that it is scarcely necessary to remind the reader here, as well as throughout this chapter, that I am speaking, not of the Federal governments, but of the several governments of each State, which the majority controls at its pleasure.

the weaker individual is not secured against the violence of the stronger: and as, in the latter state, even the stronger individuals are prompted by the uncertainty of their condition to submit to a government which may protect the weak as well as themselves, so, in the former state, will the more powerful factions be gradually induced by a like motive to wish for a government which will protect all parties, the weaker as well as the more powerful. It can be little doubted, that, if the State of Rhode Island was separated from the Confederacy and left to itself, the insecurity of right under the popular form of government within such narrow limits would be displayed by such reiterated oppressions of the factious majorities, that some power altogether independent of the people would soon be called for by the voice of the very factions whose misrule had proved the necessity of it."

Jefferson also said: "The executive power in our government is not the only, perhaps not even the principal, object of my solicitude.[9] The tyranny of the legislature is really the danger most to be feared, and will continue to be so for many years to come. The tyranny of the executive power will come in its turn, but at a more distant period."

I am glad to cite the opinion of Jefferson upon this subject rather than that of any other, because I consider him the most powerful advocate democracy has ever had.

QUESTIONS FOR DISCUSSION

1. What seems to be the purpose of this piece? Who is the audience?
2. What is the "tyranny of the majority"? How does it threaten democracy according to de Tocqueville?
3. Do you agree or disagree with de Tocqueville's analysis of democracy? Cite examples to support your position.
4. How does de Tocqueville view European monarchy? American republican government? How is oppression different in these forms of government?
5. How is the final quote from Jefferson relevant today?
6. De Tocqueville states that Americans tend to conform to the majority opinion. To what extent are Americans conformists? Explain.

KARL MARX AND FRIEDRICH ENGELS
Bourgeois and Proletarians

In 1848, with revolutions arising throughout Europe, the Communist League, a group of organized tailors in London, asked the political organizer and philosopher Karl Marx (1818–1883) to write a declaration of principles, which he named The Communist Manifesto. *While his life-long friend and supporter Friedrich Engels contributed some of his ideas to the* Manifesto, *Marx did all of the*

[9]**solicitude** Concern. [Ed. note.]

writing. Part of its purpose was to create a communist party and to capitalize on conservative rhetoric that labeled almost any opposition group "communist." The Manifesto *addresses these fears in the famous opening line, "A specter is haunting Europe." A student of the philosopher Hegel, Marx rejected Hegel's idealism—a philosophy in which ideas precede and form reality—in favor of a materialist view of history.* Materialism *asserts that economic causes, and not ideas, create social and political systems. Having observed the textile factories in the north of England, Marx concluded that the class that controls the means of production can also control the state. This first chapter of the* Manifesto *can be compared to the writings of Jefferson (p. 210) and Nyerere (p. 207).*

A specter is haunting Europe—the specter of Communism. All the powers of old Europe have entered into a holy alliance to exorcise this specter: Pope and Czar, Metternich and Guizot, French Radicals[1] and German police-spies.

Where is the party in opposition that has not been decried as communistic by its opponents in power? Where the Opposition that has not hurled back the branding reproach of Communism, against the more advanced opposition parties, as well as against its reactionary adversaries?

Two things result from this fact:

I. Communism is already acknowledged by all European powers to be itself a power.

II. It is high time that Communists should openly, in the face of the whole world, publish their views, their aims, their tendencies, and meet this nursery tale of the specter of Communism with a manifesto of the party itself.

To this end, Communists of various nationalities have assembled in London, and sketched the following manifesto, to be published in the English, French, German, Italian, Flemish, and Danish languages.

BOURGEOIS AND PROLETARIANS[2]

The history of all hitherto existing society[3] is the history of class struggles.

Freeman and slave, patrician and plebeian, lord and serf, guild-master[4] and journeyman, in a word, oppressor and oppressed, stood in constant opposition to one another, carried on an uninterrupted, now hidden, now open fight, a fight that each time ended, either in a revolutionary reconstitution of society at large, or in the common ruin of the contending classes.

---

[1] Metternich (1773–1859).—Chancellor of the Austrian empire and acknowledged leader of the European reaction. Guizot (1787–1874) was the French intellectual protagonist of high finance and of the industrial bourgeoisie and the irreconcilable foe of the proletariat. The French Radicals, Marrast (1802–1852), Carnot (1801–1888), and Marie (1795–1870) waged polemic warfare against the Socialists and Communists. [Ed. note.]

[2] By bourgeoisie is meant the class of modern capitalists, owners of the means of social production and employers of wage-labor; by proletariat, the class of modern wage-laborers who, having no means of production of their own, are reduced to selling their labor power in order to live.

[3] That is, all *written* history. In 1837, the pre-history of society, the social organization existing previous to recorded history, was all but unknown. Since then Haxthausen [August von, 1792–1866] discovered common ownership of land in Russia, Maurer [Georg Ludwig von] proved it to be the social foundation from which all Teutonic races started in history, and, by and by, village communities were found to be, or to have been, the primitive form of society everywhere from India to Ireland. The inner organization of this primitive communistic society was laid bare, in its typical form, by Morgan's [Lewis H., 1818–1881] crowning discovery of the true nature of the *gens* and its relation to the *tribe*. With the dissolution of these primeval communities, society begins to be differentiated into separate and finally antagonistic classes. I have attempted to retrace this process of dissolution in *The Origin of the Family, Private Property and the State.*

[4] Guild-master, that is a full member of a guild, a master within, not a head of a guild.

In the earlier epochs of history, we find almost everywhere a complicated arrangement of society into various orders, a manifold gradation of social rank. In ancient Rome we have patricians, knights, plebeians, slaves; in the Middle Ages, feudal lords, vassals, guild-masters, journeymen, apprentices, serfs; in almost all of these classes, again, subordinate gradations.

The modern bourgeois society that has sprouted from the ruins of feudal society, has not done away with class antagonisms. It has but established new classes, new conditions of oppression, new forms of struggle in place of the old ones.

Our epoch, the epoch of the bourgeoisie, possesses, however, this distinctive feature: It has simplified the class antagonisms. Society as a whole is more and more splitting up into two great hostile camps, into two great classes directly facing each other—bourgeoisie and proletariat.

From the serfs of the Middle Ages sprang the chartered burghers[5] of the earliest towns. From these burgesses the first elements of the bourgeoisie were developed.

The discovery of America, the rounding of the Cape, opened up fresh ground for the rising bourgeoisie. The East Indian and Chinese markets, the colonization of America, trade with the colonies, the increase in the means of exchange and in commodities generally, gave to commerce, to navigation, to industry, an impulse never before known, and thereby, to the revolutionary element in the tottering feudal society, a rapid development.

The feudal system of industry in which industrial production was monopolized by closed guilds,[6] now no longer sufficed for the growing wants of the new markets. The manufacturing system took its place. The guild-masters were pushed aside by the manufacturing middle class; division of labor between the different corporate guilds vanished in the face of division of labor in each single workshop.

Meantime the markets kept ever growing, the demand ever rising. Even manufacture no longer sufficed. Thereupon, steam and machinery revolutionized industrial production. The place of manufacture was taken by the giant, modern industry, the place of the industrial middle class, by industrial millionaires—the leaders of whole industrial armies, the modern bourgeois.

Modern industry has established the world market, for which the discovery of America paved the way. This market has given an immense development to commerce, to navigation, to communication by land. This development has, in its turn, reacted on the extension of industry; and in proportion as industry, commerce, navigation, railways extended, in the same proportion the bourgeoisie developed, increased its capital, and pushed into the background every class handed down from the Middle Ages.

We see, therefore, how the modern bourgeoisie is itself the product of a long course of development, of a series of revolutions in the modes of production and of exchange.

Each step in the development of the bourgeoisie was accompanied by a corresponding political advance of that class. An oppressed class under the sway of the

---

[5]Chartered burghers were freemen who had been admitted to the privileges of a chartered borough thus possessing full political rights. [Ed. note.]

[6]Craft guilds, made up of exclusive and privileged groups of artisans were, during the feudal period, granted monopoly rights to markets by municipal authorities. The guilds imposed minute regulations on their members controlling such matters as working hours, wages, prices, tools, and the hiring of workers. [Ed. note.]

feudal nobility, it became an armed and self-governing association in the medieval commune;[7] here independent urban republic (as in Italy and Germany), there taxable "third estate" of the monarchy (as in France); afterwards, in the period of manufacture proper, serving either the semi-feudal or the absolute monarchy as a counterpoise against the nobility, and, in fact, cornerstone of the great monarchies in general—the bourgeoisie has at last, since the establishment of modern industry and of the world market, conquered for itself, in the modern representative state, exclusive political sway. The executive of the modern state is but a committee for managing the common affairs of the whole bourgeoisie.

The bourgeoisie has played a most revolutionary role in history.

The bourgeoisie, wherever it has got the upper hand, has put an end to all feudal, patriarchal, idyllic relations. It has pitilessly torn asunder the motley feudal ties that bound man to his "natural superiors," and has left no other bond between man and man than naked self-interest, than callous "cash payment." It has drowned the most heavenly ecstasies of religious fervor, of chivalrous enthusiasm, of philistine sentimentalism, in the icy water of egotistical calculation. It has resolved personal worth into exchange value, and in place of the numberless indefeasible chartered freedoms, has set up that single, unconscionable freedom—Free Trade. In one word, for exploitation, veiled by religious and political illusions, it has substituted naked, shameless, direct, brutal exploitation.

The bourgeoisie has stripped of its halo every occupation hitherto honored and looked up to with reverent awe. It has converted the physician, the lawyer, the priest, the poet, the man of science, into its paid wage-laborers.

The bourgeoisie has torn away from the family its sentimental veil, and has reduced the family relation to a mere money relation.

The bourgeoisie has disclosed how it came to pass that the brutal display of vigor in the Middle Ages, which reactionaries so much admire, found its fitting complement in the most slothful indolence. It has been the first to show what man's activity can bring about. It has accomplished wonders far surpassing Egyptian pyramids, Roman aqueducts, and Gothic cathedrals; it has conducted expeditions that put in the shade all former migrations of nations and crusades.

The bourgeoisie cannot exist without constantly revolutionizing the instruments of production, and thereby the relations of production, and with them the whole relations of society. Conservation of the old modes of production in unaltered form, was, on the contrary, the first condition of existence for all earlier industrial classes. Constant revolutionizing of production, uninterrupted disturbance of all social conditions, everlasting uncertainty and agitation distinguish the bourgeois epoch from all earlier ones. All fixed, fast-frozen relations, with their train of ancient and venerable prejudices and opinions, are swept away, all new-formed ones become antiquated before they can ossify. All that is solid melts into air, all that is holy is profaned, and man is at last compelled to face with sober senses his real conditions of life and his relations with his kind.

---

[7]"Commune" was the name taken in France by the nascent towns even before they had conquered from their feudal lords and masters local self-government and political rights as the "Third Estate." Generally speaking, for the economic development of the bourgeoisie, England is here taken as the typical country, for its political development, France.

The need of a constantly expanding market for its products chases the bourgeoisie over the whole surface of the globe. It must nestle everywhere, settle everywhere, establish connections everywhere.

The bourgeoisie has through its exploitation of the world market given a cosmopolitan character to production and consumption in every country. To the great chagrin of reactionaries, it has drawn from under the feet of industry the national ground on which it stood. All old-established national industries have been destroyed or are daily being destroyed. They are dislodged by new industries, whose introduction becomes a life and death question for all civilized nations, by industries that no longer work up indigenous raw material, but raw material drawn from the remotest zones; industries whose products are consumed, not only at home, but in every quarter of the globe. In place of the old wants, satisfied by the production of the country, we find new wants, requiring for their satisfaction the products of distant lands and climes. In place of the old local and national seclusion and self-sufficiency, we have intercourse in every direction, universal inter-dependence of nations. And as in material, so also in intellectual production. The intellectual creations of individual nations become common property. National one-sidedness and narrow-mindedness become more and more impossible, and from the numerous national and local literatures there arises a world literature.

The bourgeoisie, by the rapid improvement of all instruments of production, by the immensely facilitated means of communication, draws all nations, even the most barbarian, into civilization. The cheap prices of its commodities are the heavy artillery with which it batters down all Chinese walls, with which it forces the barbarians' intensely obstinate hatred of foreigners to capitulate. It compels all nations, on pain of extinction, to adopt the bourgeois mode of production; it compels them to introduce what it calls civilization into their midst, i.e., to become bourgeois themselves. In a word, it creates a world after its own image.

The bourgeoisie has subjected the country to the rule of the towns. It has created enormous cities, has greatly increased the urban population as compared with the rural, and has thus rescued a considerable part of the population from the idiocy of rural life. Just as it has made the country dependent on the towns, so it has made barbarian and semi-barbarian countries dependent on the civilized ones, nations of peasants on nations of bourgeois, the East on the West.

More and more the bourgeoisie keeps doing away with the scattered state of the population, of the means of production, and of property. It has agglomerated population, centralized means of production, and has concentrated property in a few hands. The necessary consequence of this was political centralization. Independent, or but loosely connected provinces, with separate interests, laws, governments, and systems of taxation, became lumped together into one nation, with one government, one code of laws, one national class interest, one frontier, and one customs tariff.

The bourgeoisie, during its rule of scarce one hundred years, has created more massive and more colossal productive forces than have all preceding generations together. Subjection of nature's forces to man, machinery, application of chemistry to industry and agriculture, steam-navigation, railways, electric telegraphs, clearing of whole continents for cultivation, canalisation of rivers, whole populations conjured out of the ground—what earlier century had even a presentiment that such productive forces slumbered in the lap of social labour?

We see then that the means of production and of exchange, which served as the foundation for the growth of the bourgeoisie, were generated in feudal society. At a certain stage in the development of these means of production and of exchange, the conditions under which feudal society produced and exchanged, the feudal organisation of agriculture and manufacturing industry, in a word, the feudal relations of property became no longer compatible with the already developed productive forces; they became so many fetters. They had to be burst asunder; they were burst asunder.

Into their place stepped free competition, accompanied by a social and political constitution adapted to it, and by the economic and political sway of the bourgeois class.

A similar movement is going on before our own eyes. Modern bourgeois society with its relations of production, of exchange and of property, a society that has conjured up such gigantic means of production and of exchange, is like the sorcerer who is no longer able to control the powers of the nether world whom he has called up by his spells. For many a decade past the history of industry and commerce is but the history of the revolt of modern productive forces against modern conditions of production, against the property relations that are the conditions for the existence of the bourgeoisie and of its rule. It is enough to mention the commercial crises that by their periodical return put the existence of the entire bourgeois society on trial, each time more threateningly. In these crises a great part not only of the existing products, but also of the previously created productive forces, are periodically destroyed. In these crises there breaks out an epidemic that, in all earlier epochs, would have seemed an absurdity—the epidemic of over-production. Society suddenly finds itself put back into a state of momentary barbarism; it appears as if a famine, a universal war of devastation had cut off the supply of every means of subsistence; industry and commerce seem to be destroyed. And why? Because there is too much civilization, too much means of subsistence, too much industry, too much commerce. The productive forces at the disposal of society no longer tend to further the development of the conditions of bourgeois property; on the contrary, they have become too powerful for these conditions, by which they are fettered, and no sooner do they overcome these fetters than they bring disorder into the whole of bourgeois society, endanger the existence of bourgeois property. The conditions of bourgeois society are too narrow to comprise the wealth created by them. And how does the bourgeoisie get over these crises? On the one hand, by enforced destruction of a mass of productive forces; on the other, by the conquest of new markets, and by the more thorough exploitation of the old ones. That is to say, by paving the way for more extensive and more destructive crises, and by diminishing the means whereby crises are prevented.

The weapons with which the bourgeoisie felled feudalism to the ground are now turned against the bourgeoisie itself.

But not only has the bourgeoisie forged the weapons that bring death to itself; it has also called into existence the men who are to wield those weapons—the modern working class—the proletarians.

In proportion as the bourgeoisie, i.e., capital, is developed, in the same proportion is the proletariat, the modern working class, developed—a class of laborers, who live only so long as they find work, and who find work only so long as their labor increases capital. These laborers, who must sell themselves piecemeal, are a commodity, like every other article of commerce, and are consequently exposed to all the vicissitudes of competition, to all the fluctuations of the market.

Owing to the extensive use of machinery and to division of labor, the work of the proletarians has lost all individual character, and, consequently, all charm for the workman. He becomes an appendage of the machine, and it is only the most simple, most monotonous, and most easily acquired knack, that is required of him. Hence, the cost of production of a workman is restricted, almost entirely, to the means of subsistence that he requires for his maintenance, and for the propagation of his race. But the price of a commodity, and therefore also of labor, is equal to its cost of production. In proportion, therefore, as the repulsiveness of the work increases, the wage decreases. Nay more, in proportion as the use of machinery and division of labor increases, in the same proportion the burden of toil also increases, whether by prolongation of the working hours, by increase of the work exacted in a given time, or by increased speed of the machinery, etc.

Modern industry has converted the little workshop of the patriarchal master into the great factory of the industrial capitalist. Masses of laborers, crowded into the factory, are organized like soldiers. As privates of the industrial army they are placed under the command of a perfect hierarchy of officers and sergeants. Not only are they slaves of the bourgeois class, and of the bourgeois state; they are daily and hourly enslaved by the machine, by the over-looker, and, above all, by the individual bourgeois manufacturer himself. The more openly this despotism proclaims gain to be its end and aim, the more petty, the more hateful and the more embittering it is.

The less the skill and exertion of strength implied in manual labor, in other words, the more modern industry develops, the more is the labor of men superseded by that of women. Differences of age and sex have no longer any distinctive social validity for the working class. All are instruments of labor, more or less expensive to use, according to their age and sex.

No sooner has the laborer received his wages in cash, for the moment escaping exploitation by the manufacturer, than he is set upon by the other portions of the bourgeoisie, the landlord, the shopkeeper, the pawnbroker, etc.

The lower strata of the middle class—the small tradespeople, shopkeepers, and retired tradesmen generally, the handicraftsmen and peasants—all these sink gradually into the proletariat, partly because their diminutive capital does not suffice for the scale on which modern industry is carried on, and is swamped in the competition with the large capitalists, partly because their specialized skill is rendered worthless by new methods of production. Thus the proletariat is recruited from all classes of the population.

The proletariat goes through various stages of development. With its birth begins its struggle with the bourgeoisie. At first the contest is carried on by individual laborers, then by the work people of a factory, then by the operatives of one trade, in one locality, against the individual bourgeois who directly exploits them. They direct their attacks not against the bourgeois conditions of production, but against the instruments of production themselves; they destroy imported wares that compete with their labor, they smash machinery to pieces, they set factories ablaze, they seek to restore by force the vanished status of the workman of the Middle Ages.

At this stage the laborers still form an incoherent mass scattered over the whole country, and broken up by their mutual competition. If anywhere they unite to form more compact bodies, this is not yet the consequence of their own active union, but of the union of the bourgeoisie, which class, in order to attain its own political ends, is compelled to set the whole proletariat in motion, and is moreover still able to do so for a time. At this stage, therefore, the proletarians do not fight their enemies, but the enemies of their enemies, the remnants of absolute monarchy, the landowners, the nonindustrial bourgeois, the petty bourgeoisie. Thus the whole historical movement is concentrated in the hands of the bourgeoisie; every victory so obtained is a victory for the bourgeoisie.

But with the development of industry the proletariat not only increases in number; it becomes concentrated in greater masses, its strength grows, and it feels that strength more. The various interests and conditions of life within the ranks of the proletariat are more and more equalized, in proportion as machinery obliterates all distinctions of labor and nearly everywhere reduces wages to the same low level. The growing competition among the bourgeois, and the resulting commercial crises, make the wages of the workers ever more fluctuating. The unceasing improvement of machinery, ever more rapidly developing, makes their livelihood more and more precarious; the collisions between individual workmen and individual bourgeois take more and more the character of collisions between two classes. Thereupon the workers begin to form combinations (trade unions) against the bourgeoisie; they club together in order to keep up the rate of wages; they found permanent associations in order to make provision beforehand for these occasional revolts. Here and there the contest breaks out into riots.

Now and then the workers are victorious, but only for a time. The real fruit of their battles lies, not in the immediate result, but in the ever expanding union of the workers. This union is furthered by the improved means of communication which are created by modern industry, and which place the workers of different localities in contact with one another. It was just this contact that was needed to centralize the numerous local struggles, all of the same character, into one national struggle between classes. But every class struggle is a political struggle. And that union, to attain which the burghers of the Middle Ages, with their miserable highways, required centuries, the modern proletarians, thanks to railways, achieve in a few years.

This organization of the proletarians into a class, and consequently into a political party, is continually being upset again by the competition between the workers themselves. But it ever rises up again, stronger, firmer, mightier. It compels legislative recognition of particular interests of the workers, by taking advantage of the divisions among the bourgeoisie itself. Thus the ten-hour bill[8] in England was carried.

Altogether, collisions between the classes of the old society further the course of development of the proletariat in many ways. The bourgeoisie finds itself involved in a constant battle. At first with the aristocracy; later on, with those portions of the bourgeoisie itself whose interests have become antagonistic to the progress of

[8]The 10-Hour Bill, for which the English workers had been fighting for 30 years, was made a law in 1847.—Ed.

industry; at all times with the bourgeoisie of foreign countries. In all these battles it sees itself compelled to appeal to the proletariat, to ask for its help, and thus, to drag it into the political arena. The bourgeoisie itself, therefore, supplies the proletariat with its own elements of political and general education, in other words, it furnishes the proletariat with weapons for fighting the bourgeoisie.

Further, as we have already seen, entire sections of the ruling classes are, by the advance of industry, precipitated into the proletariat, or are at least threatened in their conditions of existence. These also supply the proletariat with fresh elements of enlightenment and progress.

Finally, in times when the class struggle nears the decisive hour, the process of dissolution going on within the ruling class, in fact within the whole range of old society, assumes such a violent, glaring character, that a small section of the ruling class cuts itself adrift, and joins the revolutionary class, the class that holds the future in its hands. Just as, therefore, at an earlier period, a section of the nobility went over to the bourgeoisie, so now a portion of the bourgeoisie goes over to the proletariat, and in particular, a portion of the bourgeois ideologists, who have raised themselves to the level of comprehending theoretically the historical movement as a whole.

Of all the classes that stand face to face with the bourgeoisie today, the proletariat alone is a really revolutionary class. The other classes decay and finally disappear in the face of modern industry; the proletariat is its special and essential product.

The lower middle class, the small manufacturer, the shopkeeper, the artisan, the peasant, all these fight against the bourgeoisie, to save from extinction their existence as fractions of the middle class. They are therefore not revolutionary, but conservative. Nay more, they are reactionary, for they try to roll back the wheel of history. If by chance they are revolutionary, they are so only in view of their impending transfer into the proletariat; they thus defend not their present, but their future interests; they desert their own standpoint to adopt that of the proletariat.

The "dangerous class," the social scum (Lumpenproletariat), that passively rotting mass thrown off by the lowest layers of old society, may, here and there, be swept into the movement by a proletarian revolution; its conditions of life, however, prepare it far more for the part of a bribed tool of reactionary intrigue.

The social conditions of the old society no longer exist for the proletariat. The proletarian is without property; his relation to his wife and children has no longer anything in common with bourgeois family relations; modern industrial labor, modern subjection to capital, the same in England as in France, in America as in Germany, has stripped him of every trace of national character. Law, morality, religion, are to him so many bourgeois prejudices, behind which lurk in ambush just as many bourgeois interests.

All the preceding classes that got the upper hand, sought to fortify their already acquired status by subjecting society at large to their conditions of appropriation. The proletarians cannot become masters of the productive forces of society, except by abolishing their own previous mode of appropriation, and thereby also every other previous mode of appropriation. They have nothing of their own to secure and to fortify; their mission is to destroy all previous securities for, and insurances of, individual property.

All previous historical movements were movements of minorities, or in the interest of minorities. The proletarian movement is the self-conscious, independent movement of the immense majority, in the interest of the immense majority. The proletariat, the lowest stratum of our present society, cannot stir, cannot raise itself up, without the whole superincumbent strata of official society being sprung into the air.

Though not in substance, yet in form, the struggle of the proletariat with the bourgeoisie is at first a national struggle. The proletariat of each country must, of course, first of all settle matters with its own bourgeoisie.

In depicting the most general phases of the development of the proletariat, we traced the more or less veiled civil war, raging within existing society, up to the point where that war breaks out into open revolution, and where the violent overthrow of the bourgeoisie lays the foundation for the sway of the proletariat.

Hitherto, every form of society has been based, as we have already seen, on the antagonism of oppressing and oppressed classes. But in order to oppress a class, certain conditions must be assured to it under which it can, at least, continue its slavish existence. The serf, in the period of serfdom, raised himself to membership in the commune, just as the petty bourgeois, under the yoke of feudal absolutism, managed to develop into a bourgeois. The modern laborer, on the contrary, instead of rising with the progress of industry, sinks deeper and deeper below the conditions of existence of his own class. He becomes a pauper, and pauperism develops more rapidly than population and wealth. And here it becomes evident, that the bourgeoisie is unfit any longer to be the ruling class in society, and to impose its conditions of existence upon society as an overriding law. It is unfit to rule because it is incompetent to assure an existence to its slave within his slavery, because it cannot help letting him sink into such a state, that it has to feed him, instead of being fed by him. Society can no longer live under this bourgeoisie, in other words, its existence is no longer compatible with society.

The essential condition for the existence and sway of the bourgeois class, is the formation and augmentation of capital; the condition for capital is wage-labor. Wage-labor rests exclusively on competition between the laborers. The advance of industry, whose involuntary promoter is the bourgeoisie, replaces the isolation of the laborers, due to competition, by their revolutionary combination, due to association. The development of modern industry, therefore, cuts from under its feet the very foundation on which the bourgeoisie produces and appropriates products. What the bourgeoisie therefore produces, above all, are its own grave-diggers. Its fall and the victory of the proletariat are equally inevitable.

QUESTIONS FOR DISCUSSION

1. As an in-class activity, survey the reading by quickly reading the main points. Start with Marx's thesis and outline his argument. Where does Marx's selection shift from an analysis of the past to a prediction of the future?
2. According to Marx, what will cause a class struggle between the bourgeoisie and the proletariat? What is the function of the bourgeoisie and the proletariat

according to his view? What seems to be Marx's attitude (tone) toward the bourgeois and the proletariat?

3. Explain the crisis that will bring the proletariat to power.
4. What are Marx's Western biases? How does he refer to other countries and to the expansion of bourgeois industrial society to those countries?
5. Do you agree or disagree with Marx's analysis and predictions? Explain.
6. In-class essay question: Compare and contrast Marx's communism and Nyerere's "Ujamaa" (p. 200). In particular, look at the notions of class and class struggle which are at the heart of Marx's argument and look at the assumptions of ujamaa which are central to Nyerere's argument.

SIMONE DE BEAUVOIR
Women as Other

The French author and feminist Simone de Beauvoir (1908–1986) wrote the influential feminist classic The Second Sex *(1949), from which this portion of the introduction is excerpted. De Beauvoir studied philosophy at the Sorbonne, and wrote several novels; the most well-known of these works,* The Mandarins *(1954), won the prestigious Prix Goncourt. She wrote* The Second Sex *after a visit to the United States, where she was struck by the diminishing opportunities for women after World War II (when working women were fired so that returning soldiers would have jobs). The notion that "femininity" is a social construct—that, in de Beauvoir's words "one is not born, but rather becomes, a woman"—is familiar today, but was at that time original and to some, scandalous. In the selection given here, de Beauvoir compares the oppression of blacks and Jews to the oppression of women, and explains how the attitudes of men and women define women only in relation to men. As the "Other," a woman is of secondary importance. Ironically enough, de Beauvoir herself is often defined by those who write about her solely in terms of her long relationship with existentialist philosopher Jean-Paul Sartre.*

We must face the question: what is a woman?

To state the question is, to me, to suggest, at once, a preliminary answer. The fact that I ask it is in itself significant. A man would never get the notion of writing a book on the peculiar situation of the human male.[1] But if I wish to define myself, I must first of all say: "I am a woman"; on this truth must be based all further discussion. A man never begins by presenting himself as an individual of a certain sex; it goes without saying that he is a man. The terms *masculine* and *feminine* are used symmetrically only as a matter of form, as on legal papers. In actuality the relation of the two sexes is not quite like that of two electrical poles, for man represents both the positive and the neutral, as is indicated by the common use of *man* to designate human beings in general; whereas woman represents only the negative, defined by

---

[1] The Kinsey Report [Alfred C. Kinsey and others: *Sexual Behavior in the Human Male* (W. B. Saunders Co., 1948)] is no exception, for it is limited to describing the sexual characteristics of American men, which is quite a different matter.

limiting criteria, without reciprocity. In the midst of an abstract discussion it is vexing to hear a man say: "You think thus and so because you are a woman"; but I know that my only defense is to reply: "I think thus and so because it is true," thereby removing my subjective self from the argument. It would be out of the question to reply: "And you think the contrary because you are a man," for it is understood that the fact of being a man is no peculiarity. A man is in the right in being a man; it is the woman who is in the wrong. It amounts to this: just as for the ancients there was an absolute vertical with reference to which the oblique was defined, so there is an absolute human type, the masculine. Woman has ovaries, a uterus; these peculiarities imprison her in her subjectivity, circumscribe her within the limits of her own nature. It is often said that she thinks with her glands. Man superbly ignores the fact that his anatomy also includes glands, such as the testicles, and that they secrete hormones. He thinks of his body as a direct and normal connection with the world, which he believes he apprehends objectively, whereas he regards the body of woman as a hindrance, a prison, weighed down by everything peculiar to it. "The female is a female by virtue of a certain *lack* of qualities," said Aristotle; "we should regard the female nature as afflicted with a natural defectiveness." And St. Thomas for his part pronounced woman to be an "imperfect man," an "incidental" being. This is symbolized in Genesis where Eve is depicted as made from what Bossuet called "a supernumerary bone" of Adam.

Thus humanity is male and man defines woman not in herself but as relative to him; she is not regarded as an autonomous being. Michelet writes: "Woman, the relative being. . . ." And Benda is most positive in his *Rapport d'Uriel*: "The body of man makes sense in itself quite apart from that of woman, whereas the latter seems wanting in significance by itself. . . . Man can think of himself without woman. She cannot think of herself without man." And she is simply what man decrees; thus she is called "the sex," by which is meant that she appears essentially to the male as a sexual being. For him she is sex—absolute sex, no less. She is defined and differentiated with reference to man and not he with reference to her; she is the incidental, the inessential as opposed to the essential. He is the Subject, he is the Absolute—she is the Other.[2]

The category of the *Other* is as primordial as consciousness itself. In the most primitive societies, in the most ancient mythologies, one finds the expression of a duality—that of the Self and the Other. This duality was not originally attached to the division of the sexes; it was not dependent upon any empirical facts. It is revealed in such works as that of Granet on Chinese thought and those of Dumézil on the East Indies and Rome. The feminine element was at first no more involved in

---

[2]E. Lévinas expresses this idea most explicitly in his essay *Temps et l'Autre*. "Is there not a case in which otherness, alterity [*altérité*], unquestionably marks the nature of a being, as its essence, an instance of otherness not consisting purely and simply in the opposition of two species of the same genus? I think that the feminine represents the contrary in its absolute sense, this contrariness being in no wise affected by any relation between it and its correlative and thus remaining absolutely other. Sex is not a certain specific difference . . . no more is the sexual difference a mere contradiction. . . . Nor does this difference lie in the duality of two complementary terms, for two complementary terms imply a pre-existing whole. . . . Otherness reaches its full flowering in the feminine, a term of the same rank as consciousness but of opposite meaning."

I suppose that Lévinas does not forget that woman, too, is aware of her own consciousness, or ego. But it is striking that he deliberately takes a man's point of view, disregarding the reciprocity of subject and object. When he writes that woman is mystery, he implies that she is mystery for man. Thus his description, which is intended to be objective, is in fact an assertion of masculine privilege.

such pairs as Varuna-Mitra, Uranus-Zeus, Sun-Moon, and Day-Night than it was in the contrasts between Good and Evil, lucky and unlucky auspices, right and left, God and Lucifer. Otherness is a fundamental category of human thought.

Thus it is that no group ever sets itself up as the One without at once setting up the Other over against itself. If three travelers chance to occupy the same compartment, that is enough to make vaguely hostile "others" out of all the rest of the passengers on the train. In small-town eyes all persons not belonging to the village are "strangers" and suspect; to the native of a country all who inhabit other countries are "foreigners"; Jews are "different" for the anti-Semite, Negroes are "inferior" for American racists, aborigines are "natives" for colonists, proletarians are the "lower class" for the privileged.

Lévi-Strauss, at the end of a profound work on the various forms of primitive societies, reaches the following conclusion: "Passage from the state of Nature to the state of Culture is marked by man's ability to view biological relations as a series of contrasts; duality, alternation, opposition, and symmetry, whether under definite or vague forms, constitute not so much phenomena to be explained as fundamental and immediately given data of social reality."[3] These phenomena would be incomprehensible if in fact human society were simply a *Mitsein* or fellowship based on solidarity and friendliness. Things become clear, on the contrary, if, following Hegel, we find in consciousness itself a fundamental hostility toward every other consciousness; the subject can be posed only in being opposed—he sets himself up as the essential, as opposed to the other, the inessential, the object.

But the other consciousness, the other ego, sets up a reciprocal claim. The native traveling abroad is shocked to find himself in turn regarded as a "stranger" by the natives of neighboring countries. As a matter of fact, wars, festivals, trading, treaties, and contests among tribes, nations, and classes tend to deprive the concept *Other* of its absolute sense and to make manifest its relativity; willy-nilly, individuals and groups are forced to realize the reciprocity of their relations. How is it, then, that this reciprocity has not been recognized between the sexes, that one of the contrasting terms is set up as the sole essential, denying any relativity in regard to its correlative and defining the latter as pure otherness? Why is it that women do not dispute male sovereignty? No subject will readily volunteer to become the object, the inessential; it is not the Other who, in defining himself as the Other, establishes the One. The Other is posed as such by the One in defining himself as the One. But if the Other is not to regain the status of being the One, he must be submissive enough to accept this alien point of view. Whence comes this submission in the case of woman?

There are, to be sure, other cases in which a certain category has been able to dominate another completely for a time. Very often this privilege depends upon inequality of numbers—the majority imposes its rule upon the minority or persecutes it. But women are not a minority, like the American Negroes or the Jews; there are as many women as men on earth. Again, the two groups concerned have often been originally independent; they may have been formerly unaware of each other's existence, or perhaps they recognized each other's autonomy. But a histori-

---

[3]See C. Lévi-Strauss: *Les Structures élémentaires de la parenté.* My thanks are due to C. Lévi-Strauss for his kindness in furnishing me with the proofs of his work, which, among others, I have used liberally in Part II.

cal event has resulted in the subjugation of the weaker by the stronger. The scattering of the Jews, the introduction of slavery into America, the conquests of imperialism are examples in point. In these cases the oppressed retained at least the memory of former days; they possessed in common a past, a tradition, sometimes a religion or a culture.

The parallel drawn by Bebel between women and the proletariat is valid in that neither ever formed a minority or a separate collective unit of mankind. And instead of a single historical event it is in both cases a historical development that explains their status as a class and accounts for the membership of *particular individuals* in that class. But proletarians have not always existed, whereas there have always been women. They are women in virtue of their anatomy and physiology. Throughout history they have always been subordinated to men,[4] and hence their dependency is not the result of a historical event or a social change—it was not something that *occurred*. The reason why otherness in this case seems to be an absolute is in part that it lacks the contingent or incidental nature of historical facts. A condition brought about at a certain time can be abolished at some other time, as the Negroes of Haiti and others have proved; but it might seem that a natural condition is beyond the possibility of change. In truth, however, the nature of things is no more immutably given, once for all, than is historical reality. If woman seems to be the inessential which never becomes the essential, it is because she herself fails to bring about this change. Proletarians say "We"; Negroes also. Regarding themselves as subjects, they transform the bourgeois, the whites, into "others." But women do not say "We," except at some congress of feminists or similar formal demonstration; men say "women," and women use the same word in referring to themselves. They do not authentically assume a subjective attitude. The proletarians have accomplished the revolution in Russia, the Negroes in Haiti, the Indo-Chinese are battling for it in Indo-China; but the women's effort has never been anything more than a symbolic agitation. They have gained only what men have been willing to grant; they have taken nothing, they have only received.[5]

The reason for this is that women lack concrete means for organizing themselves into a unit which can stand face to face with the correlative unit. They have no past, no history, no religion of their own; and they have no such solidarity of work and interest as that of the proletariat. They are not even promiscuously herded together in the way that creates community feeling among the American Negroes, the ghetto Jews, the workers of Saint-Denis, or the factory hands of Renault. They live dispersed among the males, attached through residence, housework, economic condition, and social standing to certain men—fathers or husbands—more firmly than they are to other women. If they belong to the bourgeoisie, they feel solidarity with men of that class, not with proletarian women; if they are white, their allegiance is to white men, not to Negro women. The proletariat can propose to massacre the ruling class, and a sufficiently fanatical Jew or Negro might dream of getting sole possession of the atomic bomb and making humanity wholly Jewish or black; but woman cannot even dream of exterminating the males. The bond that unites her to her oppressors is not comparable to any other. The division of the sexes is a

---

[4]With rare exceptions, perhaps, like certain matriarchal rulers, queens, and the like.—TR.
[5]See Part II, ch. viii.

biological fact, not an event in human history. Male and female stand opposed within a primordial *Mitsein*, and woman has not broken it. The couple is a fundamental unity with its two halves riveted together, and the cleavage of society along the line of sex is impossible. Here is to be found the basic trait of woman: she is the Other in a totality of which the two components are necessary to one another.

One could suppose that this reciprocity might have facilitated the liberation of woman. When Hercules sat at the feet of Omphale and helped with her spinning, his desire for her held him captive; but why did she fail to gain a lasting power? To revenge herself on Jason, Medea killed their children; and this grim legend would seem to suggest that she might have obtained a formidable influence over him through his love for his offspring. In *Lysistrata* Aristophanes gaily depicts a band of women who joined forces to gain social ends through the sexual needs of their men; but this is only a play. In the legend of the Sabine women, the latter soon abandoned their plan of remaining sterile to punish their ravishers. In truth woman has not been socially emancipated through man's need—sexual desire and the desire for offspring—which makes the male dependent for satisfaction upon the female.

Master and slave, also, are united by a reciprocal need, in this case economic, which does not liberate the slave. In the relation of master to slave the master does not make a point of the need that he has for the other; he has in his grasp the power of satisfying this need through his own action; whereas the slave, in his dependent condition, his hope and fear, is quite conscious of the need he has for his master. Even if the need is at bottom equally urgent for both, it always works in favor of the oppressor and against the oppressed. That is why the liberation of the working class, for example, has been slow.

Now, woman has always been man's dependent, if not his slave; the two sexes have never shared the world in equality. And even today woman is heavily handicapped, though her situation is beginning to change. Almost nowhere is her legal status the same as man's, and frequently it is much to her disadvantage. Even when her rights are legally recognized in the abstract, long-standing custom prevents their full expression in the mores. In the economic sphere men and women can almost be said to make up two castes; other things being equal, the former hold the better jobs, get higher wages, and have more opportunity for success than their new competitors. In industry and politics men have a great many more positions and they monopolize the most important posts. In addition to all this, they enjoy a traditional prestige that the education of children tends in every way to support, for the present enshrines the past—and in the past all history has been made by men. At the present time, when women are beginning to take part in the affairs of the world, it is still a world that belongs to men—they have no doubt of it at all and women have scarcely any. To decline to be the Other, to refuse to be a party to the deal—this would be for women to renounce all the advantages conferred upon them by their alliance with the superior caste. Man-the-sovereign will provide woman-the-liege with material protection and will undertake the moral justification of her existence; thus she can evade at once both economic risk and the metaphysical risk of a liberty in which ends and aims must be contrived without assistance. Indeed, along with the ethical urge of each individual to affirm his subjective existence, there is also the temptation to forgo liberty and become a thing. This is an inauspicious road, for he who takes it—passive, lost, ruined—becomes henceforth the creature of another's will, frustrated in his transcendence and deprived of every value. But it is an easy road; on it one avoids the strain involved in undertaking an authentic existence. When man makes of woman the *Other*, he may, then, expect her to manifest deep-seated tendencies toward complicity. Thus, woman may fail to lay claim to the status of subject because she lacks definite resources, because she feels the necessary bond that ties her to man regardless of reciprocity, and because she is often very well pleased with her role as the *Other*. . . .

QUESTIONS FOR DISCUSSION

1. In your own words, discuss the idea of women as the Other. What does the author mean by calling the concept of the Other "primordial" (par. 4)? When thinking about gender, de Beauvoir states that we create the categories of "Self" and "Other." In what other cases might we divide the world into Self versus Other? Illustrate with examples.
2. What might be the psychological and social consequences of this status of the Other for women?
3. According to de Beauvoir, why is recognizing the legal rights of women not enough for women to achieve equality?
4. How does de Beauvoir compare and contrast sexism to racism and to anti-Semitism? Also compare this selection to Albert Memmi's "Racism and Oppression" (p. 253). How might the categories of Self versus Other be useful for understanding racism and xenophobia?

AMAURY DE RIENCOURT
Women in Athens

In his introduction to Sex and Power in History, *de Riencourt argues that the conflict between the sexes is "the most significant element in the overall crisis of contemporary civilization." He states that, unlike Indian and Chinese civilizations which respected the differences between the sexes, Greek rational thought held women to be "inferior or incomplete males." Arguing that the devaluing of women provoked a feminist revolt that weakened Roman ethical values and family structure, de Riencourt fears that contemporary Western society could be similarly destroyed. He condemns those in the women's liberation movement who favor unisexual or androgynous values because these values imply "a social and cultural death-wish and the end of the civilization that endorses it." He rejects patriarchal values and calls for the creation of a new set of values "based on respect for the different specificities of the sexes and the same reverence for the creation of Life as for the creations of the Mind." In the chapter on Greece from which this selection is chosen, de Riencourt argues that, despite being patriarchal, the aristocracy of Greece's Homeric Age (10th–9th century B.C.E.) still held some respect for women and granted them considerable liberties. This was not the case in the democratic Periclean period (5th century B.C.E.), however, due in part to the Greek attitude toward love and to the discovery that males too had a part in procreation. Unlike contemporary forms of democracy, ancient Athens accepted inequality and so found no contradiction in practicing slavery and in oppressing women. This essay might be compared to Simone de Beauvoir's "Women as Other"(p. 242) and Albert Memmi's psychological analysis of racism and oppression (p. 253).*

With the development of Greek culture came a steady regression of woman's status; from Herodotus to Thucydides, she gradually faded into the home, and Plutarch takes pleasure in quoting Thucydides to the effect that "the name of a decent woman, like her person, should be shut up in the house." Greek literature was suddenly full of disparaging remarks about woman and her innumerable faults—witness the writings of Hesiod, Lucian, Aristophanes, and Semonides of Amorgos.[1] Her legal status deteriorated: inheritance through the mother disappeared; she could not make contracts or incur large debts or bring actions at law. Solon even went so far as to legislate that anything done under the influence of woman could not be legally binding. Furthermore, she did not even inherit her husband's property after his death. She retreated to a virtual purdah, locked in her home and advised not to be seen near a window; she spent most of her life in the women's quarters and never appeared when male friends visited her husband.

Such downgrading at the height of Greek cultural achievements is striking, especially in Periclean Athens. But Pericles himself approved; in his famous Funeral Speech, he summed up his views: "If I must also speak a word to those who are in widowhood on the powers and duties of women, I will cast all my advice in one brief sentence. Great will be your glory if you do not lower the nature which is within you—hers most of all whose praise or blame is least bruited on the lips of men."[2]

The strongly masculine character of Greek culture may in part account for this, but it is also a weird reversal of the basic concepts of sexual creativity. In the old days men were suitably ignorant about their creative role in life. Athenian lore claimed that before Cecrops, the legendary founder of Athens, "children did not know their own fathers."[3] The discovery of their role as sexual inseminators gave them a new pride and stimulated the patriarchal revolution. Now the Greeks went a step further. They fancied that *men alone* were endowed with generative power, women being merely empty vessels or, at best, sort of incubators designed to carry *their* child and nurse it in life's early stages. Like the Persians' divine Ohrmazd, more than one Greek sighed and uttered the famous "If only we could have children without having recourse to women!" This recurring theme of extreme misogynists was echoed again, some two thousand years later, by Thomas Browne: "I could be content that we might procreate like trees, without conjunction, or that there were any way to perpetuate the World without this trivial and vulgar way of union."[4] We shall see what Aeschylus did with this theme in his Oresteian trilogy.

Athenian women were hardly educated, in accord with Euripides' view that women were harmed by an overly developed intellect. In the sixth century B.C., women still contributed somewhat to Greek literature; by the fifth century B.C., they

[1]W. Jaeger, *Paideia, The Ideals of Greek Culture*, 3 vols., trans. by G. Highet (Oxford, 1954), 122.
[2]A. Zimmern, *The Greek Commonwealth* (Oxford, 1924), 338.
[3]J. E. Harrison, *Prolegomena to the Study of Greek Religion* (Cambridge, 1922), 260–62.
[4]Browne, in *Harvard Classics*, 50 vols., ed. by C. W. Eliot (New York, 1937), 3:323.

were culturally barren. Having turned their respectable women into bores, men then searched elsewhere for entertainment and inspiration—in the extraordinary development of homosexuality and in the company of the only free women in Athens, the *hetairai*, the "companions," the most accomplished courtesans of the times. Demosthenes summed up the Athenian view of woman's uses in the following statement: "We have courtesans for the sake of pleasure, concubines for the daily health of our bodies, and wives to bear us lawful offspring and be the faithful guardians of our homes."

The only attractive—and therefore influential—women were the *hetairai*, women of some social standing, endowed with a veneer of culture, and capable of witty and learned conversation. They were denied civil rights but were entitled to the protection of their special goddess, Aphrodite Pandemos. Many of them left some mark on Greek history and literature—Aspasia, one of the precursors, who seduced Pericles and opened a school of rhetoric and philosophy; the famous Clepsydra, who timed her lovers' visits with an hourglass; Thargelia, the great spy for the account of the Persians; Danae, who influenced Epicurus in his philosophic views; Archeanassa and Theoris, who amused respectively Plato and Sophocles; and countless others. Some, whose plastic beauty was breathtaking, inspired artists and served as models—Phryne, who appeared stark naked at the Eleusinian festival and posed for Praxiteles' "Aphrodite"; and also Lais of Corinth, one of the great beauties of all time, whose eccentric adventures stunned her contemporaries. In fact, nothing symbolizes more aptly the Greek view of the female sex's social role and value as Praxiteles' two antipodal statues, "The Weeping Wife" and "The Laughing Hetairai."[5]

Greek men held a contemptuous view of the opposite sex; even the best-endowed *hetairai* had a difficult time competing with their clients' male lovers. Even in Sparta, where women enjoyed more prestige and influence than in the rest of Greece, Alcman could pay no greater compliment to his women companions than to call them his "female boy-friends!"[6] The poet-politician Critias stated that girls were charming only to the extent that they were slightly boyish—and vice versa.[7] Homosexuality was both a cause and a consequence of this steady downgrading of the female of the species; and rave against it as they might, the *hetairai* proved unable to curb it. At any rate, the Greek example makes it plain that the prevalence of male homosexuality in any given society is tightly linked with increasing misogyny and the social repression of woman; a kind of *horror feminae* pervades the social atmosphere, springing from the fact that the typical feminine attributes—maternal procreativity and sexual-libidinal endowments—are no longer appreciated. Havelock Ellis quite rightly pointed out the close connection between infanticide (birth control) and homosexuality, a connection that is stamped by an incipient death-wish on the part of any society where they prevail.[8] When the point is reached that woman is rejected, even as a sex object, this society is, psychologically, committing suicide—as the Greek example made plain a few generations after Pericles.

[5]C. C. Zimmerman and S. J. Cervantes, *Marriage and the Family* (Chicago, 1956), 450.
[6]H. Ellis, *Studies in the Psychology of Sex*, 6 vols. (Philadelphia, 1911), 6:134.
[7]Jaeger, *Paideia*, 1:346.
[8]Zimmerman and Cervantes, *Marriage and the Family*, 451.

If we dig further, it becomes clear that one main reason for this degradation of the female sex is that, whereas we put the emphasis of love on its object and think of it in terms of the worthiness of the object, the ancient Greeks put it on the urge itself, honoring the feeling even if it happened to focus on an unworthy recipient. This made it easier for the Greeks to restrict their eroticism largely to homosexual relations. Its prevalence was such that it became part of public education in Sparta and Crete; it became the essential element in Greek military formations where pairs of lovers and male beloved ones formed the basic tactical unit, fighting side by side—the Sacred Band at Thebes, presumed to be the finest fighting force in the Hellenic world, was made up entirely of homosexuals.

Most Greeks had only pity for those few men who could fall in love with women with the same passion as with members of their own sex. Even the famous Platonic love is, in fact, sublimated love of an exclusively homosexual nature. In the *Symposium*, Pausanias states:

> There are two goddesses of love, and therefore, also two forms of Eros. The Eros of the earthly Aphrodite is earthly, universal, common and casual. And everything common worships her. Both sexes, man and woman, had part in the creation and birth of the earthly Aphrodite. The higher love comes from the heavenly Aphrodite and she is the creation of man. Therefore all youths and men who are seized with this love strive after their own sex, full of longing for the manly; they love the stronger nature and the higher mind.[9]

Such an outlook was devastating to feminine status, dignity, and influence.

QUESTIONS FOR DISCUSSION

1. What is the purpose of this article? Who might be the audience?
2. How did ancient Athens view the role of women in procreation and sexual relations? How might this have been used to justify Athenian patriarchy (male rule)?
3. What sources of evidence does this article use to justify its claims? What other kinds of evidence could a historian use?
4. One of de Riencourt's claims is that women's loss of status is both a cause and a consequence of the rise of homosexuality in Athenian society. What evidence does de Riencourt use to support this claim? Is it convincing? Explain.
5. Review de Beauvoir's concept of the Other (p. 242). How were women treated as the Other in ancient Athens? What were the consequences of this? Are women in contemporary America also the Other? In what ways? What are the consequences of this?
6. Review the concept of the Other in de Beauvoir. How might de Riencourt treat homosexuals as the Other? In what ways does our society view homosexuals as the Other?

[9]E. Friedell, *A Cultural History of the Modern Age*, 3 vols. (New York, 1953), 2:348–49.

NANCY BARRETT
Women and the Economy

Labor economist Nancy Barrett currently is a professor in the Department of Economics at American University, Washington, D.C. She has written and contributed to several college textbooks on microeconomic and macroeconomic policies and on prices and wages in American manufacturing. She also has written articles on the economic condition of American women. During the Carter administration she served as the Deputy Assistant Secretary of Labor for Policy, Evaluation, and Research. The following "Highlights," from the longer article "Women and the Economy," suggest both improvements for women in the past twenty-five years and the persistence of discrimination inside and outside the home.

HIGHLIGHTS

The increase in women's labor force participation over the last 25 years has brought with it questions of equal employment opportunity, pay equity, and family services that were less frequently raised when the paid labor force comprised largely males and single women, and child care and other household duties were managed by full-time homemakers.

- The number of women working or looking for work has increased by roughly 28 million over the past 25 years.
- The huge shift of labor resources out of the household economy and into other sectors such as manufacturing and services is not due to an influx of new workers, but to women who are remaining in the workforce rather than dropping out upon marriage or a first pregnancy.
- The most dramatic increase in labor force participation has been among middle-class, well-educated women who formerly would have dropped out of the labor force during their childrearing years.
- In 1960, fewer than 20 percent of married women with pre-school-age children were working outside the home, compared with more than 50 percent today.
- Seventy percent of married women with college degrees were either employed or looking for work in 1981, compared with 50 percent in 1971.
- The percentage of women pursuing advanced professional degrees has increased substantially. From 1970 to 1979, the percentage of graduates earning degrees in law who were women jumped from 5.4 to 28.5 percent, and in medicine from 8.4 to 23.0 percent.
- Despite advances made in women's educational attainment and employment opportunities, women remain overwhelmingly concentrated in low-paying female occupations.
- In 1985, 70 percent of all full-time employed women were working in occupations in which over three-quarters of the employees were females.
- Over one-third of all employed women work in clerical jobs.
- Women tend to be employed in low-paying jobs with no on-the-job training and little security, and thus they are often among the first fired.

- In almost all areas of employment, women are overrepresented at the bottom and underrepresented at the top.
- The average female worker is gaining in experience and should be progressing more rapidly up the job ladder than is actually the case.
- Women college graduates who work full time, year round, have earnings roughly on a par with male high school dropouts.
- The concentration of women in low-paying occupations, their ghettoization within male-dominated professions, and their lack of upward mobility translates into a lower average wage for women than for men.
- The median earnings for women working full time, year round, in 1985 were 68 percent of men's earnings, up from 61 percent in 1978.
- The slight improvement in the wage gap is not due to women moving into higher-paying jobs but to a recession that has had a disproportionately negative effect on the high-wage, male-dominated sectors of the economy.
- The wage gap between men and women increases with age. Younger workers of both sexes enter the labor force in the lowest pay categories, but men are more likely to advance in earnings while women remain behind. A 45- to 55-year-old woman makes approximately the same wage as a woman of 25.
- During the 1970s, adult women experienced higher unemployment rates than adult men: 6.0 percent for women compared to 4.5 percent for men.
- In the 1980s, the average unemployment rates for both women and men rose and were virtually identical at 7.2 and 7.1 percent, respectively. Between 1980 and 1985, 6.9 million new jobs were created in the female-dominated sectors of sales and services, while 500,000 jobs were lost in the male-dominated sectors of manufacturing, mining, construction, and transportation.
- The decline of full-time homemaking as the predominant occupation for married women has been accompanied by a rapid increase in the number of women seeking part-time jobs. Roughly one-third of the shift out of homemaking has been into part-time employment.
- About three-quarters of women working part time are in the low-paying sales, clerical, and service occupations.
- Women workers' low part-time pay is accompanied by the virtual absence of fringe benefits or opportunity for advancement.
- Female jobs have traditionally been and remain undervalued because of their association with unpaid work in the home and because women are not seen as important economic providers.
- Although women, on average, earn less than men, their contributions to the economic resources of families are substantial.
- For all families, and especially for black families, a second paycheck makes a significant difference in living standards and substantially reduces the incidence of poverty.
- Women with paid jobs still bear most of the responsibility for housework. The shift to paid employment has not meant an offsetting decline in the number of hours most women spend in the household economy. Thus, women now contribute more total hours to the economy (both paid and unpaid) than they did before the shift.

QUESTIONS FOR DISCUSSION

1. After reading this selection, what generalizations can you make about the inequalities for women that still exist in America? What seems to be improving for women? What seems to be unchanging and/or worsening for women? Why?
2. Why has the wage gap between men and women lessened in the last few years? Does this signal an improvement in women's wages?
3. Why might women choose to work outside the home?
4. How do Barrett's findings suggest that women are still second-class citizens in America?
5. What experiences have you had that support or contradict Barrett's findings?

ALBERT MEMMI
Racism and Oppression

The persistence of racism is not unique to America; it is a global problem. Drawing upon his experience in Tunisia in North Africa, the French author Albert Memmi (1920–   ) looks at both economic and psychological factors that account for the continued survival of racism. Racism appears to feed upon a circular logic in which social, political, and economic factors all reinforce racist stereotypes. Thus, according to Memmi, people often interpret poverty and powerlessness as signs of inferiority and incompetence; this rationalization then serves to justify discrimination and to perpetuate racism by excluding the oppressed from social, economic, and political power. In Dominated Man, *Memmi sees this process of racism as a symbol for other kinds of oppression that discriminate against the colonized, Jews, workers, women, and domestic servants.*

Everyone seems to be against racism. At least no one says openly that he himself is a racist. Even those who practice discrimination, in both words and actions, do not defend it as a philosophy. They are almost unanimous in explaining those words and those actions in a way which, they insist, has nothing to do with racism.

Of course we could accept this at face value. Or we could try to understand the phenomenon of racism, even if comprehension is likely to prove more disturbing than general indignation, in the long run. In this approach racism is taken as a topic for study; for the time being any moral issues must be left aside, and so, to some extent, must any concern with taking action.

Having chosen the second approach, we have discovered a certain number of characteristics of racism; they seem fairly decisive and, as we suspected, not so reassuring:

1. *Everyone, or nearly everyone, is an unconscious racist,* or a semi-conscious one, or even a conscious one. The degrees range from the man who starts out, "I don't have any prejudice against any race, but . . ." to the one who claims the black man has a peculiar smell or the Jew a "concentration camp" look. From the

man who professes to be anti-racist and yet cannot help feeling uncomfortably hesitant, to the defiant attitude of the nearly-avowed racist, who embraces everything about racism except the label. From the European who criticizes segregation in America but would avoid renting a room to a black student, to the Frenchman who upholds the methods of the Ku Klux Klan and would apply them in his own country if he could. All of these people offer ways to interpret and rationalize the attitudes they take and the speeches they make, but all of them, in the last analysis, share a *common denominator*. The man who speaks up for the Ku Klux Klan asserts that the hooded Americans want to defend their country, the virtue of their women and the color of their children's skin. Similarly, the man who merely refuses to rent a room to a black man and admits that he feels uneasy—even if he admits that he shouldn't—at seeing a black man walking with a white woman is also thinking, in a confused way, of the purity of women and the color of his country's children yet unborn.

While from one to the other the interpretation differs, becoming an explanation, a travesty, or an alibi, it always refers back to the same fact. It may be more or less out in the open, or more or less disguised, but it is always discernible.

2. In short, *racism is one of the most widespread attitudes in the world*. Racial prejudice is a *social fact*. This in itself is enough to explain why it is so important, so varied, so extensive, so deep and so general. This also means that it pre-exists, imposing itself on the individual.

In still other words, before taking root in the individual, racism has taken root in the institutions and ideologies all around him, in the education he receives and the culture he acquires.

It would be interesting to film one of these cultural circuits: the way the ideologists create ideologies from relations between forces and institutions; the way journalists vulgarize those ideologies and the newspaper reader swallows their diluted poison in such repeated doses that it soaks into him completely. Never has it been adequately pointed out that writers and literature of even the highest sort play an insidious role in propagating racist themes and images.[1] Religions themselves are not sinless in this respect. And lastly, the family circle is an extraordinary *culture medium* for prejudices, fears and resentments from which few children emerge wholly uncontaminated. First and foremost, racism is as intimate a part of the child's familial and social upbringing as the milk he sucks in infancy.

3. Why is this? Why is an attitude so negative and so obviously detrimental to the communal life of men so universal?

We promised that we would try to understand, instead of trying to reassure ourselves at all costs or merely waxing indignant over some people's unexpected wickedness. The truth is that the *racist explanation is convenient*. That is why it is so easily and so commonly used both by individuals and by the group: it is too tempting to be resisted.

---

[1] See *Portrait of a Jew*, chapter 6, part I.

Because it corresponds somehow to what is evident and is somehow confirmed, the racist accusation is a widespread and persuasive social fact. *It is a psycho-social fact, because racism is an institutional fact.*

The colonized was not only accused of being a second-class man. *He was in fact just that:* he did not have the same rights as the colonizer himself. The black American is not only described as a misfit: far too often he *is just that.* The Jew *is* genuinely separate and is placed under a more or less discreet form of quarantine.

Since it is a matter for observation that the *object of racism* is inferior and is ground down, isn't it tempting to look on the *racist ideology as an adequate expression of that objective situation?* To say that if the Jew is separate, it is probably because something in him naturally alienates others and deserves to be kept separate? To explain that if the fate of the colonized is so overwhelming and so miserable, it is because he was ripe to become the target of colonialism?

Of course one could stand up and say the situation is the other way around: it is the ideology, the accusation inflated to mythical proportions which explains and legitimatizes the iniquitous situation of the *person discriminated against.* But whoever spoke out so boldly would immediately have to blame himself, his family and his entire universe for having made the victim such a *victim*—and who would have strength enough to do that? It would take lucidity, honesty and courage such as even so-called highly cultured men are scarcely capable of. It is more "natural," more spontaneous, and so much more *convenient* to look for an explanation which soothes the deep-lying guilt felt by both individual and group toward the *victim of racism.*

4. The racist explanation is, after all, the most *effective.* "Euphoria-inducing," as the psychologists put it, it is a great help to the anxious and avid Narcissus[2] concealed in each one of us. It reassures and flatters the racist, excuses and strengthens him by reinforcing his individual and collective ego.

   And so economically too! By making the other people pay! The racist finds joy, solace and vindication at the expense of others. He doesn't even have to boast; he merely belittles the others to set off his own qualities. His superiority does not have to be proven, since it is implied in the other man's inferiority.

   The racist temptation is certainly the one least resisted—such an inexpensive vice, that does not even appear to be bad for the sinner's health, since it is practiced to *other* people's detriment. Why not give in to a craving so easy to satisfy and so common, for that matter?

5. *To be big, all the racist need do is climb on someone else's back.*

   It is easy to understand why he chooses for this purpose the most obvious and resigned of victims, the one who submits to blows in silence, the victim who is already the most victimized: the most convenient step in the whole very convenient process.

---

[2]**Narcissus** A young man in Greek and Roman mythology who fell in love with his own reflection in a pool of water. [Ed. note.]

You never hear of anti-American or anti-British, or even anti-German racism: these are men who are historically strong, backed up by powerful nations. Whereas the racist wrings his triumph only out of men whom history has already defeated, the weaker links in the chain of humanity. *The racist instinctively chooses the oppressed*, heaping more misfortune on the unfortunate.

6. For this reason the foreigner is choice prey for the racist, a promising and unhoped-for rung on which the posturing victor can place his foot to climb higher. *Which explains the obvious, intimate relationship between racism and xenophobia*. The vulnerability of the foreigner arouses racism, just as infirmity arouses sarcasm and scorn.

7. This accounts for the surprising *racism practiced by the oppressed man himself*. Sure enough, the proletarian, the colonized, the Negro, the black man—all can turn around and be racists too. How can one victim attack another? Simply enough: by the same process and in response to the same temptation. If the French proletarian wants to feel a little taller, whom is he to step on if not on the immigrant worker, who has been North African so far but might also be Italian, Spanish or Polish—in other words, of the same so-called race as himself? Proof, if proof were needed, that racism is not always directly connected with race. If the modest colonizer, himself so taken advantage of and so disinherited, wanted to take revenge, what other target was there than the colonized, whom he could look down upon from the limited height of those meager privileges which the colonial system gave him? So it is that the American Jew may be tempted to scorn the American black, who reciprocates heartily.

Everyone looks for an inferior rank compared to which he appears relatively lofty and grand. Racism offers everyone the solution that suits him best; he need only find someone smaller, more humiliated than himself, and there he has his victim, the target for his scorn and prejudice. *Racism is a pleasure within everyone's reach.*

8. But do men really have such a terrible urge to reassure and reassert themselves, even at the cost of humiliating others, to justify themselves even by accusing others? Once we realize how extensive this compulsion is, how often this solution is adopted, then we are forced to realize that the answer is yes.

Certainly the solution is false, the compensation vain, small and above all unjust, distorting criteria and warping perspectives, self-deceiving, destroying one man's dignity to give another the illusion of dignity. But it must be admitted that it *is a sort of a solution to genuine problems*, a tranquilizer for disturbances so manifest and so common that we would be surprised if we did not find them.

The sick man consoles himself with the thought that others are even more sick than he; he has a vague idea that there are still several degrees between himself and death and that, compared to so-and-so, he is not so badly off after all. It is a fact that misery consoles misery. Is it surprising then that the racist takes a rest from his own misery by looking at the next man's? He even goes one step further, claiming that the next man is more miserable, unfortunate and perverse than he really is.

This is made all the easier by the fact that the next man is virtually never neutral. Not enough emphasis has been placed on a particular ingredient of racism, which is the uneasiness and *fear aroused by differentness*. The foreigner, or even merely a man of another social class, is always somewhat strange and frightening. It is only a few short steps from fear to hostility, and from hostility to aggression. Loving means relaxing, yielding, forgetting oneself in the other person, identifying with him more or less. You do not forgive a foreigner until you have managed to adopt him. Otherwise he continues to be inscrutable, to resist, as it were, and your reaction is one of anxiety and irritation. How can you help resenting people who force you to remain on the defensive? And now affective logic, that misnamed upside-down reasoning, comes into play: how can these people you suspect and sentence beforehand help but turn around and resent you?

9. From this point on, the passions whirl around in a vicious circle of "reasoning" like this: since these people probably detest us, they certainly deserve to have us hate them, and mustn't we take precautions against their possible acts of aggression by acting aggressively against them if necessary, etc., etc. . . . ? Any number of battles, both individual and collective, grow chiefly out of such mean and devious arguments, designed to exorcise fear of the next man and soothe a troubled conscience.

Guilt feelings constitute one of the most powerful driving forces in the racist mechanism. Why do privilege and oppression arouse such a strong racist reaction? Because racism is undoubtedly one way of combating that inner misery which is remorse. If there is oppression it must be because someone is guilty, and if the oppressor himself does not plead guilty—a situation which would soon become intolerable—then it must be the oppressed man who is guilty. *In short, by means of racism, the victim is blamed for the real or imaginary crimes of the racist.*

10. In that case, what can be done? What indeed, if the evil is so deeply rooted and so widespread, so much a part of our institutions and our collective thoughts, so tempting and seemingly so inexpensive? But I don't believe it really is inexpensive; I maintain that like any other oppression, racism deforms the racist himself, both his appearance and his behavior, just as imperialism transformed even Europeans of good will into imperialists. But here again, tremendous lucidity would be required to realize the harm done to oneself by fear, authority and privileges. What can actually be done to wipe out the creeping infection?

It seems that we must *bring our sympathy into action*,[3] that we must make the painstaking effort *to put ourselves in the other man's place*. This sort of wisdom is as old as time; it is the best way of understanding how someone

---

[3]Or we must "empathize," to borrow the precise expression of my friend and colleague, the French sociologist, P. H. Maucorps.

else suffers, how insults and blows humiliate and pain him. Through our thoughts, at least, we achieve a kind of empathy. The ultimate effort is to try to live certain situations ourselves—to live in the black man's skin, as in the astounding experiment carried out by the white American, Griffith, or actually to share the daily existence of the working man, as certain political militants or the worker-priests compel themselves to do. There can be no doubt, in such a case, that when led by the body and the mind, the imagination, usually so lazy where others are concerned, is made to participate. No doubt either that this is the most effective form of mental hygiene to prevent racism from setting in.

11. But precisely because this process is so noble and demands so much of the individual, it should be completed by more *collective measures. Education* will certainly continue to be the best technique for training and liberating mankind. Because it is a slow process, and a preventive one, because it reaches out to the young, because it acts continuously on the individual and at the same time influences great masses, education (which should be accompanied by a campaign for *adult enlightenment*) must always aim to discover what needs to be done so that men will cease to carry arms against one another and their natural aggressiveness can be put to a different use.

12. But the main point, I think, is this. *The fight against racism coincides, at least partly, with the fight against oppression.* For fight there will be, necessarily. Racism is not only a perverted feeling; it is also the result, the expression, and the adjunct of a *de facto* situation which must be changed if racism is to be defeated. This means that the *oppressed man must cease to be oppressed*, to be the easily victimized embodiment of the oppressor's guilt feelings. The counterpart is that *the oppressor must stop being an oppressor*, stop having a convenient victim, needing to have one and needing to find an excuse for that need.

Of course the idea is not to strip man entirely of his aggressiveness, as some racists sarcastically claim it is. They hide behind a poor excuse for philosophy, allegedly virile but actually based on disdain for the human being and his possible destruction. A man needs a certain amount of aggressiveness. It would be unhealthful and even dangerous if a man were never able to hate and even, on occasion, to strike.

But his quasi-normal hesitation in the face of differentness must not become the instrument and the alibi for his injustice. Prejudice must not turn into myth. He must not feel entitled to bully any individual because that person belongs to a group covered by a blanket accusation of depravity.

Many anti-racists, swept away by an oversimplifying generosity, maintain that every real difference between men must be denied. But this is not necessary. On the contrary, *the differences must be luckily acknowledged*, admitted and respected as such. Once the other man is recognized as another man, such differences can even become a source of self-enrichment, as recognition encourages dialogue and brings it about. Whereas denying the differences, closing one's eyes to an undeniable aspect of human reality is liable to result in dangerous astonishment and a spectacular about-face the day those differences are finally brought home to even the most generous of humanists: a painful experience to which many of them, and many teachers in the colonies, can already testify.[4]

When face to face with differentness, and the problems it inevitably creates, there are two possible reactions: war, or dialogue. The temptation to defeat someone else, reduce him to servitude, and find some ideological pretext for doing so is certainly very common, and seems more worthwhile than beginning a dialogue and deciding on measures of equitable reciprocity.

13. Here is where an ethical and political *option* comes into play. Until now we have deliberately left it aside. A choice must be made between an attitude and a type of behavior which crush and humiliate certain men in order to exalt others, and an attitude and behavior which originate in the belief that all men are of equal dignity. Here is the dividing line between racists and anti-racists. The racist accepts this type of primitive violence and claims to justify it; the end result is undeniably a certain philosophy of man and of human relationships. The anti-racist rejects such a rupture between men and refuses to place them in two categories from which there is no appeal: the inferior and the superior. He believes dialogue is possible and is willing to reconsider existing situations and privileges. *In the last analysis, the dividing line runs between two views of man and two philosophies.*

14. One final word: *there is no denying the difficulty of the fight against racism.*

It is not easy to put oneself in the place of the oppressed man, whoever he may be; the difficulty of "taking part" in someone else becomes greater as the oppressed man becomes more oppressed, i.e., as the social and psychological *distance* between himself and other men increases. Often the gap between the colonized and even the best-intentioned colonizer was so wide that the white European had no notion of what was going on within the soul of his "impenetrable" native servant. Moreover, the victim of oppression feels that there is no way out; no man who is not oppressed has experienced despair and anguish to this degree. The non-oppressed man who tries to put himself in the victim's place can, by definition, call a halt to his experiment. No matter how sincere Griffith, the white American, was in dyeing his skin and living as a black among blacks in the South, he knew that whenever he wanted to he could go back up North, announce "I'm white," and bring his voluntary nightmare to an end. No one can ever put himself completely in the place of a black man nor in that of a Jew whose family has been exterminated in a crematory.

---

[4]I take this opportunity to clarify a point concerning humanism: in recent decades, humanism has been the object of a great many attacks, and I myself have mocked the humanists. But a distinction must be made among different sorts of attack. The fascists too violently condemned the humanists and sneered at them, because the humanists fought against the image of man which the fascists had drawn.

Our own impatience had a different meaning, of course. We simply regretted that the humanists were so carried away by their generous impulse towards universal man, towards brotherhood based on reason and on a denominator common to all men that they neglected the concrete, specific problems of such and such individual man. Not to mention that the man involved was often a man in a difficult historical situation, such as the colonized or the Jew. A serious oversight, since humanism was in danger of becoming the philosophy of an alibi.

This is not to say, by any means, that I deny the humanist ideal. It should be furthered. It leads the way.

At the same time, what is taught in the schools must overcome what is taught in the home and the street. It will have to uproot the entire cultural tradition which, being vague and incoherent, offers that much more resistance.

Only by transforming the objective conditions of existence can an end be put to the various forms of oppression, and this transformation will not happen overnight. It does not depend on the strength of the anti-racists alone. Nor is there any guarantee that once a much-fought-for political order has been established, it will not, during some social crisis, turn around and use the time-tested racist alibi itself.

The struggle to combat racism is long and arduous, an attack to be launched again and again, a campaign that will probably never be ended.

Yet for that very reason it is a fight which should be fought without respite and without concession. We cannot be indulgent towards racism any more than we would deliberately bring a monster into our house even—still less—if the monster were disguised. Doing that would mean giving it a chance, putting the animal and the humane sides of ourselves and other men into the scales, and finding that they came down on the side of the animal. What would it mean to accept the racist's way of thinking, even just slightly? It would mean endorsing fear, injustice and violence. Agreeing that no light is to pierce the dimness and obscurity in which we are still largely accustomed to living. Agreeing that the foreigner is to remain a potential victim. (But what man is not a foreigner—to someone else?) In short, racism illustrates the totally negative condition of subjugated man and in a certain way sheds light on the entire human condition. While the fight against racism is demanding and its outcome always uncertain, it is one of the indispensable preliminaries to the progress from animality to humanity. *We cannot afford not to take up the racist challenge.*

QUESTIONS FOR DISCUSSION

1. Why is almost everyone a racist according to Memmi? What types of racists exist?
2. How is the racist explanation psychologically "convenient" and "effective"? (See numbers 3 and 4.)
3. Explain how victims of racism can also be racists themselves. How might racism perpetuate itself?
4. How can people's reactions to "differentness" contribute to racism?
5. What is the psychological process that leads to racism? What is the relationship between guilt and racism? (See numbers 8 and 9.)
6. List the solutions needed according to Memmi. Why does the author say that oppressive "conditions of existence" must change? What are the relationships between racism, poverty, and oppression?
7. What ethical and political alternatives to racism exist? Why are these alternatives and solutions discussed at the end of this reading? Is this effective? Why or why not?

8. Because of the date of this selection, the language does not reflect the guidelines most publishers now use for inclusive language (e.g., pronouns that include women). Find three examples of noninclusive pronouns in this reading and suggest inclusive pronouns to replace these examples.
9. What racist stereotypes have you seen on T.V. or in the movies? List examples.
10. Discuss examples of racism in your community. What do you think are the causes and consequences of this?

GEORGE ORWELL
Shooting an Elephant

The English author George Orwell (the pseudonym for Eric Arthur Blair, 1903–1950) is well known for Animal Farm, *a satire on Stalinism, and* Nineteen Eighty-Four, *a warning against the growing totalitarianism in both the East and the West. Orwell's political development began in the 1920s when he spent five years in Burma as a member of the Indian imperial police. As recorded in this well-known essay, his experience gave him an insider's view of British colonialism, the occupation of another people's land, and imperialism, the use of cultural, political, and economic domination to control another country.*

In Moulmein, in lower Burma, I was hated by large numbers of people—the only time in my life that I have been important enough for this to happen to me. I was sub-divisional police officer of the town, and in an aimless, petty kind of way anti-European feeling was very bitter. No one had the guts to raise a riot, but if a European woman went through the bazaars alone somebody would probably spit betel juice over her dress. As a police officer I was an obvious target and was baited whenever it seemed safe to do so. When a nimble Burman tripped me up on the football field and the referee (another Burman) looked the other way, the crowd yelled with hideous laughter. This happened more than once. In the end the sneering yellow faces of young men that met me everywhere, the insults hooted after me when I was at a safe distance, got badly on my nerves. The young Buddhist priests were the worst of all. There were several thousands of them in the town and none of them seemed to have anything to do except stand on street corners and jeer at Europeans.

All this was perplexing and upsetting. For at that time I had already made up my mind that imperialism was an evil thing and the sooner I chucked up my job and got out of it the better. Theoretically—and secretly, of course—I was all for the Burmese and all against their oppressors, the British. As for the job I was doing, I hated it more bitterly than I can perhaps make clear. In a job like that you see the dirty work of Empire at close quarters. The wretched prisoners huddling in the stinking cages of the lock-ups, the grey, cowed faces of the long-term convicts, the scarred buttocks of the men who had been flogged with bamboos—all these oppressed me with an intolerable sense of guilt. But I could get nothing into perspective. I was young and ill-educated and I had had to think out my problems in the utter silence that is imposed on every Englishman in the East. I did not even know that the British Empire is dying, still less did I know that it is a great deal better than the younger empires that are going to supplant it. All I knew was that I was stuck between my hatred of the empire I served and my rage against the evil-spirited little beasts who tried to make my job impossible. With one part of my mind I thought of the British Raj as an unbreakable tyranny, as something clamped down, in *saecula saeculorum*,[1] upon the will of prostrate peoples; with another part I thought that the greatest joy in the world would be to drive a bayonet into a Buddhist priest's guts. Feelings like these are the normal by-products of imperialism; ask any Anglo-Indian official, if you can catch him off duty.

One day something happened which in a roundabout way was enlightening. It was a tiny incident in itself, but it gave me a better glimpse than I had had before of the real nature of imperialism—the real motives for which despotic governments act. Early one morning the sub-inspector at a police station the other end of the town rang me up on the 'phone and said that an elephant was ravaging the bazaar. Would I please come and do something about it? I did not know what I could do, but I wanted to see what was happening and I got on to a pony and started out. I took my rifle, an old .44 Winchester and much too small to kill an elephant, but I thought the noise might be useful *in terrorem*. Various Burmans stopped me on the way and told me about the elephant's doings. It was not, of course, a wild elephant, but a tame one which had gone "must." It had been chained up, as tame elephants always are when their attack of "must" is due, but on the previous night it had broken its chain and escaped. Its mahout, the only person who could manage it when it was in that state, had set out in pursuit, but had taken the wrong direction and was now twelve hours' journey away, and in the morning the elephant had suddenly reappeared in the town. The Burmese population had no weapons and were quite helpless against it. It had already destroyed somebody's bamboo hut, killed a cow and raided some fruit-stalls and devoured the stock; also it had met the municipal rubbish van and, when the driver jumped out and took to his heels, had turned the van over and inflicted violences upon it.

The Burmese sub-inspector and some Indian constables were waiting for me in the quarter where the elephant had been seen. It was a very poor quarter, a labyrinth of squalid bamboo huts, thatched with palm-leaf, winding all over a steep hillside. I remember that it was a cloudy, stuffy morning at the beginning of the rains. We began questioning the people as to where the elephant had gone and, as usual, failed to get any definite information. That is invariably the case in the East; a story always sounds clear enough at a distance, but the nearer you get to the scene of events the vaguer it becomes. Some of the people said that the elephant had gone in one direction, some said that he had gone in another, some professed not even to have heard of any elephant. I had almost made up my mind that the whole story was a pack of lies, when we heard yells a little distance away. There was a loud, scan-

---

[1] **saecula saeculorum** For ever and ever. [Ed. note.]

dalized cry of "Go away, child! Go away this instant!" and an old woman with a switch in her hand came round the corner of a hut, violently shooing away a crowd of naked children. Some more women followed, clicking their tongues and exclaiming; evidently there was something that the children ought not to have seen. I rounded the hut and saw a man's dead body sprawling in the mud. He was an Indian, a black Dravidian coolie, almost naked, and he could not have been dead many minutes. The people said that the elephant had come suddenly upon him round the corner of the hut, caught him with its trunk, put its foot on his back and ground him into the earth. This was the rainy season and the ground was soft, and his face had scored a trench a foot deep and a couple of yards long. He was lying on his belly with arms crucified and head sharply twisted to one side. His face was coated with mud, the eyes wide open, the teeth bared and grinning with an expression of unendurable agony. (Never tell me, by the way, that the dead look peaceful. Most of the corpses I have seen looked devilish.) The friction of the great beast's foot had stripped the skin from his back as neatly as one skins a rabbit. As soon as I saw the dead man I sent an orderly to a friend's house nearby to borrow an elephant rifle. I had already sent back the pony, not wanting it to go mad with fright and throw me if it smelt the elephant.

The orderly came back in a few minutes with a rifle and five cartridges, and meanwhile some Burmans had arrived and told us that the elephant was in the paddy fields below, only a few hundred yards away. As I started forward practically the whole population of the quarter flocked out of the houses and followed me. They had seen the rifle and were all shouting excitedly that I was going to shoot the elephant. They had not shown much interest in the elephant when he was merely ravaging their homes, but it was different now that he was going to be shot. It was a bit of fun to them, as it would be to an English crowd; besides they wanted the meat. It made me vaguely uneasy. I had no intention of shooting the elephant—I had merely sent for the rifle to defend myself if necessary—and it is always unnerving to have a crowd following you. I marched down the hill, looking and feeling a fool, with the rifle over my shoulder and an ever-growing army of people jostling at my heels. At the bottom, when you got away from the huts, there was a metalled road and beyond that a miry waste of paddy fields a thousand yards across, not yet ploughed but soggy from the first rains and dotted with coarse grass. The elephant was standing eight yards from the road, his left side towards us. He took not the slightest notice of the crowd's approach. He was tearing up bunches of grass, beating them against his knees to clean them and stuffing them into his mouth.

I had halted on the road. As soon as I saw the elephant I knew with perfect certainty that I ought not to shoot him. It is a serious matter to shoot a working elephant—it is comparable to destroying a huge and costly piece of machinery—and obviously one ought not to do it if it can possibly be avoided. And at that distance, peacefully eating, the elephant looked no more dangerous than a cow. I thought then and I think now that his attack of "must" was already passing off; in which case he would merely wander harmlessly about until the mahout came back and caught him. Moreover, I did not in the least want to shoot him. I decided that I would watch him for a little while to make sure that he did not turn savage again, and then go home.

But at that moment I glanced round at the crowd that had followed me. It was an immense crowd, two thousand at the least and growing every minute. It blocked the road for a long distance on either side. I looked at the sea of yellow faces above the garish clothes—faces all happy and excited over this bit of fun, all certain that the elephant was going to be shot. They were watching me as they would watch a conjurer about to perform a trick. They did not like me, but with the magical rifle in my hands I was momentarily worth watching. And suddenly I realized that I should have to shoot the elephant after all. The people expected it of me and I had got to do it; I could feel their two thousand wills pressing me forward, irresistibly. And it was at this moment, as I stood there with the rifle in my hands, that I first grasped the hollowness, the futility of the white man's dominion in the East. Here was I, the white man with his gun, standing in front of the unarmed native crowd—seemingly the leading actor of the piece; but in reality I was only an absurd puppet pushed to and fro by the will of those yellow faces behind. I perceived in this moment that when the white man turns tyrant it is his own freedom that he destroys. He becomes a sort of hollow, posing dummy, the conventionalized figure of a sahib. For it is the condition of his rule that he shall spend his life in trying to impress the "natives," and so in every crisis he has got to do what the "natives" expect of him. He wears a mask, and his face grows to fit it. I had got to shoot the elephant. I had committed myself to doing it when I sent for the rifle. A sahib has got to act like a sahib; he has got to appear resolute, to know his own mind and do definite things. To come all that way, rifle in hand, with two thousand people marching at my heels, and then to trail feebly away, having done nothing—no, that was impossible. The crowd would laugh at me. And my whole life, every white man's life in the East, was one long struggle not to be laughed at.

But I did not want to shoot the elephant. I watched him beating his bunch of grass against his knees, with that preoccupied grandmotherly air that elephants have. It seemed to me that it would be murder to shoot him. At that age I was not squeamish about killing animals, but I had never shot an elephant and never wanted to. (Somehow it always seems worse to kill a *large* animal.) Besides, there was the beast's owner to be considered. Alive, the elephant was worth at least a hundred pounds; dead, he would only be worth the value of his tusks, five pounds, possibly. But I had got to act quickly. I turned to some experienced-looking Burmans who had been there when we arrived, and asked them how the elephant had been behaving. They all said the same thing: he took no notice of you if you left him alone, but he might charge if you went too close to him.

It was perfectly clear to me what I ought to do. I ought to walk up to within, say, twenty-five yards of the elephant and test his behavior. If he charged, I could shoot; if he took no notice of me, it would be safe to leave him until the mahout came back. But also I knew that I was going to do no such thing. I was a poor shot with a rifle and the ground was soft mud into which one would sink at every step. If the elephant charged and I missed him, I should have about as much chance as a toad under a steam-roller. But even then I was not thinking particularly of my own skin, only of the watchful yellow faces behind. For at that moment, with the crowd watching me, I was not afraid in the ordinary sense, as I would have been if I had been alone. A white man mustn't be frightened in front of "natives"; and so, in general, he isn't frightened. The sole thought in my mind was that if anything went wrong those two thousand Burmans would see me pursued, caught, trampled on and reduced to a grinning corpse like that Indian up the hill. And if that happened it was quite probable that some of them would laugh. That would never do. There was only one alternative. I shoved the cartridges into the magazine and lay down on the road to get a better aim.

The crowd grew very still, and a deep, low, happy sigh, as of people who see the theatre curtain go up at last, breathed from innumerable throats. They were going to have their bit of fun after all. The rifle was a beautiful German thing with cross-hair sights. I did not then know that in shooting an elephant one would shoot to cut an imaginary bar running from ear-hole to ear-hole. I ought, therefore, as the elephant was sideways on, to have aimed straight at his ear-hole; actually I aimed several inches in front of this, thinking the brain would be further forward.

When I pulled the trigger I did not hear the bang or feel the kick—one never does when a shot goes home—but I heard the devilish roar of glee that went up from the crowd. In that instant, in too short a time, one would have thought, even for the bullet to get there, a mysterious, terrible change had come over the elephant. He neither stirred nor fell, but every line of his body had altered. He looked suddenly stricken, shrunken, immensely old, as though the frightful impact of the bullet had paralysed him without knocking him down. At last, after what seemed a long time—it might have been five seconds, I dare say—he sagged flabbily to his knees. His mouth slobbered. An enormous senility seemed to have settled upon him. One could have imagined him thousands of years old. I fired again into the same spot. At the second shot he did not collapse but climbed with desperate slowness to his feet and stood weakly upright, with legs sagging and head drooping. I fired a third time. That was the shot that did for him. You could see the agony of it jolt his whole body and knock the last remnant of strength from his legs. But in falling he seemed for a moment to rise, for as his hind legs collapsed beneath him he seemed to tower upward like a huge rock toppling, his trunk reaching skywards like a tree. He trumpeted, for the first and only time. And then down he came, his belly towards me, with a crash that seemed to shake the ground even where I lay.

I got up. The Burmans were already racing past me across the mud. It was obvious that the elephant would never rise again, but he was not dead. He was breathing very rhythmically with long rattling gasps, his great mound of a side painfully rising and falling. His mouth was wide open—I could see far down into caverns of pale pink throat. I waited a long time for him to die, but his breathing did not weaken. Finally I fired my two remaining shots into the spot where I thought his heart must be. The thick blood welled out of him like red velvet, but still he did not die. His body did not even jerk when the shots hit him, the tortured breathing continued without a pause. He was dying, very slowly and in great agony, but in some world remote from me where not even a bullet could damage him further. I felt that I had got to put an end to that dreadful noise. It seemed dreadful to see the great beast lying there, powerless to move and yet powerless to die, and not even to be able to finish him. I sent back for my small rifle and poured shot after shot into his heart and down his throat. They seemed to make no impression. The tortured gasps continued as steadily as the ticking of a clock.

In the end I could not stand it any longer and went away. I heard later that it took him half an hour to die. Burmans were bringing dahs and baskets even before I left, and I was told they had stripped his body almost to the bones by the afternoon.

Afterwards, of course, there were endless discussions about the shooting of the elephant. The owner was furious, but he was only an Indian and could do nothing. Besides, legally I had done the right thing, for a mad elephant has to be killed, like a mad dog, if its owner fails to control it. Among the Europeans opinion was divided. The older men said I was right, the younger men said it was a damn shame to shoot an elephant for killing a coolie, because an elephant was worth more than any damn Coringhee coolie. And afterwards I was very glad that the coolie had been killed; it put me legally in the right and it gave me a sufficient pretext for shooting the elephant. I often wondered whether any of the others grasped that I had done it solely to avoid looking a fool.

QUESTIONS FOR DISCUSSION

1. What is the purpose of this reading and who is the audience?
2. Why is the Burmese citizens' behavior towards the narrator "perplexing and upsetting" to him? Look up the definition of imperialism in a dictionary or encyclopedia. How might the narrator's desire to drive "a bayonet into a Buddhist priest's guts" (par. 2) be caused by imperialism?
3. The narrator refers to his own role as master. How is the narrator both a master and a slave? How might this comment on the British presence in Burma?
4. How is the psychology of imperialism and of ethnocentrism similar to that of racism (see Memmi, p. 253) and/or sexism (de Beauvoir, p. 242)?
5. What might the elephant's slow death symbolize?
6. How is the final paragraph ironic?
7. Choose a descriptive passage. What purpose does it serve in Orwell's narrative? What is your reaction to it?
8. Narration is the telling of a story. How does Orwell's use of narrative persuade?
9. This is a historical event, but many historians would not consider this essay to be history. Why?

MOHANDAS K. GANDHI
Satyagraha

Mohandas K. Gandhi (1869–1948), the Indian leader of nonviolent resistance in South Africa and against British colonial rule in India, was influenced by a variety of traditions and writers. Hindu religion, Henry David Thoreau's classic essay "Civil Disobedience," Tolstoy's writings and letters to Gandhi, and Jesus' "Sermon on the Mount" are some of the sources that contributed to Gandhi's thought. He first applied "Satyagraha" (literally, "insistence on truth") before World War I in South Africa when the government began to legislate against the Indian minority there. This strategy included strikes, boycotts, mass demonstrations, peaceful picketing, noncooperation, and civil disobedience. Upon his return to India, Gandhi organized another wave of civil disobedience. In 1919, he fasted to protest the British imprisonment of Indians without trial. In Satyagraha, religion, truth, and politics are inseparable. According to Gandhi, living by eternal "Truth" (that which he calls "truly real" as opposed to the material world) requires people to develop their selflessness, their independence from material possessions, and their courage to resist using violence even when their opponents use it. Gandhi's nonviolent means are intended to achieve justice by appealing to the conscience of the oppressor. Since Martin Luther King was greatly influenced by Gandhi's ideas, this reading can be compared to King's "Letter from Birmingham Jail" (p. 272). Likewise, Gandhi's nonviolent protest can be contrasted to Nelson Mandela's justification of using sabotage (p. 286), a form of violence which is not directed against people.

Section First: What Satyagraha Is

1
SATYAGRAHA, CIVIL DISOBEDIENCE
PASSIVE RESISTANCE, NON-CO-OPERATION

Satyagraha is literally holding on to Truth and it means, therefore, Truth-force. Truth is soul or spirit. It is, therefore, known as soul-force. It excludes the use of violence because man is not capable of knowing the absolute truth and, therefore, not competent to punish. The word was coined in South Africa to distinguish the non-violent resistance of the Indians of South Africa from the contemporary 'passive resistance' of the suffragettes and others. It is not conceived as a weapon of the weak.

Passive resistance is used in the orthodox English sense and covers the suffragette movement as well as the resistance of the Non-conformists. Passive resistance has been conceived and is regarded as a weapon of the weak. Whilst it avoids violence, being not open to the weak, it does not exclude its use if, in the opinion of a passive resister, the occasion demands it. However, it has always been distinguished from armed resistance and its application was at one time confined to Christian martyrs.

Civil Disobedience is civil breach of unmoral statutory enactments. The expression was, so far as I am aware, coined by Thoreau to signify his own resistance to the laws of a slave State. He has left a masterly treatise on the duty of Civil Disobedience. But Thoreau was not perhaps an out and out champion of non-violence. Probably, also, Thoreau limited his breach of statutory laws to the revenue law, i.e., payment of taxes. Whereas the term Civil Disobedience as practised in 1919 covered a breach of any statutory and unmoral law. It signified the resister's outlawry in a civil, i.e., non-violent manner. He invoked the sanctions of the law and cheerfully suffered imprisonment. It is a branch of Satyagraha.

Non-co-operation predominantly implies withdrawing of co-operation from the State that in the non-co-operator's view has become corrupt and excludes Civil Disobedience of the fierce type described above. By its very nature, non-co-operation is even open to children of understanding and can be safely practised by the masses. Civil Disobedience presupposes the habit of willing obedience to laws without fear of their sanctions. It can, therefore, be practised only as a last resort and by a select few in the first instance at any rate. Non-co-operation, too, like Civil Disobedience is a branch of Satyagraha which includes all non-violent resistance for the vindication of Truth.

5

SATYAGRAHA OR PASSIVE RESISTANCE[1]

Reader: Is there any historical evidence as to the success of what you have called soul-force or truth-force? No instance seems to have happened of any nation having risen through soul-force. I still think that the evil-doers will not cease doing evil without physical punishment.

Editor: The poet Tulsidas has said: "Of religion, pity, or love, is the root, as egotism of the body. Therefore, we should not abandon pity so long as we are alive." This appears to me to be a scientific truth. I believe in it as much as I believe in two and two being four. The force of love is the same as the force of the soul or truth. We have evidence of its working at every step. The universe would disappear without the existence of that force. But you ask for historical evidence. It is, therefore, necessary to know what history means. The Gujarati equivalent means: "It so happened." If that is the meaning of history, it is possible to give copious evidence. But, if it means the doings of kings and emperors, there can be no evidence of soul-force or passive resistance in such history. You cannot expect silver ore in a tin mine. History, as we know it, is a record of the wars of the world, and so there is a proverb among Englishmen that a nation which has no history, that is, no wars, is a happy nation. How kings played, how they became enemies of one another, how they murdered one another, is found accurately recorded in history, and if this were all that had happened in the world, it would have been ended long ago. If the story of the universe had commenced with wars, not a man would have been found alive today. Those people who have been warred against have disappeared as, for instance, the natives of Australia of whom hardly a man was left alive by the intruders. Mark, please, that these natives did not use soul-force in self-defence, and it does not require much foresight to know that the Australians will share the same fate as their victims. "Those that take the sword shall perish by the Sword." With us the proverb is that professional swimmers will find a watery grave.

The fact that there are so many men still alive in the world shows that it is based not on the force of arms but on the force of truth or love. Therefore, the greatest and most unimpeachable evidence of the success of this force is to be found in the fact that, in spite of the wars of the world, it still lives on.

Thousands, indeed tens of thousands, depend for their existence on a very active working of this force. Little quarrels of millions of families in their daily lives disappear before the exercise of this force. Hundreds of nations live in peace. History does not and cannot take note of this fact. History is really a record of every interruption of the even working of the force of love or of the soul. Two brothers quarrel; one of them repents and re-awakens the love that was lying dormant in him; the two again begin to live in peace; nobody takes note of this. But if the two

---

[1] In this section Gandhi as editor answers questions he thinks a reader might raise. [Ed. note.]

brothers, through the intervention of solicitors or some other reason, take up arms or go to law—which is another form of the exhibition of brute force—their doing would be immediately noticed in the press, they would be the talk of their neighbours and would probably go down to history. And what is true of families and communities is true of nations. There is no reason to believe that there is one law for families and another for nations. History, then, is a record of an interruption of the course of nature. Soul-force, being natural, is not noted in history.

Reader: According to what you say, it is plain that instances of this kind of passive resistance are not to be found in history. It is necessary to understand this passive resistance more fully. It will be better, therefore, if you enlarge upon it.

Editor: Passive resistance is a method of securing rights by personal suffering; it is the reverse of resistance by arms. When I refuse to do a thing that is repugnant to my conscience, I use soul-force. For instance, the Government of the day has passed a law which is applicable to me. I do not like it. If by using violence I force the Government to repeal the law, I am employing what may be termed body-force. If I do not obey the law and accept the penalty for its breach, I use soul-force. It involves sacrifice of self.

Everybody admits that sacrifice of self is infinitely superior to sacrifice of others. Moreover, if this kind of force is used in a cause that is unjust, only the person using it suffers. He does not make others suffer for his mistakes. Men have before now done many things which were subsequently found to have been wrong. No man can claim that he is absolutely in the right or that a particular thing is wrong because he thinks so, but it is wrong for him so long as that is his deliberate judgment. It is therefore meet that he should not do that which he knows to be wrong, and suffer the consequence whatever it may be. This is the key to the use of soul-force.

Reader: You would then disregard laws—this is rank disloyalty. We have always been considered a law-abiding nation. You seem to be going even beyond the extremists. They say that we must obey the laws that have been passed, but that if the laws be bad, we must drive out the law-givers even by force.

Editor: Whether I go beyond them or whether I do not is a matter of no consequence to either of us. We simply want to find out what is right and to act accordingly. The real meaning of the statement that we are a law-abiding nation is that we are passive resisters. When we do not like certain laws, we do not break the heads of law-givers but we suffer and do not submit to the laws. That we should obey laws whether good or bad is a newfangled notion. There was no such thing in former days. The people disregarded those laws they did not like and suffered the penalties for their breach. It is contrary to our manhood if we obey laws repugnant to our conscience. Such teaching is opposed to religion and means slavery. If the Government were to ask us to go about without any clothing, should we do so? If I were a passive resister, I would say to them that I would have nothing to do with their law. But we have so forgotten ourselves and become so compliant that we do not mind any degrading law.

A man who has realized his manhood, who fears only God, will fear no one else. Man-made laws are not necessarily binding on him. Even the Government does not expect any such thing from us. They do not say: "You must do such and such a thing," but they say: "If you do not do it, we will punish you." We are sunk so low that we fancy that it is our duty and our religion to do what the law lays down. If man will only realize that it is unmanly to obey laws that are unjust, no man's tyranny will enslave him. This is the key to self-rule or home-rule.

It is a superstition and ungodly thing to believe that an act of a majority binds a minority. Many examples can be given in which acts of majorities will be found to have been wrong and those of minorities to have been right. All reforms owe their origin to the initiation of minorities in opposition to majorities. If among a band of robbers a knowledge of robbing is obligatory, is a pious man to accept the obligation? So long as the superstition that men should obey unjust laws exists, so long will their slavery exist. And a passive resister alone can remove such a superstition.

To use brute-force, to use gunpowder, is contrary to passive resistance, for it means that we want our opponent to do by force that which we desire but he does not. And, if such a use of force is justifiable, surely he is entitled to do likewise by us. And so we should never come to an agreement. We may simply fancy, like the blind horse moving in a circle round a mill, that we are making progress. Those who believe that they are not bound to obey laws which are repugnant to their conscience have only the remedy of passive resistance open to them. Any other must lead to disaster.

12

CONDITIONS FOR SUCCESSFUL SATYAGRAHA

There can be no Satyagraha in an unjust cause. Satyagraha in a just cause is vain, if the men espousing it are not determined and capable of fighting and suffering to the end; and the slightest use of violence often defeats a just cause. Satyagraha excludes the use of violence in any shape or form, whether in thought, speech, or deed. Given a just cause, capacity for endless suffering and avoidance of violence, victory is a certainty.

13

NON-RETALIATION

Victory is impossible until we are able to keep our temper under the gravest provocation. Calmness under fire is a soldier's indispensable quality. A non-co-operator is nothing if he cannot remain calm and unperturbed under a fierce fire of provocation.

There should be no mistake. There is no civil disobedience possible, until the crowds behave like disciplined soldiers. And we cannot resort to civil disobedience, unless we can assure every Englishman that he is as safe in India as he is in his own home. It is not enough that we give the assurance. Every Englishman and Englishwoman must feel safe, not by reason of the bayonet at their disposal but by reason of our living creed of non-violence. That is the condition not only of success but our own ability to carry on the movement in its present form. There is no other way of conducting the campaign of non-co-operation.

14
COURAGE AND DISCIPLINE NECESSARY

The pledge of non-violence does not require us to co-operate in our humiliation. It, therefore, does not require us to crawl on our bellies or to draw lines with our noses or to walk to salute the Union Jack or to do anything degrading at the dictation of officials. On the contrary our creed requires us to refuse to do any of these things even though we should be shot. It was, therefore, for instance, no part of the duty of the Jalianwala Bagh people to run away or even to turn their backs when they were fired upon. If the message of non-violence had reached them, they would have been expected when fire was opened on them to march towards it with bare breasts and die rejoicing in the belief that it meant the freedom of their country. Non-violence laughs at the might of the tyrant and stultifies him by non-retaliation and non-retiral. We played into General Dyer's[1] hands because we acted as he had expected. He wanted us to run away from his fire, he wanted us to crawl on our bellies and to draw lines with our noses. That was a part of the game of 'frightfulness'. When we face it with eyes front, it vanishes like an apparition. We may not all evolve that type of courage. But I am certain that Swaraj[2] is unattainable this year if some of us have not the courage which enables us to stand firm like a rock without retaliating. The might of the tyrant recoils upon himself when it meets with no response, even as an arm violently waved in the air suffers dislocation.

And just as we need the cool courage described above, we need perfect discipline and training in voluntary obedience to be able to offer civil disobedience. Civil disobedience is the active expression of non-violence. Civil disobedience distinguishes the non-violence of the strong from the passive, i.e., negative non-violence of the weak. And as weakness cannot lead to Swaraj, negative non-violence must fail to achieve our purpose.

Have we then the requisite discipline? Have we, a friend asked me, evolved the spirit of obedience to our own rules and resolutions? Whilst we have made tremendous headway during the past twelve months, we have certainly not made enough to warrant us in embarking upon civil disobedience with easy confidence. Rules voluntarily passed by us and rules which carry no sanction save the disapproval of our own conscience must be like debts of honour held far more binding than rules superimposed upon us or rules whose breach we can purge by paying the penalty thereof. It follows that if we have not learnt the discipline of obeying our own rules, in other words carrying out our own promises, we are ill adapted for disobedience that can be at all described as civil. I do, therefore, suggest to every Congressman, every non-co-operator, and above all to every member of the All India Congress Committee to set himself or herself right with the Congress and his or her creed by carrying on the strictest self-examination and by correcting himself or herself wherever he or she might have failed.

[1] In this passage Gandhi is referring to the Massacre at Amritsar. He had organized a Satyagraha in 1919 to protest British laws that imprisoned, without trial, those Indians suspected of sedition. At a public rally in Amritsar, British soldiers, under General Dyer, opened fire and killed nearly 400 Indians. [Ed. note.]
[2] **Swaraj** Self-government or home rule. [Ed. note.]

QUESTIONS FOR DISCUSSION

1. Summarize the key characteristics of Gandhi's "Satyagraha" and the concept of "soul force." What are his definitions of these ideas?
2. Compare the role of religion in Gandhi's and King's (p. 272) beliefs. How does each use religion to distinguish between just and unjust laws?
3. Discuss Gandhi's different definitions of history. How does his definition differ from a history of wars and the "doings of kings and emperors" (par. 6)? How does this contribute to his argument?
4. Using current examples, discuss Gandhi's statement that "All reforms owe their origin to the initiation of minorities in opposition to majorities" (par. 15).
5. Discuss why you would or would not apply Satyagraha in your own life.

MARTIN LUTHER KING, JR.
Letter from Birmingham Jail

Martin Luther King (1929–1968), winner of the Nobel Peace Prize, clergyman, and civil rights leader, organized the 1956 boycott of public buses in Montgomery, Alabama, that led the Supreme Court to outlaw segregation on intrastate and interstate transportation. He also organized the Southern Christian Leadership Conference (SCLC) as a means to create a mass civil rights movement. In the spring of 1963, he campaigned to end segregation at lunch counters in Birmingham, Alabama, and wrote "Letter from Birmingham Jail" after he was arrested in this campaign. "Letter from Birmingham Jail," written in the epistolary tradition that goes back to St. Paul, is King's response to black and white clergymen who argued, in "Public Statement by Eight Alabama Clergymen," against public demonstrations. Greatly influenced by Gandhi, King justifies the need for nonviolent direct action as a last resort to challenge unjust laws. King's efforts contributed to the passage of the Civil Rights Acts of 1964 which legally desegregated public housing and the work place. But, despite legal changes, the persistence of social, political, and economic discrimination against blacks frustrated King and many others in the civil rights movement. Since nonviolent methods often did not solve more deeply entrenched forms of racism, after 1965 Malcolm X, Stokely Carmichael, and others advocated a separatist black nationalism and the use of violence to combat the violence leveled against blacks.

Public Statement by Eight Alabama Clergymen
(April 12, 1963)

We the undersigned clergymen are among those who, in January, issued "An Appeal for Law and Order and Common Sense," in dealing with racial problems in Alabama. We expressed understanding that honest convictions in racial matters could properly be pursued in the courts, but urged that decisions of those courts should in the meantime be peacefully obeyed.

Since that time there has been some evidence of increased forbearance and a willingness to face facts. Responsible citizens have undertaken to work on various problems which cause racial friction and unrest. In Birmingham, recent public events have given indication that we all have opportunity for a new constructive and realistic approach to racial problems.

However, we are now confronted by a series of demonstrations by some of our Negro citizens, directed and led in part by outsiders. We recognize the natural impatience of people who feel that their hopes are slow in being realized. But we are convinced that these demonstrations are unwise and untimely.

We agree rather with certain local Negro leadership which has called for honest and open negotiation of racial issues in our area. And we believe this kind of facing of issues can best be accomplished by citizens of our own metropolitan area, white and Negro, meeting with their knowledge and experience of the local situation. All of us need to face that responsibility and find proper channels for its accomplishment.

Just as we formerly pointed out that "hatred and violence have no sanction in our religious and political traditions," we also point out that such actions as incite to hatred and violence, however technically peaceful those actions may be, have not contributed to the resolution of our local problems. We do not believe that these days of new hope are days when extreme measures are justified in Birmingham.

We commend the community as a whole, and the local news media and law enforcement officials in particular, on the calm manner in which these demonstrations have been handled. We urge the public to continue to show restraint should the demonstrations continue, and the law enforcement officials to remain calm and continue to protect our city from violence.

We further strongly urge our own Negro community to withdraw support from these demonstrations, and to unite locally in working peacefully for a better Birmingham. When rights are consistently denied, a cause should be pressed in the courts and in negotiations among local leaders, and not in the streets. We appeal to both our white and Negro citizenry to observe the principles of law and order and common sense.

Signed by:

C. C. J. CARPENTER, D.D., LL.D., *Bishop of Alabama*

JOSEPH A. DURICK, D.D., *Auxiliary Bishop, Diocese of Mobile, Birmingham*

Rabbi MILTON L. GRAFMAN, *Temple Emanu-El, Birmingham, Alabama*

Bishop PAUL HARDIN, *Bishop of the Alabama-West Florida Conference of the Methodist Church*

Bishop NOLAN B. HARMON, *Bishop of the North Alabama Conference of the Methodist Church*

GEORGE M. MURRAY, D.D., LL.D., *Bishop Coadjutor, Episcopal Diocese of Alabama*

EDWARD V. RAMAGE, *Moderator, Synod of the Alabama Presbyterian Church in the United States*

EARL STALLINGS, *Pastor, First Baptist Church, Birmingham, Alabama*

Letter from Birmingham Jail

MARTIN LUTHER KING, JR.
Birmingham City Jail
April 16, 1963

Bishop C. C. J. CARPENTER
Bishop JOSEPH A. DURICK
Rabbi MILTON L. GRAFMAN
Bishop PAUL HARDIN
Bishop NOLAN B. HARMON
The Rev. GEORGE M. MURRAY
The Rev. EDWARD V. RAMAGE
The Rev. EARL STALLINGS

My Dear Fellow Clergymen:[1]

While confined here in the Birmingham city jail, I came across your recent statement calling my present activities "unwise and untimely." Seldom do I pause to answer criticism of my work and ideas. If I sought to answer all the criticisms that cross my desk, my secretaries would have little time for anything other than such correspondence in the course of the day, and I would have no time for constructive work. But since I feel that you are men of genuine good will and that your criticisms are sincerely set forth, I want to try to answer your statement in what I hope will be patient and reasonable terms.

I think I should indicate why I am here in Birmingham, since you have been influenced by the view which argues against "outsiders coming in." I have the honor of serving as president of the Southern Christian Leadership Conference, an organization operating in every southern state, with headquarters in Atlanta, Georgia. We have some eighty-five affiliated organizations across the South, and one of them is the Alabama Christian Movement for Human Rights. Frequently we share staff, educational, and financial resources with our affiliates. Several months ago the affiliate here in Birmingham asked us to be on call to engage in a nonviolent direct-action program if such were deemed necessary. We readily consented, and when the hour came we lived up to our promise. So I, along with several members of my staff, am here because I was invited here. I am here because I have organizational ties here. . . .

But more basically, I am in Birmingham because injustice is here. Just as the prophets of the eighth century B.C. left their villages and carried their "thus saith the Lord" far beyond the boundaries of their home towns, and just as the Apostle Paul left his village of Tarsus and carried the gospel of Jesus Christ to the far corners of the

---

[1]This response to a published statement by eight fellow clergymen from Alabama . . . was composed under somewhat constricting circumstances. Begun on the margins of the newspaper in which the statement appeared while I was in jail, the letter was continued on scraps of writing paper supplied by a friendly Negro trusty, and concluded on a pad my attorneys were eventually permitted to leave me. Although the text remains in substance unaltered, I have indulged in the author's prerogative of polishing it for publication.

Greco-Roman world, so am I compelled to carry the gospel of freedom beyond my own home town. Like Paul, I must constantly respond to the Macedonian call for aid.

Moreover, I am cognizant of the interrelatedness of all communities and states. I cannot sit idly by in Atlanta and not be concerned about what happens in Birmingham. Injustice anywhere is a threat to justice everywhere. We are caught in an inescapable network of mutuality, tied in a single garment of destiny. Whatever affects one directly, affects all indirectly. Never again can we afford to live with the narrow, provincial "outside agitator" idea. Anyone who lives inside the United States can never be considered an outsider anywhere within its bounds.

You deplore the demonstrations taking place in Birmingham. But your statement, I am sorry to say, fails to express a similar concern for the conditions that brought about the demonstrations. I am sure that none of you would want to rest content with the superficial kind of social analysis that deals merely with effects and does not grapple with underlying causes. It is unfortunate that demonstrations are taking place in Birmingham, but it is even more unfortunate that the city's white power structure left the Negro community with no alternative.

In any nonviolent campaign there are four basic steps: collection of the facts to determine whether injustices exist; negotiation; self-purification; and direct action. We have gone through all these steps in Birmingham. There can be no gainsaying the fact that racial injustice engulfs this community. Birmingham is probably the most thoroughly segregated city in the United States. Its ugly record of brutality is widely known. Negroes have experienced grossly unjust treatment in the courts. There have been more unsolved bombings of Negro homes and churches in Birmingham than in any other city in the nation. These are the hard, brutal facts of the case. On the basis of these conditions, Negro leaders sought to negotiate with the city fathers. But the latter consistently refused to engage in good-faith negotiation.

Then, last September, came the opportunity to talk with leaders of Birmingham's economic community. In the course of the negotiations, certain promises were made by the merchants—for example, to remove the stores' humiliating racial signs. On the basis of these promises, the Reverend Fred Shuttlesworth and the leaders of the Alabama Christian Movement for Human Rights agreed to a moratorium on all demonstrations. As the weeks and months went by, we realized that we were the victims of a broken promise. A few signs, briefly removed, returned; the others remained.

As in so many past experiences, our hopes had been blasted, and the shadow of deep disappointment settled upon us. We had no alternative except to prepare for direct action, whereby we would present our very bodies as a means of laying our case before the conscience of the local and the national community. Mindful of the difficulties involved, we decided to undertake a process of self-purification. We began a series of workshops on nonviolence, and we repeatedly asked ourselves: "Are you able to accept blows without retaliating?" "Are you able to endure the ordeal of jail?" We decided to schedule our direct-action program for the Easter season, realizing that except for Christmas, this is the main shopping period of the year. Knowing that a strong economic-withdrawal program would be the by-product of direct action, we felt that this would be the best time to bring pressure to bear on the merchants for the needed change.

Then it occurred to us that Birmingham's mayoral election was coming up in March, and we speedily decided to postpone action until after election day. When we discovered that the Commissioner of Public Safety, Eugene "Bull" Connor, had piled up enough votes to be in the run-off, we decided again to postpone action until the day after the run-off so that the demonstrations could not be used to cloud the issues. Like many others, we waited to see Mr. Connor defeated, and to this end we endured postponement after postponement. Having aided in this community need, we felt that our direct-action program could be delayed no longer.

You may well ask: "Why direct action? Why sit-ins, marches and so forth? Isn't negotiation a better path?" You are quite right in calling for negotiation. Indeed, this is the very purpose of direct action. Nonviolent direct action seeks to create such a crisis and foster such a tension that a community which has constantly refused to negotiate is forced to confront the issue. It seeks so to dramatize the issue that it can no longer be ignored. My citing the creation of tension as part of the work of the nonviolent-resister may sound rather shocking. But I must confess that I am not afraid of the word "tension." I have earnestly opposed violent tension, but there is a type of constructive, nonviolent tension which is necessary for growth. Just as Socrates felt that it was necessary to create a tension in the mind so that individuals could rise from the bondage of myths and half-truths to the unfettered realm of creative analysis and objective appraisal, so must we see the need for nonviolent gadflies to create the kind of tension in society that will help men rise from the dark depths of prejudice and racism to the majestic heights of understanding and brotherhood.

The purpose of our direct-action program is to create a situation so crisis-packed that it will inevitably open the door to negotiation. I therefore concur with you in your call for negotiation. Too long has our beloved Southland been bogged down in a tragic effort to live in monologue rather than dialogue.

One of the basic points in your statement is that the action that I and my associates have taken in Birmingham is untimely. Some have asked: "Why didn't you give the new city administration time to act?" The only answer that I can give to this query is that the new Birmingham administration must be prodded about as much as the outgoing one, before it will act. We are sadly mistaken if we feel that the election of Albert Boutwell as mayor will bring the millennium to Birmingham. While Mr. Boutwell is a much more gentle person than Mr. Connor, they are both segregationists, dedicated to maintenance of the status quo. I have hope that Mr. Boutwell will be reasonable enough to see the futility of massive resistance to desegregation. But he will not see this without pressure from devotees of civil rights. My friends, I must say to you that we have not made a single gain in civil rights without determined legal and nonviolent pressure. Lamentably, it is an historical fact that privileged groups seldom give up their privileges voluntarily. Individuals may see the moral light and voluntarily give up their unjust posture; but, as Reinhold Niebuhr has reminded us, groups tend to be more immoral than individuals.

We know through painful experience that freedom is never voluntarily given by the oppressor; it must be demanded by the oppressed. Frankly, I have yet to engage in a direct-action campaign that was "well timed" in the view of those who have not suffered unduly from the disease of segregation. For years now I have heard the word "Wait!" It rings in the ear of every Negro with piercing familiarity. This "Wait" has almost always meant "Never." We must come to see, with one of our distinguished jurists, that "justice too long delayed is justice denied."

We have waited for more than 340 years for our constitutional and God-given rights. The nations of Asia and Africa are moving with jetlike speed toward gaining political independence, but we still creep at horse-and-buggy pace toward gaining a cup of coffee at a lunch counter. Perhaps it is easy for those who have never felt the stinging darts of segregation to say, "Wait." But when you have seen vicious mobs lynch your mothers and fathers at will and drown your sisters and brothers at whim; when you have seen hate-filled policemen curse, kick and even kill your black brothers and sisters; when you see the vast majority of your twenty million Negro brothers smothering in an airtight cage of poverty in the midst of an affluent society; when you suddenly find your tongue twisted and your speech stammering as you seek to explain to your six-year-old daughter why she can't go to the public amusement park that has just been advertised on television, and see tears welling up in her eyes when she is told that Funtown is closed to colored children, and see ominous clouds of inferiority beginning to form in her little mental sky, and see her beginning to distort her personality by developing an unconscious bitterness toward white people; when you have to concoct an answer for a five-year-old son who is asking: "Daddy, why do white people treat colored people so mean?"; when you take a cross-country drive and find it necessary to sleep night after night in the uncomfortable corners of your automobile because no motel will accept you; when you are humiliated day in and day out by nagging signs reading "white" and "colored"; when your first name becomes "nigger," your middle name becomes "boy" (however old you are) and your last name becomes "John," and your wife and mother are never given the respected title "Mrs."; when you are harried by day and haunted by night by the fact that you are a Negro, living constantly at tiptoe stance, never quite knowing what to expect next, and are plagued with inner fears and outer resentments; when you are forever fighting a degenerating sense of "nobodiness"—then you will understand why we find it difficult to wait. There comes a time when the cup of endurance runs over, and men are no longer willing to be plunged into the abyss of despair. I hope, sirs, you can understand our legitimate and unavoidable impatience.

You express a great deal of anxiety over our willingness to break laws. This is certainly a legitimate concern. Since we so diligently urge people to obey the Supreme Court's decision of 1954 outlawing segregation in the public schools, at first glance it may seem rather paradoxical for us consciously to break laws. One may well ask: "How can you advocate breaking some laws and obeying others?" The answer lies in the fact that there are two types of laws: just and unjust. I would be the first to advocate obeying just laws. One has not only a legal but a moral responsibility to obey just laws. Conversely, one has a moral responsibility to disobey unjust laws. I would agree with St. Augustine that "an unjust law is no law at all."

Now, what is the difference between the two? How does one determine whether a law is just or unjust? A just law is a man-made code that squares with the moral law or the law of God. An unjust law is a code that is out of harmony with the moral law. To put it in the terms of St. Thomas Aquinas: An unjust law is a human law that is not rooted in eternal law and natural law. Any law that uplifts human personality is just. Any law that degrades human personality is unjust. All segregation statutes are unjust because segregation distorts the soul and damages the personality. It gives the segregator a false sense of superiority and the segregated a false sense of inferiority. Segregation, to use the terminology of the Jewish philosopher Martin Buber, substitutes an "I–it" relationship for an "I–thou" relationship and ends up relegating persons to the status of things. Hence segregation is not only politically, economically and sociologically unsound, it is morally wrong and sinful. Paul Tillich has said that sin is separation. Is not segregation an existential expression of man's tragic separation, his awful estrangement, his terrible sinfulness? Thus it is that I can urge men to obey the 1954 decision of the Supreme Court, for it is morally right; and I can urge them to disobey segregation ordinances, for they are morally wrong.

Let us consider a more concrete example of just and unjust laws. An unjust law is a code that a numerical or power majority group compels a minority group to obey but does not make binding on itself. This is *difference* made legal. By the same token, a just law is a code that a majority compels a minority to follow and that it is willing to follow itself. This is *sameness* made legal.

Let me give another explanation. A law is unjust if it is inflicted on a minority that, as a result of being denied the right to vote, had no part in enacting or devising the law. Who can say that the legislature of Alabama which set up that state's segregation laws was democratically elected? Throughout Alabama all sorts of devious methods are used to prevent Negroes from becoming registered voters, and there are some counties in which, even though Negroes constitute a majority of the population, not a single Negro is registered. Can any law enacted under such circumstances be considered democratically structured?

Sometimes a law is just on its face and unjust in its application. For instance, I have been arrested on a charge of parading without a permit. Now, there is nothing wrong in having an ordinance which requires a permit for a parade. But such an ordinance becomes unjust when it is used to maintain segregation and to deny citizens the First-Amendment privilege of peaceful assembly and protest.

I hope you are able to see the distinction I am trying to point out. In no sense do I advocate evading or defying the law, as would the rabid segregationist. That would lead to anarchy. One who breaks an unjust law must do so openly, lovingly, and with a willingness to accept the penalty. I submit that an individual who breaks a law that conscience tells him is unjust, and who willingly accepts the penalty of imprisonment in order to arouse the conscience of the community over its injustice, is in reality expressing the highest respect for law.

Of course, there is nothing new about this kind of civil disobedience. It was evidenced sublimely in the refusal of Shadrach, Meshach and Abednego to obey the laws of Nebuchadnezzar, on the ground that a higher moral law was at stake. It was practiced superbly by the Early Christians, who were willing to face hungry lions and the excruciating pain of chopping blocks rather than submit to certain unjust laws of the Roman Empire. To a degree, academic freedom is a reality today because Socrates practiced civil disobedience. In our own nation, the Boston Tea Party represented a massive act of civil disobedience.

We should never forget that everything Adolf Hitler did in Germany was "legal" and everything the Hungarian freedom fighters did in Hungary was "illegal." It was "illegal" to aid and comfort a Jew in Hitler's Germany. Even so, I am sure that, had I lived in Germany at the time, I would have aided and comforted my Jewish brothers. If today I lived in a Communist country where certain principles dear to the Christian faith are suppressed, I would openly advocate disobeying that country's antireligious laws.

I must make two honest confessions to you, my Christian and Jewish brothers. First, I must confess that over the past few years I have been gravely disappointed with the white moderate. I have almost reached the regrettable conclusion that the Negro's great stumbling block in his stride toward freedom is not the White Citizen's Counciler or the Ku Klux Klanner, but the white moderate, who is more devoted to "order" than to justice; who prefers a negative peace which is the absence of tension to a positive peace which is the presence of justice; who constantly says: "I agree with you in the goal you seek, but I cannot agree with your methods of direct action"; who paternalistically believes he can set the timetable for another man's freedom; who lives by a mythical concept of time and who constantly advises the Negro to wait for a "more convenient season." Shallow understanding from people of good will is more frustrating than absolute misunderstanding from people of ill will. Lukewarm acceptance is much more bewildering than outright rejection.

I had hoped that the white moderate would understand that law and order exist for the purpose of establishing justice and that when they fail in this purpose they become the dangerously structured dams that block the flow of social progress. I had hoped that the white moderate would understand that the present tension in the South is a necessary phase of the transition from an obnoxious negative peace, in which the Negro passively accepted his unjust plight, to a substantive and positive peace, in which all men will respect the dignity and worth of human personality. Actually, we who engage in nonviolent direct action are not the creators of tension. We merely bring to the surface the hidden tension that is already alive. We bring it out in the open, where it can be seen and dealt with. Like a boil that can never be cured so long as it is covered up but must be opened with all its ugliness to the natural medicines of air and light, injustice must be exposed, with all the tension its exposure creates, to the light of human conscience and the air of national opinion before it can be cured.

In your statement you assert that our actions, even though peaceful, must be condemned because they precipitate violence. But is this a logical assertion? Isn't this like condemning a robbed man because his possession of money precipitated the evil act of robbery? Isn't this like condemning Socrates because his unswerving commitment to truth and his philosophical inquiries precipitated the act by the misguided populace in which they made him drink hemlock? Isn't this like condemning Jesus because his unique God-consciousness and never-ceasing devotion to God's will precipitated the evil act of crucifixion? We must come to see that, as the federal courts have consistently affirmed, it is wrong to urge an individual to cease his efforts to gain his basic constitutional rights because the quest may precipitate violence. Society must protect the robbed and punish the robber.

I had also hoped that the white moderate would reject the myth concerning time in relation to the struggle for freedom. I have just received a letter from a white brother in Texas. He writes: "All Christians know that the colored people will receive equal rights eventually, but it is possible that you are in too great a religious hurry. It has taken Christianity almost two thousand years to accomplish what it has. The teachings of Christ take time to come to earth." Such an attitude stems from a tragic misconception of time, from the strangely irrational notion that there is something in the very flow of time that will inevitably cure all ills. Actually, time itself is neutral; it can be used either destructively or constructively. More and more I feel that the people of ill will have used time much more effectively than have the people of good will. We will have to repent in this generation not merely for the hateful words and actions of the bad people but for the appalling silence of the good people. Human progress never rolls in on wheels of inevitability; it comes through the tireless efforts of men willing to be co-workers with God, and without this hard work, time itself becomes an ally of the forces of social stagnation. We must use time creatively, in the knowledge that the time is always ripe to do right. Now is the time to make real the promise of democracy and transform our pending national elegy into a creative psalm of brotherhood. Now is the time to lift our national policy from the quicksand of racial injustice to the solid rock of human dignity.

You speak of our activity in Birmingham as extreme. At first I was rather disappointed that fellow clergymen would see my nonviolent efforts as those of an extremist. I began thinking about the fact that I stand in the middle of two opposing forces in the Negro community. One is a force of complacency, made up in part of Negroes who, as a result of long years of oppression, are so drained of self-respect and a sense of "somebodiness" that they have adjusted to segregation; and in part of a few middle-class Negroes who, because of a degree of academic and economic security and because in some ways they profit by segregation, have become insensitive to the problems of the masses. The other force is one of bitterness and hatred, and it comes perilously close to advocating violence. It is expressed in the various black nationalist groups that are springing up across the nation, the largest and best-known being Elijah Muhammad's Muslim movement. Nourished by the Negro's frustration over the continued existence of racial discrimination, this movement is made up of people who have lost faith in America, who have absolutely repudiated Christianity, and who have concluded that the white man is an incorrigible "devil."

I have tried to stand between these two forces, saying that we need emulate neither the "do-nothingism" of the complacent nor the hatred and despair of the black nationalist. For there is the more excellent way of love and nonviolent protest. I am grateful to God that, through the influence of the Negro church, the way of nonviolence became an integral part of our struggle.

If this philosophy had not emerged, by now many streets of the South would, I am convinced, be flowing with blood. And I am further convinced that if our white brothers dismiss as "rabble-rousers" and "outside agitators" those of us who employ nonviolent direct action, and if they refuse to support our nonviolent efforts, millions of Negroes will, out of frustration and despair, seek solace and security in black-nationalist ideologies—a development that would inevitably lead to a frightening racial nightmare.

Oppressed people cannot remain oppressed forever. The yearning for freedom eventually manifests itself, and that is what has happened to the American Negro. Something within has reminded him of his birthright of freedom, and something without has reminded him that it can be gained. Consciously or unconsciously, he has been caught up by the *Zeitgeist*,[2] and with his black brothers of Africa and his brown and yellow brothers of Asia, South America and the Caribbean, the United States Negro is moving with a sense of great urgency toward the promised land of racial justice. If one recognizes this vital urge that has engulfed the Negro community, one should readily understand why public demonstrations are taking place. The Negro has many pent-up resentments and latent frustrations, and he must release them. So let him march; let him make prayer pilgrimages to the city hall; let him go on freedom rides—and try to understand why he must do so. If his repressed emotions are not released in nonviolent ways, they will seek expression through violence; this is not a threat but a fact of history. So I have not said to my people: "Get rid of your discontent." Rather, I have tried to say that this normal and healthy discontent can be channeled into the creative outlet of nonviolent direct action. And now this approach is being termed extremist.

But though I was initially disappointed at being categorized as an extremist, as I continued to think about the matter I gradually gained a measure of satisfaction from the label. Was not Jesus an extremist for love: "Love your enemies, bless them that curse you, do good to them that hate you, and pray for them which despitefully use you, and persecute you." Was not Amos an extremist for justice: "Let justice roll down like waters and righteousness like an ever-flowing stream." Was not Paul an extremist for the Christian gospel: "I bear in my body the marks of the Lord Jesus." Was not Martin Luther an extremist: "Here I stand; I cannot do otherwise, so help me God." And John Bunyan: "I will stay in jail to the end of my days before I make a butchery of my conscience." And Abraham Lincoln: "This nation cannot survive half slave and half free." And Thomas Jefferson: "We hold these truths to be self-evident, that all men are created equal. . . ." So the question is not whether we will be extremists, but what kind of extremists we will be. Will we be extremists for hate or for love? Will we be extremists for the preservation of injustice or for the extension of justice? In that dramatic scene on Calvary's hill three men were crucified. We must never forget that all three were crucified for the same crime—the crime of extremism. Two were extremists for immorality, and thus fell below their environment. The other, Jesus Christ, was an extremist for love, truth and goodness, and thereby rose above his environment. Perhaps the South, the nation and the world are in dire need of creative extremists.

I had hoped that the white moderate would see this need. Perhaps I was too optimistic; perhaps I expected too much. I suppose I should have realized that few members of the oppressor race can understand the deep groans and passionate yearnings of the oppressed race, and still fewer have the vision to see that injustice must be rooted out by strong, persistent and determined action. I am thankful, however, that some of our white brothers in the South have grasped the meaning of this social revolution and committed themselves to it. They are still all too few in

---

[2]*Zeitgeist* Spirit of the age. [Ed. note.]

quantity, but they are big in quality. Some—such as Ralph McGill, Lillian Smith, Harry Golden, James McBride Dabbs, Ann Braden and Sarah Patton Boyle—have written about our struggle in eloquent and prophetic terms. Others have marched with us down nameless streets of the South. They have languished in filthy, roach-infested jails, suffering the abuse and brutality of policemen who view them as "dirty nigger-lovers." Unlike so many of their moderate brothers and sisters, they have recognized the urgency of the moment and sensed the need for powerful "action" antidotes to combat the disease of segregation.

Let me take note of my other major disappointment. I have been so greatly disappointed with the white church and its leadership. Of course, there are some notable exceptions. I am not unmindful of the fact that each of you has taken some significant stands on this issue. I commend you, Reverend Stallings, for your Christian stand on this past Sunday, in welcoming Negroes to your worship service on a nonsegregated basis. I commend the Catholic leaders of this state for integrating Spring Hill College several years ago.

But despite these notable exceptions, I must honestly reiterate that I have been disappointed with the church. I do not say this as one of those negative critics who can always find something wrong with the church. I say this as a minister of the gospel, who loves the church; who was nurtured in its bosom; who has been sustained by its spiritual blessings and who will remain true to it as long as the cord of life shall lengthen.

When I was suddenly catapulted into the leadership of the bus protest in Montgomery, Alabama, a few years ago, I felt we would be supported by the white church. I felt that the white ministers, priests and rabbis of the South would be among our strongest allies. Instead, some have been outright opponents, refusing to understand the freedom movement and misrepresenting its leaders; all too many others have been more cautious than courageous and have remained silent behind the anesthetizing security of stained-glass windows.

In spite of my shattered dreams, I came to Birmingham with the hope that the white religious leadership of this community would see the justice of our cause and, with deep moral concern, would serve as the channel through which our just grievances could reach the power structure. I had hoped that each of you would understand. But again I have been disappointed.

I have heard numerous southern religious leaders admonish their worshipers to comply with a desegregation decision because it is the law, but I have longed to hear white ministers declare: "Follow this decree because integration is morally right and because the Negro is your brother." In the midst of blatant injustices inflicted upon the Negro, I have watched white churchmen stand on the sideline and mouth pious irrelevancies and sanctimonious trivialities. In the midst of a mighty struggle to rid our nation of racial and economic injustice, I have heard many ministers say: "Those are social issues, with which the gospel has no real concern." And I have watched many churches commit themselves to a completely otherworldly religion which makes a strange, un-Biblical distinction between body and soul, between the sacred and the secular.

I have traveled the length and breadth of Alabama, Mississippi and all the other southern states. On sweltering summer days and crisp autumn mornings I have looked at the South's beautiful churches with their lofty spires pointing heavenward. I have beheld the impressive outlines of her massive religious-education buildings. Over and over I have found myself asking: "What kind of people worship here? Who is their God? Where were their voices when the lips of Governor Barnett dripped with words of interposition and nullification? Where were they when Governor Wallace gave a clarion call for defiance and hatred? Where were their voices of support when bruised and weary Negro men and women decided to rise from the dark dungeons of complacency to the bright hills of creative protest?

Yes, these questions are still in my mind. In deep disappointment I have wept over the laxity of the church. But be assured that my tears have been tears of love. There can be no deep disappointment where there is not deep love. Yes, I love the church. How could I do otherwise? I am in the rather unique position of being the son, the grandson and the great-grandson of preachers. Yes, I see the church as the body of Christ. But, oh! How we have blemished and scarred that body through social neglect and through fear of being nonconformists.

There was a time when the church was very powerful—in the time when the early Christians rejoiced at being deemed worthy to suffer for what they believed. In those days the church was not merely a thermometer that recorded the ideas and principles of popular opinion; it was a thermostat that transformed the mores of society. Whenever the early Christians entered a town, the people in power became disturbed and immediately sought to convict the Christians for being "disturbers of the peace" and "outside agitators." But the Christians pressed on, in the conviction that they were "a colony of heaven," called to obey God rather than man. Small in number, they were big in commitment. They were too God-intoxicated to be "astronomically intimidated." By their effort and example they brought an end to such ancient evils as infanticide and gladiatorial contests.

Things are different now. So often the contemporary church is a weak, ineffectual voice with an uncertain sound. So often it is an archdefender of the status quo. Far from being disturbed by the presence of the church, the power structure of the average community is consoled by the church's silent—and often even vocal—sanction of things as they are.

But the judgment of God is upon the church as never before. If today's church does not recapture the sacrificial spirit of the early church, it will lose its authenticity, forfeit the loyalty of millions, and be dismissed as an irrelevant social club with no meaning for the twentieth century. Every day I meet young people whose disappointment with the church has turned into outright disgust.

Perhaps I have once again been too optimistic. Is organized religion too inextricably bound to the status quo to save our nation and the world? Perhaps I must turn my faith to the inner spiritual church, the church within the church, as the true *ekklesia* and the hope of the world. But again I am thankful to God that some noble souls from the ranks of organized religion have broken loose from the paralyzing chains of conformity and joined us as active partners in the struggle for freedom. They have left their secure congregations and walked the streets of Albany, Georgia, with us. They have gone down the highways of the South on tortuous rides for freedom. Yes, they have gone to jail with us. Some have been dismissed from their churches, have lost the support of their bishops and fellow ministers. But they have acted in the faith that right defeated is stronger than evil triumphant. Their witness has been the spiritual salt that has preserved the true meaning of the gospel in these troubled times. They have carved a tunnel of hope through the dark mountain of disappointment.

I hope the church as a whole will meet the challenge of this decisive hour. But even if the church does not come to the aid of justice, I have no despair about the future. I have no fear about the outcome of our struggle in Birmingham, even if our motives are at present misunderstood. We will reach the goal of freedom in Birmingham and all over the nation, because the goal of America is freedom. Abused and scorned though we may be, our destiny is tied up with America's destiny. Before the pilgrims landed at Plymouth, we were here. Before the pen of Jefferson etched the majestic words of the Declaration of Independence across the pages of history, we were here. For more than two centuries our forebears labored in this country without wages; they made cotton king; they built the homes of their masters while suffering gross injustice and shameful humiliation—and yet out of a bottomless vitality they continued to thrive and develop. If the inexpressible cruelties of slavery could not stop us, the opposition we now face will surely fail. We will win our freedom because the sacred heritage of our nation and the eternal will of God are embodied in our echoing demands.

Before closing I feel impelled to mention one other point in your statement that has troubled me profoundly. You warmly commended the Birmingham police force for keeping "order" and "preventing violence." I doubt that you would have so warmly commended the police force if you had seen its dogs sinking their teeth into unarmed, nonviolent Negroes. I doubt that you would so quickly commend the policemen if you were to observe their ugly and inhumane treatment of Negroes here in the city jail; if you were to watch them push and curse old Negro women and young Negro girls; if you were to see them slap and kick old Negro men and young boys; if you were to observe them, as they did on two occasions, refuse to give us food because we wanted to sing our grace together. I cannot join you in your praise of the Birmingham police department.

It is true that the police have exercised a degree of discipline in handling the demonstrators. In this sense they have conducted themselves rather "nonviolently" in public. But for what purpose? To preserve the evil system of segregation. Over the past few years I have consistently preached that nonviolence demands that the means we use must be as pure as the ends we seek. I have tried to make clear that it is wrong to use immoral means to attain moral ends. But now I must affirm that it is just as wrong, or perhaps even more so, to use moral means to preserve immoral ends. Perhaps Mr. Connor and his policemen have been rather nonviolent in public, as was Chief Pritchett in Albany, Georgia, but they have used the moral means of nonviolence to maintain the immoral end of racial injustice. As T. S. Eliot has said: "The last temptation is the greatest treason: To do the right deed for the wrong reason."

I wish you had commended the Negro sit-inners and demonstrators of Birmingham for their sublime courage, their willingness to suffer and their amazing discipline in the midst of great provocation. One day the South will recognize its real heroes. They will be the James Merediths, with the noble sense of purpose that enables them to face jeering and hostile mobs, and with the agonizing loneliness that characterizes the life of the pioneer. They will be old, oppressed, battered Negro women, symbolized in a seventy-two-year-old woman in Montgomery, Alabama, who rose up with a sense of dignity and with her people decided not to ride segregated buses, and who responded with ungrammatical profundity to one who inquired about her weariness: "My feets is tired, but my soul is at rest." They will be the young high school and college students, the young ministers of the gospel and a host of their elders, courageously and nonviolently sitting in at lunch counters and willingly going to jail for conscience' sake. One day the South will know that when these disinherited children of God sat down at lunch counters, they were in reality standing up for what is best in the American dream and for the most sacred values in our Judaeo-Christian heritage, thereby bringing our nation back to those great wells of democracy which were dug deep by the founding fathers in their formulation of the Constitution and the Declaration of Independence.

Never before have I written so long a letter. I'm afraid it is much too long to take your precious time. I can assure you that it would have been much shorter if I had been writing from a comfortable desk, but what else can one do when he is alone in a narrow jail cell, other than write long letters, think long thoughts and pray long prayers?

If I have said anything in this letter that overstates the truth and indicates an unreasonable impatience, I beg you to forgive me. If I have said anything that understates the truth and indicates my having a patience that allows me to settle for anything less than brotherhood, I beg God to forgive me.

I hope this letter finds you strong in the faith. I also hope that circumstances will soon make it possible for me to meet each of you, not as an integrationist or a civil-rights leader but as a fellow clergyman and a Christian brother. Let us all hope that the dark clouds of racial prejudice will soon pass away and the deep fog of misunderstanding will be lifted from our fear-drenched communities, and in some not too distant tomorrow the radiant stars of love and brotherhood will shine over our great nation with all their scintillating beauty.

Yours for the cause of Peace and Brotherhood,
MARTIN LUTHER KING, JR.

QUESTIONS FOR DISCUSSION

1. Martin Luther King, by choosing a letter format for his communication from jail, places this essay in the tradition of St. Paul writing to various Christian communities from jail. How does this choice of form add strength to his argument?
2. Who is King's audience? How does King justify his nonviolent protest to them? What type of authority does he appeal to? How is this appropriate?
3. What are the strategies and goals of a nonviolent campaign? Considering King's argument, why is the order of the four steps important?
4. How does King justify breaking some laws and not others? How does he support the distinction between just and unjust laws? Is it convincing? Why or why not?

5. Outline King's argument. How does the argument build?
6. Martin Luther King was a practicing minister. What elements of the text are like an oral delivery of a sermon? Are these devices effective? Why or why not?
7. How does he make use of what is called a rhetorical question (a question that is asked and is then answered)?
8. King states, "Anyone who lives inside the United States can never be considered an outsider anywhere within its bounds" (par. 5). Do you agree? Why or why not?

NELSON MANDELA
I Am Prepared to Die

Considered by black South Africans to be their leader, the black nationalist Nelson R. Mandela (1918–   ), until February 11, 1990, had been serving a life sentence imposed in 1964 for forming Umkonto We Sizwe (Spear of the Nation), a group which advocates violence as a means to topple apartheid. While in prison he was elected the president general of the African National Congress (ANC) and later refused President P. W. Botha's offer to release him if he renounced the use of violence against the apartheid system. Apartheid, a policy of segregating people based on race, is a recent phenomenon in South African history. In 1948 the Nationalist Party of South Africa passed the Mixed Marriage Act of 1949 and the Immorality Amendment Act of 1950, which outlawed marriage and sexual relations between different races. The Reservation of Separate Amenities Act in 1953 segregated transportation and public places, such as restrooms, theaters, and parks. The white-controlled national government then created separate local administrations according to the government's definitions of the following racial groups: Whites, Coloureds, Asians, and Africans. To keep "Africans" away from white centers of power, the Bantu Self-Government Act of 1959 allowed the white-ruled government to move "Africans," depending upon government classifications of their "tribes," to one of ten different areas, called "Bantu Homelands." While these homelands are independent on paper, South Africa retains military and economic control over them and no other government has recognized their independence.

SECOND COURT STATEMENT, 1964

Mandela's statement from the dock in Pretoria Supreme Court, 20 April 1964, at the opening of the defence case.

I am the First Accused.

I hold a Bachelor's Degree in Arts and practised as an attorney in Johannesburg for a number of years in partnership with Oliver Tambo. I am a convicted prisoner serving five years for leaving the country without a permit and for inciting people to go on strike at the end of May 1961.

At the outset, I want to say that the suggestion made by the State in its opening that the struggle in South Africa is under the influence of foreigners or communists is wholly incorrect. I have done whatever I did, both as an individual and as a leader of my people, because of my experience in South Africa and my own proudly felt African background, and not because of what any outsider might have said.

In my youth in the Transkei I listened to the elders of my tribe telling stories of the old days. Amongst the tales they related to me were those of wars fought by our ancestors in defence of the fatherland. The names of Dingane and Bambata, Hintsa and Makana, Squngthi and Dalasile, Moshoeshoe and Sekhukhuni, were praised as the glory of the entire African nation. I hoped then that life might offer me the opportunity to serve my people and make my own humble contribution to their freedom struggle. This is what has motivated me in all that I have done in relation to the charges made against me in this case.

Having said this, I must deal immediately and at some length with the question of violence. Some of the things so far told to the Court are true and some are untrue. I do not, however, deny that I planned sabotage. I did not plan it in a spirit of recklessness, nor because I have any love of violence. I planned it as a result of a calm and sober assessment of the political situation that had arisen after many years of tyranny, exploitation, and oppression of my people by the Whites.

I admit immediately that I was one of the persons who helped to form Umkhonto we Sizwe, and that I played a prominent role in its affairs until I was arrested in August 1962.

In the statement which I am about to make I shall correct certain false impressions which have been created by State witnesses. Amongst other things, I will demonstrate that certain of the acts referred to in the evidence were not and could not have been committed by Umkhonto. I will also deal with the relationship between the African National Congress and Umkhonto, and with the part which I personally have played in the affairs of both organizations. I shall deal also with the part played by the Communist Party. In order to explain these matters properly, I will have to explain what Umkhonto set out to achieve; what methods it prescribed for the achievement of these objects, and why these methods were chosen. I will also have to explain how I became involved in the activities of these organizations.

I deny that Umkhonto was responsible for a number of acts which clearly fell outside the policy of the organization, and which have been charged in the indictment against us. I do not know what justification there was for these acts, but to demonstrate that they could not have been authorized by Umkhonto, I want to refer briefly to the roots and policy of the organization.

I have already mentioned that I was one of the persons who helped to form Umkhonto. I, and the others who started the organization, did so for two reasons. Firstly, we believed that as a result of Government policy, violence by the African people had become inevitable, and that unless responsible leadership was given to canalize and control the feelings of our people, there would be outbreaks of terrorism which would produce an intensity of bitterness and hostility between the various races of this country which is not produced even by war. Secondly, we felt that without violence there would be no way open to the African people to succeed in their struggle against the principle of white supremacy. All lawful modes of expressing opposition to this principle had been closed by legislation, and we were placed in a position in which we had either to accept a permanent state of inferiority, or to defy the Government. We chose to defy the law. We first broke the law in a way which avoided any recourse to violence; when this form was legislated against, and then the Government resorted to a show of force to crush opposition to its policies, only then did we decide to answer violence with violence.

But the violence which we chose to adopt was not terrorism. We who formed Umkhonto were all members of the African National Congress, and had behind us the ANC tradition of non-violence and negotiation as a means of solving political disputes. We believe that South Africa belongs to all the people who live in it, and not to one group, be it black or white. We did not want an interracial war, and tried to avoid it to the last minute. If the Court is in doubt about this, it will be seen that the whole history of our organization bears out what I have said, and what I will subsequently say, when I describe the tactics which Umkhonto decided to adopt. I want, therefore, to say something about the African National Congress.

The African National Congress was formed in 1912 to defend the rights of the African people which had been seriously curtailed by the South Africa Act, and which were then being threatened by the Native Land Act. For thirty-seven years— that is until 1949—it adhered strictly to a constitutional struggle. It put forward demands and resolutions; it sent delegations to the Government in the belief that African grievances could be settled through peaceful discussion and that Africans could advance gradually to full political rights. But White Governments remained unmoved, and the rights of Africans became less instead of becoming greater. In the words of my leader, Chief Lutuli, who became President of the ANC in 1952, and who was later awarded the Nobel Peace Prize:

> Who will deny that thirty years of my life have been spent knocking in vain, patiently, moderately, and modestly at a closed and barred door? What have been the fruits of moderation? The past thirty years have seen the greatest number of laws restricting our rights and progress, until today we have reached a stage where we have almost no rights at all.

Even after 1949, the ANC remained determined to avoid violence. At this time, however, there was a change from the strictly constitutional means of protest which had been employed in the past. The change was embodied in a decision which was taken to protest against apartheid legislation by peaceful, but unlawful, demonstrations against certain laws. Pursuant to this policy the ANC launched the Defiance Campaign, in which I was placed in charge of volunteers. This campaign was based on the principles of passive resistance. More than 8,500 people defied apartheid laws and went to jail. Yet there was not a single instance of violence in the course of this campaign on the part of any defier. I and nineteen colleagues were convicted for the role which we played in organizing the campaign, but our sentences were suspended mainly because the Judge found that discipline and non-violence had been stressed throughout. This was the time when the volunteer section of the ANC was established, and when the word 'Amadelakufa'[1] was first used: this was the time when the volunteers were asked to take a pledge to uphold certain principles. Evidence dealing with volunteers and their pledges has been introduced into this case,

---

[1] **Amadelakufa** Those who are prepared to make sacrifices.

but completely out of context. The volunteers were not, and are not, the soldiers of a black army pledged to fight a civil war against the whites. They were, and are, dedicated workers who are prepared to lead campaigns initiated by the ANC to distribute leaflets, to organize strikes, or do whatever the particular campaign required. They are called volunteers because they volunteer to face the penalties of imprisonment and whipping which are now prescribed by the legislature for such acts.

During the Defiance Campaign, the Public Safety Act and the Criminal Law Amendment Act were passed. These Statutes provided harsher penalties for offences committed by way of protests against laws. Despite this, the protests continued and the ANC adhered to its policy of non-violence. In 1956, 156 leading members of the Congress Alliance, including myself, were arrested on a charge of high treason and charges under the Suppression of Communism Act. The non-violent policy of the ANC was put in issue by the State, but when the Court gave judgement some five years later, it found that the ANC did not have a policy of violence. We were acquitted on all counts, which included a count that the ANC sought to set up a communist state in place of the existing regime. The Government has always sought to label all its opponents as communists. This allegation has been repeated in the present case, but as I will show, the ANC is not, and never has been, a communist organization.

In 1960 there was the shooting at Sharpeville,[2] which resulted in the proclamation of a state of emergency and the declaration of the ANC as an unlawful organization. My colleagues and I, after careful consideration, decided that we would not obey this decree. The African people were not part of the Government and did not make the laws by which they were governed. We believed in the words of the Universal Declaration of Human Rights, that 'the will of the people shall be the basis of authority of the Government', and for us to accept the banning was equivalent to accepting the silencing of the Africans for all time. The ANC refused to dissolve, but instead went underground. We believed it was our duty to preserve this organization which had been built up with almost fifty years of unremitting toil. I have no doubt that no self-respecting White political organization would disband itself if declared illegal by a government in which it had no say.

In 1960 the Government held a referendum which led to the establishment of the Republic. Africans, who constituted approximately 70 per cent of the population of South Africa, were not entitled to vote, and were not even consulted about the proposed constitutional change. All of us were apprehensive of our future under the proposed White Republic, and a resolution was taken to hold an All-In African Conference to call for a National Convention, and to organize mass demonstrations on the eve of the unwanted Republic, if the Government failed to call the Convention. The conference was attended by Africans of various political persuasions. I was the Secretary of the conference and undertook to be responsible for organizing the national stay-at-home which was subsequently called to coincide with the declaration of the Republic. As all strikes by Africans are illegal, the person organizing such a strike must avoid arrest. I was chosen to be this person, and consequently I had to leave my home and family and my practice and go into hiding to avoid arrest.

[2]**Sharpeville** The location where South African police killed 69 and wounded 178 demonstrators who were protesting South Africa's pass laws. [Ed. note.]

The stay-at-home, in accordance with ANC policy, was to be a peaceful demonstration. Careful instructions were given to organizers and members to avoid any recourse to violence. The Government's answer was to introduce new and harsher laws, to mobilize its armed forces, and to send Saracens[3], armed vehicles, and soldiers into the townships in a massive show of force designed to intimidate the people. This was an indication that the Government had decided to rule by force alone, and this decision was a milestone on the road to Umkhonto.

Some of this may appear irrelevant to this trial. In fact, I believe none of it is irrelevant because it will, I hope, enable the Court to appreciate the attitude eventually adopted by the various persons and bodies concerned in the National Liberation Movement. When I went to jail in 1962, the dominant idea was that loss of life should be avoided. I now know that this was still so in 1963.

I must return to June 1961. What were we, the leaders of our people, to do? Were we to give in to the show of force and the implied threat against future action, or were we to fight it and, if so, how?

We had no doubt that we had to continue the fight. Anything else would have been abject surrender. Our problem was not whether to fight, but was how to continue the fight. We of the ANC had always stood for a non-racial democracy, and we shrank from any action which might drive the races further apart than they already were. But the hard facts were that fifty years of non-violence had brought the African people nothing but more and more repressive legislation, and fewer and fewer rights. It may not be easy for this Court to understand, but it is a fact that for a long time the people had been talking of violence—of the day when they would fight the White man and win back their country—and we, the leaders of the ANC, had nevertheless always prevailed upon them to avoid violence and to pursue peaceful methods. When some of us discussed this in May and June of 1961, it could not be denied that our policy to achieve a non-racial State by non-violence had achieved nothing, and that our followers were beginning to lose confidence in this policy and were developing disturbing ideas of terrorism.

It must not be forgotten that by this time violence had, in fact, become a feature of the South African political scene. There had been violence in 1957 when the women of Zeerust were ordered to carry passes; there was violence in 1958 with the enforcement of cattle culling in Sekhukhuniland; there was violence in 1959 when the people of Cato Manor protested against pass raids; there was violence in 1960 when the Government attempted to impose Bantu Authorities in Pondoland. Thirty-nine Africans died in these disturbances. In 1961 there had been riots in Warmbaths, and all this time the Transkei had been a seething mass of unrest. Each disturbance pointed clearly to the inevitable growth among Africans of the belief that violence was the only way out—it showed that a Government which uses force to maintain its rule teaches the oppressed to use force to oppose it. Already small groups had arisen in the urban areas and were spontaneously making plans for violent forms of political struggle. There now arose a danger that these groups would adopt terrorism against Africans, as well as Whites, if not properly directed. Particularly disturbing was the type of violence engendered in places such as Zeerust, Sekhukhuniland, and Pondoland amongst Africans. It was increasingly

[3]**Saracens** British-made military troop carriers.

taking the form, not of struggle against the Government—though this is wʜ.. prompted it—but of civil strife amongst themselves, conducted in such a way that it could not hope to achieve anything other than a loss of life and bitterness.

At the beginning of June 1961, after a long and anxious assessment of the South African situation, I, and some colleagues, came to the conclusion that as violence in this country was inevitable, it would be unrealistic and wrong for African leaders to continue preaching peace and non-violence at a time when the Government met our peaceful demands with force.

This conclusion was not easily arrived at. It was only when all else had failed, when all channels of peaceful protest had been barred to us, that the decision was made to embark on violent forms of political struggle, and to form Umkhonto we Sizwe. We did so not because we desired such a course, but solely because the Government had left us with no other choice. In the Manifesto of Umkhonto published on 16 December 1961, which is Exhibit AD, we said:

> The time comes in the life of any nation when there remain only two choices—submit or fight. That time has now come to South Africa. We shall not submit and we have no choice but to hit back by all means in our power in defence of our people, our future, and our freedom.

This was our feeling in June of 1961 when we decided to press for a change in the policy of the National Liberation Movement. I can only say that I felt morally obliged to do what I did.

We who had taken this decision started to consult leaders of various organizations, including the ANC. I will not say whom we spoke to, or what they said, but I wish to deal with the role of the African National Congress in this phase of the struggle, and with the policy and objectives of Umkhonto we Sizwe.

As far as the ANC was concerned, it formed a clear view which can be summarized as follows:

a. It was a mass political organization with a political function to fulfil. Its members had joined on the express policy of non-violence.
b. Because of all this, it could not and would not undertake violence. This must be stressed. One cannot turn such a body into the small, closely knit organization required for sabotage. Nor would this be politically correct, because it would result in members ceasing to carry out this essential activity: political propaganda and organization. Nor was it permissible to change the whole nature of the organization.
c. On the other hand, in view of this situation I have described, the ANC was prepared to depart from its fifty-year-old policy of non-violence to this extent that it would no longer disapprove of properly controlled violence. Hence members who undertook such activity would not be subject to disciplinary action by the ANC.

I say 'properly controlled violence' because I made it clear that if I formed the organization I would at all times subject it to the political guidance of the ANC and would not undertake any different form of activity from that contemplated without the consent of the ANC. And I shall now tell the Court how that form of violence came to be determined.

As a result of this decision, Umkhonto was formed in November 1961. When we took this decision, and subsequently formulated our plans, the ANC heritage of non-violence and racial harmony was very much with us. We felt that the country was drifting towards a civil war in which Blacks and Whites would fight each other. We viewed the situation with alarm. Civil war could mean the destruction of what the ANC stood for; with civil war, racial peace would be more difficult than ever to achieve. We already have examples in South African history of the results of war. It has taken more than fifty years for the scars of the South African War to disappear. How much longer would it take to eradicate the scars of inter-racial civil war, which could not be fought without a great loss of life on both sides?

The avoidance of civil war had dominated our thinking for many years, but when we decided to adopt violence as part of our policy, we realized that we might one day have to face the prospect of such a war. This had to be taken into account in formulating our plans. We required a plan which was flexible and which permitted us to act in accordance with the needs of the times; above all, the plan had to be one which recognized civil war as the last resort, and left the decision on this question to the future. We did not want to be committed to civil war, but we wanted to be ready if it became inevitable.

Four forms of violence were possible. There is sabotage, there is guerrilla warfare, there is terrorism, and there is open revolution. We chose to adopt the first method and to exhaust it before taking any other decision.

In the light of our political background the choice was a logical one. Sabotage did not involve loss of life, and it offered the best hope for future race relations. Bitterness would be kept to a minimum and, if the policy bore fruit, democratic government could become a reality. This is what we felt at the time, and this is what we said in our Manifesto (Exhibit AD):

> We of Umkhonto We Sizwe have always sought to achieve liberation without bloodshed and civil clash. We hope, even at this late hour, that our first actions will awaken everyone to a realization of the disastrous situation to which the Nationalist policy is leading. We hope that we will bring the Government and its supporters to their senses before it is too late, so that both the Government and its policies can be changed before matters reach the desperate stage of civil war.

The initial plan was based on a careful analysis of the political and economic situation of our country. We believed that South Africa depended to a large extent on foreign capital and foreign trade. We felt that planned destruction of power plants, and interference with rail and telephone communications, would tend to scare away capital from the country, make it more difficult for goods from the industrial areas to reach the seaports on schedule, and would in the long run be a heavy drain on the economic life of the country, thus compelling the voters of the country to reconsider their position.

Attacks on the economic life lines of the country were to be linked with sabotage on Government buildings and other symbols of apartheid. These attacks would serve as a source of inspiration to our people. In addition, they would provide an outlet for those people who were urging the adoption of violent methods and would enable us to give concrete proof to our followers that we had adopted a stronger line and were fighting back against Government violence.

In addition, if mass action were successfully organized, and mass reprisals taken, we felt that sympathy for our cause would be roused in other countries, and that greater pressure would be brought to bear on the South African Government.

This then was the plan. Umkhonto was to perform sabotage, and strict instructions were given to its members right from the start, that on no account were they to injure or kill people in planning or carrying out operations. These instructions have been referred to in the evidence of 'Mr. X' and 'Mr. Z'.[4]

The affairs of the Umkhonto were controlled and directed by a National High Command, which had powers of co-option and which could, and did, appoint Regional Commands. The High Command was the body which determined tactics and targets and was in charge of training and finance. Under the High Command there were Regional Commands which were responsible for the direction of the local sabotage groups. Within the framework of the policy laid down by the National High Command, the Regional Commands had authority to select the targets to be attacked. They had no authority to go beyond the prescribed framework and thus had no authority to embark upon acts which endangered life, or which did not fit into the overall plan of sabotage. For instance, Umkhonto members were forbidden ever to go armed into operation. Incidentally, the terms High Command and Regional Command were an importation from the Jewish national underground organization Irgun Zvai Leumi, which operated in Israel between 1944 and 1948.

Umkhonto had its first operation on 16 December 1961, when Government buildings in Johannesburg, Port Elizabeth and Durban were attacked. The selection of targets is proof of the policy to which I have referred. Had we intended to attack life we would have selected targets where people congregated and not empty buildings and power stations. The sabotage which was committed before 16 December 1961 was the work of isolated groups and had no connection whatever with Umkhonto. In fact, some of these and a number of later acts were claimed by other organizations.

The Manifesto of Umkhonto was issued on the day that operations commenced. The response to our actions and Manifesto among the white population was characteristically violent. The Government threatened to take strong action, and called upon its supporters to stand firm and to ignore the demands of the Africans. The Whites failed to respond by suggesting change; they responded to our call by suggesting the laager.

In contrast, the response of the Africans was one of encouragement. Suddenly there was hope again. Things were happening. People in the townships became eager for political news. A great deal of enthusiasm was generated by the initial successes, and people began to speculate on how soon freedom would be obtained.

But we in Umkhonto weighed up the white response with anxiety. The lines were being drawn. The whites and blacks were moving into separate camps, and the

---

[4]State witnesses in the trial whose names were withheld for their protection.

prospects of avoiding a civil war were made less. The white newspapers carried reports that sabotage would be punished by death. If this was so, how could we continue to keep Africans away from terrorism?

Already scores of Africans had died as a result of racial friction. In 1920 when the famous leader, Masabala, was held in Port Elizabeth jail, twenty-four of a group of Africans who had gathered to demand his release were killed by the police and white civilians. In 1921, more than one hundred Africans died in the Bulhoek affair. In 1924 over two hundred Africans were killed when the Administrator of South-West Africa led a force against a group which had rebelled against the imposition of dog tax. On 1 May 1950, eighteen Africans died as a result of police shootings during the strike. On 21 March 1960, sixty-nine unarmed Africans died at Sharpeville.

How many more Sharpevilles would there be in the history of our country? And how many more Sharpevilles could the country stand without violence and terror becoming the order of the day? And what would happen to our people when that stage was reached? In the long run we felt certain we must succeed, but at what cost to ourselves and the rest of the country? And if this happened, how could black and white ever live together again in peace and harmony? These were the problems that faced us, and these were our decisions.

Experience convinced us that rebellion would offer the Government limitless opportunities for the indiscriminate slaughter of our people. But it was precisely because the soil of South Africa is already drenched with the blood of innocent Africans that we felt it our duty to make preparations as a long-term undertaking to use force in order to defend ourselves against force. If war were inevitable, we wanted the fight to be conducted on terms most favourable to our people. The fight which held out prospects best for us and the least risk of life to both sides was guerrilla warfare. We decided, therefore, in our preparations for the future, to make provision for the possibility of guerrilla warfare.

All whites undergo compulsory military training, but no such training was given to Africans. It was in our view essential to build up a nucleus of trained men who would be able to provide the leadership which would be required if guerrilla warfare started. We had to prepare for such a situation before it became too late to make proper preparations. It was also necessary to build up a nucleus of men trained in civil administration and other professions, so that Africans would be equipped to participate in the government of this country as soon as they were allowed to do so.

At this stage it was decided that I should attend the Conference of the Pan-African Freedom Movement for Central, East, and Southern Africa, which was to be held early in 1962 in Addis Ababa, and, because of our need for preparation, it was also decided that, after the conference, I would undertake a tour of the African States with a view to obtaining facilities for the training of soldiers, and that I would also solicit scholarships for the higher education of matriculated Africans. Training in both fields would be necessary, even if changes came about by peaceful means. Administrators would be necessary who would be willing and able to administer a non-racial State and so would men be necessary to control the army and police force of such a State.

It was on this note that I left South Africa to proceed to Addis Ababa as a delegate of the ANC. My tour was a success. Wherever I went I met sympathy for our cause and promises of help. All Africa was united against the stand of White South Africa, and even in London I was received with great sympathy by political leaders, such as Mr. Gaitskell and Mr. Grimond. In Africa I was promised support by such men as Julius Nyerere, now President of Tanganyika; Mr. Kawawa, then Prime Minister of Tanganyika; Emperor Haile Selassie of Ethiopia; General Abboud, President of the Sudan; Habib Bourguiba, President of Tunisia; Ben Bella, now President of Algeria; Modibo Keita, President of Mali; Leopold Senghor, President of Senegal; Sékou Touré, President of Guinea; President Tubman of Liberia; and Milton Obote, Prime Minister of Uganda. It was Ben Bella who invited me to visit Oujda, the Headquarters of the Algerian Army of National Liberation, the visit which is described in my diary, one of the Exhibits.

I started to make a study of the art of war and revolution and, whilst abroad, underwent a course in military training. If there was to be guerrilla warfare, I wanted to be able to stand and fight with my people and to share the hazards of war with them. Notes of lectures which I received in Algeria are contained in Exhibit 16, produced in evidence. Summaries of books on guerrilla warfare and military strategy have also been produced. I have already admitted that these documents are in my writing, and I acknowledge that I made these studies to equip myself for the role which I might have to play if the struggle drifted into guerrilla warfare. I approached this question as every African Nationalist should do. I was completely objective. The Court will see that I attempted to examine all types of authority on the subject—from the East and from the West, going back to the classic work of Clausewitz, and covering such a variety as Mao Tse Tung and Che Guevara on the one hand, and the writings on the Anglo-Boer War on the other. Of course, these notes are merely summaries of the books I read and do not contain my personal views.

I also made arrangements for our recruits to undergo military training. But here it was impossible to organize any scheme without the co-operation of the ANC offices in Africa. I consequently obtained the permission of the ANC in South Africa to do this. To this extent then there was a departure from the original decision of the ANC, but it applied outside South Africa only. The first batch of recruits actually arrived in Tanganyika when I was passing through that country on my way back to South Africa.

I returned to South Africa and reported to my colleagues on the results of my trip. On my return I found that there had been little alteration in the political scene save that the threat of a death penalty for sabotage had now become a fact. The attitude of my colleagues in Umkhonto was much the same as it had been before I left. They were feeling their way cautiously and felt that it would be a long time before the possibilities of sabotage were exhausted. In fact, the view was expressed by some that the training of recruits was premature. This is recorded by me in the document which is Exhibit R.14. After a full discussion, however, it was decided to go ahead with the plans for military training because of the fact that it would take many years to build up a sufficient nucleus of trained soldiers to start a guerrilla campaign, and whatever happened the training would be of value.

I wish to turn now to certain general allegations made in this case by the State. . . .

[One] of the allegations made by the State is that the aims and objects of the ANC and the Communist Party are the same. I wish to deal with this and with my own political position, because I must assume that the State may try to argue from certain Exhibits that I tried to introduce Marxism into the ANC. The allegation as to the ANC is false. This is an old allegation which was disproved at the Treason Trial and which has again reared its head. But since the allegation has been made again, I shall deal with it as well as with the relationship between the ANC and the Communist Party and Umkhonto and that party.

The ideological creed of the ANC is, and always has been, the creed of African Nationalism. It is not the concept of African Nationalism expressed in the cry, 'Drive the White man into the sea'. The African Nationalism for which the ANC stands is the concept of freedom and fulfilment for the African people in their own land. The most important political document ever adopted by the ANC is the 'Freedom Charter'. It is by no means a blueprint for a socialist state. It calls for redistribution, but not nationalization, of land; it provides for nationalization of mines, banks, and monopoly industry, because big monopolies are owned by one race only, and without such nationalization racial domination would be perpetuated despite the spread of political power. It would be a hollow gesture to repeal the Gold Law prohibitions against Africans when all gold mines are owned by European companies. In this respect the ANC's policy corresponds with the old policy of the present Nationalist Party which, for many years, had as part of its programme the nationalization of the gold mines which, at that time, were controlled by foreign capital. Under the Freedom Charter, nationalization would take place in an economy based on private enterprise. The realization of the Freedom Charter would open up fresh fields for a prosperous African population of all classes, including the middle class. The ANC has never at any period of its history advocated a revolutionary change in the economic structure of the country, nor has it, to the best of my recollection, ever condemned capitalist society.

As far as the Communist Party is concerned, and if I understand its policy correctly, it stands for the establishment of a State based on the principles of Marxism. Although it is prepared to work for the Freedom Charter, as a short-term solution to the problems created by white supremacy, it regards the Freedom Charter as the beginning, and not the end, of its programme.

The ANC, unlike the Communist Party, admitted Africans only as members. Its chief goal was, and is, for the African people to win unity and full political rights. The Communist Party's main aim, on the other hand, was to remove the capitalists and to replace them with a working-class government. The Communist Party sought to emphasize class distinctions whilst the ANC seeks to harmonize them. This is a vital distinction.

It is true that there has often been close co-operation between the ANC and the Communist Party. But co-operation is merely proof of a common goal—in this case the removal of white supremacy—and is not proof of a complete community of interests.

The history of the world is full of similar examples. Perhaps the most striking illustration is to be found in the co-operation between Great Britain, the United States of America, and the Soviet Union in the fight against Hitler. Nobody but Hitler would have dared to suggest that such co-operation turned Churchill or Roosevelt into communists or communist tools, or that Britain and America were working to bring about a communist world.

Another instance of such co-operation is to be found precisely in Umkhonto. Shortly after Umkhonto was constituted, I was informed by some of its members that the Communist Party would support Umkhonto, and this then occurred. At a later stage the support was made openly.

I believe that communists have always played an active role in the fight by colonial countries for their freedom, because the short-term objects of communism would always correspond with the long-term objects of freedom movements. Thus communists have played an important role in the freedom struggles fought in countries such as Malaya, Algeria, and Indonesia, yet none of these States today are communist countries. Similarly in the underground resistance movements which sprung up in Europe during the last World War, communists played an important role. Even General Chiang Kai-Shek, today one of the bitterest enemies of communism, fought together with the communists against the ruling class in the struggle which led to his assumption of power in China in the 1930s.

This pattern of co-operation between communists and non-communists has been repeated in the National Liberation Movement of South Africa. Prior to the banning of the Communist Party, joint campaigns involving the Communist Party and the Congress movements were accepted practice. African communists could, and did, become members of the ANC, and some served on the National, Provincial, and local committees. Amongst those who served on the National Executive are Albert Nzula, a former Secretary of the Communist Party; Moses Kotane, another former Secretary; and J. B. Marks, a former member of the Central Committee.

I joined the ANC in 1944, and in my younger days I held the view that the policy of admitting communists to the ANC, and the close co-operation which existed at times on specific issues between the ANC and the Communist Party, would lead to a watering down of the concept of African Nationalism. At that stage I was a member of the African National Congress Youth League, and was one of a group which moved for the expulsion of communists from the ANC. This proposal was heavily defeated. Amongst those who voted against the proposal were some of the most conservative sections of African political opinion. They defended the policy on the ground that from its inception the ANC was formed and built up, not as a political party with one school of political thought, but as a Parliament of the African people, accommodating people of various political convictions, all united by the common goal of national liberation. I was eventually won over to this point of view and I have upheld it ever since.

It is perhaps difficult for white South Africans, with an ingrained prejudice against communism, to understand why experienced African politicians so readily accept communists as their friends. But to us the reason is obvious. Theoretical differences amongst those fighting against oppression is a luxury we cannot afford at this stage. What is more, for many decades communists were the only political group in South Africa who were prepared to treat Africans as human beings and their equals; who were prepared to eat with us; talk with us, live with us, and work with us. They were the only political group which was prepared to work with the Africans for the attainment of political rights and a stake in society. Because of this, there are many Africans who, today, tend to equate freedom with communism. They are supported in this belief by a legislature which brands all exponents of democratic government and African freedom as communists and bans many of them (who are not communists) under the Suppression of Communism Act. Although I have never been a member of the Communist Party, I myself have been named under that pernicious Act because of the role I played in the Defiance Campaign. I have also been banned and imprisoned under that Act.

It is not only in internal politics that we count communists as amongst those who support our cause. In the international field, communist countries have always come to our aid. In the United Nations and other Councils of the world the communist *bloc* has supported the Afro-Asian struggle against colonialism and often seems to be more sympathetic to our plight than some of the Western powers. Although there is a universal condemnation of apartheid, the communist *bloc* speaks out against it with a louder voice than most of the white world. In these circumstances, it would take a brash young politician, such as I was in 1949, to proclaim that the Communists are our enemies.

I turn now to my own position. I have denied that I am a communist, and I think that in the circumstances I am obliged to state exactly what my political beliefs are.

I have always regarded myself, in the first place, as an African patriot. After all, I was born in Umtata, forty-six years ago. My guardian was my cousin, who was the acting paramount chief of Tembuland, and I am related both to the present paramount chief of Tembuland, Sabata Dalindyebo, and to Kaizer Matanzima, the Chief Minister of the Transkei.

Today I am attracted by the idea of a classless society, an attraction which springs in part from Marxist reading and, in part, from my admiration of the structure and organization of early African societies in this country. The land, then the main means of production, belonged to the tribe. There were no rich or poor and there was no exploitation.

It is true, as I have already stated, that I have been influenced by Marxist thought. But this is also true of many of the leaders of the new independent States. Such widely different persons as Gandhi, Nehru, Nkrumah, and Nasser all acknowledge this fact. We all accept the need for some form of socialism to enable our people to catch up with the advanced countries of this world and to overcome their legacy of extreme poverty. But this does not mean we are Marxists.

Indeed, for my own part, I believe that it is open to debate whether the Communist Party has any specific role to play at this particular stage of our political struggle. The basic task at the present moment is the removal of race discrimination and the attainment of democratic rights on the basis of the Freedom Charter. In so far as that Party furthers this task, I welcome its assistance. I realize that it is one of the means by which people of all races can be drawn into our struggle.

From my reading of Marxist literature and from conversations with Marxists, I have gained the impression that communists regard the parliamentary system of the West as undemocratic and reactionary. But, on the contrary, I am an admirer of such a system.

The Magna Charta, the Petition of Rights, and the Bill of Rights are documents which are held in veneration by democrats throughout the world.

I have great respect for British political institutions, and for the country's system of justice. I regard the British Parliament as the most democratic institution in the world, and the independence and impartiality of its judiciary never fail to arouse my admiration.

The American Congress, that country's doctrine of separation of powers, as well as the independence of its judiciary, arouses in me similar sentiments.

I have been influenced in my thinking by both West and East. All this has led me to feel that in my search for a political formula, I should be absolutely impartial and objective. I should tie myself to no particular system of society other than of socialism. I must leave myself free to borrow the best from the West and from the East. . . .

There are certain Exhibits which suggest that we received financial support from abroad, and I wish to deal with this question.

Our political struggle has always been financed from internal sources—from funds raised by our own people and by our own supporters. Whenever we had a special campaign or an important political case—for example, the Treason Trial—we received financial assistance from sympathetic individuals and organizations in the Western countries. We had never felt it necessary to go beyond these sources.

But when in 1961 the Umkhonto was formed, and a new phase of struggle introduced, we realized that these events would make a heavy call on our slender resources, and that the scale of our activities would be hampered by the lack of funds. One of my instructions, as I went abroad in January 1962, was to raise funds from the African states.

I must add that, whilst abroad, I had discussions with leaders of political movements in Africa and discovered that almost every single one of them, in areas which had still not attained independence, had received all forms of assistance from the socialist countries, as well as from the West, including that of financial support. I also discovered that some well-known African states, all of them non-communists, and even anti-communists, had received similar assistance.

On my return to the Republic, I made a strong recommendation to the ANC that we should not confine ourselves to Africa and the Western countries, but that we should also send a mission to the socialist countries to raise the funds which we so urgently needed.

I have been told that after I was convicted such a mission was sent, but I am not prepared to name any countries to which it went, nor am I at liberty to disclose the names of the organizations and countries which gave us support or promised to do so.

As I understand the State case, and in particular the evidence of 'Mr. X', the suggestion is that Umkhonto was the inspiration of the Communist Party which sought by playing upon imaginary grievances to enrol the African people into an army which ostensibly was to fight for African freedom, but in reality was fighting for a communist state. Nothing could be further from the truth. In fact the suggestion is preposterous. Umkhonto was formed by Africans to further their struggle for freedom in their own land. Communists and others supported the movement, and we only wish that more sections of the community would join us.

Our fight is against real, and not imaginary, hardships or, to use the language of the State Prosecutor, 'so-called hardships'. Basically, we fight against two features which are the hallmarks of African life in South Africa and which are entrenched by legislation which we seek to have repealed. These features are poverty and lack of human dignity, and we do not need communists or so-called 'agitators' to teach us about these things.

South Africa is the richest country in Africa, and could be one of the richest countries in the world. But it is a land of extremes and remarkable contrasts. The whites enjoy what may well be the highest standard of living in the world, whilst Africans live in poverty and misery. Forty per cent of the Africans live in hopelessly overcrowded and, in some cases, drought-stricken Reserves, where soil erosion and the overworking of the soil makes it impossible for them to live properly off the land. Thirty per cent are labourers, labour tenants, and squatters on white farms and work and live under conditions similar to those of the serfs of the Middle Ages. The other 30 per cent live in towns where they have developed economic and social habits which bring them closer in many respects to white standards. Yet most Africans, even in this group, are impoverished by low incomes and high cost of living.

The highest-paid and the most prosperous section of urban African life is in Johannesburg. Yet their actual position is desperate. The latest figures were given on 25 March 1964 by Mr. Carr, Manager of the Johannesburg Non-European Affairs Department. The poverty datum line for the average African family in Johannesburg (according to Mr. Carr's department) is R42.84 per month. He showed that the average monthly wage is R32.24 and that 46 per cent of all African families in Johannesburg do not earn enough to keep them going.

Poverty goes hand in hand with malnutrition and disease. The incidence of malnutrition and deficiency diseases is very high amongst Africans. Tuberculosis, pellagra, kwashiorkor, gastro-enteritis, and scurvy bring death and destruction of health. The incidence of infant mortality is one of the highest in the world. According to the Medical Officer of Health for Pretoria, tuberculosis kills forty people a day (almost all Africans), and in 1961 there were 58,491 new cases reported. These diseases not only destroy the vital organs of the body, but they result in retarded mental conditions and lack of initiative, and reduce powers of concentration. The secondary results of such conditions affect the whole community and the standard of work performed by African labourers.

The complaint of Africans, however, is not only that they are poor and the whites are rich, but that the laws which are made by the whites are designed to preserve this situation. There are two ways to break out of poverty. The first is by formal education, and the second is by the worker acquiring a greater skill at his work and thus higher wages. As far as Africans are concerned, both these avenues of advancement are deliberately curtailed by legislation.

The present Government has always sought to hamper Africans in their search for education. One of their early acts, after coming into power, was to stop subsidies for African school feeding. Many African children who attended schools depended on this supplement to their diet. This was a cruel act.

There is compulsory education for all white children at virtually no cost to their parents, be they rich or poor. Similar facilities are not provided for the African children, though there are some who receive such assistance. African children, however, generally have to pay more for their schooling than whites. According to figures quoted by the South African Institute of Race Relations in its 1963 journal, approximately 40 per cent of African children in the age group between seven to fourteen do not attend school. For those who do attend school, the standards are vastly different from those afforded to white children. In 1960–61 the *per capita* Government spending on African students at State-aided schools was estimated at R12.46. In the same years, the *per capita* spending on white children in the Cape Province (which are the only figures available to me) was R144.57. Although there are no figures available to me, it can be stated, without doubt, that the white children on whom R144.57 per head was being spent all came from wealthier homes than African children on whom R12.46 per head was being spent.

The quality of education is also different. According to the Bantu Educational Journal, only 5,660 African children in the whole of South Africa passed their Junior Certificate in 1962, and in that year only 362 passed matric.[5] This is presumably consistent with the policy of Bantu education about which the present Prime Minister said, during the debate on the Bantu Education Bill in 1953:

> When I have control of Native education I will reform it so that Natives will be taught from childhood to realize that equality with Europeans is not for them. . . . People who believe in equality are not desirable teachers for Natives. When my Department controls Native education it will know for what class of higher education a Native is fitted, and whether he will have a chance in life to use his knowledge.

The other main obstacle to the economic advancement of the African is the industrial colour-bar under which all the better jobs of industry are reserved for Whites only. Moreover, Africans who do obtain employment in the unskilled and semi-skilled occupations which are open to them are not allowed to form trade unions which have recognition under the Industrial Conciliation Act. This means that strikes of African workers are illegal, and that they are denied the right of collective bargaining which is permitted to the better-paid White workers. The discrimination in the policy of successive South African Governments towards African workers is demonstrated by the so-called 'civilized labour policy' under which sheltered, unskilled Government jobs are found for those white workers who cannot make the grade in industry, at wages which far exceed the earnings of the average African employee in industry.

The Government often answers its critics by saying that Africans in South Africa are economically better off than the inhabitants of the other countries in Africa. I do not know whether this statement is true and doubt whether any comparison can be made without having regard to the cost-of-living index in such countries. But even if it is true, as far as the African people are concerned it is irrelevant.

[5]The Junior Certificate examination was generally taken by white children at the age of 15, and they cannot normally leave school before this. Matriculation is taken two years later and qualifies students for higher education. The educational system, however, ensures that very few Africans reach Junior Certificate level, so that what represents a basic standard for whites is one of achievement for Africans. Even fewer attain matriculation level.

Our complaint is not that we are poor by comparison with people in other countries, but that we are poor by comparison with the white people in our own country, and that we are prevented by legislation from altering this imbalance.

The lack of human dignity experienced by Africans is the direct result of the policy of white supremacy. White supremacy implies black inferiority. Legislation designed to preserve white supremacy entrenches this notion. Menial tasks in South Africa are invariably performed by Africans. When anything has to be carried or cleaned the white man will look around for an African to do it for him, whether the African is employed by him or not. Because of this sort of attitude, whites tend to regard Africans as a separate breed. They do not look upon them as people with families of their own; they do not realize that they have emotions—that they fall in love like white people do; that they want to be with their wives and children like white people want to be with theirs; that they want to earn enough money to support their families properly, to feed and clothe them and send them to school. And what 'house-boy' or 'garden-boy' or labourer can ever hope to do this?

Pass laws, which to the Africans are among the most hated bits of legislation in South Africa, render any African liable to police surveillance at any time. I doubt whether there is a single African male in South Africa who has not at some stage had a brush with the police over his pass. Hundreds and thousands of Africans are thrown into jail each year under pass laws. Even worse than this is the fact that pass laws keep husband and wife apart and lead to the breakdown of family life.

Poverty and the breakdown of family life have secondary effects. Children wander about the streets of the townships because they have no schools to go to, or no money to enable them to go to school, or no parents at home to see that they go to school, because both parents (if there be two) have to work to keep the family alive. This leads to a breakdown in moral standards, to an alarming rise in illegitimacy, and to growing violence which erupts not only politically, but everywhere. Life in the townships is dangerous. There is not a day that goes by without somebody being stabbed or assaulted. And violence is carried out of the townships in the white living areas. People are afraid to walk alone in the streets after dark. Housebreakings and robberies are increasing, despite the fact that the death sentence can now be imposed for such offences. Death sentences cannot cure the festering sore.

Africans want to be paid a living wage. Africans want to perform work which they are capable of doing, and not work which the Government declares them to be capable of. Africans want to be allowed to live where they obtain work, and not be endorsed out of an area because they were not born there. Africans want to be allowed to own land in places where they work, and not to be obliged to live in rented houses which they can never call their own. Africans want to be part of the general population, and not confined to living in their own ghettoes. African men want to have their wives and children to live with them where they work, and not be forced into an unnatural existence in men's hostels. African women want to be with their menfolk and not be left permanently widowed in the Reserves. Africans want to be allowed out after eleven o'clock at night and not to be confined to their rooms like little children. Africans want to be allowed to travel in their own country and to seek work where they want to and not where the Labour Bureau tells them to.

Africans want a just share in the whole of South Africa; they want security and a stake in society.

Above all, we want equal political rights, because without them our disabilities will be permanent. I know this sounds revolutionary to the whites in this country, because the majority of voters will be Africans. This makes the white man fear democracy.

But this fear cannot be allowed to stand in the way of the only solution which will guarantee racial harmony and freedom for all. It is not true that the enfranchisement of all will result in racial domination. Political division, based on colour, is entirely artificial and, when it disappears, so will the domination of one colour group by another. The ANC has spent half a century fighting against racialism. When it triumphs it will not change that policy.

This then is what the ANC is fighting. Their struggle is a truly national one. It is a struggle of the African people, inspired by their own suffering and their own experience. It is a struggle for the right to live.

During my lifetime I have dedicated myself to this struggle of the African people. I have fought against white domination, and I have fought against black domination. I have cherished the ideal of a democratic and free society in which all persons live together in harmony and with equal opportunities. It is an ideal which I hope to live for and to achieve. But if needs be, it is an ideal for which I am prepared to die.

On 11 June 1964, at the conclusion of the trial, Mandela and seven others—Walter Sisulu, Govan Mbeki, Raymond Mhlaba, Elias Motsoaledi, Andrew Mlangeni, Ahmed Kathrada and Denis Goldberg—were convicted. Mandela was found guilty on four charges of sabotage and, like the others, was sentenced to life imprisonment.

QUESTIONS FOR DISCUSSION

1. Nelson Mandela's piece was also written in jail. Look at the style, purpose, and audience. How are these different from King's (p. 272)?
2. Why did the African National Congress (ANC), after using nonviolent methods, choose violent protest?
3. What types of violence does Mandela list? Which did the ANC choose and why?
4. What is the ideology of the ANC? What does the South African government claim about it? How can it cooperate with the communists in South Africa and yet not be communist? How did Mandela's views on communism change?
5. Compare the social and political conditions of Mandela and King. How might this account for their different means to achieve similar ends?

PART 3

Art and Literature

I n some respects it is misleading to have a separate part of this book titled "Art and Literature," for, as the following selections illustrate, art is a result of humans responding to their societies, and these responses are very often not only "artistic," but political, religious, or scientific, as well. A political poem or story, such as "The United Fruit Co." or "The Master of Doornvlei," can be as powerful as a political essay; and people often have found that they can best express their religious feelings in the figurative language of poetry, as Rabindranath Tagore does in "The Evermoving." This part includes essays that emphasize the vast range of theories, uses, and forms of art across cultures, as well as poems and short stories that exemplify the universal qualities of art and the human emotions that art embodies. The artists represented in this part (all highly respected both in their own cultures and around the world) provide a sampling of art's endless possibilities.

The texts in the definition section of this part, "What Use Is Art" from a Royal Bank of Canada Newsletter, "The Cultural Importance of the Arts" by Susanne K. Langer, and "Tlilli, Tlapalli: The Path of the Red and Black Ink" by Gloria Anzaldúa, encourage us to begin thinking carefully about the role of art in life. The author of "What Use Is Art" explains how art "raises [our] minds"; it gives us a degree of control over life, helps us "subdue its turbulence." By sharing for even a brief moment the vision and emotions of another person, our own lives can be enriched and expanded. In her essay "The Cultural Importance of the Arts," Susanne K. Langer makes the similar claim that art nourishes the imagination, which she feels to be "the source of all insight and true beliefs." Through the experience of art we give form to our emotions and feelings, and only by doing this can we begin to understand them. Gloria Anzaldúa writes of life on the U.S.–Mexican border, a place where Anglo, Mexican, and Indian cultures meet. In "Tlilli, Tlapalli" she describes how art, in this case storytelling, is intrinsic to her culture and to her own life.

The next section examines the role of art in a number of different societies. E. H. Gombrich's "Art for Eternity" is a detailed study of the art of ancient Egypt. Ananda K. Coomaraswamy compares the theories of art of India and the West, and Hermann List, in "Chinese Painting," explains how Chinese religion and philosophy are reflected in the art of China. The often subtle, yet very real connections between art and politics are illustrated in two pieces on Russian art, the first by J. P. Hodin, which reflects the official "party line" attitude toward art in the Stalinist era, and the second by Sylvia Hochfield, which discusses the rapidly evolving status of art and the artist in contemporary Soviet society. In "Traditional Arts of Black Africa," Roy Sieber describes some distinguishing characteristics of African art and emphasizes its sophistication. Philip Rawson discusses the significance of calligraphy to the Islamic religion.

The next section of this part includes a wide range of literary texts from a wide variety of cultures. Yet the emotions these artists express, the themes that pervade their works, are not divided by cultural boundaries. Rather, here we find similarities of theme, symbol, and form that go deeper than the division and diversity that sometimes obscure our vision.

The first five works in this part explore the definition and value of art from the artist's point of view. Jon Stallworthy's "Letter to a Friend" is a poem about the "proper" subject matter of poetry, in which he explains and defends his own poetic themes. Archibald MacLeish's famous "Ars Poetica" uses a series of masterful symbols and images to define an ideal poetry. In his poem of the same title, Javier Heraud celebrates the artistry of the poet and the power of poetry. The two "Ars Poeticas" offer an interesting opportunity for comparison of subject matter and theme. Marianne Moore's "Poetry," with its startling first line, goes on to examine what it is that makes poetry genuine and important; and Alice Walker honors the legacy of her forebears, a creative spirit that could not be destroyed, even by the horrors of slavery.

Throughout history poets often have acted as the voice of the oppressed, and the next group of poems in this part is unified by the theme of struggle against oppression. Wole Soyinka's "Chimes of Silence" chronicles the terrors of political imprisonment; Pablo Neruda, in "The United Fruit Co.," deplores the treatment of his people and country by foreign investors and the "dictatorship of flies" they engender. In "We Wear the Mask" Paul Laurence Dunbar laments the oppression and exploitation of his people; in much the same way, Ezekiel Mphahlele's short story "The Master of Doornvlei" explores the evil and injustice of South Africa's system of apartheid, and Ellen Wright Prendergast's "Famous Are the Flowers" protests the domination of one culture or society over another. Anthony Hecht's chilling portrayal of a representative event from the Holocaust, Muriel Rukeyser's excerpt from "Letter to the Front," and William Butler Yeats's account of the "Easter 1916" rebellion in Dublin, Ireland, illustrate the struggle of people, although not always successful, to overcome injustice and oppression. A less violent, but perhaps no less destructive form of oppression, is examined in W. H. Auden's "The Unknown Citizen"; but the section concludes with "The People, Yes," Carl Sandburg's admiring appraisal of humanity, of the people who have faced so much adversity and yet continue to press on.

The next group of selections, each touching in some way on the subject of science, illustrates the frequently uneasy relation between art and science. "Men of Science Say Their Say," a second selection by Carl Sandburg, echoes the themes of "The People, Yes." Morris Bishop's "$E = mc^2$" offers a humorous look at the layman's [our's?] often unquestioning acceptance of scientific "facts"; and "A Poem About Intelligence for My Brothers and Sisters," by June Jordan, examines the popular conception of intelligence and some of the consequences of this definition for African-Americans. In the dreamlike "Buffalo," Barry Lopez examines the white man's destruction of the world of the Native American and the buffalo in the mid-1800s; at the same time, he compares the Western scientific world view to the Indians' visionary, mythological understanding of reality.

The next group of poems and chapters from novels revolves around the themes of gender and sexual inequality. Marzieh Ahmadi Oskooii, in "I'm a Woman," seeks to break free of the traditional, limiting definition of "woman." Yu Hsüan-chi, too, laments the fact that in her society many paths were forbidden to females. Sor Juana Inés de la Cruz and Maxine Hong Kingston criticize their respective cultures for manipulating women and forcing them into the role of second-class citizens. Yet despite the hardships female artists have faced throughout history, their accomplishments remain extraordinary. Sappho was one of the most highly praised and respected poets of the ancient Western world. Her invocation to Aphrodite exemplifies the ancient belief that art is a link between the earthly world and the realm of the gods. "Lavender," from Murasaki Shikibu's *Tale of Genji*, details the life of the nobility of Heian Japan. Although the women of *Genji's* Japan are clearly socially inferior to the men, Murasaki Shikibu herself was a literary genius who created a masterpiece, considered by many to be the world's first novel.

Poetry, with its endless capacity for allusion and symbol, is also unsurpassed as a means of religious expression, as demonstrated in the final group of selections. Rabindranath Tagore, the great Indian poet and spiritualist, exposes the bigotry and violence that are fed by "False Religion" and, in "The Evermoving," offers a spiritual vision of peace, serenity, and unity. In "The Brahmin's Son," an excerpt from Hermann Hesse's *Siddhartha*, the young Siddhartha sets out on a religious quest for the answers to the most profound questions of human life. As he describes Siddhartha's search for meaning, Hesse, like Tagore, explores some of the great themes of Eastern religion.

The hope, the anger, the visions expressed by all of these artists are human, as much as they are Iranian, African, or Japanese or political, scientific, or spiritual; and it is very often here, in art, that we can see how the diverse cultures of our world are truly interconnected.

ROYAL BANK OF CANADA NEWSLETTER
What Use Is Art?

Many people think of art as something that is useless and difficult to understand, something only "artistic types" can really enjoy. But "What Use Is Art?" discusses some of the ways art can help each of us enjoy the human experience more fully. The author claims that understanding and appreciating art gives us the opportunity to rise above everyday life; to experience the world from many perspectives instead of just one; and to become more complex, more complete, and perhaps even more satisfied human beings.

Some people will say that art is real when it shows sound knowledge, mastered craft, vivid imagination, strong common sense, truth, and wise meaning. Others will say that the distinguishing characteristic of a work of art is that it serves no practical end, but is an end in itself. The human test of worth is: does it give pleasure? To arouse the powers of enjoyment, of yielding to beauty, is the legitimate end of art.

Tolstoy said in his essay on art: "Art is a human activity consisting in this, that one man consciously, by means of certain external signs, hands on to others feelings he has lived through, and that others are infected by these feelings and also experience them." If one does not feel deeply stirred in the presence of great pictures, great sculpture or great music, he can be certain that he is living a vastly lower and more restricted life than he could be living. The mechanical world is of our own making, but the real world is one of deep emotional experience.

The term "Fine Arts" is conventionally used to designate those arts which are concerned with line, colour and form (painting, sculpture and architecture); with sound (music) and with the exploitation of words for both their musical and expressive values (prose and poetry). Architecture, sculpture, painting, music and poetry are by common consent the five principal or greater fine arts.

Fine art addresses itself not only to the eye but also to the imagination. The eye takes notice of ten different qualities of objects: light and darkness, colour and substance, form and position, distance and nearness, movement and rest. It is through his depiction of these in his work that the artist reaches our minds and animates our thoughts.

Art changes its outlook, just as so many other parts of life do. It is the expression of an age, perhaps even a revolt against the civilization of the age. One generation despises what its predecessor applauded, yet it would be a great mistake to suppose that the latest is always the best.

We should not approach our adventure into art without some preparation. The acuteness of our perception and of our judgment depends on the wealth of our knowledge. The more comparisons we are able to make, the more qualified we are to enjoy art and to express our opinions.

In addition to being open-minded when appraising art, you need to be independent. "To know what you prefer," said Robert Louis Stevenson, "instead of humbly saying 'Amen' to what the world tells you you ought to prefer, is to have kept your soul alive."

Appreciation of an art releases us from our claustrophobia and gives us a wider outlook. It helps us to rise above life's trivialities and to subdue its turbulence. Its purpose is not to help us escape from life but to enter into a larger life.

Art is useful because it raises men's minds to a level higher than merely existing. Here are activities that men and women put forth not because they need but because they like. In an age when material things have such prominence and such a deep influence on people's minds, it is increasingly important to be able to seek the relief to be found in aesthetic activity. It releases us from the arbitrariness of life.

QUESTIONS FOR DISCUSSION

1. What are the purpose and the audience for this piece?
2. Look at the definition of art given. How does it differ from Tolstoy's definition?
3. Outline the argument for the usefulness of art. Do you agree that art is useful? Why or why not?
4. According to the definition given here, is T.V. art? Movies? Tattoos? Jewelry?
5. Do you agree that you need to know a lot about art in order to enjoy it?

SUSANNE K. LANGER
The Cultural Importance of the Arts

Susanne K. Langer (1895–1985) was educated at Radcliffe and Harvard universities and the University of Vienna (where her husband, William, also studied). During her long career as philosopher and teacher she taught at such institutions as Columbia University, Connecticut College, Northwestern University, Ohio University, the University of Washington, and the University of Michigan. She wrote extensively on linguistic analysis and on aesthetics. Her best-known work, Philosophy in a New Key: A Study in the Symbolism of Reason, Rite and Art *(1942), argues that art is a form of expression that symbolizes intuitive knowledge of certain feelings or emotions which language by itself cannot express; an accomplished cellist, she was particularly interested in music as such a form of expression. In this essay, which was first given as a lecture in 1958, Langer defines art and explains her view of its importance. Because art can give us insight into our feelings in a way that logic and reason cannot, those societies in which art flourishes tend to develop vital and creative ways of understanding this inward experience. This, Langer states, "is the beginning of a cultural age."*

Every culture develops some kind of art as surely as it develops language. Some primitive cultures have no real mythology or religion, but all have some art—dance, song, design (sometimes only on tools or on the human body). Dance, above all, seems to be the oldest elaborated art.

The ancient ubiquitous character of art contrasts sharply with the prevalent idea that art is a luxury product of civilization, a cultural frill, a piece of social veneer.

It fits better with the conviction held by most artists, that art is the epitome of human life, the truest record of insight and feeling, and that the strongest military or economic society without art is poor in comparison with the most primitive tribe of savage painters, dancers, or idol-carvers. Wherever a society has really achieved culture (in the ethnological sense, not the popular sense of "social form") it has begotten art, not late in its career, but at the very inception of it.

Art is, indeed, the spearhead of human development, social and individual. The vulgarization of art is the surest symptom of ethnic decline. The growth of a new art or even a great and radically new style always bespeaks a young and vigorous mind, whether collective or single.

What sort of thing is art, that it should play such a leading role in human development? It is not an intellectual pursuit, but is necessary to intellectual life; it is not religion, but grows up with religion, serves it and in large measure determines it.

We cannot enter here on a long discussion of what has been claimed as the essence of art, the true nature of art, or its defining function; in a single lecture dealing with one aspect of art, namely its cultural influence, I can only give you by way of preamble my own definition of art, with categorical brevity. This does not mean that I set up this definition in a categorical spirit, but only that we have no time to debate it, so you are asked to accept it as an assumption underlying these reflections.

Art, in the sense here intended—that is, the generic term subsuming painting, sculpture, architecture, music, dance, literature, drama, and film—may be defined as the practice of creating perceptible forms expressive of human feeling. I say "perceptible" rather than "sensuous" forms because some works of art are given to imagination rather than to the outward senses. A novel, for instance, usually is read silently with the eye, but is not made for vision, as a painting is; and though sound plays a vital part in poetry, words even in poetry are not essentially sonorous structures like music. Dance requires to be seen, but its appeal is to deeper centers of sensation. The difference between dance and mobile sculpture makes this immediately apparent. But all works of art are purely perceptible forms that seem to embody some sort of feeling.

"Feeling" as I am using it here covers much more than it does in the technical vocabulary of psychology, where it denotes only pleasure and pain, or even in the shifting limits of ordinary discourse, where it sometimes means sensation (as when one says a paralyzed limb has no feeling in it), sometimes sensibility (as we speak of hurting someone's feelings), sometimes emotion (e.g., as a situation is said to harrow your feelings, or to evoke tender feeling), or a directed emotional attitude (we say we feel strongly *about* something), or even our general mental or physical condition, feeling well or ill, blue, or a bit above ourselves. As I use the word, in defining art as the creation of perceptible forms expressive of human feeling, it takes in all those meanings; it applies to everything that may be felt.

Another word in the definition that might be questioned is "creation." I think it is justified, not pretentious, as perhaps it sounds; but that issue is slightly beside the point here, so let us shelve it. If anyone prefers to speak of the "making" or "construction" of expressive forms that will do here just as well.

What does have to be understood is the meaning of "form," and more particularly "expressive form"; for that involves the very nature of art and therefore the question of its cultural importance.

The word "form" has several current uses; most of them have some relation to the sense in which I am using it here, though a few, such as: "a form to be filled in for tax purposes" or "a mere matter of form" are fairly remote, being quite specialized. Since we are speaking of art, it might be good to point out that the meaning of stylistic pattern—"the sonata form," "the sonnet form"—is not the one I am assuming here.

I am using the word in a simpler sense, which it has when you say, on a foggy night, that you see dimly moving forms in the mist; one of them emerges clearly, and is the form of a man. The trees are gigantic forms; the rills of rain trace sinuous forms on the window pane. The rills are not fixed things; they are forms of motion. When you watch gnats weaving in the air, or flocks of birds wheeling overhead, you see dynamic forms—forms made by motion.

It is in this sense of an apparition given to our perception, that a work of art is a form. It may be a permanent form like a building or a vase or a picture, or a transient, dynamic form like a melody or a dance, or even a form given to imagination, like the passage of purely imaginary, apparent events that constitutes a literary work. But it is always a perceptible, self-identical whole; like a natural being, it has a character of organic unity, self-sufficiency, individual reality. And it is thus, as an appearance, that a work of art is good or bad or perhaps only rather poor; as an appearance, not as a comment on things beyond it in the world, nor as a reminder of them.

This, then, is what I mean by "form"; but what is meant by calling such forms "expressive of human feeling"? How do apparitions "express" anything—feeling or anything else? First of all, let us ask just what is meant here by "express"; what sort of "expression" we are talking about.

The word "expression" has two principal meanings: in one sense it means self-expression—giving vent to our feelings. In this sense it refers to a symptom of what we feel. Self-expression is a spontaneous reaction to an actual, present situation, an event, the company we are in, things people say, or what the weather does to us; it bespeaks the physical and mental state we are in and the emotions that stir us.

In another sense, however, "expression" means the presentation of an idea, usually by the proper and apt use of words. But a device for presenting an idea is what we call a symbol, not a symptom. Thus a word is a symbol, and so is a meaningful combination of words.

A sentence, which is a special combination of words, expresses the idea of some state of affairs, real or imagined. Sentences are complicated symbols. Language will formulate new ideas as well as communicate old ones, so that all people know a lot of things that they have merely heard or read about. Symbolic expression, therefore, extends our knowledge beyond the scope of our actual experience.

If an idea is clearly conveyed by means of symbols we say it is well expressed. A person may work for a long time to give his statement the best possible form, to find the exact words for what he means to say, and to carry his account or his argument most directly from one point to another. But a discourse so worked out is certainly not a spontaneous reaction. Giving expression to an idea is obviously a different thing from giving expression to feelings. You do not say of a man in a rage that his anger is well expressed. The symptoms just are what they are, there is no critical standard for symptoms. If, on the other hand, the angry man tries to tell you what he is fuming about, he will have to collect himself, curtail his emotional expression, and find words to express his ideas. For to tell a story coherently involves "expression" in quite a different sense: this sort of expression is not "self-expression," but may be called "conceptual expression."

Language, of course, is our prime instrument of conceptual expression. The things we can say are in effect the things we can think. Words are the terms of our thinking as well as the terms in which we present our thoughts, because they present the objects of thought to the thinker himself. Before language communicates ideas, it gives them form, makes them clear, and in fact makes them what they are. Whatever has a name is an object for thought. Without words, sense experience is only a flow of impressions, as subjective as our feelings; words make it objective, and carve it up into *things* and *facts* that we can note, remember, and think about. Language gives outward experience its form, and makes it definite and clear.

There is, however, an important part of reality that is quite inaccessible to the formative influence of language: that is the realm of so-called "inner experience," the life of feeling and emotion. The reason why language is so powerless here is not, as many people suppose, that feeling and emotion are irrational; on the contrary, they seem irrational because language does not help to make them conceivable, and most people cannot conceive anything without the logical scaffolding of words. The unfitness of language to convey subjective experience is a somewhat technical subject, easier for logicians to understand than for artists; but the gist of it is that the form of language does not reflect the natural form of feeling, so we cannot shape any extensive concepts of feeling with the help of ordinary, discursive language. Therefore the words whereby we refer to feeling only name very general kinds of inner experience—excitement, calm, joy, sorrow, love, hate, etc. But there is no language to describe just how one joy differs, sometimes radically, from another. The real nature of feeling is something language as such—as discursive symbolism—cannot render.

For this reason, the phenomena of feeling and emotion are usually treated by philosophers as irrational. The only pattern discursive thought can find in them is the pattern of outward events that occasion them. There are different degrees of fear, but they are thought of as so many degrees of the same simple feeling.

But human feeling is a fabric, not a vague mass. It has an intricate dynamic pattern, possible combinations and new emergent phenomena. It is a pattern of organically interdependent and interdetermined tensions and resolutions; a pattern of almost infinitely complex activation and cadence. To it belongs the whole gamut of our sensibility, the sense of straining thought, all mental attitude and motor set. Those are the deeper reaches that underlie the surface waves of our emotion, and make human life a life of feeling instead of an unconscious metabolic existence interrupted by feelings.

It is, I think, this dynamic pattern that finds its formal expression in the arts. The expressiveness of art is like that of a symbol, not that of an emotional symptom; it is as a formulation of feeling for our conception that a work of art is properly said to be expressive. It may serve somebody's need of self-expression besides; but that is not what makes it good or bad art. In a special sense one may call a work of art a symbol of feeling, for, like a symbol, it formulates our ideas of inward experience, as discourse formulates our ideas of things and facts in the outside world. A work of art differs from a genuine symbol—that is, a symbol in the full and usual sense—in that it does not point beyond itself to something else. Its relation to feeling is a rather special one that we cannot undertake to analyze here; in effect, the feeling it expresses appears to be directly given with it—as the sense of a true metaphor, or the value of a religious myth—and is not separable from its expression. We speak of the feeling *of*, or the feeling *in*, a work of art, not the feeling it means. And we speak truly; a work of art presents something like a direct vision of vitality, emotion, subjective reality.

The primary function of art is to objectify feeling so we can contemplate and understand it. It is the formulation of so-called "inward experience," the "inner life," that is impossible to achieve by discursive thought, because its forms are incommensurable with the forms of language and all its derivatives (e.g., mathematics, symbolic logic). Art objectifies the sentience and desire, self-consciousness and world-consciousness, emotions and moods that are generally regarded as irrational because words cannot give us clear ideas of them. But the premise tacitly assumed in such a judgment—namely, that anything language cannot express is formless and irrational—seems to me to be an error. I believe the life of feeling is not irrational; its logical forms are merely very different from the structures of discourse. But they are so much like the dynamic forms of art that art is their natural symbol. Through plastic works, music, fiction, dance, or dramatic forms we can conceive what vitality and emotion feel like.

This brings us, at last, to the question of the cultural importance of the arts. Why is art so apt to be the vanguard of cultural advance, as it was in Egypt, in Greece, in Christian Europe (think of Gregorian music and Gothic architecture), in Renaissance Italy—not to speculate about ancient cavemen, whose art is all that we know of them? One thinks of culture as economic increase, social organization, the gradual ascendancy of rational thinking and scientific control of nature over superstitious imagination and magical practices. But art is not practical; it is neither philosophy nor science; it is not religion, morality, nor even social comment (as many drama critics take comedy to be). What does it contribute to culture that could be of major importance?

It merely presents forms—sometimes intangible forms—to imagination. Its direct appeal is to that faculty, or function, that Lord Bacon considered the chief stumbling block in the way of reason, that enlightened writers like Stuart Chase never tire of condemning as the source of all nonsense and bizarre erroneous beliefs. And so it is; but it is also the source of all insight and true beliefs. Imagination is probably the oldest mental trait that is typically human—older than discursive reason; it is probably the common source of dream, reason, religion, and all true general observation. It is this primitive human power—imagination—that engenders the arts and is in turn directly affected by their products.

Somewhere at the animalian starting line of human evolution lie the beginnings of that supreme instrument of the mind—language. We think of it as a device for communication among the members of a society. But communication is only one, and perhaps not even the first, of its functions. The first thing it does is to break up what William James called the "blooming, buzzing confusion" of sense perception into units and groups, events and chains of events—things and relations, causes and effects. All these patterns are imposed on our experience by language. We think, as we speak, in terms of objects and their relations.

But the process of breaking up our sense experience in this way, making reality conceivable, memorable, sometimes even predictable, is a process of imagination. Primitive conception is imagination. Language and imagination grow up together in a reciprocal tutelage.

What discursive symbolism—language in its literal use—does for our awareness of things about us and our own relation to them, the arts do for our awareness of subjective reality, feeling and emotion; they give form to inward experiences and thus make them conceivable. The only way we can really envisage vital movement, the stirring and growth and passage of emotion, and ultimately the whole direct sense of human life, is in artistic terms. A musical person thinks of emotions musically. They cannot be discursively talked about above a very general level. But they may nonetheless be known—objectively set forth, publicly known—and there is nothing necessarily confused or formless about emotions.

As soon as the natural forms of subjective experience are abstracted to the point of symbolic presentation, we can use those forms to imagine feeling and understand its nature. Self-knowledge, insight into all phases of life and mind, springs from artistic imagination. That is the cognitive value of the arts.

But their influence on human life goes deeper than the intellectual level. As language actually gives form to our sense-experience, grouping our impressions around those things which have names, and fitting sensations to the qualities that have adjectival names, and so on, the arts we live with—our picture books and stories and the music we hear—actually form our emotive experience. Every generation has its styles of feeling. One age shudders and blushes and faints, another swaggers, still another is godlike in a universal indifference. These styles in actual emotion are not insincere. They are largely unconscious—determined by many social causes, but *shaped* by artists, usually popular artists of the screen, the juke-box, the shop window, and the picture magazine. (That, rather than incitement to crime, is my objection to the comics.) Irwin Edman remarks in one of his books that our emotions are largely Shakespeare's poetry.

This influence of art on life gives us an indication why a period of efflorescence in the arts is apt to lead a cultural advance: it formulates a new way of feeling, and that is the beginning of a cultural age. It suggests another matter for reflection, too: that a wide neglect of artistic education is a neglect in the education of feeling. Most people are so imbued with the idea that feeling is a formless total organic excitement in men as in animals, that the idea of educating feeling, developing its scope and quality, seems odd to them, if not absurd. It is really, I think, at the very heart of personal education.

There is one other function of the arts that benefits not so much the advance of culture as its stabilization; an influence on individual lives. This function is the converse and complement of the objectification of feeling, the driving force of creation in art: it is the education of vision that we receive in seeing, hearing, reading works of art—the development of the artist's eye, that assimilates ordinary sights (or sounds, motions, or events) to inward vision, and lends expressiveness and emotional import to the world. Wherever art takes a motif from actuality—a flowering branch, a bit of landscape, a historic event or a personal memory, any model or theme from life—it transforms it into a piece of imagination, and imbues its image with artistic vitality. The result is an impregnation of ordinary reality with the significance of created form. This is the subjectification of nature, that makes reality itself a symbol of life and feeling.

The arts objectify subjective reality, and subjectify outward experience of nature. Art education is the education of feeling, and a society that neglects it gives itself up to formless emotion. Bad art is corruption of feeling. This is a large factor in the irrationalism which dictators and demagogues exploit.

QUESTIONS FOR DISCUSSION

1. What is the audience and the purpose of this piece? What specific words or phrases tell you this? How would a cultural anthropologist react to the second sentence of the first paragraph?
2. How does Langer define art? Compare her definition to that of "What Use Is Art" (p. 308). What does she believe to be its function?
3. Why does Langer believe art is important? Outline her argument as she develops it in her essay.

4. Taking Langer's definition, what is the difference between an art and a craft? For example, would she define quilting as an art? Pottery making? Why or why not?
5. List as many things as you can from your own life that you would consider "art." Do the definitions you have read apply to these things? How would strangers describe you if they could see only the art in your room (posters, music, and so on)?
6. How would you define art? How do you judge art? What makes a piece of art good or bad?

GLORIA ANZALDÚA
Tlilli, Tlapalli: The Path of the Red and Black Ink

Gloria Anzaldúa, who describes herself as a Tejana (native Texan) Chicana writer, is a poet and feminist theorist now affiliated with the University of California, Santa Cruz. Her book, Borderlands/La Frontera: The New Mestiza, *from which this selection is taken, explores her Spanish and Indian (in particular, Aztec) heritage in poetry and prose. The borderlands she describes are cultural and political as well as physical, existing wherever cultures touch one another. "Tlilli, Tlapalli: The Path of the Red and Black Ink" presents a view of art that is opposed in many ways to the view expressed in Susanne Langer's essay (p. 310), and gives an insight into the way Anzaldúa works as an artist. The title refers, as she explains in the piece, to ancient Aztec codices (manuscripts), which were written in red and black ink, the colors symbolizing writing and wisdom.*

> *"Out of poverty, poetry;*
> *out of suffering, song."*
> —a Mexican saying

When I was seven, eight, nine, fifteen, sixteen years old, I would read in bed with a flashlight under the covers, hiding my self-imposed insomnia from my mother. I preferred the world of the imagination to the death of sleep. My sister, Hilda, who slept in the same bed with me, would threaten to tell my mother unless I told her a story.

I was familiar with *cuentos*—my grandmother told stories like the one about her getting on top of the roof while down below rabid coyotes were ravaging the place and wanting to get at her. My father told stories about a phantom giant dog that appeared out of nowhere and sped along the side of the pickup no matter how fast he was driving.

Nudge a Mexican and she or he will break out with a story. So, huddling under the covers, I made up stories for my sister night after night. After a while she wanted two stories per night. I learned to give her installments, building up the suspense with convoluted complications until the story climaxed several nights later. It must have been then that I decided to put stories on paper. It must have been then that working with images and writing became connected to night.

INVOKING ART

In the ethno-poetics and performance of the shaman, my people, the Indians, did not split the artistic from the functional, the sacred from the secular, art from every-day life. The religious, social and aesthetic purposes of art were all intertwined. Before the Conquest, poets gathered to play music, dance, sing and read poetry in open-air places around the *Xochicuahuitl, el Árbol Florido*, Tree-in-Flower. (The *Coaxi-huitl* or morning glory is called the snake plant and its seeds, known as *ololiuhqui*, are hallucinogenic.[1]) The ability of story (prose and poetry) to transform the storyteller and the listener into something or someone else is shamanistic. The writer, as shape-changer, is a *nahual*, a shaman.

In looking at this book that I'm almost finished writing, I see a mosaic pattern (Aztec-like) emerging, a weaving pattern, thin here, thick there. I see a preoccupa-tion with the deep structure, the underlying structure, with the gesso underpaint-ing that is red earth, black earth. I can see the deep structure, the scaffolding. If I can get the bone structure right, then putting flesh on it proceeds without too many hitches. The problem is that the bones often do not exist prior to the flesh, but are shaped after a vague and broad shadow of its form is discerned or uncovered during beginning, middle and final stages of the writing. Numerous overlays of paint, rough surfaces, smooth surfaces make me realize I am preoccupied with texture as well. Too, I see the barely contained color threatening to spill over the boundaries of the object it represents and into other "objects" and over the borders of the frame. I see a hybridization of metaphor, different species of ideas popping up here, pop-ping up there, full of variations and seeming contradictions, though I believe in an ordered, structured universe where all phenomena are interrelated and imbued with spirit. This almost finished product seems an assemblage, a montage, a beaded work with several leitmotifs and with a central core, now appearing, now disap-pearing in a crazy dance. The whole thing has had a mind of its own, escaping me and insisting on putting together the pieces of its own puzzle with minimal direction from my will. It is a rebellious, willful entity, a precocious girl-child forced to grow up too quickly, rough, unyielding, with pieces of feather sticking out here and there, fur, twigs, clay. My child, but not for much longer. This female being is angry, sad, joyful, is *Coatlicue*, dove, horse, serpent, cactus. Though it is a flawed thing—a clumsy, complex, groping blind thing—for me it is alive, infused with spirit. I talk to it; it talks to me.

I make my offerings of incense and cracked corn, light my candle. In my head I sometimes will say a prayer—an affirmation and a voicing of intent. Then I run water, wash the dishes or my underthings, take a bath, or mop the kitchen floor.

---

[1] R. Gordon Wasson, *The Wondrous Mushroom: Mycolatry in Mesoamerica* (New York, NY: McGraw-Hill Book Company, 1980), 59, 103.

This "induction" period sometimes takes a few minutes, sometimes hours. But always I go against a resistance. Something in me does not want to do this writing. Yet once I'm immersed in it, I can go fifteen to seventeen hours in one sitting and I don't want to leave it.

My "stories" are acts encapsulated in time, "enacted" every time they are spoken aloud or read silently. I like to think of them as performances and not as inert and "dead" objects (as the aesthetics of Western culture think of art works). Instead, the work has an identity; it is a "who" or a "what" and contains the presences of persons, that is, incarnations of gods or ancestors or natural and cosmic powers. The work manifests the same needs as a person, it needs to be "fed," *la tengo que bañar y vestir*.[2]

When invoked in rite, the object/event is "present"; that is, "enacted," it is both a physical thing and the power that infuses it. It is metaphysical in that it "spins its energies between gods and humans" and its task is to move the gods. This type of work dedicates itself to managing the universe and its energies. I'm not sure what it is when it is at rest (not in performance). It may or may not be a "work" then. A mask may only have the power of presence during a ritual dance and the rest of the time it may merely be a "thing." Some works exist forever invoked, always in performance. I'm thinking of totem poles, cave paintings. Invoked art is communal and speaks of everyday life. It is dedicated to the validation of humans; that is, it makes people hopeful, happy, secure, and it can have negative effects as well, which propel one towards a search for validation.[3]

The aesthetic of virtuosity, art typical of Western European cultures, attempts to manage the energies of its own internal system such as conflicts, harmonies, resolutions and balances. It bears the presences of qualities and internal meanings. It is dedicated to the validation of itself. Its task is to move humans by means of achieving mastery in content, technique, feeling. Western art is always whole and always "in power." It is individual (not communal). It is "psychological" in that it spins its energies between itself and its witness.[4]

Western cultures behave differently toward works of art than do tribal cultures. The "sacrifices" Western cultures make are in housing their art works in the best structures designed by the best architects; and in servicing them with insurance, guards to protect them, conservators to maintain them, specialists to mount and display them, and the educated and upper classes to "view" them. Tribal cultures keep art works in honored and sacred places in the home and elsewhere. They attend them by making sacrifices of blood (goat or chicken), libations of wine. They bathe, feed, and clothe them. The works are treated not just as objects, but also as persons. The "witness" is a participant in the enactment of the work in a ritual, and not a member of the privileged classes.[5]

---

[2] I have to bathe it and dress it. [Ed. trans.]
[3] Robert Plant Armstrong, *The Powers of Presence: Consciousness, Myth, and Affecting Presence* (Philadelphia, PA: University of Pennsylvania Press, 1981), 11, 20.
[4] Armstrong, 10.
[5] Armstrong, 4.

Ethnocentrism is the tyranny of Western aesthetics. An Indian mask in an American museum is transposed into an alien aesthetic system where what is missing is the presence of power invoked through performance ritual. It has become a conquered thing, a dead "thing" separated from nature and, therefore, its power.

Modern Western painters have "borrowed," copied, or otherwise extrapolated the art of tribal cultures and called it cubism, surrealism, symbolism. The music, the beat of the drum, the Blacks' jive talk. All taken over. Whites, along with a good number of our own people, have cut themselves off from their spiritual roots, and they take our spiritual art objects in an unconscious attempt to get them back. If they're going to do it, I'd like them to be aware of what they are doing and to go about doing it the right way. Let's all stop importing Greek myths and the Western Cartesian split point of view and root ourselves in the mythological soil and soul of this continent. White America has only attended to the body of the earth in order to exploit it, never to succor it or to be nurtured in it. Instead of surreptitiously ripping off the vital energy of people of color and putting it to commercial use, whites could allow themselves to share and exchange and learn from us in a respectful way. By taking up *curanderismo*, Santeria, shamanism, Taoism, Zen and otherwise delving into the spiritual life and ceremonies of multi-colored people, Anglos would perhaps lose the white sterility they have in their kitchens, bathrooms, hospitals, mortuaries and missile bases. Though in the conscious mind, black and dark may be associated with death, evil and destruction, in the subconscious mind and in our dreams, white is associated with disease, death and hopelessness. Let us hope that the left hand, that of darkness, of femaleness, of "primitiveness," can divert the indifferent, right-handed, "rational" suicidal drive that, unchecked, could blow us into acid rain in a fraction of a millisecond.

NI CUICANI: I, THE SINGER

For the ancient Aztecs, *tlilli, tlapalli, la tinta negra y roja de sus códices* (the black and red ink painted on codices) were the colors symbolizing *escritura y sabiduría* (writing and wisdom).[6] They believed that through metaphor and symbol, by means of poetry and truth, communication with the Divine could be attained, and *topan* (that which is above—the gods and spirit world) could be bridged with *mictlán* (that which is below—the underworld and the region of the dead).

> Poet: she pours water from the mouth of the pump, lowers the handle then lifts it, lowers, lifts. Her hands begin to feel the pull from the entrails, the live animal resisting. A sigh rises up from the depths, the handle becomes a wild thing in her hands, the cold sweet water gushes out, splashing her face, the shock of night-light filling the bucket.

An image is a bridge between evoked emotion and conscious knowledge; words are the cables that hold up the bridge. Images are more direct, more immediate than

[6]Miguel Leon-Portilla, *Los Antiguos Mexicanos: A través de sus crónicas y cantares* (México, D.F.: Fondo de Cultura Económica, 1961), 19, 22.

words, and closer to the unconscious. Picture language precedes thinking in words; the metaphorical mind precedes analytical consciousness.

THE SHAMANIC STATE

When I create stories in my head, that is, allow the voices and scenes to be projected in the inner screen of my mind, I "trance." I used to think I was going crazy or that I was having hallucinations. But now I realize it is my job, my calling, to traffic in images. Some of these film-like narratives I write down; most are lost, forgotten. When I don't write the images down for several days or weeks or months, I get physically ill. Because writing invokes images from my unconscious, and because some of the images are residues of trauma which I then have to reconstruct, I sometimes get sick when I *do* write. I can't stomach it, become nauseous, or burn with fever, worsen. But, in reconstructing the traumas behind the images, I make "sense" of them, and once they have "meaning" they are changed, transformed. It is then that writing heals me, brings me great joy.

To facilitate the "movies" with soundtracks, I need to be alone, or in a sensory-deprived state. I plug up my ears with wax, put on my black cloth eye-shades, lie horizontal and unmoving, in a state between sleeping and waking, mind and body locked into my fantasy. I am held prisoner by it. My body is experiencing events. In the beginning it is like being in a movie theater, as pure spectator. Gradually I become so engrossed with the activities, the conversations, that I become a participant in the drama. I have to struggle to "disengage" or escape from my "animated story," I have to get some sleep so I can write tomorrow. Yet I am gripped by a story which won't let me go. Outside the frame, I am film director, screenwriter, camera operator. Inside the frame, I am the actors—male and female—I am desert sand, mountain, I am dog, mosquito. I can sustain a four- to six-hour "movie." Once I am up, I can sustain several "shorts" of anywhere between five and thirty minutes. Usually these "narratives" are the offspring of stories acted out in my head during periods of sensory deprivation.

My "awakened dreams" are about shifts. Thought shifts, reality shifts, gender shifts: one person metamorphoses into another in a world where people fly through the air, heal from mortal wounds. I am playing with my Self, I am playing with the world's soul, I am the dialogue between my Self and *el espíritu del mundo*.[7] I change myself, I change the world.

Sometimes I put the imagination to a more rare use. I choose words, images, and body sensations and animate them to impress them on my consciousness, thereby making changes in my belief system and reprogramming my consciousness. This involves looking my inner demons in the face, then deciding which I want in my psyche. Those I don't want, I starve; I feed them no words, no images, no feelings. I spend no time with them, share not my home with them. Neglected, they leave. This is harder to do than to merely generate "stories." I can only sustain this activity for a few minutes.

---

[7]The spirit of the world. [Ed. trans.]

I write the myths in me, the myths I am, the myths I want to become. The word, the image and the feeling have a palatable energy, a kind of power. *Con imagenes domo mi miedo, cruzo los abismos que tengo por dentro. Con palabras me hago piedra, pájaro, puente de serpientes arrastrando a ras del suelo todo lo que soy, todo lo que algún día seré.*[8]

Los que están mirando (leyendo),
los que cuentan (o refieren lo que leen).
Los que vuelven ruidosamente las hojas de los códices.
Los que tienen en su poder
la tinta negra y roja (la sabiduría)
y lo pintado,
ellos nos llevan, nos guían,
nos dicen el camino.[9]

WRITING IS A SENSUOUS ACT

Tallo mi cuerpo como si estuviera lavando un trapo. Toco las saltadas venas de mis manos, mis chichis adormecidas como pájaras a la anochecer. Estoy encorbada sobre la cama. Las imagenes aleteán alrededor de mi cama como murciélagos, la sábana como que tuviese alas. El ruido de los trenes subterráneos en mi sentido como conchas. Parece que las paredes del cuarto se me arriman cada vez más cerquita.[10]

Picking out images from my soul's eye, fishing for the right words to recreate the images. Words are blades of grass pushing past the obstacles, sprouting on the page; the spirit of the words moving in the body is as concrete as flesh and as palpable; the hunger to create is as substantial as fingers and hand.

I look at my fingers, see plumes growing there. From the fingers, my feathers, black and red ink drips across the page. *Escribo con la tinta de mi sangre.*[11] I write in red ink. Intimately knowing the smooth touch of paper, its speechlessness before I spill myself on the insides of trees. Daily, I battle the silence and the red. Daily, I take my throat in my hands and squeeze until the cries pour out, my larynx and soul sore from the constant struggle.

---

[8]With images I conquer my fear, I cross the abysses that I have inside. With words I make myself stone, bird, bridge of serpents crawling over the ground of all that I am, all that someday I will be. [Ed. trans.]
[9]Those that are looking (reading),
those that tell (or relate what they read)
Those that noisily turn the pages of the codices.
Those that have in their power
the black and red ink (wisdom)
and what is painted,
they lead us, they guide us,
they show us the road. (Leon-Portilla, 125) [Ed. trans.]
[10]I run my hands over my body as if I were washing a rag. I touch the projecting veins of my hands, my sleeping nipples like birds at dusk. I lie curved over the bed. Images flutter around my bed like bats, the sheet as if it had wings. The noise of the subway trains in my ears is like shells. It seems that the walls of the room are constantly creeping closer. [Ed. trans.]
[11]I write with the ink of my blood. [Ed. trans.]

SOMETHING TO DO WITH THE DARK

Quien canta, sus males espanta.
—un dicho[12]

The toad comes out of its hiding place inside the lobes of my brain. It's going to happen again. The ghost of the toad that betrayed me—I hold it in my hand. The toad is sipping the strength from my veins, it is sucking my pale heart. I am a dried serpent skin, wind scuttling me across the hard ground, pieces of me scattered over the countryside. And there in the dark I meet the crippled spider crawling in the gutter, the day-old newspaper fluttering in the dirty rain water.

Musa bruja, venga. Cubrese con una sábana y espante mis demonios que a rempujones y a cachetadas me roban la pluma me rompen el sueño. Musa, ¡misericordia!

Óigame, musa bruja. ¿Porqué huye uste' en mi cara? Su grito me desarrolla de mi caracola, me sacude el alma. Vieja, quítese de aquí con sus alas de navaja. Ya no me despedaze mi cara. Vaya con sus pinche uñas que me desgarran de los ojos hasta los talones. Váyese a la tiznada. Que no me coman, le digo. Que no me coman sus nueve dedos caníbales.

Hija negra de la noche, carnala, ¿Porqué me sacas las tripas, porqué cardas mis entrañas? Este hilvanando palabras con tripas me está matando. Jija de la noche ¡vete a la chingada![13]

Writing produces anxiety. Looking inside myself and my experience, looking at my conflicts, engenders anxiety in me. Being a writer feels very much like being a Chicana, or being queer—a lot of squirming, coming up against all sorts of walls. Or its opposite: nothing defined or definite, a boundless, floating state of limbo where I kick my heels, brood, percolate, hibernate and wait for something to happen.

Living in a state of psychic unrest, in a Borderland, is what makes poets write and artists create. It is like a cactus needle embedded in the flesh. It worries itself deeper and deeper, and I keep aggravating it by poking at it. When it begins to fester I have to do something to put an end to the aggravation and to figure out why I have it. I get deep down into the place where it's rooted in my skin and pluck away at it, playing it like a musical instrument—the fingers pressing, making the pain worse before it can get better. Then out it comes. No more discomfort, no more ambivalence. Until another needle pierces the skin. That's what writing is for me, an end-

---

[12]"Those who sing scare away their troubles."—a proverb. [Ed. trans.]
[13]Witch-muse, come to me. Cover yourself with a sheet and scare my demons that, pushing and slapping, steal my pen, break my sleep. Have pity on me, muse!
    Hear me, witch-muse. Why do you fly in my face? Your cry pulls me from my shell, shakes my soul out of me. Old friend, get out of here with your wings of knives. Don't slash my face to pieces any more. Get away with your wretched claws that pull my eyes out from their sockets. Go to hellfire. I tell you, don't let them eat me. Don't let your nine cannibal fingers eat me.
    Black daughter of the night, dear sister, why do you pull out my guts, why do you comb my intestines? This sewing together of words with guts is killing me. Go to hell, daughter of the night! [Ed. trans.]

less cycle of making it worse, making it better, but always making meaning out of the experience, whatever it may be.

> My flowers shall not cease to live;
> my songs shall never end:
> I, a singer, intone them;
> they become scattered, they are spread about.
> —*Cantares mexicanos*

To write, to be a writer, I have to trust and believe in myself as a speaker, as a voice for the images. I have to believe that I can communicate with images and words and that I can do it well. A lack of belief in my creative self is a lack of belief in my total self and vice versa—I cannot separate my writing from any part of my life. It is all one.

When I write it feels like I'm carving bone. It feels like I'm creating my own face, my own heart—a Nahuatl concept. My soul makes itself through the creative act. It is constantly remaking and giving birth to itself through my body. It is this learning to live with *la Coatlicue* that transforms living in the Borderlands from a nightmare into a numinous experience. It is always a path/state to something else.

In *Xóchilt* in *Cuícatl*[14]

She writes while other people sleep. Something is trying to come out. She fights the words, pushes them down, down, a woman with morning sickness in the middle of the night. How much easier it would be to carry a baby for nine months and then expel it permanently. These continuous multiple pregnancies are going to kill her. She is the battlefield for the pitched fight between the inner image and the words trying to recreate it. *La musa bruja*[15] has no manners. Doesn't she know, nights are for sleeping?

She is getting too close to the mouth of the abyss. She is teetering on the edge, trying to balance while she makes up her mind whether to jump in or to find a safer way down. That's why she makes herself sick— to postpone having to jump blindfolded into the abyss of her own being and there in the depths confront her face, the face underneath the mask.

To be a mouth—the cost is too high—her whole life enslaved to that devouring mouth. *Todo pasaba por esa boca, el viento, el fuego, los mares y la Tierra.*[16] Her body, a crossroads, a fragile bridge, cannot support the tons of cargo passing through it. She wants to install 'stop' and 'go' signal lights, instigate a curfew, police Poetry. But something wants to come out.

---

[14]In *Xóchitl* in *Cuícatl* is Nahuatl for flower and song, *flor y canto.*
[15]Witch-muse. [Ed. trans.]
[16]Everything passed through that mouth, wind, fire, seas, and Earth. [Ed. trans.]

Blocks (*Coatlicue* states) are related to my cultural identity. The painful periods of confusion that I suffer from are symptomatic of a larger creative process: cultural shifts. The stress of living with cultural ambiguity both compels me to write and blocks me. It isn't until I'm almost at the end of the blocked state that I remember and recognize it for what it is. As soon as this happens, the piercing light of awareness melts the block and I accept the deep and the darkness and I hear one of my voices saying, "I am tired of fighting. I surrender. I give up, let go, let the walls fall. On this night of the hearing of faults, *Tlazolteotl, diosa de la cara negra*,[17] let fall the cockroaches that live in my hair, the rats that nestle in my skull. Gouge out my lame eyes, rout my demon from its nocturnal cave. Set torch to the tiger that stalks me. Loosen the dead faces gnawing my cheekbones. I am tired of resisting. I surrender. I give up, let go, let the walls fall."

And in descending to the depths I realize that down is up, and I rise up from and into the deep. And once again I recognize that the internal tension of oppositions can propel (if it doesn't tear apart) the mestiza writer out of the *metate* where she is being ground with corn and water, eject her out as *nahual*, an agent of transformation, able to modify and shape primordial energy and therefore able to change herself and others into turkey, coyote, tree, or human.

I sit here before my computer, *Amiguita*, my altar on top of the monitor with the *Virgen de Coatlalopeuh* candle and copal incense burning. My companion, a wooden serpent staff with feathers, is to my right while I ponder the ways metaphor and symbol concretize the spirit and etherealize the body. The Writing is my whole life, it is my obsession. This vampire which is my talent does not suffer other suitors.[18] Daily I court it, offer my neck to its teeth. This is the sacrifice that the act of creation requires, a blood sacrifice. For only through the body, through the pulling of flesh, can the human soul be transformed. And for images, words, stories to have this transformative power, they must arise from the human body—flesh and bone—and from the Earth's body—stone, sky, liquid, soil. This work, these images, piercing tongue or ear lobes with cactus needle, are my offerings, are my Aztecan blood sacrifices.

QUESTIONS FOR DISCUSSION

1. How would you describe the tone and language of this essay? What seems to be the audience for the piece?
2. What is the significance of the red and black ink of the title?
3. What does the author dislike about the Western European view of art? How does it differ from the view of what she calls "tribal people"? Compare her view to the views expressed in the selections on Soviet art (p. 338–344) and on Indian and African art (p. 333 and p. 344).
4. What does she mean when she writes, "The stress of living with cultural ambiguity both compels me to write and blocks me" (par. 34)?
5. Why might the author have interspersed sections of Spanish dialect throughout her writing?

---

[17]Tlazolteotl, goddess of the black face. [Ed. trans.]
[18]Nietzsche, in *The Will to Power*, says that the artist lives under a curse of being vampirized by his talent.

6. What are some of the images the author has used for the process of writing (for example, writing is like "carving bone")? Choose a passage that strikes you as particularly powerful and analyze its symbolism. What makes the symbolism effective?
7. Throughout this essay Anzaldúa vividly describes the simultaneous joy and pain that writing brings to her. How does she explain this paradox? What other paradoxes can you find in this piece? Explain these paradoxes.
8. Discuss the role of "transformation," of shape-changing, in Anzaldúa's conception of art/literature. Do you agree that literature can have the powers she attributes to it? Why or why not?

E. H. GOMBRICH
Art for Eternity:
Egypt, Mesopotamia, and Crete

Art historian Sir Ernst Hans Gombrich was born in Vienna in 1909; he was educated in Vienna, and has received honorary degrees from institutions all over the world, including Oxford, Cambridge, and Harvard. He was director of the Warburg Institute and Professor of History of the Classical Tradition at the University of London, 1959–1976. In his writings, Gombrich has tried to take the study of art out of isolation and to look at it in the context of cultural history, asking questions about how culture influences artistic expression. His introduction to art history, The Story of Art *(now in its fifteenth edition), is one of the most popular art textbooks ever written. In this selection, Gombrich explains the theory behind the unique forms of painting, relief, and sculpture developed in ancient Egypt.*

Some form of art exists everywhere on the globe, but the story of art as a continuous effort does not begin in the caves of southern France or among the North American Indians. There is no direct tradition which links these strange beginnings with our own days, but there is a direct tradition, handed down from master to pupil, and from pupil to admirer or copyist, which links the art of our own days, any house or any poster, with the art of the Nile Valley of some five thousand years ago. For we shall see that the Greek masters went to school with the Egyptians, and we are all the pupils of the Greeks. Thus the art of Egypt has a tremendous importance for us.

Everyone knows that Egypt is the land of the pyramids, those mountains of stone which stand like weathered landmarks on the distant horizon of history. However remote and mysterious they seem, they tell us much of their own story. They tell us of a land which was so thoroughly organized that it was possible to pile up these gigantic mounds in the lifetime of a single king, and they tell us of kings who were so rich and powerful that they could force thousands and thousands of workers or slaves to toil for them year in, year out, to quarry the stones, to drag them to the building site, and to shift them with the most primitive means till the tomb was ready to receive the king. No king and no people would have gone to such expense, and taken so much trouble, for the creation of a mere monument. In fact, we know that the pyramids had their practical importance in the eyes of the kings and their subjects. The king was considered a divine being who held sway over them, and on his departure from this earth he would again ascend to the gods whence he had come. The pyramids soaring up to the sky would probably help him to make his ascent. In any case they would preserve his sacred body from decay. For the Egyptians believed that the body must be preserved if the soul is to live on in the beyond. That is why they prevented the corpse from decaying by an elaborate method of embalming it, and binding it up in strips of cloth. It was for the mummy of the king that the pyramid had been piled up, and his body was laid right in the centre of the huge mountain of stone in a stone coffin. Everywhere round the burial chamber, spells and incantations were written to help him on his journey to the other world.

But it is not only these oldest relics of human architecture which tell of the role played by age-old beliefs in the story of art. The Egyptians held the belief that the preservation of the body was not enough. If the likeness of the king was also preserved, it was doubly sure that he would continue to exist for ever. So they ordered sculptors to chisel the king's head out of hard, imperishable granite, and put it in the tomb where no one saw it, there to work its spell and to help his soul to keep alive in and through the image. One Egyptian word for sculptor was actually 'He-who-keeps-alive'.

At first these rites were reserved for kings, but soon the nobles of the royal household had their minor tombs grouped in neat rows round the king's mound; and gradually every self-respecting person had to make provision for his after-life by ordering a costly grave which would house his mummy and his likeness, and where his soul could dwell and receive the offerings of food and drink which were given to the dead. Some of these early portraits from the pyramid age, the fourth 'dynasty' of the 'Old Kingdom', are among the most beautiful works of Egyptian art. . . . There is a solemnity and simplicity about them which one does not easily forget. One sees that the sculptor was not trying to flatter his sitter, or to preserve a fleeting expression. He was concerned only with essentials. Every lesser detail he left out. Perhaps it is just because of this strict concentration on the basic forms of the human head that these portraits remain so impressive. For, despite their almost geometrical rigidity, they are not primitive. . . . Nor are they as lifelike as the naturalistic portraits of the artists of Nigeria. . . . The observation of nature, and the regularity of the whole, are so evenly balanced that they impress us as being lifelike and yet remote and enduring.

This combination of geometric regularity and keen observation of nature is characteristic of all Egyptian art. We can study it best in the reliefs and paintings that adorned the walls of the tombs. The word 'adorned', it is true, may hardly fit an art which was meant to be seen by no one but the dead man's soul. In fact, these works were not intended to be enjoyed. They, too, were meant to 'keep alive'. Once, in a grim distant past, it had been the custom when a powerful man died to let his servants and slaves accompany him into the grave. They were sacrificed so that he should arrive in the beyond with a suitable train. Later, these horrors were considered either too cruel or too costly, and art came to the rescue. Instead of real servants, the great ones of this earth were given images as substitutes. The pictures and models found in Egyptian tombs were connected with the idea of providing the soul with helpmates in the other world.

To us these reliefs and wall-paintings provide an extraordinarily vivid picture of life as it was lived in Egypt thousands of years ago. And yet, looking at them for the first time, one may find them rather bewildering. The reason is that the Egyptian painters had quite a different way from ours of representing real life. Perhaps this is connected with the different purpose their paintings had to serve. What mattered most was not prettiness but completeness. It was the artists' task to preserve everything as clearly and permanently as possible. So they did not set out to sketch nature as it appeared to them from any fortuitous angle. They drew from memory, according to strict rules which ensured that everything that had to go into the picture would stand out in perfect clarity. Their method, in fact, resembled that of the mapmaker rather than that of the painter. . . . If we had to draw . . . a [garden (see Fig. 1)]

Figure 1. This painting of a garden with a pond illustrates how Egyptian artists strove to represent their art as clearly as possible. *From a tomb in Thebes, ca. 1400 B.C.E.*

we might wonder from which angle to approach it. The shape and character of the trees could be seen clearly only from the sides, the shape of the pond would be visible only if seen from above. The Egyptians had no compunction about this problem. They would simply draw the pond as if it were seen from above, and the trees from the side. The fishes and birds in the pond, on the other hand, would hardly look recognizable as seen from above, so they were drawn in profile.

In such a simple picture, we can easily understand the artist's procedure. A similar method is often used by children. But the Egyptians were much more consistent in their application of these methods than children ever are. Everything had to be represented from its most characteristic angle. Fig. 2 shows the effect which this idea had on the representation of the human body. The head was most easily seen in profile so they drew it sideways. But if we think of the human eye we think of it as seen from the front. Accordingly, a full-face eye was planted into the side view of the face. The top half of the body, the shoulders and chest, are best seen from the front, for then we see how the arms are hinged to the body. But arms and legs in movement are much more clearly seen sideways. That is the reason why Egyptians in these pictures look so strangely flat and contorted. Moreover the Egyptian artists found it hard to visualize either foot seen from the outside. They preferred the clear outline from the big toe upwards. So both feet are seen from the inside, and the man on the relief looks as if he had two left feet. It must not be supposed that Egyptian artists thought that human beings looked like that. They merely followed a rule which allowed them to include everything in the human form that they considered important. Perhaps this strict adherence to the rule had something to do with their magic purpose. For how could a man with his arm 'foreshortened' or 'cut off' bring or receive the required offerings to the dead?

Here as always, Egyptian art is not based on what the artist could see at a given moment, but rather on what he knew belonged to a person or a scene. It was out of these forms which he had learned, and which he knew, that he built his representations, much as the tribal artist builds his figures out of the forms he can master. It is not only his knowledge of forms and shapes that the artist embodies in his picture, but also his knowledge of their significance. We sometimes call a man a 'big boss'. The Egyptian drew the boss bigger than his servants or even his wife. . . .

It is one of the greatest things in Egyptian art that all the statues, paintings and architectural forms seem to fall into place as if they obeyed one law. We call such a law, which all creations of a people seem to obey, a 'style'. It is very difficult to explain in words what makes a style, but it is far less difficult to see. The rules which govern all Egyptian art give every individual work the effect of poise and austere harmony.

The Egyptian style comprised a set of very strict laws, which every artist had to learn from his earliest youth. Seated statues had to have their hands on their knees; men had to be painted with darker skin than women; the appearance of every Egyptian god was strictly laid down: Horus, the sun-god, had to be shown as a falcon or with a falcon's head, Anubis, the god of death, as a jackal or with a jackal's head. Every artist also had to learn the art of beautiful script. He had to cut the images and symbols of the hieroglyphs clearly and accurately in stone. But once he had mas-

Figure 2. Egyptian artists strove to preserve the human body from its most characteristic angles. Hence, they presented the head in profile, the top half of the body from the front, and the bottom half of the body in profile. *Portrait of Hesire from a wooden door in his tomb. Carved ca. 2700 B.C.E.*

tered all these rules he had finished his apprenticeship. No one wanted anything different, no one asked him to be 'original'. On the contrary, he was probably considered the best artist who could make his statues most like the admired monuments of the past. So it happened that in the course of three thousand years or more Egyptian art changed very little. Everything that was considered good and beautiful in the age of the pyramids was held to be just as excellent a thousand years later. True, new fashions appeared, and new subjects were demanded of the artists, but their mode of representing man and nature remained essentially the same.

Only one man ever shook the iron bars of the Egyptian style. He was a king of the Eighteenth Dynasty, in the period known as the 'New Kingdom', which was founded after a catastrophic invasion of Egypt. This king, called Amenophis IV, was a heretic. He broke with many of the customs hallowed by age-old tradition. He did not wish to pay homage to the many strangely shaped gods of his people. For him only one god was supreme, Aton, whom he worshipped and whom he had represented in the shape of the sun. He called himself Akhnaton, after his god, and he moved his court out of reach of the priests of the other gods, to a place which is now called El-Amarna.

The pictures which he commissioned must have shocked the Egyptians of his day by their novelty. In them none of the solemn and rigid dignity of the earlier Pharaohs was to be found. Instead, he had himself depicted lifting his daughter on to his knees, walking with his wife in the garden, leaning on his stick. Some of his portraits show him as an ugly man . . .—perhaps he wanted the artists to portray him in all his human frailty or, perhaps, he was so convinced of his unique importance as a prophet that he insisted on a true likeness. Akhnaton's successor was Tutankhamen, whose tomb with its treasures was discovered in 1922. Some of these works are still in the modern style of the Aton religion—particularly the back of the king's throne . . . , which shows the king and queen in a homely idyll. He is sitting on his chair in an attitude which might have scandalized the strict Egyptian conservative—almost lolling, by Egyptian standards. His wife is no smaller than he is, and gently puts her hand on his shoulder while the Sun-god, represented as a golden orb, is stretching his hands in blessing down to them.

It is not impossible that this reform of art in the Eighteenth Dynasty was made easier for the king because he could point to foreign works that were much less strict and rigid than the Egyptian products. On an island overseas, in Crete, there dwelt a gifted people whose artists delighted in the representation of swift movement. When the palace of their king at Knossos was excavated at the end of the nineteenth century, people could hardly believe that such a free and graceful style could have been developed in the second millennium before our era. Works in this style were also found on the Greek mainland. . . .

But this opening of Egyptian art did not last long. Already during the reign of Tutankhamen the old beliefs were restored, and the window to the outside world was shut again. The Egyptian style, as it had existed for more than a thousand years before his time, continued to exist for another thousand years or more, and the Egyptians doubtless believed it would continue for all eternity. Many Egyptian works in our museums date from this later period, and so do nearly all Egyptian buildings such as temples and palaces. New themes were introduced, new tasks performed, but nothing essentially new was added to the achievement of art.

Egypt, of course, was only one of the great and powerful empires which existed in the Near East for many a thousand years. We all know from the Bible that little Palestine lay between the Egyptian kingdom of the Nile and the Babylonian and Assyrian empires, which had developed in the valley of the two rivers Euphrates and Tigris. The art of Mesopotamia, as the valley of the two rivers was called in Greek, is less well known to us than the art of Egypt. This is at least partly due to accident. There were no stone quarries in these valleys, and most buildings were made of baked brick which, in course of time, weathered away and fell to dust. Even sculpture in stone was comparatively rare. But this is not the only explanation of the fact that relatively few early works of that art have come down to us. The main reason is probably that these people did not share the religious belief of the Egyptians that the human body and its likeness must be preserved if the soul is to continue. In the very early times, when a people called the Sumerians ruled in the capital of Ur, kings were still buried with their whole household, slaves and all, so that they should not lack a following in the world beyond. Graves of this period have been discovered, and we can admire some of the household goods of these ancient, barbarous kings in the British Museum. We see how much refinement and artistic skill can go together with primitive superstition and cruelty. There was, for instance, a harp in one of the tombs, decorated with fabulous animals. . . . They look rather like our heraldic beasts, not only in their general appearance but also in their arrangement, for the Sumerians had a taste for symmetry and precision. We do not know exactly what these fabulous animals were meant to signify, but it is almost certain that they were figures from the mythology of these early days, and that the scenes which look to us like pages from a children's book had a very solemn and serious meaning.

Though artists in Mesopotamia were not called upon to decorate the walls of tombs, they, too, had to ensure, in a different way, that the image helped to keep the mighty alive. From early times onwards it was the custom of Mesopotamian kings to commission monuments to their victories in war, which told of the tribes that had been defeated, and the booty that had been taken. . . . Perhaps the idea behind these monuments was not only to keep the memory of these victories alive. In early times, at least, the ancient beliefs in the power of the image may still have influenced those who ordered them. Perhaps they thought that, as long as the picture of their king with his foot on the neck of the prostrate enemy stood there, the defeated tribe would not be able to rise again.

In later times such monuments developed into complete picture-chronicles of the king's campaign. The best preserved of these chronicles date from a relatively late period, the reign of King Asurnasirpal II of Assyria, who lived in the ninth century BC, a little later than the biblical King Solomon. They are kept in the British Museum. There we see all the episodes of a well-organized campaign; we see the army crossing rivers and attacking fortresses . . . , their camps and their meals. The way in which these scenes are represented is rather similar to Egyptian methods, but perhaps a little less tidy and rigid. As one looks at them, one feels as if one were watching a newsreel of 2,000 years ago. It all looks so real and convincing. But as we look more carefully we discover a curious fact: there are plenty of dead and wounded in these gruesome wars—but not one of them is an Assyrian. The art of boasting and propaganda was well advanced in these early days. But perhaps we can take a slightly more charitable view of these Assyrians. Perhaps even they were still ruled by the old superstition which has come into this story so often: the superstition that there is more in a picture than a mere picture. Perhaps they did not want to represent wounded Assyrians for some such reason. In any case, the tradition which then began had a very long life. On all the monuments which glorify the warlords of the past, war is no trouble at all. You just appear, and the enemy is scattered like chaff in the wind.

QUESTIONS FOR DISCUSSION

1. As an art historian, Gombrich must interpret as well as narrate the past. Examine the text for words and phrases that show interpretation as well as description of Egyptian art. What is his interpretation?
2. What is the purpose of art in ancient Egypt according to Gombrich? Compare Gombrich's interpretation to the purpose of art according to some of the other readings, for example: "The Cultural Importance of the Arts" (p. 310), "Tlilli Tlapalli: The Path of the Red and Black Ink" (p. 316), "Understanding Indian Art" (p. 333), "What Use Is Art?" (p. 308), "Traditional Arts of Black Africa" (p. 344), "Chinese Painting" (p. 337), "The Soviet Attitude to Art" (p. 338), "Soviet Art: New Freedom, New Directions" (p. 340), and "Islamic Art" (p. 348).
3. What are some of the "rules" of ancient Egyptian art? Why was it important for the artist strictly to follow a traditional style?
4. Using the definition of "naturalism" from the list of art terms, explain how the forms and shapes of Egyptian art differ from naturalistic art.
5. What effects do the images have on you as the viewer? Do you agree with Gombrich's assertions about the effects of this art?
6. Which Egyptians are the subject of ancient Egyptian art? What might we infer about their lives?
7. Why was Amenophis IV (Akhnaton) considered a heretic? How was art during his rule different from previous periods? How might art from outside of Egypt have influenced this period?
8. What functions did art serve in the Mesopotamian empires? How is this similar to and different from the Egyptian art that Gombrich describes?

ANANDA K. COOMARASWAMY
Understanding Indian Art

Ananda K. Coomaraswamy (1877–1947) was born in Ceylon (now Sri Lanka), and attended the
University of London, where he received a doctoral degree in geology. His interest in Indian art, at
first incidental to his work as a scientist, soon became the focus of his career, and he spent the last
thirty years of his life as Keeper of Indian and Muhammadan Art in the Museum of Fine Arts,
Boston. When Coomaraswamy first began to study Indian art, it was still viewed by most art critics
*as primitive, savage, and worthy only of anthropological study. His many books (*Medieval
Sinhalese Art, The Indian Craftsman, History of Indian and Indonesian Art, Indian
Drawings, The Arts and Crafts of India and Ceylon, The Dance of Siva, Bronzes of Ceylon,
to name just a few) helped to change that view of the Indian aesthetic. His writings display an
encyclopedic knowledge of his subject, a deep understanding of the religious traditions behind the
art under discussion, and an objectivity born of his scientific training. In the selection here,
Coomaraswamy compares and contrasts European and Indian artistic theories to show that the two
cultures hold very different philosophies of art. A brief history of Indian art follows, concluding with
an examination of the impact of European influences on that art.

Works of art have been thought of in two very different ways. According to the
modern view the artist is a special or even abnormal kind of man, endowed with a
peculiar emotional sensibility which enables him to see what we call beauty; moved
by a mysterious aesthetic urge he produces paintings, sculpture, poetry or music.
These are regarded as a spectacle for the eyes or a gratification for the ear; they can
only be enjoyed by those who are called lovers of art and these are understood to be
temperamentally related to the artist but without his technical ability. Other men are
called workmen and make things which everyone needs for use; these workmen are
expected to enjoy art, if they are able, only in their spare time.

In ideal art, the artist tries to improve upon nature. For the rest, the truth of the
work of art is held to be its truth to an external world which we call nature, and
expect the artist to observe. In this kind of art there is always a demand for novelty.
The artist is an individual, expressing himself, and so it has become necessary to
have books written about every artist individually, for since each makes use of an
individual language, each requires explanation. Very often a biography is substituted for the explanation. Great importance is attached to what we call genius, and
less to training. Art history is chiefly a matter of finding out the names of artists and
considering their relation to one another. The work of art itself is an arrangement of
colours or sounds, adjudged good or bad according to whether these arrangements
are pleasing or otherwise. The meaning of the work of art is of no significance; those
who are interested in such merely human matters are called Philistines.

This point of view belongs only to the last few centuries in Europe, and to the
decadence of classical civilization in the Mediterranean. It has not been endorsed by
humanity at large, and may be quite a false view. According to another and quite
different assumption, which prevailed throughout the Middle Ages in Europe and
is in fact proper to the Christian as well as the Hindu philosophy of life, art is primarily an intellectual act; it is the conception of form, corresponding to an idea in the

mind of the artist. It is not when he observes nature with curiosity, but when the intellect is self-poised, that the forms of art are conceived. The artist is not a special kind of man, but every man is a special kind of artist or else is something less than a man. The engineer and the cook, the mathematician and the surgeon are also artists. Everything made by man or done skilfully is a work of art, a thing made by art, artificial.

The things to be made by art in imitation of the imagined forms in the mind of the artist are called true when these imagined forms are really embodied and reproduced in the wood or stone or in the sounds which are the artist's material. He has always in view to make some definite thing, not merely something beautiful, no matter what; what he loves is the particular thing he is making; he knows that anything well and truly made will be beautiful. Just what is to be made is a matter for the patron to decide; the artist himself if he is building his own house, or another person who needs a house, or in the broadest sense the patron, is the artist's whole human environment, for example when he is building a temple or laying out a city. In unanimous societies, as in India, there is general agreement as to what is most needed; the artist's work is therefore generally understood; where everyone makes daily use of works of art there is little occasion for museums, books or lectures on the appreciation of art.

The thing to be made, then, is always something humanly useful. No rational being works for indefinite ends. If the artist makes a table, it is to put things on; if he makes an image, it is as a support for contemplation. There is no division of fine or useless from decorative and useful arts; the table is made to give intellectual pleasure as well as to support a weight, the image gives sensual, or as some prefer to call it, aesthetic pleasure at the same time that it provides a support for contemplation. There is no caste division of the artist from the workman such as we are inured to in industrial societies where, as Ruskin so well expressed it, "Industry without art is brutality."

In this kind of art there is no demand for novelty, because the fundamental needs of humanity are always and everywhere the same. What is required is originality, or vitality. What we mean by "original" is "coming from its source within," like water from a spring. The artist can only express what is in him, what he is. It makes no difference whether or not the same thing has been expressed a thousand times before. There can be no property in ideas. The individual does not make them, but finds them; let him only see to it that he really takes possession of them, and his work will be original in the same sense that the recurrent seasons, sunrise and sunset are ever new although in name the same. The highest purpose of Christian and Eastern art alike is to reveal that one and the same principle of life that is manifested in all variety. Only modern art, reflecting modern interests, pursues variety for its own sake and ignores the sameness on which it depends.

Finally, the Indian artist, although a person, is not a personality; his personal idiosyncracy is at the most a part of his equipment, and never the occasion of his art. All of the greatest Indian works are anonymous, and all that we know of the lives of Indian artists in any field could be printed in a tract of a dozen pages.

Let us now consider for a short time the history of Indian art. Our knowledge of it begins about 3000 B.C. with what is known as the Indus Valley culture. Extensive cities with well-built houses and an elaborate drainage system have been excavated and studied. The highest degree of artistic ability can be recognized in the engraved seals, sculptured figures in the round, finely wrought jewellery, silver and bronze vessels and painted pottery. From the *Rgveda*, the Bible of India, datable in its present form about 1000 B.C., we learn a good deal about the arts of the carpenter, weaver and jeweller.

The more familiar Indian art of the historical period has been preserved abundantly from the third century B.C. onwards. The greater part of what has survived consists of religious architecture and sculpture, together with some paintings, coins, and engraved seals. The sculptures have been executed in the hardest stone with steel tools. From the sculptures and paintings themselves we can gather a more detailed knowledge of the other arts. The temples are often as large as European cathedrals. Almost peculiar to India has been the practice of carving out such churches in the living rock, the monolithic forms repeating those of the structural buildings. Amongst notable principles developed early in India which have had a marked influence on the development of architecture in the world at large are those of the horse-shoe arch and transverse vault.

An increasing use is made of sculpture. As in other countries, there is a stylistic sequence of primitive, classical, and baroque types. The primitive style of Bhārhut and Sāñcī can hardly be surpassed in significance and may well be preferred for the very reason that it restricts itself to the statement of absolute essentials and is content to point out a direction which the spectator must follow for himself. Nevertheless, in many ways, the Gupta period, from the fourth to the sixth centuries A.D., may be said to represent the zenith of Indian art. By this time the artist is in full and facile command of all his resources. The paintings of Ajaṇṭā, approximately comparable to those of the very early Renaissance in Europe, depict with irresistible enchantment a civilization in which the conflict of spirit and matter has been resolved in an accord such as has hardly been realised anywhere else, unless perhaps in the Far East and in Egypt. Spirituality and sensuality are here inseparably linked and seem to be merely the inner and outer aspects of one and the same expanding life. The art of this age is classical, not merely within the geographical limits of India proper, but for the whole of the Far East, where all the types of Buddhist art are of Indian origin.

There follows a mediaeval period which was essentially an age of devotion, learning and chivalry; the patronage of art and literature moving together as a matter of course.

From the twelfth century onwards, the situation is profoundly modified so far as the North of India is concerned by the impact of Muhammadan invasions of Persian and Central Asian origin. But while the effects of these invasions were to an appalling extent destructive, the Islamic art added something real and valuable to that of India; and finally, though only for a short time, under the Great Mughals in the 16th and 17th centuries, there developed in India a new kind of life which found expression in a magnificent architecture and a great school of painting. Just because of its more humanistic and worldly preoccupations, this art is better known to and better appreciated by Europeans at the present day than is the more profound art of Hindu India. Everyone has heard of the Taj Mahal, a wonder of inlaid marble built by Shāh Jahān to be the tomb of a beloved wife; everyone can easily understand and therefore admire the Mughal paintings that provide us with a faithful portrait gallery of all the great men of Northern India during a period of two centuries. This is a kind of art that really corresponds to that of the late Renaissance, with all its personal, historic and romantic interests.

In the meantime, Hindu culture persisted almost unchanged in the South. In the great temple cities of the South both the reality and the outward aspects of the ancient world have survived until now and the world has no more wonderful spectacle to offer than can be seen here. In the North, Hindu culture survived too in Rajputana and the Punjab Himalayas and here, in direct continuity with ancient tradition, there developed the two schools of Rajput painting that are the last great expressions of the Indian spirit in painting or sculpture. Modern developments in Bengal and Bombay represent attempts either to recover a lost tradition or for the development of an eclectic style, neither wholly Indian nor wholly European. At the present day the Indian genius is finding expression rather in the field of conduct than in art.

European influence on Indian art has been almost purely destructive: in the first place, by undermining the bases of patronage, removing by default the traditional responsibilities of wealth to learning. Secondly, the impact of industrialism, similarly undermining the status of the responsible craftsman, has left the consumer at the mercy of the profiteer and no better off than he is in Europe. Thirdly, by the introduction of new styles and fashions, imposed by the prestige of power, which the Indian people have not been in a position to resist. A reaction against these influences is taking place at the present day, but can never replace what has been lost; India has been profoundly impoverished, intellectually as well as economically, within the last hundred years.

Even in India, an understanding of the art of India has to be rewon; and for this, just as in Europe where the modern man is as far from understanding the art of the Middle Ages as he is from that of the East, a veritable intellectual rectification is required. What is needed in either case is to place oneself in the position of the artist by whom the unfamiliar work was actually made and in the position of the patron for whom the work was made: to think their thoughts and to see with their eyes. For so long as the work of art appears to us in any way exotic, bizarre, quaint or arbitrary, we cannot pretend to have understood it. It is not to enlarge our collection of bric-a-brac that we ought to study ancient or foreign arts, but to enlarge our own consciousness of being.

As regards India, it has been said that "East is East and West is West and never the twain shall meet." This is a counsel of despair that can only have been born of the most profound disillusion and the deepest conviction of impotence. I say on the contrary that human nature is an unchanging and everlasting principle; and that whoever possesses such a nature—and not merely the outward form and habits of the human animal—is endowed with the power of understanding all that belongs to that nature, without respect to time or place.

QUESTIONS FOR DISCUSSION

1. How does the author define art? How does this definition differ from that of Gombrich in "Art for Eternity" (p. 325) and Anzaldúa in "Tlilli, Tlapalli" (p. 316)?
2. What are the two contrasting views of art described by Coomaraswamy?

3. Which view does he endorse? What are his reasons? Outline his argument.
4. How have other cultures influenced Indian art?
5. Of what use is art, according to this author?
6. Why, according to the author, is the identity of the artist unimportant in Indian art? How important is the identity of the author in Western European art?

HERMANN LIST
Chinese Painting

In this brief passage, art historian Hermann List explains an interesting element of Chinese painting and the philosophical concept behind it. The Chinese painter's stress on inner reality rather than outward appearance is an outgrowth of Eastern religions such as Hinduism, Buddhism, and Taoism, which are based on this same concept. Art, as this essay and the others in this section illustrate, often reflects the social, religious, or political system of the society in which it is created. Art clearly cannot be separated from the rest of life—it is a vital, essential, and interconnected element of society.

Another peculiarity of Chinese painting is that reflections of objects in water are never represented, however natural it seems to us to do so. There are creatures of all kinds on the shore, and the mountains rise beyond rivers and lakes, but there is no image of them in the water. Nor does the Chinese artist paint shadows. Even in the brightest sunlight, a tree, or a man in the middle of the road, or a building, casts no shadow, though the Chinese painter does see the shadows *in* an object—the dark rift in the cliff, the underside of a bridge, and so forth. The lighting of a picture is usually uniform: very often a moonlight scene can only be recognised because the moon is visible somewhere in the sky. Such an art could never take for its subject sunrise or sunset, with their sharp contrasts of light and shade.

The Chinese explain this absence of shadows and reflections by saying that their paintings represent the inner reality of things, while shadows and reflections are merely impalpable appearances. By European standards of superficial, representational realism Chinese painting does seem at first sight indifferent to reality; but Su Tung-po declared that he who judges a picture by its resemblance to the subject judges it as a child, and a widely-read classical treatise on painting tells us that art creates something that lies beyond form.

QUESTIONS FOR DISCUSSION

1. Some might argue that art should represent visual reality as exactly as possible. How does Chinese art present an alternate view of reality?
2. How does Chinese art visually illustrate Chinese philosophy?
3. What are some ways in which Western European art illustrates Western European philosophy?

J. P. HODIN
The Soviet Attitude to Art

SYLVIA HOCHFIELD
Soviet Art: New Freedom, New Directions

The following two selections, "The Soviet Attitude to Art" and "Soviet Art: New Freedom, New Directions," show the connection between politics and art. The first piece, taken from a 1952 speech by Professor Vladimir Kemenov (then director of the Tretjakov Gallery in Moscow), reflects the "party line" attitude toward art from the Stalinist era, when realism was supposed to be the guiding principle of art. This theory, influenced heavily by the Russian political climate during the Cold War era, held that art must be "truthful" and nonindividualistic, serving national interests rather than being a personal expression. How politics can influence art may be seen in the changes that have recently taken place in the Soviet Union as a result of "glasnost" or openness. Russian artists, as documented in the second selection by Sylvia Hochfield (editor-at-large of ARTnews in New York) now have increasing freedom to go beyond the realistic forms imposed in an earlier era, to express personal visions as well as nationalistic ones.

J. P. HODIN
The Soviet Attitude to Art

Professor Kemenov's statement began with a description of the conditions under which artists live and work in the Soviet Union today. Professor Kemenov made it clear that this question had two sides. The one was aesthetic, namely, the relationship of form and content in the work of art; the other was social—the material well-being of the artist, his position in Soviet society, the conditions under which he works, and the possibilities of work. The question of the conditions and the organization of the artist's work in Soviet Russia has, however, a close connection with questions of principle, remarked Professor Kemenov.

"A brief account of Soviet aesthetics at the present time reads as follows: The basic principle is the principle of Realism. This principle of Realism is not worked out by a few artists or critics, it is worked out by us of the Soviet Union on the basis of our knowledge of world art history, of the history of Russian painting, and on our understanding of it.

"Art's first duty, we believe, is truthfully to depict life. In the famous scene in which Hamlet encounters the actors, Shakespeare says of playing that its end 'both at the first and now, was and is, to hold as 'twere, the mirror up to nature, to show virtue her own feature, scorn her own image, and the very age and body of the time his form and pressure.'

"In holding up this mirror to nature, the actor reflects accurately all the qualities of his age. This statement seems to me to have a direct connection with other forms of art. You will certainly find many quotations of all ages, proclaiming that the aim of art is truthfully to depict reality in its entirety. We in the Soviet Union feel that those artists and critics who do not take notice of this development, who are hostile to it are hostile to a truthful depiction of reality. The question naturally arises: What is a truthful picture of reality? Every person might perhaps find something different to be truthful. We however regard such a view as incorrect. It is solipsism. We reject it. In trying to reveal the inner reality in such a way, the artist would never take into account how other people see it. According to our conviction it is quite impossible for an artist not to take into account the feelings, the knowledge, the ideas of the people around him. An endless number of examples can be given of how artists have not only expressed their own inner feelings but the people's. Some English examples: Shakespeare, Robert Burns. Some Russian: Pushkin, Leo Tolstoi. They have all truthfully depicted society. In the work of the artist the task is not only to reflect what is around him. The work must be creative. The people itself is creative. It creates images and metaphors. It sings, it shapes ornaments, it has a tremendous contribution to make. And here we approach an important principle. The great artist takes his inspiration from the people and works it out in finer, higher forms. We regard those painters who take no notice of the people as being incorrect in their approach. They are not doing their work, which is to raise the creative opportunities of the people.

"All this leads us to two conclusions in the conception of our art: its Realism and its popularity, that is, the quality derived from the people. Realism is the foundation of all true art throughout the ages, and not just the basis of one style like Naturalism, Romanticism, or Expressionism. The problem for the art historian is to understand Realism and the place it holds in the history of art. It is possible to find the realist kernel in a Romantic or Expressionistic work of art. Now let us approach a third aspect. We call it Humanism. [Professor Kemenov avoided any reference here to Communism or Socialism.] It is primitive and incorrect to regard the people as being a grey, shapeless mass. The collectivity is made up of individuals. It makes the growth of the individual possible within the framework of the whole. In different periods of history the development of the individual took on a different shape. Sometimes it was rich, in other periods it occurred in much more narrow limits. The artists were also limited. Our Soviet artists realize that the most important field of development is the development of the individual, of his many-sided possibilities. Man is the highest living being in nature.

"The next aspect we wish to approach is the national form of the work of art. The people who look at paintings experience them in a visual way. What the artist represents are not abstract forms. They are concrete. They have developed in their concrete form through circumstances. In other countries they attain a different form. We speak of the national characteristics of any people and say that each people has its own national characteristics. The artist has to accept them whether he likes it or not. . . . The question of national form arises from the realistic approach and from that of the people. The people form the nation. The Soviet artists and writers regard it therefore as a weakening of their creative possibilities if they take no account of the national characteristics of the nation's individuals. We reject the cosmopolitan attitude."

SYLVIA HOCHFIELD
Soviet Art: New Freedom, New Directions

At an exhibition in Moscow last March sponsored by the elite Academy of Artists, there was one picture—the first one visitors saw when they entered the hall—that made people gasp with surprise. Entitled simply *1937*, it was a huge painting by Dmitrii Zhilinskii of a man about to be arrested. In the Soviet Union, you need only mention the year and everyone over 40 knows that you're referring to Stalin's purges, but the young don't know because Stalin's crimes are neither talked about in public nor taught in schools. There was nothing formally experimental about the painting; it was the subject, powerfully rendered, and the fact that it was shown at all, that made people catch their breath.

Zhilinskii's indictment of an era was only one of the works exhibited this year in Moscow that surprised, shocked, and delighted exhibition-goers. According to cultural figures in the Soviet Union and Western observers familiar with the Soviet scene, artists today have greater freedom to exhibit a wide variety of expressions and to deal with forbidden subjects than they have enjoyed since the 1920s, before the Stalinist crackdown put an end to the exuberant experimentation of the post-revolutionary period. Artists who were not allowed to exhibit for years, even decades, are now being shown. The question today, observers say, is not whether *glasnost* (openness) and *perestroika* (restructuring) are real in the cultural sphere but whether they will last. Everyone remembers that the thaw of the Khrushchev era was followed by years of renewed repression.

Nobody is quite sure these days what the new limits are. Official and unofficial artists alike are testing the boundaries. Even those whose careers have never been controversial are exhibiting or hoping to exhibit very different kinds of work than they have shown in the past. "Generally I feel a new climate, but personally I don't," said painter Gennadi Dobrov in his Moscow studio. . . . Dobrov is an official artist, a member of the Moscow Federation of the Artists Union, and a practitioner of conventional realism. But his large, harsh pencil drawings of people mutilated in World War II have so far been rejected for exhibition by the union's committees (although a few have been shown under other sponsorship). In a country where memories of the "Great Patriotic War" remain vivid, and old men still proudly wear their medals, these drawings, Dobrov speculated, were considered too pacifist and even unpatriotic. He said he thought the new climate might make them more acceptable.

The most significant recent development for visual artists has been "the tendency since the beginning of this year to virtually lift all external controls on the decisions on what can be displayed," said Vladimir Padunov, a fellow at the Institute of Current World Affairs in Hanover, New Hampshire. Padunov and his wife, Nancy Condee, chair of the Russian department at Wheaton College, are experts on Soviet cultural policy. According to Padunov, the Moscow Federation of the Artists Union sponsored an exhibition of young painters in January, and the "decision was made by someone who works for the state censorship agency, Glavlit, that they would no longer have to approve every individual piece prior to its being shown."

That was a decision of momentous significance. Glavlit must give prior approval to everything that is printed in the country, from *Pravda* to matchboxes, and—until the recent decision—it approved everything that was shown to the public. What did Glavlit's bowing out mean for artists?

"You begin," said Padunov, "by changing the strictures governing what can be displayed and how it can be displayed. That very quickly begins to affect what it is that is made to be displayed or to be sold or simply to validate someone's creative activity. The very fact of having new opportunities or new rules—or the absence of rules—will determine what you make."

But the absence of Glavlit doesn't mean that all censorship is off. What it means, Padunov said, "is that greater responsibility for that process is thrown on the organizers of an exhibition; in other words, they would have to exercise that function. And, on the other hand, the tendency is to throw even more of that function onto the viewers." Exhibition-goers are urged to respond in writing in visitors' books. Press conferences are held at openings—though that doesn't mean they are printed or broadcast—and dialogues between artists and members of the public are encouraged.

"What you have, in fact," added Condee, "is a definition of *glasnost* that is embodied not so much in a daring picture of some awful event that's been hidden from the public, but rather *glasnost* that comes in the form of the camera and the microphone, which is presented to the viewer, who is asked what he thinks. He can say, 'I think this is trash; this shouldn't be exhibited,' or he can say, 'I think it's about time this type of experimentation was supported.' A result of this kind of *glasnost*, in which the comments come from the viewer, is that artists are spending a great deal of time at exhibitions trying to solicit opinions that will be supportive of what they're doing. In an odd sort of way, it produces, even among the most experimental artists, an impetus toward a kind of populist art."

At the State Russian Museum in Leningrad, senior research curator Nina Barabanova turned aside questions about *glasnost* or *perestroika*, although she was amused that the whole world now seems to understand these words. She preferred to talk about the museum's fine 20th-century collection, much of which has never been on exhibition, and about its preservation in difficult times. Although the works were not shown, they were lovingly cared for, she said proudly, and "not a single piece was destroyed during the war."

But Barabanova readily agreed that there *is* something different about the major exhibition she is preparing of Soviet art from the '20s and '30s, drawn from the museum's reserves. (It was previewed in January at a huge and very popular show, which included about 150 avant-garde works.) "There were no such exhibitions in the past," she said. "Pieces will be shown that were not widely exhibited in the past." To be more precise, most of these works haven't been seen in public in the Soviet Union (some were sent abroad, to the West and to Japan) since the early '30s, before Socialist Realism became the only acceptable form of artistic expression. Many have never been seen in public at all, like the large group of paintings by Pavel Filonov that were recently bequeathed to the museum by the artist's sister. Filonov became a recluse during the '30s and continued to paint until he died, in Leningrad in 1941. The museum now has about 300 of his paintings and graphic works, along with about 100 by Malevich and prime examples of Kandinsky, Chagall, Goncharova, Popova, Larionov, Rozanova, Rodchenko, Tatlin, Lebedev, and a host of lesser-known artists of the period.

"If you ask why such exhibitions were not held in the past," Barabanova said carefully, "you must understand that estimations are changing. I've worked at the museum for 30 years. At a certain period, some of these works were considered not very interesting; some were considered too formalistic. But I think our outlook now is wider, more objective, and, if you want, not so passionate. Points of view are changing."

Another recent development on the contemporary scene has been the further blurring of the line between "official" and "unofficial" artists. Not only have unofficial artists been given unprecedented opportunities to exhibit—and to sell their work directly to the public—but they have also been granted a kind of power they didn't have before. This was demonstrated in February with the still-talked-about "exhibition at Kashirskaia" (many Moscow locations are known only by their street names or, as in this case, the nearest metro stop). The show of 67 painters aroused tremendous interest and was even given the cover story in *Ogonyuk*, the Soviet equivalent of *Life* magazine. It continued the policy of prior nonreview, but it also introduced a new twist: it consisted of works by members of the Moscow Federation of the Artists Union and those by members of an independent group called the First Creative Society. The formation of independent groups is permitted, but what was highly irregular was the exhibition of official works side-by-side with unofficial works—none of which had been given prior approval.

According to Padunov, the second feature of this exhibition "that was even harder to make sense of is that the four sections of the exhibition hall were organized by two people each, at least one of whom in each category was an absolutely unofficial artist. So you had a situation in which unofficial artists were the organizers, and therefore the screening mechanism, for works even by official artists."

The show coincided with the presence of a number of Western delegations in Moscow. Film director Milos Forman saw it and purchased a large work by Grisha Bruskin, an unofficial artist whose painterly mocking of touchy social issues—the Jewish question and the legacy of Stalin—made him one of the most controversial in the show. Bruskin paints small canvases of character types drawn from Jewish religion and folklore and then assembles them into huge canvases. He uses the same assemblage technique with pictures of wholesome boys and girls engaged in sports or patriotic activities, painted as if they were white marble statues in the Stalinist style. It was one of the latter works, *Fundamental Lexicon*, that Forman bought.

There seem to be many new directions in Soviet art, and there are abundant signs that certain kinds of derivative "nonconformist" painting based on Western models are played out. Another exhibition that aroused excitement opened at the end of May at the semi-official gallery on Malaia Gruzinskaia Street. This alternative space was opened to placate artists after the notorious bulldozer exhibition in 1974, when police goon squads moved in to beat up artists and mow down the easels they had set up in a Moscow park. Although Malaia Gruzinskaia was intended to give unofficial artists an exhibition space, it has been a stronghold of the tame and the derivative: Wyeth imitations (Wyeth is enormously popular in the Soviet Union), de Chirico imitations, Picasso imitations, soppy large-eyed children, sentimental Christian motifs.

The May exhibition was very different. Called simply "Object," it featured such works as a pair of television sets placed on chairs facing each other and conversing in video. There were also a number of scatalogical objects, which caused something of a stir since official Soviet attitudes toward sexuality are extremely puritanical. A few of the works disappeared in the course of the show, for reasons that were hard to determine. According to some, Padunov said, it was because public criticism was so harsh that the organizers decided to avoid a confrontation and remove the offending pieces. Others insisted that the works were removed because they had been damaged, and still others speculated, rather mysteriously, that the changes were "an organic process" of the exhibition itself.

The Soviet art scene is much more varied and more complex than an outsider expects. There are official artists who do interesting work, and plenty of unofficial art is no more interesting than what you'd expect to see in New York at an outdoor art fair. Although it's theoretically impossible to make a career outside of the Artists Union, in fact a number of people are said to do so, selling their works to members of the foreign community. There are even a few Soviet dignitaries who are known or rumored to collect unofficial art.

The Glazunov phenomenon, however, is completely inexplicable in Western terms. Ilya Glazunov, 57, is probably the best known and most popular artist in the Soviet Union—and undoubtedly one of the richest. His paintings of the heroes, saints, and martyrs of Old Russia, executed in a bright, decorative style that communicates with the force and directness of an icon, are wildly popular with the public. He is a celebrity portraitist as well, whose disparate subjects have included Leonid Brezhnev, Indira Gandhi, Gina Lollobrigida, and Baron Thyssen-Bornemisza. Very much a Russian nationalist, his bleak vision of the Soviet state contrasts the onion domes of old churches with the drab anonymity of modern high rises. To many of his fellow artists, Glazunov is a purveyor of technically accomplished kitsch, but to his millions of admirers he expresses the Russian soul.

Glazunov is a dominating, flamboyant, articulate man who frequently entertains Westerners in his lavishly decorated Moscow apartment and speaks with what seems to be daring frankness about Soviet life. He is very bitter about the art establishment, insisting that he was kept out of the Artists Union for 13 years after his first exhibition because he refused to paint in a Socialist Realist style—naturalism, he said, is as much the enemy of art as the avant-garde—and complaining that he has not been elected to the Academy of Artists despite his phenomenal popularity.

As if to prove his nonconformity, Glazunov shows off the huge canvas in his studio that he considers his masterpiece, which he has never been allowed to exhibit. This panorama of the modern world, called *The Mystery of the Twentieth Century*, begins with the Russian Revolution and proceeds through World War II and the rise of the Third World to modern times. It's perfectly clear why it has never been exhibited: the forbidden Trotsky is shown among the figures of the revolutionary period; Stalin lies in a blood-red bier; Mao and Golda Meir are among the postwar leaders; a dwarfish figure of Khrushchev dances on a missile, holding in one hand an ear of the corn he promised the Soviet people and in the other the shoe he pounded on the podium at the United Nations; Solzhenitsyn, dressed in prison uniform, symbolizes the soul of modern Russia.

Even though it can't be shown, the picture is useful to Glazunov because it seems to vouch for his independence and deflects attention from the persistent rumors that surround him, despite his denials, that his career has been made, in the face of the hostility of the art establishment, by friends in high places who are sympathetic to his Russian nationalism. He is, it is said, not a nonconformist at all but the regime's court painter, whose "dissidence" is strictly for Western consumption. Whatever one believes, of him or his work, he sums up the difficulty for a foreigner who tries to penetrate the paradoxes of Soviet life and art.

QUESTIONS FOR DISCUSSION

1. Why would the more repressive Soviet government of previous years require its artists to work within the limitations of Socialist Realism?
2. Explain what is meant by the statement "We reject the cosmopolitan attitude" (final paragraph) in Hodin's "The Soviet Attitude to Art."
3. As Hochfield indicates, the Soviet government has, until very recently, placed strict limitations on the kinds of works Soviet artists were allowed to produce and display. Explain how the status of Soviet artists during the past fifty years compares with their situation today. How does the officially sanctioned art of each of these periods reflect the political milieu of the time?
4. How would you describe the relationship between art and politics? Support your response with examples from several cultures.
5. Explain what Hochfield means by "the paradoxes of Soviet life and art" (final paragraph).
6. Who do you believe should have the final say on what kinds of art, and which particular pieces, will be displayed? The government? The public? Artists themselves? Why?

ROY SIEBER
Traditional Arts of Black Africa

Roy Sieber, professor of art history at Indiana University, spent considerable time in Africa. He was a Ford Foundation Fellow in Nigeria, then visiting professor at the University of Ghana and visiting research professor at the University of Ife in Nigeria. He was instrumental in developing his own university's museum collection of African, Pacific, and pre-Columbian art, emphasizing not only masterpieces but also examples of art from which one could learn the significance of the objects for the people who created and used them. He has written widely on African art. In this selection he explains some of the general styles and the cultural importance of such art, showing that it is more complex and sophisticated than we might at first realize, given our orientation toward Western European art.

To understand the traditional arts of Africa south of the Sahara it is necessary to set aside several popularly held assumptions. First, African arts are not primitive, if by primitive is meant simple, crude, or original in the sense of being without a history. The arts of Africa are, in fact, sophisticated and possess a long history. Second, African art is not produced solely for aesthetic ends—that is, it is not art for art's sake, as is so much of recent Western art; rather, it is deeply embedded in the belief patterns of the society. Third, and this refers to more than the arts, Africa's history, although difficult to reconstruct at times, is certainly as long and as rich in texture and fabric as is that of any other world area.

STYLE AND FORM

African art may be characterized as conservative, for it lay at the core of commonly held traditional belief patterns and strongly reflected those shared values, at the same time reinforcing and symbolizing them. It was radical in the sense that it was at the root of all beliefs and values. It was symbolic or representative rather than abstract or representational. Viewed from Western traditions of realism or naturalism, African sculpture seems not to be "correct." The human body is presented most frequently in a 1:3 or 1:4 proportion of head to body, whereas accurate measurement would be approximately 1:5 and Hellenistic and Mannerist proportions edged past 1:6. Thus, to Western eyes, African figure carvings tend to appear head-heavy, and this tendency is combined with an emphasis on balance and symmetry (see Fig. 1). There is no easy explanation for the style characteristics of African art, or indeed for the arts of any other culture. The proportions appear and become accepted; once accepted they become required and expected. The result for Africa is a norm that is frontal and symmetrical and that gives an impression of fixed austerity, which is reinforced by the absence of transitory facial expression. Masks and figures, for the most part, present expressionless, cool countenances; facial twitches of rage, pleasure, or horror are absent. Bodies exhibit long torsos and short legs, bent at hip and knee; arms, often bent at the elbow, are usually placed calmly against the belly or side and only rarely indulge in emphatic gestures. Stance, gesture, and expression combine to lend a strong sense of calm and austere power to most African figurative sculpture.

Despite these abstract and often simplified forms, details are accurate: characteristic hair styles, body ornaments, or scarification patterns are depicted with clarity and correctness, probably because they describe lineage affiliation or social condition as well as local fashion.

This "basic" style is combined with a limited number of figure . . . types. Like the basic style, the types appear broadly in sub-Saharan Africa. Essentially, figure types are limited to standing, seated, occasionally equestrian, and more rarely kneeling postures. Women with children are frequently depicted, expressing the great emphasis on continuity of the family and of the group. . . .

Figure 1. African art presents the human body in a head to body ratio of 1:3 or 1:4. *Oni (King) of Ife, Southwestern Nigeria, Classic phase.*

To survey African figure carving across West and Central Africa, the area where figurative art appeared most frequently, is to experience more than a single style and a limited number of types, however. Rather, a rich and amazing diversity of area, tribal, and subtribal styles can be discerned.

This complex body of styles and types amazed Western artists and critics early in this century and aroused their often extravagant admiration, but it also proved a snare and a delusion. Artists, seeking to break with the conventionalities of Western art, classicism and idealism, naturalism and materialism, assumed, quite inaccurately, that African art was highly inventive and innovative, whereas it was in fact extremely conservative in style as well as in meaning. An example of this conservatism is the continuity of the "basic" style over centuries: over-size head, short legs, detailed coiffure, expressionless and calm balance describe equally well the art of the Nok culture of two thousand years ago . . . or that of the Dogon of a few centuries ago . . . , as it does Lulua . . . or Yoruba . . . figures made in the last century.

Recent scholarship has tended to emphasize the differences of styles and forms and the multiplicity of uses of African art; in short, it has tended to dwell on a rich variety of trees while ignoring the forest. In the broadest sense there does seem to be an African figure style, quite possibly developed in perishable materials, usually wood. Grafted on this general style is the particular style of an area. For example, figure carving from the western Sudan tends to be tall, vertical, spare, and austere. . . . The body and arms become vertical cylinders. At the same time, the surfaces are carefully, often delicately worked with reference to scar patterns and bangles. Other variations of the basic African style can be found in other geographical areas. The forms of the sculptures of the Yoruba of the rain forest of southwestern Nigeria, for example . . . , tend to be rounder and fuller than the more spare forms of the arid western Sudan. Such large geographic area styles are discernible not only for the western Sudan and the Guinea coast, but also for the equatorial rain forest and for the northern and southern Congo River basins.

Within these larger geographic areas, "tribal" styles have also developed. The term *tribe* in African art studies refers to an ethnic and cultural base for a discrete style. In a sense, these tribal styles are the most visible because they are the most easily identifiable, and indeed, most survey books of African sculpture emphasize the styles of "tribal" groups.

In addition to the larger style areas and the tribal styles, still smaller units may be found. In fact, if one examines African sculptural forms closely, it is possible to determine "subtribal" styles, village styles, and even the styles of individual carvers. Thus the style of the Dogon or the Yoruba reflects both the larger style area and the increasingly smaller, specific style areas to which it belongs, and ultimately it is possible to identify the "hand" of the particular sculptor. Unfortunately the names of these artists are too often lost. At times they have been forgotten by the owners and users of the carvings, but more frequently the scholars who collected the pieces neglected to establish the identity of the artists, for they assumed, incorrectly, that the sculptors were anonymous. The opposite of this assumption is far more often true. Where we do have evidence, it becomes clear that the individual sculptors were known, their works were admired, and their genius was celebrated.

QUESTIONS FOR DISCUSSION

1. Explain the distinction the authors make between "primitive" and sophisticated art. How would Susanne K. Langer view this distinction?
2. How, according to this essay, is African art different from much Western European art?
3. How do the authors support their claim that African art is "conservative"?
4. How does the figure of the Nigerian king (Fig. 1) exemplify the principles of African art as Sieber explains them? What is your reaction to this piece?

PHILIP RAWSON
Islamic Art: Calligraphy

Geometric art was part of the Roman and Byzantine tradition. Islamic art built upon this tradition, in part because of the prohibition against the portrayal of human figures in Islamic art as a way of preventing the worship of idols. This preference for geometric design in art coincided with the Islamic reverence for the written word in the form of the Koran (sometimes spelled Quran), the holy book of Islam. Because the Koran was considered to be holy word only in Arabic, the language itself took on great importance, and calligraphy became the highest art form; some of the most important artists in the Islamic world have devoted themselves to the art. The following piece describes the art of calligraphy in the Islamic world, along with some of the religious ideas behind the art.

The doctrines of Islam, rigidly governing every aspect of religious and secular life, are enshrined chiefly in the Koran, the word of Allah dictated through Muhammad, and also in a large collection of maxims and sermons, the *Traditions*, supposedly spoken by the Prophet. The Arabic text of the Koran was probably established in definitive, edited form by the middle of the ninth century. Its text was always written with a slant-cut reed-pen, in a calligraphy intended not only to convey His message but also, in its beauty, to reflect the glory of God. Calligraphy, the art of writing the sacred book, was regarded as the highest of all the arts, and the calligraphic forms of Arabic letters were soon used as ornament on textiles, metalwork, ceramics, furnishings and architecture (Fig. 1). As the art of the scribe developed, other forms of decoration, chiefly arabesque and geometric, were introduced to provide elaborate frames for chapter headings and "rubrics"—emphasized phrases.

The earliest scripts used to transcribe the Koran were the Kufic group, developed in the seventh century. They stress the horizontal and vertical strokes, but use loops sparingly. Then the ends of the horizontals and verticals were greatly extended, and even "foliated" with elaborate serifs—a mode probably invented in Egypt in the eighth century. During the tenth century the use of the more curvilinear Naskh script became widespread, and by the fifteenth century six other kinds of script had been developed. To write any of these scripts well demands, according to Islamic tradition, special qualities of personal purity, concentration and

Figure 1. A manuscript page from a Koran (1691–1692) of the Hilyah, a description of Muhammad the Prophet.

even divine inspiration. In its developed form the calligraphy corresponded to the rhythms and cadences of chanted speech, so that the lengths and proportions of the letters were altered, not only to enrich the visual pattern, but also to embody the musical phrasing in which the words were sung. Though much less individual than Chinese calligraphy, written with the brush, Islamic calligraphy permits the writer some freedom of expression, by allowing him to follow the promptings of his inner ear—within the recognized canons of perfection for each type of script. It was perhaps the scribe's personal urge to express praise and reverence for the sacred book that carried him beyond the forms of the letters themselves into abstract decoration, usually developed out of the calligraphic forms, but also incorporating the geometric and arabesque patterns originating in other arts; once they had been introduced, it was chiefly in manuscripts that these patterns were developed and transmitted.

The arabesque is essentially an S curve, composed of opposing spirals. The relative proportions of the spirals may vary considerably, and the foliage and flowers forming its original basis are usually stylized out of recognition. As in calligraphy, the Islamic aesthetic demands that the hand be schooled to execute the arabesque without any of those tremors or linear faults which indicate a failure of concentration. Beside, or instead of, the arabesque, which was used as a background linking together the sequences of lines, a repeating geometric pattern—interwoven combinations of circles, squares, pentagons, hexagons, octagons or stars—was used for the frontispieces, especially of Korans of the thirteenth and fourteenth centuries. These are often strikingly reminiscent of masterpieces of Christian Celtic art. . . .

Geometrical shapes have a profoundly important role to play in Islamic art, since they are considered as the archetypes of all form, symbolizing the divinely ordained pattern of the universe. A generalized, "all-over" geometric design was even felt to be superior to the idiosyncratic variations of calligraphy or arabesque, and to represent the closest approach of the human understanding to God's Nature. Though the educated Muslim recognizes that geometrical forms are not in themselves divine, but merely symbols of divinity, nevertheless a kind of geometrical complacency has been the particular disease to which Muslim art has sometimes succumbed. Islam, however, seems to have preserved a continuing consciousness of the sacred function of ornament which other decorative traditions once possessed, but usually have lost.

QUESTIONS FOR DISCUSSION

1. Why did calligraphy become the highest art form in the Islamic world?
2. Discuss how Islam views the artist. How does this compare to the view of the artist in the selections on Soviet art (p. 338–344)?
3. Discuss the relationship of art and religion as described in this text, as compared to the same relationship as described in "Chinese Painting" (p. 337), "Art for Eternity" (p. 325), and "Understanding Indian Art" (p. 333).

JON STALLWORTHY
Letter to a Friend

Jon Stallworthy (1935–   ), poet and scholar, expresses in his work a fascination with the power of the creative imagination and the poet's ability to project a personal vision and affect the life of the reader. Unlike many modern poets, Stallworthy does not always directly address pressing social and political issues, and in "Letter to a Friend" he justifies his own poetic themes. He claims that he wants his poetry to do more than just mirror the pain and misery of the world; instead, he strives to expand the reader's imaginative understanding of the world, to create a perspective from which the world's beauty can be seen.

You blame me that I do not write
With the accent of the age:
The eunuch voice of scholarship,
Or the reformer's rage
(Blurred by a fag-end[1] in the twisted lip).   5
You blame me that I do not call
Truculent nations to unite.
I answer that my poems all
Are woven out of love's loose ends;
For myself and for my friends.   10

You blame me that I do not face
The banner-headline fact
Of rape and death in bungalows,
Cities and workmen sacked.
Tomorrow's time enough to rant of those,   15
When the whirlpool sucks us in.
Turn away from the bitter farce,
Or have you now forgotten
That cloud, star, leaf, and water's dance
Are facts of life, and worth your glance?   20

You blame me that I do not look
At cities, swivelled, from
The eye of the crazy gunman, or
The man who drops the bomb.
Twenty years watching from an ivory tower,   25
Taller than your chimney-stack,
I have seen fields beyond the smoke:
And think it better that I make
In the sloganed wall the people pass,
A window—not a looking-glass.   30

                                                               1961

---

[1] **fag-end** The end of a cigarette; a worthless remnant. [Ed. note.]

QUESTIONS FOR DISCUSSION

1. According to the speaker of the poem, what do others say he should write about? Why does he write his "letter" as a poem?
2. Does he feel that his own poems, which often treat subjects such as love and nature, are less valuable? Why? (Cite specific passages from the text.)
3. Do you agree? Does art have a social purpose? Would Langer in "The Cultural Importance of the Arts" (p. 310) agree?
4. Restate the theme of this poem in your own words.

ARCHIBALD MACLEISH
Ars Poetica[1]

Archibald MacLeish (1892–1982) was born in Illinois and graduated from Yale and Harvard Law School. Always possessed of a strong social conscience, he volunteered as an ambulance driver and captain of Field Artillery during World War I; after the war he practiced law in Boston. His interests, however, lay in writing rather than law, so in 1923 he took his family to France where he could concentrate fully on his poetry. He published several volumes of poems while in France, and moved back to America a few years later. He worked for Fortune *magazine during the Depression and, as World War II approached, he devoted much of his time to writing and speaking on the dangers of Fascism and the possibility of war. President Roosevelt named him Librarian of Congress in 1939; he was appointed director of the Office of Facts and Figures (a wartime department which dealt in part with propaganda) in 1941; and from 1944–1945, Assistant Secretary of State. He returned to academia in 1949 to become a professor of English at Harvard. He retired from teaching in 1962, but continued to write poetry and drama, often centering his works on the theme of the creation of beauty and meaning in the face of death and nothingness. "Ars Poetica" ("Art of Poetry"), like the other poems about poetry in this section, seeks to define poetry, to examine and express its unique qualities and powers.*

A POEM should be palpable and mute
As a globed fruit

Dumb
As old medallions to the thumb

---

[1] **The Art of Poetry** A poem by the Roman poet Horace (68–8 B.C.E.).

Silent as the sleeve-worn stone   5
Of casement ledges where the moss has grown—

A poem should be wordless
As the flight of birds

                    * * *

A poem should be motionless in time
As the moon climbs   10

Leaving, as the moon releases
Twig by twig the night-entangled trees,

Leaving, as the moon behind the winter leaves,
Memory by memory the mind—

A poem should be motionless in time   15
As the moon climbs

                    * * *

A poem should be equal to:
Not true

For all the history of grief
An empty doorway and a maple leaf   20

For love
The leaning grasses and two lights above the sea—

A poem should not mean
But be

                                                                       1926

QUESTIONS FOR DISCUSSION

1. How would you describe MacLeish's attitude toward poetry, his opinion of the value and usefulness of poetry?
2. In your own words, explain what MacLeish means by the line, "A poem should be equal to: / Not true."
3. Compare and contrast this poem with Marianne Moore's "Poetry" (p. 355). Where do you think the two poets would agree and disagree about the nature and definition of poetry?
4. Carefully examine MacLeish's extensive use of figurative language in this poem. How do you respond to the imagery he uses? What do you feel gives the poetic symbol its power?
5. This poem is divided into three main sections. What do you think was MacLeish's purpose in making these divisions? What do you see as the theme, important imagery, and purpose of each section? How do they work together?

JAVIER HERAUD
Ars Poetica

Javier Heraud (1942–1963) was born in Lima, Peru. At sixteen he began studying at the Catholic
University of Lima, and later he attended the National University of San Marcos. After a brief period
of teaching literature and English, he turned his attention to poetry and in 1960 he was awarded
the title of Young Poet of Peru. The next year he traveled to Cuba to continue his studies, but
quickly became intensely involved in the Revolution and joined the Peruvian Army of National
Liberation. In 1963, while trying secretly to cross the Rio Maranon back into Peru, he was killed by
government troops.

In truth, and frankly speaking,
poetry is a difficult job
that's won or lost
to the rhythm of the autumnal years.

(When one is young   5
and the flowers that fall are never gathered up,
one writes on and on at night,
at times filling hundreds and hundreds
of useless sheets of paper.
One can boast and say: 10
"I write without revising,
poems leave my hand
like Spring discarded
by the cypresses on my street.")
But as time passes   15
and the years filter in between the temples,
poetry becomes
the potter's art:
clay fired in the hands,
clay shaped by the quick flames.   20

And poetry is a marvelous lightning,
a rain of silent words,
a forest of throbbings and hopes,
the song of oppressed peoples,
the new song of liberated peoples.   25

So poetry, then,
is love, is death,
is man's redemption.

Madrid, 1961   *Havana, 1962*

QUESTIONS FOR DISCUSSION

1. Trace the images of nature throughout the poem. How does this imagery affect your response to this piece?
2. Discuss the distinction Heraud makes between the young poet and the older, more experienced poet. What are the motivations and the contributions of each?
3. What connection does Heraud make in this poem between poetry and politics? What does he mean when he says poetry "is love, is death, / is man's redemption"?
4. Contrast this poem to MacLeish's poem (p. 352) on poetry and its function. What are the differences?

MARIANNE MOORE
Poetry

Marianne Moore (1887–1972) has received numerous awards for her poetry. She was born in St. Louis in 1887 and received her degree from Bryn Mawr in 1909. She was subsequently a teacher of stenography for several years at an Indian school in Carlisle, Pennsylvania, after which she moved to New York and worked as a secretary, a tutor, and an assistant at the New York Public Library. She was editor of the Dial, a respected review journal, from 1926–1929, and continued to write and give readings of her poems throughout the rest of her life. Her work is witty, ironic, insightful; it is a unique blend of prose and poetry, filled with animal imagery, sprinkled with seemingly unpoetic facts and quotations, and intensified by a concern for the "genuineness" of true poetry.

I, too, dislike it: there are things that are important beyond all this fiddle.
   Reading it, however, with a perfect contempt for it, one discovers in
      it, after all, a place for the genuine.
         Hands that can grasp, eyes
         that can dilate, hair that can rise   5
            if it must, these things are important not because a

high-sounding interpretation can be put upon them but because they are
   useful. When they become so derivative as to become unintelligible,
      the same thing may be said for all of us, that we
         do not admire what   10
         we cannot understand:the bat
            holding on upside down or in quest of something to

eat, elephants pushing, a wild horse talking a roll, a tireless wolf under
   a tree, the immovable critic twitching his skin like a horse that feels a flea,
      the base-
      ball fan, the statistician—   15
         nor is it valid
            to discriminate against "business documents and

school-books;'' all these phenomena are important. One must make a
    distinction
however: when dragged into prominence by half poets, the result is not poetry,
nor till the poets among us can be   20
    ''literalists of
    the imagination''—above
        insolence and triviality and can present

for inspection, imaginary gardens with real toads in them, shall we have
    it. In the meantime, if you demand on the one hand,   25
    the raw material of poetry in
        all its rawness and
        that which is on the other hand
            genuine, then you are interested in poetry.

QUESTIONS FOR DISCUSSION

1. Marianne Moore's tone in this piece is very complex. How would you describe it?
   What are her feelings about poetry? Discuss the words, phrases, and images that
   give you this impression.
2. Compare and contrast the tone of Moore's piece with the tone of the two ''Ars
   Poetica'' poems (p. 352–354) and of Stallworthy's ''Letter to a Friend'' (p. 351).
   How do the attitudes expressed in these poems seem similar or different?
3. What is it, according to Moore, that distinguishes good poetry from bad poetry,
   ''half poets'' from genuine poets?
4. What does Moore feel is the proper subject matter for poetry? Which of the other
   poets you have read in this part would agree with this claim? Which would disagree? Use specific examples from their poems to support your opinion.

ALICE WALKER
In Search of Our Mothers' Gardens

Alice Walker (1944–   ), probably best known as the author of The Color Purple, *has created a body
of fiction, nonfiction, and poetry that has done much to restore to African-Americans the history of
their experiences here—a history which previously had been lost, forgotten, or relegated to library
basements. Walker was born in Eatonton, Georgia, the youngest child in a large sharecropping
family. In 1965 she graduated from Sarah Lawrence College and went on to teach at several schools,
among them Wellesley College, Yale University, and the University of California, Berkeley. She also
worked as an editor of* Ms. *magazine. Her writings have earned her the highest respect, as well as a
Guggenheim Fellowship and a fellowship from the National Endowment for the Arts. The essay*

reprinted here touches upon many important issues raised elsewhere in this anthology: the experience of African-Americans (especially women) in America, the power and value of art, the oppression of women and their struggle for self-expression, and the significance of the family and its transmission of a cultural heritage.

> I described her own nature and temperament. Told how they needed a larger life for their expression. . . . I pointed out that in lieu of proper channels, her emotions had overflowed into paths that dissipated them. I talked, beautifully I thought, about an art that would be born, an art that would open the way for women the likes of her. I asked her to hope, and build up an inner life against the coming of that day. . . . I sang, with a strange quiver in my voice, a promise song.
>
> —"Avey," JEAN TOOMER, *Cane*
> *The poet speaking to a prostitute who falls asleep while he's talking*

When the poet Jean Toomer walked through the South in the early twenties, he discovered a curious thing: black women whose spirituality was so intense, so deep, so *unconscious*, they were themselves unaware of the richness they held. They stumbled blindly through their lives: creatures so abused and mutilated in body, so dimmed and confused by pain, that they considered themselves unworthy even of hope. In the selfless abstractions their bodies became to the men who used them, they became more than "sexual objects," more even than mere women: they became "Saints." Instead of being perceived as whole persons, their bodies became shrines: what was thought to be their minds became temples suitable for worship. These crazy Saints stared out at the world, wildly, like lunatics—or quietly, like suicides; and the "God" that was in their gaze was as mute as a great stone.

Who were these Saints? These crazy, loony, pitiful women?

Some of them, without a doubt, were our mothers and grandmothers.

In the still heat of the post-Reconstruction South, this is how they seemed to Jean Toomer: exquisite butterflies trapped in an evil honey, toiling away their lives in an era, a century, that did not acknowledge them, except as "the *mule* of the world." They dreamed dreams that no one knew—not even themselves, in any coherent fashion—and saw visions no one could understand. They wandered or sat about the countryside crooning lullabies to ghosts, and drawing the mother of Christ in charcoal on courthouse walls.

They forced their minds to desert their bodies and their striving spirits sought to rise, like frail whirlwinds from the hard red clay. And when those frail whirlwinds fell, in scattered particles, upon the ground, no one mourned. Instead, men lit candles to celebrate the emptiness that remained, as people do who enter a beautiful but vacant space to resurrect a God.

Our mothers and grandmothers, some of them: moving to music not yet written. And they waited.

They waited for a day when the unknown thing that was in them would be made known; but guessed, somehow in their darkness, that on the day of their revelation they would be long dead. Therefore to Toomer they walked, and even ran, in slow motion. For they were going nowhere immediate, and the future was not yet within their grasp. And men took our mothers and grandmothers, "but got no pleasure from it." So complex was their passion and their calm.

To Toomer, they lay vacant and fallow as autumn fields, with harvest time never in sight: and he saw them enter loveless marriages, without joy; and become prostitutes, without resistance; and become mothers of children, without fulfillment.

For these grandmothers and mothers of ours were not Saints, but Artists; driven to a numb and bleeding madness by the springs of creativity in them for which there was no release. They were Creators, who lived lives of spiritual waste, because they were so rich in spirituality—which is the basis of Art—that the strain of enduring their unused and unwanted talent drove them insane. Throwing away this spirituality was their pathetic attempt to lighten the soul to a weight their work-worn, sexually abused bodies could bear.

What did it mean for a black woman to be an artist in our grandmothers' time? In our great-grandmothers' day? It is a question with an answer cruel enough to stop the blood.

Did you have a genius of a great-great-grandmother who died under some ignorant and depraved white overseer's lash? Or was she required to bake biscuits for a lazy backwater tramp, when she cried out in her soul to paint watercolors of sunsets, or the rain falling on the green and peaceful pasturelands? Or was her body broken and forced to bear children (who were more often than not sold away from her)—eight, ten, fifteen, twenty children—when her one joy was the thought of modeling heroic figures of rebellion, in stone or clay?

How was the creativity of the black woman kept alive, year after year and century after century, when for most of the years black people have been in America, it was a punishable crime for a black person to read or write? And the freedom to paint, to sculpt, to expand the mind with action did not exist. Consider, if you can bear to imagine it, what might have been the result if singing, too, had been forbidden by law. Listen to the voices of Bessie Smith, Billie Holiday, Nina Simone, Roberta Flack, and Aretha Franklin, among others, and imagine those voices muzzled for life. Then you may begin to comprehend the lives of our "crazy," "Sainted" mothers and grandmothers. The agony of the lives of women who might have been Poets, Novelists, Essayists, and Short-Story Writers (over a period of centuries), who died with their real gifts stifled within them.

And, if this were the end of the story, we would have cause to cry out in my paraphrase of Okot p'Bitek's great poem:

O, my clanswomen
Let us all cry together!
Come,
Let us mourn the death of our mother,
The death of a Queen
The ash that was produced
By a great fire!

O, this homestead is utterly dead
Close the gates
With *lacari* thorns,
For our mother
The creator of the Stool is lost!
And all the young men
Have perished in the wilderness!

But this is not the end of the story, for all the young women—our mothers and grandmothers, *ourselves*—have not perished in the wilderness. And if we ask ourselves why, and search for and find the answer, we will know beyond all efforts to erase it from our minds, just exactly who, and of what, we black American women are.

One example, perhaps the most pathetic, most misunderstood one, can provide a backdrop for our mothers' work: Phillis Wheatley, a slave in the 1700s.

Virginia Woolf, in her book *A Room of One's Own*, wrote that in order for a woman to write fiction she must have two things, certainly: a room of her own (with key and lock) and enough money to support herself.

What then are we to make of Phillis Wheatley, a slave, who owned not even herself? This sickly, frail black girl who required a servant of her own at times—her health was so precarious—and who, had she been white, would have been easily considered the intellectual superior of all the women and most of the men in the society of her day.

Virginia Woolf wrote further, speaking of course not of our Phillis, that "any woman born with a great gift in the sixteenth century [insert "eighteenth century," insert "black woman," insert "born or made a slave"] would certainly have gone crazed, shot herself, or ended her days in some lonely cottage outside the village, half witch, half wizard [insert "Saint"], feared and mocked at. For it needs little skill and psychology to be sure that a highly gifted girl who had tried to use her gift of poetry would have been so thwarted and hindered by contrary instincts [add "chains, guns, the lash, the ownership of one's body by someone else, submission to an alien religion"], that she must have lost her health and sanity to a certainty."

The key words, as they relate to Phillis, are "contrary instincts." For when we read the poetry of Phillis Wheatley—as when we read the novels of Nella Larsen or the oddly false-sounding autobiography of that freest of all black women writers, Zora Hurston—evidence of "contrary instincts" is everywhere. Her loyalties were completely divided, as was, without question, her mind.

But how could this be otherwise? Captured at seven, a slave of wealthy, doting whites who instilled in her the "savagery" of the Africa they "rescued" her from . . . one wonders if she was even able to remember her homeland as she had known it, or as it really was.

Yet, because she did try to use her gift for poetry in a world that made her a slave, she was "so thwarted and hindered by . . . contrary instincts, that she . . . lost her health. . . ." In the last years of her brief life, burdened not only with the need to express her gift but also with a penniless, friendless "freedom" and several small children for whom she was forced to do strenuous work to feed, she lost her health, certainly. Suffering from malnutrition and neglect and who knows what mental agonies, Phillis Wheatley died.

So torn by "contrary instincts" was black, kidnapped, enslaved Phillis that her description of "the Goddess"—as she poetically called the Liberty she did not have—is ironically, cruelly humorous. And, in fact, has held Phillis up to ridicule for more than a century. It is usually read prior to hanging Phillis's memory as that of a fool. She wrote:

The Goddess comes, she moves divinely fair,
Olive and laurel binds her *golden* hair.
Wherever shines this native of the skies,
Unnumber'd charms and recent graces rise. [My italics]

It is obvious that Phillis, the slave, combed the "Goddess's" hair every morning; prior, perhaps, to bringing in the milk, or fixing her mistress's lunch. She took her imagery from the one thing she saw elevated above all others.

With the benefit of hindsight we ask, "How could she?"

But at last, Phillis, we understand. No more snickering when your stiff, struggling, ambivalent lines are forced on us. We know now that you were not an idiot or a traitor; only a sickly little black girl, snatched from your home and country and made a slave; a woman who still struggled to sing the song that was your gift, although in a land of barbarians who praised you for your bewildered tongue. It is not so much what you sang, as that you kept alive, in so many of our ancestors, *the notion of song*.

Black women are called, in the folklore that so aptly identified one's status society, "the *mule* of the world," because we have been handed the burdens that everyone else—*everyone* else—refused to carry. We have also been called "Matriarchs," "Superwomen," and "Mean and Evil Bitches." Not to mention "Castraters" and "Sapphire's Mama." When we have pleaded for understanding, our character has been distorted; when we have asked for simple caring, we have been handed empty inspirational appellations, then stuck in the farthest corner. When we have asked for love, we have been given children. In short, even our plainer gifts, our labors of fidelity and love, have been knocked down our throats. To be an artist and a black woman, even today, lowers our status in many respects, rather than raises it: and yet, artists we will be.

Therefore we must fearlessly pull out of ourselves and look at and identify with our lives the living creativity some of our great-grandmothers were not allowed to know. I stress *some* of them because it is well known that the majority of our great-grandmothers knew, even without "knowing" it, the reality of their spirituality, even if they didn't recognize it beyond what happened in the singing at church— and they never had any intention of giving it up.

How they did it—those millions of black women who were not Phillis Wheatley, or Lucy Terry or Frances Harper or Zora Hurston or Nella Larsen or Bessie Smith; or Elizabeth Catlett, or Katherine Dunham, either—brings me to the title of this essay, "In Search of Our Mothers' Gardens," which is a personal account that is yet shared, in its theme and its meaning, by all of us. I found, while thinking about the far-reaching world of the creative black woman, that often the truest answer to a question that really matters can be found very close.

In the late 1920s my mother ran away from home to marry my father. Marriage, if not running away, was expected of seventeen-year-old girls. By the time she was twenty, she had two children and was pregnant with a third. Five children later, I was born. And this is how I came to know my mother: she seemed a large, soft, loving-eyed woman who was rarely impatient in our home. Her quick, violent temper was on view only a few times a year, when she battled with the white landlord who had the misfortune to suggest to her that her children did not need to go to school.

She made all the clothes we wore, even my brothers' overalls. She made all the towels and sheets we used. She spent the summers canning vegetables and fruits. She spent the winter evenings making quilts enough to cover all our beds.

During the "working" day, she labored beside—not behind—my father in the fields. Her day began before sunup, and did not end until late at night. There was never a moment for her to sit down, undisturbed, to unravel her own private thoughts; never a time free from interruption—by work or the noisy inquiries of her many children. And yet, it is to my mother—and all our mothers who were not famous—that I went in search of the secret of what has fed that muzzled and often mutilated, but vibrant, creative spirit that the black woman has inherited, and that pops out in wild and unlikely places to this day.

But when, you will ask, did my overworked mother have time to know or care about feeding the creative spirit?

The answer is so simple that many of us have spent years discovering it. We have constantly looked high, when we should have looked high—and low.

For example: in the Smithsonian Institution in Washington, D.C., there hangs a quilt unlike any other in the world. In fanciful, inspired, and yet simple and identifiable figures, it portrays the story of the Crucifixion. It is considered rare, beyond price. Though it follows no known pattern of quilt-making, and though it is made of bits and pieces of worthless rags, it is obviously the work of a person of powerful imagination and deep spiritual feeling. Below this quilt I saw a note that says it was made by "an anonymous Black woman in Alabama, a hundred years ago."

If we could locate this "anonymous" black woman from Alabama, she would turn out to be one of our grandmothers—an artist who left her mark in the only materials she could afford, and in the only medium her position in society allowed her to use.

As Virginia Woolf wrote further, in *A Room of One's Own*:

> Yet genius of a sort must have existed among women as it must have existed among the working class. [Change this to "slaves" and "the wives and daughters of sharecroppers."] Now and again an Emily Brontë or a Robert Burns [change this to "a Zora Hurston or a Richard Wright"] blazes out and proves its presence. But certainly it never got itself on to paper. When, however, one reads of a witch being ducked, of a woman possessed by devils [or "Sainthood"], of a wise

woman selling herbs [our root workers], or even a very remarkable man who had a mother, then I think we are on the track of a lost novelist, a suppressed poet, or some mute and inglorious Jane Austen. . . . Indeed, I would venture to guess that Anon, who wrote so many poems without signing them, was often a woman. . . .

And so our mothers and grandmothers have, more often than not anonymously, handed on the creative spark, the seed of the flower they themselves never hoped to see: or like a sealed letter they could not plainly read.

And so it is, certainly, with my own mother. Unlike "Ma" Rainey's songs, which retained their creator's name even while blasting forth from Bessie Smith's mouth, no song or poem will bear my mother's name. Yet so many of the stories that I write, that we all write, are my mother's stories. Only recently did I fully realize this: that through years of listening to my mother's stories of her life, I have absorbed not only the stories themselves, but something of the manner in which she spoke, something of the urgency that involves the knowledge that her stories—like her life—must be recorded. It is probably for this reason that so much of what I have written is about characters whose counterparts in real life are so much older than I am.

But the telling of these stories, which came from my mother's lips as naturally as breathing, was not the only way my mother showed herself as an artist. For stories, too, were subject to being distracted, to dying without conclusion. Dinners must be started, and cotton must be gathered before the big rains. The artist that was and is my mother showed itself to me only after many years. This is what I finally noticed:

Like Mem, a character in *The Third Life of Grange Copeland*, my mother adorned with flowers whatever shabby house we were forced to live in. And not just your typical straggly country stand of zinnias, either. She planted ambitious gardens—and still does—with over fifty different varieties of plants that bloom profusely from early March until late November. Before she left home for the fields, she watered her flowers, chopped up the grass, and laid out new beds. When she returned from the fields she might divide clumps of bulbs, dig a cold pit, uproot and replant roses, or prune branches from her taller bushes or trees—until night came and it was too dark to see.

Whatever she planted grew as if by magic, and her fame as a grower of flowers spread over three counties. Because of her creativity with her flowers, even my memories of poverty are seen through a screen of blooms—sunflowers, petunias, roses, dahlias, forsythia, spirea, delphiniums, verbena . . . and on and on.

And I remember people coming to my mother's yard to be given cuttings from her flowers; I hear again the praise showered on her because whatever rocky soil she landed on, she turned into a garden. A garden so brilliant with colors, so original in its design, so magnificent with life and creativity, that to this day people drive by our house in Georgia—perfect strangers and imperfect strangers—and ask to stand or walk among my mother's art.

I notice that it is only when my mother is working in her flowers that she is radiant, almost to the point of being invisible—except as Creator: hand and eye. She is involved in work her soul must have. Ordering the universe in the image of her personal conception of Beauty.

Her face, as she prepares the Art that is her gift, is a legacy of respect she leaves to me, for all that illuminates and cherishes life. She has handed down respect for the possibilities—and the will to grasp them.

For her, so hindered and intruded upon in so many ways, being an artist has still been a daily part of her life. This ability to hold on, even in very simple ways, is work black women have done for a very long time.

This poem is not enough, but it is something, for the woman who literally covered the holes in our walls with sunflowers:

They were women then
My mama's generation
Husky of voice—Stout of
Step
With fists as well as
Hands
How they battered down
Doors
And ironed
Starched white
Shirts
How they led
Armies
Headragged Generals
Across mined
Fields
Booby-trapped
Kitchens
To discover books
Desks
A place for us
How they knew that we
Must know
Without knowing a page
Of it
Themselves

Guided by my heritage of a love of beauty and a respect for strength—in search of my mother's garden, I found my own.

And perhaps in Africa over two hundred years ago, there was just such a mother; perhaps she painted vivid and daring decorations in oranges and yellows and greens on the walls of her hut; perhaps she sang—in a voice like Roberta Flack's—*sweetly* over the compounds of her village; perhaps she wove the most stunning mats or told the most ingenious stories of all the village storytellers.

Perhaps she was herself a poet—though only her daughter's name is signed to the poems that we know.

Perhaps Phillis Wheatley's mother was also an artist.

Perhaps in more than Phillis Wheatley's biological life is her mother's signature made clear.

QUESTIONS FOR DISCUSSION

1. What does Walker mean when she says spirituality "is the basis of Art" (par. 9)?
2. What role does the story of Phillis Wheatley play in this essay? How do her experiences illustrate the "contrary instincts" faced by African-American women in their struggle for freedom and self-expression?
3. Describe the "Goddess" Phillis Wheatley esteemed so highly. How is this Goddess different from Alice Walker's heroines?
4. How did Walker's mother teach her about art? How might Walker define art? Support your answer with examples from her essay.
5. How would Walker agree or disagree with the definitions of poetry represented by Jon Stallworthy's "Letter to a Friend" (p. 351), Marianne Moore's "Poetry" (p. 355), and Javier Heraud's "Ars Poetica" (p. 354)?

WOLE SOYINKA
Chimes of Silence

Wole Soyinka is a Nigerian poet, playwright, and Pulitzer Prize winner. He was imprisoned (in solitary confinement) from 1967–1969 because of his political writings, and "Chimes of Silence" is one of many prose-poems he secretly wrote while suffering the isolation of prison. Poetry was his weapon against the horrors, both physical and emotional, that he experienced. "Chimes of Silence" expresses Soyinka's response to his loss of human contact, to the palpable presence of death, to the fact that one group of humans could impose such suffering upon others. Central to the poem is the imagery of weaving, the symbol of the shuttle (the device that dispenses the thread that is woven through the strands attached to the loom)—suggesting a seed, life, creativity—things the poet needed in order to survive in "the home of death." Like other poems in this section, such as "The United Fruit Co." (p. 366), "I'm a Woman" (p. 397), and "Famous Are the Flowers" (p. 377), "Chimes of Silence" expresses a strong sociopolitical statement.

At first there is a peep-hole on the living.

It sneaks into the yard of lunatics, lifers, violent and violated nerves, cripples, tuberculars, victims of power sadism safely hidden from questions. A little square hole cut in the door, enough for a gaoler's fist to pass through and manipulate the bolt from either side. Enough also for me to—casually, oh so casually—steal a quick look at the rare flash of a hand, a face, a gesture; more often a blur of khaki, the square planted rear of the guard on the other side.

Until one day, a noise of hammering. All morning an assault of blows multiplied and magnified by the unique echoing powers of my crypt. (When it thunders, my skull *is* the anvil of gods.) By noon that breach is sealed. Only the sky is now open, a sky the size of a napkin trapped by tall spikes and broken bottles, but a sky. Vultures perch on a roof just visible from another yard. And crows. Egrets overfly my crypt and bats swarm at sunset. Albino bats, sickly pale, emitting radio pips to prowl the echo chamber. But the world is dead, suddenly. For an eternity after ceasing the hammers sustain their vehemence. Even the sky retracts, dead.

Buried alive? No. Only something men read of. Buoys and landmarks vanish. Slowly, remorselessly, reality dissolves and certitude betrays the mind.

Days weeks months, then as suddenly as that first death, a new sound, a procession. Feet approach, dragging to the clank of chains. And now another breach that has long remained indifferent, blank, a floodhole cut in the base of the wall, this emptiness slowly, gracelessly, begins to frame manacled feet. Nothing has ever passed so close, so ponderously across the floodhole of the Wailing Wall. (I named it that, because it overlooks the yard where a voice cried out in agony all of one night and died at dawn, unattended. It is the yard from which hymns and prayers rise with a constancy matched only by the vigil of crows and vultures.) And now, feet. Bare except for two pairs of boots which consciously walk deadweight to match the pace of manacles on the others. Towards noon the same procession passes the other way. Some days later the procession again goes by and I count. Eleven. The third day of this procession wakes into the longest dawn that ever was born and died of silence, a silence replete and awesome. My counting stops brusquely at six. No more. In that instant the ritual is laid bare, the silence, the furtive conspiracy of dawn, the muffled secrets hammer louder than manacles in my head, all is bared in one paralysing understanding. Five men are walking the other way, five men walking even more slowly, wearily, with the weight of the world on each foot, on each step towards eternity. I hear them pause at every scrap of life, at every beat of the silence, at every mote in the sun, those five for whom the world is about to die.

Sounds. Sounds acquire a fourth dimension in a living crypt. A definition which, as in the case of thunder becomes physically unbearable. In the case of the awaited but unheard, psychically punishing. Pips from albino bats pock the babble of evensong—moslem and christian, pagan and unclassifiable. My crypt they turn into a cauldron, an inverted bell of faiths whose sonorities are gathered, stirred, skimmed, sieved in the warp and weft of sooty mildew on walls, of green velvet fungus woven by the rain's cunning fingers. From beyond the Wall of Mists the perverse piety of women, that inhuman patience to which they are born drifts across to lash the anguish from the Wall of Purgatory. A clap of wings—a white-and-ochre bolt, a wood-pigeon diving and crossing, a restless shuttle threading sun-patches through this darkest of looms. Beyond and above the outside wall, a rustle of leaves—a boy's face! A guileless hunter unmasks, in innocence—an evil labyrinth. I shall know his voice when children's songs invade the cauldron of sounds at twilight, this pulse intrusion in the home of death.

The sun is rising behind him. His head dissolves in the pool, a shuttle sinking in a fiery loom.

QUESTIONS FOR DISCUSSION

1. This piece has been called a "prose-poem." In what ways is it similar to your definition of poetry?
2. What is the significance of the small hole in the door being boarded up? Of the procession of feet? The boy who appears over the wall?
3. What are the central images of this piece? What do they suggest?

PABLO NERUDA
The United Fruit Co.

Pablo Neruda (1903–1973) of Chile won the Nobel Prize for literature in 1971. He is admired for his innovative style and the thematic variety of his work, which ranges from sensuous love poems to odes in praise of everyday objects (such as "Ode to an Onion" and "Ode to Socks") to passionate and forceful political poetry. The following poem, "The United Fruit Co.," illustrates Neruda's social concerns: his sympathy for the exploited and oppressed laboring class and his anger at the foreign powers who, he feels, are primarily responsible for this exploitation. The poem is unified by the imagery of ripe fruit symbolizing the wealth, the people, and the dignity of his land, resources that are appropriated or discarded at will by outsiders like the United Fruit Co.

Cuando sonó la trompeta, estuvo
todo preparado en la tierra,
y Jehová repartió el mundo
a Coca-Cola Inc., Anaconda,
Ford Motors, y otras entidades: 5
la Compañía Frutera Inc.
se reservó lo más jugoso,
la costa central de mi tierra,
la dulce cintura de América.

Bautizó de nuevo sus tierras
como "Repúblicas Bananas," 10
y sobre los muertos dormidos,
sobre los héroes inquietos
que conquistaron la grandeza,
la libertad y las banderas,
estableció la ópera bufa: 15
enajenó los albedríos,
regaló coronas de César,
desenvainó la envidia, atrajo
la dictadura de las moscas,
moscas Trujillos, moscas Tachos, 20
moscas Carías, moscas Martínez,
moscas Ubico, moscas húmedas
de sangre humilde y mermelada,
moscas borrachas que zumban 25
sobre las tumbas populares,
moscas de circo, sabias moscas
entendidas en tiranía.

Entre las moscas sanguinarias
la Frutera desembarca, 30
arrasando el café y las frutas,
en sus barcos que deslizaron
como bandejas el tesoro
de nuestras tierras sumergidas.

Mientras tanto, por los abismos 35
azucarados de los puertos,
caían indios sepultados
en el vapor de la mañana:
un cuerpo rueda, una cosa
sin nombre, un número caído, 40
un racimo de fruta muerta
derramada en el pudridero.

When the trumpets had sounded and all
was in readiness on the face of the earth,
Jehovah divided his universe:
Anaconda, Ford Motors,
Coca-Cola Inc., and similar entities: 5
the most succulent item of all,
The United Fruit Company Incorporated
reserved for itself: the heartland
and coasts of my country,
the delectable waist of America. 10

They rechristened their properties:
the "Banana Republics"—
and over the languishing dead,
the uneasy repose of the heroes
who harried that greatness,   15
their flags and their freedoms,
they established an *opéra bouffe:*
they ravished all enterprise,
awarded the laurels like Caesars,
unleashed all the covetous, and contrived   20
the tyrannical Reign of the Flies—
Trujillo the fly, and Tacho the fly,
the flies called Carias, Martinez,
Ubico[1]—all of them flies, flies
dank with the blood of their marmalade   25
vassalage, flies buzzing drunkenly
on the populous middens:
the fly-circus fly and the scholarly
kind, case-hardened in tyranny.

Then in the bloody domain of the flies   30
The United Fruit Company Incorporated
unloaded with a booty of coffee and fruits
brimming its cargo boats, gliding
like trays with the spoils
of our drowning dominions.   35

And all the while, somewhere, in the sugary
hells of our seaports,
smothered by gases, an Indian
fell in the morning:
a body spun off, an anonymous   40
chattel, some numeral tumbling,
a branch with its death running out of it
in the vat of the carrion, fruit laden and foul.

QUESTIONS FOR DISCUSSION

1. What is the theme of this poem?
2. What effective metaphors and similes does Neruda use? Discuss how this imagery unifies the poem.
3. What does Neruda see as the threat of foreign powers in Chile?
4. Compare this poem to the description of torture in the Amnesty International essay "Chile" (p. 190). What are the differences in the use of language? Why?

---

[1]Names of dictators who were closely associated with U.S. business interests. [Ed. note.]

PAUL LAURENCE DUNBAR
We Wear the Mask

Paul Laurence Dunbar (1872–1906) was one of the most well-known African-American writers of his century. He was class poet and editor of his high school paper in Dayton, Ohio, and his interest in fiction and poetry continued after his graduation. With the encouragement and public praise of writer William Dean Howells, Dunbar's poetry soon brought him fame. Unlike most African-American poets of the time, Dunbar was able to support himself financially with his writing. His dialect poems were especially popular, though he felt constrained by their popularity and would rather have written more of his serious (but less lucrative) poetry. Dunbar has received some criticism for not dealing more extensively in his writings with racial problems; but as the following poem reveals, he was not unaware of the injustices faced by blacks in America.

We wear the mask that grins and lies,
It hides our cheeks and shades our eyes,—
This debt we pay to human guile;
With torn and bleeding hearts we smile,
And mouth with myriad subtleties.   5

Why should the world be overwise,
In counting all our tears and sighs?
Nay, let them only see us, while
  We wear the mask.

We smile, but, O great Christ, our cries   10
To thee from tortured souls arise.
We sing, but oh the clay is vile
Beneath our feet, and long the mile;
But let the world dream otherwise,
  We wear the mask!   15

1895

QUESTIONS FOR DISCUSSION

1. Discuss Dunbar's metaphor of the mask. What kinds of associations do you think he wants us to make with the mask he and his people wear?
2. The poet says the souls of his people are "tortured." Why would he want the world to "dream otherwise"?
3. Describe the tone of this poem. Who is its audience?
4. How would you summarize its theme? What other pieces in this section are similar in terms of theme and purpose?

EZEKIEL MPHAHLELE
The Master of Doornvlei

Ezekiel Mphahlele (1919–   ), South African journalist, social worker, and now teacher, has spent most of his life in the struggle against apartheid. "The Master of Doornvlei" is a vivid, harsh, and perhaps hopeful description of apartheid at work—the destructive power of this minority-rule form of government is evidenced in the misery of each character, the hatred and fear they cannot escape. The oppressed blacks, trapped in a cruel and unjust social system, are symbolized by the circling bird trapped in the church; the black foreman Mfukeri, alienated from the farm-workers of his own race, can never be accepted by the farm owner Sarel Britz, who fears and distrusts all blacks as threats to his supremacy; and the climactic fight between Mfukeri's bull and Sarel Britz's stallion foreshadows an impending confrontation between blacks and whites in South Africa.

The early summer rain was pouring fiercely.

In the mud-and-grass church house a bird flitted from one rafter to another, trapped. All was silent in the church except for a cough now and again that punctuated the preacher's sermon. Now and then, to relieve the gravity of the devotional moment, a few members of the congregation allowed themselves to be ensnared by the circling movements of the bird.

But only a few of them. Most of the people had their eyes fixed on the elderly preacher, as if they were following the motion of every line on each lip as he gave his sermon. In any case, he did not have a booming voice, like his deacon's (a point on which the old man was often plagued by a feeling of inferiority). So his listeners always watched his lips. One or two older women at the back screwed up their faces to see him better.

A nine-year-old boy was particularly charmed by the lost bird, and his eyes roved with it. Then he felt pity for it and wished he could catch it and let it out through the window which it missed several times. But the preacher went on, and his listeners soared on the wings of his sermon to regions where there was no labour or sweat and care.

Suddenly the boy saw the bird make straight for a closed window and hit against the glass and flutter to the floor. It tried to fly but could not. He went to pick it up. He hugged it and stroked it. He looked about, but the people's faces looked ahead, like stolid clay figures. Why are they so cold and quiet when a bird is in pain? he asked himself.

It lay quiet in his hand, and he could feel the slight beat of the heart in the little feathered form.

'And so, brothers and sisters,' the preacher concluded, 'the Holy Word bids us love one another, and do to others as we would that they do to us. Amen.' He asked his flock to kneel for prayer.

At this time Mfukeri, the foreman of Doornvlei Farm on which the makeshift church was built, came in. He looked around and spotted his target—a puny wisp of a boy with scraggy legs, the boy with the bird in his hand.

When he took the boy out the people continued to kneel, unperturbed, except for the raising of a head here and there; perhaps just to make sure who the victim was this time. As the two went out the boy's rather big waistcoat that dangled loosely from his shoulders, flapped about.

It was common for Mfukeri to butt in at a prayer session to fetch a man or woman or child for a job that needed urgent attention. The congregants were labour tenants, who in return for their work earned the few square yards of earth on which they lived, and a ration of mealie-meal, sugar, and an occasional piece of meat.

When they complained about such disturbances to the farmer, Sarel Britz, he said: 'I'm just to my labourers. I favour nobody above the rest. Farm work is farm work; I often have to give up my church service myself.'

The boy tried to protect the bird. He could not keep it on his person, so he put it in under a tin in the fowlrun before he went about the work Mfukeri had directed him to do. The rain continued to pour.

The following day the boy took ill with pneumonia. He had got soaked in the rain. On such days the little mud-and-grass houses of the labourers looked wretched: as if they might cave in any time under some unseen load. The nearest hospital was fifty miles away, and if the workers wanted to see the district surgeon, they would have to travel 25 miles there and back. The district surgeon could only be seen once a week.

The boy ran a high temperature. When he was able to speak he asked his mother to go and see how his bird fared in the fowlrun. She came back to tell him that the bird had been found under a tin, dead. That same night the boy died.

When the news went round, the workers seemed to run berserk.

'It has happened before. . . .'

'My child—not even ten yet . . .!'

'Come, let's go to Sarel Britz . . .!'

'No, wait, he'll be angry with us, very angry. . . .'

'Yes, but the White man is very powerful. . . .'

'And truly so—where do we get work if he drives us off the farm . . .?'

'He wants our hands and our sweat—he cannot do that. . . .'

'He beats us, and now he wants to kill us. . . .'

'Send him back to Rhodesia—this Mfukeri . . .!'

'Yes, we don't do such things on this farm. . . .'

'By the spirits, we don't work tomorrow until we see this thing out . . .!'

'Give us our trek-passes . . .! Save our children . . .!'

'Ho friends! I am not going with you. I have children to look after . . .!'

'That is why we are going to Sarel Britz . . .!'

'Come, friends, let's talk first before we march to the master of Doornvlei.'

Tau Rathebe, who could read and write, rallied the workers to an open spot not far from the main gate. Grim and rugged farm workers shaggy; none with extra flesh on him; young and old; with tough sinewy limbs. Those who were too scared to join the march kept in the bushes nearby to watch. Women remained behind.

The men were angry and impatient. 'We want Mfukeri away from Doornvlei, or we go, trek-pass or none!' was the general cry, echoed and re-echoed.

And they marched, as they had never done before, to the master's house.

Britz and Mfukeri were standing on the front verandah, waiting. It was to be expected: the foreman had already gone to warn Britz. Apart from what knowledge he had about Tau Rathebe, it was plain from the early morning that the workers were not prepared to work.

'What is it, men?'

'The people want Mfukeri sent away,' said Tau. 'He has been using his sjambok on some workers, and now old Petrus Sechele's son is dead, because Mfukeri took him out in the rain. I've warned him about this before.'

'I'll think about it. You're asking me to do a difficult thing; you must give me time to think.'

'How long?' asked Tau.

Sarel Britz felt annoyed at the implied ultimatum and Tau's insolent manner; but he restrained himself.

'Till noon today. Just now I want you to go to your work. I'm just, and to show it, Mfukeri is not going to the fields until I've decided.'

They dispersed, each to his work, discontented and surly. When Mfukeri left Sarel Britz in conference with his mother, the usually smooth and slippery texture on the foreman's face, peculiar to Rhodesian Africans, looked flabby.

'I've told him not to use the sjambok, but he insists on doing it, just because I forbid it,' said Britz when he had gone.

'Reason?' Marta Britz asked.

'Just to make me feel I depend on him.'

'He never behaved like this when your father was alive. Once he was told he must do a thing or mustn't he obeyed.'

There was a pause during which mother and son almost heard each other's thoughts.

'You know, Mamma, when I was at university—on the experimental farm—I knew many Black and Coloured folk. Thinking back on the time, now, makes me feel Pa was wrong.'

'Wrong about what?'

'About Kaffirs being children.'

'But they are, my son. Your father himself said so.'

'No, one has to be on the alert with them. One can't afford to take things for granted.'

'How are they grown up?'

Sarel went and stood right in front of her. 'Yes, Ma, they're fully grown up; some of them are cleverer and wiser than a lot of us Whites. Their damned patience makes them all the more dangerous. Maybe Mfukeri's still somewhat of a child. But certainly not the others. Take today, for instance. A coming together like this has never been heard of on a White man's farm. And they've left everything in the hands of their leader. No disorder. They're serpent's eggs, and I'm going to crush them.' He paused.

'I didn't tell you that Mfukeri has been keeping an eye on this Tau Rathebe. We've found out he was deported from Johannesburg. Somehow slipped into this farm. And now he's been having secret meetings with three or four of our Kaffirs at a time, to teach them what to do—like today.'

'So! Hemel!'

'So you see, Ma, Papa was wrong. I'm going to keep a sharp eye on the black swine. But first thing, I'm ready now to drive Rathebe away; out with him tomorrow.'

At noon the master of Doornvlei made his double decision known: that Tau Rathebe was to leave the farm the following morning, and that Mfukeri had been warned and would be given another chance—the last.

This caused a stir among the labourers, but Tau Rathebe asked them to keep calm. They wanted to leave with him.

'No. The police will take you as soon as you leave here. You can't go from one farm to another without a trek-pass,' he reminded them.

He left Doornvlei. . . .

Sarel Britz felt confused. He kept repeating to himself what he had said to his mother earlier. 'These are no children, no children . . . they are men. . . . I'm dealing with the minds of men. . . . My father was wrong. . . . All my boyhood he led me to believe that black people were children. . . . O Hemel, they aren't . . .!'

He had begun to see the weakness of his father's theory during his university years, but it was the incident with Rathebe that had stamped that weakness on his mind.

Harvest time came, and Doornvlei became a little world of intense life and work. The maize triangle of South Africa was buzzing with talk of a surplus crop and the threat of low prices.

'A big crop again, Mfukeri, what do you say?' said Britz.

'Yes, baas,' he grinned consent, 'little bit better than last year.'

'You know you're a good worker and foreman, Mfukeri. Without you I don't know how I'd run this farm.'

'Yes, baas. If baas is happy I'm happy.'

'Since Rathebe left there's peace here, not so.'

'Yes, baas, he makes too much trouble. Long time I tell baas he always meet the men by the valley. They talk a long time there. Sometime one man tell me they want more money and food. I'm happy for you baas. The old baas he say I must help you all the time because I work for him fifteen years. I want him to rest in peace in his grave.'

Britz nodded several times.

The Rhodesian foreman worked as hard as ever to retain the master's praise. He did not spare himself; and the other workers had to keep up with his almost inhuman pace.

'Hey you!' Mfukeri shouted often. 'You there, you're not working fast enough.' He drove them on, and some worked in panic, breaking off mealie cobs and throwing them with the dexterity of a juggler into sacks hanging from the shoulder. Mfukeri did not beat the workers any more. On this Sarel Britz had put his foot down. 'Beat your workers and you lose them,' his father had often said. But every servant felt the foreman's presence and became jittery. And the army of black sweating labourers spread out among the mealie stalks after the systematic fashion of a battle strategy.

Sometimes they sang their songs of grief and hope while reaping in the autumn sun. Sometimes they were too tired even to sing of grief; then they just went on sweating and thinking; then there was a Sunday afternoon to look forward to, when they would go to the village for a drink and song and dance and lovemaking.

Sarel Britz became sterner and more exacting. And his moods and attitude were always reflected in his trusty Mfukeri. Britz kept reminding his tenants that he was just; he favoured no one above the others; he repeated it often to Mfukeri and to his mother. He leant more and more on his foreman, who realized it and made the most of it.

Back at university the students had had endless talks about the Blacks. Britz had discussed with them his father's theory about allowing the Black man a few rungs to climb up at a time; because he was still a child. Most of his colleagues had laughed at this. Gradually he accepted their line of thinking: the White man must be vigilant.

Often when he did his accounts and books, Sarel Britz would stop in the middle of his work, thinking and wondering what he would do if he lost much of his labour, like the other farmers. What if the towns continued to attract the Black labourer by offering him jobs once preserved for the White man. Would the Black workers continue to flow into the towns, or would the law come to the farmer's rescue by stopping the influx?

Sarel Britz lived in this fear. At the same time, he thought, it would break him if he paid his workers more than forty shillings a month in order to keep them. A mighty heap of troubles rose before his eyes, and he could almost hear the shouts and yells of labour tenants from all the farms rising against their masters. . . .

The threat became more and more real to Britz. But Mfukeri consoled him. Britz had lately been inviting him to the house quite often for a chat about doings on the farm. If only that Kaffir didn't know so much about the farm so that he, Britz, had to depend on him more than he cared to. . . . 'Come to the house tonight, Mfukeri, and let's talk,' he said, one afternoon in late autumn.

'All right, baas.'

Mfukeri went to see his master. He wondered what the master had to say. He found him reclining comfortably on his chair. Mfukeri could not dare to take a chair before he was told to sit down—in the same chair he always sat on.

'Thank you, baas.'

After a moment of silence, 'What do you think of me, Mfukeri?'

'Why do you ask me, baas?'—after looking about.

'Don't be afraid to say your mind.'

'You're all right, baas.'

'Sure?'

'Yes, baas.' They smoked silently.

'You still like this farm?'

'Very much baas.'

'I'm glad. You're a good foreman—the only man I trust here.'

Mfukeri understood Britz. He wanted to assure his master that he would never desert him, that he was capable of keeping the tenants together. Hadn't he spied cleverly on Tau Rathebe and avoided an upheaval?

The foreman felt triumphant. He had never in his life dreamt he would work his way into a White man's trust. He had always felt so inferior before a White man that he despised himself. The more he despised himself the sterner and more ruth-less he became towards his fellow-workers. At least he could retain a certain amount of self-respect and the feeling that he was a man, now that his master looked so helpless.

As the foreman sat smoking his pipe, he thought: 'How pitiable they look when they're at a Black man's mercy . . . I wonder now. . . .'

'All right, Mfukeri,' said the master. The Rhodesian rose and stood erect, like a bluegum tree, over the White man; and the White man thought how indifferent his servant looked; just like a tree. To assert his authority once more Britz gave a few orders.

'Attend to that compost manure first thing tomorrow morning. And also the cleaning up of the chicken hospital; see to that fanbelt in the threshing machine.'

'Yes, baas, goodnight.'

He was moving towards the door when Britz said, 'Before I forget, be careful about Donker mixing with the cows. It wasn't your fault, of course, but you'll take care, won't you?'

'Yes.' He knew his master regarded his bull Donker as inferior stock, and felt hurt.

It was a bewildered Britz the foreman left behind. The farmer thought how overwhelming his servant was when he stood before him. Something in him quaked. He was sensitive enough to catch the tone of the last 'baas' when Mfukeri left: it was such an indifferent echo of what 'baas' sounded like years before.

Mfukeri kept a bull with a squatter family on a farm adjoining Doornvlei. La-bour tenants were not allowed to keep livestock on the farm on which they them-selves worked, because they were paid and received food rations. Mfukeri's friend agreed to keep Donker, the bull, for him. It was a good bull, though scrub.

Two days later Sarel Britz was roused from his lunch hour sleep by noise outside. He ran out and saw workers hurrying towards a common point. In a few moments he found himself standing near Mfukeri and a group of workers. In front of the barn Britz's pedigree stallion, Kasper, was kicking out at Donker, Mfukeri's bull. Donker had the horse against the barn wall, and was roaring and pawing the earth.

Kasper kicked, a quick barrage of hoofs landing a square on the bull's fore-head. But the stocky Donker kept coming in and slashing out with his short horns. Normally, there would be ecstatic shouting from the workers. They stood in silence weaving and ducking to follow the movements of the fighters. They couldn't ex-press their attitude towards either side, because they hated both Britz and Mfukeri; and yet the foreman was one of them.

The stallion tried to turn round, which was almost fatal; for Donker charged and unleashed more furious lightning kicks. Master and foreman watched, each feeling that he was entangled in this strife between their animals; more so than they dared to show outwardly. Sarel Britz bit his lower lip as he watched the rage of the bull. He seemed to see scalding fury in the very slime that came from the mouth of the bull to mix with the earth.

He didn't like the slime mixing with the sand: it looked as if Donker were invoking a mystic power in the earth to keep his fore-hoofs from slipping. Once the hoofs were planted in the ground the bull found an opening and gored Kasper in the stomach, ripping the skin with the upward motion of the horn.

Sarel Britz gave a shout, and walked away hurriedly.

When Mfukeri saw Kasper tottering, and his beloved bull drawing back, an overwhelming feeling of victory shot through every nerve in him. What he had been suppressing all through the fight came out in a gasp and, with tears in his eyes, he shouted: 'Donker! Donker!'

There was a murmur among some of the onlookers who said what a pity it was the horse's hoofs weren't shod; otherwise the ending would have been different.

Kasper was giving his last dying kicks when Britz came back with a rifle in his hand. His face was set. The workers stood aside. Two shots from the rifle finished off the stallion.

'Here, destroy the bull!' he ordered Mfukeri, handing him the gun. The foreman hesitated. 'I said shoot that bull!'

'Why do you want me to shoot my bull, baas?'

'If you don't want to do it, then you must leave this farm, at once!'

Mfukeri did not answer. They both knew the moment had come. He stood still and looked at Britz. Then he walked off, and coaxed his bull out of the premises.

'I gave him a choice,' Sarel said to his mother, telling her the whole story.

'You shouldn't have, Sarel. He has worked for us these fifteen years.'

Sarel knew he had been right. As he looked out of the window to the empty paddock, he was stricken with grief. And then he was glad. He had got rid of yet another threat to his authority.

But the fear remained.

QUESTIONS FOR DISCUSSION

1. Describe the main characters (Sarel Britz, Mfukeri, Tau Rathebe, the farm workers) and their functions in the story.
2. Describe Mfukeri's relationship with Sarel Britz and his relationship with the farm workers.
3. What does the bird symbolize? The fight between the bull and the stallion?
4. Compare and contrast the two attitudes toward blacks held by Sarel Britz and his mother.
5. Summarize the plot of this story. What is the theme?
6. This story is a fictional representation of the situation described in Mandela's "I Am Prepared to Die" (p. 286). Discuss the differences in presentation of some of the same ideas in the two pieces. Does the fictional form change the impact on the reader?

ELLEN WRIGHT PRENDERGAST
Famous Are the Flowers (Patriot's Song)

The following poem, which was considered sacred by the Hawaiians, is said to have been written in 1892 by Ellen Wright Prendergast, a friend of the Hawaiian royal family. It voices the Hawaiian native's opposition to the "greedy document," a treaty that called for the annexation of Hawaii to the United States. In 1887 white owners of sugar plantations and other businesses successfully created a new constitution that prevented 75% of the population (native Hawaiians and Japanese and Chinese laborers) from voting. With the help of American marines, the white minority led by the businessman and politician Sanford Dole overthrew Queen Liliuokalani (spelled "Lili'u-lani" in this song), who had sought to promote the rights of her people. Hawaii was later annexed in 1898, becoming a territory in 1900 and a state in 1959. Keawe, Pi'ilani, Mano, and Kakuhihewa were famous chiefs who here symbolize their respective lands. This song and its popularity illustrate the power of music to bind people together, to strengthen their sense of group identity and value. This power is also evident in other political and social works like "The United Fruit Co." (p. 366) and "I'm a Woman" (p. 397).

Kaulana nā pua a'o Hawai'i
Kūpa'a mahope o ka 'āina
Hiki mai ka 'elele o ka loko 'ino
Palapala 'ānunu me ka pākaha.

Pane mai Hawai'i moku o Keawe.   5
Kōkua nā Hono a'o Pi'ilani.
Kāko'o mai Kaua'i o Mano
Pa'apū me ke one Kakuhihewa.

'A'ole 'a'e kau i ka pūlima
Maluna o ka pepa o ka 'enemi   10
Ho'ohui 'āina kū'ai hewa
I ka pono sivila a'o ke kanaka.

'A'ole mākou a'e minamina
I ka pu'ukālā a ke aupuni.
Ua lawa mākou i ka pōhaku,   15
I ka 'ai kamaha'o o ka 'āina.

Mahope mākou o Lili'u-lani
A loa'a 'ē ka pono a ka 'āina.
(A kau hou 'ia e ke kalaunu)
Ha'ina 'ia mai ana ka puana   20
Ka po'e i aloha i ka 'āina.

Famous are the children of Hawaii
Ever loyal to the land
When the evil-hearted messenger comes
With his greedy document of extortion.

Hawaii, land of Keawe answers.   5
Pi'ilani's bays help.
Mano's Kauai lends support
And so do the sands of Kakuhihewa.

No one will fix a signature
To the paper of the enemy   10
With its sin of annexation
And sale of native civil rights.

We do not value
The government's sums of money.
We are satisfied with the stones,   15
Astonishing food of the land.

We back Lili'u-lani
Who has won the rights of the land.
(She will be crowned again)
Tell the story   20
Of the people who love their land.

QUESTIONS FOR DISCUSSION

1. What is the singer of this song protesting? Why?
2. Would a letter expressing the message of this song have a different effect? Why or why not? In what contexts would a letter be more appropriate? An essay?

ANTHONY HECHT
More Light! More Light![1]

Anthony Hecht's (1923–   ) early poetry is acclaimed for its technical brilliance and inventiveness, but it is in his later poems, such as "More Light! More Light!," that Hecht begins seriously to examine the themes and subjects he finds moving and important. A New York native and graduate of Bard College, Hecht served in Europe and Japan during World War II. He was appalled by what he witnessed there, and the following poem expresses his horror at the atrocities of the Holocaust.

[1]The last words of the German poet Goethe (1749–1832).

For Heinrich Blücher and Hannah Arendt[2]

Composed in the Tower before his execution
These moving verses, and being brought at that time
Painfully to the stake, submitted, declaring thus:
"I implore my God to witness that I have made no crime."

Nor was he forsaken of courage, but the death was horrible,   5
The sack of gunpowder failing to ignite.
His legs were blistered sticks on which the black sap
Bubbled and burst as he howled for the Kindly Light.[3]

And that was but one, and by no means one of the worst;
Permitted at least his pitiful dignity;   10
And such as were by made prayers in the name of Christ,
That shall judge all men, for his soul's tranquillity.

We move now to outside a German wood[4]
Three men are there commanded to dig a hole
In which the two Jews are ordered to lie down   15
And be buried alive by the third, who is a Pole.

Not light from the shrine at Weimar[5] beyond the hill
Nor light from heaven appeared. But he did refuse.
A Lüger settled back deeply in its glove.
He was ordered to change places with the Jews.   20

Much casual death had drained away their souls.
The thick dirt mounted toward the quivering chin.
When only the head was exposed the order came
To dig him out again and to get back in.

No light, no light in the blue Polish eye.   25
When he finished a riding boot packed down the earth.
The Lüger hovered lightly in its glove.
He was shot in the belly and in three hours bled to death.

[2]Hannah Arendt, author of a number of books on anti-Semitism and totalitarianism (including *Eichmann in Jerusalem: A Report of the Banality of Evil*) emigrated from Germany to the United States with her husband Heinrich Blucher in 1941.
[3]"The details are conflated from several executions, including Latimer and Ridley [Bishops of the Anglican Church who were executed in 1555 for their religious beliefs] whose deaths at the stake are described by Foxe in *Acts and Monuments*. But neither of them wrote poems just before their deaths, as others did" (Hecht's note).
[4]The place described is the Nazi concentration camp Buchenwald. The incident described took place in 1944, and is documented in Eugen Kogon's *The Theory and Practice of Hell* (New York, 1958).
[5]Weimar is the city where Goethe lived most of his life. The German government between the two world wars was called the Weimar Republic; it was so named because the national assembly drawing up the new constitution after World War I met in the town identified with Goethe to symbolize the break with Prussian militarism.

No prayers or incense rose up in those hours
Which grew to be years, and every day came mute   *30*
Ghosts from the ovens, sifting through crisp air,
And settled upon his eyes in a black soot.

1967

QUESTIONS FOR DISCUSSION

1. Discuss Hecht's use of the word "light" in this poem. What different meanings and connotations does it have with each use?
2. Describe the two different executions Hecht presents. What similarities and differences do you see? Does he seem to think one of the executions is worse than the other? If so, in what way?
3. In line 21 Hecht says of the Jews that "Much casual death had drained away their souls." Do you think he feels this excuses their actions?
4. Describe the change the Pole undergoes. How would you characterize Hecht's attitude toward him?
5. In your own words, explain the metaphor of the final stanza.

MURIEL RUKEYSER
Letter to the Front

Muriel Rukeyser (1913–1980) was born in New York to wealthy parents, and attended prestigious schools, including Vassar College and Columbia University. Much of Rukeyser's poetry expresses her strong socialist interests and her protest against social injustice. Among her many poetic subjects are women's rights, religious oppression, and the injustices of Western capitalism. In the following excerpt from "Letter to the Front," Rukeyser examines her Jewish heritage, especially in light of the horrors of the Holocaust.

VII
To be a Jew in the twentieth century
Is to be offered a gift. If you refuse,
Wishing to be invisible, you choose
Death of the spirit, the stone insanity.
Accepting, take full life. Full agonies: *5*
Your evening deep in labyrinthine blood
Of those who resist, fail, and resist; and God
Reduced to a hostage among hostages.

The gift is torment. Not alone the still
Torture, isolation; or torture of the flesh.   *10*
That may come also. But the accepting wish,
The whole and fertile spirit as guarantee
For every human freedom, suffering to be free,
Daring to live for the impossible.

1944

QUESTIONS FOR DISCUSSION

1. What, according to Rukeyser, are the rewards and difficulties for a Jew of accepting the Jewish heritage? Of rejecting Judaism? Which choice is portrayed more positively? Explain, using examples from the poem.
2. Explain what Rukeyser might mean by the final image of stanza 1, "and God / Reduced to a hostage among hostages."
3. What is "the impossible" of the last line of the poem?
4. What do you think was Rukeyser's purpose in writing this poem? Who is her audience? What is her relationship to this audience?
5. Discuss this poem in relation to Anthony Hecht's "More Light! More Light!" (p. 378). What themes are common to both? What are the similarities and differences in image, tone, and purpose?

WILLIAM BUTLER YEATS
Easter 1916[1]

Nobel Prize-winning Irish poet William Butler Yeats (1865–1939) is one of the more important poets of the 20th century. He also has remained one of the more controversial, accused of fascism by some and ridiculed for his preoccupation with the occult. His writing displays a body of knowledge that is impressively large and eclectic, a combination of Eastern and Western culture, ancient and modern thought; yet he always remains an Irish poet, longing for a free Ireland independent of British rule. The following poem is Yeats's tribute to the demonstration of Easter 1916 in which a group of Irish nationalists briefly took control of a post office and some other buildings in Dublin. The rebels, some of whom are named in lines 75 and 76 of the poem, were captured and executed by authorities. Yeats was acquainted with several of these people before the rebellion, and in his poem he traces the "transformation" they have achieved by their actions.

[1]In the Easter Rebellion (April 24, 1916) Irish republicans seized several buildings in Dublin, protesting English rule. The leaders of the uprising were captured and executed in May.

I have met them at close of day
Coming with vivid faces
From counter or desk among grey
Eighteenth-century houses.
I have passed with a nod of the head   5
Or polite meaningless words,
Or have lingered awhile and said
Polite meaningless words,
And thought before I had done
Of a mocking tale or a gibe   10
To please a companion
Around the fire at the club,
Being certain that they and I
But lived where motley is worn:
All changed, changed utterly: 15
A terrible beauty is born.[2]

That woman's days were spent
In ignorant good-will,
Her nights in argument
Until her voice grew shrill.   20
What voice more sweet than hers
When, young and beautiful,
She rode to harriers?[3]

This man had kept a school
And rode our wingèd horse;[4]   25
This other his helper and friend[5]
Was coming into his force;
He might have won fame in the end,
So sensitive his nature seemed,
So daring and sweet his thought.   30
This other man I had dreamed
A drunken, vainglorious lout.[6]
He had done most bitter wrong
To some who are near my heart,
Yet I number him in the song;   35

[2]The "terrible beauty" refers to the sacrifice of the rebel leaders as it coincides with the day celebrating Christ's resurrection.
[3]Countess Markiewicz (Constance Gore-Booth, 1868–1927), who took part in the rebellion. A harrier is a hound used for hunting rabbits.
[4]Patrick Pearse (1879–1916) founded a school for boys near Dublin and wrote poetry (Pegasus is the winged horse of Greek mythology, a symbol of immortality). He was the leader of the rebellion.
[5]Thomas MacDonagh (1878–1916) was Pearse's friend, and also a poet.
[6]Major John MacBride, the estranged husband of Maud Gonne (the Irish nationalist and actress, with whom Yeats was in love).

He, too, has resigned his part
In the casual comedy;
He, too, has been changed in his turn,
Transformed utterly:
A terrible beauty is born.   40

Hearts with one purpose alone
Through summer and winter seem
Enchanted to a stone
To trouble the living stream.
The horse that comes from the road,   45
The rider, the birds that range
From cloud to tumbling cloud,
Minute by minute they change;
A shadow of cloud on the stream
Changes minute by minute;   50
A horse-hoof slides on the brim,
And a horse plashes within it;
The long-legged moor-hens dive,
And hens to moor-cocks call;
Minute by minute they live: 55
The stone's in the midst of all.

Too long a sacrifice
Can make a stone of the heart.
O when may it suffice?
That is Heaven's part, our part   60
To murmur name upon name,
As a mother names her child
When sleep at last has come
On limbs that had run wild.
What is it but nightfall?   65
No, no, not night but death;
Was it needless death after all?
For England may keep faith

For all that is done and said.[7]
We know their dream; enough   70
To know they dreamed and are dead;
And what if excess of love
Bewildered[8] them till they died?
I write it out in a verse—

---

[7]England had promised Ireland home rule.
[8]This word can mean "made wild" as well as "confused."

MacDonagh and MacBride   *75*
And Connolly and Pearse
Now and in time to be,
Wherever green is worn,
Are changed, changed utterly:
A terrible beauty is born.   *80*

                                                                         1916

QUESTIONS FOR DISCUSSION

1. Describe the progress of Yeats's attitude toward the leaders of the Easter Rebellion, as related in this poem. How does he feel about each of them before the demonstration? Afterwards?
2. Given the fate of these Irish nationalists (line 66), what is the significance of the refrain, "A terrible beauty is born"? How does Yeats connect Dublin's Easter Rebellion with the events of the first Easter?
3. Although the title of this poem is "Easter 1916," the poem barely touches on the actual events that occurred on this day. What might have been Yeats' purpose in focusing on the leaders of the rebellion rather than on the event itself?
4. Compare and contrast the theme of change and transformation in this poem with the imagery of stones. What does Yeats associate with each of these ideas? What connotations are they given?

W. H. AUDEN
The Unknown Citizen

W. H. Auden (1907–1973) was born in York, England. A doctor's son, he was shaped from an early age by the scientific world of the physician: his work often seeks to expose untruths and illusions, to make plain the mysterious, to heal society's ills. Auden was educated at private schools, and then entered Christ Church, Oxford, where he wrote extensively. His first book of poems was published in 1928, the year he received his degree from the university. Auden taught occasionally and traveled widely after completing his studies. In 1939 he moved to America, where he lived (and eventually became a citizen) until 1972. During these years he also spent a good deal of time at his second residence in Austria. In 1972 he returned to live at Christ Church. Auden has left a body of verse that searches for the unusual and profound in the everyday world, yet avoids romanticism. "The Unknown Citizen," his scathing look at the modern state, exemplifies his ironic, understated poetic style.

(To JS/07/M/378   This Marble Monument Is Erected by the State)

He was found by the Bureau of Statistics to be
One against whom there was no official complaint,

And all the reports on his conduct agree
That, in the modern sense of an old-fashioned word, he was a saint,
For in everything he did he served the Greater Community.   5
Except for the War till the day he retired
He worked in a factory and never got fired,
But satisfied his employers, Fudge Motors Inc.
Yet he wasn't a scab or odd in his views,
For his Union reports that he paid his dues,   10
(Our report on his Union shows it was sound)
And our Social Psychology workers found
That he was popular with his mates and liked a drink.
The Press are convinced that he bought a paper every day
And that his reactions to advertisements were normal in every way.   15
Policies taken out in his name prove that he was fully insured,
And his Health-card shows he was once in hospital but left it cured.
Both Producers Research and High-Grade Living declare
He was fully sensible to the advantages of the Instalment Plan
And had everything necessary to the Modern Man,   20
A phonograph, a radio, a car and a frigidaire.
Our researchers into Public Opinion are content
That he held the proper opinions for the time of year;
When there was peace, he was for peace; when there was war, he went.
He was married and added five children to the population,   25
Which our Eugenist says was the right number for a parent of his generation,
And our teachers report that he never interfered with their education.
Was he free? Was he happy? The question is absurd:
Had anything been wrong, we should certainly have heard.

QUESTIONS FOR DISCUSSION

1. What is the tone of this poem? Discuss the techniques Auden uses to achieve this tone.
2. What is the attitude of the state toward the Unknown Citizen? How would you describe Auden's opinion of him? How does Auden convey both of these opinions at once?
3. Do you admire the citizen for his conformity and obedience? If so, why? If not, how do you feel he should have acted differently? How might Auden answer this question?
4. According to Auden, what is the price of conforming to the rules of a society run by faceless bureaucrats and committees? Do you agree? Do you feel that you live your own life in a manner similar to that of the Unknown Citizen? Explain.
5. How would you describe the political statement Auden is making here? Compare and contrast "The Unknown Citizen" with other works in this part, such as "The Master of Doornvlei" (p. 370) and "Chimes of Silence" (p. 364).

CARL SANDBURG
The People, Yes
Men of Science Say Their Say

Carl Sandburg (1878–1967) was fascinated by the strength, passion, and vitality of America and its people. A first-generation American born of Swedish working-class parents, Sandburg wrote for and about the common person rather than the refined upper classes. He attended school only through the eighth grade, at which point he left school to work at a series of odd jobs. At twenty, he enlisted in the Spanish-American War. Upon returning home he applied to West Point, but his dismal entrance exam scores in grammar and math kept him from being accepted. He enrolled instead at Lombard College in Illinois where he received extensive recognition for his literary and journalistic talents, though he did not complete a degree before he left. After several years of writing, lecturing, and traveling, he was finally able to make a living solely as a writer. The style of Sandburg's poetry often seems rough—his interest tended more toward the subject matter of his poems than the style—yet his work has won him much honor, even during his own lifetime. The following two poems are Sandburg's testament to the resilience of humanity, the power of people to sustain themselves with strength and hope in the face of great obstacles.

The People, Yes

   The people will live on.
The learning and blundering people will live on.
   They will be tricked and sold and again sold
And go back to the nourishing earth for rootholds,
   The people so peculiar in renewal and comeback,   5
   You can't laugh off their capacity to take it.
The mammoth rests between his cyclonic dramas.

The people so often sleepy, weary, enigmatic,
is a vast huddle with many units saying:
   "I earn my living.   10
   I make enough to get by
   and it takes all my time.
   If I had more time
   I could do more for myself
   and maybe for others.   15
   I could read and study
   and talk things over
   and find out about things.
   It takes time.
   I wish I had the time."   20

The people is a tragic and comic two-face: hero and hoodlum: phantom and
   gorilla twisting to moan with a gargoyle mouth: "They buy me and sell me . . .
   it's a game . . . sometime I'll break loose . . ."

   Once having marched
Over the margins of animal necessity,
Over the grim line of sheer subsistence
   Then man came   25
To the deeper rituals of his bones,
To the lights lighter than any bones,
To the time for thinking things over,
To the dance, the song, the story,
Or the hours given over to dreaming,   30
   Once having so marched.

Between the finite limitations of the five senses
and the endless yearnings of man for the beyond
the people hold to the humdrum bidding of work and food
while reaching out when it comes their way   35
for lights beyond the prison of the five senses,
for keepsakes lasting beyond any hunger or death.
   This reaching is alive.
The panderers and liars have violated and smutted it.
   Yet this reaching is alive yet   40
   for lights and keepsakes.

   The people know the salt of the sea
   and the strength of the winds
   lashing the corners of the earth.
   The people take the earth   45
   as a tomb of rest and a cradle of hope.
   Who else speaks for the Family of Man?

   They are in tune and step
   with constellations of universal law.
   The people is a polychrome,   50
   a spectrum and a prism
   held in a moving monolith,
   a console organ of changing themes,
   a clavilux[1] of color poems
   wherein the sea offers fog   55
   and the fog moves off in rain
   and the labrador sunset shortens

---

[1] **clavilux** A color organ; an instrument for throwing on a screen combinations of colors analogous to combinations of
musical sounds. [Ed. note.]

to a nocturne of clear stars
serene over the shot spray
of northern lights.   *60*

The steel mill sky is alive.
The fire breaks white and zigzag
shot on a gun-metal gloaming.
Man is a long time coming.
Man will yet win.   *65*
Brother may yet line up with brother:

This old anvil laughs at many broken hammers.
    There are men who can't be bought.
    The fireborn are at home in fire.
    The stars make no noise.   *70*
    You can't hinder the wind from blowing.
    Time is a great teacher.
    Who can live without hope?

In the darkness with a great bundle of grief
    the people march.   *75*
In the night, and overhead a shovel of stars for keeps, the people march:
    "Where to? what next?"

                                                    1936

Men of Science Say Their Say

men of science say their say:
there will be people left over
enough inhabitants among the Eskimos
among jungle folk
denizens of plains and plateaus   *5*
cities and towns synthetic miasma missed
enough for a census
enough to call it still a world
though definitely   my friends   my good friends
definitely not the same old world   *10*
the vanquished saying, "What happened?"
the victors saying, "We planned it so."
if it should be at the end
in the smoke   the mist   the silence of the end
if it should be one side lost   the other side won   *15*
the changes among those leftover people
the scattered ones the miasma missed
their programs of living   their books and music

they will be simple and conclusive
in the ways and manners of early men and women   20
the children having playroom
rulers and diplomats finding affairs less complex
new types of cripples here and there
and indescribable babbling survivors
listening to plain scholars saying,   25
should a few plain scholars have come through,
"As after other wars the peace is something else again."

amid the devastated areas and the untouched
the historians will take an interest
finding amid the ruins and shambles   30
tokens of contrast and surprise
testimonies here curious   there monstrous
nuclear fission corpses having one face
radioactivity cadavers another look
bacteriological victims not unfamiliar   35
scenes and outlooks nevertheless surpassing
    those of the First World War
    and those of the Second or Global War
    —the historians will take an interest
    fill their note-books   pick their way   40
    amid burned and tattered documents
    and say to each other,
    "What the hell! it isn't worth writing,
    posterity won't give a damn what we write."

in the Dark Ages many there and then   45
had fun and took love and made visions
and listened when Voices came.
then as now were the Unafraid.
then as now, "What if I am dropped into levels
        of ambiguous dust and covered   50
        over and forgotten? Have I in my
        time taken worse?"
then as now, "What if I am poured into numbers
        of the multitudinous sea and sunk
        in massive swarming fathoms? Have   55
        I gone through this last year
        and the year before?"
in either Dark Ages or Renascence have there
been ever the Immeasurable Men, the Incalculable
Women, their outlooks timeless?   60
of Rabelais, is it admissible he threw an excellent laughter and his flagons and
    ovens made him a name?

of Piers Plowman, is it permissible he made sad
lovable songs out of stubborn land, straw and
hoe-handles, barefoot folk treading dirt floors?
should it be the Dark Ages recur, will there be   65
again the Immeasurable Men, the Incalculable
Women?

QUESTIONS FOR DISCUSSION

1. After reading "The People, Yes," what kind of political system do you think Sandburg would advocate?
2. Describe Sandburg's tone in both pieces. How would you summarize his opinion
   of "the people" and their future? Of science and its contribution to society?
3. In what ways do you agree or disagree with Sandburg's characterization of
   humanity?
4. What is the role of figurative language in both poems? Discuss what you consider
   to be the most important symbols and metaphors. Explain the line in "Men of
   Science Say Their Say": "As after other wars, the peace is something else again"
   (line 27).
5. How do these two poems comment on each other in terms of subject matter and
   theme?

MORRIS BISHOP
$E = mc^2$

*Morris Bishop (1893–1973) was born in New York in a mental institution, where his father was a
physician at the hospital. He entered Cornell in 1910, and received his M.A. in 1914. He was a
distinguished student, a Phi Beta Kappa scholar, and a recipient of the Morrison Poetry Prize. After
his studies he served in World War I as a liaison officer in the U.S. Infantry; upon returning home he
became a professor at Cornell. He also served in World War II, where he performed civilian liaison
work. Bishop is probably best known for his light verse, which was frequently published in* Life, The
Saturday Evening Post, *and* The New Yorker. *He also has left an extensive body of essays and
longer works on subjects ranging from Dante, Machiavelli, and St. Francis, to the ideal university
and* The History of Cornell. *The following poem is a playful look at our ideas about science.*

What was our trust, we trust not;
   What was our faith, we doubt;
Whether we must or must not,
   We may debate about.
The soul, perhaps, is a gust of gas   5
   And wrong is a form of right—
But we know that Energy equals Mass
   By the Square of the Speed of Light.

What we have known, we know not;
  What we have proved, abjure;   *10*
Life is a tangled bowknot,
  But one thing still is sure.
Come, little lad; come, little lass—
  Your docile creed recite:
"We know that Energy equals Mass   *15*
  By the Square of the Speed of Light."

QUESTIONS FOR DISCUSSION

1. The term "light verse" is somewhat misleading; though such poems are generally short and humorous, they often slyly make serious comments on society or human beliefs and behavior. What might be the value of a light-hearted treatment of a serious subject?
2. Do you think Bishop is making a serious comment in "$E = mc^2$"? If so, what do you believe he is implying?
3. What are the things we now "doubt," according to this poem?
4. How would you describe the attitude toward science expressed here?

JUNE JORDAN
A Poem About Intelligence for My Brothers and Sisters

June Jordan was born in Harlem in 1936. She attended private schools and, in 1953, entered Barnard College. She married Michael Meyer, a white student, in 1955; her own education was interrupted so that he could continue his studies. This interracial marriage was not well accepted by society (in fact, it was illegal in 43 states), and Jordan experienced a great deal of verbal abuse when she and her husband were together in public. They were divorced in 1965. In 1967 she began her teaching career, which led to a tenured professorship at the State University of New York, Stony Brook. In 1969 she published her first book, Who Look at Me, *and since then her many volumes of poems and essays have earned her an honored place among African-American writers. The schools she had attended, and the writers she had studied there, were predominantly white. The language and themes of these poets and essayists seemed remote from her own, and weakened her faith in the value of her own young poetic voice. But her deep feelings of responsibility toward her race led her to develop a literary style that has become a powerful and significant expression of her activism. The poem reprinted here is Jordan's indictment of the labels society often imposes on minorities, and the effects of such labeling.*

A few year back and they told me Black
means a hole where other folks
got brain/it was like the cells in the heads

of Black children was out to every hour on the hour naps
Scientists called the phenomenon the Notorious   5
Jensen Lapse, remember?[1]
Anyway I was thinking
about how to devise
a test for the wise
like a Stanford-Binet   10
for the C.I.A.
you know?
Take Einstein
being the most the unquestionable the outstanding
the maximal mind of the century   15
right?

And I'm struggling against this lapse leftover
from my Black childhood to fathom why
anybody should say so:
$E = mc\ squared?$ 20
I try that on this old lady live on my block:
She sweeping away Saturday night from the stoop
and mad as can be because some absolute
jackass have left a kingsize mattress where
she have to sweep around it stains and all she   25
don't want to know nothing about in the first place
"Mrs. Johnson!" I say, leaning on the gate
between us: "What you think about somebody come up with an E equals
   $M\ C\ 2$?"

"How you doin," she answer me, sideways, like she don't   30
want to let on she know I ain
combed my hair yet and here it is
Sunday morning but still I have the nerve
to be bothering serious work with these crazy
questions about   35
"E equals what you say again, dear?"
Then I tell her, "Well
also this same guy? I think
he was undisputed Father of the Atom Bomb!"
"That right." She mumbles or grumbles, not too politely   40
"And dint remember to wear socks when he put on
his shoes!" I add on (getting desperate)
at which point Mrs. Johnson take herself and her broom
a very big step down the stoop away from me

---

[1] Arthur Robert Jensen is a psychologist who has argued that the poor scholastic achievement of blacks is due to
   genetic inferiority rather than to cultural factors. [Ed. note.]

"And never did nothing for nobody in particular 45
lessen it was a committee
and
used to say, 'What time is it?'
and
you'd say, 'Six o'clock.' 50
and
he'd say, 'Day or night?'
and
and he never made nobody a cup of tea
in his whole brilliant life!" 55
"and
(my voice rises slightly)
and
he dint never boogie neither: never!"

"Well," say Mrs. Johnson, "Well, honey, 60
I do guess
that's genius for you."

1980

QUESTIONS FOR DISCUSSION

1. Jordan is often admired for her skilled use of voice. How is the voice of this poem essential to its subject matter and theme?
2. What is the significance of the group of facts about Einstein the narrator relates to Mrs. Johnson? How would you describe the narrator's attitude toward Einstein? Toward her own intelligence?
3. What exactly does Jordan seem to be criticizing in this piece? Support your answer with specific passages from the poem.

BARRY LOPEZ
Buffalo

Oregon resident Barry Lopez (1945–   ) has written extensively about North American nature and folklore. In 1978 he received the John Burroughs Medal for excellence in natural history writing. "Buffalo," a strange, almost mystical piece, deals with the white man's destruction of the world of the Indian and the buffalo in the mid-nineteenth century. The narrator of this essay/short story is portrayed as empirical, rationalistic, and narrow-minded; perhaps he represents the white people who arrogantly and ignorantly destroyed a civilization which they could not understand, and thus considered to be "ignorant." Lopez's narrator scientifically examines the stories of the Indians, trying

unsuccessfully (and a little ridiculously) to determine their "truth." Lopez seems to imply that the
dream vision of the Indians, their prophetic expression of Truth, may be more authentic, meaningful,
and satisfying than the scientific worldview which condemns it. The Indian mythology embodies
reality in a way that the empirical method is inadequate to understand and unable to appreciate.

In January 1845, after a week of cold but brilliantly clear weather, it began to snow in southern Wyoming. Snow accumulated on the flat in a dead calm to a depth of four feet in only a few days. The day following the storm was breezy and warm—chinook weather. A party of Cheyenne camped in a river bottom spent the day tramping the snow down, felling cottonwood trees for their horses, and securing game, in response to a dream by one of them, a thirty-year-old man called Blue Feather on the Side of His Head, that they would be trapped by a sudden freeze.

That evening the temperature fell fifty degrees and an ice crust as rigid, as easily broken, as sharp as window glass formed over the snow. The crust held for weeks.

Access across the pane of ice to game and pasturage on the clear, wind-blown slopes of the adjacent Medicine Bow Mountains was impossible for both Indian hunters and a buffalo herd trapped nearby. The buffalo, exhausted from digging in the deep snow, went to their knees by the thousands, their legs slashed by the razor ice, glistening red in the bright sunlight. Their woolly carcasses lay scattered like black boulders over the blinding white of the prairie, connected by a thin cross-hatching of bloody red trails.

Winds moaned for days in the thick fur of the dead and dying buffalo, broken by the agonized bellows of the animals themselves. Coyotes would not draw near. The Cheyenne camped in the river bottom were terrified. As soon as they were able to move they departed. No Cheyenne ever camped there again.

The following summer the storm and the death of the herd were depicted on a buffalo robe by one of the Cheyenne, a man called Raven on His Back. Above the scene, in the sky, he drew a white buffalo. The day they had left camp a man was supposed to have seen a small herd of buffalo, fewer than twenty, leaving the plains and lumbering up the Medicine Bow River into the mountains. He said they were all white, and each seemed to him larger than any bull he had ever seen. There is no record of this man's name, but another Cheyenne in the party, a medicine man called Walks Toward the Two Rivers, carried the story of the surviving white buffalo to Crow and Teton Sioux in an effort to learn its meaning. In spite of the enmity among these tribes their leaders agreed that the incident was a common and disturbing augury. They gathered on the Box Elder River in southeastern Montana in the spring of 1846 to decipher its meaning. No one was able to plumb it, though many had fasted and bathed in preparation.

Buffalo were never seen again on the Laramie Plains after 1845, in spite of the richness of the grasses there and the size of the buffalo herds nearby in those days. The belief that there were still buffalo in the Medicine Bow Mountains, however, survivors of the storm, persisted for years, long after the disappearance of buffalo (some 60 million animals) from Wyoming and neighboring territories by the 1880s.

In the closing years of the nineteenth century, Arapaho and Shoshoni warriors who went into the Medicine Bow to dream say they did, indeed, see buffalo up there then. The animals lived among the barren rocks above timberline, far from any vegetation. They stood more than eight feet at the shoulder; their coats were white as winter ermine and their huge eyes were light blue. At the approach of men they would perch motionless on the granite boulders, like mountain goats. Since fogs are common in these high valleys in spring and summer it was impossible, they say, to tell how many buffalo there were.

In May 1887 a Shoshoni called Long Otter came on two of these buffalo in the Snowy Range. As he watched they watched him. They began raising and lowering their hooves, started drumming softly on the rocks. They began singing a death song, way back in the throat like the sound of wind moaning in a canyon. The man, Long Otter, later lost his mind and was killed in a buckboard accident the following year. As far as I know this is the last report of living buffalo in the Medicine Bow.

It is curious to me that in view of the value of the hides no white man ever tried to find and kill one of these buffalo. But that is the case. No detail of the terrible storm of that winter, or of the presence of a herd of enormous white buffalo in the Medicine Bow, has ever been found among the papers of whites who lived in the area or who might have passed through in the years following.

It should be noted, however, by way of verification, that a geology student from Illinois called Fritiof Fryxell came upon two buffalo skeletons in the Snowy Range in the summer of 1925. Thinking these barren heights an extraordinary elevation at which to find buffalo, he carefully marked the location on a topographic map. He measured the largest of the skeletons, found the size staggering, and later wrote up the incident in the May 1926 issue of the *Journal of Mammalogy*.

In 1955, a related incident came to light. In the fall of 1911, at the request of the Colorado Mountain Club, a party of Arapaho Indians were brought into the Rocky Mountains in the northern part of the state to relate to white residents the history of the area prior to 1859. The settlers were concerned that during the years when the white man was moving into the area, and the Indian was being extirpated, a conflict in historical records arose such that the white record was incomplete and possibly in error.

The Arapaho were at first reluctant to speak; they made up stories of the sort they believed the whites would like to hear. But the interest and persistence of the white listeners made an impression upon them and they began to tell what had really happened.

Among the incidents the Arapaho revealed was that in the winter of 1845 (when news of white settlers coming in covered wagons first reached them) there was a terrible storm. A herd of buffalo wintering in Brainard Valley (called then Bear in the Hole Valley) began singing a death song. At first it was barely audible, and it was believed the wind was making the sound until it got louder and more distinct. As the snow got deeper the buffalo left the valley and began to climb into the mountains. For four days they climbed, still singing the moaning death song, followed by Arapaho warriors, until they reached the top of the mountain. This was the highest place but it had no name. Now it is called Thatchtop Mountain.

During the time the buffalo climbed they did not stop singing. They turned red all over; their eyes became smooth white. The singing became louder. It sounded like thunder that would not stop. Everyone who heard it, even people four or five days' journey away, was terrified.

At the top of the mountain the buffalo stopped singing. They stood motionless in the snow, the wind blowing clouds around them. The Arapaho men who had followed had not eaten for four days. One, wandering into the clouds with his hands outstretched and a rawhide string connecting him to the others, grabbed hold of one of the buffalo and killed it. The remaining buffalo disappeared into the clouds; the death song began again, very softly, and remained behind them. The wind was like the singing of the buffalo. When the clouds cleared the men went down the mountain.

The white people at the 1911 meeting said they did not understand the purpose of telling such a story. The Arapaho said this was the first time the buffalo tried to show them how to climb out through the sky.

The notes of this meeting in 1911 have been lost, but what happened there remained clear in the mind of the son of one of the Indians who was present. It was brought to my attention by accident one evening in the library of the university where I teach. I was reading an article on the introduction of fallow deer in Nebraska in the August 1955 issue of the *Journal of Mammalogy* when this man, who was apparently just walking by, stopped and, pointing at the opposite page, said, "This is not what this is about." The article he indicated was called "An Altitudinal Record for Bison in Northern Colorado." He spoke briefly of it, as if to himself, and then departed.

Excited by this encounter I began to research the incident. I have been able to verify what I have written here. In view of the similarity between the events in the Medicine Bow and those in Colorado, I suspect that there were others in the winter of 1845 who began, as the Arapaho believe, trying to get away from what was coming, and that subsequent attention to this phenomenon is of some importance.

I recently slept among weathered cottonwoods on the Laramie Plains in the vicinity of the Medicine Bow Mountains. I awoke in the morning to find my legs broken.

QUESTIONS FOR DISCUSSION

1. What is the story the Native Americans tell?
2. How does the narrator respond to the dream vision of the white buffalo? (Do not confuse the narrator with the author.) With whom does the narrator seem to sympathize?
3. What meaning did the Indians attribute to the stories? What did the Arapaho mean when they said the buffalo were "trying to get away from what was coming" (par. 18)?
4. Can the scientific worldview, here represented by the narrator and the other white people, accept these stories as the Indians do? Why? What might be the limits of the scientific worldview?
5. What effect does the final sentence have on the reader? What might the narrator mean?

6. This story implies that Native American cultures traditionally have not separated myth from history in the same way Western cultures tend to do. How do you think the author feels about the Native Americans' "prophetic" expression of truth?
7. What are the similarities between this piece and the selection attributed to Chief Seattle (p. 58)? The differences?

MARZIEH AHMADI OSKOOII
I'm a Woman

Marzieh Ahmadi Oskooii was born in 1945 in Oskoo (Iran). Throughout her life she was involved in fighting against social injustices in Iran. She was imprisoned for her anti-government involvement, and, in 1973 she was shot and killed by government forces. The social and political poems she left behind were an inspiration to the people to continue their fight for justice. The following poem is, in a sense, a definition poem in which Oskooii claims that the reality of woman in society is much greater and more complex than the mere word "woman" implies—"woman" can, in fact, mean anything from mother to Iranian revolutionary.

I'm a mother,
I'm a sister,
faithful spouse,
woman—
a woman, who, from the beginning   5
with bare feet,
has run hither and thither over the steaming hot sands
of the deserts.

I'm from the small villages of the North,
a woman, who from the beginning,   10
has worked to the limits of her power
in the rice paddies and tea plantations, who
along with my skinny cow in the
threshing field, from dawn to dusk,
has felt the weight of pain.   15
A woman who gives birth to her babe
in the mountains,
loses her goat in the expanse of
the plains,
to sit mourning.   20

I'm a woman,
worker whose hands turn
the great machines of the factory,
which each day,
tear to bits my strength,   25
in the threads of the wheels,
in front of my eyes,

A woman from whose life's blood,
the carcass of the blood-sucker bloats
and from the loss of whose blood,   30
the profit of the usurer increases.

A woman, for whom, in your shameless lexicon,
there is no word
corresponding to her significance.
Your vocabulary speaks only of woman,   35
whose hands are white,
whose body is supple,
whose skin soft,
the hair perfumed.

I'm a woman,   40
a woman whose skin is the mirror of the deserts
and whose hair smells of factory smoke.
I'm a woman—
hands full of wounds,
from the cutting blades of giant pain.   45

How shameless of you to announce
that my hunger is an illusion,
my nakedness
a make-believe.

A woman for whom   50
in your shameless lexicon,
is no word
corresponding to her significance.
A woman in whose chest
is a heart   55
full of the festering
wounds of wrath,
in whose eyes
the red
reflection of the arrows   60

of liberty is flying.
It is she whose hands have
been trained
through all her sorrows, to also man
the gun.   *65*

QUESTIONS FOR DISCUSSION

1. Who seems to be the intended audience for this poem?
2. What is its purpose?
3. According to Oskooii, what does the word "woman" mean to her reader?
4. What is *her* definition of the word "woman"?
5. Discuss what she means by the phrase "shameless lexicon" (line 32).
6. How would an American rewrite this poem to fit American culture? How much would change?

YÜ HSÜAN-CHI
On a Visit to Ch'ung Chên Taoist Temple I See in the South Hall the List of Successful Candidates in the Imperial Examinations

The Chinese poet Yü Hsüan-Chi (ca. 843–868), a well-educated and highly sophisticated woman, was taken as a concubine by an official, Li Yi, to whom many of her poems are addressed. He later abandoned her at the insistence of his wife, and Yü Hsüan-Chi became a Taoist nun. In great poverty she began to take lovers once more, and was finally charged (very probably falsely) with killing her maid. Although her poet friends tried to intervene, she was executed. Her intense, symbolic, and subtly passionate poetry conveys a keen awareness of the fact that, as a woman, she is considered inferior to and dependent upon men. In the following poem she expresses her resentment that only men were allowed to take the Imperial examinations.

Cloud capped peaks fill the eyes
In the Spring sunshine.
Their names are written in beautiful characters
And posted in order of merit.
How I hate this silk dress   5
That conceals a poet.
I lift my head and read their names
In powerless envy.

QUESTIONS FOR DISCUSSION

1. The Imperial examinations were, in a sense, entrance examinations. By doing well on these exams, a young man could be chosen for a coveted government position. Even if he wasn't chosen for government service, he became part of the powerful intellectual elite of the culture. Part of the examination had to do with writing poetry. How does this fact relate to the lines, "How I hate this silk dress / That conceals a poet"?
2. What does the first image of the poem, the "cloud capped peaks" in the spring sunshine, have to do with the rest of the poem?
3. Contrast this poem with "I'm a Woman" (p. 397). What are the main differences?

SOR JUANA INÉS DE LA CRUZ
She Proves the Inconsistency of the Desires and Criticism of Men Who Accuse Women of What They Themselves Cause

Mexican poet Sor (Sister) Juana Inés de la Cruz (1648 or 1651–1695) was one of the earliest writers of the Americas, and also among the earliest champions of women's rights. Her intellectual curiosity was exceptional: she learned to read as a child by secretly following her sister to school, and by the age of 13 she was famed for her extensive learning (both in the arts and the sciences) and her intellectual capacity. Church records indicate that Sor Juana was an illegitimate child—apparently the reason for the controversy surrounding her date of birth—born in the small village of Nepantla. She was raised with her mother's family under the eye of her learned and appreciative grandfather. Soon after his death she went to Mexico City to live with wealthy relatives. She became a favorite of the nobility there, and spent two years in the Mexican court before entering a convent. From the convent, Sor Juana continued her correspondence with members of the court, often writing poems for important courtly events. She also continued to study fervently until, in 1691, the church demanded that she give up her writing, her studies, and her other worldly attachments. It is very likely that church officials were motivated by jealousy rather than spiritual concerns, for Sor Juana's beauty and accomplishments were legendary. She wrote an eloquent response to their demands, the "Respuesta a Sor Filotea," which is the New World's first affirmation of the right of women to learn and to write; but in the end she obeyed the church's orders and, in documents signed with her own blood, reaffirmed her vows. She died in 1695 while helping the sick during a plague.

Foolish men who accuse
women unreasonably,
you blame yet never see
you cause what you abuse.

You crawl before her, sad,   5
begging for a quick cure;
why ask her to be pure
when you have made her bad?

You combat her resistance
and then with gravity,   10
you call frivolity
the fruit of your intents.

In one heroic breath
your reason fails, like a wild
bogeyman made up by a child   15
who then is scared to death.

With idiotic pride
you hope to find your prize:
a regal whore like Thaïs
and Lucretia for a bride.   20

Has anyone ever seen
a stranger moral fervor:
you who dirty the mirror
regret it is not clean?

You treat favor and disdain   25
with the same shallow mock-
ing voice: love you and you squawk,
demur and you complain.

No answer at her door
will be a proper part: 30
say no—she has no heart,
say yes—and she's a whore.

Two levels to your game
in which *you* are the fool:
one you blame as cruel,   35
one who yields, you shame.

How can one not be bad
the way your love pretends
to be? Say no and she offends.
Consent and you are mad.   40

With all the fury and pain
your whims cause her, it's good
for her who has withstood
you. Now go and complain!

You let her grief take flight   *45*
and free her with new wings.
Then after sordid things
you say she's not upright.

Who is at fault in all
this errant passion? She   *50*
who falls for his pleas, or he
who pleads for her to fall?

Whose guilt is greater in
this raw erotic play?
The girl who sins for pay   *55*
or man who pays for sin?

So why be shocked or taunt
her for the steps you take?
Care for her as you make
her, or shape her as you want,   *60*

but do not come with pleas
and later throw them in
her face, screaming of sin
when you were at her knees.

You fight us from birth   *65*
with weapons of arrogance.
Between promise and pleading stance,
you are devil, flesh, and earth.

QUESTIONS FOR DISCUSSION

1. What is the theme of this poem? What audience do you imagine Sor Juana had in mind when she wrote it?
2. What is the speaker's attitude toward men at the beginning of the poem? Does her opinion undergo any changes by the end?
3. Compare this poem to Hsüan-Chi's "On a Visit to Chi'ung Chên . . ." (p. 399) and Alice Walker's "In Search of Our Mothers' Gardens" (p. 356). These three women wrote in very different times and cultures; how are their experiences and responses to these experiences similar?
4. Do you agree with Sor Juana's accusations? Do you feel that her poem is still relevant today? Think of examples from your own experiences and culture (television, film, advertising) that in your opinion confirm or disprove Sor Juana's argument.

MAXINE HONG KINGSTON
No Name Woman

Maxine Hong Kingston was born in 1940 in Stockton, California, of Chinese immigrant parents. She graduated from the University of California at Berkeley in 1962, and held various high school and college teaching positions in California and Hawaii; she gave up teaching after the success of her first book, The Woman Warrior. *She now lives in Honolulu with her husband and son. From a very early age she was aware of the conflicting cultures of her dual heritage. The following chapter from her book* The Woman Warrior *illustrates Kingston's highly acclaimed ability to weave together myth, history, and legend. This selection tells the story of the tragic fate of the narrator's Chinese aunt while at the same time emphasizing the narrator's own struggle to come to terms with both her Chinese and her American culture, particularly their respective treatment of women. Like Neruda, Prendergast, Mphahlele, and others in Part 3, Kingston deals with the complexities that result when two very different cultures meet.*

"You must not tell anyone," my mother said, "what I am about to tell you. In China your father had a sister who killed herself. She jumped into the family well. We say that your father has all brothers because it is as if she had never been born.

"In 1924 just a few days after our village celebrated seventeen hurry-up weddings—to make sure that every young man who went 'out on the road' would responsibly come home—your father and his brothers and your grandfather and his brothers and your aunt's new husband sailed for America, the Gold Mountain. It was your grandfather's last trip. Those lucky enough to get contracts waved good-bye from the decks. They fed and guarded the stowaways and helped them off in Cuba, New York, Bali, Hawaii. 'We'll meet in California next year,' they said. All of them sent money home.

"I remember looking at your aunt one day when she and I were dressing; I had not noticed before that she had such a protruding melon of a stomach. But I did not think, 'She's pregnant,' until she began to look like other pregnant women, her shirt pulling and the white tops of her black pants showing. She could not have been pregnant, you see, because her husband had been gone for years. No one said anything. We did not discuss it. In early summer she was ready to have the child, long after the time when it could have been possible.

"The village had also been counting. On the night the baby was to be born the villagers raided our house. Some were crying. Like a great saw, teeth strung with lights, files of people walked zigzag across our land, tearing the rice. Their lanterns doubled in the disturbed black water, which drained away through the broken bunds. As the villagers closed in, we could see that some of them, probably men and women we knew well, wore white masks. The people with long hair hung it over their faces. Women with short hair made it stand up on end. Some had tied white bands around their foreheads, arms, and legs.

"At first they threw mud and rocks at the house. Then they threw eggs and began slaughtering our stock. We could hear the animals scream their deaths—the roosters, the pigs, a last great roar from the ox. Familiar wild heads flared in our night windows; the villagers encircled us. Some of the faces stopped to peer at us, their eyes rushing like searchlights. The hands flattened against the panes, framed heads, and left red prints.

"The villagers broke in the front and the back doors at the same time, even though we had not locked the doors against them. Their knives dripped with the blood of our animals. They smeared blood on the doors and walls. One woman swung a chicken, whose throat she had slit, splattering blood in red arcs about her. We stood together in the middle of our house, in the family hall with the pictures and tables of the ancestors around us, and looked straight ahead.

"At that time the house had only two wings. When the men came back, we would build two more to enclose our courtyard and a third one to begin a second courtyard. The villagers pushed through both wings, even your grandparents' rooms, to find your aunt's, which was also mine until the men returned. From this room a new wing for one of the younger families would grow. They ripped up her clothes and shoes and broke her combs, grinding them underfoot. They tore her work from the loom. They scattered the cooking fire and rolled the new weaving in it. We could hear them in the kitchen breaking our bowls and banging the pots. They overturned the great waist-high earthenware jugs; duck eggs, pickled fruits, vegetables burst out and mixed in acrid torrents. The old woman from the next field swept a broom through the air and loosed the spirits-of-the-broom over our heads. 'Pig.' 'Ghost.' 'Pig,' they sobbed and scolded while they ruined our house.

"When they left, they took sugar and oranges to bless themselves. They cut pieces from the dead animals. Some of them took bowls that were not broken and clothes that were not torn. Afterward we swept up the rice and sewed it back up into sacks. But the smells from the spilled preserves lasted. Your aunt gave birth in the pigsty that night. The next morning when I went for the water, I found her and the baby plugging up the family well.

"Don't let your father know that I told you. He denies her. Now that you have started to menstruate, what happened to her could happen to you. Don't humiliate us. You wouldn't like to be forgotten as if you had never been born. The villagers are watchful."

Whenever she had to warn us about life, my mother told stories that ran like this one, a story to grow up on. She tested our strength to establish realities. Those in the emigrant generations who could not reassert brute survival died young and far from home. Those of us in the first American generations have had to figure out how the invisible world the emigrants built around our childhoods fits in solid America.

The emigrants confused the gods by diverting their curses, misleading them with crooked streets and false names. They must try to confuse their offspring as well, who, I suppose, threaten them in similar ways—always trying to get things straight, always trying to name the unspeakable. The Chinese I know hide their names; sojourners take new names when their lives change and guard their real names with silence.

Chinese-Americans, when you try to understand what things in you are Chinese, how do you separate what is peculiar to childhood, to poverty, insanities, one family, your mother who marked your growing with stories, from what is Chinese? What is Chinese tradition and what is the movies?

If I want to learn what clothes my aunt wore, whether flashy or ordinary, I would have to begin, "Remember Father's drowned-in-the-well sister?" I cannot ask that. My mother has told me once and for all the useful parts. She will add nothing unless powered by Necessity, a riverbank that guides her life. She plants vegetable gardens rather than lawns; she carries the odd-shaped tomatoes home from the fields and eats food left for the gods.

Whenever we did frivolous things, we used up energy; we flew high kites. We children came up off the ground over the melting cones our parents brought home from work and the American movie on New Year's Day—*Oh, You Beautiful Doll* with Betty Grable one year, and *She Wore a Yellow Ribbon* with John Wayne another year. After the one carnival ride each, we paid in guilt; our tired father counted his change on the dark walk home.

Adultery is extravagance. Could people who hatch their own chicks and eat the embryos and the heads for delicacies and boil the feet in vinegar for party food, leaving only the gravel, eating even the gizzard lining—could such people engender a prodigal aunt? To be a woman, to have a daughter in starvation time was a waste enough. My aunt could not have been the lone romantic who gave up everything for sex. Women in the old China did not choose. Some man had commanded her to lie with him and be his secret evil. I wonder whether he masked himself when he joined the raid on her family.

Perhaps she had encountered him in the fields or on the mountain where the daughters-in-law collected fuel. Or perhaps he first noticed her in the marketplace. He was not a stranger because the village housed no strangers. She had to have dealings with him other than sex. Perhaps he worked an adjoining field, or he sold her the cloth for the dress she sewed and wore. His demand must have surprised, then terrified her. She obeyed him; she always did as she was told.

When the family found a young man in the next village to be her husband, she had stood tractably beside the best rooster, his proxy, and promised before they met that she would be his forever. She was lucky that he was her age and she would be the first wife, an advantage secure now. The night she first saw him, he had sex with her. Then he left for America. She had almost forgotten what he looked like. When she tried to envision him, she only saw the black and white face in the group photograph the men had had taken before leaving.

The other man was not, after all, much different from her husband. They both gave orders: she followed. "If you tell your family, I'll beat you. I'll kill you. Be here again next week." No one talked sex, ever. And she might have separated the rapes from the rest of living if only she did not have to buy her oil from him or gather wood in the same forest. I want her fear to have lasted just as long as rape lasted so that the fear could have been contained. No drawn-out fear. But women at sex hazarded birth and hence lifetimes. The fear did not stop but permeated everywhere. She told the man, "I think I'm pregnant." He organized the raid against her.

On nights when my mother and father talked about their life back home, sometimes they mentioned an "outcast table" whose business they still seemed to be settling, their voices tight. In a commensal tradition, where food is precious, the powerful older people made wrongdoers eat alone. Instead of letting them start separate new lives like the Japanese, who could become samurais and geishas, the Chinese family, faces averted but eyes glowering sideways, hung on to the offenders and fed them leftovers. My aunt must have lived in the same house as my parents and eaten at an outcast table. My mother spoke about the raid as if she had seen it, when she and my aunt, a daughter-in-law to a different household, should not have been living together at all. Daughters-in-law lived with their husbands' parents, not their own; a synonym for marriage in Chinese is "taking a daughter-in-law." Her husband's parents could have sold her, mortgaged her, stoned her. But they had sent her back to her own mother and father, a mysterious act hinting at disgraces not told me. Perhaps they had thrown her out to deflect the avengers.

She was the only daughter; her four brothers went with her father, husband, and uncles "out on the road" and for some years became western men. When the goods were divided among the family, three of the brothers took land, and the youngest, my father, chose an education. After my grandparents gave their daughter away to her husband's family, they had dispensed all the adventure and all the property. They expected her alone to keep the traditional ways, which her brothers, now among the barbarians, could fumble without detection. The heavy, deep-rooted women were to maintain the past against the flood, safe for returning. But the rare urge west had fixed upon our family, and so my aunt crossed boundaries not delineated in space.

The work of preservation demands that the feelings playing about in one's guts not be turned into action. Just watch their passing like cherry blossoms. But perhaps my aunt, my forerunner, caught in a slow life, let dreams grow and fade and after some months or years went toward what persisted. Fear at the enormities of the forbidden kept her desires delicate, wire and bone. She looked at a man because she liked the way the hair was tucked behind his ears, or she liked the question-mark line of a long torso curving at the shoulder and straight at the hip. For warm eyes or a soft voice or a slow walk—that's all –a few hairs, a line, a brightness, a sound, a pace, she gave up family. She offered us up for a charm that vanished with tiredness, a pigtail that didn't toss when the wind died. Why, the wrong lighting could erase the dearest thing about him.

It could very well have been, however, that my aunt did not take subtle enjoyment of her friend, but, a wild woman, kept rollicking company. Imagining her free with sex doesn't fit, though. I don't know any women like that, or men either. Unless I see her life branching into mine, she gives me no ancestral help.

To sustain her being in love, she often worked at herself in the mirror, guessing at the colors and shapes that would interest him, changing them frequently in order to hit on the right combination. She wanted him to look back.

On a farm near the sea, a woman who tended her appearance reaped a reputation for eccentricity. All the married women blunt-cut their hair in flaps about their ears or pulled it back in tight buns. No nonsense. Neither style blew easily into heart-catching tangles. And at their weddings they displayed themselves in their long hair for the last time. "It brushed the backs of my knees," my mother tells me. "It was braided, and even so, it brushed the backs of my knees."

At the mirror my aunt combed individuality into her bob. A bun could have been contrived to escape into black streamers blowing in the wind or in quiet wisps about her face, but only the older women in our picture album wear buns. She brushed her hair back from her forehead, tucking the flaps behind her ears. She looped a piece of thread, knotted into a circle between her index fingers and thumbs, and ran the double strand across her forehead. When she closed her fingers as if she were making a pair of shadow geese bite, the string twisted together catching the little hairs. Then she pulled the thread away from her skin, ripping the hairs out neatly, her eyes watering from the needles of pain. Opening her fingers, she cleaned the thread, then rolled it along her hairline and the tops of her eyebrows. My mother did the same to me and my sisters and herself. I used to believe that the expression "caught by the short hairs" meant a captive held with a depilatory string. It especially hurt at the temples, but my mother said we were lucky we didn't have to have our feet bound when we were seven. Sisters used to sit on their beds and cry together, she said, as their mothers or their slave removed the bandages for a few minutes each night and let the blood gush back into their veins. I hope that the man my aunt loved appreciated a smooth brow, that he wasn't just a tits-and-ass man.

Once my aunt found a freckle on her chin, at a spot that the almanac said predestined her for unhappiness. She dug it out with a hot needle and washed the wound with peroxide.

More attention to her looks than these pullings of hairs and pickings at spots would have caused gossip among the villagers. They owned work clothes and good clothes, and they wore good clothes for feasting the new seasons. But since a woman combing her hair hexes beginnings, my aunt rarely found an occasion to look her best. Women looked like great sea snails—the corded wood, babies, and laundry they carried were the whorls on their backs. The Chinese did not admire a bent back; goddesses and warriors stood straight. Still there must have been a marvelous freeing of beauty when a worker laid down her burden and stretched and arched.

Such commonplace loveliness, however, was not enough for my aunt. She dreamed of a lover for the fifteen days of New Year's, the time for families to exchange visits, money, and food. She plied her secret comb. And sure enough she cursed the year, the family, the village, and herself.

Even as her hair lured her imminent lover, many other men looked at her. Uncles, cousins, nephews, brothers would have looked, too, had they been home between journeys. Perhaps they had already been restraining their curiosity, and they left, fearful that their glances, like a field of nesting birds, might be startled and caught. Poverty hurt, and that was their first reason for leaving. But another, final reason for leaving the crowded house was the never-said.

She may have been unusually beloved, the precious only daughter, spoiled and mirror gazing because of the affection the family lavished on her. When her husband left, they welcomed the chance to take her back from the in-laws; she could live like the little daughter for just a while longer. There are stories that my grandfather was different from other people, "crazy ever since the little Jap bayoneted him in the head." He used to put his naked penis on the dinner table, laughing. And one day he brought home a baby girl, wrapped up inside his brown western-style greatcoat. He had traded one of his sons, probably my father, the youngest, for her. My grandmother made him trade back. When he finally got a daughter of his own, he doted on her. They must have all loved her, except perhaps my father, the only brother who never went back to China, having once been traded for a girl.

Brothers and sisters, newly men and women, had to efface their sexual color and present plain miens. Disturbing hair and eyes, a smile like no other, threatened the ideal of five generations living under one roof. To focus blurs, people shouted face to face and yelled from room to room. The immigrants I know have loud voices, unmodulated to American tones even after years away from the village where they called their friendships out across the fields. I have not been able to stop my mother's screams in public libraries or over telephones. Walking erect (knees straight, toes pointed forward, not pigeon-toed, which is Chinese-feminine) and speaking in an inaudible voice, I have tried to turn myself American-feminine. Chinese communication was loud, public. Only sick people had to whisper. But at the dinner table, where the family members came nearest one another, no one could talk, not the outcasts nor any eaters. Every word that falls from the mouth is a coin lost. Silently they gave and accepted food with both hands. A preoccupied child who took his bowl with one hand got a sideways glare. A complete moment of total attention is due everyone alike. Children and lovers have no singularity here, but my aunt used a secret voice, a separate attentiveness.

She kept the man's name to herself throughout her labor and dying; she did not accuse him that he be punished with her. To save her inseminator's name she gave silent birth.

He may have been somebody in her own household, but intercourse with a man outside the family would have been no less abhorrent. All the village were kinsmen, and the titles shouted in loud country voices never let kinship be forgotten. Any man within visiting distance would have been neutralized as a lover—"brother," "younger brother," "older brother"—one hundred and fifteen relationship titles. Parents researched birth charts probably not so much to assure good fortune as to circumvent incest in a population that has but one hundred surnames. Everybody has eight million relatives. How useless then sexual mannerisms, how dangerous.

As if it came from an atavism deeper than fear, I used to add "brother" silently to boys' names. It hexed the boys, who would or would not ask me to dance, and made them less scary and as familiar and deserving of benevolence as girls.

But, of course, I hexed myself also—no dates. I should have stood up, both arms waving, and shouted out across libraries, "Hey, you! Love me back." I had no idea, though, how to make attraction selective, how to control its direction and magnitude. If I made myself American-pretty so that the five or six Chinese boys in the class fell in love with me, everyone else—the Caucasian, Negro, and Japanese boys—would too. Sisterliness, dignified and honorable, made much more sense.

Attraction eludes control so stubbornly that whole societies designed to organize relationships among people cannot keep order, not even when they bind people to one another from childhood and raise them together. Among the very poor and the wealthy, brothers married their adopted sisters, like doves. Our family allowed some romance, paying adult brides' prices and providing dowries so that their sons and daughters could marry strangers. Marriage promises to turn strangers into friendly relatives—a nation of siblings.

In the village structure, spirits shimmered among the live creatures, balanced and held in equilibrium by time and land. But one human being flaring up into violence could open up a black hole, a maelstrom that pulled in the sky. The frightened villagers, who depended on one another to maintain the real, went to my aunt to show her a personal, physical representation of the break she had made in the "roundness." Misallying couples snapped off the future, which was to be embodied in true offspring. The villagers punished her for acting as if she could have a private life, secret and apart from them.

If my aunt had betrayed the family at a time of large grain yields and peace, when many boys were born, and wings were being built on many houses, perhaps she might have escaped such severe punishment. But the men—hungry, greedy, tired of planting in dry soil—had been forced to leave the village in order to send food-money home. There were ghost plagues, bandit plagues, wars with the Japanese, floods. My Chinese brother and sister had died of an unknown sickness. Adultery, perhaps only a mistake during good times, became a crime when the village needed food.

The round moon cakes and round doorways, the round tables of graduated size that fit one roundness inside another, round windows and rice bowls—these talismans had lost their power to warn this family of the law: a family must be whole, faithfully keeping the descent line by having sons to feed the old and the dead, who in turn look after the family. The villagers came to show my aunt and her lover-in-hiding a broken house. The villagers were speeding up the circling of events because she was too shortsighted to see that her infidelity had already harmed the village, that waves of consequences would return unpredictably, sometimes in disguise, as now, to hurt her. This roundness had to be made coin-sized so that she would see its circumference: punish her at the birth of her baby. Awaken her to the inexorable. People who refused fatalism because they could invent small resources insisted on culpability. Deny accidents and wrest fault from the stars.

After the villagers left, their lanterns now scattering in various directions toward home, the family broke their silence and cursed her. "Aiaa, we're going to die. Death is coming. Death is coming. Look what you've done. You've killed us. Ghost! Dead ghost! Ghost! You've never been born." She ran out into the fields, far enough from the house so that she could no longer hear their voices, and pressed herself against the earth, her own land no more. When she felt the birth coming, she thought that she had been hurt. Her body seized together. "They've hurt me too much," she thought. "This is gall, and it will kill me." With forehead and knees against the earth, her body convulsed and then relaxed. She turned on her back, lay on the ground. The black well of sky and stars went out and out and out forever; her body and her complexity seemed to disappear. She was one of the stars, a bright dot in blackness, without home, without a companion, in eternal cold and silence. An agoraphobia rose in her, speeding higher and higher, bigger and bigger; she would not be able to contain it; there would be no end to fear.

Flayed, unprotected against space, she felt pain return, focusing her body. This pain chilled her—a cold, steady kind of surface pain. Inside, spasmodically, the other pain, the pain of the child, heated her. For hours she lay on the ground, alternately body and space. Sometimes a vision of normal comfort obliterated reality: she saw the family in the evening gambling at the dinner table, the young people massaging their elders' backs. She saw them congratulating one another, high joy on the mornings the rice shoots came up. When these pictures burst, the stars drew yet further apart. Black space opened.

She got to her feet to fight better and remembered that old-fashioned women gave birth in their pigsties to fool the jealous, pain-dealing gods, who do not snatch piglets. Before the next spasms could stop her, she ran to the pigsty, each step a rushing out into emptiness. She climbed over the fence and knelt in the dirt. It was good to have a fence enclosing her, a tribal person alone.

Laboring, this woman who had carried her child as a foreign growth that sickened her every day, expelled it at last. She reached down to touch the hot, wet, moving mass, surely smaller than anything human, and could feel that it was human after all—fingers, toes, nails, nose. She pulled it up on to her belly, and it lay curled there, butt in the air, feet precisely tucked one under the other. She opened her loose shirt and buttoned the child inside. After resting, it squirmed and thrashed and she pushed it up to her breast. It turned its head this way and that until it found her nipple. There, it made little snuffling noises. She clenched her teeth at its preciousness, lovely as a young calf, a piglet, a little dog.

She may have gone to the pigsty as a last act of responsibility: she would protect this child as she had protected its father. It would look after her soul, leaving supplies on her grave. But how would this tiny child without family find her grave when there would be no marker for her anywhere, neither in the earth nor the family hall? No one would give her a family hall name. She had taken the child with her into the wastes. At its birth the two of them had felt the same raw pain of separation, a wound that only the family pressing tight could close. A child with no descent line would not soften her life but only trail after her, ghostlike, begging her to give it purpose. At dawn the villagers on their way to the fields would stand around the fence and look.

Full of milk, the little ghost slept. When it awoke, she hardened her breasts against the milk that crying loosens. Toward morning she picked up the baby and walked to the well.

Carrying the baby to the well shows loving. Otherwise abandon it. Turn its face into the mud. Mothers who love their children take them along. It was probably a girl; there is some hope of forgiveness for boys.

"Don't tell anyone you had an aunt. Your father does not want to hear her name. She has never born." I have believed that sex was unspeakable and words so strong and fathers so frail that "aunt" would do my father mysterious harm. I have thought that my family, having settled among immigrants who had also been their neighbors in the ancestral land, needed to clean their name, and a wrong word would incite the kinspeople even here. But there is more to this silence: they want me to participate in her punishment. And I have.

In the twenty years since I heard this story I have not asked for details nor said my aunt's name; I do not know it. People who can comfort the dead can also chase after them to hurt them further—a reverse ancestor worship. The real punishment was not the raid swiftly inflicted by the villagers, but the family's deliberately forgetting her. Her betrayal so maddened them, they saw to it that she would suffer forever, even after death. Always hungry, always needing, she would have to beg food from other ghosts, snatch and steal it from those whose living descendants give them gifts. She would have to fight the ghosts massed at crossroads for the buns a few thoughtful citizens leave to decoy her away from village and home so that the ancestral spirits could feast unharassed. At peace, they could act like gods, not ghosts, their descent lines providing them with paper suits and dresses, spirit money, paper houses, paper automobiles, chicken, meat, and rice into eternity— essences delivered up in smoke and flames, steam and incense rising from each rice bowl. In an attempt to make the Chinese care for people outside the family, Chairman Mao encourages us now to give our paper replicas to the spirits of outstanding soldiers and workers, no matter whose ancestors they may be. My aunt remains forever hungry. Goods are not distributed evenly among the dead.

My aunt haunts me—her ghost drawn to me because now, after fifty years of neglect, I alone devote pages of paper to her, though not origamied into houses and clothes. I do not think she always means me well. I am telling on her, and she was a spite suicide, drowning herself in the drinking water. The Chinese are always very frightened of the drowned one, whose weeping ghost, wet hair hanging and skin bloated, waits silently by the water to pull down a substitute.

QUESTIONS FOR DISCUSSION

1. The narrator says her mother told stories to "warn us about life." What might the mother have been trying to teach her daughter with this story? What clues are there that the mother has interpreted events to fit her purpose?
2. How does the daughter reinterpret the story her mother tells? Why? How does this change its meaning?
3. One of the central themes of ethnic literature in America is the theme of identity. What difficulties does the narrator face in coming to terms with her Chinese-American heritage?
4. Where does the daughter receive her information about China? How reliable are these sources?
5. How does this fictional text illustrate the concept of woman as "Other," as discussed in the selection by Simone de Beauvoir (p. 342)?
6. The publishers originally called this piece autobiography, but the author calls it fiction. What makes it fiction? What is the difference between fiction and autobiography?

SAPPHO
Invocation to Aphrodite

Sappho was born ca. 630 B.C.E. on the island of Lesbos. Her lyric poetry was famous among the ancients, and she was often referred to as the tenth Muse. Unfortunately, of the thousands of lines she wrote, only one or two short poems and various fragments have survived; but these are clearly worthy of the praise they received from the classical critics, and they have established Sappho's poetic genius for modern readers. She wrote most often of the life of women in Greece: of youth, marriage, and love, especially love between young women. (In Sappho's time this love was considered a natural stage in a girl's life between her childhood and her role as wife and mother). In the following poem the speaker prays to Aphrodite, the goddess of love; like Yü Hsüan-Chi in her lyric poem "On a Visit to Ch'ung Chên . . ." (p. 399), Sappho is expressing an intense moment of feeling.

Throned in splendor, deathless, O Aphrodite,
child of Zeus, charm-fashioner, I entreat you
not with griefs and bitternesses to break my
      spirit, O goddess;

standing by me rather, if once before now   5
far away you heard, when I called upon you,
left your father's dwelling place and descended,
      yoking the golden

chariot to sparrows, who fairly drew you
down in speed aslant the black world, the bright air   10
trembling at the heart to the pulse of countless
      fluttering wingbeats.

Swiftly then they came, and you, blessed lady,
smiling on me out of immortal beauty,
asked me what affliction was on me, why I   15
      called thus upon you,

what beyond all else I would have befall my
tortured heart: "Whom then would you have Persuasion
force to serve desire in your heart? Who is it,
      Sappho, that hurt you?   20

Though she now escape you, she soon will follow;
though she take not gifts from you, she will give them:
though she love not, yet she will surely love you
      even unwilling."

In such guise come even again and set me   25
free from doubt and sorrow; accomplish all those
things my heart desires to be done; appear and
      stand at my shoulder.

QUESTIONS FOR DISCUSSION

1. What is the speaker of this poem asking of Aphrodite?
2. This poem implies a relationship between love and pain. What is that relationship? Do you agree?
3. How does this poem fit the definitions of art in the essays "What Use Is Art?" (p. 308) and "The Cultural Importance of the Arts" (p. 310)?
4. Contrast the attitude toward women expressed in this poem with that explained in "Women in Athens" (p. 247).

MURASAKI SHIKIBU
Lavender

The Tale of Genji was probably written early in the eleventh century by Murasaki Shikibu, a court woman of Heian Japan (794–1185 C.E.). The Genji, which is surprisingly "modern" in characterization and theme, is considered by many critics to be the world's first novel. Most of this complex and sophisticated romance revolves around the adventures of a nobleman named Genji. "Lavender," the third chapter of the work, describes Genji's relationship with the beautiful young girl Murasaki. He falls in love with her at first sight, adopts her, and, later in the novel, marries her. This romance is of special interest for its complex characters, its abundant and fascinating details of Japanese life in this period, and its nostalgic tone.

Genji was suffering from repeated attacks of malaria. All manner of religious services were commissioned, but they did no good.

In a certain temple in the northern hills, someone reported, there lived a sage who was a most accomplished worker of cures. "During the epidemic last summer all sorts of people went to him. He was able to cure them immediately when all other treatment had failed. You must not let it have its way. You must summon him at once."

Genji sent off a messenger, but the sage replied that he was old and bent and unable to leave his cave.

There was no help for it, thought Genji: he must quietly visit the man. He set out before dawn, taking four or five trusted attendants with him.

The temple was fairly deep in the northern hills. Though the cherry blossoms had already fallen in the city, it being late in the Third Month, the mountain cherries were at their best. The deepening mist as the party entered the hills delighted him. He did not often go on such expeditions, for he was of such rank that freedom of movement was not permitted him.

The temple itself was a sad place. The old man's cave was surrounded by rocks, high in the hills behind. Making his way up to it, Genji did not at first reveal his identity. He was in rough disguise, but the holy man immediately saw that he was someone of importance.

"This is a very great honor. You will be the gentleman who sent for me? My mind has left the world, and I have so neglected the ritual that it has quite gone out of my head. I fear that your journey has been in vain." Yet he got busily to work, and he smiled his pleasure at the visit.

He prepared medicines and had Genji drink them, and as he went through his spells and incantations the sun rose higher. Genji walked a few steps from the cave and surveyed the scene. The cave was on a height with priestly cells spread out below it. Down a winding path he saw a wattled fence of better workmanship than similar fences nearby. The halls and galleries within were nicely disposed and there were fine trees in the garden.

"Whose house might that be?"

"A certain bishop, I am told, has been living there in seclusion for the last two years or so."

"Someone who calls for ceremony—and ceremony is hardly possible in these clothes. He must not know that I am here."

Several pretty little girls had come out to draw water and cut flowers for the altar.

"And I have been told that a lady is in residence too. The bishop can hardly be keeping a mistress. I wonder who she might be."

Several of his men went down to investigate, and reported upon what they had seen. "Some very pretty young ladies and some older women too, and some little girls."

Despite the sage's ministrations, which still continued, Genji feared a new seizure as the sun rose higher.

"It is too much on your mind," said the sage. "You must try to think of something else."

Genji climbed the hill behind the temple and looked off toward the city. The forests receded into a spring haze.

"Like a painting," he said. "People who live in such a place can hardly want to be anywhere else."

The evening was long. He took advantage of a dense haze to have a look at the house behind the wattled fence. Sending back everyone except Koremitsu, he took up a position at the fence. In the west room sat a nun[1] who had a holy image before her. The blinds were slightly raised and she seemed to be offering flowers. She was leaning against a pillar and had a text spread out on an armrest. The effort to read seemed to take all her strength. Perhaps in her forties, she had a fair, delicate skin and a pleasantly full face, though the effects of illness were apparent. The features suggested breeding and cultivation. Cut cleanly at the shoulders, her hair seemed to him far more pleasing than if it had been permitted to trail the usual length. Beside her were two attractive women, and little girls scampered in and out. Much the prettiest was a girl of perhaps ten in a soft white singlet and a russet robe. He saw how lovely she would one day be. Rich hair spread over her shoulders like a fan. Her face was flushed from weeping.

---

[1] **nun** "Nun" and "bishop" are used here in the Buddhist, rather than the Christian, sense. Often in the Buddhist religion ordinary people will, in the final stage of life, renounce earthly attachments in preparation for death and a higher rebirth. [Ed. note.]

"What is it?" The nun looked up. "Another fight?" He thought he saw a resemblance. Perhaps they were mother and daughter.

"Inuki let my baby sparrows loose." The child was very angry. "I had them in
a basket."

"That stupid child," said a rather handsome woman with rich hair who
seemed to be called Shōnagon and was apparently the girl's nurse. "She always
manages to do the wrong thing, and we are forever scolding her. Where will they
have flown off to? They were getting to be such sweet little things too! How awful if
the crows find them." She went out.

"What a silly child you are, really too silly," said the nun. "I can't be sure I will
last out the day, and here you are worrying about sparrows. I've told you so many
times that it's a sin to put birds in a cage. Come here."

The child knelt down beside her. She was charming, with rich, unplucked
eyebrows and hair pushed childishly back from the forehead. How he would like to
see her in a few years! And a sudden realization brought him close to tears: the
resemblance to Fujitsubo,[2] for whom he so yearned, was astonishing.

The nun stroked the girl's hair. "You will not comb it and still it's so pretty. I
worry about you, you do seem so very young. Others are much more grown up at
your age. Your poor dead mother: she was only ten when her father died, and she
understood everything. What will become of you when I am gone?"

She was weeping, and a vague sadness had come over Genji too. The girl
gazed attentively at her and then looked down. The hair that fell over her forehead
was thick and lustrous.

> *"Are these tender grasses to grow without the dew*
> *Which holds itself back from the heavens that would receive it?"[3]*

There were tears in the nun's voice, and the other woman seemed also to be
speaking through tears:

> *"It cannot be that the dew will vanish away*
> *Ere summer comes to these early grasses of spring."*

The bishop came in. "What is this? Your blinds up? And today of all days you
are out at the veranda? I have just been told that General Genji is up at the hermitage
being treated for malaria. He came in disguise and I was not told in time to pay a call."

"And what a sight we are. You don't suppose he saw us?" She lowered the blinds.

"The shining one of whom the whole world talks. Wouldn't you like to see
him? Enough to make a saint throw off the last traces of the vulgar world, they say,
and feel as if new years had been added to his life. I will get off a note."

---

[2]**Fujitsubo** The mistress of Genji's father the emperor. It was common for courtiers of the period to have one official
wife and then take a number of mistresses. Fujitsubo herself was said to resemble Genji's mother Kiritsubo, who
died when Genji was a young boy. [Ed. note.]

[3]For the people of Heian Japan, poetry functioned as a refined form of communication. The poet was admired
according to the degree of subtlety, sensitivity, and delicacy of emotion expressed in his or her poem. [Ed. note.]

He hurried away, and Genji too withdrew. What a discovery! It was for such unforeseen rewards that his amorous followers were so constantly on the prowl. Such a rare outing for him, and it had brought such a find! She was a perfectly beautiful child. Who might she be? He was beginning to make plans: the child must stand in the place of the one whom she so resembled.

As he lay down to sleep, an acolyte came asking for Koremitsu.[4] The cell was a narrow one and Genji could hear everything that was said.

"Though somewhat startled to learn that your lord had passed us by, we should have come immediately. The fact is that his secrecy rather upset us. We might, you know, have been able to offer shabby accommodations."

Genji sent back that he had been suffering from malaria since about the middle of the month and had been persuaded to seek the services of the sage, of whom he had only recently heard. "Such is his reputation that I hated to risk marring it by failing to recover. That is the reason for my secrecy. We shall come down immediately."

The bishop himself appeared. He was a man of the cloth, to be sure, but an unusual one, of great courtliness and considerable fame. Genji was ashamed of his own rough disguise.

The bishop spoke of his secluded life in the hills. Again and again he urged Genji to honor his house. "It is a log hut, no better than this, but you may find the stream cool and pleasant."

Genji went with him, though somewhat embarrassed at the extravagant terms in which he had been described to women who had not seen him. He wanted to know more about the little girl. The flowers and grasses in the bishop's garden, though of the familiar varieties, had a charm all their own. The night being dark, flares had been set out along the brook, and there were lanterns at the eaves. A delicate fragrance drifted through the air, mixing with the stronger incense from the altar and the very special scent which had been burnt into Genji's robes. The ladies within must have found the blend unsettling.

The bishop talked of this ephemeral world and of the world to come. His own burden of sin was heavy, thought Genji, that he had been lured into an illicit and profitless affair.[5] He would regret it all his life and suffer even more terribly in the life to come. What joy to withdraw to such a place as this! But with the thought came thoughts of the young face he had seen earlier in the evening.

"Do you have someone with you here? I had a dream that suddenly begins to make sense."

"How quick you are with your dreams, sir! I fear my answer will disappoint you. It has been a very long time since the Lord Inspector died. I don't suppose you will even have heard of him. He was my brother-in-law. His widow turned her back on the world and recently she has been ill, and since I do not go down to the city she has come to stay with me here. It was her thought that I might be able to help her."

"I have heard that your sister had a daughter. I ask from no more than idle curiosity, you must believe me."

---

[4]**Koremitsu** Genji's favorite servant. [Ed. note.]
[5]**profitless affair** That is, with Fujitsubo, his father's mistress. [Ed. note.]

"There was an only daughter. She too has been dead these ten years and more. He took very great pains with her education and hoped to send her to court; but he died before that ambition could be realized, and the nun, my sister, was left to look after her. I do not know through whose offices it was that Prince Hyōbu began visiting the daughter in secret. His wife is from a very proud family, you know, sir, and there were unpleasant incidents, which finally drove the poor thing into a fatal decline. I saw before my own eyes how worry can destroy a person."

So the child he had seen would be the daughter of Prince Hyōbu and the unfortunate lady; and it was Fujitsubo, the prince's sister, whom she so resembled. He wanted more than ever to meet her. She was an elegant child, and she did not seem at all spoiled. What a delight if he could take her into his house and make her his ideal!

"A very sad story." He wished to be completely sure. "Did she leave no one behind?"

"She had a child just before she died, a girl, a great source of worry for my poor sister in her declining years."

There could be no further doubt. "What I am about to say will, I fear, startle you—but might I have charge of the child? I have reasons. I am not alone, and yet my life is lonely. If you are telling yourself that she is too young—well, sir, you are doing me an injustice. Other men may have improper motives, but I do not."

"Your words quite fill me with delight. But she is indeed young, so very young that we could not possibly think even in jest of asking you to take responsibility for her. Only the man who is presently to be her husband can take that responsibility. In a matter of such import I am not competent to give an answer. I must discuss the matter with my sister." He was suddenly remote and chilly.

Genji had spoken with youthful impulsiveness and could not think what to do next.

"It is my practice to conduct services in the chapel of Lord Amitābha." The bishop got up to leave. "I have not yet said vespers. I shall come again when they are over."

Genji was not feeling well. A shower passed on a chilly mountain wind, and the sound of the waterfall was higher. Intermittently came a rather sleepy voice, solemn and somehow ominous, reading a sacred text. The most insensitive of men would have been aroused by the scene. Genji was unable to sleep. The vespers were very long and it was growing late. There was evidence that the women in the inner rooms were still up. They were being quiet, but he heard a rosary brush against an armrest and, to give him a sense of elegant companionship, a faint rustling of silk. Screens lined the inside wall, very near at hand. He pushed one of the center panels some inches aside and rustled his fan. Though they must have thought it odd, the women could not ignore it. One of them came forward, then retreated a step or two.

"This is very strange indeed. Is there some mistake?"

"The guiding hand of the Blessed One makes no mistakes on the darkest nights." His was an aristocratic young voice.

"And in what direction does it lead?" the woman replied hesitantly. "This is most confusing."

"Very sudden and confusing, I am sure.

"Since first the wanderer glimpsed the fresh young grasses
His sleeves have known no respite from the dew.

"Might I ask you to pass my words on to your lady?"

"There is no one in this house to whom such a message can possibly seem appropriate."

"I have my reasons. You must believe me."

The woman withdrew to the rear of the house.

The nun was of course rather startled. "How very forward of him. He must think the child older than she is. And he must have heard our poems about the grasses. What can they have meant to him?" She hesitated for rather a long time. Persuaded that too long a delay would be rude, she finally sent back:

"The dew of a night of travel—do not compare it
With the dew that soaks the sleeves of the mountain dweller.

"It is this last that refuses to dry."

"I am not used to communicating through messengers. I wish to speak to you directly and in all seriousness."

Again the old nun hesitated. "There has been a misunderstanding, surely. I can hardly be expected to converse with such a fine young gentleman."

But the women insisted that it would be rude and unfeeling not to reply.

"Yes, I suppose you youngsters are not up to addressing him. As for me, I am awed by his earnestness." And she came forward.

"You will think me headstrong and frivolous for having addressed you without warning, but the Blessed One knows that my intent is not frivolous at all." He found the nun's quiet dignity somewhat daunting.

"I quite agree with you. This unexpected conversation can hardly be called frivolous."

"I have heard the sad story, and wonder if I might offer myself as a substitute for your late daughter. I was very young when I lost the one who was dearest to me,[6] and all through the years since I have had strange feelings of aimlessness and futility. We share the same fate, and I wonder if I might not ask that we be companions in it. The opportunity is not likely to come again. I have spoken, I am sure you see, quite without reserve."

"What you say would delight me did I not fear a mistake. It is true that there is someone here who is under my inadequate protection; but she is very young, and you could not possibly be asked to accept her deficiencies. I must decline your very kind proposal."

"I repeat that I have heard the whole story. Your admirable reticence does not permit you to understand that my feelings are of no ordinary sort."

But to her they seemed, though she did not say so, quite outrageous.

The bishop came out.

[6]**the one who was dearest to me** His mother. [Ed. note.]

Figure 1. This illustration conveys the Japanese style of living. In this picture, Genji speaks with the nun in an effort to meet Murasaki.

"Very well, then. I have made a beginning, and it has given me strength." And Genji pushed the screen back in place.

In the Lotus Hall, voices raised in an act of contrition mingled solemnly with the roar of the waterfall and the wind that came down from the mountain. Dawn was approaching.

This was Genji's poem, addressed to the bishop:

"A wind strays down from the hills to end my dream,
And tears well forth at these voices upon the waters."

And this the bishop's reply:

"These waters wet your sleeves. Our own are dry,
And tranquil our hearts, washed clean by mountain waters.

"Such is the effect of familiarity with these scenes."

There were heavy mists in the dawn sky, and bird songs came from Genji knew not where. Flowering trees and grasses which he could not identify spread like a tapestry before him. The deer that now paused to feed by the house and now wandered on were for him a strange and wonderful sight. He quite forgot his illness. Though it was not easy for the sage to leave his retreat, he made his way down for final services. His husky voice, emerging uncertainly from a toothless mouth, had behind it long years of discipline, and the mystic incantations suggested deep and awesome powers.

An escort arrived from the city, delighted to see Genji so improved, and a message was delivered from his father. The bishop had a breakfast of unfamiliar fruits and berries brought from far down in the valley.

"I have vowed to stay in these mountains until the end of the year, and cannot see you home." He pressed wine upon Genji. "And so a holy vow has the perverse effect of inspiring regrets."

"I hate to leave your mountains and streams, but my father seems worried and I must obey his summons. I shall come again before the cherry blossoms have fallen.

"I shall say to my city friends: 'Make haste to see
Those mountain blossoms. The winds may see them first.'"

His manner and voice were beautiful beyond description.
The bishop replied:

"In thirty hundreds of years it blooms but once.
My eyes have seen it, and spurn these mountain cherries."[7]

"A very great rarity indeed," Genji said, smiling, "a blossom with so long and short a span."

---

[7]The *udumbara* was believed to bloom only once in three thousand years, and announce the appearance of the Buddha or a king of like powers.

The sage offered a verse of thanks as Genji filled his cup:

*"My mountain door of pine has opened briefly
To see a radiant flower not seen before."*

There were tears in his eyes. His farewell present was a sacred mace[8] which had special protective powers. The bishop too gave farewell presents: a rosary of carved ebony[9] which Prince Shōtoku had obtained in Korea, still in the original Chinese box, wrapped in a netting and attached to a branch of cinquefoil pine; several medicine bottles of indigo decorated with sprays of cherry and wisteria and the like; and other gifts as well, all of them appropriate to the mountain setting. Genji's escort had brought gifts for the priests who had helped with the services, the sage himself and the rest, and for all the mountain rustics too. And so Genji started out.

The bishop went to the inner apartments to tell his sister of Genji's proposal.

"It is very premature. If in four or five years he has not changed his mind we can perhaps give it some thought."

The bishop agreed, and passed her words on without comment.

Much disappointed, Genji sent in a poem through an acolyte:

*"Having come upon an evening blossom,
The mist is loath to go without the morning sun."*

She sent back:

*"Can we believe the mist to be so reluctant?
We shall watch the morning sky for signs of truth."*

It was in a casual, cursive style, but the hand was a distinguished one.

He was about to get into his carriage when a large party arrived from the house of his father-in-law,[10] protesting the skill with which he had eluded them. Several of his brothers-in-law, including the oldest, Tō no Chūjō, were among them.

"You know very well that this is the sort of expedition we like best. You could at least have told us. Well, here we are, and we shall stay and enjoy the cherries you have discovered."

They took seats on the moss below the rocks and wine was brought out. It was a pleasant spot, beside cascading waters. Tō no Chūjō took out a flute, and one of his brothers, marking time with a fan, sang "To the West of the Toyora Temple."[11] They

[8]*Toko*, a sort of double-pointed spike used in esoteric Shingon rites.
[9]*Kongōji*, literally "diamond seed," thought to be the seed of a tree of the fig family.
[10]**father-in-law** As a youth Genji was wed in an arranged marriage to Princess Aoi, daughter of the Minister of the Left. [Ed. note.]
[11]"Katsuragi," a Saibara:

*See, by the Temple of Katsuragi,
To the west of the Toyora Temple,
White jewels in the Cypress Well,
Bring them forth and the land will prosper,
And we will prosper too.*

were handsome young men, all of them, but it was the ailing Genji whom everyone was looking at, so handsome a figure as he leaned against a rock that he brought a shudder of apprehension. Always in such a company there is an adept at the flageolet, and a fancier of the *shō* pipes[12] as well.

The bishop brought out a seven-stringed Chinese koto and pressed Genji to play it. "Just one tune, to give our mountain birds a pleasant surprise."

Genji protested that he was altogether too unwell, but he played a passable tune all the same. And so they set forth. The nameless priests and acolytes shed tears of regret, and the aged nuns within, who had never before seen such a fine gentleman, asked whether he might not be a visitor from another world.

"How can it be," said the bishop, brushing away a tear, "that such a one has been born into the confusion and corruption in which we live?"

The little girl too thought him very grand. "Even handsomer than Father," she said.

"So why don't you be his little girl?"

She nodded, accepting the offer; and her favorite doll, the one with the finest wardrobe, and the handsomest gentleman in her pictures too were thereupon named "Genji."

Back in the city, Genji first reported to his father upon his excursion. The emperor was shocked. It had been no ordinary indisposition.

He asked about the qualifications of the sage, and Genji replied in great detail.

"I must see that he is promoted. Such a remarkable record and I had not even heard of him."

Genji's father-in-law, the Minister of the Left, chanced to be in attendance. "I thought of going for you, but you did after all go off in secret. Suppose you have a few days' rest at Sanjō. I will go with you, immediately."

Genji was not enthusiastic, but he left with his father-in-law all the same. The minister had his own carriage brought up and insisted that Genji get in first. This solicitude rather embarrassed him.

At the minister's Sanjō mansion everything was in readiness. It had been polished and refitted until it was a jeweled pavilion, perfect to the last detail. As always, Genji's wife secluded herself in her private apartments, and it was only at her father's urging that she came forth; and so Genji had her before him, immobile, like a princess in an illustration for a romance. It would have been a great pleasure, he was sure, to have pertinent remarks from her upon his account of the mountain journey. She seemed the stiffest, remotest person in the world. How odd that the aloofness seemed only to grow as time went by.

"It would be nice, I sometimes think, if you could be a little more wifely. I have been very ill, and I am hurt, but not really surprised, that you have not inquired after my health."

"Like the pain, perhaps, of awaiting a visitor who does not come?"[13]

She cast a sidelong glance at him as she spoke, and her cold beauty was very intimidating indeed.

---

[12] A kind of mouth organ.
[13] A poetic allusion, apparently, not satisfactorily identified.

"You so rarely speak to me, and when you do you say such unpleasant things. 'A visitor who does not come'—that is hardly an appropriate way to describe a husband, and indeed it is hardly civil. I try this approach and I try that, hoping to break through, but you seem intent on defending all the approaches. Well, one of these years, perhaps, if I live long enough."

He withdrew to the bedchamber. She did not follow. Though there were things he would have liked to say, he lay down with a sigh. He closed his eyes, but there was too much on his mind to permit sleep.

He thought of the little girl and how he would like to see her grown into a woman. Her grandmother was of course right when she said that the girl was still too young for him. He must not seem insistent. And yet—was there not some way to bring her quietly to Nijō and have her beside him, a comfort and a companion? Prince Hyōbu was a dashing and stylish man, but no one could have called him remarkably handsome. Why did the girl so take after her aunt? Perhaps because aunt and father were children of the same empress. These thoughts seemed to bring the girl closer, and he longed to have her for his own.

The next day he wrote to the nun. He would also seem to have communicated his thoughts in a casual way to the bishop. To the nun he said:

"I fear that, taken somewhat aback by your sternness, I did not express myself very well. I find strength in the hope that something of the resolve demanded of me to write this letter will have conveyed itself to you."

With it was a tightly folded note for the girl:

"The mountain blossoms are here beside me still.
All of myself I left behind with them.

"I am fearful of what the night winds might have done."[14]

The writing, of course, and even the informal elegance of the folding, quite dazzled the superannuated women who received the letter. Somewhat overpowering, thought the grandmother.

She finally sent back: "I did not take your farewell remarks seriously; and now so soon to have a letter from you—I scarcely know how to reply. She cannot even write 'Naniwa'[15] properly, and how are we to expect that she give you a proper answer?

"Brief as the time till the autumn tempests come
To scatter the flowers—so brief your thoughts of her.

"I am deeply troubled."

The bishop's answer was in the same vein. Two or three days later Genji sent Koremitsu off to the northern hills.

[14]Prince Mototoshi, *Shūishū* 29:

Fearful of what the night winds might have done,
I rose at dawn—were my plum trees yet in bloom?

[15]A poem said to have been composed by the Korean Wani upon the accession of the emperor Nintoku, making congratulatory reference to the cherry blossoms of Naniwa, seems to have been used as a beginning lesson in calligraphy.

"There is her nurse, the woman called Shōnagon. Have a good talk with her."

How very farsighted, thought Koremitsu, smiling at the thought of the girl they had seen that evening.

The bishop said that he was much honored to be in correspondence with Genji. Koremitsu was received by Shōnagon, and described Genji's apparent state of mind in great detail. He was a persuasive young man and he made a convincing case, but to the nun and the others this suit for the hand of a mere child continued to seem merely capricious. Genji's letter was warm and earnest. There was a note too for the girl:

"Let me see your first exercises at the brush.

"No Shallow Spring, this heart of mine, believe me.[16]
And why must the mountain spring then seem so distant?"

This was the nun's reply:

"The shallow mountain spring but brings regrets.
Do you see something there, O shallow one?"

Koremitsu's report was no more encouraging. Shōnagon had said that they would be returning to the city when the nun was a little stronger and would answer him them.

Fujitsubo was ill and had gone home to her family. Genji managed a sympathetic thought or two for his lonely father, but his thoughts were chiefly on the possibility of seeing Fujitsubo. He quite halted his visits to other ladies. All through the day, at home and at court, he sat gazing off into space, and in the evening he would press Omyōbu[17] to be his intermediary. How she did it I do not know; but she contrived a meeting. It is sad to have to say that his earlier attentions, so unwelcome, no longer seemed real, and the mere thought that they had been successful was for Fujitsubo a torment.[18] Determined that there would not be another meeting, she was shocked to find him in her presence again. She did not seek to hide her distress, and her efforts to turn him away delighted him even as they put him to shame. There was no one else quite like her. In that fact was his undoing: he would be less a prey to longing if he could find in her even a trace of the ordinary. And the tumult of thoughts and feelings that now assailed him—he would have liked to consign it to the Mountain of Obscurity.[19] It might have been better, he sighed, so short was the night, if he had not come at all.

"So few and scattered the nights, so few the dreams.
Would that the dream tonight might take me with it."

[16] Anonymous, *Manyōshū* 3807:

Image of Shallow Mount upon Shallow Spring.
No such shallowness in this heart of mine.

[17] **Omyōbu** Fujitsubo's maid. [Ed. note.]
[18] No earlier meeting has been described.
[19] Kurabunoyama, thought to have been either in Yamashiro or in Omi.

He was in tears, and she did, after all, have to feel sorry for him.

"Were I to disappear in the last of dreams
Would yet my name live on in infamy?"

She had every right to be unhappy, and he was sad for her. Omyōbu gathered his clothes and brought them out to him.

Back at Nijō he spent a tearful day in bed. He had word from Omyōbu that her lady had not read his letter. So it always was, and yet he was hurt. He remained in distraught seclusion for several days. The thought that his father might be wondering about his absence filled him with terror.

Lamenting the burden of sin that seemed to be hers, Fujitsubo was more and more unwell, and could not bestir herself, despite repeated messages summoning her back to court. She was not at all her usual self—and what was to become of her? She took to her bed as the weather turned warmer. Three months had now passed and her condition was clear; and the burden of sin now seemed to have made it necessary that she submit to curious and reproving stares. Her women thought her behavior very curious indeed. Why had she let so much time pass without informing the emperor? There was of course a crucial matter of which she spoke to no one. Ben, the daughter of her old nurse, and Omyōbu, both of whom were very close to her and attended her in the bath, had ample opportunity to observe her condition. Omyōbu was aghast. Her lady had been trapped by the harshest of fates. The emperor would seem to have been informed that a malign spirit had possession of her, and to have believed the story, as did the court in general. He sent a constant stream of messengers, which terrified her and allowed no pause in her sufferings.

Genji had a strange, rather awful dream. He consulted a soothsayer, who said that it portended events so extraordinary as to be almost unthinkable.

"It contains bad omens as well. You must be careful."

"It was not my own dream but a friend's. We will see whether it comes true, and in the meantime you must keep it to yourself."

What could it mean? He heard of Fujitsubo's condition, thought of their night together, and wondered whether the two might be related. He exhausted his stock of pleas for another meeting. Horrified that matters were so out of hand, Omyōbu could do nothing for him. He had on rare occasions had a brief note, no more than a line or two; but now even these messages ceased coming.

Fujitsubo returned to court in the Seventh Month. The emperor's affection for her had only grown in her absence. Her condition was now apparent to everyone. A slight emaciation made her beauty seem if anything nearer perfection, and the emperor kept her always at his side. The skies as autumn approached called more insistently for music. Keeping Genji too beside him, the emperor had him try his hand at this and that instrument. Genji struggled to control himself, but now and then a sign of his scarcely bearable feelings did show through, to remind the lady of what she wanted more than anything to forget.

Somewhat improved, the nun had returned to the city. Genji had someone make inquiry about her residence and wrote from time to time. It was natural that her replies should show no lessening of her opposition, but it did not worry Genji as it once had. He had more considerable worries. His gloom was deeper as autumn came to a close. One beautiful moonlit night he collected himself for a visit to a place he had been visiting in secret. A cold, wintry shower passed. The address was in Rokujō, near the eastern limits of the city, and since he had set out from the palace the way seemed a long one. He passed a badly neglected house, the garden dark with ancient trees.

"The inspector's house," said Koremitsu, who was always with him. "I called there with a message not long ago. The old lady has declined so shockingly that they can't think what to do for her."

"You should have told me. I should have looked in on her. Ask, please, if she will see me."

Koremitsu sent a man in with the message.

The women had not been expecting a caller, least of all such a grand one. For some days the old lady had seemed beyond helping, and they feared that she would be unable to receive him. But they could hardly turn such a gentleman away—and so a cushion was put out for him in the south room.

"My lady says that she fears you will find it cluttered and dirty, but she is determined at least to thank you for coming. You must find the darkness and gloom unlike anything you have known."

And indeed he could not have denied that he was used to something rather different.

"You have been constantly on my mind, but your reserve has made it difficult for me to call. I am sorry that I did not know sooner of your illness."

"I have been ill for a very long time, but in this last extremity—it was good of him to come." He caught the sad, faltering tones as she gave the message to one of her women. "I am sorry that I cannot receive him properly. As for the matter he has raised, I hope that he will still count the child among those important to him when she is no longer a child. The thought of leaving her uncared for must, I fear, create obstacles along the road I yearn to travel. But tell him, please, how good it was of him. I wish the child were old enough to thank him too."

"Can you believe," he sent back, "that I would put myself in this embarrassing position if I were less than serious? There must be a bond between us, that I should have been so drawn to her since I first heard of her. It all seems so strange. The beginnings of it must have been in a different world. I will feel that I have come in vain if I cannot hear the sound of her young voice."

"She is asleep. She did not of course know that you were coming."

But just then someone came scampering into the room. "Grandmother, they say the gentleman we saw at the temple is here. Why don't you go out and talk to him?"

The woman tried to silence her.

"But why? She said the very sight of him made her feel better. I heard her." The girl seemed very pleased with the information she brought.

Though much amused, Genji pretended not to hear. After proper statements of sympathy he made his departure. Yes, she did seem little more than an infant. He would be her teacher.

The next day he sent a letter inquiring after the old lady, and with it a tightly folded note for the girl:

"Seeking to follow the call of the nestling crane
The open boat is lost among the reeds.

"And comes again and again to you?"[20]

He wrote it in a childish hand, which delighted the women. The child was to model her own hand upon it, no detail changed, they said.

Shōnagon sent a very sad answer: "It seems doubtful that my lady, after whom you were so kind as to inquire, will last the day. We are on the point of sending her off to the mountains once more. I know that she will thank you from another world."

In the autumn evening, his thoughts on his unattainable love, he longed more than ever, unnatural though the wish may have seemed, for the company of the little girl who sprang from the same roots. The thought of the evening when the old nun had described herself as dew holding back from the heavens made him even more impatient—and at the same time he feared that if he were to bring the girl to Nijō he would be disappointed in her.

"I long to have it, to bring it in from the moor,
The lavender[21] that shares its roots with another."

In the Tenth Month the emperor was to visit the Suzaku Palace.[22] From all the great families and the middle and upper courtly ranks the most accomplished musicians and dancers were selected to go with him, and grandees and princes of the blood were busy at the practice that best suited their talents. Caught up in the excitement, Genji was somewhat remiss in inquiring after the nun.

When, finally, he sent off a messenger to the northern hills, a sad reply came from the bishop: "We lost her toward the end of last month. It is the way of the world, I know, and yet I am sad."

If the news shocked even him into a new awareness of evanescence, thought Genji, how must it be for the little girl who had so occupied the nun's thoughts? Young though she was, she must feel utterly lost. He remembered, though dimly, how it had been when his mother died, and he sent off an earnest letter of sympathy. Shōnagon's answer seemed rather warmer. He went calling on an evening when he had nothing else to occupy him, some days after he learned that the girl had come out of mourning and returned to the city. The house was badly kept and almost deserted. The poor child must be terrified, he thought. He was shown to the same room as before. Sobbing, Shōnagon told him of the old lady's last days. Genji too was in tears.

"My young lady's father would seem to have indicated a willingness to take her in, but she is at such an uncomfortable age, not quite a child and still without the

---

[20]Anonymous, *Kokinshū* 732:

Like the open boat that plies the familiar canal,
I find that I come again and again to you.

[21]*Murasaki*, a gromwell from the roots of which a lavender dye is extracted. Lavender, in general the color of affinity or intimacy, suggests more specifically the *fuji* of Fujitsubo, "Wisteria Court." It is because of this poem that the girl is presently to be called Murasaki. The name Murasaki Shikibu also derives from it.

[22]South of the main palace.

discernment of an adult; and the thought of having her in the custody of the lady who was so cruel to her mother is too awful.[23] Her sisters will persecute her dreadfully, I know. The fear of it never left my lady's mind, and we have had too much evidence that the fear was not groundless. We have been grateful for your expressions of interest, though we have hesitated to take them seriously. I must emphasize that my young lady is not at all what you must think her to be. I fear that we have done badly by her, and that our methods have left her childish even for her years."

"Must you continue to be so reticent and apologetic? I have made my own feelings clear, over and over again. It is precisely the childlike quality that delights me most and makes me think I must have her for my own. You may think me complacent and self-satisfied for saying so, but I feel sure that we were joined in a former life. Let me speak to her, please.

"Rushes hide the sea grass at Wakanoura.
Will the waves that seek it out turn back to sea?[24]

"That would be too much to ask of them."

"The grass at Wakanoura were rash indeed
To follow waves that go it knows not whither.

"It would be far, far too much to ask."

The easy skill with which she turned her poem made it possible for him to forgive its less than encouraging significance. "After so many years," he whispered, "the gate still holds me back."[25]

The girl lay weeping for her grandmother. Her playmates came to tell her that a gentleman in court dress was with Shōnagon. Perhaps it would be her father?

She came running in. "Where is the gentleman, Shōnagon? Is Father here?"

What a sweet voice she had!

"I'm not your father, but I'm someone just as important. Come here."

She saw that it was the other gentleman, and child though she was, she flushed at having spoken out of turn. "Let's go." She tugged at Shōnagon's sleeve. "Let's go. I'm sleepy."

"Do you have to keep hiding yourself from me? Come here. You can sleep on my knee."

"She is really very young, sir." But Shōnagon urged the child forward, and she knelt obediently just inside the blinds.

He ran his hand over a soft, rumpled robe, and, a delight to the touch, hair full and rich to its farthest ends. He took her hand. She pulled away—for he was, after all, a stranger.

---

[23]**her mother is too awful** As the bishop mentioned to Genji earlier, Murasaki's mother, a mistress of Prince Hyobu, was driven into a "fatal decline" by the cruelty of the Prince's wife. [Ed. note.]
[24]There is a pun on *mirume*, "seeing" and "sea grass."
[25]Fujiwara Koretada, *Gosenshū* 732:

Alone, in secret, I hurry to Meeting Hill.
After so many years, the gate still holds me back.

"I said I'm sleepy." She went back to Shōnagon.

He slipped in after her. "I am the one you must look to now. You must not be shy with me."

"Please, sir. You forget yourself. You forget yourself completely. She is simply not old enough to understand what you have in mind."

"It is you who do not understand. I see how young she is, and I have nothing of the sort in mind. I must again ask you to be witness to the depth and purity of my feelings."

It was a stormy night. Sleet was pounding against the roof.

"How can she bear to live in such a lonely place? It must be awful for her." Tears came to his eyes. He could not leave her. "Close the shutters. I will be your watchman. You need one on a night like this. Come close to me, all of you."

Quite as if he belonged there, he slipped into the girl's bedroom. The women were astounded, Shōnagon more than the rest. He must be mad! But she was in no position to protest. Genji pulled a singlet over the girl, who was trembling like a leaf. Yes, he had to admit that his behavior must seem odd; but, trying very hard not to frighten her, he talked of things he thought would interest her.

"You must come to my house. I have all sorts of pictures, and there are dolls for you to play with."

She was less frightened than at first, but she still could not sleep. The storm blew all through the night, and Shōnagon quite refused to budge from their side. They would surely have perished of fright, whispered the women, if they had not had him with them. What a pity their lady was not a little older!

It was still dark when the wind began to subside and he made his departure, and all the appearances were as of an amorous expedition. "What I have seen makes me very sad and convinces me that she must not be out of my sight. She must come and live with me and share my lonely days. This place is quite impossible. You must be in constant terror."

"Her father has said that he will come for her. I believe it is to be after the memorial services."

"Yes, we must think of him. But they have lived apart, and he must be as much of a stranger as I am. I really do believe that in this very short time my feelings for her are stronger than his." He patted the girl on the head and looked back smiling as he left.

There was a heavy mist and the ground was white. Had he been on his way from a visit to a woman, he would have found the scene very affecting; but as it was he was vaguely depressed. Passing the house of a woman he had been seeing in secret, he had someone knock on the gate. There was no answer, and so he had someone else from his retinue, a man of very good voice, chant this poem twice in tones that could not fail to attract attention:

"Lost though I seem to be in the mists of dawn,
I see your gate, and cannot pass it by."

She sent out an ordinary maid who seemed, however, to be a woman of some sensibility:

*"So difficult to pass? Then do come in.
No obstacle at all, this gate of grass."*

Something more was needed to end the night, but dawn was approaching. Back at Nijō, he lay smiling at the memory of the girl. The sun was high when he arose and set about composing a letter. A rather special sort of poem seemed called for, but he laid his brush aside and deliberated for a time, and presently sent some pictures.

Looking in on his daughter that same day, Prince Hyōbu found the house vaster and more cavernous than he had remembered it, and the decay astonishingly advanced since the grandmother's death.

"How can you bear it for even a moment? You must come and live with me. I have plenty of room. And Nurse here can have a room of her own. There are other little girls, and I am sure you will get on beautifully together." Genji's perfume had been transferred to the child. "What a beautiful smell. But see how rumpled and ragged you are. I did not like the idea of having you with an ailing lady and wanted you to come and live with me. But you held back so, and I have to admit that the lady who is to be your mother has not been happy at the idea herself. It seems very sad that we should have waited for this to happen."

"Please, my lord. We may be lonely, but it will be better for us to remain as we are at least for a time. It will be better for us to wait until she is a little older and understands things better. She grieves for her grandmother and quite refuses to eat."

She was indeed thinner, but more graceful and elegant.

"Why must she go on grieving? Her grandmother is gone, and that is that. She still has me." It was growing dark. The girl wept to see him go, and he too was in tears. "You mustn't be sad. Please. You mustn't be sad. I will send for you tomorrow at the very latest."

She was inconsolable when he had gone, and beyond thinking about her own future. She was old enough to know what it meant, that the lady who had never left her was now gone. Her playmates no longer interested her. She somehow got through the daylight hours, but in the evening she gave herself up to tears, and Shōnagon and the others wept at their inability to comfort her. How, they asked one another, could they possibly go on?

Genji sent Koremitsu to make excuses. He wanted very much to call, but he had received an ill-timed summons from the palace.

"Has he quite forgotten his manners?" said Shōnagon. "I know very well that this is not as serious an affair for him as for us, but a man is expected to call regularly at the beginning of any affair. Her father, if he hears of it, will think that we have managed very badly indeed. You are young, my lady, but you must not speak of it to anyone." But the girl was not listening as attentively as Shōnagon would have wished.

Koremitsu was permitted a hint or two of their worries. "Perhaps when the time comes we will be able to tell ourselves that what must be must be, but at the moment the incompatibility overshadows everything. And your lord says and does such extraordinary things. Her father came today and did not improve matters by telling us that nothing must be permitted to happen. What could be worse than your lord's way of doing things?" She was keeping her objections to a minimum, however, for she did not want Koremitsu to think that anything of real importance had occurred.

Puzzled, Koremitsu returned to Nijō and reported upon what he had seen and heard. Genji was touched, though not moved to pay a visit. He was worried about rumors and the imputation of recklessness and frivolity that was certain to go with them. He must bring the girl to Nijō.

He sent several notes, and in the evening dispatched Koremitsu, his most faithful and reliable messenger. Certain obstacles prevented Genji's calling in person, said Koremitsu, but they must not be taken to suggest a want of seriousness.

"Her royal father has said that he will come for her tomorrow. We are feeling rather pressed. It is sad, after all, to leave a familiar place, however shabby and weedy it may be. You must forgive us. We are not entirely ourselves."

She gave him short shrift. He could see that they were busy at needlework and other preparations.

Genji was at his father-in-law's house in Sanjō. His wife was as always slow to receive him. In his boredom and annoyance he took out a Japanese koto and pleasantly hummed. "The Field in Hitachi."[26] Then came Koremitsu's unsettling report. He must act. If he were to take her from her father's house, he would be called a lecher and a child thief. He must swear the women to secrecy and bring her to Nijō immediately.

"I will go early in the morning. Have my carriage left as it is, and order a guard, no more than a man or two."

Koremitsu went to see that these instructions were carried out. Genji knew that he was taking risks. People would say that his appetites were altogether too varied. If the girl were a little older he would be credited with having made a conquest, and that would be that. Though Prince Hyōbu would be very upset indeed, Genji knew that he must not let the child go. It was still dark when he set out. His wife had no more than usual to say to him.

"I have just remembered some business at Nijō that absolutely has to be taken care of. I should not be long."

Her women did not even know that he had gone. He went to his own rooms and changed to informal court dress. Koremitsu alone was on horseback.

When they reached their destination one of his men pounded on the gate. Ignorant of what was afoot, the porter allowed Genji's carriage to be pulled inside. Koremitsu went to a corner door and knocked. Shōnagon came out.

"My lord is here."

"And my lady is asleep. You pick strange hours for your visits." Shōnagon suspected that he was on his way home from an amorous adventure.

Genji had joined Koremitsu.

"There is something I must say to her before she goes to her father's."

---

[26] A Saibara:

I plow my field in Hitachi.
You have made your way, this rainy night,
Over mountain and over moor,
To see if I have a lover.

Shōnagon smiled. "And no doubt she will have many interesting things to say in reply."

He pushed his way inside.

"Please, sir. We were not expecting anyone. The old women are a dreadful sight."

"I will go wake her. The morning mist is too beautiful for sleep."

He went into her bedroom, where the women were too surprised to cry out. He took her in his arms and smoothed her hair. Her father had come for her, she thought, only half awake.

"Let's go. I have come from your father's." She was terrified when she saw that it was not after all her father. "You are not being nice. I have told you that you must think of me as your father." And he carried her out.

A chorus of protests now came from Shōnagon and the others.

"I have explained things quite well enough. I have told you how difficult it is for me to visit her and how I want to have her in a more comfortable and accessible spot; and your way of making things easier is to send her off to her father. One of you may come along, if you wish."

"Please, sir." Shōnagon was wringing her hands. "You could not have chosen a worse time. What are we to say when her father comes? If it is her fate to be your lady, then perhaps something can be done when the time comes. This is too sudden, and you put us in an extremely difficult position."

"You can come later if you wish."

His carriage had been brought up. The women were fluttering about helplessly and the child was sobbing. Seeing at last that there was nothing else to be done, Shōnagon took up several of the robes they had been at work on the night before, changed to presentable clothes of her own, and got into the carriage.

It was still dark when they reached Nijō, only a short distance away. Genji ordered the carriage brought up to the west wing and took the girl inside.

"It is like a nightmare," said Shōnagon. "What am I to do?"

"Whatever you like. I can have someone see you home if you wish."

A bitter smile on her lips, Shōnagon got out of the carriage. What would her lady's father think when he came for her? And what did they now have to look forward to? The saddest thing was to be left behind by one's protectors. But tears did not augur well for the new life. With an effort she pulled herself together.

Since no one was living in this west wing, there was no curtained bedchamber. Genji had Koremitsu put up screens and curtains, sent someone else to the east wing for bedding, and lay down. Though trembling violently, the girl managed to keep from sobbing aloud.

"I always sleep with Shōnagon," she said softly in childish accents.

"Imagine a big girl like you still sleeping with her nurse."

Weeping quietly, the girl lay down.

Shōnagon sat up beside them, looking out over the garden as dawn came on. The buildings and grounds were magnificent, and the sand in the garden was like jewels. Not used to such affluence, she was glad there were no other women in this west wing. It was here that Genji received occasional callers. A few guards beyond the blinds were the only attendants.

They were speculating on the identity of the lady he had brought with him. "Someone worth looking at, you can bet."

Water pitchers and breakfast were brought in. The sun was high when Genji arose. "You will need someone to take care of you. Suppose you send this evening for the ones you like best." He asked that children be sent from the east wing to play with her. "Pretty little girls, please." Four little girls came in, very pretty indeed.

The new girl, his Murasaki, still lay huddled under the singlet he had thrown over her.

"You are not to sulk, now, and make me unhappy. Would I have done all this for you if I were not a nice man? Young ladies should do as they are told." And so the lessons began.

She seemed even prettier here beside him than from afar. His manner warm and fatherly, he sought to amuse her with pictures and toys he had sent for from the east wing. Finally she came over to him. Her dark mourning robes were soft and unstarched, and when she smiled, innocently and unprotestingly, he had to smile back. She went out to look at the trees and pond after he had departed for the east wing. The flowers in the foreground, delicately touched by frost, were like a picture. Streams of courtiers, of the medium ranks and new to her experience, passed back and forth. Yes, it was an interesting place. She looked at the pictures on screens and elsewhere and (so it is with a child) soon forgot her troubles.

Staying away from court for several days, Genji worked hard to make her feel at home. He wrote down all manner of poems for her to copy, and drew all manner of pictures, some of them very good. "I sigh, though I have not seen Musashi,"[27] he wrote on a bit of lavender paper. She took it up, and thought the hand marvelous. In a tiny hand he wrote beside it:

> *"Not yet mine, these grasses of Musashi,*
> *So near to dew-drenched grasses I cannot have."*

"Now you must write something."

"But I can't." She looked up at him, so completely without affectation that he had to smile.

"You can't write as well as you would like to, perhaps, but it would be wrong of you not to write at all. You must think of me as your teacher."

It was strange that even her awkward, childish way of holding the brush should so delight him. Afraid she had made a mistake, she sought to conceal what she had written. He took it from her.

> *"I do not know what it is that makes you sigh.*
> *And whatever grass can it be I am so near to?"*

The hand was very immature indeed, and yet it had strength, and character. It was very much like her grandmother's. A touch of the modern and it would not be at all unacceptable. He ordered dollhouses and as the two of them played together he found himself for the first time neglecting his sorrows.

---

[27] Anonymous, *Kokin Rokujō, Zoku Kokka Taikan* 34353:

I sigh at its name, though I have not seen Musashi.
And know that my sigh is for those lavender grasses.

Prince Hyōbu went for his daughter on schedule. The women were acutely embarrassed, for there was next to nothing they could say to him. Genji wished to keep the girl's presence at Nijō secret, and Shōnagon had enjoined the strictest silence. They could only say that Shōnagon had spirited the girl away, they did not know where.

He was aghast. "Her grandmother did not want me to have her, and so I suppose Shōnagon took it upon herself, somewhat sneakily I must say, to hide her away rather than give her to me." In tears, he added: "Let me know if you hear anything."

Which request only intensified their confusion.

The prince inquired of the bishop in the northern hills and came away no better informed. By now he was beginning to feel some sense of loss (such a pretty child); and his wife had overcome her bitterness and, happy at the thought of a little girl to do with as she pleased, was similarly regretful.

Presently Murasaki had all her women with her. She was a bright, lively child, and the boys and girls who were to be her playmates felt quite at home with her. Sometimes on lonely nights when Genji was away she would weep for her grandmother. She thought little of her father. They had lived apart and she scarcely knew him. She was by now extremely fond of her new father. She would be the first to run out and greet him when he came home, and she would climb on his lap, and they would talk happily together, without the least constraint or embarrassment. He was delighted with her. A clever and watchful woman can create all manner of difficulties. A man must be always on his guard, and jealousy can have the most unwelcome consequences. Murasaki was the perfect companion, a toy for him to play with. He could not have been so free and uninhibited with a daughter of his own. There are restraints upon paternal intimacy. Yes, he had come upon a remarkable little treasure.

QUESTIONS FOR DISCUSSION

1. Summarize the plot of this episode. Note that this selection shows Genji's relationship to three women: Fujitsubo (his stepmother), his wife, and Murasaki. What is the nature of each relationship? How might one analyze them in terms of Freudian psychology?
2. It is important to understand that in medieval times, in Europe as well as in the Orient, child betrothals were not uncommon. Sometimes young girls would be betrothed to princes and sent to their courts to be raised until they were of an age to be married. It also is important to understand that a Japanese courtier usually had many wives, and that his relationships with women were not limited to these wives. Discuss how an understanding of these cultural attitudes towards women and marriage might change your reaction to the piece.
3. Describe the male–female roles and the parent–child relationships in this story. How do these compare to the roles described in "No Name Woman" (p. 403) and "The Brahmin's Son" (p. 438)?
4. Discuss the role of poetry in *Genji*. How does the poetry help establish the mood of the piece?
5. Genji is often said to represent the ideal Heian courtier. How would you describe this ideal? Compare this ideal to the ideal of the hero in modern American culture.

6. The mood of this novel has been described as melancholy and nostalgic. Compare how the author establishes the mood to the establishment of mood in other pieces, for example in "Night" (p. 599), "The Master of Doornvlei" (p. 370), and "Chimes of Silence" (p. 364).

RABINDRANATH TAGORE
False Religion
The Evermoving

Rabindranath Tagore (1861–1941) was born in Calcutta and is the most famous member of a prestigious and artistically gifted family. At 17 he traveled to London to study English literature; after completing his education he returned to India. Tagore is renowned for his spirituality and advocation of religious tolerance, his powers of literary expression, and his dedication to the revival of India's cultural heritage. In the following poems Tagore expresses his feelings about religion. "False Religion" is his lament on the corruption of religion and on the atrocities committed "in the name of Faith." In "The Evermoving" Tagore presents his personal spirituality, which was influenced by Hinduism and Buddhism, based on the Eastern concept that the material world is illusory, and that desire for the transitory things of this world will lead only to "fear and grief." Instead, one must look beyond earthly change and embrace Brahma, the Infinite that "exists in the heart of the universe." Like many of the poets represented in Part 3, Tagore is voicing concerns about his society: spirituality, which should bring us peace and harmony, is too often used to justify hate, cruelty, and war.

False Religion

Those who in the name of Faith embrace illusion,
Kill and are killed.
Even the atheist gets God's blessings—
Does not boast of his religion;
With reverence he lights the lamp of Reason   5
And pays his homage not to scriptures,
But to the good in man.

The bigot insults his own religion
When he slays a man of another faith.
Conduct he judges not in the light of Reason;   10
In the temple he raises the blood-stained banner
And worships the devil in the name of God.

All that is shameful and barbarous through the Ages,
Has found a shelter in their temples—

Those they turn into prisons;   *15*
O, I hear the trumpet call of Destruction!
Time comes with her great broom
Sweeping all refuse away.

That which should make man free,
They turn into fetters;   *20*
That which should unite,
They turn into a sword;
That which should bring love
From the fountain of the Eternal,
They turn into prison   *25*
And with its waves they flood the world.
They try to cross the river
In a bark riddled with holes;
And yet, in their anguish, whom do they blame?

O Lord, breaking false religion,   *30*
Save the blind!
Break! O break
The altar that is drowned in blood.
Let your thunder strike
Into the prison of false religion,   *35*
And bring to this unhappy land
The light of Knowledge.

The Evermoving

With the hopeless cry
'Do not go!'
Whom do you call back?
Where is that bond
That can make the limitless, limited?   *5*
The world is like a flooded stream
That flows away, carrying everything
In laughter and tears.
'No! no! no!'
This cry is heard over the great sea of Time,   *10*
And resounds in the drum of *Rudra*,[1] the Terrible!
O Mind,
Leave behind all desire, fear and grief—
The river of creation
Is but the endless flow of destruction.   *15*

---

[1]**Rudra** The ancient Vedic god of the tempest (literally, "the roarer"), associated with thunder and lightning, who later became known as Shiva. [Ed. note.]

Everything shall pass away—
Yet I love,
When in its joyous flow
The smile of existence gleams
In the midst of destruction.   20
From the *vina*² of death
Pours forth the song of life,
Lovely in its restlessness.
From time to time, quivers the lamp of eternity
Illuminating the mirage of a moment.   25
The unplumbed river of tears bears on its current
The mother's love,
And the beloved's message;
In the battlefield of destruction.
The hero's courage is earth's treasure of beauty.   30
Time's duration measures not the worth of the gift,
Which the Infinite pours
Into the cupped hands of the transitory.

As long as it lasts
Value it with your whole life.   35
When the chariot of farewell sweeps past,
Forgetting self, make free the path,
Singing paeans of victory.
In the little earth you possess
Grieve not for what lies beyond—   40
It exists in the heart of the universe,
If not in one form, then in another;
Come out of your dark well—
Under heavens dome,
See destruction's blissful form.   45
O Sorrowful One,
The bubble of your grief shall float away
In the ocean of the Unsorrowing.

QUESTIONS FOR DISCUSSION

False Religion

1. What is Tagore criticizing in this poem? (Cite specific passages.)
2. What is the danger of false religion? The value of true religion?
3. Summarize each stanza of the poem in your own words.
4. In what ways is this criticism of religion similar to Voltaire's criticism in "Of Universal Tolerance" (p. 581)?
5. Why does Tagore capitalize words that are not usually capitalized?

²**vina** A stringed instrument, rather like a lute or guitar, still used by Indian musicians. [Ed. note.]

The Evermoving

1. In this poem the speaker presents his personal spirituality, which is strongly influenced by Buddhism and Hinduism. The first three lines express an inescapable element of life. Describe this quality in your own words.
2. Discuss the image of the river; how does it change in each stanza?
3. The speaker stresses that all things in this world shall pass away. Do you feel that the message of this poem is pessimistic? Explain, using evidence from the text to support your argument.
4. Explain the last lines of the poem.
5. What spiritual advice does this poem give to the reader?
6. How does this poem reflect the basic tenets of Buddhism, as reflected in "Introduction to Buddhism" (p. 459)?

HERMANN HESSE
The Brahmin's Son

The works of Nobel Prize-winning Swiss author Hermann Hesse (1877–1962) embody his life-long search for the "Way," the philosophy of life that would offer him spiritual fulfillment. His novels explore the mysteries of the human soul from many perspectives, Eastern and Western, and capture the anguish, the joy, and the serenity that characterize the struggle to discover Truth. In "The Brahmin's Son," the first chapter of Siddhartha, *the young Siddhartha is unsatisfied with the teachings of Hinduism, for they leave many of his fundamental questions unanswered. As the chapter concludes, he sets out with his friend Govinda to join a group of wandering ascetics. The rest of the novel describes his disillusionment with the Samanas's way of life and his subsequent attempt to find satisfaction in a life of sensuality and earthly love. He realizes that he is only being distracted from his search for true self. Finally, with the help of a simple ferryman, he discovers that true wisdom can only be found within, and at last he achieves the peace and transcendence he has sought after for so many years.*

In the shade of the house, in the sunshine on the river bank by the boats, in the shade of the sallow wood and the fig tree, Siddhartha, the handsome Brahmin's son, grew up with his friend Govinda. The sun browned his slender shoulders on the river bank, while bathing at the holy ablutions, at the holy sacrifices. Shadows passed across his eyes in the mango grove during play, while his mother sang, during his father's teachings, when with the learned men. Siddhartha had already long taken part in the learned men's conversations, had engaged in debate with Govinda and had practiced the art of contemplation and meditation with him. Already he knew how to pronounce Om silently—this word of words, to say it inwardly with the intake of breath, when breathing out with all his soul, his brow radiating the glow of pure spirit. Already he knew how to recognize Atman within the depth of his being, indestructible, at one with the universe.

There was happiness in his father's heart because of his son who was intelligent and thirsty for knowledge; he saw him growing up to be a great learned man, a priest, a prince among Brahmins.

There was pride in his mother's breast when she saw him walking, sitting down and rising: Siddhartha—strong, handsome, supple-limbed, greeting her with complete grace.

Love stirred in the hearts of the young Brahmins' daughters when Siddhartha walked through the streets of the town, with his lofty brow, his king-like eyes and his slim figure.

Govinda, his friend, the Brahmin's son, loved him more than anybody else. He loved Siddhartha's eyes and clear voice. He loved the way he walked, his complete grace of movement; he loved everything that Siddhartha did and said, and above all he loved his intellect, his fine ardent thoughts, his strong will, his high vocation. Govinda knew that he would not become an ordinary Brahmin, a lazy sacrificial official, an avaricious dealer in magic sayings, a conceited worthless orator, a wicked sly priest, or just a good stupid sheep amongst a large herd. No, and he, Govinda, did not want to become any of these, not a Brahmin like ten thousand others of their kind. He wanted to follow Siddhartha, the beloved, the magnificent. And if he ever became a god, if he ever entered the All-Radiant, then Govinda wanted to follow him as his friend, his companion, his servant, his lance bearer, his shadow.

That was how everybody loved Siddhartha. He delighted and made everybody happy.

But Siddhartha himself was not happy. Wandering along the rosy paths of the fig garden, sitting in contemplation in the bluish shade of the grove, washing his limbs in the daily bath of atonement, offering sacrifices in the depths of the shady mango wood with complete grace of manner, beloved by all, a joy to all, there was yet no joy in his own heart. Dreams and restless thoughts came flowing to him from the river, from the twinkling stars at night, from the sun's melting rays. Dreams and a restlessness of the soul came to him, arising from the smoke of the sacrifices, emanating from the verses of the Rig-Veda, trickling through from the teachings of the old Brahmins.

Siddhartha had begun to feel the seeds of discontent within him. He had begun to feel that the love of his father and mother, and also the love of his friend Govinda, would not always make him happy, give him peace, satisfy and suffice him. He had begun to suspect that his worthy father and his other teachers, the wise Brahmins, had already passed on to him the bulk and best of their wisdom, that they had already poured the sum total of their knowledge into his waiting vessel; and the vessel was not full, his intellect was not satisfied, his soul was not at peace, his heart was not still. The ablutions were good, but they were water; they did not wash sins away, they did not relieve the distressed heart. The sacrifices and the supplication of the gods were excellent—but were they everything? Did the sacrifices give happiness? And what about the gods? Was it really Prajapati who had created the world? Was it not Atman, He alone, who had created it? Were not the gods forms created like me and you, mortal, transient? Was it therefore good and right, was it a sensible and worthy act to offer sacrifices to the gods? To whom else should one offer sacrifices, to whom else should one pay honor, but to Him, Atman, the Only One? And where was Atman to be found, where did He dwell, where did His eternal heart beat, if not within the Self, in the innermost, in the eternal which each person carried within him? But where was this Self, this innermost? It was not flesh and bone, it was not thought or consciousness. That was what the wise men taught. Where, then, was it? To press towards the Self, towards Atman—was there another way that was worth seeking? Nobody showed the way, nobody knew it—neither his father, nor the teachers and wise men, nor the holy songs. The Brahmins and their holy books knew everything, everything; they had gone into everything—the creation of the world, the origin of speech, food, inhalation, exhalation, the arrangement of the senses, the acts of the gods. They knew a tremendous number of things—but was it worth while knowing all these things if they did not know the one important thing, the only important thing?

Many verses of the holy books, above all the Upanishads of Sama-Veda spoke of this innermost thing. It is written: "Your soul is the whole world." It says that when a man is asleep, he penetrates his innermost and dwells in Atman. There was wonderful wisdom in these verses; all the knowledge of the sages was told here in enchanting language, pure as honey collected by the bees. No, this tremendous amount of knowledge, collected and preserved by successive generations of wise Brahmins could not be easily overlooked. But where were the Brahmins, the priests, the wise men, who were successful not only in having this most profound knowledge, but in experiencing it? Where were the initiated who, attaining Atman in sleep, could retain it in consciousness, in life, everywhere, in speech and in action? Siddhartha knew many worthy Brahmins, above all his father—holy, learned, of highest esteem. His father was worthy of admiration; his manner was quiet and noble. He lived a good life, his words were wise; fine and noble thoughts dwelt in his head—but even he who knew so much, did he live in bliss, was he at peace? Was he not also a seeker, insatiable? Did he not go continually to the holy springs with an insatiable thirst, to the sacrifices, to books, to the Brahmins' discourses? Why must he, the blameless one, wash away his sins and endeavor to cleanse himself anew each day? Was Atman then not within him? Was not then the source within his own heart? One must find the source within one's own Self, one must possess it. Everything else was seeking—a detour, error.

These were Siddhartha's thoughts; this was his thirst, his sorrow.

He often repeated to himself the words from one of the Chandogya-Upanishads. "In truth, the name of Brahman is Satya. Indeed, he who knows it enters the heavenly world each day." It often seemed near—the heavenly world—but never had he quite reached it, never had he quenched the final thirst. And among the wise men that he knew and whose teachings he enjoyed, there was not one who had entirely reached it—the heavenly world—not one who had completely quenched the eternal thirst.

"Govinda," said Siddhartha to his friend, "Govinda, come with me to the banyan tree. We will practice meditation."

They went to the banyan tree and sat down, twenty paces apart. As he sat down ready to pronounce the Om, Siddhartha softly recited the verse:

"Om is the bow, the arrow is the soul,
Brahman is the arrow's goal
At which one aims unflinchingly."

When the customary time for the practice of meditation had passed, Govinda rose. It was now evening. It was time to perform the evening ablutions. He called Siddhartha by his name; he did not reply. Siddhartha sat absorbed, his eyes staring as if directed at a distant goal, the tip of his tongue showing a little between his teeth. He did not seem to be breathing. He sat thus, lost in meditation, thinking Om, his soul as the arrow directed at Brahman.

Some Samanas once passed through Siddhartha's town. Wandering ascetics, they were three thin worn-out men, neither old nor young, with dusty and bleeding shoulders, practically naked, scorched by the sun, solitary, strange and hostile— lean jackals in the world of men. Around them hovered an atmosphere of still passion, of devastating service, of unpitying self-denial.

In the evening, after the hour of contemplation, Siddhartha said to Govinda: "Tomorrow morning, my friend, Siddhartha is going to join the Samanas. He is going to become a Samana."

Govinda blanched as he heard these words and read the decision in his friend's determined face, undeviating as the released arrow from the bow. Govinda realized from the first glance at his friend's face that now it was beginning. Siddhartha was going his own way; his destiny was beginning to unfold itself, and with his destiny, his own. And he became as pale as a dried banana skin.

"Oh, Siddhartha," he cried, "will your father permit it?"

Siddhartha looked at him like one who had just awakened. As quick as lightning he read Govinda's soul, read the anxiety, the resignation.

"We will not waste words, Govinda," he said softly. "Tomorrow at daybreak I will begin the life of the Samanas. Let us not discuss it again."

Siddhartha went into the room where his father was sitting on a mat made of bast. He went up behind his father and remained standing there until his father felt his presence. "Is it you, Siddhartha?" the Brahmin asked. "Then speak what is in your mind."

Siddhartha said: "With your permission, Father, I have come to tell you that I wish to leave your house tomorrow and join the ascetics. I wish to become a Samana. I trust my father will not object."

The Brahmin was silent so long that the stars passed across the small window and changed their design before the silence in the room was finally broken. His son stood silent and motionless with his arms folded. The father, silent and motionless, sat on the mat, and the stars passed across the sky. Then his father said: "It is not seemly for Brahmins to utter forceful and angry words, but there is displeasure in my heart. I should not like to hear you make this request a second time."

The Brahmin rose slowly. Siddhartha remained silent with folded arms.

"Why are you waiting?" asked his father.

"You know why," answered Siddhartha.

His father left the room displeased and lay down on his bed.

As an hour passed by and he could not sleep, the Brahmin rose, wandered up and down and then left the house. He looked through the small window of the room and saw Siddhartha standing there with his arms folded, unmoving. He could see his pale robe shimmering. His heart troubled, the father returned to his bed.

As another hour passed and the Brahmin could not sleep, he rose again, walked up and down, left the house and saw the moon had risen. He looked through the window. Siddhartha stood there unmoving, his arms folded; the moon shone on his bare shinbones. His heart troubled, the father went to bed.

He returned again after an hour and again after two hours, looked through the window and saw Siddhartha standing there in the moonlight, in the starlight, in the dark. And he came silently again, hour after hour, looked into the room, and saw him standing unmoving. His heart filled with anger, with anxiety, with fear, with sorrow.

And in the last hour of the night, before daybreak, he returned again, entered the room and saw the youth standing there. He seemed tall and a stranger to him.

"Siddhartha," he said, "why are you waiting?"

"You know why."

"Will you go on standing and waiting until it is day, noon, evening?"

"I will stand and wait."

"You will grow tired, Siddhartha."

"I will grow tired."

"You will fall asleep, Siddhartha."

"I will not fall asleep."

"You will die, Siddhartha."

"I will die."

"And would you rather die than obey your father?"

"Siddhartha has always obeyed his father."

"So you will give up your project?"

"Siddhartha will do what his father tells him."

The first light of day entered the room. The Brahmin saw that Siddhartha's knees trembled slightly, but there was no trembling in Siddhartha's face; his eyes looked far away. Then the father realized that Siddhartha could no longer remain with him at home—that he had already left him.

The father touched Siddhartha's shoulder.

"You will go into the forest," he said, "and become a Samana. If you find bliss in the forest, come back and teach it to me. If you find disillusionment, come back, and we shall again offer sacrifices to the gods together. Now go, kiss your mother and tell her where you are going. For me, however, it is time to go to the river and perform the first ablution."

He dropped his hand from his son's shoulder and went out. Siddhartha swayed as he tried to walk. He controlled himself, bowed to his father and went to his mother to do what had been told to him.

As, with benumbed legs, he slowly left the still sleeping town at daybreak, a crouching shadow emerged from the last hut and joined the pilgrim. It was Govinda.

"You have come," said Siddhartha and smiled.

"I have come," said Govinda.

QUESTIONS FOR DISCUSSION

1. Describe the concept of "Atman" (see "Muṇḍaka Upanishad" on p. 473).
2. Who are the Brahmins?
3. Describe the role of sacrifice and ritual in Hindu life. How does Siddhartha feel about the rituals he performs?
4. Why is Siddhartha dissatisfied with Hinduism?
5. What does he hope to find with the Samanas?
6. Describe Siddhartha's relationship with his father and compare it to the relationship of mother and daughter in "No Name Woman" (p. 403). Discuss the sorts of conflicts young adults have with their parents today. How are these problems like the one Siddhartha experiences? How are they different?

PART 4

Religion and Philosophy

At the heart of human civilization is the concept of order. Science and technology represent human efforts first to understand and then to master the discoverable order of the natural world. Governmental and political institutions attempt to bring order to interactions within and between societies. Even art and literature can be understood as efforts to create structure and sense in a world that often appears ugly, meaningless, and chaotic. Religion and philosophy hold an important place of their own in humanity's effort to surround itself with an ordered and comprehensible universe. Inherent in each is an underlying concern with the ultimate disorder posed by the very nature of mortal existence. Mortal means subject to death. Death threatens attempts at order with an ultimate undoing of human reality, a state that modern thinkers have described as the absurdity of existence. Philosophy attempts to understand and to explain the meaning of life in spite of death; most major religions undertake to carry order and meaning on into a world beyond death. Both are unique in that they look beyond the day-to-day problems of the human condition to the ultimate dilemma of human existence.

The readings that compose this part of the book offer students the opportunity to explore a diversity of philosophic and religious ideas. These readings are organized into three sections: the first defines religion and philosophy, the second explores their diversity, and the third examines important issues they raise in modern times. The overall goal of this part is to give students a starting point from which to explore through their own writing the wealth of ideas in the world of philosophy and religion. Primary and secondary sources are juxtaposed whenever possible so as to give readers exposure to original ideas and writings, while providing necessary background information and interpretations to make these ideas both comprehensible and relevant to students' own thinking and writing processes.

The first section contains three essays that go beyond simply defining religion and philosophy to a study of the differences between the two. In an excerpt from *The Elementary Forms of the Religious Life*, the French sociologist of religion, Émile Durkheim, identifies the roots of religiousness as the human division of the world into "profane" and "sacred" phenomena. This sheds light upon the possible meanings of the word "religion" itself, which is related to the Latin *religare*, meaning "to hold back" or "to bind fast." In primitive societies, humans tended to view sacred religious rituals as a means for holding back or binding fast the threatening forces of the world around them. Will Durant's selection from *The Story of Philosophy* outlines another approach to making sense of the human world using human thought rather than human belief. Philosophy, meaning in Greek the "love of wisdom," took earliest form about 600 B.C.E. when Greek thinkers first undertook the study of the ultimate principles, causes, and reality of being and thought. They were the first in the Western world to do so in an approach that broke away from religious and theological creeds to replace faith with intellectual speculation. Ultimately, however, the distinction between "philosophy" and "religion" may be much more of a Western concept than a global one, as Winston King explains in the "Foreword" to *Religion and Nothingness*. King illustrates how differently the Eastern world and the Western world conceptualize "philosophy" and "religion." This problem becomes most obvious as one examines the texts on Taoism in this part. Its Chinese founder, Lao Tzu, sought to find harmony with the eternal nature of the universe through a deeper vision of reality and self-control. Most textbooks categorize Taoism as a religion because of the supernatural symbols it contains, but Lao Tzu's philosophy parallels in many ways the efforts of Socrates to define more clearly the nature of reality. Thus, Lao Tzu is commonly listed as an important Chinese philosopher in dictionaries of world philosophy as well.

The large variety of selections following the definitions by Durkheim, Durant, and King trace directions religions and philosophies have taken over time. Texts on Buddhism, Hinduism, Taoism, the Judeo-Christian tradition, and Islam are organized into secondary and primary sources. A secondary text is presented first in each case to supply background information, and then a primary document is given to put students in touch with the actual expression of original ideas upon which to base their own writing. Other articles on Confucian thought, Socratic thought, Nihilism, and Existentialism offer some of the important ideas that have shaped the human world both in the past and the present. The text on Nihilism underscores one philosophical issue that is constantly present in today's world. Charles Glicksberg describes it as a "spiritual crisis" or an "archetypal experience" through which virtually all major philosophers, writers, and artists in history have passed as they questioned the reality and the meaning of the world around them. In a time of shifting values, ongoing tensions between belief and reason, and an increasingly diverse, global view of what makes life meaningful, it is growing more difficult for educated people to avoid a reevaluation of the cultures in which they are born. Two poems by Gwendolyn Brooks follow up on this questioning of culture through the eyes of an American black woman. The prolific French author and philosopher Jean Paul Sartre would surely be on Glicksberg's list of important intellectuals who passed through an archetypal experience of searching for the meaning of their own existence. His text, "Existentialism," departs, however, from a nihilistic rejection of human existence as meaningless by taking the position that each individual is responsible for defining the purpose and meaning of his or her own life.

At a time when women increasingly are indeed assuming the responsibility to define the nature of their own lives, we have given particular emphasis to the issue of religion and gender. Two creation texts placing a female deity at the origin of the natural world are juxtaposed with the image of the male, patriarchal God of the Old Testament. This is followed by a selection showing the position of privilege given the male gender in another major world religion—Buddhism. In contrast to this view of religion dominated by male imagery is Riane Eisler's "Our Lost Heritage: New Facts on How God Became a Man," which takes an archaeological approach to reinterpreting a tradition of Goddess worship in Europe eight thousand years ago. Finally, the issue of gender bias in religion takes on a modern relevance in the readings by Mary Daly and Phyllis Schlafly. As a spokeswoman for the Women's Liberation Movement in America, Daly suggests that the dominance of males in the world of religion has led to acceptance of male dominance in society overall. As a conservative Christian, Schlafly takes a quite different stance on the role she feels deity has ordained for women in modern society.

The remaining texts in this part explore other issues of major significance and of particular relevance to the present. Harvey Cox's "Understanding Islam: No More Holy Wars" sets the stage for students to grapple with Christianity's historical crusade against Islam in light of the next text on the current revival of Islamic jihad or holy war by certain Moslem radicals against both Christian and non-Christian adversaries. Written in Tehran, Iran, Murtuza Mutahery's *The Martyr* presents insight from a Moslem point of view into Islamic jihad and the glory of dying for religious causes. At the heart of holy war, but capable of much milder forms of expression, is religious intolerance. Joseph Smith's "The First Vision" presents a modern case of religious particularism (that is, the view that one belief system is right and all others are wrong), which is contrasted to a call by Voltaire for universal tolerance among all citizens of the world. Essays by the more recent intellectuals Bertrand Russell and C. S. Lewis debate the place of Christian belief in a modern, secularized, and increasingly scientific world. The final selection presented shows the profound questioning of the very existence of a divine being by the 1986 Nobel Peace Prize winner, Elie Wiesel, who recounts his experiences as a young Jewish prisoner in the Nazi death camps of Auschwich and Buchenwald during World War II.

What the World Believes

This map shows the major religions of the world by geographical area. As you read selections from and about various religious traditions, the map will help you place those traditions geographically.

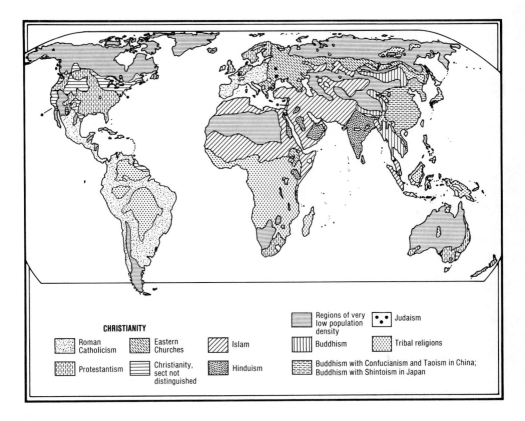

CHRISTIANITY

Roman Catholicism

Protestantism

Eastern Churches

Christianity, sect not distinguished

Islam

Hinduism

Regions of very low population density

Buddhism

Buddhism with Confucianism and Taoism in China; Buddhism with Shintoism in Japan

Judaism

Tribal religions

ÉMILE DURKHEIM
The Elementary Forms of the Religious Life

Émile Durkheim (1858–1917) is considered to be the founder of the French school of sociology. His family expected him to become a rabbi like his father, but after study at the most prestigious teacher's college in France (the École Normale Supérieure in Paris), he elected to teach philosophy, first in the state secondary schools, then at the University of Bordeaux and the University of Paris. His 1895 work, The Rules of Sociological Method, *set forth a rigorous methodology for the new "science of society," and made him both famous and influential. Later in his career he became concerned with education and religion as two of the most important ways to reform institutional structures in*

*society. In the following selection, published in 1915, Durkheim attempts to define religion in its
simplest forms. He identifies the most basic element of the religious life as a common set of beliefs
among a given group of people. Out of these beliefs grows a system of rites giving the beliefs artistic
expression, often within the confines of an institutional (or church) organization. One other essential
characteristic of religion Durkheim notes is the division of the world into sacred and profane,
forbidden and allowed, good and evil.*

Religious phenomena are naturally arranged into two fundamental categories: beliefs and rites. The first are states of opinion, and consist in representations; the
second are determined modes of action. Between these two classes of facts there is
all the difference which separates thought from action.

The rites can be defined and distinguished from other human practices, moral
practices, for example, only by the special nature of their object. A moral rule prescribes certain manners of acting to us, just as a rite does, but which are addressed to
a different class of objects. So it is the object of the rite which must be characterized,
if we are to characterize the rite itself. Now it is in the beliefs that the special nature
of this object is expressed. It is possible to define the rite only after we have defined
the belief.

All known religious beliefs, whether simple or complex, present one common
characteristic: they presuppose a classification of all the things, real and ideal, of
which men think, into two classes or opposed groups, generally designated by two
distinct terms which are translated well enough by the words *profane* and *sacred*
(profane, sacré). This division of the world into two domains, the one containing all
that is sacred, the other all that is profane, is the distinctive trait of religious thought;
the beliefs, myths, dogmas, and legends are either representations or systems of
representations which express the nature of sacred things, the virtues and powers
which are attributed to them, or their relations with each other and with profane
things. But by sacred things one must not understand simply those personal beings
which are called gods or spirits; a rock, a tree, a spring, a pebble, a piece of wood, a
house, in a word, anything can be sacred. A rite can have this character; in fact, the
rite does not exist which does not have it to a certain degree. There are words,
expressions, and formulae which can be pronounced only by the mouths of consecrated persons; there are gestures and movements which everybody cannot perform. If the Vedic sacrifice has had such an efficacy that, according to mythology, it
was the creator of the gods, and not merely a means of winning their favor, it is
because it possessed a virtue comparable to that of the most sacred beings. The circle
of sacred objects cannot be determined, then, once for all. Its extent varies infinitely,
according to the different religions. That is how Buddhism is a religion: in default of
gods, it admits the existence of sacred things, namely, the four noble truths and the
practices derived from them. . . .

. . . The real characteristic of religious phenomena is that they always suppose
a bipartite division of the whole universe, known and knowable, into two classes
which embrace all that exists, but which radically exclude each other. Sacred things
are those which the interdictions protect and isolate; profane things, those to which
these interdictions are applied and which must remain at a distance from the first.
Religious beliefs are the representations which express the nature of sacred things

and the relations which they sustain, either with each other or with profane things. Finally, rites are the rules of conduct which prescribe how a man should comport himself in the presence of these sacred objects. . . .

The really religious beliefs are always common to a determined group, which makes profession of adhering to them and of practicing the rites connected with them. They are not merely received individually by all the members of this group; they are something belonging to the group, and they make its unity. The individuals which compose it feel themselves united to each other by the simple fact that they have a common faith. A society whose members are united by the fact that they think in the same way in regard to the sacred world and its relations with the profane world, and by the fact that they translate these common ideas into common practices, is what is called a "Church." In all history, we do not find a single religion without a Church. Sometimes the Church is strictly national, sometimes it passes the frontiers; sometimes it embraces an entire people (Rome, Athens, the Hebrews), sometimes it embraces only a part of them (the Christian societies since the advent of Protestantism); sometimes it is directed by a corps of priests, sometimes it is almost completely devoid of any official directing body. But wherever we observe the religious life, we find that it has a definite group as its foundation. Even the so-called "private" cults, such as the domestic cult or the cult of a corporation, satisfy this condition; for they are always celebrated by a group, the family, or the corporation. Moreover, even these particular religions are ordinarily only special forms of a more general religion which embraces all; these restricted Churches are in reality only chapels of a vaster Church which, by reason of this very extent, merits this name still more.

It is quite another matter with magic. To be sure, the belief in magic is always more or less general; it is very frequently diffused in large masses of the population, and there are even peoples where it has as many adherents as the real religion. But it does not result in binding together those who adhere to it, nor in uniting them into a group leading a common life. *There is no Church of magic.* Between the magician and the individuals who consult him, as between these individuals themselves, there are no lasting bonds which make them members of the same moral community, comparable to that formed by the believers in the same god or the observers of the same cult. The magician has a clientele and not a Church, and it is very possible that his clients have no other relations between each other, or even do not know each other; even the relations which they have with him are generally accidental and transient; they are just like those of a sick man with his physician. The official and public character with which he is sometimes invested changes nothing in this situation; the fact that he works openly does not unite him more regularly or more durably to those who have recourse to his services. . . .

Thus we arrive at the following definition: *A religion is a unified system of beliefs and practices relative to sacred things, that is to say, things set apart and forbidden—beliefs and practices which unite into one single moral community called a Church, all those who adhere to them.* The second element which thus finds a place in our definition is no less essential than the first; for by showing that the idea of religion is inseparable from that of the Church, it makes it clear that religion should be an eminently collective thing.

QUESTIONS FOR DISCUSSION

1. How does Durkheim define religion? And church? How does this compare with Bertrand Russell's definition of religion in "Religion and Science" (p. 90)? What are some other possible definitions of these words?
2. According to Durkheim, all religions classify the world into two opposing domains. What are these domains and what kinds of activities or objects might go into each?
3. As humans organize things, ideas, and actions into categories of "sacred" and "profane," can you think of possible conflicts that might result between groups because of differences?
4. Some people suggest that as long as there are religions, there will be wars within and between religions. Do you agree? Why or why not?
5. Durkheim writes of religion in scientific, anthropological terms. His conclusions are founded upon observations and analysis of existing religious groups. But in this essay, he does not attempt to explore possible reasons why human beings create religions in the first place. In your opinion, why do they?

WILL DURANT
The Story of Philosophy

During a prolific writing career (in collaboration with his wife, Ariel) that began with The Story of Philosophy *in 1926, Will Durant (1885–1981) made the world of philosophy more accessible to the average American than any other scholar of this century. In an age that places much value upon technological and scientific solutions to life's problems and upon material and economic success as a measure of meaningful existence, Durant argues that philosophy is still the key to meaningful understanding of human existence. Though science offers knowledge, he felt that only philosophy could teach us how that knowledge relates to the whole picture of purposeful living. As he presents his five-part definition of philosophy, note the constant reference to the word "ideal." Contrast this approach to forming an ideal world with the religious quest as suggested in Durkheim's* The Elementary Forms of the Religious Life *(p. 449).*

ON THE USES OF PHILOSOPHY

There is a pleasure in philosophy, and a lure even in the mirages of metaphysics, which every student feels until the coarse necessities of physical existence drag him from the heights of thought into the mart of economic strife and gain. Most of us have known some golden days in the June of life when philosophy was in fact what Plato calls it, "that dear delight"; when the love of a modestly elusive Truth seemed more glorious, incomparably, than the lust for the ways of the flesh and the dross of the world. And there is always some wistful remnant in us of that early wooing of wisdom. "Life has meaning," we feel with Browning—"to find its meaning is my meat and drink." So much of our lives is meaningless, a self-cancelling vacillation and futility; we strive with the chaos about us and within; but we would believe all the while that there is something vital and significant in us, could we but decipher our own souls. We want to understand; "life means for us constantly to transform into light and flame all that we are or meet with";[1] we are like Mitya in *The Brothers Karamazov*—"one of those who don't want millions, but an answer to their questions"; we want to seize the value and perspective of passing things, and so to pull ourselves up out of the maelstrom of daily circumstance. We want to know that the little things are little, and the big things big, before it is too late; we want to see things now as they will seem forever—"in the light of eternity." We want to learn to laugh in the face of the inevitable, to smile even at the looming of death. We want to be whole, to coördinate our energies by criticizing and harmonizing our desires; for coördinated energy is the last word in ethics and politics, and perhaps in logic and metaphysics too. "To be a philosopher," said Thoreau, "is not merely to have subtle thoughts, nor even to found a school, but so to love wisdom as to live, according to its dictates, a life of simplicity, independence, magnanimity, and trust." We may be sure that if we can but find wisdom, all things else will be added unto us. "Seek ye first the good things of the mind," Bacon admonishes us, "and the rest will either be supplied or its loss will not be felt."[2] Truth will not make us rich, but it will make us free.

Some ungentle reader will check us here by informing us that philosophy is as useless as chess, as obscure as ignorance, and as stagnant as content. "There is nothing so absurd," said Cicero, "but that it may be found in the books of the philosophers." Doubtless some philosophers have had all sorts of wisdom except common sense; and many a philosophic flight has been due to the elevating power of thin air. Let us resolve, on this voyage of ours, to put in only at the ports of light, to keep out of the muddy streams of metaphysics and the "many-sounding seas" of theological dispute. But is philosophy stagnant? Science seems always to advance, while philosophy seems always to lose ground. Yet this is only because philosophy accepts the hard and hazardous task of dealing with problems not yet open to the methods of science—problems like good and evil, beauty and ugliness, order and freedom, life and death; so soon as a field of inquiry yields knowledge susceptible of exact formulation it is called science. Every science begins as philosophy and ends as art; it arises in hypothesis and flows into achievement. Philosophy is a hypothetical interpretation of the unknown (as in metaphysics), or of the inexactly known (as in ethics or political philosophy); it is the front trench in the siege of truth. Science is the captured territory; and behind it are those secure regions in which knowledge and art build our imperfect and marvelous world. Philosophy seems to stand still, perplexed; but only because she leaves the fruits of victory to her daughters the sciences, and herself passes on, divinely discontent, to the uncertain and unexplored.

Shall we be more technical? Science is analytical description, philosophy is synthetic interpretation. Science wishes to resolve the whole into parts, the organism into organs, the obscure into the known. It does not inquire into the values and ideal possibilities of things, nor into their total and final significance; it is content to

---

[1] Nietzsche, *The Joyful Wisdom*, pref.
[2] *De Augmentis Scientiarum*, VIII, 2.

show their present actuality and operation, it narrows its gaze resolutely to the nature and process of things as they are. The scientist is as impartial as Nature in Turgenev's poem: he is as interested in the leg of a flea as in the creative throes of a genius. But the philosopher is not content to describe the fact; he wishes to ascertain its relation to experience in general, and thereby to get at its meaning and its worth; he combines things in interpretive synthesis; he tries to put together, better than before, that great universe-watch which the inquisitive scientist has analytically taken apart. Science tells us how to heal and how to kill; it reduces the death rate in retail and then kills us wholesale in war; but only wisdom—desire coördinated in the light of all experience—can tell us when to heal and when to kill. To observe processes and to construct means is science; to criticize and coördinate ends is philosophy: and because in these days our means and instruments have multiplied beyond our interpretation and synthesis of ideals and ends, our life is full of sound and fury, signifying nothing. For a fact is nothing except in relation to desire; it is not complete except in relation to a purpose and a whole. Science without philosophy, facts without perspective and valuation, cannot save us from havoc and despair. Science gives us knowledge, but only philosophy can give us wisdom.

Specifically, philosophy means and includes five fields of study and discourse: logic, esthetics, ethics, politics, and metaphysics. *Logic* is the study of ideal method in thought and research: observation and introspection, deduction and induction, hypothesis and experiment, analysis and synthesis—such are the forms of human activity which logic tries to understand and guide; it is a dull study for most of us, and yet the great events in the history of thought are the improvements men have made in their methods of thinking and research. *Esthetics* is the study of ideal form, or beauty; it is the philosophy of art. *Ethics* is the study of ideal conduct; the highest knowledge, said Socrates, is the knowledge of good and evil, the knowledge of the wisdom of life. *Politics* is the study of ideal social organization (it is not, as one might suppose, the art and science of capturing and keeping office); monarchy, aristocracy, democracy, socialism, anarchism, feminism—these are the *dramatis personae* of political philosophy. And lastly, *metaphysics* (which gets into so much trouble because it is not, like the other forms of philosophy, an attempt to coördinate the real in the light of the ideal) is the study of the "ultimate reality" of all things: of the real and final nature of "matter" (ontology), of "mind" (philosophical psychology), and of the interrelation of "mind" and "matter" in the processes of perception and knowledge (epistemology).

These are the parts of philosophy; but so dismembered it loses its beauty and its joy. We shall seek it not in its shrivelled abstractness and formality, but clothed in the living form of genius; we shall study not merely philosophies, but philosophers; we shall spend our time with the saints and martyrs of thought, letting their radiant spirit play about us until perhaps we too, in some measure, shall partake of what Leonardo called "the noblest pleasure, the joy of understanding." Each of these philosophers has some lesson for us, if we approach him properly. "Do you know," asks Emerson, "the secret of the true scholar? In every man there is something wherein I may learn of him; and in that I am his pupil." Well, surely we may take this attitude to the master minds of history without hurt to our pride! And we may flatter ourselves with that other thought of Emerson's, that when genius speaks to us we feel a ghostly reminiscence of having ourselves, in our distant youth, had vaguely this self-same thought which genius now speaks, but which we had not art or courage to clothe with form and utterance. And indeed, great men speak to us only so far as we have ears and souls to hear them; only so far as we have in us the roots, at least, of that which flowers out in them. We too have had the experiences they had, but we did not suck those experiences dry of their secret and subtle meanings: we were not sensitive to the overtones of the reality that hummed about us. Genius hears the overtones, and the music of the spheres; genius knows what Pythagoras meant when he said that philosophy is the highest music.

So let us listen to these men, ready to forgive them their passing errors, and eager to learn the lessons which they are so eager to teach. "Do you then be reasonable," said old Socrates to Crito, "and do not mind whether the teachers of philosophy are good or bad, but think only of Philosophy herself. Try to examine her well and truly; and if she be evil, seek to turn away all men from her; but if she be what I believe she is, then follow her and serve her, and be of good cheer."

QUESTIONS FOR DISCUSSION

1. What is Durant's definition of philosophy? Why does he repeatedly mention science in this definition?
2. According to Durant, science seems always to be moving forward, while philosophy appears to lose ground. Why is this, in his opinion?
3. In comparing philosophy to science, Durant sums up: "Science gives us knowledge, but only philosophy can give us wisdom"(par.3). Explain this in terms of facts and meaning.
4. Durant claims that "Truth will not make us rich, but it will make us free" (par. 1). In what sense will it make us free?
5. In modern education, few students ever actually study philosophy. Would you consider taking a course in philosophy? Why or why not?

WINSTON L. KING
Religion and Nothingness

In his "Foreword" to Religion and Nothingness, *Winston King, Emeritus Professor at Vanderbilt University, discusses the problem of approaching Eastern religious systems with Western concepts of religion and philosophy. Westerners tend to see these as distinctly different entities. In the East, religions are often deeply philosophical and philosophies often are quite religious. King briefly explores the implications these differing approaches to knowledge have in terms of the ways the East and the West see the universe and the place of humans within it.*

FOREWORD

A basic difficulty that stares us in the face immediately is the differing relation of philosophy and religion in East and West. And it is very important to keep this in mind from the beginning. For us in the West, religion and philosophy have been two ever since the time of the Greek philosophers. For though the Catholic theological tradition incorporated Aristotle into its theology and Platonism into its experience, philosophy never lost its independence, even in the Middle Ages. In the early modern period it asserted its independence anew under the impulse of humanism and the new empirical sciences. By the time of the Enlightenment it had come to qualify and question the basic foundations and assumptions of the Christian faith and ended up, as at present, occasionally in rational support of religious verities (always on the basis of its own rational foundations), more often in outright hostility toward all religion, but in any event always completely separate. And this separation has been institutionalized in the faculty structures of many universities, especially in the United States.

In the millennia-long traditions of the Hindu and Buddhist East, philosophy and religion have in effect and intent been branches of the same enterprise, that of seeking man's salvation. In India it is not uncommon for the professor of philosophy to spend the years of his retirement in personal religious quest, that is, in fully existentializing his intellectualism. In Japan since the Meiji Restoration, the Western pattern of separating the public (national and prefectural) universities from the religiously founded and supported ones has been faithfully followed, but the interchange of professors between the two systems and the similar content of the philosophico-religious courses taught in both bring them closer. After all, the Western pattern has been present in university learning for only a century, while the Buddhist cultural pattern has been dominant in all Japanese learning for fifteen centuries. Thus it is no anomaly in Japan that Nishitani should concurrently teach philosophy in Kyoto University (national) and religion in Ōtani University (a Jōdo Shinshū Buddhist institution). A Japanese friend says flatly that there would have been no difference in content between the way in which Nishitani would have taught a given course in the "philosophy" faculty of Kyoto University and in the department of "religion" in Ōtani University. . . .

There is yet another factor, Buddhist in general and Zen in particular, which is fully as central to the difficulty of East-West communication as any of the above: the differing East-West views of the universe and man's place in it. A comparison of the two by means of somewhat stereotypical models may illustrate this fundamental difference of cultural stance. The Western traditional model of the universe may be said to be a mechanical one, not too unlike an intricate piece of clockwork with the greater and lesser wheels and their movements meticulously geared to one another. The whole tends to be a more or less definite and limited system, both in time and space. The parts may be closely related to one another, but much of the causality is conceived in a somewhat mechanical single-line mode, item to item. (I recognize that modern physical theory greatly qualifies this picture; but this does not alter the general validity of the comparison here.) Relationships therein are genuine and important but tend to be discreet and external; there is no confusion of the being or individuality of any one part with that of any other.

Conjoint with this underlying conceptual model, part and parcel of the same cultural philosophical mode of awareness, are the basic building blocks of the Western thought structure—culturally inevitable, one might say. In Western religious thought there is God (prime mover, "watch" creator) who is transcendent of his creation, including man. (Judaism and all its derivates have been strongly averse to humanizing God or divinizing man.) But since man is more Godlike than any other creature, he in turn transcends them all, the little lord of creation under its Great Lord. The ultimate purpose of this subcreation, according to Christianity, is to serve man and in the end to be conducive to his eternal bliss. In post-Christian philosophy man as subject remains rather lordly in his relation to objects. Mind, soul, or consciousness alone "within" the citadel of individual selfhood looks "out" at everything else, whether human or nonhuman, as "other." As Nishitani often insists, this Cartesian division of reality into immaterial, invisible, subjective consciousness and material, visible objectivity is the epitome of Western thought, the creator of its cultures and civilization. Out of this climate has arisen the Western dichotomous type of logical assertion that A is *not*, *can*not be B. Nurtured in this atmosphere, deeply conditioned by the Christian world view, there has arisen the dualistic ethic of (absolute) good versus (absolute) evil, right versus wrong, selfishness versus unselfishness and similar sharp distinctions. On this same subject-object foundation, the human intellect, deliberately abstracting itself from all emotion and aesthetic sensibility (except perhaps the beauty of systematic order), can dispassionately and logically consider and analyze any *other*, be it man, animal, plant, rock, star, or component thereof, and thus create an immense and all-pervasive structure called science.

By contrast the Eastern and Buddhist model for conceiving the universe can be termed a biological-organic one. The East speaks of the interdependency of part upon part and of part and whole, of the internal relations of one entity to another within the organism that is the universe. There is here the amorphous unity of nondistinction, of the Taoist Great Primordial Nothingness (which is prior, perhaps temporally, certainly structurally, to all individual being in the universe) out of which beings flow in their diverse forms and to whose oceanlike womb they return upon dissolution. Hua Yen Buddhism's philosophy of totality placed all beings in what Van Bragt, using a Christian term for the interrelations within the Trinity, calls "circuminsessional interpenetration" of one another. Fa Tsang illustrated it by his hall of mirrors in which each mirror (individual being) reflects (or "contains") the central Buddha image as well as every other mirror in the hall (the universe). Thus the whole can be said to be *in* the part as truly as the part is *in* the whole. These and many similar figures clearly suggest a living body rather than an intricate machine.

It is then inevitable that a philosophy (Zen Buddhist) which had its origins and nourishment in this thought complex will characteristically portray the universe in a way radically different from the Western manner. In place of one-on-one causal sequences there will be holistic, contextual-causal interpretations. In place of a straight-line historical-causal "progress" of events to a climax of some sort in a limited time-span there will be a historical "process" wherein time is cyclical and infinite, and "purpose," "drive," and "direction" much less obvious and important. Individual entities, including man, will not be seen as so substantially separable from other entities as in Western thought, but rather as a single flowing event in which the interdependent relationships are as real as, or even more real than the related entities themselves. And man will have none of that proud, unique difference and lordship over creation which the Christian West has given him—and which he retains in post-Christian secularized form. In Eastern thought he is part and parcel of the universe in which his existence is set, one little wavelet in a vast ocean of being/non-being. And quite obviously his visceral values, existential concerns, and intuitional awareness will be fully as important in relating to and understanding the universe as his sheerly rational knowledge—if not more so.

QUESTIONS FOR DISCUSSION

1. Who is the audience for this piece? From what standpoint does Winston King write?
2. How might a feminist author like Mary Daly (p. 556) revise the use of pronouns in the last part of this essay?
3. How are philosophy and religion conceptualized in the Eastern world? Compare this to Western concepts of philosophy and religion.
4. According to King, how do people in the East view the universe and the place of human beings within it? How do Westerners view these?
5. Over the past centuries, Western nations have sent and continue to send thousands of Christian missionaries to convert Eastern peoples. Why would it be valuable for these missionaries to understand what "philosophy" and "religion" mean to Easterners?
6. What valuable contributions might Eastern and Western thought make to each other, according to this author?

JOHN JARVIS
Introduction to Buddhism

This selection, which should be read in conjunction with "The Enlightenment of the Buddha: Buddhacarita" (p. 461), briefly summarizes the events of Buddha's life as tradition has recorded them, and discusses key elements of Buddhism—in particular, the Four Noble Truths and the Holy Eightfold Path.

The life story of Siddhartha Gautama (who became Buddha, or "the enlightened one") and the origins of the religion he founded occurred in a time and a place quite different in many ways from the modern world, East or West. Most significantly for historical study of the period, it was a time when writing was not the primary means of preserving important events and ideas. Rather, the spoken word in the form of oral history and the memorization and recitation of religious doctrines served these functions. It was not until centuries after Buddha's death that his teachings began to be written down and gathered into the collections that we have today. As in the case of Jesus, we do not have the Buddha's own words about his life and ideas to draw upon, but the writings of the monks who followed the path he offered. Thus, many details in the story of this important figure remain obscure and uncertain.

The first full accounts of the life of Buddha, written some five hundred years after his death, indicate that he was born around 560 B.C.E. in Kapilavastu, a region that is now in Nepal. His father was a minor prince in the kingdom and legend tells us that he went to great lengths to raise his son, the future Buddha, in noble style, protected from the suffering and struggles of the common people outside of the court. Around the age of 29, a turning point came for the young prince as he took a series of chariot rides outside of the protected world that his father had maintained. For the first time, he saw peasants laboring in their fields for survival, and constantly facing old age, disease, and death. This affected him profoundly, and he began to meditate on the true nature of human existence. When he saw a wandering religious man on another ride in the country, he decided to abandon the safety of household life (he was now married with an infant son) and to seek the true meaning of life. In his uncompromising quest for truth, Gautama's willingness to give up his father's kingdom, as well as a wife and small son, is called the Great Renunciation. This act has served as an example for countless devotees over the last twenty-five centuries who have likewise given up worldly ways to become Buddhist monks and nuns.

For a time, Gautama wandered on his own, learning from other spiritual wise men and practicing extreme forms of vegetarianism, fasting, and meditation. He found that these practices left him too weak and confused to attain the state of philosophical insight that he sought, so he tried a "middle way" of seeking enlightenment that encouraged taking better care of the body. Then, legend has it that he seated himself under a Bodhi tree with the resolve of not rising until he had found the meaning of existence through meditation. After much effort, he succeeded on the night of a full moon, and, as the night wore on, he formulated the ideas that would become the foundation of Buddhism.

Buddha's purpose in seeking enlightenment was closely connected to the world he had discovered outside of his father's protected court. He wanted to show people the path to free themselves from the misery and pain of human existence. Buddha and other religious thinkers of his time understood one's place of birth and good or bad fortune in this life as being the result of actions in a previous life. A person who had practiced noble deeds in a past life would be reincarnated into a good family and into less painful circumstances as a reward in this life. If one continued to do good here, even better circumstances could be anticipated in the next life. The reverse was also true: doing evil in this life would only lead to being reborn into worse suffering in the life to come. Buddha's goal was to find a way to escape this unending cycle of rebirth by achieving a state of existence no longer characterized by struggle and by some degree of pain at every level.

For Buddha, the key to reaching *nirvana*, or a state of complete peace beyond human comprehension, was to take complete control of one's thoughts and actions and to cease to participate in behavior that had bad effects. He taught that, by overcoming all ignorance, low views, and inferior deeds, one could break out of the cycle of human rebirth and existence. His teachings, which offer a good example of the fine line between philosophy and religion in Eastern thought, are based upon what came to be called the Four Noble Truths: (1) life is suffering, (2) suffering comes from ignorance and low views, (3) the cycle of being reborn into human suffering can only be broken by overcoming the ignorance that causes it, and (4) there is a true path (the Noble or Holy Eightfold Path) that leads to the end of suffering.

The Noble Eightfold Path gives the devoted Buddhist a clear set of eight behaviors to master in order to reach a state of enlightenment. These are: (1) holding right views (avoiding the illusion of happiness offered by greed or the sensual pleasures of life), (2) right intentions (being entirely devoted to the quest for complete happiness and letting go of the illusionary pleasures of this world), (3) right speech (speaking only the truth), (4) right action (being honest, true and pure in all behavior), (5) right living (hurting no other creatures, human or otherwise, hence vegetarianism is often encouraged), (6) right effort (maintaining strict self-control), (7) right-mindedness (being disciplined in one's thoughts), and (8) right meditation (contemplating life deeply and using the principles employed by Buddha himself to reach enlightenment).

Buddha is said to have died at the age of eighty, which would have been around 480 B.C.E. Though Buddhism gradually faded in importance in India where Hinduism absorbed many of its major concepts, it became the major religion of China by the first century C.E., and from there spread to Japan. In both places it remains influential today. At the peak of its popularity, it attracted more followers than any other world religion, but in modern times, only about six percent of the world's population profess Buddhism as their religion. Despite its relative decline, the impact of this religion remains deeply imprinted in the cultures of the Eastern world, and it has increasingly found acceptance among Westerners in the twentieth century. Today, despite the passage of time and profound changes in the world, millions of people worldwide continue to find relevant and meaningful the view of the world and the place of human existence in that world as formulated by Siddhartha Gautama over twenty-five centuries ago. This is perhaps the truest test of the value of Buddha's contribution to the world of religion and philosophy.

QUESTIONS FOR DISCUSSION

1. How has the biography and teachings of Buddhism been preserved for more modern times? What effects do you think this way of preserving facts and ideas might have upon what we can really know about Buddhism and its founder?
2. What was Siddhartha Gautama's "Great Renunciation"?
3. According to this text, what seemed to be Buddha's main purpose in seeking enlightenment?
4. What aspects of Buddhism's Four Noble Truths seem philosophical? What elements seem more religious? Based upon these four principles and the Noble (or Holy) Eightfold Path, do you find Buddhism more a religion or a philosophy? Why?

NINIAN SMART AND RICHARD D. HECHT
The Enlightenment of the Buddha: Buddhacarita

Ninian Smart is professor of religious studies at the University of California, Santa Barbara; he has written extensively about religion and the study of religion in a worldwide context. His books include The Long Search, The Religious Experience of Mankind, Beyond Ideology, *and* Religion and the Western Mind. *The "Buddhacarita," taken from an anthology edited by Smart and his colleague Richard D. Hecht, relates the life story of the Buddha. This second century* C.E. *text is an account of Buddha's coming to awareness of the true nature and purpose of human existence. Buddha (his name in life was Siddhartha Gautama) died around 500* B.C.E., *but he left a lasting religious tradition that sees life as a painful proving ground where living creatures are born, die, and are reborn (reincarnated) again and again until they learn to overcome ignorance, low views, inferior deeds, and violent passions. Buddhism teaches that complete joy and freedom from suffering (nirvana) are the result of a religious and philosophical journey towards "enlightenment," which is defined as understanding the true nature of life. Note that in each of the watches of the night in the text, Buddha progressively comes to understand the principles that will become the foundation of his teachings. The "watches of the night" were the means by which ancient cities kept time, with the first watch corresponding to our evening hours, the second watch to the hours just before and after midnight, the third watch to our early morning hours, and the fourth watch to the time around dawn. It is from Buddha's insights in the third watch of the night that the key doctrines of the Four Noble Truths and the Noble Eightfold Path are derived.*

Now that he had defeated Māra's[1] violence by his firmness and calm, the Bodhisattva,[2] possessed of great skill in Transic meditation,[3] put himself into trance, intent of discerning both the ultimate reality of things and the final goal of existence. After he had gained complete mastery over all the degrees and kinds of trance:

1. In the first watch of the night he recollected the successive series of his former births. 'There was I so and so; that was my name; deceased from there I came here'—in this way he remembered thousands of births, as though living them over again. When he had recalled his own births and deaths in all these various lives of his, the Sage, full of pity, turned his compassionate mind towards other living beings, and he thought to himself: 'Again and again they must leave the people they regard as their own, and must go on elsewhere, and that without ever stopping. Surely this world is unprotected and helpless, and like a wheel it turns round and round.' As he continued steadily to recollect the past thus, he came to the definite conviction that this world of samsāra[4] is as unsubstantial as the pith of a plantain tree.

---

[1] **Māra** 'Death-dealer'; the Buddhist Evil One or Satan. [Ed. note.]
[2] **Bodhisattva** (i.e., a Being destined for Enlightenment) Until his Enlightenment the Buddha has the title of Bodhisattva. [Ed. note.]
[3] **Transic meditation** Disciplined progression through particular mental states, the climax of which is an experience of enhanced psychic vitality. There are usually four states: concentration of the mind on a single subject, mental and physical joy and ease, then a sense of ease only, then finally a sense of perfect equanimity. [Ed. note.]
[4] **samsāra** Changing, used to describe the unceasing round of birth, death, and rebirth. [Ed. note.]

2. Second to none in valour, he then, in the second watch of the night, acquired the supreme heavenly eye, for he himself was the best of all those who have sight. Thereupon with the perfectly pure heavenly eye he looked upon the entire world, which appeared to him as though reflected in a spotless mirror. He saw that the decease and rebirth of beings depend on whether they have done superior or inferior deeds. And his compassionateness grew still further. It became clear to him that no security can be found in this flood of samsāric existence, and that the threat of death is ever-present. Beset on all sides, creatures can find no resting place. In this way he surveyed the five places of rebirth with his heavenly eye. And he found nothing substantial in the world of becoming, just as no core of heartwood is found in a plantain tree when its layers are peeled off one by one.

3. Then, as the third watch of that night drew on, the supreme master of trance turned his meditation to the real and essential nature of this world: 'Alas, living beings wear themselves out in vain! Over and over again they are born, they age, die, pass on to a new life, and are reborn! What is more, greed and dark delusion obscure their sight, and they are blind from birth. Greatly apprehensive, they yet do not know how to get out of this great mass of ill.' He then surveyed the twelve links of conditioned co-production,[5] and saw that, beginning with ignorance, they lead to old age and death, and, beginning with the cessation of ignorance, they lead to the cessation of birth, old age, death and all kinds of ill.

   When the great seer had comprehended that where there is no ignorance whatever, there also the karma[6]-formations are stopped—then he had achieved a correct knowledge of all there is to be known, and he stood out in the world as a Buddha. He passed through the eight stages of Transic Insight, and quickly reached their highest point. From the summit of the world downwards he could detect no self anywhere. Like the fire, when its fuel is burnt up, he became tranquil. He had reached perfection, and he thought to himself: 'This is the authentic Way on which in the past so many great seers, who also knew all higher and all lower things, have travelled on to ultimate and real truth. And now I have obtained it!'

4. At that moment, in the fourth watch of the night, when dawn broke and all the ghosts that move and those that move not went to rest, the great seer took up the position which knows no more alteration, and the leader of all reached the state of all-knowledge. When, through his Buddhahood, he had cognized this fact, the earth swayed like a woman drunken with wine, the sky shone bright with the Siddhas[7] who appeared in crowds in all the directions, and the mighty drums of thunder resounded through the air. Pleasant breezes blew softly, rain fell from a cloudless sky, flowers and fruits dropped from the trees out of season—in an effort, as it were, to show reverence for him. Mandarava flowers and lotus blos-

---

[5]**conditioned co-production** These are described in full in Buddha's First Sermon, delivered to five monks who had been his companions in pursuit of the spiritual life. The word "ill" is a translation of "dukkha," which may also be translated as "suffering." [Ed. note.]

[6]**karma** In Hinduism and Buddhism, the whole ethical consequence of one's acts considered as fixing one's lot in the future existence. [Ed. note.]

[7]**Siddhas** Men who have obtained perfection. [Ed. note.]

soms, and also water lilies made of gold and beryl, fell from the sky on to the ground near the Shakya sage, so that it looked like a place in the world of the gods. At that moment no one anywhere was angry, ill, or sad; no one did evil, none was proud; the world became quite quiet, as though it had reached full perfection. Joy spread through the ranks of those gods who longed for salvation; joy also spread among those who lived in the regions below. Everywhere the virtuous were strengthened, the influence of Dharma[8] increased, and the world rose from the dirt of the passions and the darkness of ignorance. Filled with joy and wonder at the Sage's work, the seers of the solar race who had been protectors of men, who had been royal seers, who had been great seers, stood in their mansions in the heavens and showed him their reverence. The great seers among the hosts of invisible beings could be heard widely proclaiming his fame. All living things rejoiced and sensed that things went well. Māra alone felt deep displeasure, as though subjected to a sudden fall.

For seven days he dwelt there—his body gave him no trouble, his eyes never closed, and he looked into his own mind. He thought: 'Here I have found freedom', and he knew that the longings of his heart had at last come to fulfilment. Now that he had understood the principle of causation and had become certain of the lack of self in all that is, he roused himself again from his deep trance, and in his great compassion he surveyed the world with his Buddha-eye, intent on giving it peace. When, however, he saw on the one side of the world lost in low views and confused efforts, thickly covered with the dirt of the passions, and saw on the other side the exceeding subtlety of the Dharma of emancipation, he felt inclined to take no action. But when he weighed up the significance of the pledge to enlighten all beings he had taken in the past, he became again more favourable to the idea of proclaiming the path to Peace. Reflecting in his mind on this question, he also considered that, while some people have a great deal of passion, others have but little. As soon as Indra and Brahmā, the two chiefs of those who dwell in the heavens, had grasped the Sugata's[9] intention to proclaim the path to Peace, they shone brightly and came up to him, the weal of the world their concern. He remained there on his seat, free from all evil and successful in his aim. The most excellent Dharma which he had seen was his most excellent companion. His two visitors gently and reverently spoke to him these words, which were meant for the weal of the world: 'Please do not condemn all those that live as unworthy of such treasure! Oh, please engender pity in your heart for beings in this world! So varied is their endowment, and while some have much passion, others have only very little. Now that you, O Sage, have yourself crossed the ocean of the world of becoming, please rescue also the other living beings who have sunk so deep into suffering! As a generous lord shares his wealth, so may also you bestow your own virtues on others! Most of those who know what for them is good in this world and the next, act only for their own advantage. In the world of men and in heaven it is hard to find anyone

---

[8]**Dharma** Teaching of Buddha. [Ed. note.]
[9]**Sugata** Another title of the Buddha, 'One who has gone well.' [Ed. note.]

who is impelled by concern for the weal of the world.' Having made this request to the great seer, the two gods returned to their celestial abode by the way they had come. And the sage pondered over their words. In consequence he was confirmed in his decision to set the world free.

QUESTIONS FOR DISCUSSION

1. In the first and second watches of the night, what did the Buddha learn about the "ultimate reality" of earthly existence?
2. In the second and third watches of the night, the Buddha contemplated the cycle of death and rebirth that is commonly called "reincarnation." What did he discover about the way to escape from this difficult cycle?
3. Many religions are concerned with an individual's outward actions towards others. Their commandments and rules focus upon doing good to fellow human beings and respecting deity. Buddhism does not have this focus. From this text, what does the focus of Buddhism seem to be?

DIANA L. ECK
Darśan: Seeing the Divine Image in India

Diana Eck is professor of Hindu religion in the Department of Sanskrit and Indian Studies at Harvard University, where she also is affiliated with the Center for the Study of World Religions. She has published a number of studies of Hindu religion. In the selection reprinted here, she uses the Sanskrit word "darśan," meaning "seeing," to contrast the great variety of symbols and meanings in Hinduism with Western religious concepts. She points out that as the Judeo-Christian and the Islamic traditions have used sacred books and words to communicate perceptions of divine truth, the Hindu people have relied much more heavily upon visual images, giving a creative richness and variety to their religion that is often baffling and even shocking to Westerners. Also puzzling to Western observers who are used to conceiving religion in terms of one God, one divine book, and one path to truth, is the Hindu concept of many Gods, many symbols, and many paths to truth—all leading to an all-inclusive ONE.

The vivid variety of Hindu deities is visible everywhere in India. Rural India is filled with countless wayside shrines. In every town of some size there are many temples, and every major temple will contain its own panoply of shrines and images. One can see the silver mask of the goddess Durgā, or the stone shaft of the Śiva *liṅga*, or the four-armed form of the god Viṣṇu. Over the doorway of a temple or a home sits the plump, orange, elephant-headed Ganeśa or the benign and auspicious Lakṣmī. Moreover, it is not only in temples and homes that one sees the images of the deities. Small icons are mounted at the front of taxis and buses. They decorate the walls of tea stalls, sweet shops, tailors, and movie theatres. They are painted on public buildings and homes by local folk artists. They are carried through the streets in great festival processions.

It is visibly apparent to anyone who visits India or who sees something of India through the medium of film that this is a culture in which the mythic imagination has been very generative. The images and myths of the Hindu imagination consti-tute a basic cultural vocabulary and a common idiom of discourse. Since India has "written" prolifically in its images, learning to read its mythology and iconography is a primary task for the student of Hinduism. In learning about Hinduism, it might be argued that perhaps it makes more sense to begin with Ganeśa, the elephant-headed god who sits at the thresholds of space and time and who blesses all begin-nings (Fig. 1), and then proceed through the deities of the Hindu pantheon, rather than to begin with the Indus Valley civilization and proceed through the ages of Hindu history. Certainly for a student who wishes to visit India, the development of a basic iconographic vocabulary is essential, for deities such as the monkey Hanu-mān or the fierce Kālī confront one at every turn.

When the first European traders and travelers visited India, they were aston-ished at the multitude of images of the various deities which they saw there. They called them "idols" and described them with combined fascination and repug-nance. For example, Ralph Fitch, who traveled as a merchant through north India in the 1500s writes of the images of deities in Banāras: "Their chiefe idols bee blacke and evill favoured, their mouths monstrous, their eares gilded and full of jewels, their teeth and eyes of gold, silver and glasse, some having one thing in their hands and some another."[1]

Fitch had no interpretive categories, save those of a very general Western Chris-tian background, with which to make sense of what he saw. Three hundred years did little to aid interpretation. When M. A. Sherring lived in Banāras in the middle of the 1800s he could still write, after studying the city for a long time, of "the worship of uncouth idols, of monsters, of the liṅga and other indecent figures, and of a multitude of grotesque, ill-shapen, and hideous objects."[2] When Mark Twain trav-eled through India in the last decade of the nineteenth century, he brought a certain imaginative humor to the array of "idols" in Banāras, but he remained without what Arnheim would call "manageable models" for placing the visible data of India in a recognizable context. Of the "idols" he wrote, "And what a swarm of them there is! The town is a vast museum of idols—and all of them crude, misshapen, and ugly. They flock through one's dreams at night, a wild mob of nightmares."[3]

Without some interpretation, some visual hermeneutic,[4] icons and images can be alienating rather than enlightening. Instead of being keys to understanding, they can kindle xenophobia and pose barriers to understanding by appearing as a "wild mob of nightmares," utterly foreign to and unassimilable by our minds. To under-stand India, we need to raise our eyes from the book to the image, but we also need some means of interpreting and comprehending the images we see.

---

[1] William Foster, ed., *Early Travels in India 1583–1619* (London: Oxford University Press, 1921), p. 23.
[2] M. A. Sherring, *The Sacred City of the Hindus* (London: Trubner & Co., 1868), p. 37.
[3] Mark Twain, *Following the Equator* (Hartford, Connecticut: The American Publishing Company, 1898), p. 504.
[4] **hermeneutic** Interpretive, interpretation, unfolding the signification. [Ed. note.]

The bafflement of many who first behold the array of Hindu images springs from the deep-rooted Western antagonism to imaging the divine at all. The Hebraic hostility to "graven images" expressed in the Commandments is echoed repeatedly in the Hebrew Bible: "You shall not make for yourself a graven image, or any likeness of anything that is in heaven above, or that is in the earth beneath, or that is in the water under the earth."

The Hebraic resistance to imaging the divine has combined with a certain distrust of the senses in the world of the Greek tradition as well. While the Greeks were famous for their anthropomorphic images of the gods, the prevalent suspicion in the philosophies of classical Greece was that "what the eyes reported was not true."[5] Like those of dim vision in Plato's cave, it was thought that people generally accept the mere shadows of reality as "true." Nevertheless, if dim vision described human perception of the ordinary world, the Greeks continued to use the notion of true vision to describe wisdom, that which is seen directly in the full light of day rather than obliquely in the shadowy light of the cave. Arnheim writes, "The Greeks learned to distrust the senses, but they never forgot that direct vision is the first and final source of wisdom. They refined the techniques of reasoning, but they also believed that, in the words of Aristotle, 'the soul never thinks without an image.'"[6]

On the whole, it would be fair to say that the Western traditions, especially the religious traditions of the "Book"—Judaism, Christianity, and Islam—have trusted the Word more than the Image as a mediator of the divine truth. The Qur'ān and the Hebrew Bible are filled with injunctions to "proclaim" and to "hear" the word. The ears were somehow more trustworthy than the eyes. In the Christian tradition this suspicion of the eyes and the image has been a particularly Protestant position.

And yet the visible image has not been without some force in the religious thinking of the West. The verbal icon of God as "Father" or "King" has had considerable power in shaping the Judeo-Christian religious imagination. The Orthodox Christian traditions, after much debate in the eighth and ninth centuries, granted an important place to the honoring of icons as those "windows" through which one might look toward God. They were careful, however, to say that the icon should not be "realistic" and should be only two-dimensional. In the Catholic tradition as well, the art and iconography, especially of Mary and the saints, has had a long and rich history. And all three traditions of the "Book" have developed the art of embellishing the word into a virtual icon in the elaboration of calligraphic and decorative arts. Finally, it should be said that there is a great diversity within each of these traditions. The Mexican villager who comes on his knees to the Virgin of Guadalupe, leaves a bundle of beans, and lights a candle, would no doubt feel more at home in a Hindu temple than in a stark, white New England Protestant church. Similarly, the Moroccan Muslim woman who visits the shrines of Muslim saints, would find India less foreign than did the eleventh century Muslim scholar Alberuni, who wrote that "the Hindus entirely differ from us in every respect."[7]

---

[5]Arnheim, p. 5.
[6]Arnheim, p. 12.
[7]Edward C. Sachau, ed., *Alberuni's India* (Delhi: S. Chand & Co., 1964), p. 17.

Worshiping as God those "things" which are not God has been despised in the Western traditions as "idolatry," a mere bowing down to "sticks and stones." The difficulty with such a view of idolatry, however, is that anyone who bows down to such things clearly does not understand them to be sticks and stones. No people would identify themselves as "idolators," by faith. Thus, idolatry can be only an outsider's term for the symbols and visual images of some other culture. Theodore Roszak, writing in *Where the Wasteland Ends*, locates the "sin of idolatry" precisely where it belongs: in the eye of the beholder.[8]

In beginning to understand the consciousness of the Hindu worshiper who bows to "sticks and stones," an anecdote of the Indian novelist U. R. Anantha Murthy is provocative. He tells of an artist friend who was studying folk art in rural north India. Looking into one hut, he saw a stone daubed with red *kunkum* powder, and he asked the villager if he might bring the stone outside to photograph it. The villager agreed, and after the artist had photographed the stone he realized that he might have polluted this sacred object by moving it outside. Horrified, he apologized to the villager, who replied, "It doesn't matter. I will have to bring another stone and anoint *kunkum* on it." Anantha Murthy comments, "Any piece of stone on which he put *kunkum* became God for the peasant. What mattered was his faith, not the stone."[9] We might add that, of course, the stone matters too. If it did not, the peasant would not bother with a stone at all.

Unlike the zealous Protestant missionaries of a century ago, we are not much given to the use of the term "idolatry" to condemn what "other people" do. Yet those who misunderstood have still left us with the task of understanding, and they have raised an important and subtle issue in the comparative study of religion: What is the nature of the divine image? Is it considered to be intrinsically sacred? Is it a symbol of the sacred? A mediator of the sacred? How are images made, consecrated, and used, and what does this tell us about the way they are understood? But still another question remains to be addressed before we take up these topics. That is the question of the multitude of images. Why are there so many gods?

THE POLYTHEISTIC IMAGINATION

It is not only the image-making capacity of the Hindu imagination that confronts the Western student of Hinduism, but the bold Hindu polytheistic consciousness. Here too, in attempting to understand another culture, we discover one of the great myths of our own: the myth of monotheism. Myths are those "stories" we presuppose about the nature of the world and its structures of meaning. Usually we take our own myths so much for granted that it is striking to recognize them as "myths" which have shaped not only our religious viewpoint, but our ways of knowing. Even Westerners who consider themselves to be secular participate in the myth of monotheism: that in matters of ultimate importance, there is only One—one God,

[8]Theodore Roszak, *Where the Wasteland Ends* (Garden City, New York: Doubleday & Co., 1972), Chapter 4, "The Sin of Idolatry."
[9]U. R. Anantha Murthy, "Search for an Identity: A Viewpoint of a Kannada Writer," in Sudhir Kakar, ed., *Identity and Adulthood* (Delhi: Oxford University Press, 1979), pp. 109–110.

one Book, one Son, one Church, one Seal of the Prophets, one Nation under God. The psychologist James Hillman speaks of a "monotheism of consciousness" which has shaped our very habits of thinking, so that the autonomous, univocal, and independent personality is considered healthy; single-minded decision-making is considered a strength; and the concept of the independent ego as "number one" is considered normal.[10]

In entering into the Hindu world, one confronts a way of thinking which one might call "radically polytheistic," and if there is any "great divide" between the traditions of India and those of the West, it is in just this fact. Some may object that India has also affirmed Oneness as resolutely and profoundly as any culture on earth, and indeed it has. The point here, however, is that India's affirmation of Oneness is made in a context that affirms with equal vehemence the multitude of ways in which human beings have seen that Oneness and expressed their vision. Indian monotheism or monism cannot, therefore, be aptly compared with the monotheism of the West. The statement that "God is One" does not mean the same thing in India and the West.

At virtually every level of life and thought, India is polycentric and pluralistic. India, with what E. M. Forster called "her hundred mouths,"[11] has been the very exemplar of cultural multiplicity. There is geographical and racial diversity from the Pathans of the Punjab to the Dravidians of Tamilnād. There are fourteen major language groups. There is the elaborate social diversity of the caste system. There is the religious diversity of major religious traditions: the Hindus, Muslims, Sikhs, Christians, Buddhists, Jains, and Parsis. (As Mark Twain quipped in his diaries from India, "In religion, all other countries are paupers. India is the only millionaire."[12]) And even within what is loosely called "Hinduism" there are many sectarian strands: Vaiṣṇavas, Śaivas, Śāktas, Smārtas, and others. Note that the very term *Hinduism* refers only to the "ism" of the land which early Muslims called "Hind," literally, the land beyond the Indus. Hinduism is no more, no less than the "ism" of India.

The diversity of India has been so great that it has sometimes been difficult for Westerners to recognize in India any underlying unity. As the British civil servant John Strachey put it, speaking to an audience at Cambridge University in 1859, "There is no such country, and this is the first and most essential fact about India that can be learned. . . ."[13] Seeking recognizable signs of unity—common language, unifying religion, shared historical tradition—he did not see them in India.

In part, the unity of India, which Strachey and many others like him could not see, is in its cultural genius for embracing diversity, so that diversity unites, rather than divides. For example, there are the six philosophical traditions recognized as "orthodox." But they are not called "systems" in the sense in which we use that term. Rather, they are *darśanas*. Here the term means not the "seeing" of the deity, but the "seeing" of truth. There are many such *darśanas*, many "points of view" or "perspectives" on the truth. And although each has its own starting point, its own

[10]James Hillman, *Re-Visioning Psychology* (New York: Harper & Row, 1975), pp. xiv–xv, 158–9.
[11]E. M. Forster, *A Passage to India*, p. 135.
[12]Mark Twain, *Following the Equator*, p. 397.
[13]Francis G. Hutchins, *The Illusion of Permanence* (Princeton: Princeton University Press, 1967), p. 142.

theory of causation, its own accepted enumeration of the means by which one can arrive at valid knowledge, these "ways of seeing" share a common goal—liberation—and they share the understanding that all their rivals are also "orthodox." Philosophical discourse, therefore, takes the form of an ongoing dialogue, in which the views of others are explained so that one can counter them with one's own view. Any "point of view" implicitly assumes that another point of view is possible.

Moving from the philosophical to the social sphere, there is the well-known diversity of interlocking and interdependent caste groups. On a smaller scale, there is the polycentric system of family authority, which is integral to the extended, joint family. Here not only the father and mother, but grandparents, aunts, and uncles serve as different loci of family authority and fulfill different needs.

Not unrelated to this complex polycentrism of the social structure is the polycentric imaging of the pantheon of gods and goddesses. Just as the social and institutional structures of the West have tended historically to mirror the patriarchal monotheism of the religious imagination, so have the social structure and family structure of India displayed the same tendency toward diversification that is visible in the complex polytheistic imagination. At times, the ordering of the diverse parts of the whole seems best described as hierarchical;[14] yet it is also true that the parts of the whole are knotted together in interrelations that seem more like a web than a ladder. The unity of India, both socially and religiously, is that of a complex whole. In a complex whole, the presupposition upon which oneness is based is not unity or sameness, but interrelatedness and diversity.

The German Indologist Betty Heimann uses the image of a crystal to describe this multiplex whole:

> Whatever Man sees, has seen or will see, is just one facet only of a crystal. Each of these facets from its due angle provides a correct viewpoint, but none of them alone gives a true all-comprehensive picture. Each serves in its proper place to grasp the Whole, and all of them combined come nearer to its full grasp. However, even the sum of them all does not exhaust all hidden possibilities of approach.[15]

The diversity of deities is part of the earliest Vedic[16] history of the Hindu tradition. In the Ṛg Veda, the various gods are elaborately praised and in their individual hymns, each is praised as Supreme. Indra may in one hymn be called the "Sole Sovereign of Men and of Gods," and in the next hymn Varuṇa may be praised as the "Supreme Lord, Ruling the Spheres." Max Müller, who was the first great Western interpreter of the Vedas, searched for an adequate term to describe the religious spirit of this literature. It is not monotheism, although there certainly is a vision of divine supremacy as grand as the monotheistic vision. It is not really polytheism, at least if one understands this as the worship of many gods, each with partial authority and a limited sphere of influence. He saw that these Western terms did not quite fit the Hindu situation. To describe the deities of Hinduism, Müller coined the word

---

[14]The hierarchical model is the one adopted by Louis Dumont in *Homo Hierarchicus* (Chicago: University of Chicago Press, 1970).

[15]Betty Heimann, *Facets of Indian Thought* (London: George Allen & Unwin, 1964), pp. 21–22.

[16]**Vedic** Pertaining to the Vedas, the most ancient sacred literature of the Hindus. [Ed. note.]

kathenotheism—the worship of one god at a time. Each is exalted in turn. Each is praised as creator, source, and sustainer of the universe when one stands in the presence of that deity. There are many gods, but their multiplicity does not diminish the significance or power of any of them. Each of the great gods may serve as a lens through which the whole of reality is clearly seen.

The spirit which Müller saw in the Vedic hymns continues to be of great significance in many aspects of Indian religious life. To celebrate one deity, one sacred place, one temple, does not mean there is no room for the celebration of another. Each has its hour. One learns, for example, that there are three gods in the tradition today: Viṣṇu, Śiva, and the Devī. But it is clear from their hymns and rites that these deities are not regarded as having partial powers. Each is seen, by those who are devotees, as Supreme in every sense. Each is alone seen to be the creator, sustainer, and final resting place of all. Each has assembled the minor deities and autochthonous divinities of India into its own entourage. The frustration of students encountering the Hindu array of deities for the first time is, in part, the frustration of trying to get it all straight and to place the various deities and their spouses, children, and manifestations in a fixed pattern in relation to one another. But the pattern of these imaged deities is like the pattern of the kaleidoscope: one twist of the wrist and the relational pattern of the pieces changes.

In the Bṛhadāraṇyaka Upaniṣad, a seeker named Vidagdha Śākalya approaches the sage Yājñavalkya with the question, "How many gods are there, Yājñavalkya?"[17]

"Three thousand three hundred and six," he replied.

"Yes," said he, "but just how many gods are there, Yājñavalkya?"
"Thirty-three."

"Yes," said he, "but just how many gods are there, Yājñavalkya?"
"Six."

"Yes," said he, "but just how many gods are there, Yājñavalkya?"
"Three."

"Yes," said he, "but just how many gods are there, Yājñavalkya?"
"Two."

"Yes," said he, "but just how many gods are there, Yājñavalkya?"
"One and a half."

"Yes," said he, "but just how many gods are there, Yājñavalkya?"
"One."

Yājñavalkya continues by explaining the esoteric knowledge of the different enumerations of the gods. But the point he makes is hardly esoteric. It is not the secret knowledge of the forest sages, but is part of the shared presuppositions of the culture. In any Hindu temple there will be, in addition to the central sanctum, a dozen surrounding shrines to other deities: Gaṇeśa, Hanumān, Durgā, Gaurī, and so on. Were one to ask any worshiper Vidagdha Śākalya's question, "How many gods are there?" one would hear Yājñavalkya's response from even the most uneducated. "Sister, there are many gods. There is Śiva here, and there is Viṣṇu, Gaṇeśa,

---

[17]Bṛhadāraṇyaka Upaniṣad 3.9.1. Quoted here from Robert E. Hume, *The Thirteen Principal Upaniṣads* (1877, 2nd ed. revised, London: Oxford University Press, 1931).

Figure 1. This Hindu deity is Ganeśa, the elephant-headed god who blesses all beginnings.

Hanumān, Gaṅgā, Durgā, and the others. But of course, there is really only one. These many are differences of name and form."

"Name and form"—*nāma rūpa*—is a common phrase, used often to describe the visible, changing world of *saṁsāra* and the multiple world of the gods. There is one reality, but the names and forms by which it is known are different. It is like clay, which is one, but which takes on various names and forms as one sees it in bricks, earthen vessels, pots, and dishes. While some philosophers would contend that the perception of the one is a higher and clearer vision of the truth than the perception of the many, Hindu thought is most distinctive for its refusal to make the one and the many into opposites. For most, the manyness of the divine is not superseded by oneness. Rather, the two are held simultaneously and are inextricably related. As one of the great praises of the Devī puts it: "Nameless and Formless Thou art, O Thou Unknowable. All forms of the universe are Thine: thus Thou art known."[18]

The very images of the gods portray in visual form the multiplicity and the oneness of the divine, and they display the tensions and the seeming contradictions that are resolved in a single mythic image. Many of the deities are made with multiple arms, each hand bearing an emblem or a weapon, or posed in a gesture, called a *mudrā*. The emblems and *mudrās* indicate the various powers that belong to the deity. Gaṇeśa's lotus is an auspicious sign, while his hatchet assures that in his role as guardian of the threshold he is armed to prevent the passage of miscreants. The Devī Durgā has eight arms and in her many hands she holds the weapons and emblems of all the gods, who turned their weapons over to her to kill the demon of chaos. Multiple faces and eyes are common. The creator Brahmā, for example, has four faces, looking in each of the four directions. Śiva and Viṣṇu are depicted together in one body, each half with the emblems appropriate to its respective deity. Similarly, Śiva is sometimes depicted in the Ardhanārīśvara, "Half-Woman God" form, which is half Śiva and half Śakti. The androgynous image is split down the middle: one-breasted, clothed half in male garments and half in female. In a similar way, Rādhā and Kṛṣṇa are sometimes shown as entwined together in such a fashion that, while one could delineate two separate figures, they appear to the eye as inseparably one.

The variety of names and forms in which the divine has been perceived and worshiped in the Hindu tradition is virtually limitless. If one takes some of the persistent themes of Hindu creation myths as a starting point, the world is not only the embodiment of the divine, but the very body of the divine. The primal person, Puruṣa, was divided up in the original sacrifice to become the various parts of the cosmos (Ṛg Veda X.90). Or, in another instance, the original germ or egg from which the whole of creation evolved was a unitary whole, containing in a condensed form within it the whole of the potential and life of the universe (Ṛg Veda X.121; Chāndogya Upaniṣad 3.19; Aitareya Upaniṣad 1.1). If all names and forms evolved from the original seed of the universe, then all have the potential for revealing the nature of the whole. While far-sighted visionaries may describe the one Brahman by the negative statement, "Not this . . . Not this . . .," still from the standpoint of this world, one can as well describe Brahman with the infinite affirmation, "It is this . . .

---

[18]From the "Nārāyaṇīstuti" in the *Devī Māhātmya* of the *Mārkaṇḍeya Purāṇa*. Quoted in Kramrisch, *The Hindu Temple*, p. 298.

It is this. . . ." The two approaches are inseparable. As Betty Heimann put it, " . . . whenever the uninitiated outsider is surprised, embarrassed, or repulsed by the exuberant paraphernalia of materialistic display in Hindu cult, he must keep in mind that, side by side with these, stands the utmost abstraction in religious feeling and thought, the search for the *Neti-Neti* Brahman, the 'not this, not that,' which denies itself to all representations, higher or lower."[19]

QUESTIONS FOR DISCUSSION

1. In what ways might a person raised in Western Christianity be surprised by religious symbolism in Hinduism?
2. What is the historic reason that people raised in the Judeo-Christian tradition are somewhat unused to visual representations of deity?
3. Christian missionaries of the past condemned Hindus for worshipping "idols." In what ways was this a cultural misunderstanding?
4. What does it mean to say that the Hindu world is "polytheistic"? Why has one specialist labeled the Hindus "Kathenotheistic," meaning worshippers of "one god at a time"?
5. At one point, the text indicates that there are 3,306 gods in Hindu tradition. Then it goes on to say there is only one god. How would you explain this seeming contradiction?
6. This text attempts to persuade the reader to a different point of view. What is this point of view? Are you persuaded? How does the author use comparison and contrast to build her persuasive argument?
7. The footnotes indicate this writing is based upon scholarly research. In what ways does the author make the reading accessible to a wider audience?

Muṇḍaka Upanishad

The Upanishads *represent the first recorded efforts of early Indian philosophers and wise men to come to grips with "knowing" and "being." Written in Sanskrit sometime after 600 B.C.E., the* Upanishads's *purpose is summed up in the words of a chant in the "Brihad-Aranyaka Upanishad":*

From the unreal lead me to the real!
From darkness lead me to light!
From death lead me to immortality!

This collection of metaphysical writings translated by Robert Ernest Hume, shows the first systematic attempts of the Hindus to solve the mysteries of human origins and the purpose of existence. At the

[19]Heimann, p. 33.

same time, Pythagoras among the Greeks, Confucius in China, and Buddha in both India and China were formulating their own responses to these mysteries. These writings are still very much in use today after some 25 centuries. They are to the Indian believer what the New Testament is to the Christian. Perhaps their major contribution to the world of ideas is the formulation of the concept of the ultimate unity and oneness of all that exists. Called the doctrine of universal immanence or intelligent monism, it teaches that not only did the supreme Person create all that exists, but everything in existence is part of the creator. Deity is not viewed as an individual being separate from the rest of creation. Humans, animals, the wind, water, the earth, the planets, all are filled with the presence of the divine spirit, and all are part of the divine physical being. As one approaches this text or the other texts in this section on Buddhism, Taoism, Judaism, and Christianity, it is valuable to know that oral traditions were much more a part of the societies that produced these writings. The actual writing of the texts often came after traditions, beliefs, and ideas had been kept alive for centuries through oral histories and rituals. For this reason, many of the written forms reflect oral structures that could be easily memorized in short, rhythmic, sometimes even poetic language.

SECOND MUṆḌAKA: THE DOCTRINE OF BRAHMA-ĀTMAN

First Khaṇḍa

The Imperishable, the source and the goal of all beings

1. This is the truth:—

   As, from a well-blazing fire, sparks
   By the thousand issue forth of like form,
   So from the Imperishable, my friend, beings manifold
   Are produced, and thither also go.

The supreme Person

2. Heavenly (*divya*), formless (*a-mūrtta*) is the Person (Purusha).
   He is without and within, unborn,
   Breathless (*a-prāṇa*), mindless (*a-manas*), pure (*śubhra*),
   Higher than the high Imperishable.

The source of the human person and of the cosmic elements

3. From Him is produced breath (*prāṇa*),
   Mind (*manas*), and all the senses (*indriya*),
   Space (*kha*), wind, light, water,
   And earth, the supporter of all.

The macrocosmic Person

4. Fire is His head; His eyes, the moon and sun;
   The regions of space, His ears; His voice, the revealed Vedas;
   Wind, His breath (*prāṇa*); his Heart, the whole world. Out of His feet,
   The earth. Truly, He is the Inner Soul (Ātman) of all.

The source of the world and of the individual

5. From Him [proceeds] fire, whose fuel is in the sun;
   From the moon (Soma), rain; herbs, on the earth.
   The male pours seed in the female.
   Many creatures are produced from the Person (Purusha).

The source of all religious rites

6. From Him the Rig Verses, the Sāman Chant, the sacrificial formulas (*yajus*),
      the initiation rite (*dīkṣā*).
   And all the sacrifices, ceremonies, and sacrificial gifts (*dakṣiṇā*),
   The year too, and the sacrificer, the worlds
   Where the moon (Soma) shines brightly, and where the sun.[1]

The source of all forms of existence

7. From Him, too, gods are manifoldly produced,
   The celestials (Sādhyas), men, cattle, birds,
   The in-breath and the out-breath (*prāṇāpānau*), rice and barley, austerity
      (*tapas*),
   Faith (*śraddhā*), truth, chastity, and the law (*vidhi*).

The source of the activity of the senses

8. From Him come forth the seven life-breaths (*prāṇa*),[2]
   The seven flames, their fuel, the seven oblations,
   These seven worlds, wherein do move
   The life-breaths that dwell in the secret place [of the heart] placed seven and
      seven.

The source of the world—the immanent Soul of things

9. From Him, the seas and the mountains all.
   From Him roll rivers of every kind.
   And from Him all herbs, the essence, too,
   Whereby that Inner Soul (*antarātman*) dwells in beings.

The supreme Person found in the heart

10. The Person (Purusha) himself is everything here:
    Work (*karman*) and austerity (*tapas*) and Brahma, beyond death.
    He who knows That, set in the secret place [of the heart]—
    He here on earth, my friend, rends asunder the knot of ignorance.

---

[1] That is, the world of the fathers, and the world of the gods, respectively.
[2] Śaṅkara explains these seven *prāṇa* as the seven organs of sense in the head (i.e. two eyes, two ears, two nostrils, and the mouth). They are compared to seven different sacrificial oblations. The enlightenments produced by their activity are the flames of the sacrifice; the objects which supply their action, the fuel. Each sense moves in an appropriate world of its own; but they are all co-ordinated by the mind (*manas*), which is located in the heart.

Second Khaṇḍa

The all-inclusive Brahma

1. Manifest, [yet] hidden; called 'Moving-in-secret';
   The great abode! Therein is placed that
   Which moves and breathes and winks.
   What that is, know as Being (*sad*) and Non-being (*a-sad*),
   As the object of desire, higher than understanding,
   As what is the best of creatures!

2. That which is flaming, which is subtler than the subtle,
   On which the worlds are set, and their inhabitants—
   That is the imperishable Brahma.
   It is life (*prāṇa*), and It is speech and mind.
   That is the real. It is immortal.
   It is [a mark] to be penetrated. Penetrate It, my friend!

A target to be penetrated by meditation on 'Om'

3. Taking as a bow the great weapon of the Upanishad,
   One should put upon it an arrow sharpened by meditation.
   Stretching it with a thought directed to the essence of That,
   Penetrate that Imperishable as the mark, my friend.

4. The mystic syllable *Om* (*praṇava*) is the bow. The arrow is the soul (*ātman*).
   Brahma is said to be the mark (*lakṣya*).
   By the undistracted man is It to be penetrated.
   One should come to be in It, as the arrow [in the mark].

The immortal Soul, the one warp of the world and of the individual

5. He on whom the sky, the earth, and the atmosphere
   Are woven, and the mind, together with all the life-breaths (*prāṇa*),
   Him alone know as the one Soul (Ātman). Other
   Words dismiss. He is the bridge to immortality.

The great Soul to be found in the heart

6. Where the channels are brought together
   Like the spokes in the hub of a wheel—
   Therein he moves about,
   Becoming manifold.
   Om!—Thus meditate upon the Soul (Ātman).
   Success to you in crossing to the farther shore beyond darkness!

7. He who is all-knowing, all-wise,
   Whose is this greatness on the earth—
   He is in the divine Brahma city

And in the heaven established! The Soul (Atman)!
Consisting of mind, leader of the life-breaths and of the body,
He is established on food, controlling the heart.
By this knowledge the wise perceive
The blissful Immortal that gleams forth.

Deliverance gained through vision of Him

8. The knot of the heart is loosened,
   All doubts are cut off,
   And one's deeds (karman) cease
   When He is seen—both the higher and the lower.

The self-luminous light of the world

9. In the highest golden sheath
   Is Brahma, without stain, without parts.
   Brilliant is It, the light of lights—
   That which knowers of the Soul (Ātman) do know!

10. The sun shines not there, nor the moon and stars;
    These lightnings shine not, much less this [earthly] fire!
    After Him, as He shines, doth everything shine.
    This whole world is illumined with His light.

The omnipresent Brahma

11. Brahma, indeed, is this immortal. Brahma before,
    Brahma behind, to right and to left.
    Stretched forth below and above,
    Brahma, indeed, is this whole world, this widest extent.

THIRD MUNDAKA: THE WAY TO BRAHMA

First Khanda

Recognition of the Great Companion, the supreme salvation

1. Two birds, fast bound companions,
   Clasp close the self-same tree.
   Of these two, the one eats sweet fruit;
   The other looks on without eating.

2. On the self-same tree a person, sunken,
   Grieves for his impotence, deluded;
   When he sees the other, the Lord (īś), contented,
   And his greatness, he becomes freed from sorrow.

3. When a seer sees the brilliant
   Maker, Lord, Person, the Brahma-source,
   Then, being a knower, shaking off good and evil,
   Stainless, he attains supreme identity (*sāmya*) [with Him].

Delight in the Soul, the life of all things

4. Truly, it is Life (*prāṇa*) that shines forth in all things!
   Understanding this, one becomes a knower. There is no superior speaker.
   Having delight in the Soul (Ātman), having pleasure in the Soul, doing the
      rites,
   Such a one is the best of Brahma-knowers.

The pure Soul obtainable by true methods

5. This Soul (Ātman) is obtainable by truth, by austerity (*tapas*),
   By proper knowledge (*jñāna*), by the student's life of chastity (*brahmacarya*)
      constantly [practised].
   Within the body, consisting of light, pure is He
   Whom the ascetics (*yati*), with imperfections done away, behold.

6. Truth alone conquers, not falsehood.
   By truth is laid out the path leading to the gods (*devayāna*)
   By which the sages whose desire is satisfied ascend
   To where is the highest repository of truth.

The universal inner Soul

7. Vast, heavenly, of unthinkable form,
   And more minute than the minute, It shines forth.
   It is farther than the far, yet here near at hand,
   Set down in the secret place [of the heart], even here among those who
      behold [It].

Obtainable by contemplation, purified from sense

8. Not by sight is It grasped, not even by speech,
   Not by any other sense-organs (*deva*), austerity, or work.
   By the peace of knowledge (*jñāna-prasāda*), one's nature purified—
   In that way, however, by meditating, one does behold Him who is without
      parts.

9. That subtle Soul (Ātman) is to be known by thought (*cetas*)
   Wherein the senses (*prāṇa*) fivefoldly have entered.
   The whole of men's thinking is interwoven with the senses.
   When that is purified, the Soul (Ātman) shines forth.

The acquiring power of thought

10. Whatever world a man of purified nature makes clear in mind,
    And whatever desires he desires for himself—
    That world he wins, those desires too.
    Therefore he who is desirous of welfare should praise the knower of the Soul
    (Ātman).

Second Khaṇḍa

Desires as the cause of rebirth

1. He knows that Supreme Brahma-abode,
   Founded on which the whole world shines radiantly.
   They who, being without desire, worship the Person (Purusha)
   And are wise, pass beyond the seed (*śukra*) [of rebirth] here.

2. He who in fancy forms desires,
   Because of his desires is born [again] here and there.
   But of him whose desire is satisfied, who is a perfected soul (*kṛtātman*),
   All desires even here on earth vanish away.

The Soul (Ātman) known only by revelation to His own elect

3. This Soul (Ātman) is not to be obtained by instruction,
   Nor by intellect, nor by much learning.
   He is to be obtained only by the one whom He chooses;
   To such a one that Soul (Ātman) reveals His own person (*tanūm svām*).

Certain indispensable conditions, pre-eminently knowledge

4. This Soul (Ātman) is not to be obtained by one destitute of fortitude,
   Nor through heedlessness, nor through a false notion of austerity (*tapas*).
   But he who strives by these means, provided he knows—
   Into his Brahma-abode this Soul (Ātman) enters.

In tranquil union with the Soul of all is liberation from death and from all distinctions of individuality

5. Attaining Him, the seers (*ṛṣi*) who are satisfied with knowledge,
   Who are perfected souls (*kṛtātman*), from passion free (*vītarāga*), tranquil—
   Attaining Him who is the universally omnipresent, those wise,
   Devout souls (*yuktātman*) into the All itself do enter.

6. They who have ascertained the meaning of the Vedānta-knowledge,
   Ascetics (*yati*) with natures purified through the application of renunciation
   (*saṁnyāsa-yoga*)—
   They in the Brahma-worlds at the end of time
   Are all liberated beyond death.

7. Gone are the fifteen parts[3] according to their station,
   Even all the sense-organs (*deva*) in their corresponding divinities!
   One's deeds (*karman*) and the self that consists of understanding (*vijñāna-maya ātman*)—
   All become unified in the supreme Imperishable.

8. As the flowing rivers in the ocean
   Disappear, quitting name and form,[4]
   So the knower, being liberated from name and form,
   Goes unto the Heavenly Person, higher than the high.

The rewards and the requisite conditions of this knowledge of Brahma

9. He, verily, who knows that supreme Brahma, becomes very Brahma.[5] In his family no one ignorant of Brahma arises. He crosses over sorrow. He crosses over sin (*pāpman*). Liberated from the knots of the heart, he becomes immortal.

10. This very [doctrine] has been declared in the verse:—
    They who do the rites, who are learned in the Vedas, who are intent on Brahma,
    They who, possessing faith (*śraddhayan*), make oblation of themselves, even of the one seer[6]—
    To them indeed one may declare this knowledge of Brahma,
    When, however, the Muṇḍaka-vow[7] has been performed by them according to rule.'

11. This is the truth. The seer (*ṛṣi*) Aṅgiras declared it in ancient time. One who has not performed the vow does not read this.
    Adoration to the highest seers!
    Adoration to the highest seers!

QUESTIONS FOR DISCUSSION

1. A text such as this often seems confusing and awkward to Westerners when they first encounter it. What problems can you think of that might make translating this kind of writing into English especially difficult?
2. Both Hinduism and Buddhism teach that all things that exist come from the same source. This principle of oneness is based upon the idea that all creations are made from the same basic matter and draw upon the same life-giving force,

---

[3]That is, of the microcosm back into the macrocosm. Cf. Praśna, 6. 5.
[4]The Sanskrit idiom for 'individuality.'
[5]In the title to his Latin translation, 'Oupnekhat,' Anquetil Duperron set this sentence evidently as the summary of the contents of the Upanishads: 'Quisquis Deum intelligit, Deus fit,' 'whoever knows God, becomes God.'
[6]Identified with Prāṇa, 'Life,' in Praśna 2. II. The reference, then, is probably to the mystical Prāṇāgnihotra sacrifice, in which 'breath' is symbolically sacrificed for an Agnihotra ceremony.
[7]Śaṅkara explains this as 'carrying fire on the head—a well-known Vedic vow among followers of the Atharva-Veda.' But it is more likely to be 'shaving the head,' as Buddhist monks did later. This preliminary requisite to the study of the Upanishad doubtless gave it the title 'The Shaveling Upanishad,' or 'The Upanishad of the Tonsured.'

though each is a uniquely different expression of existence. What evidence of the principle of oneness can you find in the "Second Muṇḍaka"?
3. In *Religion and Nothingness* (p. 445), Winston King indicated that Eastern religions tend to view human beings as inseparably connected to a much larger, holistic, cyclical, and infinite process of being and nonbeing. In what ways does "The Doctrine of Brahma-Atman" place humans within a framework of connectedness to other parts of existence?
4. In your own words sum up a definition of "the all-inclusive Brahma."
5. The "Third Muṇḍaka" describes the way to reach one's supreme identity and perfect union with the Soul through knowledge of Brahma. In what ways is this similar to reaching "heaven" in Christianity? In what ways is it quite different?

BENJAMIN HOFF
The Tao of Pooh: The *How* of Pooh? and Nowhere and Nothing

*Benjamin Hoff, who also has edited the diary of a young woman who lived in Oregon around the turn of the century (*The Singing Creek Where the Willows Grow: The Rediscovered Diary of Opal Whiteley*), makes his home in Portland, Oregon. In *The Tao of Pooh, *he uses the characters from A. A. Milne's Winnie-the-Pooh children's stories to explain the concepts of Taoism—or, as he puts it in the foreword to the book, he explains the principles of Taoism through Winnie-the-Pooh and explains Winnie-the-Pooh through the principles of Taoism. The first excerpt ("The* How *of Pooh?") touches upon how Taoism differs from Confucianism and Buddhism, and the second ("Nowhere and Nothing") explains the concept of the Great Nothing. Both selections not only explain Taoist concepts but also illustrate the subtle humor Hoff declares to be part of even the most profound Taoist writings.*

The *How* of Pooh?

"You see, Pooh," I said, "a lot of people don't seem to know what Taoism is. . . ."
"Yes?" said Pooh, blinking his eyes.
"So that's what this chapter is for—to explain things a bit."
"Oh, I see," said Pooh.
"And the easiest way to do that would be for us to go to China for a moment."
"*What?*" said Pooh, his eyes wide open in amazement. "Right now?"
"Of course. All we need to do is lean back, relax, and there we are."
"Oh, I see," said Pooh.

Let's imagine that we have walked down a narrow street in a large Chinese city and have found a small shop that sells scrolls painted in the classic manner. We go inside and ask to be shown something allegorical—something humorous, perhaps, but with some sort of Timeless Meaning. The shopkeeper smiles. "I have just the thing," he tells us. "A copy of *The Vinegar Tasters!*" He leads us to a large table and unrolls the scroll, placing it down for us to examine. "Excuse me—I must attend to something for a moment," he says, and goes into the back of the shop, leaving us alone with the painting.

Although we can see that this is a fairly recent version, we know that the original was painted long ago; just when is uncertain. But by now, the theme of the painting is well known.

We see three men standing around a vat of vinegar. Each has dipped his finger into the vinegar and has tasted it. The expression on each man's face shows his individual reaction. Since the painting is allegorical, we are to understand that these are no ordinary vinegar tasters, but are instead representatives of the "Three Teachings" of China, and that the vinegar they are sampling represents the Essence of Life. The three masters are K'ung Fu-tse (Confucius), Buddha, and Lao-tse, author of the oldest existing book of Taoism. The first has a sour look on his face, the second wears a bitter expression, but the third man is smiling.

To K'ung Fu-tse (kung FOOdsuh), life seemed rather sour. He believed that the present was out of step with the past, and that the government of man on earth was out of harmony with the Way of Heaven, the government of the universe. Therefore, he emphasized reverence for the Ancestors, as well as for the ancient rituals and ceremonies in which the emperor, as the Son of Heaven, acted as intermediary between limitless heaven and limited earth. Under Confucianism, the use of precisely measured court music, prescribed steps, actions, and phrases all added up to an extremely complex system of rituals, each used for a particular purpose at a particular time. A saying was recorded about K'ung Fu-tse: "If the mat was not straight, the Master would not sit." This ought to give an indication of the extent to which things were carried out under Confucianism.

To Buddha, the second figure in the painting, life on earth was bitter, filled with attachments and desires that led to suffering. The world was seen as a setter of traps, a generator of illusions, a revolving wheel of pain for all creatures. In order to find peace, the Buddhist considered it necessary to transcend "the world of dust" and reach Nirvana, literally a state of "no wind." Although the essentially optimistic attitude of the Chinese altered Buddhism considerably after it was brought in from its native India, the devout Buddhist often saw the way to Nirvana interrupted all the same by the bitter wind of everyday existence.

To Lao-tse (LAOdsuh), the harmony that naturally existed between heaven and earth from the very beginning could be found by anyone at any time, but not by following the rules of the Confucianists. As he stated in his *Tao Te Ching* (DAO DEH JEENG), the "Tao Virtue Book," earth was in essence a reflection of heaven, run by the same laws—*not* by the laws of men. These laws affected not only the spinning of distant planets, but the activities of the birds in the forest and the fish in the sea. According to Lao-tse, the more man interfered with the natural balance produced and governed by the universal laws, the further away the harmony retreated into the distance. The more forcing, the more trouble. Whether heavy or light, wet or dry, fast or slow, everything had its own nature already within it, which could not be violated without causing difficulties. When abstract and arbitrary rules were imposed from the outside, struggle was inevitable. Only then did life become sour.

To Lao-tse, the world was not a setter of traps but a teacher of valuable lessons. Its lessons needed to be learned, just as its laws needed to be followed; then all would go well. Rather than turn away from "the world of dust," Lao-tse advised others to "join the dust of the world." What he saw operating behind everything in heaven and earth he called *Tao* (DAO), "the Way." A basic principle of Lao-tse's teaching was that this Way of the Universe could not be adequately described in words, and that it would be insulting both to its unlimited power and to the intelligent human mind to attempt to do so. Still, its nature could be understood, and those who cared the most about it, and the life from which it was inseparable, understood it best.

Over the centuries Lao-tse's classic teachings were developed and divided into philosophical, monastic, and folk religious forms. All of these could be included under the general heading of Taoism. But the basic Taoism that we are concerned with here is simply a particular way of appreciating, learning from, and working with whatever happens in everyday life. From the Taoist point of view, the natural result of this harmonious way of living is happiness. You might say that happy serenity is the most noticeable characteristic of the Taoist personality, and a subtle sense of humor is apparent even in the most profound Taoist writings, such as the twenty-five-hundred-year-old *Tao Te Ching*. In the writings of Taoism's second major writer, Chuang-tse (JUANGdsuh), quiet laughter seems to bubble up like water from a fountain.

"But what does that have to do with vinegar?" asked Pooh.
"I thought I had explained that," I said.
"I don't think so," said Pooh.
"Well, then, I'll explain it now."
"That's good," said Pooh.

In the painting, why is Lao-tse smiling? After all, that vinegar that represents life must certainly have an unpleasant taste, as the expressions on the faces of the other two men indicate. But, through working in harmony with life's circumstances, Taoist understanding changes what others may perceive as negative into something positive. From the Taoist point of view, sourness and bitterness come from the interfering and unappreciative mind. Life itself, when understood and utilized for what it is, is sweet. That is the message of *The Vinegar Tasters*.

"Sweet? You mean like honey?" asked Pooh.
"Well, maybe not *that* sweet," I said. "That would be overdoing it a bit."
"Are we still supposed to be in China?" Pooh asked cautiously.
"No, we're through explaining and now we're back at the writing table."
"Oh.
"Well, we're just in time for something to eat," he added, wandering over to the kitchen cupboard.

Nowhere and Nothing

"Where are we going?" said Pooh, hurrying after him, and wondering whether it was to be an Explore or a What-shall-I-do-about-you-know-what.

"Nowhere," said Christopher Robin.

So they began going there, and after they had walked a little way Christopher Robin said:

"What do you like doing best in the world, Pooh?"

(And of course, what Pooh liked doing best was going to Christopher Robin's house and eating, but since we've already quoted that, we don't think we need to quote it again.)

"I like that too," said Christopher Robin, "but what I like *doing* best is Nothing."

"How do you do Nothing?" asked Pooh, after he had wondered for a long time.

"Well, it's when people call out at you just as you're going off to do it, What are you going to do, Christopher Robin, and you say, Oh, nothing, and then you go and do it."

"Oh, I see," said Pooh.

"This is a nothing sort of thing that we're doing now."

"Oh, I see," said Pooh again.

"It means just going along, listening to all the things you can't hear, and not bothering."

Chuang-tse described it this way:

Consciousness wandered North to the land of the Dark Waters and climbed the Unnoticeable Slope, where he met Speechless Non-Doer. "I have three questions for you," Consciousness said. "First, what thoughts and efforts will lead us to understanding the Tao? Second, where must we go and what must we do to find peace in the Tao? Third, from what point must we start and which road must we follow in order to reach the Tao?" Speechless Non-Doer gave him no answer.

Consciousness traveled South to the land of the Bright Ocean and climbed the Mountain of Certainty, where he saw Impulsive Speech-Maker. He asked him the same questions. "Here are the answers," Impulsive Speech-Maker replied. But as soon as he started to speak, he became confused and forgot what he was talking about.

Consciousness returned to the palace and asked the Yellow Emperor, who told him, "To have no thought and put forth no effort is the first step towards understanding the Tao. To go nowhere and do nothing is the first step towards finding peace in the Tao. To start from no point and follow no road is the first step towards reaching the Tao."

What Chuang-tse, Christopher Robin, and Pooh are describing is the Great Secret, the key that unlocks the doors of wisdom, happiness, and truth. What is that magic, mysterious something? Nothing. To the Taoist, Nothing is *something*, and Something—at least the sort of thing that many consider to be important—is really nothing at all. Our explanation of this will attempt to give some sort of indication of what the Taoists call *T'ai Hsü*, the "Great Nothing."

We will begin with an illustration from the writings of Chuang-tse:

> On his way back from the K'un-lun Mountains, the Yellow Emperor lost the dark pearl of Tao. He sent Knowledge to find it, but Knowledge was unable to understand it. He sent Distant Vision, but Distant Vision was unable to see it. He sent Eloquence, but Eloquence was unable to describe it.
>
> Finally, he sent Empty Mind, and Empty Mind came back with the pearl.

When Eeyore lost his tail, who found it for him? Clever Rabbit? No. He was busy doing Clever Things. Scholarly Owl? No. He didn't recognize it when he saw it. Know-It-All Eeyore? No. He didn't even realize that it was missing until Pooh told him. And even then, it took a while to convince him that the tail was definitely Not There.

Then Pooh went off to find it. First, he stopped at Owl's house, and Owl told him in twenty-five thousand monotonous words or more that the Thing To Do would be to Issue a Reward, which would involve writing out a . . . (yawn) . . . notice, and putting it . . . (YAWN) . . . all over the . . . (umm). Oh, yes—where were we? All over the Forest. And then they went outside . . .

> And Pooh looked at the knocker and the notice below it, and he looked at the bell-rope and the notice below it, and the more he looked at the bell-rope, the more he felt that he had seen something like it, somewhere else, sometime before.
>
> "Handsome bell-rope, isn't it?" said Owl.
>
> Pooh nodded.
>
> "It reminds me of something," he said, "but I can't think what. Where did you get it?"
>
> "I just came across it in the Forest. It was hanging over a bush, and I thought at first somebody lived there, so I rang it, and nothing happened, and then I rang it again very loudly, and it came off in my hand, and as nobody seemed to want it, I took it home, and—"

Aha. So Pooh returned the tail to Eeyore, and after it had been put back in place, Eeyore felt much better.

For a while anyway.

An Empty sort of mind is valuable for finding pearls and tails and things because it can see what's in front of it. An Overstuffed mind is unable to. While the Clear mind listens to a bird singing, the Stuffed-Full-of-Knowledge-and-Cleverness mind wonders what *kind* of bird is singing. The more Stuffed Up it is, the less it can hear through its own ears and see through its own eyes. Knowledge and Cleverness tend to concern themselves with the wrong sorts of things, and a mind confused by Knowledge, Cleverness, and Abstract Ideas tends to go chasing off after things that don't matter, or that don't even exist, instead of seeing, appreciating, and making use of what is right in front of it.

Let's consider Emptiness in general for a moment. What is it about a Taoist landscape painting that seems so refreshing to so many different kinds of people? The Emptiness, the space that's not filled in. What is it about fresh snow, clean air, pure water? Or good music? As Claude Debussy expressed it, "Music is the space between the notes."

"Wooh *Baby*! Oooaowee *BABY*! (Wanga wanga wanga.) Baby, don't *leave* me! (Wanga wanga crash bang!) Baby, don't *LEAVE* me!" (Click.) Like silence after noise, or cool, clear water on a hot, stuffy day, Emptiness cleans out the messy mind and charges up the batteries of spiritual energy.

Many people are afraid of Emptiness, however, because it reminds them of Loneliness. Everything has to be filled in, it seems—appointment books, hillsides, vacant lots—but when all the spaces are filled, the Loneliness *really* begins. Then the Groups are joined, the Classes are signed up for, and the Gift-to-Yourself items are bought. When the Loneliness starts creeping in the door, the Television Set is turned on to make it go away. But it doesn't go away. So some of *us* do instead, and after discarding the emptiness of the Big Congested Mess, we discover the fullness of Nothing.

One of our favorite examples of the value of Nothing is an incident in the life of the Japanese emperor Hirohito. Now, being emperor in one of the most frantically Confucianist countries in the world is not necessarily all that *relaxing*. From early morning until late at night, practically every minute of the emperor's time is filled in with meetings, audiences, tours, inspections, and who-knows-what. And through a day so tightly scheduled that it would make a stone wall seem open by comparison, the emperor must glide, like a great ship sailing in a steady breeze.

In the middle of a particularly busy day, the emperor was driven to a meeting hall for an appointment of some kind. But when he arrived, there was no one there. The emperor walked into the middle of the great hall, stood silently for a moment, then bowed to the empty space. He turned to his assistants, a large smile on his face. "We must schedule more appointments like this," he told them. "I haven't enjoyed myself so much in a long time."

In the forty-eighth chapter of the *Tao Te Ching*, Lao-tse wrote, "To attain knowledge, add things every day. To attain wisdom, remove things every day." Chuang-tse described the principle in his own humorous way:

"I am learning," Yen Hui said.

"How?" the Master asked.

"I forgot the rules of Righteousness and the levels of Benevolence," he replied.

"Good, but could be better," the Master said.

A few days later, Yen Hui remarked, "I am making progress."

"How?" the Master asked.

"I forgot the Rituals and the Music," he answered.

"Better, but not perfect," the Master said.

Some time later, Yen Hui told the Master, "Now I sit down and forget everything."

The Master looked up, startled. "What do you mean, you forget everything?" he quickly asked.

"I forget my body and senses, and leave all appearance and information behind," answered Yen Hui. "In the middle of Nothing, I join the Source of All Things."

The Master bowed. "You have transcended the limitations of time and knowledge. I am far behind you. You have found the Way!"

Gathering, analyzing, sorting, and storing information—these functions and more the mind can perform so automatically, skillfully, and effortlessly that it makes the most sophisticated computer look like a plastic toy by comparison. But it can do infinitely more. To use the mind as it's all too commonly used, on the kinds of things that it's usually used on, is about as inefficient and inappropriate as using a magic sword to open up a can of beans. The power of a clear mind is beyond description. But it can be attained by anyone who can appreciate and utilize the value of Nothing.

Let's say you get an idea—or, as Pooh would more accurately say, it gets you. Where did it come from? From this something, which came from *that* something? If you are able to trace it all the way back to its source, you will discover that it came from Nothing. And chances are, the greater the idea, the more directly it came from there. "A stroke of genius! Completely unheard of! A revolutionary new approach!" Practically everyone has gotten some sort of an idea like that sometime, most likely after a sound sleep when everything was so clear and filled with Nothing that an Idea suddenly appeared in it. But we don't have to fall asleep for a few hours for that to happen. We can be awake, instead—*completely* awake. The process is very natural.

It starts when we are children, helpless but aware of things, enjoying what is around us. Then we reach adolescence, still helpless but trying to at least *appear* independent. When we outgrow that stage, we become adults—self-sufficient individuals able and mature enough to help others as we have learned to help ourselves.

But the adult is not the highest stage of development. The end of the cycle is that of the independent, clear-minded, all-seeing Child. That is the level known as wisdom. When the *Tao Te Ching* and other wise books say things like, "Return to the beginning; become a child again," that's what they're referring to. Why do the en-*light*ened seem filled with light and happiness, like children? Why do they sometimes even look and talk like children? Because they are. The wise are Children Who Know. Their minds have been emptied of the countless minute somethings of small learning, and filled with the wisdom of the Great Nothing, the Way of the Universe.

They walked on, thinking of This and That, and by-and-by they came to an enchanted place on the very top of the Forest called Galleons Lap, which is sixty-something trees in a circle; and Christopher Robin knew that it was enchanted because nobody had ever been able to count whether it was sixty-three or sixty-four, not even when he tied a piece of string round each tree after he had counted it. Being enchanted, its floor was not like the floor of the Forest, gorse and bracken and heather, but close-set grass, quiet and smooth and green. . . . Sitting there they could see the whole world spread out until it reached the sky, and whatever there was all the world over was with them in Galleons Lap.

There the Pooh books come to an end, in the Enchanted Place at the top of the Forest. We can go there at any time. It's not far away; it's not hard to find. Just take the path to Nothing, and go Nowhere until you reach it. Because the Enchanted Place is right where you are, and if you're Friendly With Bears, you can find it.

QUESTIONS FOR DISCUSSION

1. Describe the three major schools of thought represented in "The Vinegar Tasters."
2. What effect does Hoff achieve by adapting a children's story to philosophical/religious themes and ideas?
3. According to Hoff, "To the Taoist, Nothing is *something*. . . ." Explain. Contrast the concept of nothingness in Taoism with Glicksberg's explanation of nothingness in Nihilism.
4. Hoff argues that "Emptiness" is also something very real. What examples does he use to support this position? Is his argument convincing?
5. Can you draw any parallels between the Taoist principles of "Nothing" and "Something" and more general eastern ideas of "Being" and "Non-Being"?
6. Why does Taoism encourage its followers to "Return to the beginning; become a child again"?

LAO TZU
The Sayings of Lao Tzu

The Chinese philosopher Lao Tzu was born around 600 B.C.E. and lived contemporary to Confucius. "Lao Tzu" is not a name, but rather a title given him, and means "old person or old philosopher." Tradition and the first histories of his time give his original name as Li Erh, and indicate that he served as librarian in the court of the Chou dynasty. At the heart of the philosophy/religion that grew out of his teachings is the concept of the "Tao." Tao is a broad, vague term meaning the way the universe functions. Literally, it means "path"; figuratively, it describes the path followed by the natural functioning of all aspects of the seen and unseen universe. The planets move in their orbits, day is followed by night, and water runs downhill, wearing away the most rigid barriers that try to stop it. In the same way, Taoism teaches that humans can follow a natural path of harmony if they choose to do so. Lao Tzu was one of the first in China to teach that, through a meditative quest for wisdom, human beings can find the Tao and exist in a perfectly peaceful state of being, free from unproductive desires such as lust, greed, anger, fear, sorrow, regret, and the meaningless human activity that grows out of these desires. The ideal state for the Taoist is to attain the purity and simplicity of a child, or, to use another Taoist symbol, an "uncarved block." The original language of

Lao Tzu's writing shows some of the fundamental differences that can exist between cultures. Chinese characters are not based upon sounds as in English. Rather, each character is an artistic image of the idea it embodies. Instead of letters, the Chinese use "ideographs." For example, the last character in the last line of Lao Tzu's first short text (reproduced below the translation in the original Chinese) looks like a gate, and it means "gate." The challenge of translating profound philosophic insights from Chinese to English may help to explain why the following texts can seem strange and difficult upon a first reading.

I

The Tao which can be spoken of is not the eternal Tao;
The name which can be named is not the eternal Name.
'Non-Being' names this beginning of Heaven and Earth;
'Being' names the mother of the myriad things.
Therefore, some people constantly dwell in 'Non-Being'
Because they seek to perceive its mysteries,
While some constantly dwell in 'Being'
Because they seek to perceive its boundaries.
These two ['Non-Being' and 'Being'] are of the same origin,
But have different names;
Together they are called abstruse[1]—
Abstruse and again abstruse,
This is the gate of all mysteries.

道可道，非常道；
名可名，非常名。
無，名天地之始；
有，名萬物之母。
故常無，欲以觀其妙；
常有，欲以觀其徼。
此兩者，同出而異名，同謂之玄。
玄之又玄，眾妙之門。

II

Everyone understands that which makes 'beauty' beautiful,
And thus the concept of ugliness arises;
Everyone understands that which makes 'goodness' good,
And thus the concept of badness arises.
Hence, being and non-being give birth to each other;
Difficult and easy complete each other;
Long and short form each other;
High and low lean on each other;
Sound and echo are harmonious with each other;
And before and after follow each other.

---

[1]**abstruse** Difficult to be comprehended or understood. [Ed. note.]

Therefore, the Sage undertakes affairs of 'non-action'
And disseminates the 'non-spoken' teachings.
The Sage permits the myriad things to arise of themselves,
But does not attempt to be their master;
He assists the growth of things,
But does not appropriate them;
He does things to assist them,
But does not claim that they depend on him;
The achievement is accomplished,
But he does not dwell in these accomplishments himself.
Only because he does not dwell in these accomplishments
He does not forfeit his achievements.

XLVIII

In the pursuit of learning,
One must daily expand his sphere of activity,
But in the pursuit of the Tao,
One must daily reduce it—
Reduce it and reduce it again
Until one attains a state of 'non-activity'.
He attains a state of 'non-activity',
And yet there is nothing which is not accomplished.
Those who would seek to rule the empire
Must always do so through 'non-activity'.
As soon as they become active
They are no longer worthy of ruling the empire.

QUESTIONS FOR DISCUSSION

Part I

1. How might a translator go about the conceptual task of transforming Chinese characters into English language? How exact could such translations ever really be?
2. In what way does Lao Tzu express the oneness of being and nonbeing in this text?
3. Why might Lao Tzu have described "Non-Being" as filled with mystery, and "Being" as having boundaries?
4. Lao Tzu chose to write his thoughts in very short verses that seldom take up even one full page. Why might he have decided to use this particular form?

Part II

1. How do "being and nonbeing give birth to each other," according to Lao Tzu?
2. How does it become clear that Lao Tzu is attempting to teach his readers?

Part XLVIII

1. In the preceding selection on Taoism (p. 481), Benjamin Hoff translates the first four lines of this section: "To attain knowledge, add things every day. To attain wisdom, remove things every day." Which translation do you prefer? Why?
2. How does Hoff's translation help you to understand the value Lao Tsu and Taoism attach to attaining a state of "non-activity" filled with wisdom rather than a state of "activity" filled with doing and learning?
3. Why does Lao Tzu advise those who would seek to rule empires to do so through "non-activity"? What parallel does this advice have in Plato's "Allegory of the Cave"?
4. Lao Tzu's writings here are the basis for Taoism. In the Western world, Taoism is commonly considered a religion. Would Durkheim (p. 449) define it as a religion? Would Durant (p. 452)? Why or why not?

STEPHEN L. HARRIS
Understanding the Bible: A Reader's Introduction

Stephen L. Harris is professor of humanities at California State University, Sacramento; his work on understanding the Bible is a standard resource for students of religion and the history of the Judeo-Christian tradition in Western thought. This book, part of which is in a question-and-answer format, takes a scholarly approach to Biblical study, marshaling historical and textual evidence to discuss issues of religion. In the section reproduced here, Harris answers questions about how Old Testament and New Testament writers present their deity, and about Biblical depictions of the devil.

Is there a single "biblical view" of Israel's god?
How do different Old and New Testament writers present their deity?

The reader will better appreciate the Bible's portrait of the deity by remembering that each individual writer of Scripture had a personal, and therefore necessarily limited, understanding of his god. Because the Bible authors also wrote from a variety of theological viewpoints and from an ever-changing cultural perspective during the approximately 1,100 years that it took the Bible to be completed, each gave a somewhat different emphasis to the divine nature. The scriptural portrait that emerges is thus extremely complex, even contradictory, a composite portrayal to which many different personalities contributed.

To some writers the deity was primarily strength; to others he was a military leader who gave victory to his people; to still others he was an unknowable intelligence, the mysterious creator and sustainer of the universe. The highest concepts of the biblical God, in which he appears as supreme wisdom, love, and mercy, are found in the Prophets of the Old Testament and in the teachings of Jesus and the

Johannine[1] literature of the New [Testament]. Men like Isaiah, Hosea, and Micah saw God as an almighty power who could judge the world harshly but who was also kind, loving, and deeply concerned for his human creation. Jesus presented him as a gracious father ever near to those who would seek him. The author of 1 John achieved an even more essential vision: to him, God *is* love.

But John's remarkable perception is a far cry from the earliest views of God that are found in the Pentateuch and Former Prophets. The god whom Abraham, Moses, Samuel, or Jehu recognized is not precisely the same as that whom Isaiah, Jesus, or John knew. It is not, of course, that the deity changes but simply that man's ability to perceive him changes. By definition, a supreme god's qualities are infinite, while the human capacity to understand the divine is limited. It is instructive to examine a few of the characteristic ways in which Bible writers have viewed their god.

In general, it appears that men have seen in a divine being those qualities that they have themselves most needed or valued at any particular time. Thus when the early Hebrews were a poor, oppressed minority in Egypt, they looked to Yahweh[2] to show his power to deliver them from their enemies. The ten plagues that Yahweh inflicts upon pharaoh and the Egyptians are a demonstration of his irresistible might, proof that he is stronger than other gods. In the Exodus narrative there is little concern for Yahweh's objective justice or mercy, for such qualities would have been seen as irrelevant to those who needed a god with a strong arm.

From the earliest poems and songs that have survived from Israel's oral traditions, we note that Yahweh was also viewed as a fighter, a supernatural general who could crush enemy armies. As Moses exulted when pharaoh's cavalry was drowned in the Sea of Reeds:

Yahweh I sing: he has covered himself in glory,
  horse and rider he has thrown into the sea.
Yah is my strength, my song,
He is my salvation. . . .
Yahweh is a warrior;
Yahweh is his name.

(Exodus 15:1–3)

The warrior Yahweh also led Israel's armies to victory over the Canaanites. Joshua's conquest of the Promised Land occurred because his god was invisibly fighting against Israel's enemies (Josh. 5:13–15).

To the priestly writers of Leviticus and similar material, their god was holy, set apart from ordinary life and approached only through elaborate rituals and sacrifices. As presented in the New Testament, the Pharisees tended to hold a similar view. The deuteronomic writers of Israel's historical books, such as 1 and 2 Kings, saw Yahweh as the lord of history, the manipulator of human events who causes the rise and fall of nations. In this role, Yahweh is also judge of the earth, the impartial administrator of rewards and punishments according to the recipient's moral behav-

---

[1]**Johannine** Written by John. [Ed. note.]
[2]**Yahweh** Hebrew name for God; literally translated, "He is." [Ed. note.]

ior. The authors of Genesis 1, Psalm 104, and Job 38–42 saw their god as the mysterious power whose word alone was enough to create the world and whose incomparable wisdom directs the workings of nature.

In contrast, some Bible writers viewed their god as all too human, attributing to him both the virtues and defects of a human personality. At times their deity is represented as a typical Near Eastern king, powerful and fundamentally just but prone to jealousy, quick-tempered, and easily provoked to punish insubordination. This god is a destroyer as well as a creator, venting his wrath through flood, famine, plague, drought, earthquake, and fire from heaven. Since it was believed that the biblical god controlled everything that happened (Amos 3:3–8), every natural disaster was interpreted as his express will, though occasionally a Bible writer injected a note of doubt about this. For the author of Ecclesiastes, for example, the deity is remote from and uninterested in daily life, and the element of chance typically controls human affairs: "I see this too under the sun: the race does not go to the swift, nor the battle to the strong; there is no bread for the wise, wealth for the intelligent, nor favor for the learned; all are subject to time and mischance" (Eccles. 9:11).

Many of the Latter Prophets, who raised Israel's religion to its greatest heights, balanced the negative aspects of their god's strength and avenging justice by also emphasizing his compassion, kindness, and patience. Although he presents his god as severely punishing disobedience, Hosea also hears Yahweh say that his love for Israel is too great to allow him to punish her as she deserves. How can I afflict my beloved? Yahweh asks.

My heart recoils from it,
My whole being trembles at the thought.
I will not give rein to my fierce anger.
I will not destroy Ephraim [Israel] again,
    for I am God, not man:
I am the Holy One in your midst
    and I have no wish to destroy.

(Hosea 11:9)

Jesus expresses the same forbearing attitude when he rebukes his disciples' eagerness to call fire from heaven to consume a Samaritan village that had refused them hospitality (Luke 9:51–56).

Perhaps the single most sublime description of the Supreme Being in either Old or New Testament occurs in Isaiah 40, where the poet articulates a vision of Israel's god philosophically unmatched elsewhere in the Bible. All the basic tenets of ethical monotheism are made explicit: Yahweh is One—eternal, almighty, and omniscient. Like the author of Psalm 90, however, the poet exalts Yahweh's transcendent majesty at the expense of man's relative importance. Man—a grasshopper, worm, or blade of grass withered by the sun—is reduced to a nonentity.

The New Testament, with its doctrine that the son of God became flesh to reveal the Father more fully, modifies this view. Although man remains morally inferior and alienated from God, he is justified and redeemed through faith in the

Son. The New Testament god is both a personal immanent deity who answers individual prayers and the invisible omnipotent power who administers the universe. In the New Testament religious environment it would be unthinkable for God to appear in human form as Yahweh did to Adam, Abraham, Jacob, and (possibly) Moses. Instead, he is represented as appearing in the person of his mediator, Jesus, who reportedly states that "he who has seen me has seen the Father" (John 14:9). According to Paul and the Gospel writers, Jesus' submission to death on the cross is the act that reconciles the Christian god to man and opens the way not only for Israel but for all people to find him (2 Cor. 5:18–21).

In spite of the changing and developing picture of godhood projected by the various Christian writers, the deity himself is regarded as immutable: "With him there is no such thing as alteration, no shadow of a change" (James 1:17). By New Testament times the harsher qualities once attributed to God were now seen as belonging to his cosmic enemy, the Devil.

Who is the Devil? What relationship has he to the biblical deity?

From the Greek word *diabolos*, "devil" means "accuser" or "slanderer." In the Book of Revelation the Devil is identified with the serpent who misled Adam and Eve and with the Hebrew "Satan" (Rev. 12:12). The word *Satan* derives from a Hebrew root meaning "obstacle"; personified, it means "opposer" or "adversary." Throughout the New Testament it is assumed that Satan or the Devil has great power over this world, of which he is the present ruler (see, for example, Luke 4:5–8; 2 Cor. 4:4). He is the embodiment of evil, the corruptor of mankind, the source of falsehood and sin, and the archenemy of God. His time of misrule is limited, however, for he is destined to be defeated by Christ and eventually consumed in the everlasting "lake of fire" (Rev. 20:1–5).

Although the idea is extrabiblical, Christian legend holds that the Devil was originally an important angel, a "covering cherub" who through intolerable pride rebelled against God, was cast out of heaven (Isa. 14:12–19; Ezek. 28:12–19), then seduced mankind in order to reign over a rival kingdom of sin. Popular religion pictured him as the king of hell, the ultimate destination of condemned sinners. Dante's *Divine Comedy* and Milton's *Paradise Lost* most vividly depict popular beliefs about the Devil and his history.

A close reading of the biblical text gives a different story of the Devil's origin and development, however. According to some knowledgeable scholars, the Satan figure evolved from the violent destructive aspect of Yahweh's character, a development that becomes apparent on tracing the Satan concept from earliest to latest biblical references. At the outset, Bible writers saw all things, good and evil alike, as emanating from a single source—Yahweh. Israel's strict monotheistic credo decreed that Yahweh caused both joys and sorrows, prosperity and punishment. Thus we read in 1 Samuel 16:14–23 that Yahweh himself sends an "evil spirit" to torment King Saul; in 1 Kings 22:18–28 he dispatches a "lying spirit" to deceive Ahab.

Somewhat later in Israel's religious development, the source of man's troubles was seen to lie in Yahweh's henchman rather than in Yahweh himself. In Job 1–2 and Zechariah 3:1–9, Satan is a member of the heavenly court, one of the "sons of God." He is, significantly, *man's* rather than Yahweh's adversary; he acts as God's prosecuting attorney whose job it is to test the loyalty of the deity's earthly subjects. Throughout the Old Testament, Satan consistently functions as God's administrative agent and is thus a facet of the divine personality.

The clearest example of Satan's assuming the darker aspects of Yahweh's nature occurs in the two accounts of King David's census. In the first version, which dates from the tenth century B.C.E., Yahweh puts it into David's head to sin by taking a census of Israel—always hated by the people since it was done for purposes of taxation and military conscription—for which act the god punishes not David but the people with a plague (2 Sam. 24:1–25). In the second version, written hundreds of years later, it is not Yahweh but "the Satan" who inspires the census (1 Chron. 21:1–30); Yahweh only punishes. Evidently, with the passage of time and development of an expanded sense of justice, it was no longer possible to see Yahweh as both the cause and enemy of sin and as the vindictive avenger of sin as well. The negative qualities that earlier writers had assumed to be in their god were eventually transferred to Satan.

Whereas in the Old Testament Satan can do nothing without Yahweh's express permission, in the New he functions as an independent agent who competes with God for human souls. According to the temptation scenes in the Synoptic Gospels (Matthew, Mark, and Luke, which adopt a "single view" of Jesus' life), he even attempts to win the allegiance of the Messiah. Interestingly, Jesus does not dispute Satan's claim to control the world or his right to offer it to whomever he wishes (Mark 1:12–13; Matt. 4:1–11; Luke 4:1–13). According to Mark's Gospel, one of Jesus' major goals is to break up Satan's kingdom and the hold that he and his demons (lesser evil spirits) exercise on the people; hence Mark emphasizes Jesus' works of exorcising devils and dispossessing the victims of demonic control. The New Testament, then, in contrast to the Old, shows Satan as a formidably powerful figure totally opposed to the Creator God. He is the origin of lies, sin, suffering, and death— a thoroughly nasty character who merits incineration in Revelation's fiery lake.

RECOMMENDED READING

Russell, Jeffrey Burton. "Hebrew Personifications of Evil" and "The Devil in the New Testament." In *The Devil: Perceptions of Evil from Antiquity to Primitive Christianity*, pp. 174–220 and 221–49. Ithaca, N.Y.: Cornell University Press, 1978.

QUESTIONS FOR DISCUSSION

1. According to Stephen Harris, over 1,100 years, what effect have multiple authors had upon the image of deity in the Bible? What are some of the major images given of God in the Old and New Testaments?
2. Both the Old and New Testaments portray deity as unchanging and immutable (Isaiah 44:6, James 1:17). What, then, explains the warrior God of the Old Testament who has become the God of love by New Testament times?
3. What does this text suggest happened to the "harsher qualities" associated with Yahweh's nature in the Old Testament?
4. What parallels do you see in the ways people's perceptions of Yahweh and of Satan evolved over time?

Two Concepts of Deity: Exodus 32 and St. John 8

The following two texts should be read in conjunction with the previous selection by Stephen Harris, "Understanding the Bible: A Reader's Introduction" (p. 491). The texts contrast the Israelite's conceptions of deity (1200 B.C.E.) with the concept of deity taught by Jesus. In particular, the texts show differences in terms of the concepts of sin, divine anger, and punishment for misdeeds.

Exodus

CHAPTER 32

And when the people saw that Moses delayed to come down out of the mount, the people gathered themselves together unto Aaron, and said unto him, Up, make us gods, which shall go before us; for *as for* this Moses, the man that brought us up out of the land of Egypt, we wot not what is become of him.

2 And Aaron said unto them, Break off the golden earrings, which *are* in the ears of your wives, of your sons, and of your daughters, and bring *them* unto me.

3 And all the people brake off the golden earrings which *were* in their ears, and brought *them* unto Aaron.

4 And he received *them* at their hand, and fashioned it with a graving tool, after he had made it a molten calf: and they said, These *be* thy gods, O Israel, which brought thee up out of the land of Egypt.

5 And when Aaron saw *it*, he built an altar before it; and Aaron made proclamation, and said, To morrow *is* a feast to the LORD.

6 And they rose up early on the morrow, and offered burnt offerings, and brought peace offerings; and the people sat down to eat and to drink, and rose up to play.

7 And the LORD said unto Moses, Go, get thee down; for thy people, which thou broughtest out of the land of Egypt, have corrupted *themselves:*

8 They have turned aside quickly out of the way which I commanded them: they have made them a molten calf, and have worshipped it, and have sacrificed thereunto, and said, These *be* thy gods, O Israel, which have brought thee up out of the land of Egypt.

9 And the LORD said unto Moses, I have seen this people, and, behold, it *is* a stiffnecked people:

10 Now therefore let me alone, that my wrath may wax

hot against them, and that I may consume them: and I will make of thee a great nation.

11 And Moses besought the LORD his God, and said, LORD, why doth thy wrath wax hot against thy people, which thou hast brought forth out of the land of Egypt with great power, and with a mighty hand?

12 Wherefore should the Egyptians speak, and say, For mischief did he bring them out, to slay them in the mountains, and to consume them from the face of the earth? Turn from thy fierce wrath, and repent of this evil against thy people.

13 Remember Abraham, Isaac, and Israel, thy servants, to whom thou swarest by thine own self, and saidst unto them, I will multiply your seed as the stars of heaven, and all this land that I have spoken of will I give unto your seed, and they shall inherit it for ever.

14 And the LORD repented of the evil which he thought to do unto his people.

15 And Moses turned, and went down from the mount, and the two tables of the testimony were in his hand: the tables were written on both their sides; on the one side and on the other were they written.

16 And the tables were the work of God, and the writing was the writing of God, graven upon the tables.

17 And when Joshua heard the noise of the people as they shouted, he said unto Moses, There is a noise of war in the camp.

18 And he said, It is not the voice of them that shout for mastery, neither is it the voice of them that cry for being overcome: but the noise of them that sing do I hear.

19 And it came to pass, as soon as he came nigh unto the camp, that he saw the calf, and the dancing: and Moses' anger waxed hot, and he cast the tables out of his hands, and brake them beneath the mount.

20 And he took the calf which they had made, and burnt it in the fire, and ground it to powder, and strawed it upon the water, and made the children of Israel drink of it.

21 And Moses said unto Aaron, What did this people unto thee, that thou hast brought so great a sin upon them?

22 And Aaron said, Let not the anger of my lord wax hot: thou knowest the people, that they are set on mischief.

23 For they said unto me, Make us gods, which shall go before us: for as for this Moses, the man that brought us up out of the land of Egypt, we wot not what is become of him.

24 And I said unto them, Whosoever hath any gold, let them break it off. So they gave it me: then I cast it into the fire, and there came out this calf.

25 And when Moses saw that the people were naked; (for Aaron had made them naked unto their shame among their enemies:)

26 Then Moses stood in the gate of the camp, and said, Who *is* on the LORD'S side? *let him come* unto me. And all the sons of Levi gathered themselves together unto him.

27 And he said unto them, Thus saith the LORD God of Israel, Put every man his sword by his side, *and* go in and out from gate to gate throughout the camp, and slay every man his brother, and every man his companion, and every man his neighbour.

28 And the children of Levi did according to the word of Moses: and there fell of the people that day about three thousand men.

29 For Moses had said, Consecrate yourselves to day to the LORD, even every man upon his son, and upon his brother; that he may bestow upon you a blessing this day.

30 And it came to pass on the morrow, that Moses said unto the people, Ye have sinned a great sin: and now I will go up unto the LORD; peradventure I shall make an atonement for your sin.

31 And Moses returned unto the LORD, and said, Oh, this people have sinned a great sin, and have made them gods of gold.

32 Yet now, if thou wilt forgive their sin—; and if not, blot me, I pray thee, out of thy book which thou hast written.

33 And the LORD said unto Moses, Whosoever hath sinned against me, him will I blot out of my book.

34 Therefore now go, lead the people unto *the place* of which I have spoken unto thee: behold mine Angel shall go before thee: nevertheless in the day when I visit I will visit their sin upon them.

35 And the LORD plagued the people, because they made the calf, which Aaron made.

St. John

CHAPTER 8

Jesus went unto the mount of Olives.

2 And early in the morning he came again into the temple, and all the people came unto him; and he sat down, and taught them.

3 And the scribes and Pharisees brought unto him a woman taken in adultery; and when they had set her in the midst,

4 They say unto him, Master, this woman was taken in adultery, in the very act.

5 Now Moses in the law commanded us, that such should be stoned; but what sayest thou?

6 This they said, tempting him, that they might have to

accuse him. But Jesus stooped down, and with *his* finger wrote on the ground, *as though he heard them not.*

7 So when they continued asking him, he lifted up himself, and said unto them, He that is without sin among you, let him first cast a stone at her.

8 And again he stooped down, and wrote on the ground.

9 And they which heard *it*, being convicted by *their own* conscience, went out one by one, beginning at the eldest, *even* unto the last: and Jesus was left alone, and the woman standing in the midst.

10 When Jesus had lifted up himself, and saw none but the woman, he said unto her, Woman, where are those thine accusers? hath no man condemned thee?

11 She said, No man, Lord. And Jesus said unto her, Neither do I condemn thee: go, and sin no more.

QUESTIONS FOR DISCUSSION

1. What sin is committed in each selection, and why is it a sin?
2. What punishment results for the sinner in each case? Discuss the nature of divine justice as portrayed in each text.
3. After reading "Darśan: Seeing the Divine Image in India" (p. 464), discuss how the people of Moses's time viewed the golden calf differently than villagers in India viewed the sacred stone daubed with red kunkum powder.
4. After reading "The Enlightenment of the Buddha" (p. 461), discuss the results of wrongdoing (or "inferior deeds") as presented in that text. How does the Buddhist concept of divine justice differ from the two presented here?

BENGT SUNDKLER
A Black Messiah: Acts of the Nazarites

A number of new religions have developed in modern times: Mormonism and Christian Science in the United States, the Perfect Liberty Kyodan in Japan, various new sects combining Hindu and Western motifs, and the many religions of black Africa. One of the most interesting of the latter is the Ama Nazaretha, the Nazarite Church, founded by the charismatic Zulu prophet Isaiah Shembe in 1911. This religion expresses the search for a new spiritual identity among people under colonial rule; Shembe attempted to recreate in modern times the sacred world of Zion in Jesus' time, adapting Biblical names, vocabulary, and principles to an African setting. The selection reprinted here, taken from Bengt Sundkler's study of this Zulu Zion movement, is from the Acts of the Nazarites, *collected stories of conversion and testimonies of miracles compiled by Shembe's son. Ekuphakameni, where one of the miracles related here occurs, is a hill which is the holiest place of Ama Nazaretha.*

His presence amazed me. He[1] looked like Jesus, and I was thinking, I am not sleeping, nor am I drunk. Furthermore he was so pleasant, speaking in a friendly manner. I have seen Jesus in pictures. Here only the hair was different from that of Jesus. Later he said, 'Let us go.' His Jesus-like appearance began to change and slowly disappeared, and now he looked like a beautiful girl, and I have never seen a girl as beautiful as this one was.

As we walked along, people were acknowledging him and I had to ask him, 'Did Jesus really come on earth?' He said, 'He came for sure, my child, but people did not understand it and they crucified him. Today many do not see him,' and he added, 'Blessed are those who see him.'

Shembe told people to give Mngoma a chair. Mngoma said, 'Never shall I sit on a chair, like my Lord who is also sitting on a chair.' He then gave me a mat.

In a certain Church service later on, Shembe said, 'Today the witchfinder of heaven (*isangoma sasezulwini*) has come, knowing all the acts which people have committed, good and bad. Some among you do good, others do bad things. I am dividing people according to their acts.' Later, Shembe said, 'I, Shembe, am leaving with you two prophets clothed in sackcloth; they are the two olive trees about whom the Book of Revelations (11:4) is speaking. The Lord is leaving and handing over the Church to these two prophets.'

In the morning, there was a Church service, and after that the sick ones came. There was a piece of cloth with the help of which the sick ones were prayed for. The Lord gave it to us in order that we pray with it. There was a woman with a bad demon. Then Shembe called those patients and caught hold of the woman who was as dead, lying down. He said, 'Her spirit is in heaven!' We were very much afraid as we heard that she was dead, and that her spirit was in heaven.

Then I felt that the work of the Lord at that place was indeed spoiled, because they said they offered human sacrifice at Ekuphakameni, and yet they said about Jesus that he was praying for them with the help of Beelzebul. I saw him looking towards heaven and then to that person. That gave me hope, for now I noticed that the woman began to move; the one who was dead had risen.

Shembe now left for another place. As we approached, an old woman was singing praises and saying, 'Now the Saviour has come to liberate me!'

Shembe said, 'We have come here to chase away the war from this place.' Then he produced the piece of cloth and said, 'Let us pray for the sick.'

Many people assembled. The time for baptizing people had come. People said, 'There are crocodiles in that place where we are to be baptized.' They came to a small river. I brought out the word which I did not even know [beforehand] that I was to pronounce. Those who enter this water will find that their sins will remain in it, and the different kinds of illness will remain in that water. Indeed after my sermon, I entered the water and baptized them and these people who had been dragged there by hand-cart were now healed and could walk on their own.

We came from Judia and were on our way to Velabahleke [two different Nazaretha centres]. Near the dip at Emlalazi many came to see Shembe. An old

---

[1] **He** Isaiah Shembe. [Ed. note.]

man, Newanga, came and said, 'Man of God, we are dying, we and our children and cattle are killed by the sun. I pray for rain.' The man of God said, 'You have your pastors—why do you not ask them?' He replied, 'They have no rain' (*abanayo im-vula*). He said, 'Whom are you asking about rain?' He said, 'I ask you; I see you are man of God, and you will get it.'

Only one day passed, and then very heavy rain fell, continuing for two days all over the country. We left and came to Mkhwanazis, walking along praising Jehova on our dancing drum. As we walked along, a miracle happened; a Ndlanzi girl was bitten by a puff-adder. The man of God bowed down and sucked the wound, getting [the poison] out. The girl was healed and she crossed the river, walking easily on her own feet. May the name of Jehova be praised who gave us his Servant so that we should live through him.

QUESTIONS FOR DISCUSSION

1. This text is a mixture of Christian and African elements. What elements can you identify as clearly African?
2. The author is trying to convey a spiritual message parallel to accounts of the life of Jesus in the New Testament. How does his writing mix fact and personal perception so as to achieve this aim? Is he successful in portraying Isaiah Shembe as a unique individual?

JOHN B. CHRISTOPHER
The Prophet
The Teachings of Islam

John B. Christopher, Emeritus Professor of history at the University of Rochester, has published widely on Islamic culture. The following excerpts from The Islamic Tradition *demonstrate Émile Durkheim's definition of religion as a system of beliefs and practices that revolves around concepts of the sacred and the profane. Muhammad the Prophet (570–632 C.E.) brought a new system of beliefs to the clannish and violent societies of sixth and seventh century Arabia. These beliefs took active expression in what came to be called "the five pillars of the faith." Concepts of what is good (sacred) and of what is evil (profane) are tied directly to the* Koran, *the sacred book of the Islamic faith compiled by 652 C.E. People who accept its teachings are called "Muslims," meaning "those who have submitted." This book defines for Muslims what is proper belief and correct behavior and what is not. Many parallels have been drawn between Islam and the Jewish and Christian traditions, which are also religions that are founded upon a sacred book.*

The Prophet

Muhammad was born, probably about the year A.D. 570, into a family of the Banu Hashim ("sons of Hashim"), a clan of Quraish that had played a prominent role in Meccan history, and from whom the Hashimite monarchs of twentieth-century Jordan and Iraq claim descent. The great Muslim biography of the Prophet, the *Sira*,[1] which dates from the eighth century, traced the ancestry of Muhammad back to Ishmael, son of Abraham in the Book of Genesis by the concubine Hagar. Muslims believe that Ishmael was the progenitor of the Arab people, whereas Isaac, the son born later to Abraham and his wife Sarah, was the progenitor of the Jewish people. Modern scholars reject the genealogy of Muhammad and many other details of the *Sira* as extravagant embellishments in the story-telling tradition of Arabic literature, but they accept its broad outlines as sound in the main. It is generally agreed that Muhammad's great-grandfather, for whom the Banu Hashim were named, pioneered in the caravan trade with Syria, and that Muhammad's grandfather had the important privilege of furnishing food and water to pilgrims visiting the Kaaba. His grandfather is also credited with having reconstructed the sacred well of Zamzam, the waters of which, according to legend, first appeared when the angel Gabriel intervened to slake the thirst of Hagar and Ishmael after Abraham had abandoned them at the insistence of Sarah.

Muhammad's father died on a caravan journey, probably before his son was born; and the boy was brought up by his grandfather and, after his death, by Muhammad's uncle abu-Talib, the head of the Banu Hashim. At this time the Banu Hashim, though still respected in Mecca, had been surpassed in riches and influence by other clans. Because Muhammad did not inherit wealth, he had to make his own way; he apparently served as business agent for Khadija, a well-to-do widow many years his senior, whom he eventually married. The couple had six children, and their marriage seems to have been outstandingly congenial; not until after Khadija's death, in A.D. 619, did Muhammad follow Arab custom and take other wives.

The *Sira* claims that Muhammad made a journey to Syria as Khadija's agent and also an earlier trip as a lad accompanying a caravan of his uncle. These claims have prompted much speculation and controversy as to whether Muhammad must therefore have had some kind of direct experience with Syrian Christianity. But it cannot be proved that Muhammad ever traveled to Syria, and it is the consensus of scholars that, although he was aware of Christianity and Judaism, his knowledge was general and vague, based on hearsay, on the second-hand reports circulating in Mecca. There is no evidence that he had any first-hand acquaintance with Jewish or Christian worship or with the Bible. Indeed, Muslim tradition holds that Muhammad was illiterate, in spite of the fact that one would expect a business agent to have had some ability to read and write.

It is conjectured that Muhammad's religious views may have been influenced to a considerable degree by the *hanifs*, who were very critical of the pagan practices

---

[1] *Sirat Rasul Allah* ("Life of the Prophet of God"), written by ibn-Ishaq and edited by ibn-Hisham; there is an English translation by Alfred Guillaume, *A Life of Muhammad* (Oxford University Press, 1955).

and low moral tone of Meccan society. Recent scholarship, particularly Montgomery Watt's study, *Muhammad at Mecca* (Oxford University Press, 1953), stresses the significance of his personal concern over the city's increasing commercialism and materialism. Muhammad is thought to have participated in the League of the Virtuous, which linked the Banu Hashim and other less prosperous clans against attempts by the wealthy clans to exclude Yemenis from trade with Mecca. The issue here was partly economic, since the poorer clans depended on wares supplied by Yemenis for the conduct of their own little businesses. But a question of justice was also at stake, for the Yemeni merchants had a long-established and recognized position in Mecca.

THE CALL TO RECITE

As the years passed, Muhammad's sense of alienation from existing Meccan society evidently increased, and at times he retreated to a cave in a nearby mountain for meditation and prayer. During one retreat, probably about the year A.D. 610, when he was approximately 40 years old, he experienced the traumatic seizure or awakening that was to transform him into a prophet. In a dream or vision Muhammad saw a heavenly being, who may have been the angel Gabriel, he later suggested, or possibly even Allah himself. The being commanded Muhammad to recite certain messages and, when Muhammad at first refused, struggled with him until he agreed to comply. And so Muhammad memorized and then repeated the messages to his family and some of his fellow citizens as divine revelations. Here is part of the first message:

Recite: In the name of thy Lord who created,
       created Man of a blood-clot.
Recite: And thy Lord is the Most Generous,
       who taught by the Pen,
       taught Man that he knew not.
       No indeed: surely Man waxes insolent,
       for he thinks himself self-sufficient.
       Surely unto thy Lord is the Returning.[2]

During the remaining years of his life Muhammad experienced a great many additional seizures and received a host of additional revelations, usually, he believed, through the angel Gabriel. The complete roster of revelations comprises the *Koran*, a word which means *recital* and has in Arabic a sacred connotation very like that of *scripture* in English.

Until recently many non-Muslims dismissed Muhammad's alleged religious experiences as the convulsions of an epileptic, or the outbursts of a hysterical person, or the fraudulent, self-induced episodes of an opportunist. In the light of modern medical and psychological knowledge, such views no longer appear very tenable. Epileptics, for example, have no memory of what has occurred during their

[2]A. J. Arberry, *The Koran Interpreted*, II (Macmillan, 1955), sura 96, 345.

attacks, whereas Muhammad gave vivid reports of what happened to him. More-over, the very symptoms which used to be thought indicative of Muhammad's epi-lepsy are now considered quite compatible with intense religious excitement—con-vulsive movements during his seizures, foam on his lips, profuse sweating even on a cold day, complaints of hearing the clanking of chains or the ringing of bells. Do these symptoms suggest the delusions of hysteria? Most scholars today think not. It is conjectured that Muhammad seldom had visions after his initial experience, nor did he necessarily hear an actual voice relaying to him the full text of a divine mes-sage. Many a revelation apparently came to Muhammad as a sudden intuition, a flash of inspiration, an idea implanted by the angel Gabriel rather than a word-by-word communication.

The accounts of Muhammad's prolonged and anguished doubts over the source of his messages argue very strongly in favor of his sincerity. The perpetrator of a fraud could hardly have invented the crisis that engulfed Muhammad after his first revelation, when, fearing that an evil jinni had taken possession of him, he contemplated suicide. Sustained by the sympathy of Khadija, and gradually reas-sured by further revelations, he became convinced after many months had passed that he had indeed been chosen to be the Prophet or messenger of Allah.

The Teachings of Islam

The primary source of Islamic teachings is the Koran. To Muslims it is no mere book but the word of God as revealed to Muhammad, supplementing and completing the revelations of the early prophets and of Jesus; it contains in its entirety a truth of which only a part may be found in the Old Testament or the New. It is, a sympathetic Western expert notes,

> the holy of holies. It must never rest beneath other books, but always on top of them; one must never drink or smoke when it is being read aloud, and it must be listened to in silence. It is a talisman against disease and disaster. In many places children under ten years of age are required to learn by heart its 6200 odd verses. . . .
>
> There is something impressive and touching in the sight of simple people murmuring the sacred text as they travel. . . . Some people never leave their homes without having a small copy . . . on their person. The bereaved find their great consolation in reading it. No event of consequence passes without the read-ing of an appropriate passage.[1]

Recitation or chanting of selected verses is the closest Islamic approach to liturgy or to hymn-singing; and Koranic passages are much favored for the decoration of

---

[1] Alfred Guillaume, *Islam* (Penguin, 1954), p. 74.

mosques, where the depiction of human beings or other living creatures is forbidden. For Muslims the significance of the Koran is all-embracing, perhaps even surpassing that of the Bible for fundamentalist Christians.

The full text of the Koran, as we now have it, dates from about twenty years after Muhammad's death when it was pieced together, in the picturesque words of the traditional account, from "scraps of parchment and leather, tablets of stone, ribs of palm branches, camels' shoulder blades and ribs, pieces of board, and the breasts of men." By this time trained reciters had committed large portions of the Koran to memory, just as they were accustomed to do with the great poems of the sixth century. It is also probable that Muhammad himself had been so concerned with the accurate preservation of certain verses that he dictated them to secretaries.

Although there is little reason to suppose that the lag of twenty years before the completion of the Koran distorted the essence of Muhammad's message, the task of non-Muslim students of Islam has been complicated. The reasons why were admirably summarized more than a century ago by Thomas Carlyle, one of the first Western men of letters to attempt a fair-minded appraisal of Muhammad:

> Nothing but a sense of duty could carry any European through the Koran. We read in it, as we might in the State-Paper Office, masses of lumber, that perhaps we may get some glimpses of a remarkable man. It is true we have it under disadvantages: the Arabs see more method in it than we. Mahomet's followers found the Koran lying all in fractions, . . . and they published it, without any discoverable order as to time or otherwise; merely trying, . . . and this not very strictly, to put the longest chapters first. The real beginning of it, in that way, lies almost at the end: for the earliest portions were the shortest. Read in its historical sequence it perhaps would not be so bad. Much of it, too, they say is rhythmic; a kind of wild chanting song, in the original. This may be a great point; much perhaps has been lost in the Translation here. Yet with every allowance, one feels it difficult to see how any mortal ever could consider this Koran as a Book written in Heaven, too good for the Earth; as a well-written book, or indeed as a *book* at all; and not a bewildered rhapsody.[2]

The 6200 verses of the Koran are grouped in 114 chapters or suras, which vary enormously in length, from a very few lines to more than thirty pages. As Carlyle complained, the arrangement of chapters by order of decreasing length places near the end the brief, early Meccan suras, which contain the most dramatic verses of the Koran. Another source of difficulty lies in the titles assigned to the suras, some of which bear little relation to their content; a famous example is sura 2, the longest of all, called "The Cow." Four suras are titled by one or more letters of the Arabic alphabet—*Ta, Ha, Ya, Sin, Sad, Qaf*—and a few others are prefaced by groups of letters after the title—*Alif, Lam, Mim, Ra,* and so on. The reasons for this remain a mystery; perhaps the solution lies in the ingenious suggestion that the disjointed letters represent Muhammad's stammering and mumbling efforts to articulate

---

[2]Thomas Carlyle, "The Hero as Prophet," *On Heroes, Hero-Worship and the Heroic in History* (Oxford University Press [London], 1946), pp. 25–86.

immediately after the traumatic experience of receiving a revelation (M. Rodinson, *Mohammed* [Pantheon, 1971], pp. 75, 93).

Muslims justify the unique structure of the Koran on the ground that it was prescribed by Muhammad himself. A leading Western convert to Islam finds a rationale for the placement of the early Meccan suras: "The inspiration of the Prophet progressed from inmost things to outward things, whereas most people find their way through outward things to things within."[3]

The early Meccan verses are indeed concerned with inmost things—the relationship of man and God, the imminence of the Last Judgment—and are written in a crisp, rhyming prose that sounds like poetry. The verses from Medina are less poetic and more concerned with outward things, such as the administration of the *umma* and the day-to-day conduct of its members. The first Medinan suras, from the period immediately after the Hegira, include stories or parables from the Old and New Testaments, often in rather garbled form. As Muhammad's expectation of swift conversion of Jews and Christians faded, the later Medinan suras focused on Abraham, whom Muhammad called the "friend of God," because he was a pioneering *hanif* and preacher against the worship of idols. The Arabs and Jews, Muhammad believed, as descendants of Abraham through his sons Ishmael and Isaac, respectively, should fulfill their historic destiny by accepting Islam.

The Koran exemplifies in the highest degree the hypnotic qualities of early Arabic literature. In Muslim devotions the Koran is not read, in the conventional sense of the term, but recited or intoned in a fashion that stresses its poetic quality and its power to stir or grip the listener. Muslims tend to hold that it is improper—indeed, sacrilegious—to tamper with the traditional order or original language of the Koran. In deference to Muslim sensibilities some English versions bear such titles as *The Koran Interpreted* or *The Meaning of the Glorious Koran: An Explanatory Translation* to indicate that they cannot presume to be the actual words of God.[4] Other translations, however, attempt to make what Carlyle termed "a bewildered rhapsody" more intelligible to non-Muslim readers by arranging the suras and even individual verses in their proper chronological sequence.[5]

HADITHS

The Koran is not the sole source of direct information about Muhammad and his teachings. Reports of statements he had made and actions he had taken in everyday life were passed along by word of mouth from his companions to later generations; these statements are called *hadiths* or traditions. Although not claimed by Muslims to be the words of God, the hadiths have been endowed with a special importance since even the details of Muhammad's daily routine could reflect divine guidance.

---

[3]M. M. Pickthall, *The Meaning of the Glorious Koran: An Explanatory Translation* (Mentor, 1953), pp. xxviii–xxix.
[4]Arberry, *The Koran Interpreted*; Pickthall, *The Meaning of the Glorious Koran.*
[5]Examples are J. M. Rodwell, *The Koran*, first published in 1861 (Everyman's Library, 1933); Richard Bell's scholarly dissection and reconstruction, *The Qur'an, Translated with a Critical Re-arrangement of the Surahs*, 2 vols. (Edinburgh University Press, 1937; reprinted 1960); and N. J. Dawood's more readable, *The Koran: A New Translation* (Penguin, 1956).

Many hadiths were incorporated into the *Sira*, the early biography of the Prophet . . .; later, al-Bukhari (A.D. 810–870) issued a compendium of hadiths. Here is one of the thousands of traditions he included:

> Muhammad ibn Muqatil Abu'l-Hasan has related to me saying: Abdallah informed us on the authority of Humaid ibn Abd ar-Rahman, on the authority of Abu Huraira—with whom may Allah be pleased—that a man came to the Apostle of Allah—upon whom be Allah's blessing and peace—saying: "O Apostle of Allah, there is no hope for me . . . I had intercourse with my wife during Ramadan." The Prophet answered: "Then set free a slave." Said he: "I have none." The Prophet answered: "Then fast for two months on end." Said he: "But I could not." The Prophet answered: "Then feed sixty poor people." Said he: "I have not the wherewithall." Just then there was brought to the Prophet a basket of dates, so he said to the man: "Take this and distribute it as charitable alms in expiation of your sin." Said he: "O Apostle of Allah, am I to distribute it to other than my own family? when by Him in whose hands is my soul there is no one between the gateposts of the city more needy than I am." Thereat the Prophet laughed till his canine teeth showed, and he said: "Go along and take it."[6]

This text suggests the almost insoluble problems surrounding the authenticity of hadiths transmitted orally over a span of more than two centuries. Perhaps the authorities cited were not reliable, perhaps one of them might have misquoted the Prophet, perhaps the whole hadith was forged by an interested party—no one could, or can, be entirely certain. Some alleged hadiths were obviously borrowed from the Old Testament or the New; some were edifying precepts devised by good Muslims to attract errant brethren back to the path of righteousness; and some were simply tall tales made up by storytellers to elicit generous tips from their audiences. Al-Bukhari is said to have examined 600,000 hadiths (another source says 300,000) and classified each as "sound," "good," "weak," or "unsound"; he judged fewer than 3,000 to be sound, and excluded all the others from his compendium. Both al-Bukhari and the editors of other collections of hadiths that appeared in the ninth century were learned and painstaking scholars. Yet they have been widely criticized during the last hundred years for assigning undue importance to the credentials of the chain of authorities transmitting a particular hadith and paying too little heed to the intrinsic merits or plausibility of the text itself. In any case, it is often argued, the so-called science of verifying hadiths was useful chiefly for making the study of genealogy and historical biography such a prominent feature in Islamic life; sifting the evidence more than two hundred years after the event was bound to be so faulty that all hadiths might as well be considered apocryphal. The judgment of an Indian Muslim, writing in the late nineteenth century, is typical:

> The vast flood of traditions soon formed a chaotic sea. Truth and error, fact and fable mingled together in an undistinguishable confusion. Every religious, social,

---

[6]Adapted with modified spelling and punctuation from Arthur Jeffrey, ed., *Reader on Islam* (Mouton, 1962), p. 86.

and political system was defended, when necessary, to please a Khalif or an Ameer to serve his purpose, by an appeal to some oral traditions. The name of Mohammad was abused to support all manner of lies and absurdities, or to satisfy the passion, caprice, or arbitrary will of the despots, leaving out of consideration the creation of any standards of test. . . . I am seldom inclined to quote traditions having little or no belief in their genuineness, as generally they are unauthentic, unsupported, and one-sided.[7]

A generation later, a British scholar made a more generous evaluation:

But however sceptical we are with regard to the ultimate historical value of the traditions, it is hard to overrate their importance in the formation of the life of the Islamic races throughout the centuries. If we cannot accept them at their face value, they are of inestimable value as a mirror of the events which preceded the consolidation of Islam into a system. Many of the political, dynastic, religious, and social differences which agitated Islam in the days of its imperial might are illustrated in traditions promulgated by the conflicting parties in the interest of their pretensions. In them we see how the rival forces of militarism and pacifism, asceticism and materialism, mysticism and literalism, free will and determination, strove fiercely for the mastery.[8]

Even a spurious hadith may reveal an issue that aroused feelings strong enough for men to put words in the mouth of the Prophet. And traditions such as the one quoted above, with its report of the Prophet's gentle treatment of the man who broke the ban on sexual activity during the daylight hours of Ramadan, endow the austere figure of Muhammad with warmth and humor.

THE LAST JUDGMENT

There is little that is gentle or humorous, however, in the urgent warnings relayed by Muhammad in the early revelations of the Koran. Everyone must realize, he insists, especially the stubborn materialists and polytheists of Mecca, that the Last Judgment is no remote contingency but something that may have to be faced a few moments after death. The very titles of some suras are arresting: "The Terror" (56), "The Mustering" (59), "The Darkening" (81), "The Splitting" (82), "The Earthquake" (99), "The Clatterer" (101). The verses themselves convey the awfulness of the Last Day:

> When heaven is split open,
> when the stars are scattered,
> when the seas swarm over,
> when the tombs are overthrown,
> then a soul shall knows its works, the former and the latter. . . .

[7]Moulavi Cheragh Ali, *The Proposed Political Reforms in the Ottoman Empire and Other Mohammadan States* (Bombay, 1883), pp. xix and 147, as quoted by Alfred Guillaume, *The Traditions of Islam* (Oxford University Press, 1924), p. 29.
[8]Guillaume, *The Traditions of Islam*, pp. 12–13.

When the sun shall be darkened,
when the stars shall be thrown down,
when the mountains shall be set moving,
when the pregnant camels shall be neglected,
when the savage beasts shall be mustered,
when the seas shall be set boiling,
when the souls shall be coupled,
when the buried infant shall be asked for what sin she was slain,
when the scrolls shall be unrolled,
when heaven shall be stripped off,
when Hell shall be set blazing,
when Paradise shall be brought nigh,
then shall a soul know what it has produced.[9]

Souls will be consigned to eternal punishment or reward:

Faces on that day humbled,
labouring, toilworn,
roasting at a scorching fire,
watered at a boiling fountain,
no food for them but cactus thorn
unfattening, unappeasing hunger.

Faces on that day jocund,
with their striving well-pleased,
in a sublime Garden,
hearing there no babble;
therein a running fountain,
therein uplifted couches
and goblets set forth
and cushions arrayed
and carpets outspread.[10]

Many Westerners have expressed shock not so much at the gruesome punishments of the Muslim hell as at the sensual delights of the Islamic paradise with its "maidens good and comely, houris, cloistered in cool pavilions, untouched before them by any man or jinn" and its promise of indulgence in unique beverages ("no brows throbbing, no intoxication").[11] Yet, "the highest joys even there are spiritual," as Carlyle observed, and they may be summed up in the word *salaam*, "peace." *Salaam alaykum* ("peace be upon you, peace be with you") is the universal greeting among Muslims. Verse after verse in the Koran insists that the peace of paradise is

---

[9] Arberry, *The Koran Interpreted*, II, Suras 82 and 81, 328 and 326.
[10] Arberry, *The Koran Interpreted*, II, Sura 88, 336.
[11] Adapted from Arberry, *The Koran Interpreted*, II, Suras 55 and 56, 253 and 254.

reserved for those who have faith and who fear the Lord. The damned are the unbe-lievers, those who deny the Last Judgment or commit the unforgivable sin of sug-gesting that God could have partners.

MAN AND GOD

The Koran demanded that Muslims affirm the unity of God and warned Christians to abandon the doctrine of the Trinity because it violated the strict canon of mono-theism: "People of the Book, go not beyond the bounds in your religion, and say not as to God but the Truth. The Messiah, Jesus son of Mary, was only the Messenger of God, and His Word that He committed to Mary, and a Spirit from Him. So believe in God and His Messengers, and say not, 'Three.'"[12]

The Prophet, although entrusted with God's message, never claimed to have the power that lies at the heart of the Christian view of Jesus—that of interceding with God on behalf of man. Allah is, in effect, unapproachable and incomprehen-sible. This concept of the deity goes far to account for the reputation of Muslims as fatalists, accepting with equal composure good fortune or ill because both represent "the will of Allah."

But Islam is a religion of hope as well as of resignation. According to a hadith, Muhammad stated that God had 99 "most beautiful" names in addition to Allah and would admit to paradise any Muslims who had committed them all to memory. Aiding memorization is the "Islamic rosary," the "worry beads" that Muslims so often finger, which consist of a string of 99 beads, or one of 33 beads to be negotiated three times. The 99 names, drawn partly from the Koran and partly from the hadiths, stress both the stern and the gentle aspects of Allah. Here are the Koranic verses containing the 13 names heading the list:

> He is the All-merciful, the All-compassionate.
> He is the King, the All-holy, the All-peaceable.
> the All-Faithful, the All-preserver,
> the All-mighty, the All-compeller,
> the All-sublime.
> He is God,
> the Creator, the Maker, the Shaper.
> To Him belong the names Most Beautiful.[13]

QUESTIONS FOR DISCUSSION

"The Prophet"

1. In terms of modern-day conflicts between Arabs and Jews, what is significant and ironic about Muhammad the Prophet's ancestor Ishmael?

---

[12]Arberry, *The Koran Interpreted*, I, Sura 4, 125.

[13]Abridged from Sura 59. Arberry, *The Koran Interpreted*, II, 270. The complete list of the 99 may be found in *The Encyclopaedia of Islam*, new ed., s.v. al-Asma' al-Husna, and in Edwin Arnold's *Pearls of the Faith*.

"The Teachings of Islam"

1. How do the teachings of the Koran fit in with the revelations of the early Hebrew prophets and the teachings of Jesus?
2. What is the definition of "hadiths"? Do other religions tend to create their own forms of hadiths? Explain.
3. Who shall be inheritors of paradise and who shall be damned at the Last Judgment, according to the Islamic faith?
4. What does this text indicate is the proper relationship in Islam between humans and deity?

The Quran

To the Muslim believer, the Quran (sometimes spelled Koran) is more than a sacred book. Each of its verses and chapters (suras) is accepted as verbal revelation from deity to Muhammad the Prophet. Because he could not write, Muhammad memorized them word for word, and only later were they written down. Thus, the Quran is sacred to Muslims in a different way than the Bible is to Christians. To believers, it is, word for word, the will and law of Allah. Great debate still surrounds the act of translating it to other languages for fear of changing the words and meaning of divine revelation. The selections here from Sura 3 reflect Islam's acceptance of and borrowings from the Judeo-Christian heritage. The Arabic and Jewish peoples have a long, shared history since they have lived in the same lands at many points over time. Muhammad the Prophet would have been familiar with Jewish and Christian history like any other Arab of his time. However, the perspective he gives in these passages is different in significant ways from the perspective Christians hold, which, equally, is different from the perspective of the Jewish people themselves.

Surely the true religion in the estimation of Allah is Islam, that is, complete submission to Him, and those who were given the Book disagreed only, out of mutual envy, after knowledge had come to them. Whoso rejects the Signs of Allah should remember that Allah is Swift at reckoning. (20)

Now if they should dispute with thee, say to them: I have submitted myself wholly to Allah, and also those who follow me. Say to those who have been given the Book and to those to whom no revelation has been vouchsafed: Do you submit yourselves to Allah also? If they submit they will surely be guided; but if they turn away, thy duty is only to convey the message. Allah is Watchful of His servants. (21)

To those who reject the Signs of Allah and seek to kill the Prophets and those from among the people who enjoin equity, without just cause, announce thou a painful chastisement. These are they whose works shall come to naught in this world and the next, and they shall have no helpers. (22–23) . . .

Let not the believers take the disbelievers for intimate friends in preference to believers; whoever does that has no connection with Allah. Your only course is to keep away from them altogether. Allah warns you against His chastisement; and to Allah is your return. Warn them: Whether you keep hidden that which is in your minds, or disclose it, Allah knows it; and He knows whatever is in the heavens and whatever is in the earth. Allah has full power over all things. Beware of the day when everyone shall find confronting him all the good he has done and all the evil he has done. He will wish there were a great distance between him and the evil. Allah warns you against His chastisement; Allah is Most Compassionate towards His servants. (29–31) . . .

Call to mind when the angels said to Mary: Allah has exalted thee and purified thee and chosen thee from among all the women of thy time. Mary, be obedient to thy Lord and prostrate thyself before Him and worship Him alone with single-minded devotion along with those who worship. (43–44) . . .

Call to mind when the angels said to Mary: Allah, through His word, gives thee glad tidings of a son named the Messiah, Jesus son of Mary, honoured in this world and the next, and of those who are granted nearness to Allah. He shall admonish people in his early years and also in his ripe years, and he shall be of the righteous. Mary said: Lord, how shall I have a son, when no man has touched me? He answered: Such is the power of Allah, He creates what He pleases. When He decrees a thing, He says to it: Be; and it is. He will teach him the Book and the Wisdom and the Torah and the Gospel and will make him a Messenger to the children of Israel, bearing the message: I have come to you with a Sign from your Lord, that for your benefit, in the manner of a bird, I shall fashion, from among persons who are capable of receiving an impress, shapes and shall breathe into them a new spirit, then they will begin to soar like birds by the command of Allah; and I shall declare clean the blind and the leprous and shall bestow life on the spiritually dead, by the command of Allah; and shall announce to you what you will eat and what you will store up in your houses. In all this there is a Sign for you, if you will believe. I fulfil that which has been sent down before me, namely the Torah, and shall make lawful for you some of that which was forbidden you. I come to you with a Sign from your Lord; so be mindful of your duty to Allah and obey me. Verily, Allah is my Lord and your Lord; so worship Him. That is the straight path. (46–52)

When Jesus perceived their disbelief, he asked: Who will be my helpers in the cause of Allah? The disciples answered: We are helpers in the cause of Allah. We have believed in Allah, and bear thou witness we are obedient to Allah. They affirmed: Our Lord we have believed in that which Thou hast sent down and we have become the followers of this Messenger, so write us down among the witnesses. (53–54)

The enemies of Jesus devised their plans and Allah devised His plan; Allah is the best of planners. Allah reassured Jesus: I shall cause thee to die a natural death, and shall exalt thee to Myself, and shall clear thee from the calumnies of those who disbelieve, and shall place those who follow thee above those who disbelieve, until the Day of Judgment; then to Me shall be your return and I will judge between you concerning that wherein you differ. As for those who disbelieve, I will punish them with a severe punishment in this world and in the next, and they shall have no helpers; and as for those who believe and work righteousness, Allah will pay them their full desserts. Allah loves not the wrongdoers. That is what We recite unto thee of the Signs and the Wise Instructions. (55–59)

The case of Jesus in the sight of Allah is like unto the case of Adam. He created him out of dust. He said concerning him: Be; and he began to be. This is the truth from thy Lord, so be thou not of those who doubt. Then whoso should dispute with thee concerning it, after that which has come to thee of divinely revealed knowledge, say to them: Come, let us call our sons and you call your sons, and let us call our women and you call your women, and let us call our people and you call your people, then let us pray fervently for the triumph of the truth and invoke the curse of Allah on those who lie. Most certainly this is the true account. There is none worthy of worship save Allah; and surely, it is Allah Who is the Mighty, the Wise. Then if they turn away, let them remember that Allah knows well those who create mischief. (60–64)

Say to the People of the Book: Let us agree upon one matter which is the same for you and for us, namely, that we worship none but Allah, and that we associate no partner with Him, and that some of us take not others for lords beside Allah. Then, if they turn away, say to them: Bear ye witness that we have submitted to Allah. (65)

People of the Book, why do you dispute concerning Abraham, whereas the Torah and Gospel were surely not sent down till after him? Will you not then understand? Hearken, you are those who have disputed about that whereof you had some knowledge; why do you now dispute about that whereof you have no knowledge at all? Allah knows and you know not. Abraham was neither a Jew nor a Christian; he was ever inclined to Allah and obedient to Him, and he was not of those who associate partners with Allah. Surely, the people closest to Abraham are those who followed him, and this Prophet and those who believe in him. Allah is the Friend of believers. (66–69)

QUESTIONS FOR DISCUSSION

1. According to the first verse of this text, what does "Islam" signify?
2. What does the Quran indicate was the mission of Jesus, the Messiah?
3. Does Allah seem to resemble the warrior God of the Old Testament, or the God of love of the New Testament, as explained by Stephen Harris in *Understanding the Bible* (p. 491)? Explain.
4. What other elements of the Judeo-Christian tradition do you find in this text?

WILLIAM H. MCNEILL and JEAN W. SEDLAR
Introduction to Confucius
From the Analects of Confucius (Lun Yü)

The following two pieces, "Introduction to Confucius" and "From the Analects of Confucius (Lun Yü)" from The Analects of Confucius, *should be read together. In the first, historians William H. McNeill and Jean W. Sedlar briefly outline the life of Confucius as we know it, and describe the main tenants of the philosophy of Confucianism. As with many religious figures of ancient times (Jesus and Buddha, for example), Confucius wrote nothing himself; his sayings were passed on orally by his followers and written down much later. As McNeill and Sedlar point out, however, these sayings, or* Analects, *are the best source for the actual teaching of Confucius. The selections from the* Analects *reprinted here focus on education and on the concept of "jen"—goodness, or human-heartedness—which is central to Confucianism.*

Introduction to Confucius

Until very recent times in China, Confucius (K'ung Fu Tzu,[1] or Master K'ung) was generally regarded as the greatest thinker who ever lived. The complex of ideas attached to his name—human-heartedness, decorum, respect for parents and ancestors—expresses the characteristic attitude of the traditional Chinese. From about the first century B.C. until the twentieth century A.D. Confucianism was recognized, with occasional interruptions, as the official philosophy of the Chinese empire. The Confucian Classics were the basic texts of Chinese education and the subject matter of the civil service examinations, virtually ensuring that the imperial bureaucracy would be imbued with Confucian principles. The all-pervasiveness of Confucian influence in social norms and private morals, the exalted status accorded to Confucius himself, and the general acceptance of his reputed opinions as almost unquestioned truths, gave to Confucianism many of the characteristics which in other civilizations have belonged to religion rather than philosophy.

Confucius himself was born in the small state of Lu on the northeast China plain, in what was then one of the oldest centers of Chinese culture. His traditional dates, 550–479 B.C., are approximately accurate, making him a contemporary of the Buddha, the pre-Socratic philosophers of Greece, and perhaps the Persian Zoroaster. Confucius himself tells us that his background was humble. But he was well educated by the standards of his century—a fact strongly suggesting that he belonged to the lower aristocracy. As a young man he apparently held minor official

---

[1] *Tzu* is a title of respect meaning "Master." It is affixed to the names of many eminent Chinese, e.g., Meng Tzu (Mencius), Mo Tzu, Hsün Tzu, etc.

posts in his native state; his ambition was to gain a position of political influence, but this eluded him. Much of his life evidently was devoted to study and teaching; history does not record how he supported himself. He probably began to evolve his ideas in informal debates with friends, and gradually the force of his intellect and personality attracted others to his company. When nearly sixty years old, he began a series of wide-ranging travels to the various courts of China, seeking a prince who would make use of his talents. Preceded by his reputation for learning, he was everywhere received with honor. But no one offered him a position in which he could influence events; and after some ten years of wandering he returned home to Lu.

Confucius' reputation, then, rests upon his ideas rather than his statesmanship. He is said to have been the first independent teacher in China—as opposed to the tutors employed by noble houses—though this is hard to prove. Certainly teaching in his day was not recognized as a profession. The education which Confucius provided included politics, history, and literature, but ignored the aristocrats' traditional training in archery and charioteering. This emphasis on mental rather than physical prowess was undoubtedly an innovation at that time. Confucius' early followers were derided as *ju* ("weaklings"). Within a century of his death, however, the word lost its pejorative significance; and it remains to this day the standard term for "Confucian" (or "literati") in the Chinese language.

Though Confucius described himself as a transmitter rather than a creator of ideas, there can be no doubt that he was both. Certainly he loved the traditional Chinese culture and revered the legendary sage-kings of antiquity, Yao, Shun, and Yü. He liked to speak in archaic formulas and proverbs, and often disparaged the present by comparison with the past. But reverence for antiquity—then as later— was a common trait in China, and Confucius spoke far less about it than most of his followers did. His primary concern was to improve contemporary society; and, without doubt, the conditions of his day left much to be desired. The titular emperor of China exercised a purely nominal authority over all but a small area around his capital; his functions were mainly ceremonial. His supposed vassals, the *de facto* rulers of the various Chinese states, were constantly at war both with one another and with the semi-barbarian states on their borders. The north China plain—the heartland of Chinese culture—had become a vast battleground. Confucius sought to discover the means of ending this chaos.

He said little about the methods he rejected, but it is clear what they were. Obviously, he did not believe that additional warfare could serve any good purpose. At the same time, he refused to look to supernatural beings for assistance. While not denying the existence of gods or spirits—who were supposed to inhabit trees, rocks, rivers, and many other natural phenomena—he preferred not to discuss them. Heaven (*T'ien*), on the other hand, he treated as a remote, impersonal principle which did not intervene in human affairs. The positive basis of Confucius' thought was *Tao*, or the "Way." As used by the Taoist school of philosophy, the term meant something analogous to the course of Nature; Confucius regarded it as the standard of ethics in human affairs.

Conduct in harmony with Tao meant faithfulness and loyalty, reasonableness and moderation, respect for the feelings and rights of others. To the modern mind such precepts are in no way remarkable, but in China of the sixth century B.C. they represented a decided shift of emphasis. In pre-Confucian China, as in other early civilizations, the chief regulator of human behavior was the necessity of pleasing divine beings. The gods and spirits had to be provided with suitable offerings and expressions of devotion according to strictly prescribed formulae. Confucius' insistence upon an internal regulator of conduct—as opposed to the external demands of ritual—was a major innovation in his time. Confucius spoke not of propitiating the spirits, but of cultivating human character. Righteousness, in the broadest possible sense, was his standard for both private and public morals. While respecting the ancient religious ritual, he interpreted it as an aspect of propriety or decorum—a conventional form of social intercourse which directs human behavior into harmonious channels and prevents extremes of emotion.

In later centuries the followers of Confucius were known for their great devotion to book-learning, and similar habits were attributed to the Master as well. But it is unlikely that Confucius himself consulted many books, if only because in his lifetime they were expensive, hard to obtain, and clumsy to use. Legend, nonetheless, has made of him a formidable scholar, and assigned him a role in the composition or editing of the Five Confucian Classics. He is supposed to have selected the 305 poems of the *Book of Songs* from an existing collection of over three thousand, and to have put together the documents which now comprise the *Book of History*. He is similarly reputed to have inspired, if not actually composed, the *Book of Rites*, and to be the author of the *Spring and Autumn Annals* and the appendices to the *Book of Changes*. None of these assertions stands up under critical scrutiny. Most of the material in the Classics post-dates Confucius by at least several centuries; and even those portions of the *History* and the *Changes* which preceded him were arranged into the present Classics long after his death. Of the Five Classics, only the *Book of Songs* existed in approximately its present form in the sixth century B.C.; and Confucius probably had nothing to do with selecting its contents.

The one work which is accurately attributed to Confucius is the *Analects* (*Lun Yü*, or "Selected Sayings"). But even this small book—a collection of pithy and disconnected statements on a variety of subjects—did not come from the Master's own hand. It is rather a fourth-century B.C. compilation of his sayings as remembered and passed on by his followers. At one time there were probably several sets of *Analects* in existence, each the product of a different Confucian school. As we have it today, the collection consists of twenty chapters (or "books") of varying dates, of which the third through the ninth contain sayings which probably originated with Confucius himself. Other books are clearly later insertions, and in some cases they contain ideas of which he would scarcely have approved.

The *Analects* remains, nonetheless, the best extant source for the actual opinions of Confucius. Within a few centuries of his death, various notions quite alien to what we know of him became attached to his name. As the Confucian school gained popularity and attracted the patronage of emperors under the Han dynasty (206 B.C.–A.D. 220), an increasing number of ideas that derived from the rival schools of Taoism, Legalism, and Yin-Yang came to be presented under the Confucian label. The Five Classics—supposedly authentic accounts of Confucius' own ideas—are in fact an eclectic mass of divergent and sometimes discordant elements. But in ceasing to be the system of a single and rather obscure individual, Confucianism became a vast intellectual edifice embodying all the major tendencies of Chinese thought. Accepted by ordinary people for its applicability to everyday human concerns and its insistence that government exists for the common welfare, revered by the educated classes for its stress on advancement through merit and its code of gentlemanly behavior, and supported by emperors for its inherent conservatism combined with a reputation for benevolence, Confucianism remained the dominant intellectual system of China until well into the twentieth century.

From the Analects of Confucius (Lun Yü)

CONFUCIUS AS A TEACHER: ON EDUCATION

II, 15   The Master said, "'He who learns but does not think,[1] is lost.' He who thinks but does not learn is in great danger."[2]

II, 17   The Master said, "Yu,[3] shall I teach you what knowledge is? When you know a thing, to recognize that you know it, and when you do not know a thing, to recognize that you do not know it. That is knowledge."

VII, 1   The Master said, "I have 'transmitted what was taught to me without making up anything of my own.' I have been faithful to and loved the Ancients. In these respects, I make bold to think, not even our old P'eng[4] can have excelled me."

VII, 2   The Master said, "I have listened in silence and noted what was said. I have never grown tired of learning nor wearied of teaching others what I have learnt. These at least are merits which I can confidently claim."

VII, 4   In his leisure hours the Master's manner was very free and easy, and his expression alert and cheerful.

VII, 8   The Master said, "Only one who bursts with eagerness do I instruct; only one who bubbles with excitement, do I enlighten. If I hold up one corner and a man cannot come back to me with the other three,[5] I do not continue the lesson."

All quotations from the *Analects* are taken from *The Analects of Confucius*, trans. by Arthur Waley, London: George Allen & Unwin, 1958. Reprinted by permission of George Allen & Unwin, Ltd.
  [1]The word translated here as "think" (*ssu*) denotes "pay attention" or "observe" rather than "to reason."
  [2]The first clause is probably a proverbial saying; the second is Confucius' reply. "Learn" refers to learning the Way of the ancients.
  [3]The familiar name of Tzu-lu, one of Confucius' favorite disciples.
  [4]A wise old man regarded as the guardian of tradition.
  [5]Metaphor from laying out of field-plots? (Tr.)

VII, 18   The "Duke of She"[6] asked Tzu-lu about Master K'ung (Confucius). Tzu-lu did not reply. The Master said, "Why did you not say 'This is the character of the man: so intent upon enlightening the eager that he forgets his hunger, and so happy in doing so, that he forgets the bitterness of his lot and does not realize that old age is at hand. That is what he is.'"[7]

VII, 37   The Master's manner was affable yet firm, commanding but not harsh, polite but easy.

XIII, 9   When the Master was going to Wei,[8] Jan Ch'iu[9] drove him. The Master said, "What a dense population!" Jan Ch'iu said, "When the people have multiplied, what next should be done for them?" The Master said, "Enrich them." Jan Ch'iu said, "When one has enriched them, what next should be done for them?" The Master said, "Instruct them."

XV, 35   The Master said, "When it comes to Goodness one need not avoid competing with one's teacher."

ON GOODNESS

[The word *jen* in Chinese is the generic term for "human being." Here rendered as "Goodness," it is most often translated into English as "humanity" or "human-heartedness." *Jen* is perhaps the most important single concept in the *Analects*, though Confucius nowhere defines it precisely. He speaks of it in a very broad sense as the sum of the qualities which the ideal human being ought to possess, i.e., humanness in the highest degree. Courtesy, loyalty, and unselfishness lie "in its direction," though they are not the whole of it. In Confucius' use of the term, *jen* is in fact a more than human quality. He conceded that the sage-kings of antiquity had possessed it, but refused to apply the word to any living person.]

I, 3   The Master said, "'Clever talk and a pretentious manner'[10] are seldom found in the Good."

I, 6   The Master said, "A young man's duty is to behave well to his parents at home and to his elders abroad, to be cautious in giving promises and punctual in keeping them, to have kindly feelings towards everyone, but seek the intimacy of the Good. If, when all that is done, he has any energy to spare, then let him study the polite arts."[11]

II, 24   The Master said, "Just as to sacrifice to ancestors other than one's own is presumption, so to see what is right and not do it is cowardice."

---

[6]The "Duke of She" was a noble of the state of Ch'u (lived 523–475 B.C.). By reputation a man of principle, he is supposed to have discussed matters of government with Confucius. His title, however, he had invented for himself.

[7]According to the traditional chronology Confucius was sixty-two at the time this was said. (Tr.)

[8]A small state just to the west of Lu.

[9]One of the three disciples mentioned as accompanying Confucius on his travels (the others were Tzu-lu and Yen Hui).

[10]A traditional phrase. (Tr.)

[11]I.e., learn to recite the *Songs*, practice archery, deportment, and the like. (Tr.)

IV, 2   The Master said, "Without Goodness a man
Cannot for long endure adversity,
Cannot for long enjoy prosperity.

The Good Man rests content with Goodness; he that is merely wise pursues Goodness in the belief that it pays to do so."

IV, 3, 4   Of the adage "Only a Good Man knows how to like people, knows how to dislike them," the Master said, "He whose heart is in the smallest degree set upon Goodness will dislike no one."

XV, 23   Tzu-kung[12] asked saying, "Is there any single saying that one can act upon all day and every day?" The Master said, "Perhaps the saying about consideration: 'Never do to others what you would not like them to do to you.'"[13]

QUESTIONS FOR DISCUSSION

1. In what ways did the Chinese people traditionally view Confucius as more than merely a philosopher?
2. Why were Confucius's early followers considered "weaklings"? How did their identity change within the first century after their master's death?
3. What was Confucius's approach to ending the wars and social chaos of his time?
4. What does a reading of even a few of the *Analects of Confucius* reveal about the focus of his philosophical teachings?

PLATO
The Allegory of the Cave

Though Socrates (ca. 470–399 B.C.E.) is considered one of the greatest thinkers and philosophers of the Western world, he wrote nothing. We know of him primarily through the writings of Plato (ca. 427–348 B.C.E.), his pupil. Socrates' method of teaching, as is evidenced in Plato's text below, was in dialogue form. He would ask questions and let the student develop wisdom and insight by formulating answers. Socrates sought to teach his students that the answers to life's essential questions are already in their own minds if they will only seek them. Thus, for him, self-knowledge through constant examination of one's own life was the basis for true understanding. The following selection is an allegory, meaning a story with symbolic meaning reaching far beyond the story itself. Life in "the cave" represents a world of ignorance and illusion that the mass of people accept as reality and truth because they do not bother to question it. A philosopher is one who climbs from the cave by questioning and discovers true light and life outside. He or she then faces the difficult task of returning to those trapped in the cave and attempting to convince them that a better world exists outside of the darkness in which they live.

---

[12]Tzu-kung was one of Confucius' most successful followers: he held important diplomatic positions between 495 and 468 B.C.

[13]The same sentiment in different words appears in *Analects* V, 11 and in XII, 2.

"Next, then," I said, "take the following parable of education and ignorance as a picture of the condition of our nature. Imagine mankind as dwelling in an underground cave with a long entrance open to the light across the whole width of the cave; in this they have been from childhood, with necks and legs fettered, so they have to stay where they are. They cannot move their heads round because of the fetters, and they can only look forward, but light comes to them from fire burning behind them higher up at a distance. Between the fire and the prisoners is a road above their level, and along it imagine a low wall has been built, as puppet showmen have screens in front of their people over which they work their puppets."

"I see," he said.

"See, then, bearers carrying along this wall all sorts of articles which they hold projecting above the wall, statues of men and other living things,[1] made of stone or wood and all kinds of stuff, some of the bearers speaking and some silent, as you might expect."

"What a remarkable image," he said, "and what remarkable prisoners!"

"Just like ourselves," I said. "For, first of all, tell me this: What do you think such people would have seen of themselves and each other except their shadows, which the fire cast on the opposite wall of the cave?"

"I don't see how they could see anything else," said he, "if they were compelled to keep their heads unmoving all their lives!"

"Very well, what of the things being carried along? Would not this be the same?"

"Of course it would."

"Suppose the prisoners were able to talk together, don't you think that when they named the shadows which they saw passing they would believe they were naming things?"[2]

"Necessarily."

"Then if their prison had an echo from the opposite wall, whenever one of the passing bearers uttered a sound, would they not suppose that the passing shadow must be making the sound? Don't you think so?"

"Indeed I do," he said.

"If so," said I, "such persons would certainly believe that there were no realities except those shadows of handmade things."[3]

"So it must be," said he.

"Now consider," said I, "what their release would be like, and their cure from these fetters and their folly; let us imagine whether it might naturally be something like this. One might be released, and compelled suddenly to stand up and turn his neck round, and to walk and look towards the firelight; all this would hurt him, and he would be too much dazzled to see distinctly those things whose shadows he had seen before. What do you think he would say, if someone told him that what he saw before was foolery, but now he saw more rightly, being a bit nearer reality and turned towards what was a little more real? What if he were shown each of the

---

[1]Including models of trees, etc.
[2]Which they had never seen. They would say "tree" when it was only a shadow of the model of a tree.
[3]Shadows of artificial things, not even the shadow of a growing tree: another stage from reality.

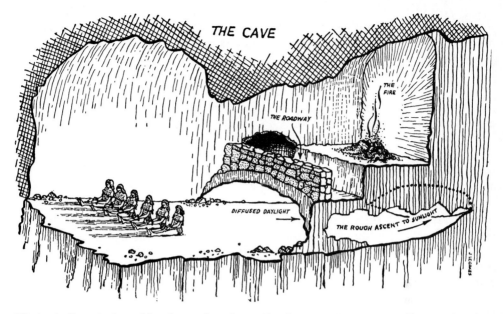

Figure 1. Socrates' parable of our education and subsequent ignorance is illustrated in this drawing of the Cave.

passing things, and compelled by questions to answer what each one was? Don't you think he would be puzzled, and believe what he saw before was more true than what was shown to him now?"

"Far more," he said.

"Then suppose he were compelled to look towards the real light, it would hurt his eyes, and he would escape by turning them away to the things which he was able to look at, and these he would believe to be clearer than what was being shown to him."

"Just so," said he.

"Suppose, now," said I, "that someone should drag him thence by force, up the rough ascent, the steep way up, and never stop until he could drag him out into the light of the sun, would he not be distressed and furious at being dragged; and when he came into the light, the brilliance would fill his eyes and he would not be able to see even one of the things now called real?"[4]

"That he would not," said he, "all of a sudden."

"He would have to get used to it, surely, I think, if he is to see the things above. First he would most easily look at shadows, after that images of mankind and the rest in water, lastly the things themselves. After this he would find it easier to survey by night the heavens themselves and all that is in them, gazing at the light of the stars and moon, rather than by day the sun and the sun's light."

"Of course."

---

[4]To the next stage of knowledge: the real thing, not the artificial puppet.

"Last of all, I suppose, the sun; he could look on the sun itself by itself in its own place, and see what it is like, not reflections of it in water or as it appears in some alien setting."

"Necessarily," said he.

"And only after all this he might reason about it, how this is he who provides seasons and years, and is set over all there is in the visible region, and he is in a manner the cause of all things which they saw."

"Yes, it is clear," said he, "that after all that, he would come to this last."

"Very good. Let him be reminded of his first habitation, and what was wisdom in that place, and of his fellow-prisoners there; don't you think he would bless himself for the change, and pity them?"

"Yes, indeed."

"And if there were honours and praises among them and prizes for the one who saw the passing things most sharply and remembered best which of them used to come before and which after and which together, and from these was best able to prophesy accordingly what was going to come—do you believe he would set his desire on that, and envy those who were honoured men or potentates among them? Would he not feel as Homer says,[5] and heartily desire rather to be serf of some landless man on earth and to endure anything in the world, rather than to opine as they did and to live in that way?"

"Yes indeed," said he, "he would rather accept anything than live like that."

"Then again," I said, "just consider; if such a one should go down again and sit on his old seat, would he not get his eyes full of darkness coming in suddenly out of the sun?"

"Very much so," said he.

"And if he should have to compete with those who had been always prisoners, by laying down the law about those shadows while he was blinking before his eyes were settled down—and it would take a good long time to get used to things— wouldn't they all laugh at him and say he had spoiled his eyesight by going up there, and it was not worth-while so much as to try to go up? And would they not kill anyone who tried to release them and take them up, if they could somehow lay hands on him and kill him?"[6]

"That they would!" said he.

"Then we must apply this image, my dear Glaucon," said I, "to all we have been saying. The world of our sight is like the habitation in prison, the firelight there to the sunlight here, the ascent and the view of the upper world is the rising of the soul into the world of mind; put it so and you will not be far from my own surmise, since that is what you want to hear; but God knows if it is really true. At least, what appears to me is, that in the world of the known, last of all,[7] is the idea of the good, and with what toil to be seen! And seen, this must be inferred to be the cause of all right and beautiful things for all, which gives birth to light and the king of light in the

---

[5]*Odyssey* xi. 489.
[6]Plato probably alludes to the death of Socrates. See *Apology*, p. 444.
[7]The end of our search.

world of sight, and, in the world of mind, herself the queen produces truth and reason; and she must be seen by one who is to act with reason publicly or privately."

"I believe as you do," he said, "in so far as I am able."

"Then believe also, as I do," said I, "and do not be surprised, that those who come thither are not willing to have part in the affairs of men, but their souls ever strive to remain above; for that surely may be expected if our parable fits the case."

"Quite so," he said.

"Well then," said I, "do you think it surprising if one leaving divine contemplations and passing to the evils of men is awkward and appears to be a great fool, while he is still blinking—not yet accustomed to the darkness around him, but compelled to struggle in law courts or elsewhere about shadows of justice, or the images which make the shadows, and to quarrel about notions of justice in those who have never seen justice itself?"

"Not surprising at all," said he.

"But any man of sense," I said, "would remember that the eyes are doubly confused from two different causes, both in passing from light to darkness and from darkness to light; and believing that the same things happen with regard to the soul also, whenever he sees a soul confused and unable to discern anything he would not just laugh carelessly; he would examine whether it had come out of a more brilliant life, and if it were darkened by the strangeness; or whether it had come out of greater ignorance into a more brilliant light, and if it were dazzled with the brighter illumination. Then only would he congratulate the one soul upon its happy experience and way of life, and pity the other; but if he must laugh, his laugh would be a less downright laugh than his laughter at the soul which came out of the light above."

"That is fairly put," said he.

"Then if this is true," I said, "our belief about these matters must be this, that the nature of education is not really such as some of its professors say it is; as you know, they say that there is not understanding in the soul, but they put it in, as if they were putting sight into blind eyes."

"They do say so," said he.

"But our reasoning indicates," I said, "that this power is already in the soul of each, and is the instrument by which each learns; thus if the eye could not see without being turned with the whole body from the dark towards the light, so this instrument must be turned round with the whole soul away from the world of becoming until it is able to endure the sight of being and the most brilliant light of being: and this we say is the good, don't we?"

"Yes."

"Then this instrument," said I, "must have its own art, for the circumturning or conversion, to show how the turn can be most easily and successfully made; not an art of putting sight into an eye, which we say has it already, but since the instrument has not been turned aright and does not look where it ought to look—that's what must be managed."

"So it seems," he said.

"Now most of the virtues which are said to belong to the soul are really something near to those of the body; for in fact they are not already there, but they are put later into it by habits and practices; but the virtue of understanding everything really belongs to something certainly more divine, as it seems, for it never loses its power, but becomes useful and helpful or, again, useless and harmful, by the direction in which it is turned. Have you not noticed men who are called worthless but clever, and how keen and sharp is the sight of their petty soul, and how it sees through the things towards which it is turned? Its sight is clear enough, but it is compelled to be the servant of vice, so that the clearer it sees the more evil it does."

"Certainly," said he.

"Yet if this part of such a nature," said I, "had been hammered at from childhood, and all those leaden weights of the world of becoming knocked off—the weights, I mean, which grow into the soul from gorging and gluttony and such pleasures, and twist the soul's eye downwards—if, I say, it had shaken these off and been turned round towards what is real and true, that same instrument of those same men would have seen those higher things most clearly, just as now it sees those towards which it is turned."

"Quite likely," said he.

"Very well," said I, "isn't it equally likely, indeed, necessary, after what has been said, that men uneducated and without experience of truth could never properly supervise a city, nor can those who are allowed to spend all their lives in education right to the end? The first have no single object in life, which they must always aim at in doing everything they do, public or private; the second will never do anything if they can help it, believing that they have already found mansions abroad in the Islands of the Blest."[8]

"True," said he.

"Then it is the task of us founders," I said, "to compel the best natures to attain that learning which we said was the greatest, both to see the good, and to ascend that ascent; and when they have ascended and properly seen, we must never allow them what is allowed now."

"What is that, pray?" he asked.

"To stay there," I said, "and not be willing to descend again to those prisoners, and to share their troubles and their honours, whether they are worth having or not."

"What!" said he, "are we to wrong them and make them live badly, when they might live better?"

"You have forgotten again, my friend," said I, "that the law is not concerned how any one class in a city is to prosper above the rest; it tries to contrive prosperity in the city as a whole, fitting the citizens into a pattern by persuasion and compulsion, making them give of their help to one another wherever each class is able to help the community. The law itself creates men like this in the city, not in order to allow each one to turn by any way he likes, but in order to use them itself to the full for binding the city together."

"True," said he, "I did forget."

"Notice then, Glaucon," I said, "we shall not wrong the philosophers who grow up among us, but we shall treat them fairly when we compel them to add to

[8]Cf. *Banquet*, p. 77, n. 3.

their duties the care and guardianship of the other people. We shall tell them that those who grow up philosophers in other cities have reason in taking no part in public labours there; for they grow up there of themselves, though none of the city governments wants them; a wild growth has its rights, it owes nurture to no one, and need not trouble to pay anyone for its food. But you we have engendered, like king bees[9] in hives, as leaders and kings over yourselves and the rest of the city; you have been better and more perfectly educated than the others, and are better able to share in both ways of life. Down you must go then, in turn, to the habitation of the others, and accustom yourselves to their darkness; for when you have grown accustomed you will see a thousand times better than those who live there, and you will know what the images are and what they are images of, because you have seen the realities behind just and beautiful and good things. And so our city will be managed wide awake for us and for you, not in a dream, as most are now, by people fighting together for shadows, and quarrelling to be rulers, as if that were a great good. But the truth is more or less that the city where those who are to rule are least anxious to be rulers is of necessity best managed and has least faction in it; while the city which gets rulers who want it most is worst managed."

"Certainly," said he.

"Then will our fosterlings disobey us when they hear this? Will they refuse to help, each group in its turn, in the labours of the city, and want to spend most of their time dwelling in the pure air?"

"Impossible," said he, "for we shall only be laying just commands on just men. No, but undoubtedly each man of them will go to the ruler's place as to a grim necessity, exactly the opposite of those who now rule in cities."

"For the truth is, my friend," I said, "that only if you can find for your future rulers a way of life better than ruling, is it possible for you to have a well-managed city; since in that city alone those will rule who are truly rich, not rich in gold, but in that which is necessary for a happy man, the riches of a good and wise life: but if beggared and hungry, for want of goods of their own, they hasten to public affairs, thinking that they must snatch goods for themselves from there, it is not possible. Then rule becomes a thing to be fought for; and a war of such a kind, being between citizens and within them, destroys both them and the rest of the city also."

"Most true," said he.

"Well, then," said I, "have you any other life despising political office except the life of true philosophy?"

"No, by heaven," said he.

"But again," said I, "they must not go awooing office like so many lovers! If they do, their rival lovers will fight them."

"Of course they will!"

"Then what persons will you compel to accept guardianship of the city other than those who are wisest in the things which enable a city to be best managed, who also have honours of another kind and a life better than the political life?"

"No others," he answered.

---

[9]Both the Greeks and Romans spoke always of "king," not "queen," of a hive.

"Would you like us, then, to consider next how such men are to be produced in a city, and how they shall be brought up into the light, as you know some are said to go up from Hades to heaven?"

"Of course I should," said he. "Remember that this, as it seems, is no spinning of a shell,[10] it's more than a game; the turning of a soul round from a day which is like night to a true day—this is the ascent into real being, which we shall say is true philosophy."

"Undoubtedly."

"We must consider, then, which of the studies has a power like that."

"Of course."

"Then, my dear Glaucon, what study could draw the soul from the world of becoming to the world of being? But stay, I have just thought of something while speaking—surely we said that these men must of necessity be athletes of war in their youth."

"We did say so."

"Then the study we seek must have something else in addition."

"What?"

"Not to be useless for men of war."

"Oh yes, it must," he said, "if possible."

"Gymnastic and music[11] we used before to educate them."

"That is true," said he.

"Gymnastic, I take it, is devoted to what becomes and perishes, for it presides over bodily growth and decay."

"So it appears."

"Then this, I suppose, could not be the study we seek."

"No indeed."

"Is it music, then, as far as we described that?"

"But if you remember," said he, "music was the counter-balance of gymnastic. Music educated the guardians by habits, and taught them no science, but a fine concord by song and a fine rhythm by tune, and the words they used had in them qualities akin to these, whether the words were fabulous tales or true. But a study! There was nothing in it which led to any such good as you now seek."

"Thanks for reminding me," said I. "What you say is quite accurate; it had nothing of that sort in it. But, my dear man, Glaucon, what study could there be of that sort? For all the arts and crafts were vulgar, at least we thought so."

"Certainly we did, but what study is left apart from gymnastic and music and the arts and crafts?"

"Look here," I said; "if we can't find anything more outside these, let us take one that extends to them all."

"Which?" he asked.

"This, which they have in common, which is used in addition by all arts and all sciences and ways of thinking, which is one of the first things every man must learn of necessity."

---

[10] A game. Boys in two groups would spin a shell, black on one side and white on the other, and according as it fell, one party would run and the other chase. The one who tossed called out, "Night or Day!"

[11] In their wide meanings, of course.

"What's that?" he asked again.

"Just this trifle," I said—"to distinguish between one and two and three: I mean, in short, number and calculation. Is it not always true that every art and science is forced to partake of these?"

"Most certainly," he said.

"Even the art of war?"

"So it must," said he.

"At least," I said, "Palamedes[12] in the plays is always making out Agamemnon to be a perfectly ridiculous general. Haven't you noticed that Palamedes claims to have invented number, and with this arranged the ranks in the encampment before Troy, and counted the ships and everything else, as if they had not been counted before and as if before this Agamemnon did not know how many feet he had, as it seems if he really could not count? Then what sort of general do you think he was?"

"Odd enough," said he, "if that was true!"

"Then shall we not put down this," I said, "as a study necessary for a soldier, to be able to calculate and count?"

"Nothing more so," said he, "if he is to understand anything at all about his own ranks, or, rather, if he is to be even anything of a man."

"I wonder," said I, "if you notice what I do about this study."

"And what may that be?"

"It is really one of those we are looking for, those which lead naturally to thinking; but no one uses it rightly, although it draws wholly towards real being."

"What do you mean?" he asked.

"I will try to explain," said I, "what I, at least, believe. Whatever points I distinguish in my own mind as leading in favour of or against what we are speaking of, pray look at them with me and agree or disagree; then we shall see more clearly if this study is what I divine it to be."

"Do indicate them," said he.

"That is what I am doing," I said. "If you observe, some things which the senses perceive do not invite the intelligence to examine them, because they seem to be judged satisfactorily by the sense; but some altogether urge it to examine them because the sense appears to produce no sound result."

QUESTIONS FOR DISCUSSION

1. How does Plato's use of dialogue contribute to his purpose of instructing his audience?
2. How does Socrates characterize the world of physical sight in the text? To what does he compare "the world of the mind" (par. 34)? Which of the two would this suggest is more real, true, and good?

---

[12] A chief in the Grecian army before Troy, and a proverbial master of inventions. All three tragedians brought him into their plays, and he was credited with the invention of number, among other things. Plato is bored with Palamedes.

3. Would Socrates agree that the process of education means putting education into souls like "putting sight into blind eyes" (par. 42)?
4. Who are the philosophers Socrates speaks of? Why does he feel they would make good rulers?
5. Define what the text means by "true philosophy" (par. 66).

CHARLES I. GLICKSBERG
The Literature of Nihilism

"Nihilism" comes from the Latin word "nihil," meaning "nothing." Nihilists believe in nothing, claiming that concepts of God and morality are all of human invention. In its most intense form among nineteenth century European thinkers and revolutionaries, it developed a four-part code: (1) annihilate the idea of God, or there can be no freedom; (2) annihilate the idea of right, which is only might; (3) annihilate civilization, property, marriage, morality, and justice; and (4) let your own happiness be your only law. Because nihilists reject ideas of God and right and wrong, their literature constantly reflects a troubled search for the purpose in living. As long as belief in a divine being and in divine truth have existed, the possibility of doubting also has existed. Nihilism carries doubt to its logical extreme. In many ways, the punk movement of the late 1980s is one example of nihilistic tendencies expressed on a societal level.

The decisive point is not only that nihilism asserts the vacuum, the *nihil*, the nothing, but that the assertor himself is oppressed and afflicted by his own nothingness.[1]

Almost all the questions of most interest to speculative minds are such as science cannot answer, and the confident answers of theologians no longer seem so convincing as they did in former centuries. Is the world divided into mind and matter, and, if so, what is mind and what is matter? Is mind subject to matter, or is it possessed of independent powers? Has the universe any unity or purpose? Is it evolving towards some goal? Are there really laws of nature, or do we believe in them only because of our innate love of order? Is man what he seems to the astronomer, a tiny lump of impure carbon and water impotently crawling on a small and unimportant planet? Or is he what he appears to Hamlet? Is he perhaps both at once? Is there a way of living that is noble and another that is base, or are all ways of living merely futile?[2]

The supreme paradox of all thought is the attempt to discover something that thought cannot think.[3]

[1]Helmut Thielicke, *Nihilism*, trans. John W. Doberstein (New York: Harper & Brothers, 1961), p. 54.
[2]Bertrand Russell, *A History of Western Philosophy* (New York: Simon and Schuster, 1945), p. xiii.
[3]Søren Kierkegaard, *Philosophical Fragments*, trans. David Swenson (Princeton, N.J.: Princeton University Press, 1962), p. 46.

No one with any insight will still deny today that nihilism is in the most varied and most hidden forms "the normal state" of man.[4]

For, why is the triumph of Nihilism *inevitable* now? Because the very values current amongst us to-day will arrive at their logical conclusion in Nihilism, because Nihilism is the only possible outcome of our greatest values and ideals, because we must first experience Nihilism before we can realise what the actual worth of these "values" was. . . . Sooner or later we shall be in need of *new values*.[5]

We feel that even when *all possible* scientific questions have been answered, the problems of life remain completely untouched. Of course there are then no questions left, and this itself is the answer.[6]

1. THE PARADOX OF NIHILISM

The aim of this book is to analyze some of the ways in which nihilism makes itself felt, obtrusively or obliquely, in the literature of the modern age. This presents a formidably complex problem of interpretation, for nihilism does not—in literature at least—exist in a pure state. Differently put, the nihilist, both as author and persona, is plagued by internal contradictions; he is rarely, if ever, altogether consistent in his beliefs and behavior. In "Problems of the Theatre," Dürrenmatt takes up the often-heard charge that literature today is nihilistic in content. This is the answer he gives:

> Today, of course, there exists a nihilistic art, but not every art that seems nihilistic is so. True nihilistic art does not appear to be nihilistic at all; usually it is considered to be especially humane and supremely worthy of being read by our more mature young people. A man must be a pretty bungling sort of nihilist to be recognized as such by the world at large. People call nihilistic what is merely uncomfortable.[7]

Not that nihilistic writers invariably disguise or conceal their nihilistic outlook. Indeed, some boldly identify themselves as such, yet their writing still bears the marks of conflict and contradiction. For to undertake a work of art, no matter how much it may be infected with the blight of radical pessimism, is in effect to affirm a value, to live for the sake of the work that is being produced. Even the psychopathological genius of a Céline demands that the truth, no matter how horrible it turns out to be, be told: the truth about the human animal and his homicidal manias, the unflinching truth about his journey to the end of the night. Thiher calls Céline a nihilist by default; Céline's rejection of the destructive powers in life "proclaims a thirst for affirmation and perhaps for transcendence. . . ."[8]

---

[4]Martin Heidegger, *The Question of Being*, trans. William Kluback and Jean T. Wilde (New York: Twayne Publishers, 1958), p. 47.
[5]Friedrich Nietzsche, *The Complete Works of Friedrich Nietzsche*, ed. Oscar Levy. Vol. 14. *The Will to Power*, trans. Anthony M. Ludovici (Edinburgh and London: T. N. Foulis, 1910), 1:2.
[6]Quoted in George Pitcher, *The Philosophy of Wittgenstein* (Englewood Cliffs, N.J.: Prentice-Hall, 1964), p. 161.
[7]Friedrich Dürrenmatt, *Four Plays: 1957–62* (London: Jonathan Cape, 1964), p. 39.
[8]Allen Thiher, *Céline: The Novel as Delirium* (New Brunswick, N.J.: Rutgers University Press, 1972), p. 43.

What, then, is generally meant by nihilism? Nihilism is difficult to define because it takes so many different forms, but it is a real enough experience. It is a spiritual crisis through which all thinking men pass at some time in their lives; and very few come through this ordeal unscathed. There is the passive nihilism of the Buddhist variety: life is an empty dream, action is futile, and striving for happiness, fulfillment, or perfection betrays the fact that one is still the slave of illusion.[9] The second type, the nihilism of negativity, is derived from the special brand of nihilism that sprang up in Europe, especially in Russia, in the nineteenth century; it was a nihilism that, despite its professed rejection of all belief, rested its faith in the scientific method.

Then there is a species of nihilism that is active, Dionysian: Nietzsche speaks of ecstatic nihilism. Nietzsche's nihilism is metaphysical rather than ideological. His attitude toward science is therefore not worshipful; science is no more than a body of fictions, a set of conventions; it did not presuppose that it was based on truth. Nietzsche's nihilism was all-inclusive. He perceived no meaning in the world, no ultimate purpose, no sustaining principle of order. Man is saddled with the task of imposing order on a senseless universe.[10] There is also the type of nihilism that is carried to the logical extreme of suicide. Finally, there is the nihilism that promotes and justifies an unconscionable struggle for power. Life on earth is completely amoral in character; categorical imperatives are human constructs; no law exists to prevent the rule of the strong—a doctrine that motivated the Nazi reign of terror.[11]

Webster's New International Dictionary defines nihilism as "a viewpoint that all traditional values and beliefs are unfounded and that all existence is consequently senseless and useless: a denial of intrinsic meaning and value in life." Another definition that this dictionary gives is that nihilism is "a doctrine that denies or is taken as denying any objective or real ground of truth. In a more specific context

[9]"Nihilism' connotes negativity and emptiness; in fact, it denotes two bodies of thought that, although distinct from Nietzsche's, nevertheless bear it some partial resemblance. The Nihilism of Emptiness is essentially that of Buddhist or Hindu teaching, both of which hold that the world we live in and seem to know has no ultimate reality, and that our attachment to it is an attachment to an illusion. Reality itself has neither name nor form, and what has name and form is but a painful dreaming from which all reasonable men would wish to escape if they knew the way and knew that their attachment was nothingness. Life is without sense or point, there is a ceaseless alternation of birth and death and birth again, the constantly turning wheel of existence going nowhere eternally: if we wish salvation, it is salvation from life that we must seek." (Arthur C. Donato, *Nietzsche as Philosopher* [New York: The Macmillan Company, 1965], p. 28.) This is the Buddhist outlook that both Schopenhauer and Nietzsche incorporated in their work, but there is a pronounced difference in their attitude toward this type of unmitigated pessimism. Nietzsche fought against its seductive, enervating appeal, searching desperately for an ideal that would affirm and justify life.

[10]By nihilism Nietzsche "had in mind a thoroughly disillusioned conception of a world which is as hostile to human aspiration as he could imagine it to be. It is hostile, not because it, or anything other than us, has goals of its own, but because it is utterly indifferent to what we either believe or hope. The recognition of this negative fact should not lead us to 'a negation, a no, a will to nothingness.' Rather, he felt, it is an intoxicating fact to know that the world is devoid of form and meaning. . . . To be able to accept and affirm such a view he thought required considerable courage, for it meant that we must abandon hopes and expectations which had comforted man, through religions and philosophies, from the beginning." *Ibid.*, p. 33.

[11]In *Nihilism*, Stanley Rosen directs his attack on the nihilists as the enemies of reason. "Not the least element in the origin of contemporary nihilism is that, when the pride and confidence in the project to master nature evaporated, the light of God was extinguished, and man saw himself altogether in the shadow of the beast." (Stanley Rosen, *Nihilism*. [New Haven and London: Yale University Press, 1969], p. 66.) Nihilism, he goes on to say, "is fundamentally an attempt to overcome or to repudiate the past on behalf of an unknown and unknowable yet hoped-for future." (*Ibid.*, p. 140.) Such a Promethean ambition entails a disregard, if not downright contempt, for the problematical present. "The nihilist perseveres in the face of despair not because he has a reason for so doing, but because his ostensible comprehension of the worthlessness of all reasons is understood by him as freedom." (*Ibid.*, p. 142.) The nihilist "despairs because he is fully enlightened . . . or free from all illusions. His despair is the sign of his enlightenment or freedom, the seal of his integrity." (*Ibid.*)

this includes the philosophy of moral nihilism, which denies the objective ground of morality."[12]

Literary nihilism manifests itself chiefly in the recurrent effort to break out of this spiritual impasse. Nihilism is universally recognized as a lethal evil that must be resisted and finally overcome if mankind is to survive. It is virtually impossible, the nihilist finds, to endure the pains and perils of life while inwardly convinced that life serves no purpose at all and is therefore not worth living. The nihilist comes to believe that life is a senseless nightmare, a thing of sound and fury signifying nothing, and then struggles desperately to prove that his reasoning or intuition is all wrong. Thus does Professor Teufelsdröckh cry out in anguish when he is in the infernal grip of the Everlasting No: "To me the Universe was void of Life, of Purpose, of Volition, even of Hostility: it was one huge, dead, immeasurable Steam-Engine, rolling on, in its dead indifference, to grind me limb from limb. O, the vast, gloomy, solitary Golgotha, and Mill of Death! Why was the Living banished thither companionless, conscious?"[13] Like Carlyle's hero, the modern nihilist refuses to believe that he is fatherless, outcast, and that the universe belongs to the Devil. On the other hand, he will not allow himself to be deceived by fantasies, religious or metaphysical, of wish-fulfillment. He strives to keep faith with the sorry logic of his position: if all is illusion, then perhaps his anguished crisis of consciousness is also compounded of illusion.

But if the truth that man pursues so eagerly is only a solipsist illusion, then he finds himself trapped in a vicious circle of contradictions. Why speak? Why recommend one illusion as vastly superior to another? If truth is a myth, then all distinctions are abolished, and one might as well follow the erratic guidance of instinct and feeling instead of the promptings of reason. When the writer as nihilist exposes the ridiculous limitations of thought and comes to believe that truth is a will-o'-the-wisp that the mind vainly chases in a phantasmagoria of locked-in subjectivity, how can he mobilize the energy to go ahead with his creative effort? How nerve himself for the enterprise of art? If all things begin and end in naught, then why strive, why live, why perpetuate the race?

This is the bind of the absurd from which the nihilist is unable to extricate himself. We shall examine the different strategies a number of modern writers employ in order to defeat the nihilism that afflicts them. Unamuno counteracts the paralyzing constriction of nada by affirming a supernatural faith that assures him of personal immortality. The Russian writer Leonid Andreyev violently denounces the God in whom he does not believe for imposing a cruel and incomprehensible fate on his human victims. In *Breaking-Point*, Artzybashef ironically hails death as liberator and seems to recommend the grace of salvation that suicide affords. Kafka, the most complex and prophetic of the modern nihilists, closely questions the sphinx of the infinite, but can provide no answer to its riddle. In France, Sartre describes the

---

[12]"Nietzsche's Nihilism—his idea that there is no order or structure objectively present in the world and antecedent to the form we ourselves give it—has, he believed, the consequence that the men who accept it will have no temptation to disesteem human life by contrasting it with something eternal, inalterable, or intrinsically good. As a metaphysician, he sought to provide a picture of the world as it actually is . . . so that men might have no illusions either about it or about themselves, and, unimpeded by mistaken views, might set about their proper task, which was to make of humankind something more than it had been." Donato, *Nietzsche as Philosopher*, p. 195.

[13]Thomas Carlyle, *Sartor Resartus* (London: J. M. Dent & Sons, 1948), pp. 125–26.

demoralizing experience of Nausea and then attempts to negate the void of Being by affiliating himself with the revolutionary movement. Camus rises above the myth of the absurd by espousing the humanistic ethic of rebellion. Kazantzakis, who frankly proclaims that he is a nihilist, accepts the challenge posed by a world without divine or ultimate meaning but remains undaunted and commits himself the more resolutely to the creative quest.

Though the writers discussed in this book have produced work that in part or as a whole is steeped in the destructive element of nihilism, they represent no organized body of thought. Profoundly influenced as they have been by the disasters of history in their age, they derive from no common ideological ancestry. The horror born of the explosion of two world wars has intensified their despair and accounts in large measure for their nihilistic outlook. As Lewis Mumford remarks, the cult of nihilism tends swiftly to grow into a cult of violence and terror on the political scene, "expressing a total contempt for life. . . . In an active or latent state, nihilism is at work throughout our civilization."[14] Important, however, as is the social and historical background in charting the course of literary development, it does not appear that nihilism is the special creation of the twentieth century, this age of crisis and catastrophe. The historical crisis of our time colors and accentuates the dominant motif of doom that crops up, but the nihilist strain has made itself felt in other cultures during the past, though in a less virulent manner. Before the advent of the horrors of the holocaust, there were poets, dramatists, and philosophers, who faced the nihilist dilemma. From Sophocles and Lucretius to Schopenhauer, Nietzsche, Dostoevski, Kierkegaard, and Tolstoy, there is scarcely an important creative figure who has not at some time been stricken with the fever of nihilism. It is always there to be faced—and overcome.[15]

I am assuming that the spiritual conflict that culminates in nihilism, far from being the mark of an unhinged mind or craven temperament or the characteristic but short-lived product of a time of trouble, is an archetypal experience. The writer either passes through the dark night of the soul and beholds finally the glimmer of the light beyond, however ambiguously it shines forth, or he never emerges from the darkness that hems him in. Though the nihilist has presumably abandoned the quest for ultimate meaning, he never actually ceases to question or cry out or seek a solution to the mystery of being. If he did so, he would have to give up entirely his career as a writer. The dialectic of nihilism is charged with unresolvable elements of complexity. It is not the formal expression of a philosophical position nor is it a logically elaborated system of thought. If it embodies a world vision that is in the end forced to say No to life, it utters this categorical negation with different accents of conviction. The writer as nihilist may, in his work as in his life, be at odds with himself. He believes and disbelieves at the same time. Like Camus, he loves life even

---

[14]Lewis Mumford, *The Conduct of Life* (New York: Harcourt, Brace and Company, 1951), p. 150.

[15]When one considers the hazards of the human condition, it is indeed surprising that the history of world literature affords so few instances of writers overwhelmingly committed to some form of nihilism. Is this failure to find literary champions of the first rank *prima facie* evidence that the nihilistic cause is too restrictive in scope, too starkly negative in its implications, to serve as the vehicle of a universal vision of life, a vision that must include the glory and the triumph as well as anguish of being?

in those moments of utter despair when he condemns it as absurd. He may, like Bertolt Brecht, be a nihilist in his youth and then become a man with a cause to support, the founder of the epic theater. He may suspend judgment completely as he conducts an interminable monologue, a debate in which, like Kafka, he espouses both sides of the case without ever arriving at any positive conclusion.

The creative nihilist is thus engaged in a struggle that is never ended. It is hard to envisage a *militant* nihilist. What is there for him, be it a Nietzsche or a Kazantzakis, to be militant about? So long as he writes, he affirms the value of the project to which he is committed, even though he continues to hurl imprecations at a world that fails to conform to the heart's desire. On whatever ground he chooses to conduct his quarrel with God or the universe, he is, as a creative being, celebrating the numinous paradox that is life. He persists in seeking the light that dwells in the heart of darkness, though he cannot silence the suspicion that whatever gods or goals he discovers along the way may be the projections of his own mind. He cannot silence the clamorous voice of doubt. His profession of "faith," whatever form it finally assumes, is instinct with a profound skepticism, but at least this provisional and qualified faith restores him temporarily to life. Only a few nihilists are permanently crucified on the cross of the negative.

The rage of the nihilist against the ineradicable absurdity of existence is an inverted expression of his love of life. Since his life goes on—he rejects, as does Camus, the expedient of suicide—he stops at some point in his career to ask himself: "How am I to live? What is to be done?" In dealing with the torments and tribulations as well as existential contradictions that characterize the nihilistic protagonist, Dostoevski is, like Nietzsche, a prophetic figure. He fights against that which tempts him most: the snares of the Devil, "the destructive element," the blasphemous denial of God's existence. The nihilistic heroes he presents, metaphysical rebels against God, are complex incarnations of his own persona. Dostoevski is Raskolnikov, Smerdyakov, Ivan Karamazov, Stavrogin, Kirillov just as much as he is Alyosha, Zossima, Shatov, Myshkin, and Sonya. If Dostoevski paints with merciless insight the extremes of evil that infect the heart of man, who is capable of the worst enormities, he also portrays the counterpointed craving of the sons of Satan for more and more of life, life everlasting, until the end of eternity. The more violently they rebel against the human condition, the greater the energy with which they love life. Kirillov, the monomaniac who is bent on disproving the existence of God, is a religious mystic.[16]

It is apparent that the nihilist and the humanist share a common body of assumptions. Both believe that man is alone, both reject faith in the supernatural. But whereas the secular humanist then proceeds to declare that man is the measure, the sole source and touchstone of value, the nihilist repudiates all such man-made values as illusions, mere as-if fictions designed to hide from human eyes the

---

[16]One critic maintains that it is impossible to answer the question whether Dostoevski was a believer. "He loved his atheists and seemed to cherish their arguments. . . . Certainly Dostoevsky was no firm believer of the naïve and unshaken kind. He had gone through 'a furnace of doubt.' But his oscillations between believing and doubting suggest a wrestling with faith alien to an avowed atheist." William Hubben, *Dostoevsky, Kierkegaard, Nietzsche, and Kafka* (New York: Collier Books, 1962), p. 86.

emptiness and futility of existence. The nihilist (he may use some other name: Jeffers, for example, called himself aptly an Inhumanist[17]) will not conceal from himself the desolating "truth" of human dereliction. He will proclaim far and wide his discovery that the idea of progress, like the romantic faith in the perfectibility of man, is a spurious myth. He harbors no revolutionary hopes; he does not look forward to the future for the redemption of mankind.

It is at this point of no return that the nihilist reverses his field, as it were, and takes up a position that, in defiance of the canons of logic, brings him to a closer understanding of the intense spiritual battle the religious Existentialist must wage before he can affirm his faith in God. Faced with the ultimate issue of death—his death—as annihilation, the nihilist wants to know how best to live the time of his life. But what is "good," what is "best"? Intellectually he is convinced that he has purged his mind of all religious traces, though his longing for God, as was true in the case of Nietzsche and Kazantzakis, never leaves him. But longing that never goes beyond that stage is not the same thing as the actuality of faith. Like Valéry, the nihilist distrusts the coinages of the mind, the stratagems of the duplicitous self, the abstractions that it creates and then hypostatizes as sacred realities. He applies the same stringent skepticism to his own negative conclusions. He turns to literature as a means of contemplating the universe through a variety of disparate perspectives, realizing as he does so that literature is in itself but a symbolic confrontation of reality that can illuminate but cannot solve his existential conflict.

The literary nihilist nevertheless persists in his search for ultimate meaning, as if to make sure he has made no error in his calculations. Invoking the law of polarity, he shadows forth that which other writers, more modest in their creative aim or less driven by demonic pride to pierce the secret of the universe, deliberately ignore or omit. If Heaven is balanced by Hell and God by the Devil, so the plenitude of being is opposed by the ever-present threat of nothingness. Eros is perpetually in conflict with Thanatos, life is gravitating toward the inorganic state of being. The nihilist suffers excruciatingly from his obsession with the dialectic of nothingness. If he actually believes that nothingness is the ultimate end of existence, then he cannot, like the humanist, be sustained by the constructive role he plays in the historic process or rest his hopes on some radiant consummation in the future order of society.

This encounter with nothingness forms the crux of nihilist literature, just as the experience of the dark night of the soul lies at the heart of Christian mysticism. Most people are sleepwalkers (to use Hermann Broch's expressive term) who take it for granted that life has a meaning beyond the mere living of it. It is this instinctive faith that the nihilist begins by questioning and then finally decides to reject. As soon as he does so, he finds himself trapped in a spiritual cul-de-sac. He is unable either to affirm or to deny. He can neither act nor refrain from acting. How shall he act on his negative beliefs?

---

[17]See "The Ironic Vision of Robinson Jeffers," in Charles I. Glicksberg, *Modern Literary Perspectivism* (Dallas, Tex.: Southern Methodist University Press, 1970), p. 100. See also Mercedes Cunningham Monjian, *Robinson Jeffers: A Study in Inhumanism* (Pittsburgh: University of Pittsburgh Press, 1958).

This life-negating dementia[18] constitutes a theme that has been pondered by poets, philosophers, mystics, and saints for over two thousand years. It is the archetypical concern of the tragic vision, the central, though not sole, preoccupation of religion. When human consciousness first arose, man must have formulated the question of questions: Who am I in relation to the cosmos? What am I doing here on earth? What purpose am I supposed to serve? What are the ancient myths but symbolic representations of the unceasing battle man must wage against the demonic powers that each winter threaten the continuity of life.

Nietzsche announced that God was dead and wrestled with the problem of what was to take the place of God. He sought to grasp the truth bearing on the human condition, without regard for the harmful consequences it might have for mankind. The relentless search for the truth at all costs is sustained by a moral principle, but it led Nietzsche to the ultimate of disillusionment. If truth is a myth, then the pursuit of truth must cease, for it leads nowhere. Nothing is to be believed, not even the empirically warranted conclusions of science. The upshot in Nietzsche's case is a nihilism that cannot be borne because it cannot be lived. As Karl Jaspers points out: "Even if his thinking appears as a self-destructive process in which no truth can last, even if the end is always nothingness, Nietzsche's own will is diametrically opposed to this nihilism. In empty space he wants to grasp the positive."[19] He endeavors to formulate a vital faith, a transcendent affirmation that can inspire human life to nobler effort. Hence he glorifies strength, the *élan vital*, the will to power, the ideal of eternal recurrence. This is a far cry, however, from any religious gospel that the general run of mankind can embrace. But the passion of striving, the stubborn hankering after the ideal, is abundantly present in his work; he is not satisfied with the finite, the merely human; he must break out of the nihilistic impasse.

QUESTIONS FOR DISCUSSION

1. How does Glicksberg define nihilism? How is this different from the definition in a standard dictionary?
2. What role does the absurdity of existence play in the nihilistic world view?
3. Based upon the opening quote by Friedrich Nietzsche, what is the nihilistic attitude towards science?
4. Could nihilism lead to destructive actions? Could it lead to creative actions?
5. What does Glicksberg indicate is the purpose of most literary nihilism?
6. What does Glicksberg mean when he describes nihilism as an "archetypal experience" (par. 15)?
7. Who are some of the world's important figures who have faced this archetypal experience, according to Glicksberg?
8. What were philosophers like Nietzsche searching for when they embraced nihilism?

[18]**dementia** Insanity, madness, craziness. [Ed. note.]
[19]Karl Jaspers, *Nietzsche and Christianity*, trans. E. B. Ashton (Chicago: Henry Regnery Company, 1961), p. 84.

GWENDOLYN BROOKS
the preacher: ruminates behind the sermon
We Real Cool

Gwendolyn Brooks (1917–   ) is an American poet whose work deals with everyday life among urban blacks. She graduated from Wilson Junior College in 1936; her early verse appeared in a newspaper written for the black community, The Chicago Defender. *In 1950, she became the first black poet to win the Pulitzer Prize (for* Annie Allen, *a collection of poems about a girl growing up in inner-city Chicago). Other works include* The Bean Eaters *(1960), which critics agree contains some of her best verse,* In the Mecca *(1968),* Primer for Blacks *(1980),* Young Poets' Primer *(1981), and* To Disembark *(1981). She also has written a book for children,* Bronzeville Boys and Girls *(1956), and published an autobiographical work,* Report from Part One *(1972). In 1968 she succeeded Carl Sandburg as Poet Laureate for Illinois State, and from 1985–1986 she was Poetry Consultant to the Library of Congress. The poems reprinted here deal with religious and philosophical aspects of life, particularly urban life.*

the preacher: ruminates behind the sermon

I think it must be lonely to be God.
Nobody loves a master. No. Despite
The bright hosannas, bright dear-Lords, and bright
Determined reverence of Sunday eyes.

Picture Jehovah striding through the hall
Of His importance, creatures running out
From servant-corners to acclaim, to shout
Appreciation of His merit's glare.

But who walks with Him?—dares to take His arm,
To slap Him on the shoulder, tweak His ear,
Buy Him a Coca-Cola or a beer,
Pooh-pooh His politics, call Him a fool?

Perhaps—who knows?—He tires of looking down.
Those eyes are never lifted. Never straight.
Perhaps sometimes He tires of being great
In solitude. Without a hand to hold.

We Real Cool

The pool players.
Seven at the golden shovel.

We real cool. We
Left school. We

Lurk late. We
Strike straight. We

Sing sin. We
Thin gin. We

Jazz June. We
Die soon.

QUESTIONS FOR DISCUSSION

"the preacher: ruminates behind the sermon"

1. What does "ruminate" mean? What does the use of this word suggest about the thoughts of the preacher?
2. Why do you think the words in the title of the poem are not capitalized?
3. What is the preacher saying about God? Why might the preacher be saying this?

"We Real Cool"

1. Read this poem aloud—how would you describe the rhythm? How does the rhythm relate to the meaning of the poem?
2. Read June Jordan's "A Poem About Intelligence for My Brothers and Sisters" (p. 391). Discuss how both Brooks and Jordan incorporate black idiomatic speech into their poetry.
3. In what sense can this poem be considered nihilistic?

JEAN PAUL SARTRE
Existentialism

Jean-Paul Sartre (1905–1980) was a French novelist and playwright, also known as a proponent of the philosophy of existentialism. He described his childhood as lonely; he lost his father early and grew up in the home of his maternal grandfather, mocked by children his age because he was cross-eyed. He attended the prestigious École Nomale Supérieure in Paris and taught for many years in French secondary schools. Rejecting what he called the "bourgeois" institution of marriage, he formed a long-lasting relationship with the writer Simone de Beauvoir; the two of them founded and edited Les Temps Modernes, *a monthly review. His philosophical work* Being and Nothingness *(1943) is one of his best-known, along with his plays (such as "No Exit," 1946), and his studies of French writer Jean Genet. He was awarded the Nobel Prize for Literature in 1964, but declined it. It is important for non-European readers to understand that Sartre's ideas on existentialism were formulated amid the tremendous social chaos brought about by two world wars, which decimated the population and ruined the economies of entire nations. Like the nihilists of the late nineteenth century, many of whom lived through the suffering caused by such chaos, he came to doubt the existence of a divine being. But while existentialists agree with nihilists that there is no divine power guiding earthly matters, they choose a radically different path in assessing what humans must do as a result. Existentialists insist that individuals must assume the moral responsibility for shaping their own lives, as Sartre explains in the selection reprinted here.*

Atheistic existentialism, which I represent, . . . states that if God does not exist, there is at least one being in whom existence precedes essence, a being who exists before he can be defined by any concept, and that this being is man, or, as Heidegger says, human reality. What is meant here by saying that existence precedes essence? It means that, first of all, man exists, turns up, appears on the scene, and, only afterwards, defines himself. If man, as the existentialist conceives him, is indefinable, it is because at first he is nothing. Only afterward will he be something, and he himself will have made what he will be. Thus, there is no human nature, since there is no God to conceive it. Not only is man what he conceives himself to be, but he is also only what he wills himself to be after this thrust toward existence.

Man is nothing else but what he makes of himself. Such is the first principle of existentialism. It is also what is called subjectivity. But what do we mean by this, if not that man has a greater dignity than a stone or table? For we mean that man first exists, that is, that man first of all is the being who hurls himself toward a future and who is conscious of imagining himself as being in the future. Man is at the start a plan which is aware of itself, rather than a patch of moss, a piece of garbage, or a cauliflower; nothing exists prior to this plan; there is nothing in heaven; man will be what he will have planned to be. Not what he will want to be. Because by the word "will" we generally mean a conscious decision, which is subsequent to what we have already made of ourselves. I may want to belong to a political party, write a book, get married; but all that is only a manifestation of an earlier, more spontaneous choice that is called "will." But if existence really does precede essence, man is responsible for what he is. Thus, existentialism's first move is to make every man aware of what he is and to make the full responsibility of his existence rest on him. And when we say that a man is responsible for himself, we do not only mean that he is responsible for his own individuality, but that he is responsible for all men.

The word "subjectivism" has two meanings. Subjectivism means, on the one hand, that an individual chooses and makes himself; and, on the other, that it is impossible for man to transcend human subjectivity. The second of these is the essential meaning of existentialism. When we say that man chooses his own self, we mean that every one of us does likewise; but we also mean by that that in making this choice he also chooses all men. In fact, in creating the man that we want to be, there is not a single one of our acts which does not at the same time create an image of man as we think he ought to be. To choose to be this or that is to affirm at the same time the value of what we choose, because we can never choose evil. We always choose the good, and nothing can be good for us without being good for all.

If, on the other hand, existence precedes essence, and if we grant that we exist and fashion our image at one and the same time, the image is valid for everybody and for our whole age. Thus, our responsibility is much greater than we might have supposed, because it involves all mankind. If I am a workingman and choose to join a Christian trade union rather than be a Communist, and if by being a member, I want to show that the best thing for a man is resignation, that the kingdom of man is not of this world, I am not only involving my own case—I want to be resigned for everyone. As a result, my action has involved all humanity. To take a more individual matter, if I want to marry, to have children, even if this marriage depends solely on my own circumstances or passion or wish, I am involving all humanity in monogamy and not merely myself. Therefore, I am responsible for myself and for everyone else. I am creating a certain image of man of my own choosing. In choosing myself, I choose man.

The existentialist thinks it very distressing that God does not exist, because all possibility of finding values in a heaven of ideas disappears along with Him; there can no longer be an a priori Good, since there is no infinite and perfect consciousness to think it. Nowhere is it written that the good exists, that we must be honest, that we must not lie; because the fact is we are on a plane where there are only men. Dostoievsky said, "If God didn't exist, everything would be possible." That is the very starting point of existentialism. Indeed, everything is permissible if God does not exist, and as a result man is forlorn, because neither within him or without does he find anything to cling to. He can't start making excuses for himself.

If existence really does precede essence, there is no explaining things away by reference to a fixed and given nature. In other words, there is no determinism, man is free, man is freedom. On the other hand, if God does not exist, we find no values or commands to turn to which legitimize our conduct. So, in the bright realm of values, we have no excuse behind us, nor justification before us. We are alone, with no excuses.

That is the idea I shall try to convey when I say that man is condemned to be free. Condemned, because he did not create himself, yet, in other respects is free; because, once thrown into the world, he is responsible for everything he does.

To give you an example which will enable you to understand forlornness better, I shall cite the case of one of my students who came to see me under the following circumstances: his father was on bad terms with his mother, and, moreover, was inclined to be a collaborationist, his older brother had been killed in the German offensive of 1940, and the young man, with somewhat immature but generous feelings, wanted to avenge him. His mother lived alone with him, very much upset by the half-treason of her husband and the death of her older son; the boy was her only consolation.

The boy was faced with the choice of leaving for England joining the Free French forces—that is, leaving his mother behind—or remaining with his mother and helping her to carry on. He was fully aware that the woman lived only for him and that his going off—and perhaps his death—would plunge her into despair. He was also aware that every act that he did for his mother's sake was a sure thing, in the sense that it was helping her to carry on, whereas every effort he made toward going off and fighting was an uncertain move which might run aground and prove completely useless; for example, on his way to England he might, while passing through Spain, be detained indefinitely in a Spanish camp; he might reach England or Algiers and be stuck in an office at a desk job. As a result, he was faced with two very different kinds of action: one, concrete, immediate, but concerning only one individual; the other concerned an incomparably vaster group, a national collectivity, but for that very reason was dubious, and might be interrupted en route. And, at the same time, he was wavering between two kinds of ethics. On the one hand, an ethics of sympathy, of personal devotion; on the other, a broader ethics, but one whose efficacy was more dubious. He had to choose between the two.

Who could help him choose? Christian doctrine? No. Christian doctrine says, "Be charitable, love your neighbor, take the more rugged path, etc., etc." But which is the more rugged path? Whom should he love as a brother? The fighting man or his mother? Which does the greater good, the vague act of fighting in a group, or the concrete one of helping a particular human being to go on living? Who can decide a priori? Nobody. No book of ethics can tell him. The Kantian ethics says, "Never treat any person as a means, but as an end." Very well, if I stay with my mother, I'll treat her as an end and not as a means; but by virtue of this very fact, I'm running the risk of treating the people around me who are fighting, as means; and conversely, if I go to join those who are fighting, I'll be treating them as an end, and, by doing that, I run the risk of treating my mother as a means.

If values are vague, and if they are always too broad for the concrete and specific case that we are considering, the only thing left for us is to trust our instincts. That's what this young man tried to do; and when I saw him, he said, "In the end, feeling is what counts. I ought to choose whichever pushes me in one direction. If I feel that I love my mother enough to sacrifice everything else for her—my desire for vengeance, for action, for adventure—then I'll stay with her. If, on the contrary, I feel that my love for my mother isn't enough, I'll leave."

But how is the value of a feeling determined? What gives his feeling for his mother value? Precisely the fact that he remained with her. I may say that I like so-and-so well enough to sacrifice a certain amount of money for him, but I may say so only if I've done it. I may say "I love my mother well enough to remain with her" if I have remained with her. The only way to determine the value of this affection is, precisely, to perform an act which confirms and defines it. But, since I require this affection to justify my act, I find myself caught in a vicious circle.

Given that men are free and that tomorrow they will freely decide what man will be, I cannot be sure that, after my death, fellow-fighters will carry on my work to bring it to its maximum perfection. Tomorrow, after my death, some men may decide to set up Fascism, and the others may be cowardly and muddled enough to let them do it. Fascism will then be the human reality, so much the worse for us.

Actually, things will be as man will have decided they are to be. Does that mean that I should abandon myself to quietism? No. First, I should involve myself; then, act on the old saw, "Nothing ventured, nothing gained." Nor does it mean that I shouldn't belong to a party, but rather that I shall have no illusions and shall do what I can. For example, suppose I ask myself, "Will socialization, as such, ever come about?" I know nothing about it. All I know is that I'm going to do everything in my power to bring it about. Beyond that, I can't count on anything. Quietism is the attitude of people who say, "Let others do what I can't do." The doctrine I am presenting is the very opposite of quietism, since it declares, "There is no reality except in action." Moreover, it goes further, since it adds, "Man is nothing else than his plan; he exists only to the extent that he fulfills himself; he is therefore nothing else than the ensemble of his acts, nothing else than his life."

Now, for the existentialist there is really no love other than one which manifests itself in a person's being in love. There is no genius other than one which is expressed in works of art; the genius of Proust is the sum of Proust's works; the genius of Racine is his series of tragedies. Outside of that, there is nothing. Why say that Racine could have written another tragedy, when he didn't write it? A man is involved in life, leaves his impress on it, and outside of that there is nothing. To be sure, this may seem a harsh thought to someone whose life hasn't been a success. But, on the other hand, it prompts people to understand that reality alone is what counts, that dreams, expectations, and hopes warrant no more than to define a man as a disappointed dream, as miscarried hopes, as vain expectations. In other words, to define him negatively and not positively. However, when we say, "You are nothing else than your life," that does not imply that the artist will be judged solely on the basis of his works of art; a thousand other things will contribute toward summing him up. What we mean is that a man is nothing else than a series of undertakings, that he is the sum, the organization, the ensemble of the relationships which make up these undertakings.

When all is said and done, what we are accused of, at bottom, is not our pessimism, but an optimistic toughness. If people throw up to us our works of fiction in which we write about people who are soft, weak, cowardly, and sometimes even downright bad, it's not because these people are soft, weak, cowardly, or bad; because if we were to say, as Zola did, that they are that way because of heredity, the workings of environment, society, because of biological or psychological determinism, people would be reassured. They would say, "Well, that's what we're like, no one can do anything about it." But when the existentialist writes about a coward, he says that this coward is responsible for his cowardice. He's not like that because he has a cowardly heart or lung or brain; he's not like that on account of his physiological make-up; but he's like that because he has made himself a coward by his acts. There's no such thing as a cowardly constitution; there are nervous constitutions; there is poor blood, as the common people say, or strong constitutions. But the man whose blood is poor is not a coward on that account, for what makes cowardice is the act of renouncing or yielding. A constitution is not an act; the coward is defined on the basis of the acts he performs. People feel, in a vague sort of way, that this coward we're talking about is guilty of being a coward, and the thought frightens them. What people would like is that a coward or a hero be born that way.

Existentialism is nothing else than an attempt to draw all the consequences of a coherent atheistic position. It isn't trying to plunge man into despair at all. But if one calls every attitude of unbelief despair, like the Christians, then the word is not being used in its original sense. Existentialism isn't so atheistic that it wears itself out showing that God doesn't exist. Rather, it declares that even if God did exist, that would change nothing. There you've got our point of view. Not that we believe that God exists, but we think that the problem of His existence is not the issue. In this sense existentialism is optimistic, a doctrine of action, and it is plain dishonesty for Christians to make no distinction between their own despair and ours and then to call us despairing.

QUESTIONS FOR DISCUSSION

1. How does Sartre explain the concept "existence precedes essence" (par. 1)?
2. Atheistic existentialism presupposes that there is no divine creator with a predetermined plan already established for the human race. Who, then, would Sartre say is responsible for what humans are and for what their purpose in existence is?
3. As an atheistic existentialist, would Sartre agree with nihilists that life is absurd and filled with despair?
4. In your opinion, how might Sartre fit into Plato's "The Allegory of the Cave" (p. 519)?
5. Would you agree that this essay is in the form of an argument? If so, who might be the audience that Sartre wishes to persuade? Does he give any indications of who might be in opposition to his point of view?

Three Concepts of Creation: Genesis 1 and 2, Nu Kwa, and Shakti

The following three texts reflect a need among developing societies to explain both their own beginnings and the origins of the world around them. In the Western world, we are most familiar with a male creator, as presented here in the book of "Genesis" (from an oral tradition dating from about 1000 B.C.E.; the word means "origin" or "beginning"), but as Riane Eisler points out in "Our Lost Heritage: New Facts on How God Became a Man" (p. 550), many early societies worshipped female creators. The selections "Nu Kwa" (from Northern China, dating from an oral tradition of about 2500 B.C.E.) and "Shakti" (dating from an oral tradition of about 3000 B.C.E.; the word means "power" or "life force") present concepts of creation by a Great Mother. These selections on creation, along with the Buddhist text "Woman and the Order" (p. 549), may be read in conjunction with Eisler's essay on female deities in ancient Western cultures.

Genesis

CHAPTER I

In the beginning God created the heaven and the earth.

2 And the earth was without form, and void; and darkness *was* upon the face of the deep. And the Spirit of God moved upon the face of the waters.

3 And God said, Let there be light: and there was light.

4 And God saw the light, that *it was* good: and God divided the light from the darkness.

5 And God called the light Day, and the darkness he called Night. And the evening and the morning were the first day.

6 And God said, Let there be a firmament in the midst of the waters, and let it divide the waters from the waters.

7 And God made the firmament, and divided the waters which *were* under the firmament from the waters which *were* above the firmament: and it was so.

8 And God called the firmament Heaven. And the evening and the morning were the second day.

9 And God said, Let the waters under the heaven be gathered together unto one place, and let the dry *land* appear: and it was so.

10 And God called the dry *land* Earth; and the gathering together of the waters called he Seas: and God saw that *it was* good.

11 And God said, Let the earth bring forth grass, the herb yielding seed, *and* the fruit tree yielding fruit after his kind, whose seed *is* in itself, upon the earth: and it was so.

12 And the earth brought forth grass, *and* herb yielding seed after his kind, and the tree yielding fruit, whose seed *was* in itself, after his kind: and God saw that *it was* good.

13 And the evening and the morning were the third day.

14 And God said, Let there be lights in the firmament of the heaven to divide the day from the night; and let them be for signs, and for seasons, and for days, and years:

15 And let them be for lights in the firmament of the heaven to give light upon the earth: and it was so.

16 And God made two great lights; the greater light to rule the day, and the lesser light to rule the night: *he made* the stars also.

17 And God set them in the firmament of the heaven to give light upon the earth,

18 And to rule over the day and over the night, and to divide the light from the darkness: and God saw that *it was* good.

19 And the evening and the morning were the fourth day.

20 And God said, Let the waters bring forth abundantly the moving creature that hath life, and fowl *that* may fly above the earth in the open firmament of heaven.

21 And God created great whales, and every living creature that moveth, which the waters brought forth abundantly, after their kind, and every winged fowl after his kind: and God saw that *it was* good.

22 And God blessed them, saying, Be fruitful, and multiply, and fill the waters in the seas, and let fowl multiply in the earth.

23 And the evening and the morning were the fifth day.

24 And God said, Let the

earth bring forth the living creature after his kind, cattle, and creeping thing, and beast of the earth after his kind: and it was so.

25 And God made the beast of the earth after his kind, and cattle after their kind, and every thing that creepeth upon the earth after his kind: and God saw that *it was* good.

26 And God said, Let us make man in our image, after our likeness: and let them have dominion over the fish of the sea, and over the fowl of the air, and over the cattle, and over all the earth, and over every creeping thing that creepeth upon the earth.

27 So God created man in his *own* image, in the image of God created he him; male and female created he them.

28 And God blessed them, and God said unto them, Be fruitful, and multiply, and replenish the earth, and subdue it: and have dominion over the fish of the sea, and over the fowl of the air, and over every living thing that moveth upon the earth.

29 And God said, Behold, I have given you every herb bearing seed, which *is* upon the face of all the earth, and every tree, in which *is* the fruit of a tree yielding seed; to you it shall be for meat.

30 And to every beast of the earth, and to every fowl of the air, and to every thing that creepeth upon the earth, wherein *there is* life, *I have given* every green herb for meat: and it was so.

31 And God saw every thing that he had made, and, behold, *it was* very good. And the evening and the morning were the sixth day.

CHAPTER 2

Thus the heavens and the earth were finished, and all the host of them.

2 And on the seventh day God ended his work which he had made; and he rested on the seventh day from all his work which he had made.

3 And God blessed the seventh day, and sanctified it: because that in it he had rested from all his work which God created and made.

4 These *are* the generations of the heavens and of the earth when they were created, in the day that the Lord God made the earth and the heavens,

5 And every plant of the field before it was in the earth, and every herb of the field before it grew: for the Lord God had not caused it to rain upon the earth, and *there was* not a man to till the ground.

6 But there went up a mist from the earth, and watered the whole face of the ground.

7 And the Lord God formed man *of* the dust of the ground, and breathed into his nostrils the breath of life; and man became a living soul.

8 And the Lord God planted a garden eastward in Eden; and there he put the man whom he had formed.

9 And out of the ground made the Lord God to grow ev-

ery tree that is pleasant to the sight, and good for food; the tree of life also in the midst of the garden, and the tree of knowledge of good and evil.

10 And a river went out of Eden to water the garden; and from thence it was parted, and became into four heads.

11 The name of the first *is* Pī'-sŏn: that *is* it which compasseth the whole land of Hăv'-ĭ-läh, where *there is* gold;

12 And the gold of that land *is* good: there *is* bdellium and the onyx stone.

13 And the name of the second river *is* Gī'-hŏn: the same *is* it that compasseth the whole land of Ē-thĭ-ō'-pĭ-ă.

14 And the name of the third river *is* Hĭd'-dĕ-kĕl: that *is* it which goeth toward the east of Assyria. And the fourth river *is* Eu-phrā'-tēs.

15 And the LORD God took the man, and put him into the garden of Eden to dress it and to keep it.

16 And the LORD God commanded the man, saying, Of every tree of the garden thou mayest freely eat:

17 But of the tree of the knowledge of good and evil, thou shalt not eat of it: for in the day that thou eatest thereof thou shalt surely die.

18 And the LORD God said, *It is* not good that the man should be alone; I will make him an help meet for him.

19 And out of the ground the LORD God formed every beast of the field, and every fowl of the air; and brought *them* unto Adam to see what he would call them: and whatsoever Adam called every living creature, that *was* the name thereof.

20 And Adam gave names to all cattle, and to the fowl of the air, and to every beast of the field; but for Adam there was not found an help meet for him.

21 And the LORD God caused a deep sleep to fall upon Adam, and he slept: and he took one of his ribs, and closed up the flesh instead thereof;

22 And the rib, which the LORD God had taken from man, made he a woman, and brought her unto the man.

23 And Adam said, This *is* now bone of my bones, and flesh of my flesh: she shall be called Woman, because she was taken out of Man.

24 Therefore shall a man leave his father and his mother, and shall cleave unto his wife: and they shall be one flesh.

25 And they were both naked, the man and his wife, and were not ashamed.

Nu Kwa

To the valleys of the wide flowing Hwang Ho, came the Goddess Nu Kwa and there from the rich golden earth, She fashioned the race of golden people, carefully working the features of each with Her skillful fingers. But so arduous was Her task that She soon tired of making these individual creations and began to pull a string through the mud. In this way She made the others, though not as carefully formed, as She had made those of the golden earth, the ancestors of the Chinese people.

From the Kun Lun mountains, sweet western paradise whose summits reach the heights of heaven, Nu Kwa sent the great winds and the life giving waters, making the earth good for planting, pouring the excess waters into the Chihli Po Hai Bay—and then She filled it with fish so that all might eat to satisfaction.

But there came a time when all the universe was in great chaos; fires raged and waters brought floods. At this time, the pillar of the north, the pillar of the south, the pillar of the east, and the pillar of the west—all of these were destroyed. The nine provinces of the earth separated from each other and even heaven and earth were no longer suited to each other, for they had blown so far apart. Everything was wrong. Animals ate the people. Vultures seized and killed the elderly and weak.

Then Great Mother Nu Kwa saw what had happened and came to repair the damage, using coloured stones to patch the heavens. Seeing the ruins of the pillars, those which had supported the four corners of heaven, She took the legs of the great turtle and used them as columns, placing them firmly at the four compass points of the world. With Her mighty arms She smothered the blazing fires and when the burning reeds had turned to ash, She piled the ashes high enough so that the wild flooding waters came to repose where they are today. When all was once again in place—only then was Mother Nu Kwa satisfied to rest.

It was then that She looked upon all that She had done. It was a time of perfect harmony when all flowed in its course, each at its own pace. The stars followed their correct paths in the heavens. The rain came only when the rain should come. Each season followed the one before—in rightful order. Mother Nu Kwa had repaired the pattern for all that occurred in the universe, so that the crops were plentiful, the people were no longer the meal of the wild animal, vultures did not prey among the weak and old, nor were serpents harmful to them either.

Life was spent in nights of peace, undisturbed by anxious dream, and waking time was carefree and untroubled. It was the time of Mother Nu Kwa, She who established the patterns of existence, the order and rhythm of the universe, the sacred way of harmony and balance.

Shakti

She who holds the Universe in Her womb,
source of all creative energies,
Maha Devi who conceives
and bears and nourishes
all that exists—
She is the ghanibuti,
the massed condensed power of energy;
She is the sphurana,
the power that burgeons forth into action;

She is purest consciousness and bliss,
inherent in the manifestation of all being.

Never can She be known
in Her perfect completeness,
for Her omnipotence is in all
that She continually does.
Do they not say
that even Shiva is unable to stir,
lies as a corpse,
until She grants him Her energies?
In the form of the coiled serpent,[1]
the Bhunjangi Kundalini,
She unwinds Herself through the chakras,[2]
through the lotuses[3] of the body,
as She creates Her cosmic serpent spiral
through the lotus chakras of the Universe.
At Her sacred shrine of Kamrupa,
they drink the kula nectar
that is the blood that passes from Her
as the moon passes from the sky,
while those who reach out to know her
sit in Her circle of worshippers,
the sacred Shakti Cakra Pravartika,
knowing that if they worship Her with full devotion,
She will appear and give what is requested,
as She maintains the many beings of the world.

Some say that there are many worlds,
each ruled by a goddess or a god,
but that there is just the One Great Mother,
the Jagad Amba, the Makara,
Shakti of all existence,
She to whom even the gods bow down
in reverent worship and respect,
anxious for even the dust of Her feet
to touch their waiting heads—
for it is Shakti who is the ultimate source,
the infinite Cosmic Energy of all that occurs,
Maha Devi[4] of the thousand petalled lotus.

---

[1]**serpent** In Kundalini yoga, energy lies coiled at the base of the spinal cord like a serpent, waiting to be awakened through yoga exercises. [Ed. note.]

[2]**chakras** Literally, "circles." The points on the body serving mystical purposes in Tantric yoga exercises. [Ed. note.]

[3]**lotuses** Hindu religious symbols roughly equivalent to the cross in Christianity. As the lotus grows in a swamp but its beautiful flower blooms untouched above the mire, so is a Hindu in the world but not of it. [Ed. note.]

[4]**Jagad Amba, the Makara . . . Maha Devi** All names for the Great Mother. [Ed. note.]

QUESTIONS FOR DISCUSSION

Chapter 1 of Genesis

1. According to this text, how did ancient Hebrew tribal societies conceive of deity?
2. Verses 26 and 27 state that God created man "in his own image." How do they suggest that women fit into this process?
3. Many modern environmentalists feel that attitudes permitting misuse and exploitation of the earth's natural resources in the Western world stem from interpretations given in verses 26 and 27 over the centuries. Explain how these verses could be interpreted in such a way.
4. Compare the attitude towards the earth implied by verses 26–27 to the attitude expressed in Chief Seattle's "Environmental Statement" (p. 58).

Chapter 2 of Genesis

1. Compare the creation story in this chapter with the one in Genesis 1. What differences do you find in terms of the beginnings of the human race, particularly the roles given women?
2. The original text of Genesis comes from nomadic Hebrew tribes in Palestine sometime before the year 250 B.C.E. What difficulties would a translator face in making a modern translation of a text arising from this kind of society?

Nu Kwa

1. Compare this creation story to the one from "Genesis" (p. 542). How are they alike? How are they different?
2. "Nu Kwa" is in many ways nature personified—"Mother Nature," as in Western culture. What are some possible reasons for cultures viewing nature as a mother rather than as a father?
3. Many religious traditions include a great disaster of some sort; here the disaster is fire as well as flood. Why might disaster involving a deity be an important part of a religious tradition?
4. This creation story ends with a depiction of a golden age when all was harmony and peace in the universe. Discuss why so many religious traditions might have a golden age or time of perfection as an important feature of their prehistory.

Shakti

1. Compare the concept of the Great Mother as depicted here with that in "Nu Kwa." How are they alike? How do they differ?
2. Compare the concept of the creator in this text and in "Genesis." How are they alike? How do they differ?
3. Discuss the concept of the creator as cosmic energy; why would ancient people see such a concept as female?

4. In what way does this text reflect the culture from which it comes? (Read Diana Eck's "Darśan: Seeing the Divine Image in India" (p. 464) to help you answer this question.) Discuss in particular the images of the lotus and of the serpent.
5. Compare the concept of the creator to that in the *Upanishads* (p. 473), which experts believe comes after the Aryan invasion of India in about 2000 B.C.E. How are the two creators different? What does this difference tell you about the Aryan invaders?

NINIAN SMART AND RICHARD D. HECHT
Women and the Order

In the following dialogue with his pupil Ānanda, the Buddha reveals his perceptions of the effect women would have upon his religion. At the time of this writing, nuns were permitted to join Buddhist monasteries, but only under certain conditions that kept them in inferior positions of authority and separated from the male monks. Buddha predicted that women would bring about the downfall of Buddhism.

Then the venerable[1] Ānanda drew near to where the Blessed One was; and having drawn near and greeted the Blessed One, he sat down respectfully at one side. And seated respectfully at one side, the venerable Ānanda spoke to the Blessed One as follows:

'Mahā-Pajāpatī of the Gautama clan, Reverend Sir, has accepted the eight weighty regulations; the sister of the mother of the Blessed One has become ordained.'

'If, Ānanda, women had not retired from household life to the houseless one, under the Doctrine and Discipline announced by the Tathāgata, religion, Ānanda, would long endure: a thousand years would the Good Doctrine abide. But since, Ānanda, women have now retired from household life to the houseless one, under the Doctrine and Discipline announced by the Tathāgata, not long, Ānanda, will religion endure; but five hundred years, Ānanda, will the Good Doctrine abide. Just as, Ānanda, those families which consist of many women and few men are easily overcome by burglars, in exactly the same way, Ānanda, when women retire from household life to the houseless one, under a doctrine and discipline, that religion does not long endure. Just as, Ānanda, when the disease called mildew falls upon a flourishing field of rice, that field of rice does not long endure, in exactly the same way, Ānanda, when women retire from household life to the houseless one, under a doctrine and discipline, that religion does not long endure. Even as, Ānanda, when

---

[1]**venerable** Worthy of honor and respect, usually due to age, achievements, or character. [Ed. note.]

the disease called rust falls upon a flourishing field of sugarcane, that field of sugarcane does not long endure in exactly the same way, Ānanda, when women retire from household life to the houseless one, under a doctrine and discipline, that religion does not long endure. And just as, Ānanda, to a large pond a man would prudently build a dyke, in order that the water might not transgress its bounds, in exactly the same way, Ānanda, have I prudently laid down eight weighty regulations, not to be transgressed as long as life shall last.'

QUESTIONS FOR DISCUSSION

1. What main conclusion does the Buddha defend in this argument?
2. What premises does he offer to support this conclusion? Is the argument convincing?
3. Can you draw parallels between the Buddha's attitude toward women and attitudes toward women in other major world religions?

RIANE EISLER
Our Lost Heritage:
New Facts on How God Became a Man

Riane Eisler (1931–   ) is codirector for the Center for Partnership Studies and a lecturer on feminist issues. She is the author of Dissolutions: No-Fault Divorce, Marriage, and the Future of Women *(1977);* What the ERA Means to Your Life, Your Rights, and the Future *(1978); and* The Chalice and the Blade: Our History, Our Future *(1987). In the selection reprinted here, from an article published in 1985, Eisler challenges traditional interpretations of the origins of Western civilization. Using archaeological evidence of goddess worship in early European agricultural communities, she proposes that male-dominated hierarchical religions and societies have not always been the norm in the Western world, and theorizes about how the change from a female to a male deity might have taken place.*

In the nineteenth century, archeological excavations began to confirm what scholars of myth had long maintained—that goddess worship preceded the worship of God. After reluctantly accepting what no longer could be ignored, religious historians proposed a number of explanations for why there had been this strange switch in divine gender. A long-standing favorite has been the so-called Big Discovery theory. This is the idea that, when men finally became aware that women did not bring forth children by themselves—in other words, when they discovered that it involved their sperm, their paternity—this inflamed them with such a new-found sense of importance that they not only enslaved women but also toppled the goddess.

Today, new archeological findings—particularly post-World War II excavations—are providing far more believable answers to this long-debated puzzle. For largely due to more scientific archeological methods, including infinitely more accurate archeological dating methods such as radiocarbon and dendrochronology,[1] there has been a veritable archeological revolution.

As James Mellaart of the London University Institute of Archeology writes, we now know that there were in fact many cradles of civilization, all of them thousands of years older than Sumer, where civilization was long said to have begun about five thousand years ago.[2] But the most fascinating discovery about these original cultural sites is that they were structured along very different lines from what we have been taught is the divinely, or naturally, ordained human order.

One of these ancient cradles of civilization is Catal Huyuk, the largest Neolithic site yet found. Located in the Anatolian plain of what is now Turkey, Catal Huyuk goes back approximately eight thousand years to about 6500 BCE—three thousand years before Sumer. As Mellaart reports, this ancient civilization "is remarkable for its wall-paintings and plaster reliefs, its sculpture in stone and clay . . . , its advanced technology in the crafts of weaving, woodwork, metallurgy . . . , its advanced religion . . . , its advanced practices in agriculture and stockbreeding, and . . . a flourishing trade. . . ."[3]

But undoubtedly the most remarkable thing about Catal Huyuk and other original sites for civilization is that they were *not* warlike, hierarchic, and male-dominated societies like ours. As Mellaart writes, over the many centuries of its existence, there were in Catal Huyuk no signs of violence or deliberate destruction, "no evidence for any sack or massacre." Moreover, while there was evidence of some social inequality, "this is never a glaring one." And most significantly—in the sharpest possible contrast to our type of social organization—"the position of women was obviously an important one . . . with a fertility cult in which a goddess was the principal deity."[4]

Now it is hardly possible to believe that in this kind of society, where, besides all their other advances, people clearly understood the principles of stockbreeding, they would not have also had to understand that procreation involves the male. So the Big Discovery theory is not only founded on the fallacious assumption that men are naturally brutes, who were only deterred from forcefully enslaving women by fear of the female's "magical" powers of procreation; the Big Discovery theory is also founded on assumptions about what happened in prehistory that are no longer tenable in light of the *really* big discoveries we are now making about our lost human heritage—about societies that, while not ideal, were clearly more harmonious than ours.

But if the replacement of a Divine Mother with a Divine Father was not due to men's discovery of paternity, how did it come to pass that all our present world religions either have no female deity or generally present them as "consorts" or subservient wives of male gods?

To try to answer that question, let us look more carefully at the new archeological findings.

---

[1] Radiocarbon dating is a method of establishing the age of prehistoric artifacts by measuring the radioactivity of carbon; dendrochronology is a dating procedure based on counting the growth rings of trees.

[2] J. Mellaart, *The Neolithic of the Near East* (New York: Charles Scribner's Sons, 1975). [Au.]

[3] J. Mellaart, *Catal Huyuk* (New York: McGraw-Hill, 1967), p. 11. [Au.]

[4] Ibid., pp. 69, 225, 553. [Au.]

Logic would lead one to expect what ancient myths have long indicated and archeology has since confirmed: that since life issues from woman, not man, the first anthropomorphic deity was female rather than male. But logical or not, this position was hardly that of the first excavators of Paleolithic caves, some of whom were monks, such as the well-known Abbé Henri Breuil. They consistently refused to see in the many finds of twenty-five-thousand-year-old stylized female sculptures what they clearly were: representations of a female divinity, a Great Mother. Instead, the large-breasted, wide-hipped, bountiful, and often obviously pregnant women these men christened "Venus figurines" were described either as sex objects (products of men's erotic fantasies) or deformed, ugly women.[5] Moreover, in order to conform to their model of history as the story of "man the hunter" and "man the warrior," they refused to see what was actually in the famous cave paintings. As Alexander Marshack has now established, not only did they insist that stylized painting of tree branches and plants were weapons, they sometimes described these pictures as backward arrows or harpoons, chronically missing their mark![6] They also, as Andre Leroi-Gourhan noted in his major study of the Paleolithic, insisted on interpreting the already quite advanced art of the period as an expression of hunting magic, a view borrowed from extremely primitive contemporary societies like the Australian aborigines.[7]

Although Leroi-Gourhan's interpretation of the objects and paintings found in Paleolithic caves is in sexually stereotyped terms, he stresses that the art of the Paleolithic was first and foremost religious art, concerned with the mysteries of life, death, and regeneration.[8] And it is again this concern that is expressed in the rich art of the Neolithic, which, as Mellaart points out, not only shows a remarkable continuity with the Paleolithic,[9] but clearly foreshadows the great goddess of later Bronze Age civilizations in her various forms of Isis, Nut, and Maat in Egypt, Ishtar, Lillith, or Astarte in the Middle East, the sun-goddess Arinna of Anatolia, as well as such later goddesses as Demeter, Artemis, and Kore in Greece, Atargatis, Ceres, and Cybele in Rome, and even Sophia or Wisdom of the Christian Middle Ages, the Shekinah of Hebrew Kabalistic tradition, and, of course, the Virgin Mary or Holy Mother of the Catholic Church about whom we read in the Bible.[10]

This same prehistoric and historic continuity is stressed by UCLA archeologist Marija Gimbutas, whose monumental work, *The Goddesses and Gods of Old Europe*, brings to life yet another Neolithic civilization: the indigenous civilization that sprang up in the Balkans and Greece long, long before the rise of Indo-European Greece.[11] Once again, the archeological findings in what Gimbutas termed the civilizations of Old Europe not only demolish the old "truism" of the "warlike Neolithic"

---

[5]See, for example, E. O. James, *The Cult of the Mother Goddess* (London: Thames and Hudson, 1959) and M. Gimbutas, "The Image of Woman in Prehistoric Art," *Quarterly Review of Archeology*, December 1981. [Au.]
[6]A. Marshack, *The Roots of Civilization* (New York: McGraw-Hill, 1972). [Au.]
[7]A. Leroi-Gourhan, *Prehistoire de l'Art Occidental* (Paris: Edition D'Art Lucien Mazenod, 1971). [Au.]
[8]Ibid. [Au.]
[9]J. Mellaart, *Catal Huyuk*, p. 11. [Au.]
[10]See, for example, R. Eisler, *The Blade and the Chalice: Beyond War, Sexual Politics, and Fear*, work in progress; M. Stone, *When God Was a Woman* (New York: Harvest, 1976); E. Neumann, *The Great Mother* (Princeton, NJ: Princeton University Press, 1955). [Au.]
[11]M. Gimbutas, *The Goddesses and Gods of Old Europe* (Berkeley, CA: University of California Press, 1982). [Au.]

but also illuminate our true past, again showing that here, too, the original direction of human civilization was in some ways far more civilized than ours, with pre-Indo-Europeans living in far greater harmony with one another and the natural environment.

Moreover, excavations in Old Europe, like those unearthed in other parts of the ancient world, show that what brought about the onset of male dominance both in heaven and on earth was not some sudden male discovery. What ushered it in was the onslaught of barbarian hordes from the arid steppes and deserts on the fringe areas of our globe. It was wave after wave of these pastoral invaders who destroyed the civilizations of the first settled agrarian societies. And it was they who brought with them the gods—and men—of war that made so much of later or recorded history the bloodbath we are now taught was the *totality* of human history.

In Old Europe, as Gimbutas painstakingly documents, there were three major invasionary waves, as the Indo-European peoples she calls the Kurgans wiped out or "Kurganized" the European populations. "The Old European and Kurgan cultures were the antithesis of one another," writes Gimbutas. She continues:

> The Old Europeans were sedentary horticulturalists prone to live in large well-planned townships. The absence of fortifications and weapons attests the peaceful coexistence of this egalitarian civilization that was probably matrilinear and matrilocal.[12] . . . The Old European belief system focused on the agricultural cycle of birth, death, and regeneration, embodied in the feminine principle, a Mother Creatrix. The Kurgan ideology, as known from comparative Indo-European mythology, exalted virile, heroic warrior gods of the shining and thunderous sky. Weapons are nonexistent in Old European imagery; whereas the dagger and battle-axe are dominant symbols of the Kurgans, who, like all historically known Indo-Europeans, glorified the lethal power of the sharp blade.[13]

So while we are still commonly taught that it was to Indo-European invaders—such as the Aechaean warriors, celebrated by Homer, who eventually sacked Troy—that we owe our Western heritage, we now know that they in fact did not bring us civilization. Rather, they destroyed, degraded, and brutalized a civilization already highly advanced along wholly different lines. And, just as the factuality of how these truly savage peoples denoted both women and goddesses to the subservient status of consort or wife has now been established, the fact [that] they brought in warfare with them is also confirmed.

Once again, as when Heinrich Schliemann defied the archeological establishment and proved that the city of Troy was not Homeric fantasy but prehistoric fact, new archeological findings verify ancient legends and myths. For instance, the Greek poet Hesiod, who wrote about the same time as Homer, tells us of a "golden race," who lived in "peaceful ease" in a time when "the fruitful earth poured forth her fruits." And he laments how they were eventually replaced by "a race of bronze"

---

[12]In anthropology, *matrilinear* refers to descent through the female line; *matrilocal* pertains to residence with the wife's family.
[13]M. Gimbutas, "The First Wave of Eurasian Steppe Pastoralists in Copper Age Europe," *Journal of Indo-European Studies,* 1977, p. 281.

who "ate not grain" (in other words, were not farmers) and instead specialized in warfare ("the all-lamented sinful works of Ares were their chief care").[14]

Perhaps one of the most fascinating legends of ancient times is, of course, that of the lost civilization of Atlantis. And here again, as with the once only legendary city of Troy, archeological findings illuminate our true past. For what new findings suggest is what the eminent Greek scholar Spyridon Martinatos already suspected in 1939: that the legend of a great civilization which sank into the Atlantic is actually the garbled folk memory of the Minoan civilization of Crete and surrounding Mediterranean islands, portions of which did indeed disappear into the sea after unprecedented volcanic eruptions sometime after 1500 BCE.[15]

First discovered at the turn of this century, the once unknown Bronze Age civilization of ancient Crete has now been far more extensively excavated. As Nicolas Platon, former superintendent of antiquities in Crete and director of the Acropolis Museum, who excavated the island for over thirty years, writes, Minoan civilization was "an astonishing achievement." It reflected "a highly sophisticated art and way of life," indeed producing some of the most beautiful art the world has ever seen. Also in this remarkable society—the only place where the worship of the goddess and the influence of women in the public sphere survived into historic times, where "the whole of life was pervaded by an ardent faith in the goddess Nature, the source of all creation and harmony"—there was still "a love of peace, a horror of tyranny, and a respect for the law."[16]

And once again, it was not men's discovery of their biological role in paternity that led to the toppling of the goddess. It was another, final Indo-European invasion: the onslaught of the Dorians, who, with their weapons of iron, as Hesiod writes, brought death and destruction in their wake.[17]

So the revolution in norms that literally stood reality on its head—that established this seemingly fundamental and sacrosanct idea that we are the creations of a Divine Father, who all by Himself brought forth all forms of life—was in fact a relatively late event in the history of human culture. Moreover, this drastic change in direction of cultural evolution, which set us on the social course that in our nuclear age threatens to destroy all life, was certainly not predetermined or, by any stretch of the imagination, inevitable. Rather than being some mystical mystery, it was the substitution of a force-based model of social organization for one in which both the female and male halves of humanity viewed the supreme power in the universe not as the "masculine" power to destroy but rather as the "feminine" power to give and nurture life.

Another popular old idea about this change was that it was the replacement of matriarchy with patriarchy. But my research of many years shows that matriarchy is simply the flip side of the coin to the *dominator* model of society, based upon the dominance of men over women that we call patriarchy. The real alternative to patri-

[14]Hesiod, quoted in J. M. Robinson, *An Introduction to Early Greek Philosophy* (Boston: Houghton Mifflin, 1968), pp. 12–14. [Au.]

[15]S. Martinatos, "The Volcanic Destruction of Minoan Crete," *Antiquity*, 1939, 13:425–439. [Au.]

[16]N. Platon, *Crete* (Geneva: Nagel, 1966), pp. 48, 148. [Au.]

[17]Hesiod, see note 14. [Au.]

archy, already foreshadowed by the original direction of human civilization, is what I have called the *partnership* model of social relations.[18] Based upon the full and equal partnership between the female and male halves of our species, this model was already well-established a long time ago, before, as the Bible has it, a male god decreed that woman be subservient to man.

The new knowledge about our true human heritage is still meeting enormous resistance, with traditional "experts" from both the religious and academic establishments crying heresy. But it is a knowledge that, in the long run, cannot be suppressed.

It is a knowledge that demolishes many old misconceptions about our past. It also raises many fascinating new questions. Is the real meaning of the legend of our fall from paradise that, rather than having transgressed in some horrible way, Eve should have obeyed the advice of the serpent (long associated with the oracular or prophetic powers of the goddess) and *continued* to eat from the tree of knowledge? Did the custom of sacrificing the first-born child develop after the destruction of this earlier world—as the Bible has it, after our expulsion from the Garden of Eden—when women had been turned into mere male-controlled technologies of reproduction, as insurance of a sort that conception had not occurred before the bride was handed over to her husband?

We may never have complete answers to such questions, since archeology only provides some of the data and ancient writings, such as the Old Testament, were rewritten so many times, each time to more firmly establish, and sanctify, male control.[19] But what we do have is far more critical in this time when the old patriarchal system is leading us ever closer to global holocaust. This is the knowledge that it was not always this way: there are viable alternatives that may not only offer us survival but also a far, far better world.

QUESTIONS FOR DISCUSSION

1. What is the "Big Discovery" (par. 1) theory? What is one concrete reason that this theory is not convincing?
2. What was, according to Eisler, one of the most remarkable things about the Neolithic ruin Catal Huyuk?
3. Why did many early archaeologists fail to understand the significance of goddess-oriented artifacts?
4. Where does Eisler indicate our male-dominated, warlike heritage comes from, and what did it replace?
5. If ancient Indo-Europeans worshipped a divine goddess who was closely associated with nature and the giving of life, why is the Western world now almost entirely dominated by the worship of a male, father-like deity?

[18]See, for example, R. Eisler, *The Blade and the Chalice*; R. Eisler, "Violence and Male-Dominance: The Ticking Time Bomb," *Humanities in Society*, Winter-Spring 1984, 7:1/2:3–18; R. Eisler and D. Loye, "The 'Failure' of Liberalism: A Reassessment of Ideology from a New Feminine-Masculine Perspective," *Political Psychology*, 1983, 4:2:375–391; R. Eisler, "Beyond Feminism: The Gylan Future," *Alternative Futures*, Spring-Summer 1981, 4:2/3:122–134. [Au.]
[19]Ibid. [Au.]

6. What does Eisler suggest is the danger of a male-dominated, warlike society in the twentieth century?
7. What is matriarchy? How does the early society described by Eisler differ from a matriarchal society?
8. In your own words, explain what type of modern society we would be if it were based on goddess worship.

MARY DALY
After the Death of God the Father

Mary Daly is a professor of theology at Boston College, and has written widely about issues of women and organized religion, and the spiritual dimension of the women's liberation movement. Her books include The Church and the Second Sex *(1968),* Beyond God the Father: Toward a Philosophy of Women's Liberation *(1973),* Gyn/Ecology: The Metaethics of Radical Feminism *(1979), and* Pure Lust: Elemental Feminist Philosophy *(1984). In the selection here, reprinted from* Beyond God the Father, *Daly discusses the challenge to organized religion of going beyond the image of deity as a patriarch (a male head of a family or tribe), and some of the reasons for going beyond such an image.*

The first step in the elevation of women under all systems of religion is to convince them that the great Spirit of the Universe is in no way responsible for any of these absurdities.

—ELIZABETH CADY STANTON

The biblical and popular image of God as a great patriarch in heaven, rewarding and punishing according to his mysterious and seemingly arbitrary will, has dominated the imagination of millions over thousands of years. The symbol of the Father God, spawned in the human imagination and sustained as plausible by patriarchy, has in turn rendered service to this type of society by making its mechanisms for the oppression of women appear right and fitting. If God in "his" heaven is a father ruling "his" people, then it is in the "nature" of things and according to divine plan and the order of the universe that society be male-dominated.

Within this context a mystification of roles takes place: the husband dominating his wife represents God "himself." The images and values of a given society have been projected into the realm of dogmas and "Articles of Faith," and these in turn justify the social structures which have given rise to them and which sustain their plausibility. The belief system becomes hardened and objectified, seeming to have an unchangeable independent existence and validity of its own. It resists social change that would rob it of its plausibility. Despite the vicious circle, however, change can occur in society, and ideologies can die, though they die hard.

As the women's movement begins to have its effect upon the fabric of society, transforming it from patriarchy into something that never existed before—into a diarchal situation that is radically new—it can become the greatest single challenge to the major religions of the world, Western and Eastern. Beliefs and values that have held sway for thousands of years will be questioned as never before. This revolution may well be also the greatest single hope for survival of spiritual consciousness on this planet. . . .

THE INADEQUATE GOD OF POPULAR PREACHING

The image of the divine Father in heaven has not always been conducive to humane behavior, as any perceptive reader of history knows. The often cruel behavior of Christians toward unbelievers and toward dissenters among themselves suggests a great deal not only about the values of the society dominated by that image, but also about how that image itself functions in relation to behavior. There has been a basic ambivalence in the image of the heavenly patriarch—a split between the God of love and the jealous God who represents the collective power of "his" chosen people. As historian Arnold Toynbee has indicated, this has reflected and perpetuated a double standard of behavior.[1] Without debating the details of his historical analysis, the insight is available on an experiential level. The character of Vito Corleone in *The Godfather* is a vivid illustration of the marriage of tenderness and violence so intricately blended in the patriarchal ideal. The worshippers of the loving Father may in a sense love their neighbors, but in fact the term applies only to those within a restricted and unstable circumference, and these worshippers can "justifiably" be intolerant and fanatic persecutors of those outside the sacred circle.

How this God operates is illustrated in contemporary American civil religion.[2] In one of the White House sermons given during the first term of Richard Nixon, Rabbi Louis Finkelstein expressed the hope that a future historian may say "that in the period of great trials and great tribulations, the finger of God pointed to Richard Milhous Nixon, giving the vision and the wisdom to save the world and civilization; and also to open the way for our country to realize the good that the twentieth century offers mankind."[3] Within this context, as Charles Henderson has shown, God is an American and Nixon is "his" annointed one.[4] The preachers carefully selected for the White House sermons stress that this nation is "under God." The

---

[1] Arnold Toynbee, *Christianity among the Religions of the World* (New York: Charles Scribner's Sons, 1957), p. 19.
[2] See Robert N. Bellah, "Civil Religion in America," *Daedalus*, XCVI (Winter 1967), pp. 1–21. Bellah points out that the inauguration of a president is an important ceremonial event in American civil religion. It involves religious legitimation of the highest political authority. At Nixon's inauguration in 1973, Cardinal Cooke of New York was reported to have used the expression "heavenly Father" approximately seven times (conversation with Janice Raymond, who counted, January 20, 1973).
[3] Rabbi Louis Finkelstein, in *White House Sermons*, edited by Ben Hibbs (New York: Harper and Row, 1972), p. 68. This sermon was delivered June 29, 1969. Similar sentiments have been expressed by the Rev. John McLaughlin, S.J., "the Catholic Billy Graham." See *National Catholic Reporter*, October 6, 1972, p. 9.
[4] Charles Henderson, *The Nixon Theology* (New York: Harper and Row, 1972). See also Henderson's article "The [Social] Gospel according to 1) Richard Nixon 2) George McGovern," *Commonweal*, XCVI (September 29, 1972), pp. 518–25.

logical conclusion is that its policies are right. Under God, the President becomes a Christ figure. In 1969, the day the astronauts would set foot on the moon, and when the President was preparing to cross the Pacific "in search of peace," one of these preachers proclaimed:

> And my hope for mankind is strengthened in the knowledge that our intrepid President himself will soon go into orbit, reaching boldly for the moon of peace. God grant that he, too, may return in glory and that countless millions of prayers that follow him shall not have been in vain.[5]

A fundamental dynamic of this "theology" was suggested by one of Nixon's speech writers, Ray Price, who wrote:

> Selection of a President has to be an act of faith. . . . This faith isn't achieved by reason: it's achieved by charisma, by a feeling of trust. . . .[6]

Price also argued that the campaign would be effective only "if we can get people to make the *emotional* leap, or what theologians call 'leap of faith.'"[7] This is, of course, precisely the inauthentic leap that Camus labeled as philosophical suicide. It is the suicide demanded by a civil religion in which "God," the Savior-President, and "our nation" more or less merge. When the "leap" is made, it is possible simply not to see what the great God-Father and his annointed one are actually doing. Among the chosen ones are scientists and professors who design perverse methods of torture and death such as flechette pellets that shred the internal organs of "the enemy" and other comparable inhumane "anti-personnel" weapons. Also among the elect are politicians and priests who justify and bestow their blessing upon the system that perpetrates such atrocities. "Under God" are included the powerful industrialists who are making the planet uninhabitable.

Sophisticated thinkers, of course, have never intellectually identified God with a Superfather in heaven. Nevertheless it is important to recognize that even when very abstract conceptualizations of God are formulated in the mind, images survive in the imagination in such a way that a person can function on two different and even apparently contradictory levels at the same time. Thus one can speak of God as spirit and at the same time imagine "him" as belonging to the male sex.[8] Such primitive images can profoundly affect conceptualizations which appear to be very refined and abstract. So too the Yahweh of the future, so cherished by the theology of hope, comes through on an imaginative level as exclusively a He-God, and it is consistent with this that theologians of hope have attempted to develop a political theology which takes no explicit cognizance of the devastation wrought by sexual politics.

---

[5]Dr. Paul S. Smith, in *White House Sermons*, pp. 82–83.
[6]Cited in Henderson, *The Nixon Theology*, p. 175.
[7]*Ibid.*, p. 176.
[8]This is exemplified in a statement of John L. McKenzie, S.J., in *The Two Edged Sword* (New York: Bruce, 1956), pp. 93–94: "God is of course masculine, but not in the sense of sexual distinction. . . ."

The widespread conception of the "Supreme Being" as an entity distinct from this world but controlling it according to plan and keeping human beings in a state of infantile subjection has been a not too subtle mask of the divine patriarch. The Supreme Being's plausibility and that of the static worldview which accompanies this projection has of course declined, at least among the more sophisticated, as Nietzsche prophesied. This was a projection grounded in specifically patriarchal societal structures and sustained as subjectively real by the usual processes of producing plausibility such as preaching, religious indoctrination, and cult. The sustaining power of the social structure has been eroded by a number of developments in recent history, including the general trend toward democratization of society and the emergence of technology. However, it is the women's movement which appears destined to play the key role in the overthrow of such oppressive elements in traditional theism, precisely because it strikes at the source of the societal dualism that is reflected in traditional beliefs. It presents a growing threat to the plausibility of the inadequate popular "God" not so much by attacking "him" as by leaving "him" behind. Few major feminists display great interest in institutional religion. Yet this disinterest can hardly be equated with lack of spiritual consciousness. Rather, in our present experience the woman-consciousness is being wrenched free to find its own religious expression.

It can legitimately be pointed out that the Judeo-Christian tradition is not entirely bereft of elements that can foster intimations of transcendence. Yet the liberating potential of these elements is choked off in the surrounding atmosphere of the images, ideas, values, and structures of patriarchy. The social change coming from radical feminism has the potential to bring about a more acute and widespread perception of qualitative differences between the conceptualizations of "God" and of the human relationship to God which have been oppressive in their connotations, and the kind of language that is spoken from and to the rising woman-consciousness.

QUESTIONS FOR DISCUSSION

1. In the quote at the beginning of the text, what concrete characteristics of society might Elizabeth Cady Stanton be referring to by the words "these absurdities"?
2. What is the main point of Daly's argument about the social effects of belief in a "Father God" (par. 1)?
3. Who is her intended audience? What might her purpose be in writing this essay?
4. What evidence does Daly use to support her argument? Is her position supported by logic and reason, by an appeal to emotion, or both? Give examples.
5. Daly suggests that the women's movement is transforming patriarchy into "a diarchal situation that is radically new" (par. 3). What does this mean? Cite examples from your own experience and/or from the media.
6. What parallels might you draw between feminist determination to reshape male images of deity and the Zulu tribe's determination in the text "A Black Messiah: Acts of the Nazarites" (p. 499) to reshape Caucasian images of a spiritual savior?

PHYLLIS SCHLAFLY
The Power of the Positive Woman

Phyllis Schlafly received an M.A. in political science from Harvard University and a J.D. from Washington University Law School. She is a member of the Illinois Bar, a popular lecturer, and has written or edited a number of books, including Child Abuse in the Classroom, Pornography's Victims, Safe—Not Sorry, A Choice Not an Echo, *and* The Power of the Positive Woman. *In this selection from the latter, Schlafly takes an opposing standpoint to writers like Mary Daly who seek to change the roles and status of women in modern society. Schlafly grounds her position in a firm belief in the major elements of the Judeo-Christian tradition. Her message is more than just religious, however; it is a mixture of religious belief, patriotic devotion, maintenance of established male/female social roles, and political fervor. Her argumentative style juxtaposes words and phrases such as "the Positive Woman," "America, the greatest country in the world," and "the American family" with images of "lesbian rights," "communist enemies," and "the destructive goal of equality."*

The Bible tells us, "Where there is no vision, the people perish." The Positive Woman must have a vision for America that gives perspective to her goals, her hopes for the future, and her commitment to her country. The Positive Woman starts with the knowledge that America is the greatest country in the world and that it is her task to do her part to keep it that way.

By common consent over nearly two centuries, the day Americans celebrate as our most important national patriotic anniversary is the Fourth of July. The bicentennial of our nation, July 4, 1976, was not the anniversary of the signing of the United States Constitution, or the ratification of the Bill of Rights, or the start or finish of the Revolutionary War—important as all these events were. The Fourth of July is the anniversary of the adoption of the Declaration of Independence on July 4, 1776.

This basic document of our national existence is the most perfect orientation of man to God and government outside of Holy Scripture. It is the most important document in American history and the most inspired writing in world history that ever flowed from the hand of man alone. Here is why:

1. The Declaration of Independence is the official and unequivocal recognition by the American people of their belief and faith in God. It is a religious document from its first sentence to its last. It affirms God's existence as a "self-evident" truth that requires no further discussion or debate. The nation it creates is God's country. The rights it defends are God given. The actions of its signers are God inspired. There are four references to God—God as Creator of all men, God as the Supreme Judge, God as the source of all rights, God as our patron and protector.

2. The Declaration of Independence declares that each of us is created equal. This means equal before God. It does not mean that all men are born with equal abilities, and so on, as some try to claim. Nor does it mean that all men can be

made equal, as Communist dogma alleges. Obviously and realistically, and as your own individuating fingerprints prove, each of God's creatures is unequal and different from every other person who has ever lived or ever will live on this earth.

3. The Declaration of Independence proclaims that life and liberty are unalienable gifts of God—natural rights—which no person or government can rightfully take away.

4. The Declaration of Independence proclaims that the purpose of government is to secure these unalienable individual rights and that government derives its powers from the consent of the governed. For the first time in history, government was reduced from master to servant.

The Declaration of Independence comes to us after 200 years in all its pristine purity. Whereas the United States Constitution has had to suffer the slings and arrows of some outrageous federal court interpretations and judicial distortions, neither the meddling judges nor the bungling bureaucrats have confused or distorted the Declaration of Independence. As the Declaration was in the beginning, it is now and ever shall be because it proclaims truth and facts that are not subject to change or amendment.

The Supreme Court that banned God from the public schools has not been able to censor Him out of the Declaration of Independence. The Supreme Court has forbidden public school children to declare their dependence upon God, but the Declaration of Independence pledges the firm reliance of the American people forever on the continued protection of God's Divine Providence.

After thus orienting our nation toward God's law, the Founding Fathers then gave us the United States Constitution—"the most wonderful work ever struck off at a given time by the brain and purpose of man." It provides the foundation for a political system that restrains the power of government through the separation of powers between the federal government and the separate states, and then among the three branches of the federal government, and also for an economic system based on private property, individual enterprise, and the use of government to maintain a free competitive system. The result has been that America has enjoyed more freedom and more material benefits than any nation in history.[1]

[1] Comparisons of standards of living and purchasing power between the United States and foreign countries usually leave me wondering about their validity because of the obvious statistical barrier posed by the different money systems. The international journal *To the Point* (February 9, 1976, p. 23) published a meaningful comparison of eight major countries by showing the buying power of wage earners in different occupations expressed in the working time required to buy common consumer items. The resulting chart is a blockbuster that provides new proof of the superiority of the American system in providing more material goods to more people than any system in history.

Compare, for example, the purchase of twenty-two pounds of sugar by a nurse. An American nurse can buy the sugar with one hour of work, an English nurse with four hours, seventeen minutes, a Japanese nurse with four hours, fifty minutes, a Polish nurse with six hours, forty-eight minutes, and a Russian nurse with sixteen hours.

What if you are a skilled laborer trying to buy a pair of men's shoes? An American can buy them with six hours of work, a Japanese with ten hours, an Englishman with fifteen hours, and a Russian with forty-three hours, or an entire week.

Now take the case of an engineer buying a man's suit. In America, it takes him twelve hours, in Japan thirty-four hours. A Russian engineer has to work 162 hours, or about a full month.

Anyone who wants to exchange our American economic system for socialism had better prepare himself for an abrupt reduction in standard of living caused by having to work up to sixteen times longer for ordinary consumer necessities.

There are those today who espouse the notion that government can solve all problems by allowing bureaucratic experts to spend more and more of our money. There is no evidence to justify this policy. Progress has been the least in those areas where government has traditionally undertaken the job, namely, the postal service, public schools, and garbage collection. Progress has been the greatest in those areas where there has been private enterprise without government interference, such as automobiles, airplanes, and computers. There is no ceiling on man's ingenuity and resourcefulness to cope with problems—so long as we operate in the American climate of freedom. The "can do" philosophy that carved our great nation out of the wilderness can build a future brighter than any of us could ever dream.

Those who are inclined to go the route of the welfare state rather than private enterprise should take a good look at what has happened to Great Britain. For the last thirty years, Britain has had nationalized electricity, gas, water, coal, steel, railroads, and long-distance trucks and buses. Because of the absence of competition, prices in nationalized industries increased much faster than those in private industries. "Bringing coals to Newcastle" used to be an expression that described England's unlimited abundance of that essential national resource. Yet after the coal mines were nationalized, the inefficiency was so great that England had to import coal.

In housing, the social planners argued that tenants should be protected from greedy landlords and that rent control would fix a "just price" for all. The result of artificially low rents is the virtual elimination of privately owned apartments or rooms to rent. Landlords sell their property whenever tenants leave because the rent does not cover the costs, and the law makes it difficult if not impossible to remove even the most objectionable tenants. Those who cannot afford to own their own homes, or whom circumstances compel to take temporary housing, must resort to public housing, which is plagued with muggings, vandalism, noise, and inconvenience.

Socialized medicine has resulted in long queues for medical care, long waiting lists to get into hospital beds (the waiting list for an operation to have eye cataracts removed is two years), and the emigration of many experienced doctors and specialists, while more and more money each year is spent on administration.

About 64 percent of the gross national product is taken by the British government. The progressive income tax rate goes up to 98 percent. The average British worker pays one-third of his wages for the welfare state. British socialism is a spectacular economic failure, and the proof is in the pound. Since 1971 when the pound was allowed to "float" against other currencies, it has suffered an effective devaluation of 45 percent.

England has been a model for America in many ways. The Positive Woman will do all she can to make sure that we do not follow England's leadership into socialism and bankruptcy. Yet, in the United States, government is taking more and more of our personal income. In 1930, government on all levels took 15 percent of the personal income of Americans. By 1950, the government bite of our personal income had risen to 32 percent. By 1976, the government's hand in our pocketbook was taking 44 percent. At the current rate of increase, by the mid-1980s, government will be taking 54 percent of our personal income.

The Positive Woman will also reject socialism because of its effect on the family through its pursuit of the destructive goal of equality. The connection was explained in a book edited by Aleksandr Solzhenitsyn:

> The basic propositions of the socialist world view have often been proclaimed: the abolition of private property, religion and the family. One of the principles which is not so often represented as fundamental, though it is no less widespread, is the demand for *equality, the destruction of the hierarchy into which society has arranged itself*. The idea of equality in socialist ideology has a special character, which is particularly important for an understanding of socialism. In the more consistent socialist systems equality is understood in so radical a way that it leads to a negation of the existence of any genuine differences between individuals: "equality" is turned into "equivalence."[2]

It will do no good, however, to have the greatest material prosperity in the world if we do not meet the challenge of the nuclear age posed by the tremendous buildup of military power by the Soviet Union. Since 1962, the year of the Cuban Missile Crisis, the Soviets have built the mightiest arsenal of weapons of destruction the world has ever known—weapons that have only one utility, the destruction or blackmail of the United States.[3]

The paramount question confronting America is: What is our national response to this challenge? Are we building the nuclear weapons we need to enable us to live in freedom and independence in the face of the Soviet threat? Make no mistake about it, our freedom of religion, speech, and press, our independence as a nation, and our entire Judeo-Christian civilization are possible only in a world defended by America's armed forces with their nuclear weapons. Without the superiority of American defenses over every potential aggressor, there can be no freedom, independence, or civilization as we know it.

If we want to hang on to the precious vitality that built our great nation, we must teach our young people that the password of freedom is Patrick Henry's eloquent "Give me liberty or give me death"—not the plea of the handout hunter, "Gimme, gimme, gimme." If we want our independence to endure, we must teach our young people to reject the lure of the Soviet appeasers who cry, "Better Red than dead"—and instead to kindle the patriotic fervor of Nathan Hale, the young teacher who said, "I regret that I have but one life to give for my country."

The Positive Woman must be a patriot and a defender of our Judeo-Christian civilization. She, therefore, must support the legislation, the legislators, and the funding necessary to defend the values of home and country against attack by aggressors who respect neither.

---

[2]Igor Shafarevich, "Socialism in Our Past and Future," published in Aleksandr Solzhenitsyn, *From Under the Rubble* (New York: Bantam Books, 1976), p. 51.
[3]The Soviet military threat and the inadequacy of the United States response have been copiously documented in the books by Phyllis Schlafly and Rear Admiral Chester Ward, USN (Ret.): *The Gravediggers* (Alton, Ill.: Pere Marquette Press, 1964), *Strike from Space* (New York: Devin-Adair Co., 1965), *The Betrayers* (Alton, Ill.: Pere Marquette Press, 1968), *Kissinger on the Couch* (New Rochelle, N.Y.: Arlington House, 1975), and *Ambush at Vladivostok* (Alton, Ill.: Pere Marquette Press, 1976).

The reason why the pressure groups pushing women's lib, more federal control, and a weakening of American military defenses have had significant successes is not that they have more persuasive arguments, not that they have history on their side, and not even that they have the support of the majority of voters. Indeed, they have none of these. The reason they have been winning is that they have developed skills in the techniques of: (1) the legislative and election process, (2) the litigating of social change through the courts by the use of lawyer specialists, (3) the placing of their agents and sympathizers in the media and the educational system, and (4) the use of *other people's money* through tax funds, tax-exempt foundations, and other tax-exempt organizations.

The Positive Woman accepts her obligation, insofar as she is able, to develop the skills and the techniques to safeguard the values of God, family, and country. In the words of Saint James, she becomes a doer of the word, and not merely a hearer:

> Be ye doers of the word, and not hearers only, deceiving your own selves.
>
> For if any be a hearer of the word, and not a doer, he is like unto a man beholding his natural face in a glass; for he beholdeth himself, and goeth his way, and straightway forgetteth what manner of man he was.
>
> But who so looketh unto the perfect law of liberty, and continueth therein, he being not a forgetful hearer, but a doer of the word, this man shall be blessed in his deed.[4]

Is a national vision too broad in scope for the average American woman? Are the problems of our military defense and private enterprise economics too complex or too controversial? Time and again, God has given women the mission to save their country. . . .

Here is a starting checklist of goals that can be restored to America if Positive Women will apply their dedicated efforts:

1. The right of a woman to be a full-time wife and mother and to have this right recognized by laws that obligate her husband to provide the primary financial support and a home for her and their children.
2. The responsibility of parents (not the government) for the care of preschool children.
3. The right of parents to insist that the schools:
   a. permit voluntary prayer,
   b. teach the "fourth R," right and wrong, according to the precepts of Holy Scriptures,
   c. use textbooks that do not offend the religious and moral values of the parents,
   d. use textbooks that honor the family, monogamous marriage, woman's role as wife and mother, and man's role as provider and protector,
   e. teach such basic educational skills as reading and arithmetic before time and money are spent on frills,

---

[4]James 1:22–25.

     f. permit children to attend school in their own neighborhood, and

     g. separate the sexes for gym classes, athletic practice and competition, and academic and vocational classes, if so desired.

4. The right of employers to give job preference (where qualifications are equal) to a wage earner supporting dependents.

5. The right of a woman engaged in physical-labor employment to be protected by laws and regulations that respect the physical differences and different family obligations of men and women.

6. The right to equal opportunity in employment and education for all persons regardless of race, creed, sex, or national origin.

7. The right to have local governments prevent the display of printed or pictorial materials that degrade women in a pornographic, perverted, or sadistic manner.

8. The right to defend the institution of the family by according certain rights to husbands and wives that are not given to those choosing immoral lifestyles.

9. The right to life of all innocent persons from conception to natural death.

10. The right of citizens to live in a community where state and local government and judges maintain law and order by a system of justice under due process and punishment that is swift and certain.

11. The right of society to protect itself by designating different roles for men and women in the armed forces and police and fire departments, where necessary.

12. The right of citizens to have the federal government adequately provide for the common defense against aggression by any other nation.

All things are possible to those who take as their text:

They that wait upon the Lord shall renew their strength; they shall mount up with wings as eagles; they shall run, and not be weary; and they shall walk, and not faint.[5]

QUESTIONS FOR DISCUSSION

1. Compare Schlafly's purpose and her intended audience to Mary Daly's article "After the Death of God the Father" (p. 556). In what ways are they the same?

2. What is the main point of Schlafly's argument about the role of the Positive Woman? Would Daly agree with this point?

3. Using the language of Schlafly's text, construct an image of the God that she constantly refers to. How would Daly react to this image of both deity and of social organization?

4. Outline the things Schlafly feels the Positive Woman will do to maintain Schlafly's image of what America should be.

5. Schlafly acknowledges that there are many Americans who do not agree with her ideas. What kind of language does she use to portray these opponents?

[5]Isaiah 40:31.

6. Early in the essay, Schlafly argues that "Progress (on social issues) has been the greatest in those areas . . . without government interference" (par. 11). In what ways is this position consistent or inconsistent with the role of government implied in her checklist of goals for America at the end of the essay? With the separation of church and state?
7. Schlafly often makes use of lists to support her positions. How does this affect you as a reader?
8. Compare Schlafly's basic argument to the argument in Voltaire's "Of Universal Tolerance" (p. 581).

HARVEY COX
Understanding Islam: No More Holy Wars

Harvey Cox is an ordained Baptist minister and professor of church and society in the Divinity School of Harvard University. He has written a number of books on the relation between theology and society at large, including The Secular City *and* Religion in the Secular City: Toward a Postmodern Theology. *He also has published articles on theology and society in such magazines as* Commonweal, Harpers, Life, Playboy, Theology Today, *and* Christian Scholar. *In this selection, originally published in the* Atlantic Monthly, *Cox discusses the intolerance among Christians towards the Islamic faith. He emphasizes the similarities between these two world religions, calling for an end to the Christian/Islam holy war through acceptance and understanding.*

> *No cask without an end stave or a head*
> *E'er gaped so wide as one shade I beheld,*
> *Cloven from chin to where the wind is voided.*
> *Between his legs his entrails hung in coils;*
> *The vitals were exposed to view, and too*
> *That sorry paunch which changes food to filth.*
> *While I stood all absorbed in watching him*
> *He looked at me and stretched his breast apart,*
> *Saying: "Behold, how I split myself!*
> *Behold, how mutilated is Mahomet!*
> *In front of me the weeping Ali goes,*
> *His face cleft through from forelock to chin;*
> *And all the others that you see about*
> *Fomenters were of discord and of schism:*
> *And that is why they are so gashed asunder."*
> Dante, *Inferno*, Canto 28

Odious Western images of Muhammad and of Islam have a long and embarrassingly honorable lineage. Dante places the prophet in that circle of hell reserved for those stained by the sin he calls *seminator di scandalo e di scisma*. As a schismatic,

Muhammad's fitting punishment is to be eternally chopped in half from his chin to his anus, spilling entrails and excrement at the door of Satan's stronghold. His loyal disciple Ali, whose sins of division were presumably on a lesser scale, is sliced only "from forelock to chin." There is scandal, too. A few lines later, Dante has Muhammad send a warning to a contemporary priest whose sect was said to advocate the community of goods and who was also suspected of having a mistress. The admonition cautions the errant padre that the same fate awaits him if he does not quickly mend his ways. Already in Dante's classic portrait, we find the image of the Moslem linked with revolting violence, distorted doctrine, a dangerous economic idea, and the tantalizing hint of illicit sensuality.

Nothing much has changed in the 600 years since. Even the current wave of interest in Eastern spirituality among many American Christians has not done much to improve the popular estimate of Islam. It is fashionable now in the West to find something of value in Buddhism or Hinduism, to peruse the *Sutras*[1] or the *Bhagavad Gita*,[2] to attend a lecture by Swami Muktananda or the Dalai Lama, even to try a little yoga or meditation. But Americans in general and Christians in particular seem unable to find much to admire in Islam. As G. H. Hansen observes, with only a modicum of hyperbole, in his book *Militant Islam*, the mental picture most Westerners hold of this faith of 750 million people is one of ". . . strange bearded men with burning eyes, hieratic figures in robes and turbans, blood dripping from the amputated hands and from the striped backs of malefactors, and piles of stones barely concealing the battered bodies of adulterous couples." Lecherous, truculent, irrational, cruel, conniving, excitable, dreaming about lascivious heavens while hypocritically enforcing oppressive legal codes: the stereotype of the Moslem is only partially softened by a Kahlil Gibran who puts it into sentimental doggerel or a Rudolph Valentino who does it with zest and good humor.

There is, of course, one important exception to the West's rejection of the religious value of Islam. This exception's most visible representatives have been Muhammad Ali and the late Malcolm X. Most Americans who seem genuinely drawn to the call of the minaret are blacks. But given the racial myopia that continues to affect almost all American cultural perceptions, this exception has probably deepened the distrust most white Christians feel toward Islam. The dominant image was summed up brilliantly in a Boston newspaper's cartoon showing a Moslem seated in prayer. Over his head the balloon contained one word: "Hate!"

This captious caricaturing of Moslems and Arabs is not confined to the popular mentality. In his *Orientalism*, Edward Said describes a study published in 1975 of Arabs in American textbooks that demonstrates how prejudices continue to be spread through respectable sources. One textbook, for example, sums up Islam in the following manner:

> The Moslem religion, called Islam, began in the seventh century. It was started by a wealthy businessman of Arabia, called Muhammad. He claimed that he was a prophet. He found followers among the other Arabs. He told them they were picked to rule the world.

[1] **Sutras** Short written statement of religious rules or laws in Buddhism and Brahmanism. [Ed. note.]

This passage is, unfortunately, not atypical. Although phrased with some degree of restraint, it coheres all too well with the popular medieval picture of Muhammad as a sly trickster or the current comic-book depictions of the sated, power-mad Arab. Moreover, Dante's unflattering portrait of the prophet was rooted in traditions that existed long before his time. These primal shadowgraphs have notoriously long half-lives, and they continue to darken our capacity to understand Islam to this day. . . .

. . . Along with study and analysis, a kind of cultural archaeology or even a collective psychoanalysis may be necessary if we are to leave Dante's Inferno behind and live in peace with our Moslem neighbors on the planet Earth. The question is, How can Westerners, and Christians in particular, begin to cut through the maze of distorting mirrors and prepare the ground for some genuine encounter with Moslems?

The first thing we probably need to recognize is that the principal source of the acrimony underlying the Christian–Moslem relationship is a historical equivalent of sibling rivalry. Christians somehow hate to admit that in many ways their faith stands closer to Islam than to any other world religion. Indeed, that may be the reason Muhammad was viewed for centuries in the West as a charlatan and an imposter. The truth is, theologically speaking at least, both faiths are the offspring of an earlier revelation through the Law and the Prophets to the people of Israel. Both honor the Virgin Mary and Jesus of Nazareth. Both received an enormous early impetus from an apostle—Paul for Christianity and Muhammad for Islam—who translated a particularistic vision into a universal faith. The word "Allah" (used in the core formula of Islam: "There is no God but Allah and Muhammad is his prophet") is not an exclusively Moslem term at all. It is merely the Arabic word for God, and is used by Arabic Christians when they refer to the God of Christian faith.

There is nothing terribly surprising about these similarities since Muhammad, whose preaching mission did not begin until he reached forty, was subjected to considerable influence from Christianity during his formative years and may have come close—according to some scholars—to becoming an Abyssinian Christian. As Arend van Leeuwen points out in his thoughtful treatment of Islam in *Christianity in World History*, "The truth is that when Islam was still in the initial stages of its development, there was nothing likely to prevent the new movement from being accepted as a peculiar version of Arabian Christianity." Maybe the traditional Christian uneasiness with Islam is that it seems just a little *too* similar. We sense the same aversion we might feel toward a twin brother who looks more like us than we want him to and whose habits remind us of some of the things we like least in ourselves.

The metaphor of a brother, or perhaps a cousin, is entirely germane. Muhammad considered himself to be in a direct line with the great biblical prophets and with Jesus. The title he preferred for himself was *alnabi al-ummi*, the "prophet of the nations" (or of the "gentiles"). He believed he was living proof that the God who had called and used previous prophets such as Abraham and Job, neither of whom was Jewish, could do the same thing again. Later on, Moslem theologians liked to trace the genealogy of Muhammad back to Hagar, the bondwoman spouse of Abraham. The Old Testament story says that Hagar's giving birth to Ishmael stirred

---

[2]**Bhagavad Gita** The most important segment of Hindu scripture and the best source for a knowledge of Hindu philosophy on the nature of deity. [Ed. note.]

up such jealousy between her and Sarah, Abraham's first wife and the mother of Isaac, that Sarah persuaded Abraham to banish the bondwoman and her child into the desert. There Hagar gave up hope and left the child under a shrub to die. But God heard the child's weeping, created a well of water in the desert to save them both, and promised Hagar that from her son also, as from Isaac, He would "create a great nation." According to the symbolism of this old saga, the Jews and the Arabs (and by extension all Moslems) are the common offspring of Abraham (called "Ibrahim" in Arabic). This makes Christians and Moslems cousins, at least by legendary lineage.

The similarity between Christians and Moslems does not stop with religious genealogy. The actual elements of the Koran's message—faith, fasting, alms, prayer, and pilgrimage—all have Christian analogues. Despite its firm refusal to recognize any divine being except God (which is the basis for its rejection of Christ's divinity), Islam appears sometimes to be a pastiche of elements from disparate forms of Christianity molded into a potent unity. Take the Calvinist emphasis on faith in an omnipotent deity, the pietistic cultivation of daily personal prayer, the medieval teaching on charity, the folk-Catholic fascination with pilgrimage, and the monastic practice of fasting, and you have all the essential ingredients of Islam. All, that is, except the confluence of forces which, through the personality of Muhammad and the movement he set off, joined these elements in the white heat of history and fused them into a coherent faith of compelling attractiveness.

Like Paul, who said his apostleship was to both Jews and gentiles, Muhammad believed his mission was twofold. He felt called by God to bring the law and the Gospel to the heretofore neglected peoples of Arabia. But he also felt he had a mission *to* those very peoples—Christians and Jews (whom he called "peoples of the book")—*from* whom the original message of salvation had come. In one important respect, therefore, Muhammad's mission was different from St. Paul's. Since Muhammad carried on his preaching in the early decades of the seventh century, he not only had to deal with a Judaism he considered corrupted (as Paul had too); he also had to face an even more corrupted form of Christianity. Fortunately for St. Paul, since the Christian movement was only a decade or so old when he lived, he had to cope only with a few legalizers and gnostics. The infant Church had not yet tasted the corruption that comes, perhaps inevitably, from power and longevity. From a certain Christian perspective, Muhammad was as much a reformer as an apostle. A prophet of the gentiles, he also saw himself as a purifier of the faith of all the "peoples of the book," Christians and Jews, calling them away from the ornate and decadent versions of the faith they had fallen into and back to its simple essence, at least as he understood it. There is always something of this urge to simplify, to return *ad fontes*, in any reformer. And Muhammad was no exception. . . .

No discussion of the relations of Moslems and Christians can proceed very far without raising the parallel question of the equally long and similarly vexed interaction of Moslems and Jews. The Jewish historian S. D. Goitein is the leading scholar in the study of what he calls the "symbiosis" between Jews and Arabs. Now at the Institute for Advanced Study in Princeton, after having taught at the Hebrew University of Jerusalem, Goitein has spent a lifetime probing Moslem religious literature, the medieval Geniza (documents written in Hebrew characters but in the Arabic language), and the fascinating histories of the so-called Oriental Jewish communities—those of the Arab and Moslem worlds. His *From the Land of Sheba* is an anthology of Yemenite literature. It would be hard to find a more reliable guide to this intricate area.

Goitein believes that Islam is actually far closer to Judaism than to Christianity in its core ideas. In taking this position, he joins a debate that has been going on for years (the other side contending that the similarity with Christianity is more important). Goitein bases his case on the obvious fact that both Islam and Judaism are religions of the Holy Law, and that Moslem law is in many respects similar to the Jewish Halakah, which he calls its "older sister." Both therefore differ, at least in this respect, from Christianity, which, with its emphasis on grace, has always harbored a certain suspicion of religious law (even though Christian theologians have managed to spin out yards of it over the years).

Goitein's "sister" image of the bond between Islam and Judaism should not be surprising when one bears in mind the saying, attributed to Muhammad, "You will follow the traditions of those who preceded you span by span and cubit by cubit— so closely that you will go after them even if they creep into the hole of a lizard." This colorful advice takes on even more significance in light of the fact that there were large Jewish settlements in the city of al-Medina, the birthplace of the first Moslem community, and that the biographers of the prophet almost all agree that these communities, far from being an obstacle to the spread of Islam, were in fact wondrous evidence of Allah's merciful and providential preparation of the people for a monotheistic faith. As with Christianity, the early years of Islam seem in retrospect to have promised mostly fraternal—or in this case sororial—congeniality with Judaism. But again, the roiling history of Jewish and Islamic peoples has often turned familial ties into tribal vendettas. Must it always be so?

In his informative book *Jews and Arabs: Their Contacts Through the Ages*, Goitein does what only a seasoned scholar ever dares to do. He compresses eons of history into one volume, risks a few well-grounded generalizations, and even hazards some guesses about the future. He divides the millennia-long give-and-take between these two peoples into four periods. The first, corresponding perhaps to the Alexandrian age of the Christian–Islam story, begins before historical memory and reaches up to the sixth century A.D. and the appearance of Islam. During this early period, a critically formative one for the Jews since it saw the compilation of both the Bible and the Talmud, Goitein believes Jews and Arabs had quite similar social patterns and religious practices. He firmly rejects any notion of a common Semitic race, however, as a modern idea concocted from the misapplication of a term invented by a German scholar in 1781 to denote a group of related languages, not "races," or even peoples. The distinction is an important one. There are several examples of peoples who for a variety of historical reasons now speak a language spoken by other peoples with whom they have no ethnic consanguinity at all. Black Americans are a case in point. Likewise, Jews and Moslem Arabs are related, according to Goitein, but by history and tradition, not by race.

The period from, roughly, 500 A.D. to 1300 A.D. is Goitein's second one. He describes it as one of "creative symbiosis," in which early Islam developed in a largely Jewish environment. Although he agrees that Christian influences, coming especially from monastic groups, played some role in this primal period, he believes that Judaism was even more important, so much so that he is willing to say—with some reservations—that Islam appears to be "an Arab recast of Israel's religion." But the influence was not one-way, and the impact of Islam and the Arabic language on Jewish thought and the Hebrew language was, he adds, at least as considerable. Goitein also reminds his readers that although Jews experienced some legal disqualifications under Moslem rule, they almost always fared better than they did under Christian dominance.

Goitein's third period begins in about 1300, when the previously high-riding Arabs began to "fade out" of world history at the same time that the Oriental Jews began to fade out of Jewish history. During this phase, which lasted until about 1900, the Arab nations fell to various conquerors until the entire Arab world had become a colony of the modern West. Meanwhile Jewish religious and intellectual life flourished in Europe, while Jews living in the beleaguered Moslem world, though they nurtured a rich internal culture, shared the suffering and obscurity of their Moslem neighbors.

The present period in Goitein's scheme begins in about 1900 with the coincidental revival of Jewish and Arab cultural and national identities, both influenced by the growing nationalism of nineteenth-century Europe. Since Zionism was an almost exclusively European (and American) movement, however, it was perceived by Arabs and other Moslems more as a new Western intrusion into the East, a pattern going back at least to the Crusades, than as something essentially Jewish, at least at the beginning. But shortly after the founding of the State of Israel, Israelis had to cope with a kind of mirror image of this "intrusion" as Jewish immigrants from Arab countries, the "forgotten Jews" of the previous period, streamed into Israel, making it less "European" with every passing day. The paradox of this apparent double intrusion was illustrated recently when an Oriental Jewish scholar living in Israel complained to a visitor about all the remarks he heard from his European colleagues lamenting the "Levantizing" of Israel. "How," he asked, "can you 'Levantize' something that is already the Levant?" His comment underscores Goitein's thoughtful prophecy that since the future of Jewish–Moslem relations has everything to do with the relations between Israel and its Arab neighbors, Israel's internal policy toward its Oriental Jews and its Arab citizens will be of decisive importance. Whether or not this turns out to be true, remembering the roller-coaster history of Jewish–Moslem relations helps one not to become too depressed about the steep decline these relations have taken in recent decades. There have been downs before, and ups, and it is not impossible that the tiny minority of Arab-Israeli citizens who are also Christians might eventually be able to play a conciliatory role. Likewise, though it seems far-fetched today, the global Jewish community, with centuries of experience in the Christian and the Moslem worlds, might someday provide an essential bridge between these two faith traditions, both in some ways its offspring. In any case, whatever happens to facilitate the conversation that must go on among Christians, Jews, and Moslems is bound to benefit all three.

Jews may help, but in the final analysis, given the role our religions play in both our cultures, no real rapport between the Arabs and the West seems possible unless Christians and Moslems make a more serious effort to understand each other. Curiously, after being warned for years that our greatest enemies in the world were godless and atheistic, Americans are now faced with a challenge that emanates from profoundly religious sources. Although Islam has never accepted the dichotomy between religion and the civil polity that has arisen in the West, there can be little doubt that the present Islamic renaissance is not a deviation but an authentic expression of the elements that were there at its origin. So we are now told that, instead of atheists, we are dealing with "fanatics," or "Moslem fundamentalists." This language is not very helpful either.

Sometime soon a real conversation must begin. Perhaps the moment has come to set aside Dante, Urban II, and the rest; to remember instead the two children of Father Abraham, from both of whom God promised to make great nations; to recall that Jesus also cast his lot with the wounded and wronged of his time; to stop caricaturing the faith of Arabia's apostle; and to try to help both Christians and Moslems to recover what is common to them in a world that is just too small for any more wars, especially holy ones.

QUESTIONS FOR DISCUSSION

1. Readers of the *Atlantic Monthly* were the original audience for this essay. Discuss how Cox shapes his argument to appeal to this particular audience.
2. What does Cox perceive as the main barrier to Christians living in peace with Moslems?
3. How does Cox justify defining the Christian–Moslem conflict as a "sibling rivalry"?
4. Compare the arguments Cox uses to those in Voltaire's "Of Universal Tolerance" (p. 581). Discuss how Cox takes the general arguments in Voltaire's piece and applies them specifically to Islam.
5. Read below "The Martyr" by Murtuza Mutahery, and discuss how the concept of jihad (holy war) has helped to shape the Christian attitude toward Islam. What holy wars have been sanctified historically by the Christian religion?
6. Cox notes that the one exception to Westerners' reactions to Islam has been among American blacks. Why might Islam appeal to black Americans?
7. Explain the reference to the "current flap with the ayatollahs" (par. 11). If he were revising this piece, how might Cox expand this reference to acknowledge the rise of Islamic fundamentalism and American reaction to it since 1981?

MURTUZA MUTAHERY
The Martyr

The concepts of Islamic holy war (jihad) and martyrdom have been increasingly in the news over the past decade as political and religious strife has intensified in the Middle East. Murtuza Mutahery, an Islamic apologist, explains in this text the Islamic point of view: martyrdom for one's religion is a heroic act, and the cause for which one gives one's life—jihad—is sacred, grounded in the word of the Quran. It is important to realize that Islam originated in a time when violence and bloodshed were common outgrowths of intertribal animosities; it is not surprising, therefore, that the language of warfare found a place in the revelations of the Prophet Muhammad. It is also important to understand that the concepts of martyrdom and holy war are not peculiar to Islam; they are part of Christian history as well.

REASONS OF SANCTITY

What is the basis of the sanctity of martyrdom? It is evident that merely being killed can have no sanctity. It is not always a matter of pride. Many a death may even be a matter of disgrace.

Let us elucidate this point a bit further. We know that there are several kinds of death:

1. Natural Death: If a man dies a natural death, after completing his normal span of life, his death is considered to be an ordinary event. It is neither a matter of pride nor of shame. It is not even a matter of much sorrow.
2. Accidental Death: Death as the result of accidents or an epidemic disease like small-pox, plague, or due to such natural disasters, as an earthquake or a flood, is considered to be premature, and hence is regarded as regrettable.
3. Criminal Death: In this case, a person kills another in cold blood simply to satisfy his own passion or because he considered the victim to be his opponent or rival. There are many instances of such murders. We often read in the daily newspapers that a particular woman killed the small child of her husband because the father loved the child while the woman wanted to monopolize his attention, or that a particular man murdered the woman who refused to accept his love. Similarly, we read in history, that a particular ruler massacred all the children of another ruler, to foil the chances of any future rivalry.

   In such cases, the action of the murderer is considered to be atrociously criminal and heinous, and the person killed is regarded as a victim of aggression and tyranny, whose life has been taken in vain. The reaction which such a murder creates, is one of horror and pity. It is evident that such a death is shocking and pitiable, but it is neither praise-worthy nor a matter of pride. The victim loses his life unnecessarily, because of malice, enmity and hatred.
4. Self-murder: In this case, the death itself constitutes a crime, and hence, it is the worst kind of death. Suicidal deaths and the deaths of those who are killed in motor accidents because of their own fault, come under this category. The same is the case of the death, of those who are killed while committing a crime.
5. Martyrdom: Martyrdom is the death of a person who, in spite of being fully conscious of the risks involved, willingly faces them for the sake of a sacred cause, or, as the Holy Qur'an says, in the way of Allah.

   It has two basic elements: (a) The life is sacrificed for a cause; and (b) the sacrifice is made consciously.

   Usually in the case of martyrdom, an element of crime is involved. As far as the victim is concerned, his death is sacred, but as far as his killers are concerned, their action is a heinous crime.

Martyrdom is heroic and admirable, because it results from a voluntary, conscious and selfless action. It is the only type of death which is higher, greater and holier than life itself.

It is regrettable that most of the zakirs who narrate the story of Karbala, call Imam Husain (P) the Doyen of the Martyrs, although they have little analytical insight into the question of martyrdom. They describe the events in such a way, as though he lost his life in vain.

Many of our people mourn Imam Husain (P) for his innocence. They regret that he was a victim of the selfishness of a power-hungry man, who shed his blood, through no fault of his. Had the fact been really so simple, Imam Husain (P) would have been regarded, only as an innocent person whom great injustice was done, but he could not have been called a martyr, let alone his being the Doyen of the Martyrs.

It is not the whole story, that Imam Husain (P) was a victim of selfish designs. No doubt the perpetrators of the tragedy, committed the crime out of their selfishness, but the Imam consciously made the supreme sacrifice. His opponents wanted him to pledge his allegiance, but he, knowing fully well the consequences, chose to resist their demand. He regarded it as a great sin to remain quiet at the juncture. The history of his martyrdom, and especially his statements, bear witness to this fact.

JIHAD OR MARTYR'S RESPONSIBILITY

The sacred cause that leads to martyrdom or the giving of one's life, has become a law in Islam. It is called Jihad. This is not the occasion to discuss its nature in detail, nor to say whether it is always defensive or offensive, and, if it is only defensive, whether it is confined to the defence of the individual or at the most, of national rights, or that its scope is so wide as to include the defence of all human rights such as freedom and justice. There are other relevant questions also, such as whether the faith in the Divine Unity is or is not a part of human rights, and whether jihad is or is not basically repugnant to the right of freedom. The discussion of these questions can be both interesting and instructive, but in its proper place.

For the present, suffice it to say, that Islam is not a religion directing that should some one slap your right cheek, offer the left one to him, nor does it say: pay unto Caesar what belongs to Caesar, and unto God what belongs to God. Similarly, it is not a religion which may have no sacred social ideal, or may not consider it necessary to defend it.

The Holy Qur'an in many of its passages, has mentioned three sacred concepts, side by side. They are faith, hijrat[1] and jihad. The man of the Qur'an is a being attached to faith and detached from everything else. To save his own faith, he migrates, and to save society he carries out jihad. It will take much of the space, if we reproduce all the verses and the hadiths on this subject. Hence we will content ourselves by quoting a few sentences from the Nahj al Balagha:[2]

---

[1] Migration.
[2] The epistle written by Imam Ali (P).

> No doubt jihad is an entrance to Paradise, which Allah has opened for His chosen friends. It is the garment of piety, Allah's impenetrable armour and trust-worthy shield. He who refrains from it because he dislikes it, Allah will clothe him in a garment of humiliation and a cloak of disaster.

Jihad is a door to Paradise, but it is not open to all and sundry. Everyone is not worthy of it; Everyone is not elected to become a mujahid. Allah has opened this door for his chosen friends only. A mujahid's position is so high that we cannot call him simply Allah's friend. He is Allah's chosen friend. The Holy Qur'an says that paradise has eight doors. Evidently, it does not have so many doors to avoid over-crowding, for there is no question of it in the next world. As Allah can check the accounts of all people instantly (the Holy Qur'an says: "He is quick at reckoning"). He can also arrange their entry into Paradise through one door. There is no question of entering in turn or forming a queue there. Similarly, these doors cannot be for different classes of people for there is no class distinction in the next world. There, the people will not be classified according to their social status or profession.

There, the people will be graded and grouped together on the basis of the degree of their faith, good deeds and piety only, and a door analogous to its spiritual development in this world, will be opened to each group, for the next world is only a heavenly embodiment of this world. The door through which the mujahids and the martyrs will enter, and the portion of Paradise set aside for them, is the one which is reserved for Allah's chosen friends, who will be graced with His special favour.

Jihad is the garment of piety. The expression, garment of piety has been used by the Holy Qur'an in the Sura al A'raf. Imam Ali (P) says that Jihad is the garment of piety. Piety consists of true purity, that is, freedom from spiritual and moral pollu-tions which are rooted in selfishness, vanity and aliveness, merely for personal profit and pleasure. On this basis, a real mujahid is the most pious. He is pure because he is free from jealousy, free from vanity, free from avarice and free from stinginess. A mujahid is the purest of all the pure. He exercises complete self-nega-tion and self-sacrifice. The door which is opened to him, is different from the doors opened to others morally undefiled. That piety has various grades, can be deduced from the Holy Qur'an itself, which says: "On those who believe and do good deeds there is no blame for what they eat, as long as they keep their duty and believe, and do good deeds then again they keep their duty and believe, and keep their duty and do good to others. And Allah loves the good."[3]

This verse implies two valuable points of the Qur'anic knowledge. The first point is that, there are various degrees on faith and piety. This is the point under discussion at present. The other point concerns the philosophy of life and human rights. The Holy Qur'an wants to say that all good things have been created for the people of faith, piety and good deeds. Man is entitled to utilize the bounties of Allah only when he marches forward on the path of evolution prescribed for him by na-ture. That is the path of faith, piety and worthy deeds.

---

[3]Sura al Maida: 93.

Muslim scholars inspired by this verse, and by what has been explicitly or implicitly stated in other Islamic texts, have classified piety into three degrees:

a. average piety,
b. above average piety; and
c. outstanding piety.

The piety of the mujahids, is one of supreme self-sacrifice. They sincerely renounce all they possess, and surrender themselves to Allah. Thus, they put on a garment of piety.

Jihad is an impenetrable armour of Allah. A Muslim community equipped with the spirit of Jihad, cannot be vulnerable to the enemy's assaults. Jihad is a reliable shield of Allah. The armour is the defensive covering worn during fighting, but the shield is a tool taken in hand, to foil the enemy's strokes and thrusts. A shield is meant to prevent a blow, and an armour is meant to neutralize its effect. Apparently, Imam Ali (P) has compared jihad to both an armour and a shield, because some forms of it have a preventive nature and prevent the onslaught of the enemy, and other forms of it have a resistive nature and render his attacks ineffective.

Allah will clothe with a garment of humiliation, a person who refrains from Jihad because he dislikes it. The people who lose the spirit of fighting and resisting the forces of evil, are doomed to humiliation, disgrace, bad-luck and helplessness. The Holy Prophet has said: "All good lies in the sword and under the shadow of the sword." He has also said: "Allah has honoured my followers, because of the hoofs of their horses, and the position of their arrows". This means that the Muslim community is the community of power and force. Islam is the religion of power. It produces mujahids. Will Durant in his book, *History of Civilization*, says that no religion has called its followers to power to the extent that Islam has.

According to another hadith, the Holy Prophet has been quoted as having said: "He who did not fight and did not even think of fighting, will die the death of a sort of hypocrite". Jihad, or at least a desire to take part in it, is an integral part of the doctrine of Islam. One's fidelity to Islam is judged by it. Another hadith reports the Holy Prophet as having said, that a martyr would not be interrogated in his grave. The Holy Prophet said that the flash of the sword over his head was enough of a test. A martyr's fidelity, having once been proved, has no need of any further interrogation.

QUESTIONS FOR DISCUSSION

1. What do the examples under number three, "Criminal Death," reveal about perceptions of male and female personalities in Islamic society?
2. What form of death is considered "higher, greater, and holier than life itself" (par. 11)? What two basic requirements must be met for this kind of death?
3. Does it seem significant that the term "sacred cause" (par. 8) is not defined or limited? What possible dangers arise from the vagueness of this term?

4. What is jihad? What is its purpose? How has it been used recently in the Middle East?
5. Jesus taught that if someone slaps your right cheek, you should offer the left. How does this differ from the teachings of Muhammad?
6. Muhammad taught that the next world is a heavenly embodiment of this world. What is your reaction to this concept?
7. What is a "mujahid" (par. 17)? Could this sort of figure exist in other religions?
8. Muhammad taught "All good lies in the sword and under the shadow of the sword," in a time of tribal warfare and violence some 1,400 years ago in Arabia. How useful is such a philosophy in this century?

JOSEPH SMITH
The First Vision

Joseph Smith (1805–1844) was the founder and first modern prophet of The Church of Jesus Christ of Latter-day Saints, commonly referred to as the Mormons. An unusual spiritual vision that he claimed to have experienced as a fourteen-year-old boy was the first step towards the eventual organization of a new religious movement upon American soil in 1830. His account of this first vision raises the question of tolerance within Christianity.

EXTRACTS FROM THE HISTORY OF JOSEPH SMITH, THE PROPHET[1]

1. Owing to the many reports which have been put in circulation by evil-disposed and designing persons, in relation to the rise and progress of the Church of Jesus Christ of Latter-day Saints, all of which have been designed by the authors thereof to militate against its character as a Church and its progress in the world—I have been induced to write this history, to disabuse the public mind, and put all inquirers after truth in possession of the facts, as they have transpired, in relation both to myself and the Church, so far as I have such facts in my possession.

2. In this history I shall present the various events in relation to this Church, in truth and righteousness, as they have transpired, or as they at present exist, being now the eighth year since the organization of the said Church.

3. I was born in the year of our Lord one thousand eight hundred and five, on the twenty-third day of December, in the town of Sharon, Windsor county, State of Vermont. . . . My father, Joseph Smith, Sen., left the State of Vermont, and moved to Palmyra, Ontario (now Wayne) county, in the State of New York, when I was in my tenth year, or thereabouts. In about four years after my father's arrival in Palmyra, he moved with his family into Manchester in the same county of Ontario—

[1]For the complete record see History of the Church, vol. 1, chaps. 1 to 5 inclusive.

4. His family consisting of eleven souls, namely, my father, Joseph Smith; my mother, Lucy Smith (whose name, previous to her marriage, was Mack, daughter of Solomon Mack); my brothers, Alvin (who died November 19th, 1824, in the 27th year of his age), Hyrum, myself, Samuel Harrison, William, Don Carlos; and my sisters, Sophronia, Catherine, and Lucy.

5. Some time in the second year after our removal to Manchester, there was in the place where we lived an unusual excitement on the subject of religion. It commenced with the Methodists, but soon became general among all the sects in that region of country. Indeed, the whole district of country seemed affected by it, and great multitudes united themselves to the different religious parties, which created no small stir and division amongst the people, some crying, "Lo, here!" and others, "Lo, there!" Some were contending for the Methodist faith, some for the Presbyterian, and some for the Baptist.

6. For, notwithstanding the great love which the converts to these different faiths expressed at the time of their conversion, and the great zeal manifested by the respective clergy, who were active in getting up and promoting this extraordinary scene of religious feeling, in order to have everybody converted, as they were pleased to call it, let them join what sect they pleased; yet when the converts began to file off, some to one party and some to another, it was seen that the seemingly good feelings of both the priests and the converts were more pretended than real; for a scene of great confusion and bad feeling ensued—priest contending against priest, and convert against convert; so that all their good feelings one for another, if they ever had any, were entirely lost in a strife of words and a contest about opinions.

7. I was at this time in my fifteenth year. My father's family was proselyted to the Presbyterian faith, and four of them joined that church, namely, my mother, Lucy; my brothers Hyrum and Samuel Harrison; and my sister Sophronia.

8. During this time of great excitement my mind was called up to serious reflection and great uneasiness; but though my feelings were deep and often poignant, still I kept myself aloof from all these parties, though I attended their several meetings as often as occasion would permit. In process of time my mind became somewhat partial to the Methodist sect, and I felt some desire to be united with them; but so great were the confusion and strife among the different denominations, that it was impossible for a person young as I was, and so unacquainted with men and things, to come to any certain conclusion who was right and who was wrong.

9. My mind at times was greatly excited, the cry and tumult were so great and incessant. The Presbyterians were most decided against the Baptists and Methodists, and used all the powers of both reason and sophistry to prove their errors, or, at least, to make the people think they were in error. On the other hand, the Baptists and Methodists in their turn were equally zealous in endeavoring to establish their own tenets and disprove all others.

10. In the midst of this war of words and tumult of opinions, I often said to myself: What is to be done? Who of all these parties are right; or, are they all wrong together? If any one of them be right, which is it, and how shall I know it?

11. While I was laboring under the extreme difficulties caused by the contests of these parties of religionists, I was one day reading the Epistle of James, first chapter and fifth verse, which reads: *If any of you lack wisdom, let him ask of God, that giveth to all men liberally, and upbraideth not; and it shall be given him.*

12. Never did any passage of scripture come with more power to the heart of man than this did at this time to mine. It seemed to enter with great force into every feeling of my heart. I reflected on it again and again knowing that if any person needed wisdom from God, I did; for how to act I did not know, and unless I could get more wisdom than I then had, I would never know; for the teachers of religion of the different sects understood the same passages of scripture so differently as to destroy all confidence in settling the question by an appeal to the Bible.

13. At length I came to the conclusion that I must either remain in darkness and confusion, or else I must do as James directs, that is, ask of God. I at length came to the determination to "ask of God," concluding that if he gave wisdom to them that lacked wisdom, and would give liberally, and not upbraid, I might venture.

14. So, in accordance with this, my determination to ask of God, I retired to the woods to make the attempt. It was on the morning of a beautiful, clear day, early in the spring of eighteen hundred and twenty. It was the first time in my life that I had made such an attempt, for amidst all my anxieties I had never as yet made the attempt to pray vocally.

15. After I had retired to the place where I had previously designed to go, having looked around me, and finding myself alone, I kneeled down and began to offer up the desire of my heart to God. I had scarcely done so, when immediately I was seized upon by some power which entirely overcame me, and had such an astonishing influence over me as to bind my tongue so that I could not speak. Thick darkness gathered around me, and it seemed to me for a time as if I were doomed to sudden destruction.

16. But, exerting all my powers to call upon God to deliver me out of the power of this enemy which had seized upon me, and at the very moment when I was ready to sink into despair and abandon myself to destruction—not to an imaginary ruin, but to the power of some actual being from the unseen world, who had such marvelous power as I had never before felt in any being—just at this moment of great alarm, I saw a pillar of light exactly over my head, above the brightness of the sun, which descended gradually until it fell upon me.

17. It no sooner appeared than I found myself delivered from the enemy which held me bound. When the light rested upon me I saw two Personages, whose brightness and glory defy all description, standing above me in the air. One of them spake unto me, calling me by name and said, pointing to the other—*This is My Beloved Son. Hear Him!*

18. My object in going to inquire of the Lord was to know which of all the sects was right, that I might know which to join. No sooner, therefore, did I get possession of myself, so as to be able to speak, than I asked the Personages who stood above me in the light, which of all the sects was right—and which I should join.

19. I was answered that I must join none of them, for they were all wrong; and the Personage who addressed me said that all their creeds were an abomination in

his sight; that those professors were all corrupt; that: "they draw near to me with their lips, but their hearts are far from me, they teach for doctrines the command-ments of men, having a form of godliness, but they deny the power thereof."

20. He again forbade me to join with any of them; and many other things did he say unto me, which I cannot write at this time. When I came to myself again, I found myself lying on my back, looking up into heaven. When the light had de-parted, I had no strength; but soon recovering in some degree, I went home. And as I leaned up to the fireplace, mother inquired what the matter was. I replied, "Never mind, all is well—I am well enough off." I then said to my mother, "I have learned for myself that Presbyterianism is not true." It seems as though the adversary was aware, at a very early period of my life, that I was destined to prove a disturber and an annoyer of his kingdom; else why should the powers of darkness combine against me? Why the opposition and persecution that arose against me, almost in my infancy?

21. Some few days after I had this vision, I happened to be in company with one of the Methodist preachers, who was very active in the before mentioned reli-gious excitement; and, conversing with him on the subject of religion, I took occa-sion to give him an account of the vision which I had had. I was greatly surprised at his behavior; he treated my communication not only lightly, but with great con-tempt, saying it was all of the devil, that there were no such things as visions or revelations in these days; that all such things had ceased with the apostles, and that there would never be any more of them.

22. I soon found, however, that my telling the story had excited a great deal of prejudice against me among professors of religion, and was the cause of great per-secution, which continued to increase; and though I was an obscure boy, only be-tween fourteen and fifteen years of age, and my circumstances in life such as to make a boy of no consequence in the world, yet men of high standing would take notice sufficient to excite the public mind against me, and create a bitter persecution; and this was common among all the sects—all united to persecute me.

23. It caused me serious reflection then, and often has since, how very strange it was that an obscure boy, of a little over fourteen years of age, and one, too, who was doomed to the necessity of obtaining a scanty maintenance by his daily labor, should be thought a character of sufficient importance to attract the attention of the great ones of the most popular sects of the day, and in a manner to create in them a spirit of the most bitter persecution and reviling. But strange or not, so it was, and it was often the cause of great sorrow to myself.

QUESTIONS FOR DISCUSSION

1. In the first verses of this text, Joseph Smith says that he and members of the young Mormon Church have been persecuted. What evidence does he give?
2. What indications do you find of a spirit of intolerance in the religious climate of nineteenth-century America in general?
3. Is the message Joseph Smith received open and tolerant of other churches and religious beliefs?

4. How might Durkheim's definition, in *The Elementary Forms of the Religious Life* (p. 449), of religions as human efforts to organize the universe into "sacred" elements and "profane" elements explain the conflict among the different churches in Smith's time?
5. Structurally, what parallels can you see between the form of this text and of other texts religions call "sacred"?

VOLTAIRE
Of Universal Tolerance

Voltaire, the pseudonym of François-Marie Arquet (1694–1777), was one of France's most famous and influential writers. He studied law for a time, but made his mark as a dramatist and as a crusader against tyranny and bigotry. Candide, *a satire on philosophical optimism, is his best-known work, and has recently been adapted for the modern stage in a musical version by Leonard Bernstein. Voltaire's liberal religious opinions and his mockery of the political order often causes him difficulty; he was imprisoned in the Bastille for a year (1717), and fled from Paris to the countryside after the publication of his* Lettres Philosophiques *(1734), in which he spoke out against established religious and political systems. His essay on Christian intolerance presented here reflects the attitudes of the eighteenth-century French Enlightenment, when reason, religious and intellectual tolerance, and freedom of expression came to be viewed as basic essentials of a civilized world. Benjamin Franklin, Tom Paine, and Thomas Jefferson were three prominent American figures who were much influenced by the Enlightenment ideas of men like Voltaire. This helps explain the deep note of tolerance in the U.S. Constitution as well as the fundamental separation of church and state in the American nation.*

It does not demand any great skill or highly developed eloquence to prove that Christians ought to show tolerance for one another. I will go a step further: I will tell you that we ought to look upon all men as our brothers. What! Call a Turk my brother? A Chinaman my brother? A Jew? A Siamese? Yes, without hesitation; are we not all children of the same father and creatures of the same God?

But these people despise us; they treat us as idolaters! And what of it? I will tell them they are quite wrong. It seems to me that I could shake up at least the arrogant assumptions of a high Moslem leader or the head of a Buddhist monastery if I were to say to them something like this:

"This little globe, which is no more than a dot, spins through space the same as countless other globes, and we are lost in this immense vastness. Mankind, at about five feet of height, is unquestionably a rather small thing in all of creation. And yet one of these insignificant beings says to a few of his neighbors in Arabia or in South Africa: 'Listen to me, for the God of all these worlds has enlightened me. There are nine hundred million little ants like us on the earth, but my anthill alone is dear to God; all the others are a source of disgust to him for all eternity; mine alone will know happiness, and all others will be forever miserable.'"

At that point they would stop me and ask who the madman was that spoke such foolishness. I would be obliged to answer them: "It is you yourselves." I would then attempt to calm them down, but that would be quite difficult.

Next I would speak to the Christians, and I would dare to tell, for example, a Dominican Inquisitor devoted to his faith: "Dear brother, you know that each province of Italy has its own way of talking and that people in Venice and Bergamo do not speak at all like those in Florence. The Academy of Crusca has set up the rules of the Italian language; its dictionary is a standard from which one must not stray, and Buonmattei's book of grammar is an infallible guide which must be followed; but do you believe that the consul of the Academy, or Buonmattei in his absence, would have been able, in good conscience, to cut the tongues out of all the Venetians and of all the Bergamese who would have persisted in speaking their own dialects?"

The Inquisitor would answer me: "There is a vast difference; here it is a question of the salvation of your soul: it is for your own good that the Grand Inquisitor orders your arrest upon the testimony of a single person, be he of the worst character and an outlaw to justice; that you have no lawyer to defend you; that the name of your accuser be not even known to you; that the Inquisitor first promise you mercy, and then condemn you; that he put you through five different tortures, and that afterwards you either be whipped, sent to the gallows, or burned at the stake. [Church leaders and influential Christian judges] are of exactly of this opinion, and this holy practice cannot suffer contradiction."

I would take the liberty of answering him: "My brother, perhaps you are right; I am convinced of the good you only wish to do me, but can I not be saved without all that?"

It is true that these absurd horrors do not stain the face of the earth every day, but they have been done frequently, and one could easily compile them into a book that would be much larger than the Gospels that condemn them. Not only is it quite cruel in this short life to persecute those who do not think like us, but I wonder if it isn't rather bold to pronounce their eternal damnation as well. It seems to me that it is not the business of momentary specks of insignificance, such as we are, to second guess the decrees of the Creator. I am far from fighting against the maxim "Outside of the Church there is no salvation"; I respect the Church and all that it teaches, but, in truth, do we know all of the ways of God and the extent of his mercy? Isn't it permitted to hope in him as much as to fear him? Isn't it enough to be faithful to the Church? Must each particular group take for themselves the rights of the Divine, and decide, in its place, the eternal fate of all men?

When we wear clothes in mourning for the king of Sweden, Denmark, England, or Prussia, do we say that we are in mourning for a damned soul that is eternally burning in hell? In Europe, there are forty million inhabitants who do not belong to the Church of Rome. Shall we say to each of them: "Sir, in light of the fact that you are infallibly damned, I will neither eat, nor converse, nor have anything to do with you?"

What ambassador of France, when given audience with a Great Lord, will say in the depths of his heart: His Highness will be infallibly burned during all of eternity because he has undergone circumcision? If he really believed that the Great Lord was a mortal enemy to God and the object of divine vengeance, would he be able to speak to him? Should he have been sent to see him? With what other man could one do business, what civil responsibilities could one carry out, if in effect one was convinced of this idea that he was dealing with the damned?

O schism-loving worshippers of a merciful God! If you have cruel hearts, if, while you adore him whose entire law consists of these words: "Love God and your neighbor," you have buried this sacred and pure law under meaningless arguments and incomprehensible disputes; if you have sown discord, here over a new word, there over a single letter of the alphabet; if you have attached eternal punishment to the omission of a few words, to the lack of a few ceremonies that other peoples could not know of, I would tell you with tears for all of mankind: "Come with me to the day where all will be judged and where God will reward each man according to his own works.

"I see all the dead from centuries past and from our own time appear together in his presence. Are you certain that our Creator and Father will say to the wise and virtuous Confucius, to the lawmaker Solon, to Pythagoras, Zaleucus, Socrates, Plato, the divine Antonians, the benevolent Trajan, to Titus, to the best of mankind, to Epictetus, and to many others, the very models of men: 'Away with you, monsters, go suffer torments that are infinite in intensity and duration; let your suffering be as eternal as I am! And you, my beloved, Jean Châtel, Ravaillac, Damiens, Cartouche, etc. [Christian leaders with reputations for corruption, evil-doing, and villainous treatment of other humans], you who died with the prescribed ceremonies, sit on my right and share endlessly both my empire and my goodness.'"

You draw back with horror at these words; and, after they have escaped me, I have nothing left to say to you.

QUESTIONS FOR DISCUSSION

1. What is satire? Discuss how this piece is satiric. (For example, what effect does the anthill comparison have?)
2. What might be Voltaire's reasons for using satire to treat a "sacred" subject?
3. Notice that Voltaire makes his argument for tolerance in part through narrative and direct address to religious and historical figures and to his readers. What effect does this approach have on you as a reader?
4. Explain the historical reference to the "Grand Inquisitor" (par. 6). How does this reference give weight to Voltaire's argument?
5. Discuss how Voltaire might react to Phyllis Schlafly's "The Power of the Positive Woman" (p. 560), Joseph Smith's "The First Vision" (p. 577), and Murtuza Mutahery's "The Martyr" (p. 572). What specific ideas or statements would he object to? Why?
6. Do you agree or disagree with Voltaire's idea of universal tolerance? Why or why not?

BERTRAND RUSSELL
Why I Am Not a Christian
C. S. LEWIS
What Christians Believe

BERTRAND RUSSELL
Why I Am Not a Christian

Bertrand Russell (1872–1970) was an English mathematician and philosopher, known also for his advocacy of political and social causes, especially pacifism and nuclear disarmament. He published more than 40 books on a wide range of topics, including works on philosophy, mathematics, science, sociology, ethics, politics, religion, education, history, and science. Early works, such as The Principles of Mathematics *(1903) and the three-volume* Principia Mathematica *(1910–1913), written in collaboration with fellow-philosopher and mathematician Alfred North Whitehead, were enormously influential among logicians for many years. During the 1920s he wrote several popular books explaining scientific concepts for nonscientists:* The ABC of Atoms *and* The ABC of Relativity, *for example, as well as the work excerpted here,* Why I Am Not a Christian. *He received the Nobel Prize for Literature in 1950. He remained politically active and influential to the end of his long life; at the age of 91, for example, he chaired the Who Killed Kennedy Committee after the publication of the Warren Report, and he was an active opponent of U.S. policies in Viet Nam during the last decade of his life. Very early in his life Russell had begun to have religious doubts, and as he matured he became not only a religious skeptic but an active opponent of Christianity and its teachings. In the selection reprinted here, he takes issue with various Christian ideas, asserts that Christian churches have actually hindered progress, and declares what we must do. Compare Russell's views with those of C. S. Lewis in the selection which follows.*

WHAT IS A CHRISTIAN?

Nowadays . . . we have to be a little more vague in our meaning of Christianity [than were people in former times]. I think, however, that there are two different items which are quite essential to anybody calling himself a Christian. The first is one of a dogmatic nature—namely, that you must believe in God and immortality. If you do not believe in those two things, I do not think that you can properly call yourself a Christian. Then, further than that, as the name implies, you must have some kind of belief about Christ. The Mohammedans, for instance, also believe in God and in immortality, and yet they would not call themselves Christians. I think you must have at the very lowest the belief that Christ was, if not divine, at least the best and wisest of men. If you are not going to believe that much about Christ, I do not think you have any right to call yourself a Christian. Of course, there is another sense, which you find in *Whitaker's Almanack* and in geography books, where the population of the world is said to be divided into Christians, Mohammedans [Muslims], Buddhists, fetish worshipers, and so on; and in that sense we are all Christians. The geography books count us all in, but that is a purely geographical sense, which I suppose we can ignore. Therefore I take it that when I tell you why I am not a Christian I have to tell you two different things: first, why I do not believe in God and in immortality; and, secondly, why I do not think that Christ was the best and wisest of men, although I grant him a very high degree of moral goodness.

But for the successful efforts of unbelievers in the past, I could not take so elastic a definition of Christianity as that. As I said before, in olden days it had a much more full-blooded sense. For instance, it included the belief in hell. Belief in eternal hell-fire was an essential item of Christian belief until pretty recent times. In this country, as you know, it ceased to be an essential item because of a decision of the Privy Council, and from that decision the Archbishop of Canterbury and the Archbishop of York dissented; but in this country our religion is settled by Act of Parliament, and therefore the Privy Council was able to override their Graces and hell was no longer necessary to a Christian. Consequently I shall not insist that a Christian must believe in hell.

THE EXISTENCE OF GOD

To come to this question of the existence of God: it is a large and serious question, and if I were to attempt to deal with it in any adequate manner I should have to keep you here until Kingdom Come, so that you will have to excuse me if I deal with it in a somewhat summary fashion. You know, of course, that the Catholic Church has laid it down as a dogma that the existence of God can be proved by the unaided reason. That is a somewhat curious dogma, but it is one of their dogmas. They had to introduce it because at one time the freethinkers adopted the habit of saying that there were such and such arguments which mere reason might urge against the existence of God, but of course they knew as a matter of faith that God did exist. The arguments and the reasons were set out at great length, and the Catholic Church felt that they must stop it. Therefore they laid it down that the existence of God can be proved by the unaided reason and they had to set up what they considered were arguments to prove it. There are, of course, a number of them, but I shall take only a few.

THE FIRST-CAUSE ARGUMENT

Perhaps the simplest and easiest to understand is the argument of the First Cause. (It is maintained that everything we see in this world has a cause, and as you go back in the chain of causes further and further you must come to a First Cause, and to that First Cause you give the name of God.) That argument, I suppose, does not carry very much weight nowadays, because, in the first place, cause is not quite what it used to be. The philosophers and the men of science have got going on cause, and it has not anything like the vitality it used to have; but, apart from that, you can see that the argument that there must be a First Cause is one that cannot have any validity. I may say that when I was a young man and was debating these questions very seriously in my mind, I for a long time accepted the argument of the First Cause, until one day, at the age of eighteen, I read John Stuart Mill's Autobiography, and I there found this sentence: "My father taught me that the question 'Who made me?' cannot be answered, since it immediately suggests the further question 'Who made God?'" That very simple sentence showed me, as I still think, the fallacy in the argument of the First Cause. If everything must have a cause, then God must have a cause. If there can be anything without a cause, it may just as well be the world as God, so that there cannot be any validity in that argument. It is exactly of the same nature as the Hindu's view, that the world rested upon an elephant and the elephant rested upon a tortoise; and when they said, "How about the tortoise?" the Indian said, "Suppose we change the subject." The argument is really no better than that. There is no reason why the world could not have come into being without a cause; nor, on the other hand, is there any reason why it should not have always existed. There is no reason to suppose that the world had a beginning at all. The idea that things must have a beginning is really due to the poverty of our imagination. Therefore, perhaps, I need not waste any more time upon the argument about the First Cause. . . .

DEFECTS IN CHRIST'S TEACHING

Historically it is quite doubtful whether Christ ever existed at all, and if He did we do not know anything about Him, so that I am not concerned with the historical question, which is a very difficult one. I am concerned with Christ as He appears in the Gospels, taking the Gospel narrative as it stands, and there one does find some things that do not seem to be very wise. For one thing, He certainly thought that His second coming would occur in clouds of glory before the death of all the people who were living at that time. There are a great many texts that prove that. He says, for instance, "Ye shall not have gone over the cities of Israel till the Son of Man be come." Then He says, "There are some standing here which shall not taste death till the Son of Man comes into His kingdom"; and there are a lot of places where it is quite clear that He believed that His second coming would happen during the lifetime of many then living. That was the belief of His earlier followers, and it was the basis of a good deal of His moral teaching. When He said, "Take no thought for the morrow," and things of that sort, it was very largely because He thought that the second coming was going to be very soon, and that all ordinary mundane affairs did not count. I have, as a matter of fact, known some Christians who did believe that the second coming was imminent. I knew a parson who frightened his congregation terribly by telling them that the second coming was very imminent indeed, but they were much consoled when they found that he was planting trees in his garden. The early Christians did really believe it, and they did abstain from such things as planting trees in their gardens, because they did accept from Christ the belief that the second coming was imminent. In that respect, clearly He was not so wise as some other people have been, and He was certainly not superlatively wise.

THE MORAL PROBLEM

Then you come to moral questions. There is one very serious defect to my mind in Christ's moral character, and that is that He believed in hell. I do not myself feel that any person who is really profoundly humane can believe in everlasting punishment. Christ certainly as depicted in the Gospels did believe in everlasting punishment, and one does find repeatedly a vindictive fury against those people who would not listen to His preaching—an attitude which is not uncommon with preachers, but which does somewhat detract from superlative excellence. You do not, for instance, find that attitude in Socrates. You find him quite bland and urbane toward the people who would not listen to him; and it is, to my mind, far more worthy of a sage to take that line than to take the line of indignation. You probably all remember the sort of things that Socrates was saying when he was dying, and the sort of things that he generally did say to people who did not agree with him.

You will find that in the Gospels Christ said, "Ye serpents, ye generation of vipers, how can ye escape the damnation of hell." That was said to people who did not like His preaching. It is not really to my mind quite the best tone, and there are a great many of these things about hell. There is, of course, the familiar text about the sin against the Holy Ghost: "Whosoever speaketh against the Holy Ghost it shall not be forgiven him neither in this World nor in the world to come." That text has caused an unspeakable amount of misery in the world, for all sorts of people have imagined that they have committed the sin against the Holy Ghost, and thought that it would not be forgiven them either in this world or in the world to come. I really do not think that a person with a proper degree of kindliness in his nature would have put fears and terrors of that sort into the world.

Then Christ says, "The Son of Man shall send forth His angels, and they shall gather out of His kingdom all things that offend, and them which do iniquity, and shall cast them into a furnace of fire; there shall be wailing and gnashing of teeth"; and He goes on about the wailing and gnashing of teeth. It comes in one verse after another, and it is quite manifest to the reader that there is a certain pleasure in contemplating wailing and gnashing of teeth, or else it would not occur so often. Then you all, of course, remember about the sheep and the goats; how at the second coming He is going to divide the sheep from the goats, and He is going to say to the goats, "Depart from me, ye cursed, into everlasting fire." He continues, "And these shall go away into everlasting fire." Then He says again, "If thy hand offend thee, cut it off; it is better for thee to enter into life maimed, than having two hands to go into hell, into the fire that never shall be quenched; where the worm dieth not and the fire is not quenched." He repeats that again and again also. I must say that I think all this doctrine, that hell-fire is a punishment for sin, is a doctrine of cruelty. It is a doctrine that put cruelty into the world and gave the world generations of cruel torture; and the Christ of the Gospels, if you could take Him as His chroniclers represent Him, would certainly have to be considered partly responsible for that.

There are other things of less importance. There is the instance of the Gadarene swine, where it certainly was not very kind to the pigs to put the devils into them and make them rush down the hill to the sea. You must remember that He was omnipotent, and He could have made the devils simply go away; but He chose to send them into the pigs. Then there is the curious story of the fig tree, which always rather puzzled me. You remember what happened about the fig tree. "He was hungry; and seeing a fig tree afar off having leaves, He came if haply He might find anything thereon; and when He came to it He found nothing but leaves, for the time of figs was not yet. And Jesus answered and said unto it: 'No man eat fruit of thee hereafter for ever' . . . and Peter . . . saith unto Him: 'Master, behold the fig tree which thou cursedst is withered away.'" This is a very curious story, because it was not the right time of year for figs, and you really could not blame the tree. I cannot myself feel that either in the matter of wisdom or in the matter of virtue Christ stands quite as high as some other people known to history. I think I should put Buddha and Socrates above Him in those respects.

THE EMOTIONAL FACTOR

As I said before, I do not think that the real reason why people accept religion has anything to do with argumentation. They accept religion on emotional grounds. One is often told that it is a very wrong thing to attack religion, because religion makes men virtuous. So I am told; I have not noticed it. You know, of course, the parody of that argument in Samuel Butler's book, *Erewhon Revisited*. You will remember that in *Erewhon* there is a certain Higgs who arrives in a remote country, and after spending some time there he escapes from that country in a balloon. Twenty years later he comes back to that country and finds a new religion in which he is worshiped under the name of the "Sun Child," and it is said that he ascended into heaven. He finds that the Feast of the Ascension is about to be celebrated, and he hears Professors Hanky and Panky say to each other that they never set eyes on the man Higgs, and they hope they never will; but they are the high priests of the religion of the Sun Child. He is very indignant, and he comes up to them, and he says, "I am going to expose all this humbug and tell the people of Erewhon that it was only I, the man Higgs, and I went up in a balloon." He was told, "You must not do that, because all the morals of this country are bound round this myth, and if they once know that you did not ascend into heaven they will all become wicked"; and so he is persuaded of that and he goes quietly away.

That is the idea—that we should all be wicked if we did not hold to the Christian religion. It seems to me that the people who have held to it have been for the most part extremely wicked. You find this curious fact, that the more intense has been the religion of any period and the more profound has been the dogmatic belief, the greater has been the cruelty and the worse has been the state of affairs. In the so-called ages of faith, when men really did believe the Christian religion in all its completeness, there was the Inquisition, with its tortures; there were millions of unfortunate women burned as witches; and there was every kind of cruelty practiced upon all sorts of people in the name of religion.

You find as you look around the world that every single bit of progress in humane feeling, every improvement in the criminal law, every step toward the diminution of war, every step toward better treatment of the colored races, or every mitigation of slavery, every moral progress that there has been in the world, has been consistently opposed by the organized churches of the world. I say quite deliberately that the Christian religion, as organized in its churches, has been and still is the principal enemy of moral progress in the world.

HOW THE CHURCHES HAVE RETARDED PROGRESS

You may think that I am going too far when I say that that is still so. I do not think that I am. Take one fact. You will bear with me if I mention it. It is not a pleasant fact, but the churches compel one to mention facts that are not pleasant. Supposing that in this world that we live in today an inexperienced girl is married to a syphilitic man; in that case the Catholic Church says, "This is an indissoluble sacrament. You must stay together for life." And no steps of any sort must be taken by that woman to prevent herself from giving birth to syphilitic children. That is what the Catholic Church says. I say that this is fiendish cruelty, and nobody whose natural sympathies have not been warped by dogma, or whose moral nature was not absolutely dead to all sense of suffering, could maintain that it is right and proper that that state of things should continue.

That is only an example. There are a great many ways in which, at the present moment, the church, by its insistence upon what it chooses to call morality, inflicts upon all sorts of people undeserved and unnecessary suffering. And of course, as we know, it is in its major part an opponent still of progress and of improvement in all the ways that diminish suffering in the world, because it has chosen to label as morality a certain narrow set of rules of conduct which have nothing to do with human happiness; and when you say that this or that ought to be done because it would make for human happiness, they think that has nothing to do with the matter at all. "What has human happiness to do with morals? The object of morals is not to make people happy."

FEAR, THE FOUNDATION OF RELIGION

Religion is based, I think, primarily and mainly upon fear. It is partly the terror of the unknown and partly, as I have said, the wish to feel that you have a kind of elder brother who will stand by you in all your troubles and disputes. Fear is the basis of the whole thing—fear of the mysterious, fear of defeat, fear of death. Fear is the parent of cruelty, and therefore it is no wonder if cruelty and religion have gone hand in hand. It is because fear is at the basis of those two things. In this world we can now begin a little to understand things, and a little to master them by help of science, which has forced its way step by step against the Christian religion, against the churches, and against the opposition of all the old precepts. Science can help us to get over this craven fear in which mankind has lived for so many generations. Science can teach us, and I think our own hearts can teach us, no longer to look around for imaginary supports, no longer to invent allies in the sky, but rather to look to our own efforts here below to make this world a fit place to live in, instead of the sort of place that the churches in all these centuries have made it.

WHAT WE MUST DO

We want to stand upon our own feet and look fair and square at the world—its good facts, its bad facts, its beauties, and its ugliness; see the world as it is and be not afraid of it. Conquer the world by intelligence and not merely by being slavishly subdued by the terror that comes from it. The whole conception of God is a conception derived from the ancient Oriental despotisms. It is a conception quite unworthy of free men. When you hear people in church debasing themselves and saying that they are miserable sinners, and all the rest of it, it seems contemptible and not worthy of self-respecting human beings. We ought to stand up and look the world frankly in the face. We ought to make the best we can of the world, and if it is not so good as we wish, after all it will still be better than what these others have made of it in all these ages. A good world needs knowledge, kindliness, and courage; it does not need a regretful hankering after the past or a fettering of the free intelligence by the words uttered long ago by ignorant men. It needs a fearless outlook and a free intelligence. It needs hope for the future, not looking back all the time toward a past that is dead, which we trust will be far surpassed by the future that our intelligence can create.

C. S. LEWIS
What Christians Believe

C. S. Lewis (1898–1963) was a classical scholar and novelist known also as a Christian apologist (that is, one who explains a doctrine or idea through reasoned argument). He served as fellow and tutor at Magdalen College, Oxford, and then as professor of medieval and renaissance English at Cambridge University. His publications include critical works, such as The Allegory of Love: A Study in Medieval Tradition *(1936), which many consider his greatest work; works as a lay expositor of Christianity, such as his best-selling fictional work* The Screwtape Letters *(1942); stories for children, such as* The Chronicles of Narnia *(1950–1956), and science-fiction works (at the time a very new genre), such as* Out of the Silent Planet *(1938). In this selection, taken from* Mere Christianity, *Lewis argues against atheism and for the Christian faith; the fact that he was an atheist in his youth and became reconverted to Christianity made Lewis particularly sensitive to the kinds of arguments he needed to convince unbelievers. This piece should be compared to the preceding essay by Bertrand Russell.*

THE RIVAL CONCEPTIONS OF GOD

I have been asked to tell you what Christians believe, and I am going to begin by telling you one thing that Christians do not need to believe. If you are a Christian you do not have to believe that all the other religions are simply wrong all through. If you are an atheist you do have to believe that the main point in all the religions of the whole world is simply one huge mistake. If you are a Christian, you are free to think that all these religions, even the queerest ones, contain at least some hint of the truth. When I was an atheist I had to try to persuade myself that most of the human race have always been wrong about the question that mattered to them most; when I became a Christian I was able to take a more liberal view. But, of course, being a Christian does mean thinking that where Christianity differs from other religions, Christianity is right and they are wrong. As in arithmetic—there is only one right answer to a sum, and all other answers are wrong: but some of the wrong answers are much nearer being right than others.

The first big division of humanity is into the majority, who believe in some kind of God or gods, and the minority who do not. On this point, Christianity lines up with the majority—lines up with ancient Greeks and Romans, modern savages, Stoics, Platonists, Hindus, Mohammedans [Muslims], etc., against the modern Western European materialist.

Now I go on to the next big division. People who all believe in God can be divided according to the sort of God they believe in. There are two very different ideas on this subject. One of them is the idea that He is beyond good and evil. We humans call one thing good and another thing bad. But according to some people that is merely our human point of view. These people would say that the wiser you become the less you would want to call anything good or bad, and the more clearly you would see that everything is good in one way and bad in another, and that nothing could have been different. Consequently, these people think that long before you got anywhere near the divine point of view the distinction would have disappeared altogether. We call a cancer bad, they would say, because it kills a man; but you might just as well call a successful surgeon bad because he kills a cancer. It all depends on the point of view. The other and opposite idea is that God is quite definitely "good" or "righteous," a God who takes sides, who loves love and hates hatred, who wants us to behave in one way and not in another. The first of these views—the one that thinks God beyond good and evil—is called Pantheism. It was held by the great Prussian philosopher Hegel and, as far as I can understand them, by the Hindus. The other view is held by Jews, Mohammedans and Christians.

And with this big difference between Pantheism and the Christian idea of God, there usually goes another. Pantheists usually believe that God, so to speak, animates the universe as you animate your body: that the universe almost *is* God, so that if it did not exist He would not exist either, and anything you find in the universe is a part of God. The Christian[s'] idea is quite different. They think God invented and made the universe—like a man making a picture or composing a tune. A painter is not a picture, and he does not die if his picture is destroyed. You may say, "He's put a lot of himself into it," but you only mean that all its beauty and interest has come out of his head. His skill is not in the picture in the same way that it is in his head, or even in his hands. I expect you see how this difference between Pantheists and Christians hangs together with the other one. If you do not take the distinction between good and bad very seriously, then it is easy to say that anything you find in this world is a part of God. But, of course, if you think some things really bad, and God really good, then you cannot talk like that. You must believe that God is separate from the world and that some of the things we see in it are contrary to His will. Confronted with a cancer or a slum the Pantheist can say, "If you could only see it from the divine point of view, you would realise that this also is God." The Christian replies, "Don't talk damned nonsense." For Christianity is a fighting religion. It thinks God made the world—that space and time, heat and cold, and all the colours and tastes, and all the animals and vegetables, are things that God "made up out of His head" as a man makes up a story. But it also thinks that a great many things have gone wrong with the world that God made and that God insists, and insists very loudly, on our putting them right again.

And, of course, that raises a very big question. If a good God made the world why has it gone wrong? And for many years I simply refused to listen to the Christian answers to this question, because I kept on feeling "whatever you say, and however clever your arguments are, isn't it much simpler and easier to say that the world was not made by any intelligent power? Aren't all your arguments simply a complicated attempt to avoid the obvious?" But then that threw me back into another difficulty.

My argument against God was that the universe seemed so cruel and unjust. But how had I got this idea of *just* and *unjust?* A man does not call a line crooked unless he has some idea of a straight line. What was I comparing this universe with when I called it unjust? If the whole show was bad and senseless from A to Z, so to speak, why did I, who was supposed to be part of the show, find myself in such violent reaction against it? A man feels wet when he falls into water, because man is not a water animal: a fish would not feel wet. Of course I could have given up my idea of justice by saying it was nothing but a private idea of my own. But if I did that, then my argument against God collapsed too—for the argument depended on saying that the world was really unjust, not simply that it did not happen to please my private fancies. Thus in the very act of trying to prove that God did not exist—in other words, that the whole of reality was senseless—I found I was forced to assume that one part of reality—namely my idea of justice—was full of sense. Consequently atheism turns out to be too simple. If the whole universe has no meaning, we should never have found out that it has no meaning: just as, if there were no light in the universe and therefore no creatures with eyes, we should never know it was dark. *Dark* would be without meaning.

THE INVASION

Very well then, atheism is too simple. And I will tell you another view that is also too simple. It is the view I call Christianity-and-water, the view which simply says there is a good God in Heaven and everything is all right—leaving out all the difficult and terrible doctrines about sin and hell and the devil, and the redemption. Both these are boys' philosophies.

It is no good asking for a simple religion. After all, real things are not simple. They look simple, but they are not. The table I am sitting at looks simple: but ask a scientist to tell you what it is really made of—all about the atoms and how the light waves rebound from them and hit my eye and what they do to the optic nerve and what it does to my brain—and, of course, you find that what we call "seeing a table" lands you in mysteries and complications which you can hardly get to the end of. A child saying a child's prayer looks simple. And if you are content to stop there, well and good. But if you are not—and the modern world usually is not—if you want to go on and ask what is really happening—then you must be prepared for something difficult. If we ask for something more than simplicity, it is silly then to complain that the something more is not simple.

Very often, however, this silly procedure is adopted by people who are not silly, but who, consciously or unconsciously, want to destroy Christianity. Such people put up a version of Christianity suitable for a child of six and make that the object of their attack. When you try to explain the Christian doctrine as it is really held by an instructed adult, they then complain that you are making their heads turn round and that it is all too complicated and that if there really were a God they are sure He would have made "religion" simple, because simplicity is so beautiful, etc. You must be on your guard against these people for they will change their ground every minute and only waste your time. Notice, too, their idea of God "making religion simple": as if "religion" were something God invented, and not His statement to us of certain quite unalterable facts about His own nature.

Besides being complicated, reality, in my experience, is usually odd. It is not neat, not obvious, not what you expect. For instance, when you have grasped that the earth and the other planets all go round the sun, you would naturally expect that all the planets were made to match—all at equal distances from each other, say, or distances that regularly increased, or all the same size, or else getting bigger or smaller as you go farther from the sun. In fact, you find no rhyme or reason (that we can see) about either the sizes or the distances; and some of them have one moon, one has four, one has two, some have none, and one has a ring.

Reality, in fact, is usually something you could not have guessed. That is one of the reasons I believe Christianity. It is a religion you could not have guessed. If it offered us just the kind of universe we had always expected, I should feel we were making it up. But, in fact, it is not the sort of thing anyone would have made up. It has just that queer twist about it that real things have. So let us leave behind all these boys' philosophies—these over-simple answers. The problem is not simple and the answer is not going to be simple either.

What is the problem? A universe that contains much that is obviously bad and apparently meaningless, but containing creatures like ourselves who know that it is bad and meaningless. There are only two views that face all the facts. One is the Christian view that this is a good world that has gone wrong, but still retains the memory of what it ought to have been. The other is the view called Dualism. Dualism means the belief that there are two equal and independent powers at the back of everything, one of them good and the other bad, and that this universe is the battlefield in which they fight out an endless war. I personally think that next to Christianity Dualism is the manliest and most sensible creed on the market. But it has a catch in it.

The two powers, or spirits, or gods—the good one and the bad one—are supposed to be quite independent. They both existed from all eternity. Neither of them made the other, neither of them has any more right than the other to call itself God. Each presumably thinks it is good and thinks the other bad. One of them likes hatred and cruelty, the other likes love and mercy, and each backs its own view. Now what do we mean when we call one of them the Good Power and the other the Bad Power? Either we are merely saying that we happen to prefer the one to the other—like preferring beer to cider—or else we are saying that, whatever the two powers think about it, and whichever we humans, at the moment, happen to like, one of them is actually wrong, actually mistaken, in regarding itself as good. Now if we mean merely that we happen to prefer the first, then we must give up talking about good and evil at all. For good means what you ought to prefer quite regardless of what you happen to like at any given moment. If "being good" meant simply joining the side you happened to fancy, for no real reason, then good would not deserve to be called good. So we must mean that one of the two powers is actually wrong and the other actually right.

But the moment you say that, you are putting into the universe a third thing in addition to the two Powers: some law or standard or rule of good which one of the powers conforms to and the other fails to conform to. But since the two powers are judged by this standard, then this standard, or the Being who made this standard, is farther back and higher up than either of them, and He will be the real God. In fact, what we meant by calling them good and bad turns out to be that one of them is in a right relation to the real ultimate God and the other in a wrong relation to Him.

The same point can be made in a different way. If Dualism is true, then the bad Power must be a being who likes badness for its own sake. But in reality we have no experience of anyone liking badness just because it is bad. The nearest we can get to it is in cruelty. But in real life people are cruel for one of two reasons—either because they are sadists, that is, because they have a sexual perversion which makes cruelty a cause of sensual pleasure to them, or else for the sake of something they are going to get out of it—money, or power, or safety. But pleasure, money, power, and safety are all, as far as they go, good things. The badness consists in pursuing them by the wrong method, or in the wrong way, or too much. I do not mean, of course, that the people who do this are not desperately wicked. I do mean that wickedness, when you examine it, turns out to be the pursuit of some good in the wrong way. You can be good for the mere sake of goodness: you cannot be bad for the mere sake of badness. You can do a kind action when you are not feeling kind and when it gives you no pleasure, simply because kindness is right; but no one ever did a cruel action simply because cruelty is wrong—only because cruelty was pleasant or useful to him. In other words badness cannot succeed even in being bad in the same way in which goodness is good. Goodness is, so to speak, itself: badness is only spoiled goodness. And there must be something good first before it can be spoiled. We called sadism a sexual perversion; but you must first have the idea of a normal sexuality before you can talk of its being perverted; and you can see which is the perversion, because you can explain the perverted from the normal, and cannot explain the normal from the perverted. It follows that this Bad Power, who is supposed to be on an equal footing with the Good Power, and to love badness in the same way as the Good Power loves goodness, is a mere bogy. In order to be bad he must have good things to want and then to pursue in the wrong way: he must have impulses which were originally good in order to be able to pervert them. But if he is bad he cannot supply himself either with good things to desire or with good impulses to pervert. He must be getting both from the Good Power. And if so, then he is not independent. He is part of the Good Power's world: he was made either by the Good Power or by some power above them both.

Put it more simply still. To be bad, he must exist and have intelligence and will. But existence, intelligence and will are in themselves good. Therefore he must be getting them from the Good Power: even to be bad he must borrow or steal from his opponent. And do you now begin to see why Christianity has always said that the devil is a fallen angel? That is not a mere story for the children. It is a real recognition of the fact that evil is a parasite, not an original thing. The powers which enable evil to carry on are powers given it by goodness. All the things which enable a bad man to be effectively bad are in themselves good things—resolution, cleverness, good looks, existence itself. That is why Dualism, in a strict sense, will not work.

But I freely admit that real Christianity (as distinct from Christianity-and-water) goes much nearer to Dualism than people think. One of the things that surprised me when I first read the New Testament seriously was that it talked so much about a Dark Power in the universe—a mighty evil spirit who was held to be the Power behind death and disease, and sin. The difference is that Christianity thinks this Dark Power was created by God, and was good when he was created, and went wrong. Christianity agrees with Dualism that this universe is at war. But it does not think this is a war between independent powers. It thinks it is a civil war, a rebellion, and that we are living in a part of the universe occupied by the rebel.

Enemy-occupied territory—that is what this world is. Christianity is the story of how the rightful king has landed, you might say landed in disguise, and is calling us all to take part in a great campaign of sabotage. When you go to church you are really listening-in to the secret wireless from our friends: that is why the enemy is so anxious to prevent us from going. He does it by playing on our conceit and laziness and intellectual snobbery. I know someone will ask me, "Do you really mean, at this time of day, to re-introduce our old friend the devil—hoofs and horns and all?" Well, what the time of day has to do with it I do not know. And I am not particular about the hoofs and horns. But in other respects my answer is "Yes, I do." I do not claim to know anything about his personal appearance. If anybody really wants to know him better I would say to that person, "Don't worry. If you really want to, you will. Whether you'll like it when you do is another question."

THE SHOCKING ALTERNATIVE

Christians, then, believe that an evil power has made himself for the present the Prince of this World. And, of course, that raises problems. Is this state of affairs in accordance with God's will or not? If it is, He is a strange God, you will say: and if it is not, how can anything happen contrary to the will of a being with absolute power?

But anyone who has been in authority knows how a thing can be in accordance with your will in one way and not in another. It may be quite sensible for a mother to say to the children, "I'm not going to go and make you tidy the schoolroom every night. You've got to learn to keep it tidy on your own." Then she goes up one night and finds the Teddy bear and the ink and the French Grammar all lying in the grate. That is against her will. She would prefer the children to be tidy. But on the other hand, it is her will which has left the children free to be untidy. The same thing arises in any regiment, or trade union, or school. You make a thing voluntary and then half the people do not do it. That is not what you willed, but your will has made it possible.

It is probably the same in the universe. God created things which had free will. That means creatures which can go either wrong or right. Some people think they can imagine a creature which was free but had no possibility of going wrong; I cannot. If a thing is free to be good it is also free to be bad. And free will is what has made evil possible. Why, then, did God give them free will? Because free will, though it makes evil possible, is also the only thing that makes possible any love or goodness or joy worth having. A world of automata—of creatures that worked like machines—would hardly be worth creating. The happiness which God designs for

His higher creatures is the happiness of being freely, voluntarily united to Him and to each other in an ecstasy of love and delight compared with which the most rapturous love between a man and a woman on this earth is mere milk and water. And for that they must be free.

Of course God knew what would happen if they used their freedom the wrong way: apparently He thought it worth the risk. Perhaps we feel inclined to disagree with Him. But there is a difficulty about disagreeing with God. He is the source from which all your reasoning power comes: you could not be right and He wrong any more than a stream can rise higher than its own source. When you are arguing against Him you are arguing against the very power that makes you able to argue at all: it is like cutting off the branch you are sitting on. If God thinks this state of war in the universe a price worth paying for free will—that is, for making a live world in which creatures can do real good or harm and something of real importance can happen, instead of a toy world which only moves when He pulls the strings—then we may take it it is worth paying.

When we have understood about free will, we shall see how silly it is to ask, as somebody once asked me: "Why did God make a creature of such rotten stuff that it went wrong?" The better stuff a creature is made of—the cleverer and stronger and freer it is—then the better it will be if it goes right, but also the worse it will be if it goes wrong. A cow cannot be very good or very bad; a dog can be both better and worse; a child better and worse still; an ordinary man, still more so; a man of genius, still more so; a superhuman spirit best—or worst—of all.

How did the Dark Power go wrong? Here, no doubt, we ask a question to which human beings cannot give an answer with any certainty. A reasonable (and traditional) guess, based on our own experiences of going wrong, can, however, be offered. The moment you have a self at all, there is a possibility of putting yourself first—wanting to be the centre—wanting to be God, in fact. That was the sin of Satan: and that was the sin he taught the human race. Some people think the fall of man had something to do with sex, but that is a mistake. (The story in the Book of Genesis rather suggests that some corruption in our sexual nature followed the fall and was its result, not its cause.) What Satan put into the heads of our remote ancestors was the idea that they could "be like gods"—could set up on their own as if they had created themselves—be their own masters—invent some sort of happiness for themselves outside God, apart from God. And out of that hopeless attempt has come nearly all that we call human history—money, poverty, ambition, war, prostitution, classes, empires, slavery—the long terrible story of man trying to find something other than God which will make him happy.

The reason why it can never succeed is this. God made us: invented us as a man invents an engine. A car is made to run on gasoline, and it would not run properly on anything else. Now God designed the human machine to run on Himself. He Himself is the fuel our spirits were designed to burn, or the food our spirits were designed to feed on. There is no other. That is why it is just no good asking God to make us happy in our own way without bothering about religion. God cannot give us a happiness and peace apart from Himself, because it is not there. There is no such thing.

That is the key to history. Terrific energy is expended—civilisations are built up—excellent institutions devised; but each time something goes wrong. Some fatal flaw always brings the selfish and cruel people to the top and it all slides back into misery and ruin. In fact, the machine conks. It seems to start up all right and runs a few yards, and then it breaks down. They are trying to run it on the wrong juice. That is what Satan has done to us humans.

And what did God do? First of all He left us conscience, the sense of right and wrong: and all through history there have been people trying (some of them very hard) to obey it. None of them ever quite succeeded. Secondly, He sent the human race what I call good dreams: I mean those queer stories scattered all through the heathen religions about a god who dies and comes to life again and, by his death, has somehow given new life to men. Thirdly, He selected one particular people and spent several centuries hammering into their heads the sort of God He was—that there was only one of Him and that He cared about right conduct. Those people were the Jews, and the Old Testament gives an account of the hammering process.

Then comes the real shock. Among these Jews there suddenly turns up a man who goes about talking as if He was God. He claims to forgive sins. He says He has always existed. He says He is coming to judge the world at the end of time. Now let us get this clear. Among Pantheists, like the Indians, anyone might say that he was a part of God, or one with God: there would be nothing very odd about it. But this man, since He was a Jew, could not mean that kind of God. God, in their language, meant the Being outside the world Who had made it and was infinitely different from anything else. And when you have grasped that, you will see that what this man said was, quite simply, the most shocking thing that has ever been uttered by human lips.

One part of the claim tends to slip past us unnoticed because we have heard it so often that we no longer see what it amounts to. I mean the claim to forgive sins: any sins. Now unless the speaker is God, this is really so preposterous as to be comic. We can all understand how a man forgives offences against himself. You tread on my toe and I forgive you, you steal my money and I forgive you. But what should we make of a man, himself unrobbed and untrodden on, who announced that he forgave you for treading on other men's toes and stealing other men's money? Asinine fatuity is the kindest description we should give of his conduct. Yet this is what Jesus did. He told people that their sins were forgiven, and never waited to consult all the other people whom their sins had undoubtedly injured. He unhesitatingly behaved as if He was the party chiefly concerned, the person chiefly offended in all offences. This makes sense only if He really was the God whose laws are broken and whose love is wounded in every sin. In the mouth of any speaker who is not God, these words would imply what I can only regard as a silliness and conceit unrivalled by any other character in history.

Yet (and this is the strange, significant thing) even His enemies, when they read the Gospels, do not usually get the impression of silliness and conceit. Still less do unprejudiced readers. Christ says that He is "humble and meek" and we believe Him; not noticing that, if He were merely a man, humility and meekness are the very last characteristics we could attribute to some of His sayings.

I am trying here to prevent anyone saying the really foolish thing that people often say about Him: "I'm ready to accept Jesus as a great moral teacher, but I don't accept His claim to be God." That is the one thing we must not say. A man who was merely a man and said the sort of things Jesus said would not be a great moral teacher. He would either be a lunatic—on a level with the man who says he is a poached egg—or else he would be the Devil of Hell. You must make your choice. Either this man was, and is, the Son of God: or else a madman or something worse. You can shut Him up for a fool, you can spit at Him and kill Him as a demon; or you can fall at His feet and call Him Lord and God. But let us not come with any patronising nonsense about His being a great human teacher. He has not left that open to us. He did not intend to.

QUESTIONS FOR DISCUSSION

"Why I Am Not a Christian"

1. What two beliefs does Russell see as essential to being Christian? Do you agree that these are the essential elements of Christianity? Explain.
2. Why doesn't Russell include "hell" in his list of essential Christian elements? Do you think a belief in hell is important to being Christian? Explain.
3. In what ways does Russell's approach to argument resemble Voltaire's (p. 581)? In what ways is it dissimilar?
4. Summarize the First Cause Argument for the existence of God. What other explanations for "cause" exist?
5. Discuss Russell's interpretation of Jesus' moral character.
6. Would you agree with Russell that people accept religion on emotional grounds? How might these people react to his rational treatment of religion?
7. Russell contends that Christianity "has been and still is the principal enemy of moral progress in the world" (par. 12). How does he support this conclusion?
8. Russell structures his essay carefully into sections with headings. What effect does this have on you, the reader?
9. Discuss the tone of Russell's piece as compared to the tone of the piece by C. S. Lewis. How does Russell achieve his tone?

"What Christians Believe"

1. Who is Lewis's audience? What is his purpose?
2. Lewis sets out to write about what Christians believe. Why, then, does he spend a great deal of space and energy outlining the beliefs and unbeliefs of other groups? How does this help him build his argument?
3. Lewis labels Christianity a "fighting religion" (par. 4). Do you see evidences of a "fight" in Lewis's approach to writing about Christianity?
4. Would Riane Eisler in "Our Lost Heritage: New Facts on How God Became a Man" (p. 550) agree that it is normal and good to have "fighting religions"?
5. What kind of deity does Lewis present in this text?
6. In The Martyr (p. 572), Mutahery stated that the next world is only a heavenly embodiment of this one. What evidence suggests that Lewis would agree in many ways with this concept?
7. Lewis suggests that Christianity is true because it is not "the sort of thing anyone would have made up" (par. 11). How does he support this point?
8. What is Dualism?

9. What different perspective does Stephen Harris's commentary on changing conceptions of God and Satan in "Understanding the Bible" (p. 491) give to Lewis's long treatment of the Good Power and the Dark Power in the universe?
10. In what ways do you find Lewis's argument convincing? In what ways do you find it unconvincing?

ELIE WIESEL
Night

Elie Wiesel (1928–   ) lived through the experience he describes below. As a young teenager, he and his family were deported from their home in Hungary to the Nazi death camps at Auschwitz and Buchenwald. His parents and a younger sister died there. He lived on to recount from a Jewish perspective the story of having to face the silence of God in a world where human suffering had been carried to the extreme. Wiesel won the Nobel Peace Prize in 1987 for his efforts to tell the world of the horror of the Holocaust.

A week later, on the way back from work, we noticed in the center of the camp, at the assembly place, a black gallows.

We were told that soup would not be distributed until after roll call. This took longer than usual. The orders were given in a sharper manner than on other days, and in the air there were strange undertones.

"Bare your heads!" yelled the head of the camp, suddenly.

Ten thousand caps were simultaneously removed.

"Cover your heads!"

Ten thousand caps went back onto their skulls, as quick as lightning.

The gate to the camp opened. An SS section appeared and surrounded us: one SS at every three paces. On the lookout towers the machine guns were trained on the assembly place.

"They fear trouble," whispered Juliek.

Two SS men had gone to the cells. They came back with the condemned man between them. He was a youth from Warsaw. He had three years of concentration camp life behind him. He was a strong, well-built boy, a giant in comparison with me.

His back to the gallows, his face turned toward his judge, who was the head of the camp, the boy was pale, but seemed more moved than afraid. His manacled hands did not tremble. His eyes gazed coldly at the hundreds of SS guards, the thousands of prisoners who surrounded him.

The head of the camp began to read his verdict, hammering out each phrase:

"In the name of Himmler . . . prisoner Number . . . stole during the alert. . . . According to the law . . . paragraph . . . prisoner Number . . . is condemned to death. May this be a warning and an example to all prisoners."

No one moved.

I could hear my heart beating. The thousands who had died daily at Auschwitz and at Birkenau in the crematory ovens no longer troubled me. But this one, leaning against his gallows—he overwhelmed me.

"Do you think this ceremony'll be over soon? I'm hungry. . . ." whispered Juliek.

At a sign from the head of the camp, the Lagerkapo advanced toward the condemned man. Two prisoners helped him in his task—for two plates of soup.

The Kapo wanted to bandage the victim's eyes, but he refused.

After a long moment of waiting, the executioner put the rope around his neck. He was on the point of motioning to his assistants to draw the chair away from the prisoner's feet, when the latter cried, in a calm, strong voice:

"Long live liberty! A curse upon Germany! A curse . . . ! A cur—"

The executioners had completed their task.

A command cleft the air like a sword.

"Bare your heads."

Ten thousand prisoners paid their last respects.

"Cover your heads!"

Then the whole camp, block after block, had to march past the hanged man and stare at the dimmed eyes, the lolling tongue of death. The Kapos and heads of each block forced everyone to look him full in the face.

After the march, we were given permission to return to the blocks for our meal. I remember that I found the soup excellent that evening. . . .

I witnessed other hangings. I never saw a single one of the victims weep. For a long time those dried-up bodies had forgotten the bitter taste of tears.

Except once. The Oberkapo of the fifty-second cable unit was a Dutchman, a giant, well over six feet. Seven hundred prisoners worked under his orders, and they all loved him like a brother. No one had ever received a blow at his hands, nor an insult from his lips.

He had a young boy under him, a *pipel*, as they were called—a child with a refined and beautiful face, unheard of in this camp.

(At Buna, the *pipel* were loathed; they were often crueller than adults. I once saw one of thirteen beating his father because the latter had not made his bed properly. The old man was crying softly while the boy shouted: "If you don't stop crying at once I shan't bring you any more bread. Do you understand?" But the Dutchman's little servant was loved by all. He had the face of a sad angel.)

One day, the electric power station at Buna was blown up. The Gestapo, summoned to the spot, suspected sabotage. They found a trail. It eventually led to the Dutch Oberkapo. And there, after a search, they found an important stock of arms.

The Oberkapo was arrested immediately. He was tortured for a period of weeks, but in vain. He would not give a single name. He was transferred to Auschwitz. We never heard of him again.

But his little servant had been left behind in the camp in prison. Also put to torture, he too would not speak. Then the SS sentenced him to death, with two other prisoners who had been discovered with arms.

One day when we came back from work, we saw three gallows rearing up in the assembly place, three black crows. Roll call. SS all round us, machine guns trained: the traditional ceremony. Three victims in chains—and one of them, the little servant, the sad-eyed angel.

The SS seemed more preoccupied, more disturbed than usual. To hang a young boy in front of thousands of spectators was no light matter. The head of the camp read the verdict. All eyes were on the child. He was lividly pale, almost calm, biting his lips. The gallows threw its shadow over him.

This time the Lagerkapo refused to act as executioner. Three SS replaced him.

The three victims mounted together onto the chairs.

The three necks were placed at the same moment within the nooses.

"Long live liberty!" cried the two adults.

But the child was silent.

"Where is God? Where is He?" someone behind me asked.

At a sign from the head of the camp, the three chairs tipped over.

Total silence throughout the camp. On the horizon, the sun was setting.

"Bare your heads!" yelled the head of the camp. His voice was raucous. We were weeping.

"Cover your heads!"

Then the march past began. The two adults were no longer alive. Their tongues hung swollen, blue-tinged. But the third rope was still moving; being so light, the child was still alive. . . .

For more than half an hour he stayed there, struggling between life and death, dying in slow agony under our eyes. And we had to look him full in the face. He was still alive when I passed in front of him. His tongue was still red, his eyes were not yet glazed.

Behind me, I heard the same man asking:

"Where is God now?"

And I heard a voice within me answer him:

"Where is He? Here He is—He is hanging here on this gallows. . . ."

That night the soup tasted of corpses.

QUESTIONS FOR DISCUSSION

1. What is Wiesel's purpose in writing this narrative? Who is his audience? Discuss what makes this piece of writing effective. Look especially at dialogue, descriptive detail, and the narrative structure.
2. How would a knowledge of Jewish history help a reader understand the prisoners' questioning of God's existence?
3. In what ways might the philosophy expressed in this text be considered existential?
4. What are some reasons Wiesel might have decided to label this piece *Night?*

APPENDIX A
Thematic Table of Contents

DIVERSITY IN SCIENCE

Shigeru Nakayama, "Two Styles of Learning"
Anne Walton, "Women Scientists: Are They Really Different?"
Raymond Dawson, "Science and China's Influence on the World"
John B. Christopher, "Science"
Fritjof Capra, *The Tao of Physics*
Carl G. Jung, "Sigmund Freud"
Chief Seattle, "Environmental Statement"

THE ENVIRONMENT

Chief Seattle, "Environmental Statement"
Rachel Carson, "The Obligation to Endure"
Mac Margolis, "Amazon Ablaze"
John W. Mellor, "The Intertwining of Environmental Problems and Poverty"
Carl Sagan, *The Dragons of Eden: Speculations on the Evolution of Human Intelligence*
Genesis 1 and 2
Carl Sandburg, "Men of Science Say Their Say"

THE CONFLICT BETWEEN RELIGION AND SCIENCE

Albert Einstein, "Religion and Science"
Bertrand Russell, "Religion and Science"
C. S. Lewis, "What Do Christians Believe?"
Will Durant, *The Story of Philosophy*
Morris Bishop, "$E = mc^2$"

SCIENTISTS ON SCIENCE

Margaret Mead, "Warfare: An Invention—Not a Biological Necessity"
Charles Darwin, "The Action of Natural Selection"

602

Julius Robert Oppenheimer, "The Scientist in Society"
Albert Einstein, "Religion and Science"
Bertrand Russell, "Religion and Science"
Carl G. Jung, "Sigmund Freud"
Rachel Carson, "The Obligation to Endure"

THE QUESTION OF HUMAN NATURE

Charles Darwin, "The Action of Natural Selection"
George E. Simpson, "Early Social Darwinism"
Cynthia Eagle Russett, *Darwin in America: The Intellectual Response, 1865–1912*
Margaret Mead, "Warfare: An Invention—Not a Biological Necessity"
Julius K. Nyerere, "Ujamaa—The Basis of African Socialism"
Karl Marx and Friedrich Engels, "Bourgeois and Proletarians"
Albert Memmi, "Racism and Oppression"
Benjamin Hoff, *The Tao of Pooh: The How of Pooh?* and *Nowhere and Nothing*
Voltaire, "Of Universal Tolerance"
Anthony Hecht, "More Light! More Light!"
June Jordan, "A Poem About Intelligence for My Brothers and Sisters"
Carl Sandburg, "The People, Yes"
Sappho, "Invocation to Aphrodite"
Niccolo Machiavelli, *The Prince*

WAR AND PEACE

Margaret Mead, "Warfare: An Invention—Not a Biological Necessity"
George E. Simpson, "Early Social Darwinism"
Niccolo Machiavelli, *The Prince*
John Connor, "The U.S. Was Right"
Gar Alperovitz, "The U.S. Was Wrong"
Sidney Shalett, "First Atomic Bomb Dropped on Japan"
Masuji Ibuse, *Black Rain*
Karl Marx and Friedrich Engels, "Bourgeois and Proletarians"
Martin Luther King, Jr., "Letter from Birmingham Jail"
Nelson Mandela, "I Am Prepared to Die"
Elie Wiesel, *Night*
Harvey Cox, "Understanding Islam: No More Holy Wars"
Anthony Hecht, "More Light! More Light!"
William Butler Yeats, "Easter 1916"
W. H. Auden, "The Unknown Citizen"

BIRTH TECHNOLOGY

Ann Snitow, "The Paradox of Birth Technology"
S. Ogbuagu, "Depo Provera—A Choice or an Imposition on the African
    Woman?"

Jo McGowan, "In India, They Abort Females"
Jeffrey Rubin *et al.*, "The Eye of the Beholder: Parents' View on Sex of Newborns"

DIVERSITY IN GOVERNMENT

Kenneth Minogue *et al.*, Definitions of Democracy, Communism, Socialism, Nationalism, and Technocracy
Kautilya, *The Arthashastra*
Niccolo Machiavelli, *The Prince*
Patricia J. Sethi, "Pinochet: Destiny Gave Me the Job"
Amnesty International, "Chile"
Plato, *The Republic*
Confucius, The Sacred Books of Confucius
Thomas Jefferson, *The Declaration of Independence*
Julius K. Nyerere, "Ujamaa—The Basis of African Socialism" and *The Arusha Declaration*
United Nations, *Universal Declaration of Human Rights*
Roderick Ogley, "Extracts from the Declaration of the Belgrade Conference of . . . Nonaligned Countries"
Alexis de Tocqueville, *Democracy in America*
Karl Marx and Friedrich Engels, "Bourgeois and Proletarians"
Mohandas Gandhi, *Satyagraha*
Margaret Mead, "Warfare: An Invention—Not a Biological Necessity"
Pablo Neruda, "The United Fruit Co."
W. H. Auden, "The Unknown Citizen"

GENDER AND POWER

Simone de Beauvoir, "Women as Other"
Amaury de Riencourt, "Women in Athens"
Nancy Barrett, "Women and the Economy"
Anne Walton, "Women Scientists: Are They Really Different?"
Jeffrey Rubin *et al.*, "The Eye of the Beholder: Parents' View on Sex of Newborns"
Marzieh Ahmadi Oskooii, "I'm a Woman"
Yü Hsüan-Chi, "On a Visit to Ch'ung Chen Taoist Temple I See . . . the Imperial Examinations"
Maxine Hong Kingston, "No Name Woman"
Sor Juana Inés de la Cruz, "She Proves the Inconsistency . . . of Men Who Accuse Women of What They Themselves Cause"
Alice Walker, "In Search of Our Mothers' Gardens"
Genesis 1 and *2*
"Nu Kwa"
"Shakti"
Ninian Smart and Richard D. Hecht, "Women and the Order"
Riane Eisler, "Our Lost Heritage: New Facts on How God Became a Man"

Mary Daly, "After the Death of God the Father"
Phyllis Schlafly, "The Power of the Positive Woman"

RACISM AND OPPRESSION
Albert Memmi, "Racism and Oppression"
George Orwell, "Shooting an Elephant"
Mohandas Gandhi, *Satyagraha*
Martin Luther King, Jr., "Letter from Birmingham Jail"
Nelson Mandela, "I Am Prepared to Die"
Wole Soyinka, "Chimes of Silence"
Paul Laurence Dunbar, "We Wear the Mask"
Ezekiel Mphahlele, "The Master of Doornvlei"
Ellen Wright Prendergast, "Famous Are the Flowers (Patriot's Song)"
Barry Lopez, "Buffalo"

DEFINITIONS OF ART
Royal Bank of Canada Newsletter, "What Use Is Art?"
Susanne K. Langer, "The Cultural Importance of the Arts"
Gloria Anzaldúa, "Tlilli, Tlapalli: The Path of the Red and Black Ink"
Jon Stallworthy, "Letter to a Friend"
Archibald MacLeish, "Ars Poetica"
Javier Heraud, "Ars Poetica"
Marianne Moore, "Poetry"

DIVERSITY IN ART
E. H. Gombrich, "Art for Eternity"
Ananda K. Coomaraswamy, "Understanding Indian Art"
Hermann List, "Chinese Painting"
J. P. Hodin, "The Soviet Attitude to Art"
Sylvia Hochfield, "Soviet Art: New Freedom, New Directions"
Roy Sieber, "Traditional Arts of Black Africa"
Philip Rawson, "Islamic Art: Calligraphy"

ART AND GENDER
Alice Walker, "In Search of Our Mothers' Gardens"
Marzieh Ahmadi Oskooii, "I'm a Woman"
Yü-Hsüan-Chi, "On a Visit to Ch'ung Chen Taoist Temple I See . . . the Imperial
    Examinations"
Murasaki Shikibu, "Lavender"
Sor Juana Inés de la Cruz, "She Proves the Inconsistency . . . of Men Who Accuse
    Women of What They Themselves Cause"
Sappho, "Invocation to Aphrodite"

DIVERSITY IN BELIEF SYSTEMS

Émile Durkheim, *The Elementary Forms of the Religious Life*
Winston L. King, *Religion and Nothingness*
John Jarvis, "Introduction to Buddhism"
Ninian Smart and Richard Hecht, "The Enlightenment of the Buddha:
     Buddhacarita"
Diana L. Eck, *Darśan: Seeing the Divine Image in India*
"Muṇḍaka Upanishad"
Benjamin Hoff, *The Tao of Pooh: The* How *of Pooh?* and *Nowhere and Nothing*
Lao Tzu, *The Sayings of Lao Tzu*
Stephen L. Harris, *Understanding the Bible: A Reader's Introduction*
Exodus 32
St. John 8
Bengt Sundkler, "A Black Messiah: Acts of the Nazerites"
John B. Christopher, "The Prophet" and "The Teachings of Islam"
The Quran
William H. McNeil and Jean W. Sedlar, "Introduction to Confucius" and "From
     the Analects of Confucius (Lun Yü)"
Fritjof Capra, *The Tao of Physics*
Chief Seattle, "Environmental Statement"

THE SEARCH FOR MEANING

W. H. Auden, "The Unknown Citizen"
Rabindranath Tagore, "False Religion" and "The Evermoving"
Hermann Hesse, "The Brahmin's Son"
Will Durant, *The Story of Philosophy*
John Jarvis, "Introduction to Buddhism"
Benjamin Hoff, *The Tao of Pooh: The* How *of Pooh?* and *Nowhere and Nothing*
Stephen L. Harris, *Understanding the Bible: A Reader's Introduction*
Plato, "The Allegory of the Cave"
Charles I. Glicksberg, "The Literature of Nihilism"
Gwendolyn Brooks, "the preacher: ruminates behind the sermon" and "We Real
     Cool"
Jean Paul Sartre, "Existentialism"
Albert Einstein, "Religion and Science"
Bertrand Russell, "Religion and Science"

GENDER AND RELIGION

St. John 8
Genesis 1 and *2*
"Nu Kwa"
"Shakti"
Ninian Smart and Richard D. Hecht, "Women and the Order"

Riane Eisler, "Our Lost Heritage: New Facts on How God Became a Man"
Mary Daly, "After the Death of God the Father"
Phyllis Schlafly, "The Power of the Positive Woman"

TOLERANCE AND INTOLERANCE
Harvey Cox, "Understanding Islam: No More Holy Wars"
Murtuza Mutahery, *The Martyr*
Joseph Smith, "The First Vision"
Voltaire, "Of Universal Tolerance"
Bertrand Russell, "Why I Am Not a Christian"
C. S. Lewis, "What Christians Believe"
Elie Wiesel, *Night*
Anthony Hecht, "More Light! More Light!"
Muriel Rukeyser, "Letter to the Front"
William Butler Yeats, "Easter 1916"
Rabindranath Tagore, "False Religion"
Hermann Hesse, "The Brahmin's Son"

APPENDIX B
Rhetorical
Table of Contents

Based on Kinneavy's Modes and Aims

By Mode

DESCRIPTION
Wole Soyinka, "Chimes of Silence"
Amnesty International, "Chile"
Nancy Barrett, "Women and the Economy"
John Jarvis, "Introduction to Buddhism"
Diana L. Eck, *Darśan: Seeing the Divine Image in India*
Lao Tzu, *The Sayings of Lao Tzu*
John B. Christopher, "The Teachings of Islam"
Mary Daly, "After the Death of God the Father"
Phyllis Schlafly, "The Power of the Positive Woman"
Murtuza Mutahery, *The Martyr*
Raymond Dawson, "Science and China's Influence on the World"
Mac Margolis, "Amazon Ablaze"
John W. Mellor, "The Intertwining of Environmental Problems and Poverty"
Charles Darwin, "The Action of Natural Selection"
George E. Simpson, "Early Social Darwinism"
Cynthia Eagle Russett, *Darwin in America: The Intellectual Response, 1865–1912*
Jeffrey Rubin *et al.*, "The Eye of the Beholder: Parents' View on Sex of Newborns"

CLASSIFICATION AND DEFINITION
Edward T. Hall, "The Anthropology of Manners"
Julius Robert Oppenheimer, "The Scientist in Society"
Shigeru Nakayama, "Two Styles of Learning"
Anne Walton, "Women Scientists: Are They Really Different?"
Albert Einstein, "Religion and Science"
Bertrand Russell, "Religion and Science"
Émile Durkheim, *The Elementary Forms of the Religious Life*
Will Durant, *The Story of Philosophy*
Stephen L. Harris, *Understanding the Bible: A Reader's Introduction*

William H. McNeill and Jean W. Sedlar, "Introduction to Confucius" and "From the Analects of Confucius (Lun Yü)"

Charles I. Glicksberg, "The Literature of Nihilism"

Jean Paul Sartre, "Existentialism"

Riane Eisler, "Our Lost Heritage: New Facts on How God Became a Man"

C. S. Lewis, "What Christians Believe"

Kenneth Minogue *et al.*, Definitions of Democracy, Communism, Socialism, Nationalism, and Technocracy

Julius K. Nyerere, "Ujamaa—The Basis of African Socialism" and *The Arusha Declaration*

United Nations, *Universal Declaration of Human Rights*

Roderick Ogley, "Extracts from the Declaration of the Belgrade Conference . . . of Nonaligned Countries"

Simone de Beauvoir, "Women as Other"

Albert Memmi, "Racism and Oppression"

Mohandas Gandhi, *Satyagraha*

Royal Bank of Canada Newsletter, "What Use Is Art?"

Susanne K. Langer, "The Cultural Importance of the Arts"

Gloria Anzaldúa, "Tlilli, Tlapalli: The Path of the Red and Black Ink"

E. H. Gombrich, "Art for Eternity"

Ananda K. Coomaraswamy, "Understanding Indian Art"

Hermann List, "Chinese Painting"

J. P. Hodin, "The Soviet Attitude to Art"

Sylvia Hochfield, "Soviet Art: New Freedom, New Directions"

Roy Sieber, "Traditional Arts of Black Africa"

Philip Rawson, "Islamic Art: Calligraphy"

Jon Stallworthy, "Letter to a Friend"

Archibald MacLeish, "Ars Poetica"

Javier Heraud, "Ars Poetica"

Marianne Moore, "Poetry"

Alice Walker, "In Search of Our Mothers' Gardens"

Marzieh Ahmadi Oskooii, "I'm a Woman"

NARRATION

Sidney Shalett, "First Atomic Bomb Dropped on Japan"

Masuji Ibuse, *Black Rain*

Suzanne H. Sankowsky, *Mainstreams of World History*

Ninian Smart and Richard D. Hecht, "The Enlightenment of Buddha: Buddhacarita"

"Muṇḍaka Upanishad"

Exodus 32

St. John 8

Bengt Sundkler, "A Black Messiah: Acts of the Nazerites"

John B. Christopher, "The Prophet"

The Quran

Plato, "The Allegory of the Cave"
Genesis 1 and 2
"Nu Kwa"
"Shakti"
Joseph Smith, "The First Vision"
Elie Wiesel, *Night*
George Orwell, "Shooting an Elephant"
Ezekiel Mphahlele, "The Master of Doornvlei"
Barry Lopez, "Buffalo"
Maxine Hong Kingston, "No Name Woman"
Murasaki Shikibu, "Lavender"
Hermann Hesse, "The Brahmin's Son"

EVALUATION

Chief Seattle, "Environmental Statement"
Rachel Carson, "The Obligation to Endure"
Margaret Mead, "Warfare: An Invention—Not a Biological Necessity"
John Connor, "The U.S. Was Right"
Gar Alperovitz, "The U.S. Was Wrong"
Ann Snitow, "The Paradox of Birth Technology"
S. Ogbuagu, "Depo Provera—A Choice or an Imposition on the African
    Woman?"
Jo McGowan, "In India, They Abort Females"
Gwendolyn Brooks, "the preacher: ruminates behind the sermon" and "We Real
    Cool"
Ninian Smart and Richard D. Hecht, "Women and the Order"
Harvey Cox, "Understanding Islam: No More Holy Wars"
Voltaire, "Of Universal Tolerance"
Bertrand Russell, "Why I Am Not a Christian"
Kautilya, *The Arthashastra*
Niccolo Machiavelli, *The Prince*
Patricia J. Sethi, "Pinochet: Destiny Gave Me the Job"
Plato, *The Republic*
Confucius, "The Sacred Books of Confucius"
Alexis de Tocqueville, *Democracy in America*
Karl Marx and Friedrich Engels, "Bourgeois and Proletarians"
Amaury de Riencourt, "Women in Athens"
Martin Luther King, Jr., "Letter from Birmingham Jail"
Nelson Mandela, "I Am Prepared to Die"
Pablo Neruda, "The United Fruit Co."
Paul Laurence Dunbar, "We Wear the Mask"
Ellen Wright Prendergast, "Famous Are the Flowers (Patriot's Song)"
Anthony Hecht, "More Light! More Light!"
Muriel Rukeyser, "Letter to the Front"

William Butler Yeats, "Easter 1916"
W. H. Auden, "The Unknown Citizen"
Morris Bishop, "*E* = *mc²*"
June Jordan, "A Poem About Intelligence for My Brothers and Sisters"
Yü Hsüan-Chi, "On a Visit to Ch'ung Chen Taoist Temple I See . . . the Imperial
    Examinations"
Sor Juana Inés de la Cruz, "She Proves the Inconsistency . . . of Men Who Accuse
    Women of What They Themselves Cause"
Sappho, "Invocation to Aphrodite"
Rabindranath Tagore, "False Religion" and "The Evermoving"

By Aim

EXPRESSIVE
Julius K. Nyerere, *The Arusha Declaration*
Thomas Jefferson, *The Declaration of Independence*
United Nations, *Universal Declaration of Human Rights*
Roderick Ogley, "Extracts from the Declaration of the Belgrade Conference of . . .
    Nonaligned Countries"
Robert Ernest Hume, "Muṇḍaka Upanishad"
Lao Tzu, *The Sayings of Lao Tzu*
The Quran
Exodus 32
Plato, "The Allegory of the Cave"
Genesis 1 and *2*
"Nu Kwa"
"Shakti"
Martin Luther King, Jr., "Letter from Birmingham Jail"
Nelson Mandela, "I Am Prepared to Die"

REFERENTIAL (OR EXPOSITORY: CONVEY INFORMATION, PROVE A POINT, EXPLORE A SUBJECT)
Edward T. Hall, "The Anthropology of Manners"
Julius Robert Oppenheimer, "The Scientist in Society"
Shigeru Nakayama, "Two Styles of Learning"
Anne Walton, "Women Scientists: Are They Really Different?"
Raymond Dawson, "Science and China's Influence on the World"
John B. Christopher, "Science"
Fritjof Capra, *The Tao of Physics*
Carl G. Jung, "Sigmund Freud"
Mac Margolis, "Amazon Ablaze"
John W. Mellor, "The Intertwining of Environmental Problems and Poverty"

Carl Sagan, *The Dragons of Eden: Speculations on the Evolution of Human Intelligence*
Albert Einstein, "Religion and Science"
Charles Darwin, "The Action of Natural Selection"
George E. Simpson, "Early Social Darwinism"
Cynthia Eagle Russett, *Darwin in America: The Intellectual Response, 1865–1912*
Sidney Shalett, "First Atomic Bomb Dropped on Japan"
Suzanne H. Sankowsky, *Mainstreams of World History*
Ann Snitow, "The Paradox of Birth Technology"
Jeffrey Rubin *et al.*, "The Eye of the Beholder: Parents' View on Sex of Newborns"
Kenneth Minogue *et al.*, Definitions of Democracy, Communism, Socialism, Nationalism, and Technocracy
Kautilya, *The Arthashastra*
Niccolo Machiavelli, *The Prince*
Patricia J. Sethi, "Pinochet: Destiny Gave Me the Job"
Amnesty International, "Chile"
Plato, *The Republic*
Confucius, "The Sacred Books of Confucius"
Julius K. Nyerere, "Ujamaa—The Basis of African Socialism"
Alexis de Tocqueville, *Democracy in America*
Karl Marx and Friedrich Engels, "Bourgeois and Proletarians"
Simone de Beauvoir, "Women as Other"
Amaury de Riencourt, "Women in Athens"
Nancy Barrett, "Women and the Economy"
Royal Bank of Canada Newsletter, "What Use Is Art?"
Susanne K. Langer, "The Cultural Importance of the Arts"
Gloria Anzaldúa, "Tlilli, Tlapalli: The Path of the Red and Black Ink"
E. H. Gombrich, "Art for Eternity"
Ananda K. Coomaraswamy, "Understanding Indian Art"
Hermann List, "Chinese Painting"
J. P. Hodin, "The Soviet Attitude to Art"
Sylvia Hochfield, "Soviet Art: New Freedom, New Directions"
Roy Sieber, "Traditional Arts of Black Africa"
Philip Rawson, "Islamic Art: Calligraphy"
Émile Durkheim, *The Elementary Forms of the Religious Life*
Will Durant, *The Story of Philosophy*
Winston L. King, *Religion and Nothingness*
John Jarvis, "Introduction to Buddhism"
Ninian Smart and Richard D. Hecht, "The Enlightenment of the Buddha: Buddhacarita"
Diana L. Eck, *Darśan: Seeing the Divine Image in India*
Benjamin Hoff, *The Tao of Pooh: The* How *of Pooh?* and *Nowhere and Nothing*
Stephen L. Harris, *Understanding the Bible: A Reader's Introduction*
Bengt Sundkler, "A Black Messiah: Acts of the Nazerites"
John B. Christopher, "The Prophet" and "The Teachings of Islam"
William H. McNeill and Jean W. Sedlar, "Introduction to Confucius" and "From the Analects of Confucius (Lun Yü)"

Charles I. Glicksberg, "The Literature of Nihilism"
Jean Paul Sartre, "Existentialism"
Riane Eisler, "Our Lost Heritage: New Facts on How God Became a Man"
Murtuza Mutahery, *The Martyr*
C. S. Lewis, "What Christians Believe"

LITERARY

Jon Stallworthy, "Letter to a Friend"
Archibald MacLeish, "Ars Poetica"
Javier Heraud, "Ars Poetica"
Marianne Moore, "Poetry"
Alice Walker, "In Search of Our Mothers' Gardens"
Wole Soyinka, "Chimes of Silence"
Pablo Neruda, "The United Fruit Co."
Paul Laurence Dunbar, "We Wear the Mask"
Ezekiel Mphahlele, "The Master of Doornvlei"
Ellen Wright Prendergast, "Famous are the Flowers (Patriot's Song)"
Anthony Hecht, "More Light! More Light!"
Muriel Rukeyser, "Letter to the Front"
William Butler Yeats, "Easter 1916"
W. H. Auden, "The Unknown Citizen"
Carl Sandburg, "The People, Yes" and "Men of Science Say Their Say"
Morris Bishop, "$E = mc^2$"
June Jordan, "A Poem About Intelligence for My Brothers and Sisters"
Barry Lopez, "Buffalo"
Marzieh Ahmadi Oskooii, "I'm a Woman"
Yü Hsüan-Chi, "On a Visit to Ch'ung Chen Taoist Temple I See . . . the Imperial
    Examinations"
Sor Juana Inés de la Cruz, "She Proves the Inconsistency . . . of Men Who Accuse
    Women of What They Themselves Cause"
Maxine Hong Kingston, "No Name Woman"
Sappho, "Invocation to Aphrodite"
Murasaki Shikibu, "Lavender"
Rabindranath Tagore, "False Religion" and "The Evermoving"
Hermann Hesse, "The Brahmin's Son"
Gwendolyn Brooks, "the preacher: ruminates behind the sermon" and "We Real
    Cool"
Elie Wiesel, *Night*
Masuji Ibuse, *Black Rain*

PERSUASIVE

John Connor, "The U.S. Was Right"
Gar Alperovitz, "The U.S. Was Wrong"
Jo McGowan, "In India, They Abort Females"

Patricia J. Sethi, "Pinochet: Destiny Gave Me the Job"
Julius K. Nyerere, "Ujamaa—The Basis of African Socialism"
St. John 8
Bengt Sundkler, "A Black Messiah: Acts of the Nazerites"
Ninian Smart and Richard D. Hecht, "Women and the Order"
Joseph Smith, "The First Vision"
Chief Seattle, "Environmental Statement"
Rachel Carson, "The Obligation to Endure"
Bertrand Russell, "Religion and Science"
Margaret Mead, "Warfare: An Invention—Not a Biological Necessity"
S. Ogbuagu, "Depo Provera—A Choice or an Imposition on the African
    Woman?"
Albert Memmi, "Racism and Oppression"
Mary Daly, "After the Death of God the Father"
Phyllis Schlafly, "The Power of the Positive Woman"
Harvey Cox, "Understanding Islam: No More Holy Wars"
Voltaire, "Of Universal Tolerance"
Bertrand Russell, "Why I Am Not a Christian"

Copyrights and Acknowledgments

Author-Title Index

"Action of Natural Selection, The," 94

"After the Death of God the Father,"
556

"Allegory of the Cave, The," 519

Alperovitz, Gar, 109

"Amazon Ablaze," 65

Amnesty International, 190

"Analects of Confucius (Lun Yü),
From the," 517

"Anthropology of Manners, The," 3

Anzaldúa, Gloria, 316

"Ars Poetica," 352, 354

"Art for Eternity," 325

Arthashastra, The, 173

Arusha Declaration, The, 207

Auden, W. H., 384

Barrett, Nancy, 251

Bishop, Morris, 390

"Black Messiah: Acts of the Nazarites,
A," 499

Black Rain, 117

"Bourgeois and Proletarians," 232

"Brahmin's Son, The," 438

Brooks, Gwendolyn, 536

"Buffalo," 393

Capra, Fritjof, 49

Carson, Rachel, 60

"Chile," 190

"Chimes of Silence," 364

"Chinese Painting," 337

Christopher, John B., 41, 501

Confucius, 195, 514

Connor, John, 109

Coomaraswamy, Ananda, 333

Cox, Harvey, 566

"Cultural Importance of the Arts,
The," 310

Daly, Mary, 556

*Darśan: Seeing the Divine Image in
India*, 464

*Darwin in America: The Intellectual
Response, 1865–1912*, 100

Darwin, Charles, 94

Dawson, Raymond, 39

de Beauvoir, Simone, 242

de la Cruz, Sor Juana Inés, 400

de Riencourt, Amaury, 247

de Tocqueville, Alexis, 226

Declaration of Independence, The, 210

Definitions of Democracy,
Communism, Socialism,
Nationalism, and
Technocracy, 162

"Democracy in America," 226

"Depo Provera—A Choice or an
Imposition on the African
Woman?," 135

*Dragons of Eden: Speculations on the
Evolution of Human Intelligence,
The*, 83

Dunbar, Paul Laurence, 369

Durant, Will, 452

Durkheim, Émile, 449

"$E = mc^2$," 390

"Early Social Darwinism," 97

"Easter 1916," 381

Eck, Diana L., 464

Einstein, Albert, 86

Eisler, Riane, 550

Elementary Forms of the Religious Life, The, 449

"Enlightenment of the Buddha: Buddhacarita, The," 461

"Environmental Statement," 58

"Evermoving, The," 436

"Existentialism," 537

Exodus 32, 496

"Extracts from the *Declaration of the Belgrade Conference of . . . Nonaligned Countries*," 222

"Eye of the Beholder: Parents' View on Sex of Newborns, The," 149

"False Religion," 435

"Famous Are the Flowers (*Patriot's Song*)," 377

"First Atomic Bomb Dropped on Japan," 113

"First Vision, The," 577

Gandhi, Mohandas, 266

Genesis 1 and *2*, 542

Glicksberg, Charles I., 528

Gombrich, E. H., 325

Hall, Edward T., 3

Harris, Stephen L., 491

Hecht, Anthony, 378

Heraud, Javier, 354

Hesse, Hermann, 438

Hochfield, Sylvia, 340

Hodin, J. P., 338

Hoff, Benjamin, 481

Hsüan-Chi, Yü, 399

"I'm a Woman," 397

"I Am Prepared to Die," 286

Ibuse, Masuji, 117

"In India, They Abort Females," 147

"In Search of Our Mothers' Gardens," 356

"Intertwining of Environmental Problems and Poverty, The," 74

"Introduction to Buddhism," 458

"Introduction to Confucius," 514

"Invocation to Aphrodite," 412

"Islamic Art: Calligraphy," 348

Jarvis, John, 458

Jefferson, Thomas, 210

Jordan, June, 391

Jung, Carl G., 53

Kautilya, 173

King, Martin Luther, Jr., 272

King, Winston L., 455

Kingston, Maxine Hong, 403

Langer, Susanne K., 310

Lao Tzu, 488

"Lavender," 413

"Letter from Birmingham Jail," 272

"Letter to a Friend," 351

"Letter to the Front," 380

Lewis, C. S., 590

List, Hermann, 337

"Literature of Nihilism, The," 528

Lopez, Barry, 393

Machiavelli, Niccolo, 180

MacLeish, Archibald, 352

Mainstreams of World History, 127

Mandela, Nelson, 286

Margolis, Mac, 65

Martyr, The, 572

Marx, Karl, 232

"Master of Doornvlei, The," 370

McGowan, Jo, 147

McNeill, William H., 514

Mead, Margaret, 104

Mellor, John W., 74

Memmi, Albert, 253

"Men of Science Say Their Say," 388

Minogue, Kenneth, 162

Moore, Marianne, 355

"More Light! More Light!," 378

Mphahlele, Ezekiel, 370

"Muṇḍaka Upanishad," 473

Mutahery, Murtuza, 572

Nakayama, Shigeru, 15

Neruda, Pablo, 366

Night, 599

"No Name Woman," 403

"Nu Kwa," 545

Nyerere, Julius K., 200

"Obligation to Endure, The," 60

Ogbuagu, S., 135

Ogley, Roderick, 222

"On a Visit to Ch'ung Chen Taoist Temple I See . . . the Imperial Examinations," 399
Oppenheimer, Julius Robert, 10
Orwell, George, 261
Oskooii, Marzieh Ahmadi, 397
"Our Lost Heritage: New Facts on How God Became a Man," 550
"Paradox of Birth Technology, The," 128
"People, Yes, The," 386
"Pinochet: Destiny Gave Me the Job," 188
Plato, 193, 519
"Poem About Intelligence for My Brothers and Sisters, A," 391
"Poetry," 355
Power of the Positive Woman, The, 560
"preacher: ruminates behind the sermon, the," 536
Prendergast, Ellen Wright, 377
Prince, The, 180
"Prophet, The," 501
Quran, The, 501
"Racism and Oppression," 253
Rawson, Philip, 348
Religion and Nothingness, 455
"Religion and Science," 86, 90
Republic, The, 193
Royal Bank of Canada Newsletter, 308
Rubin, Jeffrey, 149
Rukeyser, Muriel, 380
Russell, Bertrand, 90, 584
Russett, Cynthia Eagle, 100
"Sacred Books of Confucius, The," 195
Sagan, Carl, 83
Sandburg, Carl, 386
Sankowsky, Suzanne H., 127
Sappho, 412
Sartre, Jean Paul, 537
Satyagraha, 266
Sayings of Lao Tzu, The, 488
Schlafly, Phyllis, 560
"Science and China's Influence on the World," 39
"Science," 41

"Scientist in Society, The," 10
Seattle, Chief, 58
Sedlar, Jean W., 514
Sethi, Patricia J., 188
"Shakti," 546
Shalett, Sidney, 113
"She Proves the Inconsistency . . . of Men Who Accuse Women of What They Themselves Cause," 400
Shikibu, Murasaki, 413
"Shooting an Elephant," 261
Sieber, Roy, 344
Sigmund Freud, 52
Simpson, George E., 97
Smart, Ninian, 461
Smith, Joseph, 577
Snitow, Ann, 128
"Soviet Art: New Freedom, New Directions," 340
"Soviet Attitude to Art, The," 338
Soyinka, Wole, 364
St. John 8, 498
Stallworthy, Jon, 351
Story of Philosophy, The, 452
Sundkler, Bengt, 499
Tagore, Rabindranath, 435
Tao of Physics, The, 49
Tao of Pooh, The, 481
"Teachings of Islam, The," 504
Three Concepts of Creation, 542
"Tlilli, Tlapalli: The Path of the Red and Black Ink," 316
"Traditional Arts of Black Africa," 344
"Two Styles of Learning," 15
"U.S. Was Right, The," 109
"U.S. Was Wrong, The," 111
"Ujamaa—The Basis of African Socialism," 200
"Understanding Indian Art," 333
"Understanding Islam: No More Holy Wars," 566
Understanding the Bible: A Reader's Introduction, 491
"United Fruit Co., The," 366
United Nations, 215

Universal Declaration of Human Rights, The, 215
"Universal Tolerance, Of," 581
"Unknown Citizen, The," 384
Voltaire, 581
Walker, Alice, 356
Walton, Anne, 25
"Warfare: An Invention—Not a Biological Necessity," 104
"We Real Cool," 536
"We Wear the Mask," 369
"What Christians Believe," 590

"What the World Believes," 449
"What Use Is Art?," 308
"Why I Am Not a Christian," 584
Wiesel, Elie, 599
"Women and the Economy," 251
"Women and the Order," 549
"Women as Other," 242
"Women in Athens," 247
"Women Scientists: Are They Really Different?," 25
Yeats, William Butler, 381